T0134779

Communications
in Computer and Information Science   1681

Rationale

The CCIS series is devoted to the publication of proceedings of computer science conferences. Its aim is to efficiently disseminate original research results in informatics in printed and electronic form. While the focus is on publication of peer-reviewed full papers presenting mature work, inclusion of reviewed short papers reporting on work in progress is welcome, too. Besides globally relevant meetings with internationally representative program committees guaranteeing a strict peer-reviewing and paper selection process, conferences run by societies or of high regional or national relevance are also considered for publication.

Topics

The topical scope of CCIS spans the entire spectrum of informatics ranging from foundational topics in the theory of computing to information and communications science and technology and a broad variety of interdisciplinary application fields.

Information for Volume Editors and Authors

Publication in CCIS is free of charge. No royalties are paid, however, we offer registered conference participants temporary free access to the online version of the conference proceedings on SpringerLink (http://link.springer.com) by means of an http referrer from the conference website and/or a number of complimentary printed copies, as specified in the official acceptance email of the event.

CCIS proceedings can be published in time for distribution at conferences or as post-proceedings, and delivered in the form of printed books and/or electronically as USBs and/or e-content licenses for accessing proceedings at SpringerLink. Furthermore, CCIS proceedings are included in the CCIS electronic book series hosted in the SpringerLink digital library at http://link.springer.com/bookseries/7899. Conferences publishing in CCIS are allowed to use Online Conference Service (OCS) for managing the whole proceedings lifecycle (from submission and reviewing to preparing for publication) free of charge.

Publication process

The language of publication is exclusively English. Authors publishing in CCIS have to sign the Springer CCIS copyright transfer form, however, they are free to use their material published in CCIS for substantially changed, more elaborate subsequent publications elsewhere. For the preparation of the camera-ready papers/files, authors have to strictly adhere to the Springer CCIS Authors' Instructions and are strongly encouraged to use the CCIS LaTeX style files or templates.

Abstracting/Indexing

CCIS is abstracted/indexed in DBLP, Google Scholar, EI-Compendex, Mathematical Reviews, SCImago, Scopus. CCIS volumes are also submitted for the inclusion in ISI Proceedings.

How to start

To start the evaluation of your proposal for inclusion in the CCIS series, please send an e-mail to ccis@springer.com.

Yuqing Sun · Tun Lu · Yinzhang Guo ·
Xiaoxia Song · Hongfei Fan · Dongning Liu ·
Liping Gao · Bowen Du
Editors

Computer Supported Cooperative Work and Social Computing

17th CCF Conference, ChineseCSCW 2022
Taiyuan, China, November 25–27, 2022
Revised Selected Papers, Part I

 Springer

Editors
Yuqing Sun
Shandong University
Jinan, China

Yinzhang Guo
Taiyuan University of Science
and Technology
Taiyuan, China

Hongfei Fan
Tongji University
Shanghai, China

Liping Gao
University of Shanghai for Science
and Technology
Shanghai, China

Tun Lu
Fudan University
Shanghai, China

Xiaoxia Song
Shanxi Datong University
Datong, China

Dongning Liu
Guangdong University of Technology
Guangzhou, China

Bowen Du
Tongji University
Shanghai, China

ISSN 1865-0929   ISSN 1865-0937 (electronic)
Communications in Computer and Information Science
ISBN 978-981-99-2355-7   ISBN 978-981-99-2356-4 (eBook)
https://doi.org/10.1007/978-981-99-2356-4

This Springer imprint is published by the registered company Springer Nature Singapore Pte Ltd.
The registered company address is: 152 Beach Road, #21-01/04 Gateway East, Singapore 189721, Singapore

Preface

Welcome to the post-proceedings of ChineseCSCW 2022, the 17th CCF Conference on Computer-Supported Cooperative Work and Social Computing.

ChineseCSCW 2022 was organized by the China Computer Federation (CCF), and co-hosted by the CCF Technical Committee on Cooperative Computing (CCF TCCC), the Taiyuan University of Science and Technology, and the Shanxi Datong University, in Taiyuan, Shanxi, China, during November 25–27, 2022. The conference was also supported by SCHOLAT and Guangdong Xuanyuan Network Technology Co., Ltd. The theme of the conference was *Human-Centered Collaborative Intelligence*, which reflects the emerging trend of the combination of artificial intelligence, human-system collaboration, and AI-empowered applications.

ChineseCSCW (initially recognized as CCSCW) is a highly reputable conference series on computer-supported cooperative work (CSCW) and social computing in China, and has a long history. It aims at bridging Chinese and overseas CSCW researchers, practitioners, and educators, with a particular focus on innovative models, theories, techniques, algorithms, and methods, as well as domain-specific applications and systems, from both technical and social aspects in CSCW and social computing. The conference was initially held biennially since 1998, and has been held annually since 2014.

This year, the conference received 211 submissions, and after a rigorous double-blind peer review process, only 60 of them were eventually accepted as full papers to be orally presented, resulting in an acceptance rate of 28%. The program also included 30 short papers, which were presented as posters. In addition, the conference featured 6 keynote speeches, 5 high-level technical seminars, the ChineseCSCW Cup 2022 Collaborative Intelligence Big Data Challenge, the Forum for Outstanding Young Scholars, the Forum for Presentations of Top-Venue Papers, and an awards ceremony for senior TCCC members. We are grateful to the distinguished keynote speakers, *Changjun Jiang* (CAE Member) from *Tongji University*, *Xingshe Zhou* from *Northwestern Polytechnical University*, *Ting Liu* from *Harbin Institute of Technology*, *Xing Xie* from *Microsoft Research Asia*, *Xin Lu* from *National University of Defense Technology*, and *Tong Zhang* from *South China University of Technology*.

We hope that you enjoyed ChineseCSCW 2022.

November 2022

Yong Tang
Peikang Bai
Liying Yao

Organization

Steering Committee

Yong Tang	South China Normal University, China
Weiqing Tang	China Computer Federation, China
Ning Gu	Fudan University, China
Shaozi Li	Xiamen University, China
Bin Hu	Lanzhou University, China
Yuqing Sun	Shandong University, China
Xiaoping Liu	Hefei University of Technology, China
Zhiwen Yu	Northwestern Polytechnical University, China
Xiangwei Zheng	Shandong Normal University, China
Tun Lu	Fudan University, China

General Chairs

Yong Tang	South China Normal University, China
Peikang Bai	Taiyuan University of Science and Technology, China
Liying Yao	Shanxi Datong University, China

Program Committee Chairs

Yuqing Sun	Shandong University, China
Tun Lu	Fudan University, China
Dongning Liu	Guangdong University of Technology, China
Yinzhang Guo	Taiyuan University of Science and Technology, China
Xiaoxia Song	Shanxi Datong University, China

Organization Committee Chairs

Xiaoping Liu	Hefei University of Technology, China
Zhiwen Yu	Northwestern Polytechnical University, China

Chaoli Sun   Taiyuan University of Science and Technology,
                              China
Jifu Zhang   Taiyuan University of Science and Technology,
                              China

Publicity Chairs

Xiangwei Zheng   Shandong Normal University, China
Jianguo Li   South China Normal University, China

Publication Chairs

Bin Hu   Lanzhou University, China
Hailong Sun   Beihang University, China

CSCW Cup Competition Chairs

Chaobo He   South China Normal University, China
Yong Li   Shanxi Datong University, China

Paper Award Chairs

Shaozi Li   Xiamen University, China
Yichuan Jiang   Southeast University, China

Paper Recommendation Chairs

Honghao Gao   Shanghai University, China
Yiming Tang   Hefei University of Technology, China

Finance Chairs

Huichao Yan   Shanxi Datong University, China
Guoyou Zhang   Taiyuan University of Science and Technology,
                              China

Program Committee

Tie Bao	Jilin University, China
Zhan Bu	Nanjing University of Finance and Economics, China
Hongming Cai	Shanghai Jiao Tong University, China
Xinye Cai	Nanjing University of Aeronautics and Astronautics, China
Yongming Cai	Guangdong Pharmaceutical University, China
Yuanzheng Cai	Minjiang University, China
Zhicheng Cai	Nanjing University of Science and Technology, China
Buqing Cao	Hunan University of Science and Technology, China
Donglin Cao	Xiamen University, China
Jian Cao	Shanghai Jiao Tong University, China
Jingjing Cao	Wuhan University of Technology, China
Chao Chen	Chongqing University, China
Jianhui Chen	Beijing University of Technology, China
Long Chen	Southeast University, China
Longbiao Chen	Xiamen University, China
Liangyin Chen	Sichuan University, China
Qingkui Chen	University of Shanghai for Science and Technology, China
Ningjiang Chen	Guangxi University, China
Wang Chen	China North Vehicle Research Institute, China
Weineng Chen	South China University of Technology, China
Yang Chen	Fudan University, China
Zhen Chen	Yanshan University, China
Shiwei Cheng	Zhejiang University of Technology, China
Xiaohui Cheng	Guilin University of Technology, China
Yuan Cheng	Wuhan University, China
Lizhen Cui	Shandong University, China
Weihui Dai	Fudan University, China
Xianghua Ding	Fudan University, China
Wanchun Dou	Nanjing University, China
Bowen Du	Tongji University, China
Hongfei Fan	Tongji University, China
Yili Fang	Zhejiang Gongshang University, China
Lunke Fei	Guangdong University of Technology, China
Liang Feng	Chongqing University, China
Shanshan Feng	Shandong Normal University, China

Honghao Gao	Shanghai University, China
Jing Gao	Guangdong Hengdian Information Technology Co., Ltd., China
Ying Gao	South China University of Technology, China
Yunjun Gao	Zhejiang University, China
Liping Gao	University of Shanghai for Science and Technology, China
Ning Gu	Fudan University, China
Bin Guo	Northwestern Polytechnical University, China
Kun Guo	Fuzhou University, China
Wei Guo	Shandong University, China
Yinzhang Guo	Taiyuan University of Science and Technology, China
Tao Han	Zhejiang Gongshang University, China
Fei Hao	Shanxi Normal University, China
Chaobo He	Zhongkai University of Agriculture and Engineering, China
Fazhi He	Wuhan University, China
Haiwu He	Chinese Academy of Sciences, China
Bin Hu	Lanzhou University, China
Daning Hu	Southern University of Science and Technology, China
Wenting Hu	Jiangsu Open University, China
Yanmei Hu	Chengdu University of Technology, China
Changqin Huang	South China Normal University, China
Tao Jia	Southwest University, China
Bo Jiang	Zhejiang Gongshang University, China
Bin Jiang	Hunan University, China
Jiuchuan Jiang	Nanjing University of Finance and Economics, China
Weijin Jiang	Xiangtan University, China
Yichuan Jiang	Southeast University, China
Lu Jia	China Agricultural University, China
Miaotianzi Jin	Shenzhen Artificial Intelligence and Data Science Institute (Longhua), China
Lanju Kong	Shandong University, China
Yi Lai	Xi'an University of Posts and Telecommunications, China
Dongsheng Li	Microsoft Research, China
Guoliang Li	Tsinghua University, China
Hengjie Li	Lanzhou University of Arts and Science, China
Jianguo Li	South China Normal University, China
Jingjing Li	South China Normal University, China

Junli Li	Jinzhong University, China
Li Li	Southwest University, China
Pu Li	Zhengzhou University of Light Industry, China
Renfa Li	Hunan University, China
Shaozi Li	Xiamen University, China
Taoshen Li	Guangxi University, China
Weimin Li	Shanghai University, China
Xiaoping Li	Southeast University, China
Yong Li	Tsinghua University, China
Lu Liang	Guangdong University of Technology, China
Hao Liao	Shenzhen University, China
Bing Lin	Fujian Normal University, China
Dazhen Lin	Xiamen University, China
Cong Liu	Shandong University of Technology, China
Dongning Liu	Guangdong University of Technology, China
Hong Liu	Shandong Normal University, China
Jing Liu	Guangzhou Institute of Technology, Xidian University, China
Li Liu	Chongqing University, China
Shijun Liu	Shandong University, China
Shufen Liu	Jilin University, China
Xiaoping Liu	Hefei University of Technology, China
Yuechang Liu	Jiaying University, China
Tun Lu	Fudan University, China
Hong Lu	Shanghai Polytechnic University, China
Huijuan Lu	China Jiliang University, China
Dianjie Lu	Shandong Normal University, China
Qiang Lu	Hefei University of Technology, China
Haoyu Luo	South China Normal University, China
Zhiming Luo	Xiamen University, China
Peng Lv	Central South University, China
Pin Lv	Guangxi University, China
Xiao Lv	Naval University of Engineering, China
Li Ni	Anhui University, China
Hui Ma	University of Electronic Science and Technology of China and Zhongshan Institute, China
Keji Mao	Zhejiang University of Technology, China
Chao Min	Nanjing University, China
Haiwei Pan	Harbin Engineering University, China
Li Pan	Shandong University, China
Yinghui Pan	Shenzhen University, China
Lianyong Qi	Qufu Normal University, China

Jiaxing Shang	Chongqing University, China
Limin Shen	Yanshan University, China
Yuliang Shi	Shanda Dareway Company Limited, China
Yanjun Shi	Dalian University of Science and Technology, China
Xiaoxia Song	Datong University, China
Kehua Su	Wuhan University, China
Songzhi Su	Xiamen University, China
Hailong Sun	Beihang University, China
Ruizhi Sun	China Agricultural University, China
Yuqing Sun	Shandong University, China
Yuling Sun	East China Normal University, China
Wen'an Tan	Nanjing University of Aeronautics and Astronautics, China
Lina Tan	Hunan University of Technology and Business, China
Yong Tang	South China Normal University, China
Shan Tang	Shanghai Polytechnic University, China
Weiqing Tang	China Computer Federation, China
Yan Tang	Hohai University, China
Yiming Tang	Hefei University of Technology, China
Yizheng Tao	China Academy of Engineering Physics, China
Shaohua Teng	Guangdong University of Technology, China
Fengshi Tian	China People's Police University, China
Zhuo Tian	Institute of Software, Chinese Academy of Sciences, China
Binhui Wang	Nankai University, China
Dakuo Wang	IBM Research, USA
Hongbin Wang	Kunming University of Science and Technology, China
Hongjun Wang	Southwest Jiaotong University, China
Hongbo Wang	University of Science and Technology Beijing, China
Lei Wang	Alibaba Group, China
Lei Wang	Dalian University of Technology, China
Tao Wang	Minjiang University, China
Tianbo Wang	Beihang University, China
Tong Wang	Harbin Engineering University, China
Wanyuan Wang	Southeast University, China
Xiaogang Wang	Shanghai Dianji University, China
Yijie Wang	National University of Defense Technology, China
Yingjie Wang	Yantai University, China

Zhenxing Wang	Shanghai Polytechnic University, China
Zhiwen Wang	Guangxi University of Science and Technology, China
Zijia Wang	Guangzhou University, China
Yiping Wen	Hunan University of Science and Technology, China
Ling Wu	Fuzhou University, China
Quanwang Wu	Chongqing University, China
Wen Wu	East China Normal University, China
Zhengyang Wu	South China Normal University, China
Chunhe Xia	Beihang University, China
Fangxiong Xiao	Jinling Institute of Technology, China
Jing Xiao	South China Normal University, China
Zheng Xiao	Hunan University, China
Xiaolan Xie	Guilin University of Technology, China
Zhiqiang Xie	Harbin University of Science and Technology, China
Yu Xin	Harbin University of Science and Technology, China
Jianbo Xu	Hunan University of Science and Technology, China
Jiuyun Xu	China University of Petroleum, China
Meng Xu	Shandong Technology and Business University, China
Heyang Xu	Henan University of Technology, China
Yonghui Xu	Shandong University, China
Xiao Xue	Tianjin University, China
Yaling Xun	Taiyuan University of Science and Technology, China
Jiaqi Yan	Nanjing University, China
Xiaohu Yan	Shenzhen Polytechnic, China
Yan Yao	Qilu University of Technology, China
Bo Yang	University of Electronic Science and Technology of China, China
Chao Yang	Hunan University, China
Dingyu Yang	Shanghai Dianji University, China
Gang Yang	Northwestern Polytechnical University, China
Jing Yang	Harbin Engineering University, China
Lin Yang	Shanghai Computer Software Technology Development Center, China
Tianruo Yang	Hainan University, China
Xiaochun Yang	Northeastern University, China

Xu Yu	Qingdao University of Science and Technology, China
Shanping Yu	Beijing Institute of Technology, China
Zhiwen Yu	Northwestern Polytechnical University, China
Zhiyong Yu	Fuzhou University, China
Jianyong Yu	Hunan University of Science and Technology, China
Yang Yu	Zhongshan University, China
Zhengtao Yu	Kunming University of Science and Technology, China
Chengzhe Yuan	Guangdong Engineering and Technology Research Center for Service Computing, China
Junying Yuan	Nanfang College Guangzhou, China
An Zeng	Guangdong Polytechnical University, China
Dajun Zeng	Institute of Automation, Chinese Academy of Sciences, China
Zhihui Zhan	South China University of Technology, China
Changyou Zhang	Chinese Academy of Sciences, China
Jia Zhang	Jinan University, China
Jifu Zhang	Taiyuan University of Science and Technology, China
Jing Zhang	Nanjing University of Science and Technology, China
Liang Zhang	Fudan University, China
Libo Zhang	Southwest University, China
Miaohui Zhang	Energy Research Institute of Jiangxi Academy of Sciences, China
Peng Zhang	Fudan University, China
Senyue Zhang	Shenyang Aerospace University, China
Shaohua Zhang	Shanghai Software Technology Development Center, China
Wei Zhang	Guangdong University of Technology, China
Xin Zhang	Jiangnan University, China
Zhiqiang Zhang	Harbin Engineering University, China
Zili Zhang	Southwest University, China
Hong Zhao	Xidian University, China
Xiangwei Zheng	Shandong Normal University, China
Jinghui Zhong	South China University of Technology, China
Ning Zhong	Beijing University of Technology, China
Yifeng Zhou	Southeast University, China
Huiling Zhu	Jinan University, China
Nengjun Zhu	Shanghai University, China
Tingshao Zhu	Chinese Academy of Science, China

Xia Zhu	Southeast University, China
Xianjun Zhu	Jinling University of Science and Technology, China
Yanhua Zhu	The First Affiliated Hospital of Guangdong Pharmaceutical University, China
Jia Zhu	South China Normal University, China
Jianhua Zhu	City University of Hong Kong, China
Jie Zhu	Nanjing University of Posts and Telecommunications, China
Qiaohong Zu	Wuhan University of Technology, China

Contents – Part I

Collaborative Mechanisms, Models, Approaches, Algorithms and Systems

Contents – Part II

Crowd Intelligence and Crowd Cooperative Computing

Cooperative Evolutionary Computation and Human-Like Intelligent Collaboration

Domain-Specific Collaborative Applications

Social Media and Online Communities

Multi-step Ahead PM2.5 Prediction Based on Hybrid Machine Learning Techniques

Yulin Wang[1], Junying Yuan[2(✉)], Yiwu Xu[1], and Yun Chen[2]

[1] Guangzhou Institute of Science and Technology, Guangzhou, China
[2] Nanfang College Guangzhou, Guangzhou, China
cihisa@outlook.com

Abstract. In order to improve the accuracy of short-term PM2.5 prediction, we proposed a new hybrid solution that combines several machine learning techniques. Firstly, a set of phase space features are obtained from PM2.5 historical data based on PSR technique and combined with numerical weather prediction (NWP) data to construct a pool of candidate features. Secondly, the optimal feature subset is selected and input to the multi-step ahead prediction model based on the RReliefF feature selection algorithm. Then, K-means clustering is used to divide the input instances into a number of subsets to train ANFIS. Finally, the particle swarm optimization (PSO) algorithm is used to optimize the ANFIS network's parameters. In order to verify the effectiveness of the proposed method, two benchmark models (PSR-FS, PCA-FS) were established to compare with the hybrid model. The experimental results showed that the hybrid solution obtained the best prediction performance in short-term PM2.5 prediction.

Keywords: PM2.5 prediction · Multi-step ahead prediction · Machine learning · Hybrid model · Benchmark model

1 Introduction

PM2.5 refers to particulate matter in the atmosphere with a diameter less than or equal to 2.5 μ, which is one of the air pollutants and is harmful to humans. Therefore, there is a need for accurate monitoring and prediction of PM2.5 pollution. Due to the nonlinearity and instability of PM2.5 data, accurate prediction on different time scales (daily and hourly) and timely reporting to air quality management department is required. Short-term PM2.5 prediction a few hours in advance can provide strong support to the relevant departments for PM2.5 control.

In recent years, researchers have investigated short-term PM2.5 prediction from different perspectives, and classifying short-term PM2.5 predictions into following 3 categories: (1) Physical-based methods [1–3], focus on modeling using meteorological and geographic information, which can usually perform well over a longer range. (2) Statistical-based methods [4–6], which are based on historical data to identify internal patterns and trends in order to derive prediction results. (3) Machine learning-based

© The Author(s), under exclusive license to Springer Nature Singapore Pte Ltd. 2023
Y. Sun et al. (Eds.): ChineseCSCW 2022, CCIS 1681, pp. 3–16, 2023.
https://doi.org/10.1007/978-981-99-2356-4_1

methods [7–9] are mainly supervised learning models. However, the prediction accuracy of these models needs further improvement.

In recent years, the feature selection and analysis of PM2.5 prediction models based on machine learning have received much attention.

The prediction accuracy of the model can be improved by feeding the information obtained from PM2.5 historical data into the supervised model. For example, Jin [10] et al. used wavelet decomposition (WD) to preprocess PM2.5 data, trained a gated recursive unit (GRU) network by using the decomposition results and used the network to predict PM2.5. Teng [11] et al. combined empirical modal decomposition (EMD) method, sample entropy (SE), and bidirectional long and short-term memory neural network (Bi-LSTM) to construct a novel hybrid prediction model to predict PM2.5 concentrations in the future 1–24 h. Qin [12] et al. used the ensemble empirical modal decomposition (EEMD) for Beijing PM2.5 data and constructed support vector regression (SVR) models for prediction based on the decomposed subseries.

In addition, numerical weather prediction (NWP) data (including humidity, wind direction, atmospheric pressure, temperature, wind speed, etc.) can also be used as input variables for supervised models. It is important to note that unrelated and superfluous variables reduce the accuracy as the dimension of the input variables increases. Therefore, suitable variables need to be selected by feature selection methods. The commonly used feature selection methods mainly include filtering methods, packing methods and embedded methods. Filtering methods rank input variables based on relevance and select the top-ranked input variables to train the model and improve its predictive ability. Packing methods use prediction models to score subsets of input variables. The embedded methods are similar to the packing methods, except that it optimizes the objective function of the prediction model. In this paper, the filtering methods are chosen for feature selection, which have low computational complexity and are not prone to over-fitting.

As far as the authors know, few currently available PM2.5 prediction methods can improve the accuracy of prediction models by selecting appropriate variables while fully considering the usable information (e.g., PM2.5 historical data and NWP data). Therefore, this paper proposed a new hybrid prediction method that considers both PM2.5 historical data and NWP data and uses a filtering method to select the optimal features to train the prediction model. The basic idea of the proposed model is shown in Fig. 1.

First, the nonlinearity and instability features of the original PM2.5 data were identified and processed by using the phase space reconstruction (PSR) technique, and these features were combined with NWP data to construct a candidate feature pool; Then the most suitable features were selected from the candidate feature pool according to the RReliefF algorithm, and the instances of these features were K-means clustered to obtain subsets of different categories, which were input into the ANFIS model for training, and the particle swarm optimization (PSO) is used to optimize the model; Finally, the model is used to predict the PM2.5 concentration in the future 1–24 h.

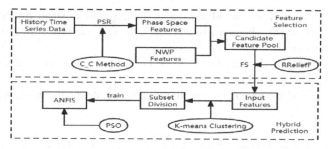

Fig. 1. Basic idea of the proposed model.

2   Feature Selection

For multi-step prediction of PM2.5, a univariate historical data of PM2.5 is known, and
the features required for the model need to be selected during modeling, i.e., feature
selection. As the chaotic characteristic of the PM2.5 historical data, its correlation with
future PM2.5 concentrations decays rapidly with increasing prediction time steps, which
leads to a decrease in prediction performance. Therefore, both PM2.5 historical data and
NWP data need to be used as features. The purpose of introducing NWP data is to provide auxiliary information for PM2.5 prediction, such as wind humidity, wind direction,
atmospheric pressure, temperature, wind speed. For different steps of prediction, these
features have different effects on the prediction objectives. Therefore, the feature selection is divided into two stages. First, the initial features are selected from the PM2.5
historical data based PSR method, and the initial features are further combined with the
NWP data to construct the candidate feature pool. Second, the optimal input variables
are filtered from the candidate feature pool based on the RReliefF algorithm.

2.1   Candidate Feature Pool Construction Based on PSR Method and NWP Data

PM2.5 as a complex spatio-temporal object is a typical chaotic time series.PSR is an
valid tool to analyze the dynamic patterns of chaotic data. Therefore, this paper used the
PSR method to identify and process the nonlinearity and instability of PM2.5 data. The
basic idea of PSR is to expand the one-dimensional data into a high-dimensional space,
so as to mine the effective information in the original data. Its key is to determine the
delay time τ and the embedding dimension m, which determine the similarity degree of
the phase space and the size of the chaotic attractor to obtain the most streamlined data
structure and the best kinetic information of PM2.5, i.e., the initial features.

There are two views on the determination of the above two parameters. The first view
is to assume that the two parameters are uncorrelated and independent of each other,
and to calculate the values of the two parameters separately. The delay time τ_d can be
calculated by auto correlation function, multiple auto correlation, mutual information,
etc. The embedding dimension m can be calculated by G-P algorithm or pseudo-nearest
neighbor algorithm. The second view is to assume that the two parameters are interdependent, so that the delay time τ_d and the embedding dimension m are calculated along
with the delay time window $\tau_\omega = (m - 1)\tau d$. The C_C method can calculate the delay

time window τ_ω, and it has the advantages of easy operation, small computation and noise immunity [13, 14]. Therefore, in this paper, the C_C method is used to determine these two parameters.

The C_C method is described as follows: For a time series $\{x(t)\}$ of length N, its phase space is reconstructed as: $\{x(i)\}(i = 1, 2, ..., M)$, $M = N - (m - 1)\tau_d$, where the time delay is τ_d and the reconstruction dimension is m, define the correlation integral as:

$$C(m, N, r, t) = \frac{2}{M(M-1)} \sum_{1 \le i \le j \le M} \theta(r - d_{ij}), r > 0 \tag{1}$$

where d_{ij} is the Euclidean distance between vectors, $d_{ij} = \|X_i - X_j\|$; Heavisible function $\theta(x) = 0(x < 0)$ or $1(x \ge 0)$, and r is the radius of the time series. The time series $\{x(t)\}$ is divided into t mutually non-overlapping sub-sequences, i.e.:

$$\begin{aligned} x_1 &= \{x(1), x(t+1), ..., x(N-t+1)\} \\ x_2 &= \{x(2), x(t+2), ..., x(N-t+2)\} \\ &... \\ x_t &= \{x(t), x(2t), ..., x(N)\} \end{aligned} \tag{2}$$

Define the test statistic of the sub-sequence as:

$$S(m, r, t) = \frac{1}{t} \sum_{s=1}^{t} [C_s(m, r, t) - C_s^m(1, r, t)], m = 2, 3, ... \tag{3}$$

According to the BDS statistical findings, the C_C method mainly calculates the values of the following 3 statistics:

$$\overline{S}(t) = \sum_{m=2}^{5} \sum_{j=1}^{4} S(m, r_j, t) \tag{4}$$

$$\Delta\overline{S}(t) = \frac{1}{4} \sum_{m=2}^{5} \Delta S(m, t) \tag{5}$$

$$S_{cor} = \Delta\overline{S}(t) + |\overline{S}(t)| \tag{6}$$

where $r_j = j\sigma/2$, σ is taken as the standard deviations of the time series, and the value of $S(m, r, t)$ is estimated using Eq. (3).

$$\Delta S(m, t) = \max\{S(m, r_j, t)\} - \min\{S(m, r_j, t)\} \tag{7}$$

After the calculation, then the optimal τ_d takes the first local minima of $\Delta S(t) \sim t$ and the optimal τ_ω takes the global minima of $Scor(t) \sim t$. In addition, the embedding dimension m can be obtained by the following equation:

$$m = \tau_\omega / \tau_d + 1 \tag{8}$$

The initial features associated with the PM2.5 historical data are obtained by estimating the delay time τ_d and the embedding dimension m by the C_C method:

Initial_Features$_{PM2.5}$(t) = [x(t), x(t − τ_d), ..., x(t − (m − 1)τ_d)], where x(t) is the PM2.5 concentration value observed at the current moment t.

The initial input variables associated with the NWP data are:

$$Initial_{Features_{NWP}}(t) = [W_S(t), W_D(t), T(t), H(t), P(t)] \tag{9}$$

where $W_S(t)$, $W_D(t)$, $T(t)$, $H(t)$, $P(t)$ denotes the values of NWP (wind speed, wind direction, temperature, humidity, and atmosphere pressure) at the moment t, respectively. Therefore, the candidate feature pool constructed based on PSR and NWP is: Candidate_Features = [Initial_Features$_{PM2.5}$(t), Initial_Features$_{NWP}$(t)] and the dimension of the candidate feature pool: |Candidate_Features| = m + 5.

2.2 Optimal Feature Selection Based on RReliefF Algorithm

In general, well-chosen features input to the model can actively improve the performance of the model. The RReliefF algorithm is a feature selection algorithm with good performance and is mainly used to solve regression problems. RReliefF algorithm is an extension of the Relief algorithm that is more powerful and can handle incomplete and noisy data [15]. RReliefF algorithm provides information about the attribute quality. Assume that W[A] is the quality of attribute A, which is an approximation of the following Bayesian rule:

$$W[A] = \frac{P_{diffC|diffA}P_{diffA}}{P_{diffC}} - \frac{(1 - P_{diffC|diffA})P_{diffA}}{1 - P_{diffC}} \tag{10}$$

W[A] can be calculated directly using the probabilities of the predicted values of two different instances, P_{diffA}, P_{diffC} and $P_{diffC|diffA}$ defined as follows:

$$P_{diffA} = P(different\ value\ of\ A|nearest\ instances) \tag{11}$$

$$P_{diffC} = P(different\ prediction|nearest\ instances) \tag{12}$$

$$P_{diffC|diffA} = P(different\ value\ of\ A|different\ value\ of\ A\ and\ nearest\ instances) \tag{13}$$

The main idea of RReliefF algorithm is that some instances are randomly selected from the training data, and then k sets of the same type are obtained by searching the nearest neighbors. Finally, the weight value of each feature is obtained and ranked. The feature with the highest weight value is selected to train the prediction model.

Therefore, in this paper, the feature selection based on RReliefF algorithm ranks the priority of all the features in the candidate feature pool and selects different numbers of top-ranked features to train the model, and based on the training results of the model, the optimal number of final features can be determined.

3 The Proposed Hybrid Prediction Model

In this paper, a hybrid method combining K-means clustering, PSO and ANFIS is applied to the prediction model.

3.1 Subset Division Based on K-means Clustering Algorithm

The K-means clustering algorithm is a division-based unsupervised learning method that is widely used in business and scientific research for its practical, simple and efficient features. It can divide the input data set into different classes of subsets, while the same class of data has similar features. Inputting these same type of data into the model for training can significantly reduce the complexity of model training.

The basic steps of the K-means clustering algorithm are as follows [16]:

(1) Data preprocessing: Normalize the data in the input data set D into the space of [0, 1] to obtain n data points p1, p2, ..., pn;
(2) Initialization: The number of clusters k is chosen, and k points c1, c2, ..., ck, as initial cluster centroids, are randomly selected from the n data points.
(3) Divide the clusters and calculate the Euclidean distance dist between each data point p1, p2, ..., pn and centroids c1, c2, ..., ck, the data points are divided into the nearest centroid clusters set S1, S2, ..., Sk; The Euclidean distance dist between data object p (with m-dimensional attributes) and the i-th($1 \leq i \leq k$) centroid of the cluster is computed as:

$$dist(c_i, p) = \sqrt{\sum_{j=1}^{m} (c_{ij} - p_j)^2} \tag{14}$$

(4) Update the cluster centroids: Calculate the mean value of data points in each cluster set Si($1 \leq i \leq k$) as:

$$c'_i = \frac{sum}{num} = \frac{\sum_{p \in S_i} p}{|S_i|} \tag{15}$$

Update the mean c'_i to the new cluster centroid of the K-means clustering algorithm and calculate the Sum of Squares Due to Error (SSE) for each cluster:

$$SSE = \sum_{i=1}^{k} \sum_{p \in S_i} (dist(c'_i, p))^2 \tag{16}$$

(5) The algorithm ends with the judgment that if the number of iterations reaches the set upper limit or the objective function SSE converges, the clustering centroid is returned and the clustering results are output; Otherwise, it returns to steps 3 to 5.

During the training process, the clustering results are used to train the ANFIS network model, thus helping to determine the parameters of the ANFIS network model. In the prediction process, the data vector closest to the center of the clustering is fed into the model for prediction.

3.2 Optimization of ANFIS Network Model Based on PSO Algorithm

ANFIS combines the ability of fuzzy systems to simulate inference processes and handle uncertainty with the learning ability and adaptability of neural networks, and compared to traditional machine learning algorithms, ANFIS is able to approximate nonlinear functions with arbitrary accuracy and is agile and efficient, without problems such as hyperparameters and kernel function selection [17].

Assume that x and y are the inputs and z is the output. For the 1st-order Sugeno fuzzy model (p, q, and r are constant parameters), with the following 2 fuzzy rules.

(1) if x is A1 and y is B1 then z1 $= $ p1*x $+ $ q1*y $+ $ r1.
(2) if x is A2 and y is B2 then z2 $= $ p2*x $+ $ q2*y $+ $ r2.

The typical structure of the 1st-order ANFIS is shown in Fig. 2. The network structure in Fig. 2 is divided into 5 layers: fuzzification layer, rule layer, normalization layer, defuzzification layer and output layer. Here the output of the i-th node in layer 1 (fuzzification layer) is denoted as $O_{1,i}$.

Layer 1: Each node i is an adaptive node in this layer and the output is given by the following equation:

$$O_{1,i} = \begin{cases} \mu_{A_i}(x), i = 1, 2 \\ \mu_{B_{i-2}}(y), i = 3, 4 \end{cases} \tag{17}$$

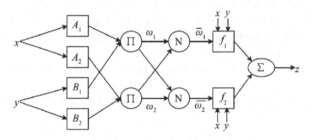

Fig. 2. Typical structure of ANFIS.

where μ is the affiliation function of ANFIS. The affiliation function has Gaussian type function, triangular function, trapezoidal function and bell-shaped function, and the Gaussian type function is usually selected as shown in the following equation:

$$\mu_A(x) = \exp\left\{-\left[\left(\frac{x - c_i}{a_i}\right)^2\right]^{b_i}\right\} \tag{18}$$

where a_i is the variance of the affiliation function; b_i is the trainable parameter; and c_i is the height of the affiliation function spikes.

Layer 2: Node i is a fixed node in this layer, marked as Π. Its output is the product of all input signals, which represents the excitation strength of a rule. The output of this layer is given by the following equation:

$$O_{2,i} = \omega_i = \mu_{A_i}(x)\mu_{B_i}(y), i = 1, 2 \tag{19}$$

Layer 3: Node i is a fixed node, marked as N. This layer is a normalization of the individual rule adaptations.

$$O_{3,i} = \overline{\omega}_i = \frac{\omega_i}{\omega_1 + \omega_2}, i = 1, 2 \tag{20}$$

Layer 4: The nodes in this layer are adaptive nodes, and each node corresponds to a fuzzy rule.

$$O_{4,i} = \overline{\omega}_i f_i = \overline{\omega}_i (p_i x + q_i y + r_i), i = 1, 2 \tag{21}$$

Layer 5: The nodes in this layer are fixed nodes, marked as Σ, which calculate the sum of all incoming signals as the final output.

$$O_{5,i} = \sum_i \overline{\omega}_i f_i = \frac{\sum_i \omega_i f_i}{\sum_i \omega_i} \tag{22}$$

In this paper, we use the ANFIS method to fit the training set, construct a prediction model, and use the PSO algorithm to heuristically optimize the ANFIS network parameters to improve the prediction accuracy of the model. The PSO algorithm, developed by Eberhart and Kennedy in 1995, was originally inspired by the regularity of flocking activity of birds of prey, which in turn led to a simplified model using group intelligence [18]. The PSO algorithm is described as a search for a spatial distribution of n particles in e-dimensional space, with the velocity and position of the i-th particle described as: $V_i = \{v_{i,1}, v_{i,2}, ..., v_{i,e}\}$ and $X_i = \{x_{i,1}, x_{i,2}, ..., x_{i,e}\}$.

The updated equations for the velocity and position of the particle are:

$$v_{i,j}(t+1) = \rho v_{i,j}(t) + c_1 r_1 \lfloor p_{besti} - x_{i,j}(t) \rfloor + c_2 r_2 \lfloor g_{besti} - x_{i,j}(t) \rfloor \tag{23}$$

$$x_i(t+1) = x_i(t) + v_i(t+1) \tag{24}$$

where ρ is the inertia weight; c_1 and c_2 are particle accelerations; r_1 and r_2 are random vectors; p_{besti} is the current particle local optimum; and g_{besti} is the global optimum.

4   Analysis of Results

To validate the reliability of the proposed method, this paper uses the PM2.5 and NWP datasets of Beijing with a time interval of 1 h (e.g., 24 observations per day). The dataset is divided into two non-overlapping parts. The first part is the dataset for the whole year of 2019, which is used for input variable selection and prediction model training. The second part is the dataset for the whole year of 2020 and is used for testing the prediction model. The proposed method is implemented in the PyCharm programming environment.

4.1   Feature Selection Analysis

Using PM2.5 historical data, the PSO parameters τ_d and m were determined by the C_C method, and the curves of $\Delta S(t) \sim t$ and $Scor(t) \sim t$ were plotted, as shown in Fig. 3.

As can be seen from Fig. 3, the optimal delay time is taken as the first local minima of the curve $\Delta S(t) \sim t$, i.e., $\tau_d = 3$ h.

The optimal delay time window is taken as the global minimum of curve $Scor(t) \sim t$, i.e., $\tau_\omega = 12$ h. From this, the delay time $\tau_d = 3$ h and the embedding dimension m = 5 can be determined.

The initial input variables associated with the PM2.5 historical data can be obtained based on the reconstructed parameters obtained by the C_C method. Assuming that the current moment is t, Then the initial input variables associated with the PM2.5 historical data are:$Initial\_Features_{PM2.5}(t) = [x(t), x(t - 3), x(t - 6), x(t - 9), x(t - 12)]$, where $x(t)$ is the observed value of PM2.5 at moment t. The set can be simplified to: {His1, His2, His3, His4, His5}. Meanwhile, the initial variables associated with the NWP data is: $Initial\_Features_{NWP}(t) = [W_S(t), W_D(t), T(t), H(t), P(t)]$, and the set can be simplified to: {Wind$_V$, Wind$_D$, Temp, Hum, ATP}; Therefore, the final candidate feature pool can be obtained as: {His1, His2, His3, His4, His5, Wind$_V$, Wind$_D$, Temp, Hum, ATP}.

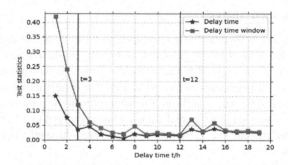

Fig. 3.   Calculation of delay time and embedding dimension by C-C method.

Then, the features in the candidate feature pool are ranked by the RReliefF algorithm, and different number of features are selected to train the model, and the error trend plot of the prediction models in different time range (6 h, 12 h, 18 h and 24 h ahead) are obtained, as shown in Fig. 4.

As can be seen from Fig. 4, when the model accuracy no longer grows or grows very slowly, this paper considers that adding further features does not improve the prediction accuracy of the model to obtain the optimal number of feature selection. Since the model have different prediction steps, the number of feature selection may change with different prediction steps.

Table 1 shows the detailed ranking and selected number of the candidate features pool in different prediction steps.

As can be seen from Table 1, the ranking of features belonging to the same time range is similar, and humidity, wind direction, and temperature are ranked the highest, historical data are in the middle, and wind speed and atmospheric pressure are ranked

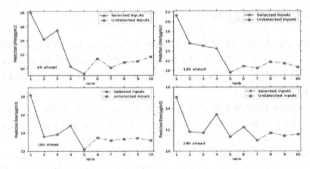

Fig. 4. Calculation of delay time and embedding dimension by C-C method.

last in all the prediction steps. For the different prediction step, the candidate feature pool is first ranked, and then the different number of top-ranked features are input into the model for training, and an optimal subset of features is selected according to the prediction accuracy of the model, thus effectively reducing the input dimension and interference information.

4.2 Feature Selection Analysis

The features selected in the training set are used to train the above hybrid prediction model, and then the trained model is used to obtain the prediction results in different time ranges (6 h, 12 h, 18 h and 24 h Ahead) on the test set, as shown in Fig. 5. Figure 5 shows the graph of the prediction results of the model in different time ranges.

From Fig. 5, it can be seen that the prediction curves of the proposed hybrid model in the range of 6 h is closer to the actual value curves compared to 12 h, 18 h and 24 h. It can be concluded that the hybrid model has a good prediction effect in the short-term PM2.5 prediction.

To evaluate the effectiveness and accuracy of the proposed hybrid prediction model, three performance metrics, such as MAE, RMSE, and MAPE, are used, as shown in Eq. (25), (26), and (27).

$$MAE = \frac{1}{N} \sum_{i=1}^{N} |(y_i - \hat{y}_i)| \tag{25}$$

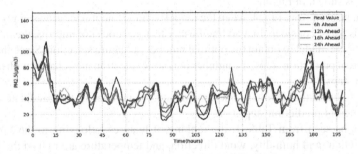

Fig. 5. Prediction results of the model at different time ranges.

Table 1. Detailed ranking and selected number of candidate feature pool in different prediction steps.

Steps	Ranked Features	num
1-step	Hum, His5, Wind$_D$, Temp, His3, His4, His1, Wind$_V$, His2, ATP	5
2-step	Hum, Temp, Wind$_D$, His5, His3, His4, His1, His2, Wind$_V$, ATP	6
3-step	Hum, Wind$_D$, Temp, His5, His4, His3, His1, His2, Wind$_V$, ATP	5
4-step	Hum, Wind$_D$, Temp, His5, His4, His3, His1, His2, Wind$_V$, ATP	5
5-step	Hum, Wind$_D$, Temp, His5, His4, His3, His1, His2, Wind$_V$, ATP	6
6-step	Hum, Wind$_D$, Temp, His4, His5, His3, His1, His2, Wind$_V$, ATP	5
7-step	Hum, Wind$_D$, Temp, His4, His5, His3, His2, His1, Wind$_V$, ATP	6
8-step	Hum, Wind$_D$, Temp, His4, His5, His2, His3, His1, Wind$_V$, ATP	6
9-step	Hum, Wind$_D$, Temp, His4, His5, His2, His3, His1, Wind$_V$, ATP	6
10-step	Hum, Wind$_D$, Temp, His4, His5, His2, His3, His1, Wind$_V$, ATP	5
11-step	Hum, Wind$_D$, Temp, His4, His5, His2, His3, His1, Wind$_V$, ATP	5
12-step	Hum, Wind$_D$, Temp, His4, His5, His2, His3, His1, Wind$_V$, ATP	5
13-step	Hum, Wind$_D$, Temp, His4, His5, His2, His1, His3, Wind$_V$, ATP	6
14-step	Hum, Wind$_D$, Temp, His4, His5, His2, His3, His1, Wind$_V$, ATP	6
15-step	Hum, Wind$_D$, Temp, His4, His5, His2, His3, His1, Wind$_V$, ATP	6
16-step	Hum, Wind$_D$, Temp, His4, His5, His3, His2, His1, Wind$_V$, ATP	6
17-step	Hum, Wind$_D$, Temp, His4, His5, His3, His1, His2, Wind$_V$, ATP	5
18-step	Hum, Wind$_D$, Temp, His4, His5, His3, His1, His2, Wind$_V$, ATP	5
19-step	Hum, Wind$_D$, Temp, His5, His4, His1, His3, His2, Wind$_V$, ATP	6
20-step	Hum, Wind$_D$, Temp, His5, His3, His4, His1, His2, Wind$_V$, ATP	7
21-step	Hum, Wind$_D$, Temp, His5, His1, His3, His4, His2, Wind$_V$, ATP	6
22-step	Hum, Wind$_D$, Temp, His5, His1, His3, His4, His2, Wind$_V$, ATP	6
23-step	Hum, Wind$_D$, Temp, His1, His5, His3, His4, His2, Wind$_V$, ATP	6
24-step	Hum, Wind$_D$, Temp, His4, His5, His2, His3, His1, Wind$_V$, ATP	7

$$RMSE = \sqrt{\frac{1}{N} \sum_{i=1}^{N} \left| (y_i - \hat{y}_i) \right|^2} \tag{26}$$

$$MAPE = \frac{1}{N} \sum_{i=1}^{N} \left| \frac{y_i - \hat{y}_i}{y_i} \right| \times 100\% \tag{27}$$

In order to evaluate the effectiveness of the proposed FS method based on the RReliefF algorithm, i.e., the RReliefF-FS model, two benchmark models for feature selection were constructed separately for comparative analysis, i.e., the PSR-based feature selection (PSR-FS) model and the PCA-based feature selection (PCA-FS) model. For the PSR-FS model, the selected features include all the PSR variables obtained by the C_C method and all the NWP variables, i.e., all the variables in the candidate feature pool, without further selection. For the PCA-FS model, the selected features are mainly the variables obtained from the candidate feature pool based on principal component analysis. Some multi-step hybrid prediction models are constructed to perform prediction based on these three feature selection methods, respectively.

The performance of the models based on these three feature selection methods was evaluated using the three performance metrics (MAE, RMSE, and MAPE) described above. Table 2 shows the comparison of the multi-step prediction performance of the different models.

Table 2. Multi-step prediction errors of different models.

Steps	RReliefF-FS			PSR-FS			PCA-FS		
	MAE	RMSE	MAPE	MAE	RMSE	MAPE	MAE	RMSE	MAPE
1-step	1.6	1.2	2.7	12.5	10.3	43.3	1.7	1.3	3.2
2-step	2.6	1.8	3.9	11.6	9.2	29.7	3.5	3.0	7.4
3-step	3.9	2.9	6.7	11.8	9.0	23.8	4.6	3.7	8.6
4-step	4.2	3.1	6.8	11.5	8.6	19.7	6.1	4.8	10.7
5-step	5.6	4.4	10.1	11.6	8.4	20.1	6.6	5.2	12.1
6-step	6.8	5.1	11.4	11.8	8.4	20.0	7.6	5.7	13.2
7-step	9.4	7.3	17.7	11.8	8.6	21.4	8.5	6.5	15.3
8-step	10.2	8.0	18.3	12.3	9.0	20.4	8.6	6.2	14.9
9-step	11.0	8.9	20.4	12.4	8.8	21.9	10.4	8.1	18.3
10-step	12.7	9.3	22.3	12.2	8.7	21.5	10.0	7.5	17.8
11-step	12.8	9.5	23.1	12.9	9.3	23.0	9.9	7.4	17.3
12-step	12.9	9.7	23.4	13.2	9.6	23.9	10.8	8.2	19.4
13-step	13.2	9.9	24.1	13.1	9.6	24.1	10.9	8.3	19.5
14-step	13.2	10.1	26.3	13.6	9.9	24.9	12.3	9.7	23.3
15-step	13.3	10.6	26.9	13.8	10.1	25.5	16.7	13.5	33.9
16-step	14.2	10.7	27.2	14.1	10.5	26.6	10.9	8.0	17.7
17-step	14.4	10.9	27.8	12.6	9.5	21.9	11.1	8.0	17.7
18-step	14.8	11.1	28.5	13.7	9.9	24.4	13.4	10.0	25.0
19-step	14.9	11.1	29.4	13.6	9.7	23.8	13.4	9.9	24.4
20-step	15.0	11.6	29.9	12.2	8.8	20.0	12.3	9.0	21.1
21-step	15.1	11.7	30.1	12.1	9.0	19.8	12.5	9.1	22.5
22-step	15.6	12.1	34.1	12.5	8.9	20.6	12.9	9.4	23.7
23-step	16.0	12.2	40.6	12.6	9.4	21.0	11.5	8.7	20.2
24-step	16.6	12.5	40.9	13.0	9.6	21.9	12.5	9.1	21.8

As shown in Table 2, the prediction errors based on the proposed method at 1–6 steps are the smallest compared to both benchmark models. This indicates that the proposed method has excellent performance in PM2.5 short-term prediction. Overall, firstly, the prediction error of the RReliefF-FS method increases with the increase of the prediction step, where the lowest value is the 1-step prediction with the values of MAE, RMSE and MAPE of 1.56, 1.2 and 2.7%, respectively. Secondly, the overall variation of the prediction error based on the PSR-FS method is not significant, where the lowest value is for the 2-step prediction with the values of MAE, RMSE and MAPE of 11.5, 8.6 and 19.7%, respectively, where the highest value is for the 16-step prediction with the values of MAE, RMSE and MAPE of 14.1, 10.5 and 26.6%. Finally, the prediction error based on the PCA-FS method also increases with the increase of the prediction step, where the lowest value is the 1-step prediction with the values of MAE, RMSE, and MAPE of 1.7, 1.3, and 3.2, respectively. Therefore, the proposed method has better performance than the benchmark model in the short-term prediction of PM2.5.

For a more visual comparison, Fig. 6 shows the curve trends of MAE, RMSE, and MAPE for the multi-step prediction models based on different feature selection methods.

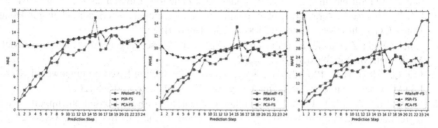

Fig. 6. Error trend of multi-step prediction models based on different feature selection methods.

As shown in Fig. 6, there are fluctuations in the curves of both benchmark models, especially in the medium-length prediction phase, while in the proposed model, the error trend increases smoothly, and the error values of the 1–6 step prediction are smaller than those of the other benchmark models, indicating that the RReliefF-FS model can effectively select appropriate features in PM2.5 short-term prediction, showing better adaptability and robustness.

5 Conclusion

In this paper, a new multi-step ahead prediction algorithm for PM2.5 based on hybrid machine learning techniques is proposed. First, the PSR method and the RReliefF algorithm are used for FS. Secondly, K-means clustering is used to divide the input instances into a number of subsets to train ANFIS, and finally, the PSO algorithm is used to optimize the parameters of the ANFIS network. The proposed method is extensively evaluated and validated by building two benchmark models for comparative analysis. The experimental results show that the proposed model is superior in short-term prediction.

The model is generalized and the accuracy of the model in medium- and long-term forecasting needs to be improved, and future work needs to be improved in these two areas.

Acknowledgments. This work is supported in part by Guangdong Province Key Construction Discipline Scientific Research Ability Promotion Project unser grant 2021ZDJS132, and in part by Guangdong Innovative Projects with Characteristics in Colleges and Universities under grants 2019KTSCX228 and 2021ZDZX4048.

References

1. Byun, D., Schere, K.L.: Review of the governing equations, computational algorithms, and other components of the models-3 community multiscale air quality (CMAQ) modeling system. Appl. Mech. Rev. **59**(2), 51–77 (2006)
2. Konopka, P., Groo, J.U., Günther, G.: Annual cycle of ozone at and above the tropical tropopause: observations versus simulations with the Chemical Lagrangian Model of the Stratosphere (CLa MS). Atmos. Chem. Phys. **10**(1), 121–132 (2010)
3. Lee, H.M., Park, R.J., Henze, D.K.: PM2.5 source attribution for Seoul in May from 2009 to 2013 using GEOS-Chem and its adjoint model. Environ. Pollut. **221**(1), 377–384 (2017)
4. Hu, Y.-S., Duan, H.-M.: Study on PM_(2.5) dispersion and prediction based on Gaussian plume and multiple linear regression model. Arid Zone Res. Environ. **29**(6), 86–92 (2016)
5. Liu, T.: Time series forecasting of air quality based on regional numerical modeling in Hong Kong. J. Geophys. Res. Atmos. **123**(8), 4175–4196 (2018)
6. Lili, L., Xuan, Z., Du, M.: Research on PM2.5 prediction based on generalized additive model. Math. Stat. Manag. **39**(5), 811–823 (2020)
7. Liu, Q., Chen, H.Y.: PM_(2.5) mass concentration prediction based on empowered KNN-LSTM model. J. Hefei Univ. Technol. Nat. Sci. Ed. **44**(12), 1690–1698 (2021)
8. Li, X., Luo, A., Li, J., Li, Y.: Air pollutant concentration forecast based on support vector regression and quantum-behaved particle swarm optimization. Environ. Model. Assess. **24**(2), 205–222 (2018). https://doi.org/10.1007/s10666-018-9633-3
9. Jing, L.A.: Estimation of monthly 1 km resolution PM 2.5 concentrations using a random forest model over "2+26" cities, China. Urban Clim. **35**(1), 95–109 (2021)
10. Jin, X.B., Zhang, J.F., Wang, S.Y.: Wavelet decomposition-based PM2.5 deep mixing prediction model. In: 31st China Process Control Conference (CPCC2020), Suzhou, China, vol. 63, pp. 1–9 (2021)
11. Teng, M., Li, S., Xing, J.: 24-Hour prediction of PM2.5 concentrations by combining empirical mode decomposition and bidirectional long short-term memory neural network. Sci. Total Environ. **821**, 153276 (2022)
12. Qin, X.W.: PM2.5 prediction in Beijing based on overall empirical modal decomposition and support vector regression. J. Jilin University (Earth Sci. Ed.) **46**(2), 563–568 (2016)
13. Lu, Z.-B., Cai, Z.-M., Jiang, K.-Y.: Parameter selection for phase space reconstruction based on improved C-C method. J. Syst. Simul. **19**(11), 2527–2538 (2007)
14. Kim, H.S., Eykholt, R., Salas, J.D.: Nonlinear dynamics, delay times, and embedding windows. Physica D **127**(1–2), 48–60 (1999)
15. Wu, J.H.: Complex network link classification based on RReliefF feature selection algorithm. Comput. Eng. **43**(8), 208–214 (2017)
16. Yuting, K., Fuxiang, T., Xin, Z.: A review of K-means algorithm optimization research based on differential privacy. Comput. Sci. **49**(2), 162–173 (2022)
17. Jang, J.-S.R.: ANFIS: adaptive- network- based fuzzy inference system. IEEE Trans. Syst. Man Cybern. **23**(4), 665–685 (1993)
18. Bai, D.D., He, J.H., Wang, X.J.: Adaptive particle swarm support vector machine wind speed combined forecasting model. Acta energiae solaris sinica **36**(4), 792–797 (2015)

A Joint Framework for Knowledge Extraction from Flight Training Comments

Yuxuan Zhang[1,2], Jiaxing Shang[1,2(✉)], Linjiang Zheng[1,2], Quanwang Wu[1,2], Weiwei Cao[3], and Hong Sun[4]

[1] College of Computer Science, Chongqing University, Chongqing, China
shangjx@cqu.edu.cn
[2] Key Laboratory of Dependable Service Computing in Cyber Physical Society, Ministry of Education, Chongqing University, Chongqing, China
{zlj_cqu,wqw}@cqu.edu.cn
[3] Key Laboratory of Flight Techniques and Flight Safety, Civil Aviation Flight University of China, Guanghan, China
ywcao@my.swjtu.edu.cn
[4] Flight Technology and Flight Safety Research Base, Civil Aviation Flight University of China, Guanghan, China

Abstract. The flight training comments are textual evaluation from the instructor to the flight training students. Extracting the assessment experience and knowledge from the flight training comments can help improve the flight training level. To this end, a joint extraction framework is proposed in this paper. For the model input, we use an end-to-end grid tagging scheme as the decoding algorithm to extract aspect terms, opinion terms and opinion pairs simultaneously. Considering the continuity of terms, we propose WoBERT as encoder, which modifies the pre-trained word segmentation based on BERT, and realizes Chinese word segmentation at word-level granularity. We conduct extensive experiments on a real flight training comments dataset. The results show that the model with WoBERT as the encoder achieves the best performance with a F1-score of 0.647, which can be used for the task of knowledge extraction from the flight training comments.

Keywords: Flight training comments · Opinion pair extraction · Word granularity · Natural language processing · WoBERT

1 Introduction

Flight training comments are textual evaluations given by the instructor to the flight students during the flight assessment. Extracting the instructors' assessment experience and knowledge from the flight training comments can help improve the flight training level of students and provide support for a scientific, effective and comprehensive initial flight training assessment, which has important research value and practical significance.

© The Author(s), under exclusive license to Springer Nature Singapore Pte Ltd. 2023
Y. Sun et al. (Eds.): ChineseCSCW 2022, CCIS 1681, pp. 17–27, 2023.
https://doi.org/10.1007/978-981-99-2356-4_2

For the unstructured flight training data represented by instructor reviews, natural language processing techniques are needed to understand the assessment knowledge embedded in them. However, there has no research in this area being reported, and the more relevant ones are research on keyword extraction and fine-grained sentiment analysis. The existing research works mainly focus on commodity reviews, film and TV reviews, etc., and no research efforts were observed for reviews related to flight training.

Aspect-based sentiment analysis (ABSA) is an important research direction in sentiment analysis task, which has attracted great attention from both academia and industry. Based on the flight training comments that have strong domain specificity, this paper proposes an joint evaluation knowledge extraction framework for flight training comments. Firstly, we perform BIO (Beginning, Inside, Outside) tagging on the data to offer convenience to the decoding algorithm. Secondly, an improved BERT model is used as the underlying encoder for training. This improved BERT model can achieve word-level Chinese word separation at the pretraining granularity to make full use of the professionalism of flight training comments. In addition, similar to Wu et al. [12], considering that the traditional pipeline approach is prone to error propagation, the paper also uses an end-to-end grid tagging scheme as the decoding algorithm to extract aspect terms, opinion terms and opinion pairs at the same time.

2   Related Work

2.1   Keyword Extraction

In keyword extraction research, Gollapalli et al. [3] proposed a method to fuse expert knowledge to improve the accuracy of keyword extraction. Zhang et al. [15] proposed the MIKE keyword extraction method by integrating multidimensional heterogeneous information into a unified model. Papagiannopoulou et al. [7] proposed an unsupervised keyword extraction method based on local word embeddings to improve the quality of keyword extraction by training word embedding vectors on a single document. Florescu et al. [2] proposed SurfKE, a keyword extraction algorithm based on graph representation learning, considering the disadvantages of traditional methods that require manual feature extraction. Qiu et al. [9] proposed OEWE, an automatic keyword extraction method based on word embedding, for documents related to the field of earth sciences. Yang et al. [14] studied the keyword extraction problem on short Chinese texts and proposed an extraction model combining a BiLSTM neural network with attention. Jing et al. [6] proposed a joint ABSA model by introducing a dual encoder design, one focusing on the classification of opinion pairs and the other on sequence labeling, to improve the effectiveness and robustness of the model.

2.2   Aspect Based Sentiment Analysis

The pipeline approach firstly extracts evaluation objects in the text, and then extracts opinions based on the aspects. Hu et al. [5] used association mining to identify aspects and extract adjacent adjectives as opinions. Peng et al. [8] used a graph neural network to extract syntactic dependencies of the text while extracting opinions and sentiment polarity to construct connections between aspects and opinions.

However, the results of pipeline approaches depend heavily on the accuracy of evaluation object extraction and suffer from error propagation. In order to avoid the error propagation problem, recent studies have proposed the joint approach. The joint approach models the task uniformly and obtains aspect terms and opinion terms at once. Wang et al. [11] used coupled multi-layer attention to simultaneously extract aspects and opinions, with bidirectional propagation via interactive learning. Zhao et al. [16] proposed a span-based multi-task framework SpanMlt to jointly extract aspects and opinions, considering the disadvantages of sequence annotation methods that are difficult to extract in one-to-many and many-to-one situations. Wu et al. [12] designed a novel grid tagging method, GTS, which represents the task using a unified label, continuously updates the grid tagging in an iterative manner, and decodes the final grid tagging to obtain opinion pairs.

3 Model Architecture

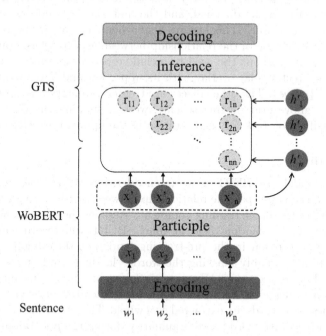

Fig. 1. Overview of the joint framework for evaluation knowledge extraction.

3.1   Task Definition

As mentioned above, the paper focuses on the OPE (Opinion Pair Extraction) task on flight training comments. Given a sentence $s = \{w_1, w_2, \cdots, w_n\}$, where w_i denotes the i-th word in the sentence and the total length of the sentence is n. We use a and o to denote aspect words and opinion words, s and e to denote the start index and end index of a complete word. The goal of the OPE task is to extract the set of opinion pairs from this sentence denoted as follows (Fig. 1):

$$Pair = (w_{as} : w_{ae}), (w_{os} : w_{oe}) \tag{1}$$

where ":" indicates all words from s to e.

3.2   Grid Tagging Scheme

For the design of model inputs, we utilize the grid tagging scheme proposed by Wu [12], and make some improvements based on it.

Specifically, four tags $\{A, O, P, N\}$ are used to denote the four categories of aspect terms, opinion terms, opinion pairs and null, respectively. The upper triangular matrix is used to represent the relationship between each word and the word pairs.

The use of labels is as follows: for A and O labels, compared to the original scheme, the model specifies that they do not appear in the interior of the upper triangle, but only on the diagonal, and the first and last indexes are $\{as, ae\}$ and $\{os, oe\}$, respectively. This ensures that when calculating is error, one can focus on the calculation of the relationship between aspect terms, opinion terms and opinion pairs without the need to include errors in unimportant places. P is marked as a rectangular overlay with its upper left and lower right points as $\{as, ae\}$ and $\{os, oe\}$. The other places are treated as empty and noted as N.

With the above grid tagging scheme, we can simplify the OTE task to a tagging classification task for each position in the upper triangular matrix.

3.3   Encoding

Most of the models use BERT [1] as an encoder, but BERT does not take into consideration the non-separable relationship between words during pre-training. For example, in the flight training comment "Assume the forced landing is not turned to the forced landing field in time", BERT will record each word in the sentence as a token in the pre-training, and then do random masking in the pre-training, probably masking the words "landing" and "forced" to train the relationship between them. However, in terms of sentence meaning, "forced landing" is a professional term, and even to extract the opinion pairs in the sentence, these two words are extracted as a whole. Therefore, the original BERT model was added with word-based granularity during the pre-training stage.

The implementation of the word-based granularity model mainly relies on the change of the tokenizer [10], in which the model customizes a special word separation "WoBertTokenizer" to replace the original "Tokenizer" method. Specifically, we first build a dictionary based on the specialist terms of flight training comments. For a given sentence s, we use Chinese word separation provided by Jieba to divide the words, and get the output word list $[w_1, w_2, \cdots, w_l]$, iterate through each w_i, if w_i in the word list, then keep it, otherwise use the original word splitting again, and finally the result of each w_i is stitched together in an orderly manner as the final word splitting result. The details of the word separation are shown in Algorithm 1.

Algorithm 1. Word granularity segmentation algorithm

Require:
    Flight training sentences S
Ensure:
    Result P
1: Initialize: Let $P \leftarrow \emptyset$
2: Input the sentence P
3: Pre-split the sentence to get the set $w = \{w_1, w_2, \cdots, w_n\}$
4: **for** each w_i in w **do**
5:    **if** $w_i \in Vocab$ **then**
6:       $P \leftarrow P \cup \{w_i\}$
7:    **else**
8:       $w_i \rightarrow w_{i1}, \cdot, w_{ij}$
9:       **for** each w_{ij} in w_i **do**
10:          $P \leftarrow P \cup \{w_{ij}\}$
11:       **end for**
12:    **end if**
13: **end for**
14: **return** P

3.4 Inference Strategy

As described in Sect. 3.2, there are certain constraint relationships between different opinion terms. Therefore, we add inference strategies after BERT to use these potential constraint relations to continuously and iteratively correct the model.

In the grid tagging scheme, there are three constraint relations: For position (i,j), if $i = j$, the only possible tag for the position is $\{A, O, N\}$, instead of P. Therefore, if the tag for the position is predicted to be P, we set it to N by default. If the token of position (i, i) is A, i.e., the word corresponding to this token is predicted to be an aspect term, then for any position (i, j) satisfying $j < i$, the corresponding tag can only be $\{P, N\}$, but not $\{A, O\}$. So if either A or O occurs in the tagged position of the prediction, we set it to N by default. And the previous prediction for the location (i, j) can be used to infer the tag for that location in the current round.

In summary, the inference strategy on the grid tagging scheme exploits these constraint relations by iterative prediction and inference. In the k-th round, the feature at position (i,j) is denoted as z_{ij}^k and its corresponding probability vector is p_{ij}^k, which are initialized as follows:

$$p_{ij}^0 = softmax(W_s r_{ij} + b_s) \tag{2}$$

$$z_{ij}^0 = r_{ij} \tag{3}$$

The specific calculations in the iterative are as follows:

$$p_i^{t-1} = maxpooling(p_{i,:}^{t-1}) \tag{4}$$

$$p_j^{t-1} = maxpooling(p_{j,:}^{t-1}) \tag{5}$$

$$q_{ij}^{t-1} = [z_{ij}^{t-1}; p_i^{t-1}; p_j^{t-1}; p_{ij}^{t-1}] \tag{6}$$

$$z_{ij}^t = W_q q_{ij}^{t-1} + b_q \tag{7}$$

$$p_{ij}^t = softmax(W_s z_{ij}^t + b_s) \tag{8}$$

where p_i^{t-1} denotes the vector consisting of the maximum probability values among the four labels corresponding to the i-th position and the other positions. Based on the three constraint relations mentioned above, the probability of tagging corresponding to position (i,j) is corrected in p_{ij}^t computed in continuous iterations. The predicted probability p_{ij}^T of the last round is used to obtain the index corresponding to the maximum probability value at each position (i,j), i.e., its most probable token r.

We calculate the cross-entropy loss value of the real distribution data and the label prediction data as the training loss, as shown in Eq. (9):

$$\mathcal{L} = -\sum_{i=1}^{n}\sum_{j=i}^{n}\sum_{k \in C} II(y_{ij} = k)log(p_{i,j|k}^L) \tag{9}$$

where y_{ij} represents the true labels of the word pairs (w_i, w_j), $II()$ is the indicator function and C denotes the set of tags as $\{A, O, P, N\}$.

3.5   Decoding

Through the above steps, the token prediction results for a given sentence in the grid tagging can be obtained. Then the opinion pair can be extracted directly by matching the tokens on the diagonal and strictly matching their corresponding matrix ranges. The extraction is found to be unsatisfactory through pre-experiments, and it is difficult to obtain the complete matrix to determine the opinion pairs when a sentence contains multiple opinion pairs in the comment. For this reason, a simple but effective scheme of relaxing the matching constraint to decode the opinion pairs is proposed by referring to Wu et al. [12]. The specific decoding details are shown in Algorithm 2.

Algorithm 2. Decoding Algorithm for OPE [12]
_____
Require:
    The tagging results $R_{n \times n}$
Ensure:
    Opinion pair set $\mathcal{P}$, i.e., $([as : ac], [os : oe])$
1: Initialize the aspect term set $\mathcal{A} = \emptyset$, the opinion term set $\mathcal{O} = \emptyset$, the opinion pair set $\mathcal{P} = \emptyset$
2: /* get the aspect term set and the opinion term set */
3: **while** get a span index range (l, n) **do**
4:    **if** $\forall l \leq i \leq r, R(i,i) = A$ and $R(l-1, l-1) \neq A$ and $R(r+1, r+1) \neq A$ **then**
5:      $\mathcal{A} \leftarrow \mathcal{A} \cup \{(l, r)\}$
6:    **end if**
7:    **if** $\forall l \leq i \leq r, R(i,i) = O$ and $R(l-1, l-1) \neq O$ and $R(r+1, r+1) \neq O$ **then**
8:      $\mathcal{O} \leftarrow \mathcal{O} \cup \{(l, r)\}$
9:    **end if**
10: **end while**
11: /* get the opinion pair set */
12: **while** $(as, ae) \in \mathcal{A}$ and $(os, oe) \in \mathcal{O}$ **do**
13:    Initialize $flag \leftarrow F$
14:    **for** each $as \leq i \leq ae$ **do**
15:      **for** each $os \leq j \leq oe$ **do**
16:        **if** $R(i, j) = P$ **then**
17:          $flag \leftarrow T$
18:        **end if**
19:      **end for**
20:    **end for**
21:    **if** $flag = T$ **then**
22:      $\mathcal{P} \leftarrow \mathcal{P} \cup \{([as, ae], [os, oe])\}$
23:    **end if**
24: **end while**
25: **return** $\mathcal{P}$

4 Experiment

4.1 Dataset

The data in this paper come from a large amount of flight training comments data accumulated by the Civil Aviation Flight Academy of China, which contains the information of instructor comments for a total of 208 trainees from 2015 to 2020. Firstly, with the help of a developed tagging tool, the comment data were tagged with the required labels for the model. We randomly split the dataset into the ratio of 6:1.5:2.5 as training, validation and testing set. The dataset of flight training comments used in the experiment is summarized in Table 1.

Table 1. Statistics of the dataset. $\#S$, $\#A$, $\#O$, and $\#P$ represent the number of sentences, aspect terms, opinion terms, and opinion pairs, respectively.

Datasets	#S	#A	#O	#P
Train	438	807	807	807
Val	110	197	197	197
Test	181	326	325	325

4.2   Experimental Setup

For performance evaluation, we use Precision, Recall, and F1-score to evaluate the extraction of aspect terms, opinion terms, and opinion pairs, where Precision represents the proportion of extracted correct words to all words extracted, Recall represents the proportion of extracted correct words to all words that are true, and F1-score is the summed average of Precision rate and Recall. An extracted aspect term, opinion term or opinion pair is considered correct if and only if the word span at the extraction is exactly the same as the ground truth.

Table 2. Training hyperparameter settings

Parameters	value	Instruction
learning_rate	5e−5	Learning rate
dropout	0.5	Neuron random drop probability
epochs	100	Times of training iteration
optimizer	Adam	Optimizer
b_size	8	Batch size
T	2	Times of inference

On the experimental scheme, to ensure the accuracy and stability of model training, the average value of experiment is taken as the final performance result, and the model is saved at the epoch with the highest F1-score. For model training, each training hyperparameter is taken with reference to empirical values, as shown in Table 2. Comparison experiments are conducted with structures using traditional deep learning methods DE-CNN [13], BiLSTM [4], and BERT [1] as encoders.

4.3   Experimental Results

The improved GTS model described above was applied to the flight training comment data to perform the task, and the best model were taken to save and test for extracting performance. The final performance results are shown in Tables 3, 4 and 5, with the best results shown in bold.

Table 3. Comparison of aspect extraction performance.

Model	Precision	Recall	F1-score
GTS+CNN	0.5726	0.6667	0.6161
GTS+BiLSTM	0.5855	0.6618	0.6213
GTS+BERT	0.6087	**0.6763**	**0.6407**
GTS+WoBERT	**0.6199**	0.6618	0.6402

Table 4. Comparison of opinion extraction performance.

Model	Precision	Recall	F1-score
GTS+CNN	0.5932	0.6774	0.6325
GTS+BiLSTM	0.5803	0.7226	0.6437
GTS+BERT	0.6707	**0.7097**	0.6897
GTS+WoBERT	**0.6749**	**0.7097**	**0.6918**

Table 5. Comparison of opinion pair extraction performance.

Model	Precision	Recall	F1-score
GTS+CNN	0.5079	0.6339	0.5640
GTS+BiLSTM	0.4974	0.6275	0.5549
GTS+BERT	0.6139	0.6340	0.6238
GTS+WoBERT	**0.6352**	**0.6601**	**0.6474**

From the tables we can see that the BERT model almost always outperforms the CNN and LSTM, with the WoBERT using word granularity showing a larger performance improvement, not only outperforming the results of the CNN and BiLSTM networks, but also performing slightly better than the BERT with word granularity. For aspect extraction, it can be seen that the performance of the four models is similar, with the F1-score of the model using GTS+BERT reaching 0.6407, which is slightly better than that of the GTS+WoBERT model with word granularity. For opinion extraction, a significant performance improvement can be seen with the use of WoBERT, outperforming the F1-scores of the other two models by almost 5%. The novel tagging scheme and inference strategy of the GTS model can exploit the potential relationships between different opinion factors, so it not only solves the opinion pair extraction task in an end-to-end manner, but also improves the performance of aspect and opinion sentiment word extraction. For opinion pair extraction, it can be seen that the performance of the first two models is significantly inferior to the latter two models due to the strong context modelling capability of BERT, while WoBERT with word granularity achieves better results in the opinion pair extraction task, with F1-scores outperforming word granularity BERT by around 2%. This shows that when extracting evaluation words such as flight training comments, which contain a lot of specialist terms, pre-training with some of the specialist words instead of individual words gives better results.

5   Conclusion

This paper researches and implements an evaluation knowledge extraction method for flight training comments. We simplify the OTE task to a label classification task for each position in the label matrix based on a grid tagging approach, and using the WoBERT pre-training model to encoder the comment sentences. We improved the decoding algorithm by relaxing the matching conditions, which extracts opinion pairs more accurately from the predicted tag matrix. After experimental validation, the F1-score of test set can reach 0.64744, which is about 2% better than the direct application of the original GTS model (test set F1-score of 0.62379).

However, the paper only extracted the evaluation aspect, evaluation opinion and opinion pairs from the flight training comments. However, sentiment polarity was not yet considered. Therefore, in the future the data can be further tagged with sentiment polarity to achieve the pair extraction of aspect term, opinion term, and sentiment polarity. In addition, the paper has improved the decoding of the professionalism of the flight comments, but still uses generic evaluation indicators for the assessment, which lacks some empirical evaluation from flight experts. The use of span and semantic relations between aspect and opinion words is still inadequate and needs further improvement and refinement in the future.

Acknowledgements. This work was supported in part by: National Natural Science Foundation of China (Nos. U2033213, 61966008, 61873042), Open Found of Key Laboratory of Flight Techniques and Flight Safety, CAAC (Nos. FZ2021KF01, FZ2021KF14).

References

1. Devlin, J., Chang, M.W., Lee, K., Toutanova, K.: BERT: pre-training of deep bidirectional transformers for language understanding. In: Proceedings of the 2019 Conference of the North American Chapter of the Association for Computational Linguistics: Human Language Technologies, Volume 1 (Long and Short Papers), pp. 4171–4186. Association for Computational Linguistics (2019)

2. Florescu, C., Jin, W.: A supervised Keyphrase extraction system based on graph representation learning. In: Azzopardi, L., Stein, B., Fuhr, N., Mayr, P., Hauff, C., Hiemstra, D. (eds.) ECIR 2019. LNCS, vol. 11437, pp. 197–212. Springer, Cham (2019). https://doi.org/10.1007/978-3-030-15712-8_13

3. Gollapalli, S.D., Li, X.L., Yang, P.: Incorporating expert knowledge into keyphrase extraction. In: Proceedings of the AAAI Conference on Artificial Intelligence, vol. 31 (2017)

4. Hochreiter, S., Schmidhuber, J.: Long short-term memory. Neural Comput. **9**(8), 1735–1780 (1997)

5. Hu, M., Liu, B.: Mining and summarizing customer reviews. In: Proceedings of the Tenth ACM SIGKDD International Conference on Knowledge Discovery and Data Mining, pp. 168–177 (2004)

6. Jing, H., Li, Z., Zhao, H., Jiang, S.: Seeking common but distinguishing difference, a joint aspect-based sentiment analysis model. In: Proceedings of the 2021 Conference on Empirical Methods in Natural Language Processing (EMNLP), pp. 3910–3922 (2021)

7. Papagiannopoulou, E., Tsoumakas, G.: Local word vectors guiding keyphrase extraction. Inf. Process. Manag. **54**(6), 888–902 (2018)

8. Peng, H., Xu, L., Bing, L., Huang, F., Lu, W., Si, L.: Knowing what, how and why: a near complete solution for aspect-based sentiment analysis. In: Proceedings of the AAAI Conference on Artificial Intelligence, vol. 34, pp. 8600–8607 (2020)

9. Qiu, Q., Xie, Z., Wu, L., Li, W.: Geoscience keyphrase extraction algorithm using enhanced word embedding. Expert Syst. Appl. **125**, 157–169 (2019)

10. Su, J.: WoBERT: word-based Chinese BERT model-ZhuiyiAI. Technical report, Technical report (2020)

11. Wang, W., Pan, S.J., Dahlmeier, D., Xiao, X.: Coupled multi-layer attentions for co-extraction of aspect and opinion terms. In: Proceedings of the AAAI Conference on Artificial Intelligence, vol. 31 (2017)

12. Wu, Z., Ying, C., Zhao, F., Fan, Z., Dai, X., Xia, R.: Grid tagging scheme for aspect-oriented fine-grained opinion extraction. In: Findings of the Association for Computational Linguistics: EMNLP 2020, pp. 2576–2585. Association for Computational Linguistics, Online, November 2020

13. Xu, H., Liu, B., Shu, L., Yu, P.S.: Double embeddings and CNN-based sequence labeling for aspect extraction. arXiv preprint arXiv:1805.04601 (2018)

14. Yang, D., Wu, Y., Fan, C.: A Chinese short text keyword extraction model based on attention. Comput. Sci. **47**(01), 193–198 (2020)

15. Zhang, Y., Chang, Y., Liu, X., Gollapalli, S.D., Li, X., Xiao, C.: MIKE: keyphrase extraction by integrating multidimensional information. In: Proceedings of the 2017 ACM on Conference on Information and Knowledge Management, pp. 1349–1358 (2017)

16. Zhao, H., Huang, L., Zhang, R., Lu, Q., Xue, H.: SpanMlt: a span-based multitask learning framework for pair-wise aspect and opinion terms extraction. In: Proceedings of the 58th Annual Meeting of the Association for Computational Linguistics, pp. 3239–3248 (2020)

ScholarRec: A User Recommendation System for Academic Social Network

Yu Weng[1], Wenguang Yu[1,2], Ronghua Lin[1,2], Yong Tang[1,2], and Chaobo He[1,2(✉)]

[1] South China Normal University, Guangzhou 510631, China
hechaobo@foxmail.com
[2] Pazhou Lab, Guangzhou 510330, China

Abstract. With the development of recommendation algorithms, recommendation systems are being widely used for recommendation tasks in different domains. However, most recommendation systems do not make good use of valid information, resulting in unsatisfactory recommendations. At the same time, the overly complex system design leads to slow recommendation speed, which does not meet the speed requirement. To address the above issues, we introduce a new user recommendation system based on academic social website SCHOLAT, including the key modules of the system and the key processes of the system. Then we introduce the solutions proposed to solve the system performance problem and cold start problem. Finally we introduce the social network dataset of SCHOLAT used for training model, and verify the effect of Variational Graph Normalized Auto-Encoders(VGNAE) on SCHOLAT dataset. We compare the effect of old version and new version recommendation system. The experimental results show that the new version of the recommendation system outperform the old one in terms of recommendation accuracy and relevance. And the system performance also meet the practical application requirements.

Keywords: Recommendation system · Graph convolutional network · SCHOLAT

1 Introduction

With the continuous development of the Internet, the world has ushered in the era of information explosion. The speed of information generation far exceed the speed of information processing. It is difficult for information consumers to find the information they really need. And it is also difficult for information producers to make their information stand out from the huge amount of data. To alleviate this contradiction, researchers have proposed a series of recommendation algorithms [1] and built many different kinds of recommendation systems [2]. On the one hand, the recommendation system helps information consumers to find information they are interested in. On the other hand, it helps information producers to promote their information, thus achieving a win-win situation.

Nowadays, recommendation systems are widely used in different types of websites, and it also used on academic social website SCHOLAT. System recommend scholars that may be of interest to users, which can help users quickly find friends they know but have not yet established friendships with. However, since the system has been built for a long time, the recommendation algorithm and system performance can no longer meet the needs of today. Through the analysis of the old system, we find that the system has the following shortcomings: 1) It uses only a simple collaborative filtering algorithm, which leads to a single recommendation result. 2) The speed of the algorithm is slow, especially when the user has more friends. 3) The lack of feedback mechanism, the system cannot make adjustments to the recommendation results according to the user's feedback. In order to solve the above problems, we designed a new recommendation system.

The main contributions of this paper are as follows: 1) By comparing to the recommendation algorithms proposed by scholars in recent years [3,4], we finally use the VGNAE [6] model to implement the new system. 2) To solve the problem that the model cannot be trained due to the high dimensionality of user features, we use TF-IDF algorithm and BERT cosine similarity to reduce the dimensionality of user features. 3) In order to solve the performance problem, we design a caching module, which makes the system's recommendation speed greatly improved. 4) Add feedback module, the system can adjust the recommendation results according to the user's feedback. 5) We use SCHOLAT social network dataset to evaluate the system effect and performance. Experimental results show that the new system outperforms the old system in terms of prediction accuracy and prediction speed.

2   Related Work

2.1   Collaborative Filtering Based Recommendation System

The main idea of collaborative filtering system [7–9] is to use the past behaviors of existing user groups to predict the possible future behaviors of current users. If the past behaviors of users and a group of users are similar, their future behaviors may also be similar. In social networks [10], collaborative filtering algorithms recommend users with the same features based on their existing features and personal information. Therefore, in order to ensure that the algorithm can work properly, system will ask users to provide some information when they register, such as: where they work, their interests, etc.

2.2   Content Based Recommendation System

The main idea of the content based recommendation system [10] is to use the user's previously liked items to find items that match this and recommend them to the user. Older versions of shopping sites, such as Amazon, eBay, etc., use a content-based recommendation system [11,12]. In social networks, content based algorithms recommends users who have viewed the same content. The advantage of this type of algorithm is that it does not require users to provide personal information in advance, but the disadvantage is that users must use it for a period of time in order to collect enough browsing history.

2.3 Implicit Semantics Based Recommendation System

Unlike the several recommendation systems introduced before, implicit semantics based recommendation system [13,14] does not use the explicit features of users or items for recommendation, but learns the feature representation of users or items through some algorithm or model, calculates the similarity of users or items in latent space, and takes the user or item with the highest similarity as the recommendation result. The commonly used algorithm models are: graph based [15], matrix operation [16,17], probability model [18,19], machine learning [20,21], etc. In social networks [23], algorithms or models collect information about users in different dimensions, map specific information to the latent space, and recommend users with similar characteristics. Since implicit semantics based recommendation system can use the information of users and items in different dimensions, its recommendation effect is also far better than the previous kinds of recommendation systems. However, the complex algorithms lead to slower real-time recommendations. We need to address the performance issues by caching or other techniques.

3   System Design

3.1   System Architecture

We use Python to build our recommendation system for two main reasons: 1) It is easy and convenient to build web services with Python's flask framework [24]. 2) Python makes it easy to implement machine learning models with PyTorch. The overall architecture of the system is designed as shown in the Fig. 1. The system is roughly divided into three layers: interface layer, service layer and storage layer. The interface layer is responsible for accepting and processing requests from clients. The service layer is responsible for implementing all the functions of the system. And the storage layer is responsible for storing all kinds of data needed for the operation of the system. We introduce some of the key modules in Fig. 1 as follows.

- **Recommend scholar**: Recommendation result interface. The client initiates recommendation request to the system through this interface. The system gets the recommendation result according to the user ID, and returns the recommendation result to the client after sorting.
- **Follow scholar**: User follow interface. After a user clicks "follow" button in the recommendation results section, the client notifies the system through this interface. The system records the user's following behavior and removes the followed user from the recommendation result list.

- **Dislike scholar**: User dislike interface. After a user clicks "dislike" button in the recommendation result section, the client notifies the system through this interface. The system will records the user's uninterested behavior and removes the uninterested user from the recommendation result list.

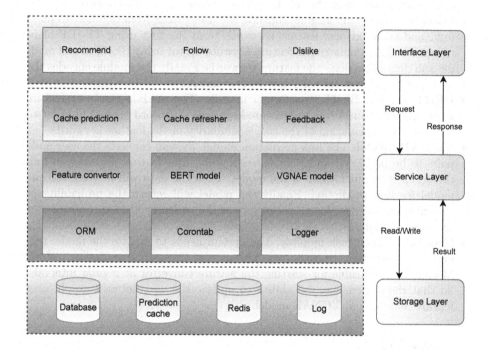

Fig. 1. System architecture

- **Cache prediction**: Read the list of cached recommended users according to the user ID. If the cache list is about to run out, system sends a request to the cache refresher module to refresh the cache. While reading the list of cached recommended users, this module requests the feedback module to update the user's activity, and adds one to the user's activity for each recommendation request.
- **Cache refresher**: Refresher uses the VGNAE model to refresh the cached list of recommended users. The module constructs pairs of user nodes to be predicted as model input. Then the module uses VGNAE model to inference, gets the probability of link existence for each pair of nodes. Finally it sorts the prediction results from highest to lowest to generate a recommendation list, writes result to the cache file. All the operation will be record to the system log.
- **Feedback**: The feedback module, which is responsible for handling operations such as follow, dislike in the interface layer and user activity updates within

the system. The system records user feedback into the storage layer's Redis database. The module ensures that the system will not recommend users who are already followed and users who have already expressed their disinterest. The user activity is used for the cold start algorithm of new users, system recommends users who are active on the website to new users so that they can be integrated into the scholar social network as soon as possible.

- **Feature convertor**: Module converts the user profile from rich text to plain text, and then extracts feature keywords from the text using TF-IDF algorithm. Then it calculates the feature keyword vector using BERT model module and dimensionalizes the feature keywords. Finally the module encodes the user features to generate the user feature matrix.
- **BERT model**: BERT transformer module. The module gets user feature keywords and transforms the feature keywords into word vectors in order to facilitate the calculation of the cosine similarity of the feature keywords.
- **VGNAE model**: The link prediction model. System converts the user node pairs to be predicted and their corresponding user feature information into the accepted input format of the model. Then the data will be feed into the model for link prediction. Finally the model will return the probability of the existence of edges for all node pairs as the recommendation result of user recommendation.
- **Crontab**: Timed task monitor. The system needs to update the model regularly to keep the accuracy and relevance of the recommendation results. Module is responsible for starting the feature convertor at regular intervals. So that the system has the ability to update the user network graph, user feature matrix, and VGNAE model.

3.2 Key Modules

In this section, we will introduce the key modules to implement the recommendation function.

Feature Convertor Module. Since SCHOLAT does not classify users by tags, we try to collect the original characteristic information of users from the following dimensions: work unit, scholar title, research field, research interest, personal profile, etc. Among them, user profiles are stored in rich text format, and it is necessary to first convert the rich text to plain text, then perform sentence cutting on the text, and finally use TF-IDF algorithm [25] to extract keywords from the text as user features. TF-IDF is a technique for user information retrieval and text mining. The algorithm consists of two parts, TF(Term Frequency) and IDF(Inverse Document Frequency), and the following are the main steps of the algorithm.

The Term Frequency, which indicates the frequency of keywords appearing in the text, calculated as follows.

$$TF_{i,j} = \frac{n_{i,j}}{\sum_k n_{k,j}} \tag{1}$$

where $n(i, j)$ denotes the number of occurrences of word i in document j. $\sum_k n_{k,j}$ denotes the total number of occurrences of all words in document j. The Inverse Document Frequency, which represent a measure of the importance of words in a document, is calculated as follows.

$$IDF_i = \log \frac{|D|}{|\{j : t_i \in d_j\}|} \tag{2}$$

$|D|$ denotes the total number of documents in the corpus, denominator denotes the number of documents containing the word t_i, and if the fewer documents contain the word t_i, the larger the IDF, indicating that the word has good class differentiation ability.

Finally, the results of the TF-IDF algorithm are obtained by multiplying the TF and IDF results, which are calculated as follows.

$$TF - IDF = TF * IDF \tag{3}$$

After statistical analysis of all the extracted user features, we found that there are 26573 different features among the 27449 valid users in SCHOLAT. If we directly construct a user feature matrix and input it into the model for training, the model will slow down or even fail to complete the training due to the excessive number of features, so we need to reduce the dimensionality of the existing features. After observation, we found that there are a large number of features with the same meaning expressed in different forms, such as: computer and computer technology, software and software engineering, etc. In this regard, we can use the BERT model [26] to convert all feature keywords into word embeddings, calculate the cosine-similarity between the embeddings, and merge feature keywords with similar features to achieve dimensionality reduction.

VGNAE Model. VGNAE was proposed in 2021 by Seong Jin Ahn and Myoung Ho Kim [6, 27]. The model mainly consisted of two parts, encoder and decoder. The encoder maps the input graph network structure and node features into the latent space. And then the decoder solves the latent space information and reduces the latent space information to the graph network information, which contains the prediction result of the node pair to be predicted. The larger the result value is, the more likely the edge exists. The model structure is shown in Fig. 2.

Firstly, we define a social network graph $G = (V, E)$, $N = |V|$ denotes the number of nodes. A denote the adjacency matrix of the graph, where we set each node connected to itself, and D denotes the degree matrix of the graph. We define Z as the hidden space matrix with dimension (N, F). Finally we define the node feature matrix as X with dimension (N, D).

The inference equation for the VGNAE encoder is as follows.

$$q(Z \mid X, A) = \prod_{i=1}^{N} q(z_i \mid X, A) \tag{4}$$

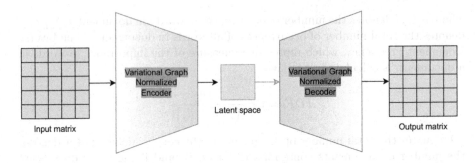

Fig. 2. VGNAE model structure

where
$$q\left(z_i \mid X, A\right) = \mathcal{N}\left(z_i \mid \mu_i, \operatorname{diag}\left(\sigma_i^2\right)\right) \tag{5}$$

where $\mu = GCN_\mu(X, A)$ denotes the mean vector of the matrix and $\log \sigma = GCN_\sigma(X, A)$ denote the similarity, both calculated from the 2-layer GCN model, which is defined as $GCN(X, A) = \tilde{A}\operatorname{ReLU}\left(\tilde{A}XW_0\right)W_1$, $\tilde{A} = D^{-\frac{1}{2}}AD^{\frac{1}{2}}$ denoted as a symmetric normalized matrix.

The inference equation for the VGNAE decoder is as follows.

$$p(A \mid Z) = \prod_{i=1}^{N}\prod_{j=1}^{N} p\left(A_{ij} \mid z_i, z_j\right) \tag{6}$$

where
$$p\left(A_{ij} = 1 \mid z_i, z_j\right) = \sigma\left(z_i^T z_j\right) \tag{7}$$

The loss function of the VGNAE model is defined as follows. Where, KL is the scatter formula to calculate the distance between two probabilities.

$$\mathcal{L} = \mathbb{E}_{q(Z|X,A)}[\log p(A \mid Z)] - KL[q(Z \mid X, A)\|p(Z)] \tag{8}$$

where
$$KL(q\|p) = \Sigma_j Q_j \log\left(\frac{Q_j}{P_j}\right) \tag{9}$$

and
$$p(Z) = \prod_{i=1}^{n} N\left(z_i \mid 0, I\right) \tag{10}$$

After the model is trained, the node pairs to be predicted are constructed as adjacency matrix. And the feature matrix are also constructed, which can be input to the model to obtain the prediction results for each pair of node edges. The results indicates the probability of the existence of edges for the node pair, with a probability distribution of $[0, 1]$.

3.3 Key Processes

In this section, we will introduce the main processes of the system.

Feature Reduction Process. The system first counts the frequency of all feature keywords, screens out the features with higher frequency and representativeness as the target of dimensionality reduction. Then it converts all feature words into word vectors using the BERT model. Finally it merges the feature words with higher similarity into the list of feature words of the dimensionality reduction target by calculating the cosine similarity of the feature words. In this paper, the dimensionality of user features is reduced to 1000. The feature reduction process is shown in Fig. 3.

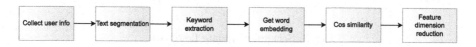

Fig. 3. Feature reduction flowchart

VGNAE Inference Process. Due to the large number of SCHOLAT users, only a portion of node pairs can be selected as the input to the model for each inference process. The system first constructs the list of users to be recommended for the users requesting recommendations, which consists of the users' K-Hop neighbors on the social network graph. If the user is an isolated node (e.g., a new enrolled), the VGNAE model inference is stopped and the cold-start algorithm is used instead to recommend for the user. The list of users to be recommended consist of two lists, S and D, where each element of S is the user ID of the requested recommendation and D is the user ID of the user to be recommended. At the same time, the system constructs all the user features to be predicted into a feature matrix. Input the two matrices into VGNAE to obtain the result matrix. The values of the result matrix are distributed on the interval $[0, 1]$, indicating the probability of the existence of links for the corresponding node pairs. The prediction results are output in the form of a list, corresponding to the input list of sparse adjacency matrix one by one. Finally, the system sorts the prediction results and stores in the recommendation cache file. The complete flow of the system from constructing inputs, model inference, output result storage is shown in Fig. 4.

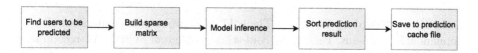

Fig. 4. VGNAE inference flowchart

Scheduled Update Process. The system will regularly collects the latest user information from the database, builds the user network graph and retrains the model. The regular update function is realized by a timer, which will be started when the system start. And the feature convertor module will be started after the timer is finished to generate the latest user network graph and user feature adjacency matrix. Then the model will be trained. The current prediction cache will be refreshed after the model training is finished. The flow of the scheduled update is shown in Fig. 5.

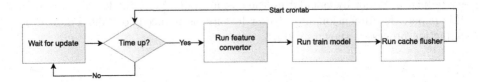

Fig. 5. Scheduled update flowchart

3.4   Critical Problem Solving

System Performance Problem Solving. When using neural network model to obtain user recommendation results in real time, all steps of VGNAE model inference need to be executed. With so many steps, it takes a lot of time and machine resources to make a real-time user recommendation, which is not performance-compliant in practical applications. Users are not willing to spend a lot of time on obtaining user recommendation results once. Therefore, in order to solve the problem of system performance and user experience, we adopt the method of advance caching of recommendation results. The specific approach is to cache the user's recommendation results in advance. When the user requests for the list of recommendation results, the system reads the cache list directly and returns the recommendation results. When the cache results are about to be exhausted, the system submits a task to the thread pool to refresh the cache results for that user. The thread pool completes a VGNAE model inference process in another thread to obtain the user recommendation results. Using the multi-threaded approach effectively prevent the system from spending too much time on waiting for the model inference and improve the system performance. The recommendation process after the system switched to the advance caching recommendation method is shown in Fig. 6.

Cold Start Problem Solving. The cold start problem is common in all recommendation systems. Facing the cold-start problem of SCHOLAT recommendation system, our solution idea is very simple but also very efficient and reliable. The idea of the cold start algorithm is as follows: 1) gets the user's activity from the system feedback module, 2) sorts the users according to the level of activity,

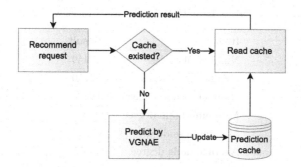

Fig. 6. Advance caching recommendation flowchart

3) if the user's personal information includes school, college, major and research interest, etc., further filter out the users with the same school, college, major and research interest, 4) ranks these users in the queue with higher recommendation priority, followed by the remaining active users. System recommends the users in the list in order. The basis of our analysis of the cold start algorithm idea is that for new users, they are more familiar with people around them generally, that is, users from the same school, college and profession, so we mark these users as users with higher recommendation priority. At the same time, in order to make users integrate into the social network faster, we can recommend users who are more active in the website, and new users may also get to know these active users. Once a user joins a social network (user nodes are no longer isolated), we can use a neural network-based recommendation algorithm to recommend more users to this user.

4   Implementation and Evaluation

4.1   SCHOLAT Social Network Dataset

We use a sparse matrix to construct the user social network, and we extract the relationship from the database. The binary of relationship (u, v), which represent the existence of friend relationship between user u and user v, is added to the sparse matrix. The details of the dataset are shown in Table 1.

4.2   Model Evaluation

The VGNAE model is set as follows: the model is optimized using the Adam optimizer with a learning rate of 0.005, an input channel of 1000 dimensions, a GCN hidden layer dimension of 128, the number of training iterations set to 300, the ratio of training set, validation set, test set is 8:1:1, and the number of positive samples is the same as the number of negative samples. The model is trained using the dataset constructed from the reduced-dimensional features, the final results of the model are compared with other link prediction algorithms as

Table 1. SCHOLAT dataset overview

Item	Result
Number of nodes	27449
Number of edges	52250
Number of node features	1000
Minimum node degree	0
Maximum node degree	1361
Average node degree	3.807

shown in Table 2. It can be observed that the VGNAE model outperforms other link prediction algorithms in all aspects of metrics. The VGNAE model achieves the best prediction results when using 80% of the data as the training set, with an AUC metric of 0.980 and an AP metric of 0.984.

Table 2. Model effect

Model	Train	Loss	AUC	AP
CN [28, 29]	80%	-	0.889	0.930
Jaccard [30]	80%	-	0.888	0.891
PA [30]	80%	-	0.828	0.800
AA [30]	80%	-	0.888	0.925
RA [31]	80%	-	0.890	0.955
GCN	20%	0.180	0.819	0.816
GCN	60%	0.322	0.847	0.886
GCN	80%	0.353	0.865	0.906
VGNAE	20%	1.127	0.969	0.972
VGNAE	60%	1.192	0.977	0.980
VGNAE	80%	1.222	**0.980**	**0.984**

4.3   Performance Comparison

The system use advance caching of recommendation results to improve the performance. The comparison of the speed of using cache to get user recommendation results and the speed of getting user recommendation results in real time is shown in Table 3. It can be easily observed that the speed of using cache to get user recommendation results is greatly improved in the same configuration of machines. The model with the biggest improvement is VGNAE, which is improved from 3140 ms to 121 ms.

Table 3. Recommendation speed comparison

Model	Real time recommendation(ms)	Cache recommendation(ms)
GCN	2940	**116**
VGNAE	3140	**121**

4.4   Demonstration Effect

Recommendation effect for new users in the old system is shown on the left side of Fig. 7, the recommendation results for new users are almost always the same, and the results will be the most active users on website. The original recommendation page is shown in the middle side of Fig. 7. Since there is no refresh button for changing a group of users, the list of recommended users can only be refreshed after refreshing the whole page. When the user does not produce any follow behavior, the recommendation results will not change much, and the system will always recommend the same group of scholars, so the recommendation module does not play its proper role.

The recommendation algorithm of the new recommendation system is implemented based on the VGNAE model, which take into account the existing personal information of users in an all-round way, and has a complete feedback mechanism. After a user requests for a recommendation, following the recommended user, and the feedback for not interested, the system will adjust the result of the next recommendation according to the user feedback in real time. As shown in the right side of Fig. 7, users can click the refresh button in the upper right corner to change a group of recommended users. If they are not interested in a certain user, they can click the not interested button to feedback to the recommendation system.

Fig. 7. Recommendation module comparison

5   Conclusion

This paper analyzes the old user recommendation system of SCHOLAT and finds that the recommendation algorithm of the old system utilizes less user information, which leads to the unsatisfactory recommendation effect. The recommendation result of the system is monotonous due to the lack of effective feedback mechanism, which is no longer suitable for today's user needs. To solve this problems, a redesigned user recommendation system is proposed, which uses the latest machine learning-based recommendation algorithm and also improves the user feedback mechanism. The experimental results show that the new system meets user requirements in terms of user recommendation effect and recommendation speed. The system design the recommendation algorithm as an independent sub-module, if the latest and best recommendation algorithm is launched, the system is also able to quickly apply the algorithm to practice with good scalability.

Acknowledgment. This work was supported in part by the National Natural Science Foundation of China under Grant U1811263 and Grant 62077045.

References

1. Lü, L.Y., Zhou, T.: Link Prediction. Higher Education Press, Beijing (2013)
2. Sun, Z., Guo, Q., Yang, J., et al.: Research commentary on recommendations with side information: a survey and research directions. Electron. Commerce Res. Appl. **37**, 100879 (2019)
3. Wei, L., Ling, C.: Link prediction in complex networks. Inform. Contr. **49**(1), 1–23 (2020)
4. Liben-Nowell, D., Kleinberg, J.: The link-prediction problem for social networks. J. Assoc. Inform. Sci. Technol. **58**(7), 1019–1031 (2007)
5. Google Scholar Google Scholar Digital Library Digital Library (2007)
6. Ahn, S.J., Kim, M.H.: Variational Graph Normalized AutoEncoders. In: Proceedings of the 30th ACM International Conference on Information Knowledge Management, pp. 2827–2831 (2021)
7. Karydi, E., Margaritis, K.: Parallel and distributed collaborative filtering: a survey. ACM Comput. Surv. (CSUR) **49**(2), 1–41 (2016)
8. Su, X., Khoshgoftaar, T.M.: A survey of collaborative filtering techniques. Adv. Artif. Intell. **12** (2009)
9. Goldberg, D., Nichols, D., Oki, B.M., et al.: Using collaborative filtering to weave an information tapestry. Commun. ACM **35**(12), 61–70 (1992)
10. Rajendran, D.P.D., Sundarraj, R.P.: Using topic models with browsing history in hybrid collaborative filtering recommender system: experiments with user ratings[J]. Int. J. Inform. Manage. Data Insights **1**(2), 100027 (2021)
11. Sarwar, B., Karypis, G., Konstan, J., et al.: Item-based collaborative filtering recommendation algorithms. In: Proceedings of the 10th International Conference on World Wide Web, pp. 285–295 (2001)
12. Linden, G., Smith, B., York, J.: Amazon.com recommendations: item-to-item collaborative filtering. In: IEEE Internet Computing, vol. 7(1), pp. 76–80 (2003) https://doi.org/10.1109/MIC.2003.1167344

13. Zhao, H., Yao, Q., Li, J., et al.: Meta-graph based recommendation fusion over heterogeneous information networks. In: Proceedings of the 23rd ACM SIGKDD International Conference on Knowledge Discovery and Data Mining, pp. 635–644 (2017)
14. Zhang, S., Yao, L., Sun, A., et al.: Deep learning based recommender system: a survey and new perspectives. ACM Comput. Surv. (CSUR) **52**(1), 1–38 (2019)
15. Peng, Z., et al.: news recommendation model based on improved label propagation algorithm. In: Milošević, D., Tang, Y., Zu, Q. (eds.) HCC 2019. LNCS, vol. 11956, pp. 315–324. Springer, Cham (2019). https://doi.org/10.1007/978-3-030-37429-7_31
16. Guo, Q., Zhuang, F., Qin, C., et al.: A survey on knowledge graph-based recommender systems. IEEE Trans. Knowl. Data Eng. PP(99), 1–1 (2020)
17. Menon, A.K., Elkan, C.: Link prediction via matrix factorization. In: European Conference on Machine Learning and Knowledge Discovery in Databases. Berlin, Germany: Springer-Verlag, pp. 437–452 (2011)
18. Ahmed, N.M., Chen, L., Wang, Y.L., et al.: DeepEye: link prediction in dynamic networks based on non-negative matrix factorization. Big Data Mining Anal. **1**(1), 19–33 (2018)
19. Pearl, J.: Probabilistic Reasoning in Intelligent Systems. Morgan Kaufmann Publishers Inc, New York, NJ, USA (1988)
20. Lü, L., Zhou, T.: Link prediction in complex networks: a survey. Physica A Stat. Mech. Appl. **390**(6), 1150–1170 (2011)
21. Kipf, T.N., Welling, M.: Semi-supervised classification with graph convolutional networks. arXiv preprint arXiv:1609.02907 (2016)
22. Grover, A., Leskovec, J.: node2vec: Scalable feature learning for networks. In: Proceedings of the 22nd ACM SIGKDD International Conference on Knowledge Discovery and Data Mining, pp. 855–864 (2016)
23. Vedavathi, N., Anil Kumar, K.M.: An efficient e-learning recommendation system for user preferences using hybrid optimization algorithm. Soft Comput. **25**(14), 9377–9388 (2021)
24. Lokhande, P.S., Aslam, F., Hawa, N., et al.: Efficient way of web development using python and flask. Int. J. Adv. Compt. Res. **6** (2015)
25. Aizawa, A.: An information-theoretic perspective of tf-idf measures. Inform. Process. Manage. **39**(1), 45–65 (2003)
26. Devlin, J., Chang, M.W., Lee, K, et al. Bert: Pre-training of deep bidirectional transformers for language understanding. arXiv preprint arXiv:1810.04805 (2018)
27. Kipf, T.N., Welling, M.: Variational graph auto-encoders. arXiv preprint arXiv:1611.07308 (2016)
28. Soundarajan, S., Hopcroft, J.: Using community information to improve the precision of link prediction methods. In: Proceedings of the 21st International Conference Companion on World Wide Web (WWW '12 Companion). ACM, New York, NY, USA, 607–608. http://doi.acm.org/10.1145/2187980.2188150
29. Ahmad, I., Akhtar, M.U., Noor, S., et al.: Missing link prediction using common neighbor and centrality based parameterized algorithm. Sci Rep **10**, 364 (2020). https://doi.org/10.1038/s41598-019-57304-y
30. Liben-Nowell, D., Kleinberg, J.: The Link Prediction Problem for Social Networks (2004)
31. Zhou, T., Lü, L., Zhang, Y.C.: Predicting missing links via local information. Europ. Phys.: J. B **71**(4), 623–630 (2009). https://doi.org/10.1140/epjb/e2009-00335-8

Incremental Evolutionary Community Discovery Method Based on Neighbor Subgraph

Yan Zhao, Chang Guo, Weimin Li[✉], Dingmei Wei, and Heng Zhu

School of Computer Engineering and Science, Shanghai University,
Shanghai 200444, China
wmli@shu.edu.cn

Abstract. With the popularity of online social networks, dynamic community discovery has received more and more attention. The existing dynamic community discovery algorithm divides the network into multiple time slices and uses the static community detection method to identify the community on each network, but its efficiency is low. How to effectively handle changes in the network structure at different periods, is the key to analyse the dynamic community evolution. Aiming at the form of dynamic network data flow, this paper based on the neighbor subgraph and put forward an incremental community discovery algorithm, which limits the influence of the increment on the network to the neighbor subgraph of the incremental node. The core nodes in the network are found through the local information of the nodes, and the update strategy is designed according to the incremental type and the type of the involved nodes to update the structure of community. Analyse the evolution of the community structure and provide dynamic community structure in real-time as the community structure changes as incremental events occur. Finally, experiments are conducted on static social networks and dynamic social network. Experimental results verify the superiority and efficiency of the algorithm.

Keywords: Community evolution · Neighbor subgraph · Incremental community discovery · Resistance distance

1 Introduction

The study found that social networks generally have a community structure, that is, there are some communities in the network, the density of nodes within the same community is higher, and the frequency of node connections between different communities is lower. Since the nodes of the same community in social networks often have similar attributes, such as interest, location, etc., identifying the community structure of the network can help people better mine network information. Therefore, in the analysis and research of social network, community discovery is a research hotspot, such as using the community to solve the recommendation of the cold start [25], maximizing the impact based on community [2], and so on.

© The Author(s), under exclusive license to Springer Nature Singapore Pte Ltd. 2023
Y. Sun et al. (Eds.): ChineseCSCW 2022, CCIS 1681, pp. 42–57, 2023.
https://doi.org/10.1007/978-981-99-2356-4_4

At present, dynamic network has attracted more and more attention in the analysis of social network. Traditional algorithms for community discovery are aimed at static networks and cannot obtain the changes in the community structure in dynamic networks. Therefore, studying the evolution of dynamic network communities can help solve this problem.

Most of the traditional dynamic evolution community discovery algorithm is a time-step method. This method divides the dynamic network into multiple continuous time step networks according to the time window. In each time slice network, the communities are determined by a static community discovery algorithm, and the communities in adjacent time steps are matched to track the community evolution. The time step method ignores the community structure that has been obtained on the previous time step and re-performs the community discovery algorithm on each time step network, so it is not efficient. To solve the time efficiency problem, and the real-time problem of the time-step method, the incremental dynamic evolution community discovery method is proposed. The incremental approach designs a progressive processing strategy to update the community structure in real-time as the network changes. The increment in a dynamic network is the change of nodes or edges in the network, which can be divided into 1) new nodes join the network. 2) the original nodes disappear from the network. 3) changes in the relationships between nodes. Different types of increments have different impacts on the network. Even the same types of increments may have varying degrees of impact. How to design a reasonable and comprehensive progressive strategy is a challenge for the implementation of the incremental method.

This paper proposes an incremental evolutionary community discovery based on the neighbor subgraph method (IECD-NS), which can analyse the community structure in time-varying networks. To limit the impact of network increments, we define a neighbor subgraph, which can be used to find core nodes by local topology information of the nodes. According to the characteristics of core nodes, the core subgraph is defined. When there are new increments in the network, we take the type of increment into account, and the types of nodes and the changes in the core sub-graph of the community are comprehensively considered. The incremental processing strategy proposed in this article can update the community structure of the network in real-time and identify the birth, death, growth, shrink, merge, and split events of the community.

2 Related Work

During dynamic community evolution, the network structure remains roughly stable, with only a small fraction of the topology changing. Therefore, the incremental method does not re-divide the entire network when the network generates dynamic increments. Instead, it designs a processing strategy based on the type of increment and makes local adjustments to the community structure of some affected nodes.

Many incremental methods implement community discovery [22] in dynamic networks by transforming traditional static community discovery algorithms.

Han J et al. [5] utilize the Adaptive Label Propagation Algorithm (ALPA) to enable detection and monitoring of communities in dynamic networks. Liu W et al. [17] proposed a bottom-up incremental community discovery framework to speed up community discovery algorithms in highly dynamic graphs. Li W et al. [16] established a dynamic community evolution tracking model based on resistance distance based on the concepts of node resistance, core nodes and dynamic contributions between nodes. DynaMo [28] is also a modularity-based adaptive incremental algorithm that is 2–5 times faster than the time-step Louvain algorithm with greater efficiency. To ensure the continuity of community structure in dynamic time, Li W et al. [15] proposed a multi-objective optimization method by fusing three characteristics of community in dynamic networks: temporal variability, stability, and continuity.

Some algorithms speed up the algorithm speed by a parallel algorithm [7] to handle large-scale dynamic networks. Zhang C et al. [27] proposed an incremental node-based parallel community discovery algorithm that uses a parallel weighted community clustering metric to handle large-scale dynamic communities. Li G et al. [10] proposed an incremental algorithm based on the MapReduce model and label propagation strategy, called parallel label propagation and incremental related vertices (PLPIRV). From the perspective of heterogeneous networks, some scholars have established some effective models [13] for dynamic community discovery.

Identifying important nodes with significant meaning can help track communities in a constantly changing dynamic network. Many scholars have proposed some methods about distance measure and structure measure [20] to find important nodes. Wang et al. [21] proposed the concept of topological potential field for community discovery. In this method, each node has an independent topological potential value that measures the node's ability to affect its surrounding nodes. In [24], a random walk is adopted to simulate the spread of information, the distance between nodes is calculated based on how often information is returned to the original node. Some other scholars find important nodes based on the influence maximization task [12]. Li W et al. [11] proposed crowd sentiment-based attribute influence maximization, which overcomes the shortcomings of the traditional method of insufficient feature consideration. DEIM [14] is a dynamic influence maximization algorithm based on cohesive entropy, which takes into account the dynamics of propagation and local aggregation factors and helps to find important nodes that influence the community.

3   Incremental Evolutionary Community Discovery Method Based on Neighbor Subgraph

The IECD-NS algorithm designs a reasonable increment processing strategy to discover and update community structures, which consider the heterogeneity of neighbor nodes, different increment types and node types. Due to the high real-time requirements of this method and the high cost of obtaining global information in the network, this paper defines a neighbor subgraph to effectively capture the local topology information of nodes. Using the resistance distance between nodes in neighbor subgraphs, the local equivalent distance is designed. The smaller the local equivalent distance, the more likely the node pair belongs to the same community. Identify the core nodes in the network according to the local equivalent distance of the passing nodes and the local information of the nodes. The core subgraph of the community is defined according to the characteristics of the core nodes. In the process of increment generation, the impact area of the increment is determined according to the type of the increment and the types of nodes involved. Processing strategies can track community structure and identify community evolution events, including merge, growth, birth, shrink, death and split events of communities.

3.1   Core Node Discovery Based on Neighbor Subgraph

A dynamic network can be formalized as a network sequence $G = \{G_1, G_2, .., G_T\}$. Let $G_t = (V^t, E^t)$ represent the network topology structure at time $t(1 \leq t)$, G_t is an unweighted and undirected network, V^t is the set of nodes in sub-network G_t, and V^t is the edge set in sub-network G_t.

Dynamic networks are often large and complex, and the acquisition of global information is costly. Based on the smoothness assumption, the dynamic network topology remains mostly unchanged for a short time, and only a small part of the structure changes. Therefore, it is not necessary to frequently re-obtain global information due to network changes. Using local information is an efficient and accurate method in dynamic networks. To mine local information, this paper defines neighbor subgraphs.

Definition 1. *Neighbor subgraph: The neighbor subgraph of node i at time t is $NeiG_i^t(NeiE_i^t, NeiV_i^t)$, where the node set $NeiV_i^t$ is composed of adjacent nodes of node i, and the edge set $NeiE_i^t$ consists of edges between nodes in $NeiE_i^t$.*

Through the neighbor subgraph, the heterogeneity of the neighbor nodes can be found, that is, the degree of affinity between the node and the neighbor node. To effectively discover the degree of affinity, we model the neighbor subgraph as a resistance network. In the neighbor subgraph, edges are treated as resistances, and the inverse of the edge weight value is the resistance value. In a weightless social network, the resistance value of the edge is 1Ω.

Definition 2. *Local resistance distance: A resistive network can be represented by the neighbor subgraph $NeiG_p^t$ of node p at time t. The equivalent resistance distance between node p and its neighbor q is called the local resistance distance R_{pq}^t of nodes p and q.*

The resistive distances can be calculated in [8]. It should be noted that since $NeiG_p^t$ and $NeiG_q^t$ are not necessarily the same, R_{pq}^t and R_{qp}^t may not be equal. The number of common neighbors between nodes reflects the degree of similarity between the nodes. To make full use of the local information of the neighbor subgraph, this paper defines a local equivalent distance by combining the local resistance distance of nodes and common neighbors.

Definition 3. *Local Equivalence Distance: The local equivalence distance between nodes shows how closely they are connected in the neighbor subgraph. The distance of the nodes is calculated as follows:*

$$D_{pq}^t = R_{pq}^t * min(1 - \frac{\sum_{u \in V_p^t \wedge u \in V_q^t} w_{pu}^t}{\sum_{u \in V_p^t} w_{pu}^t}, 1 - \frac{\sum_{u \in V_p^t \wedge u \in V_q^t} w_{qu}^t}{\sum_{u \in V_q^t} w_{qu}^t}) \qquad (1)$$

At time t, V_p^t is neighbor nodes set of node p, and w_{pu}^t is the weight of the edge(p,u). When D_{pq}^t is less than the threshold ϵ, these two nodes are possibly be neighbors. The local neighbor threshold of each node is calculated adaptively by combined with the local topology information of each node, and the local neighbor is determined by the threshold.

Definition 4. *Local neighbor threshold: At time t, the local neighbor threshold ϵ_p^t of node is calculated by calculating the mean value of the local equivalent distance between node p and all its neighbors, and its calculation formula is as follows:*

$$\epsilon_p^t = (\prod_{q \in V_p^t} D_{pq}^t)^{\frac{1}{|V_p^t|}} \qquad (2)$$

Definition 5. *Close neighbors: At time t, for the neighbor node q of node p, if the local equivalent distance D_{pq}^t is less than the node p's local neighbor threshold ϵ_p^t, or D_{qp}^t is smaller than ϵ_q^t, then node q belongs to the local close neighbor of node p. The node's local neighbor set is represented as follows:*

$$N_p^t = \{q : q \in V_p^t \wedge (D_{pq}^t < \epsilon_p^t \vee D_{qp}^t < \epsilon_p^t)\} \qquad (3)$$

The higher the number of nodes in N_p^t, the node p is more likely to be the core node. We use clustering threshold μ to determine the relationship between the number of local neighbors of a node and important nodes. Since the global clustering threshold ignores the influence of different community sizes and structures, this paper uses the local information of nodes to generate the local minimum clustering threshold of nodes to be suitable for community discovery of different scales.

Definition 6. *Local Minimum Clustering Threshold: The local minimum clustering threshold μ_p^t combines its own local information and local parameter α, and is calculated as follows:*

$$\mu_p^t = \alpha * |V_p^t| \qquad (4)$$

Where $|V_p^t|$ is the number of neighbors of node p, α is a local parameter entered by the user, which can adjust the shape of the resulted community. Based on the node's local close neighbor set and local minimum clustering threshold, it can be judged whether the node can become the core node in a community.

Definition 7. *Core node: At moment t, if the number of local neighbors of node p is greater than or equal to its local minimum clustering threshold μ_p^t, then node p is identified as a core node. The core representation is as follows:*

$$Core^t = \{p : p \in V^t \wedge |N_p^t| \geq \mu_p^t\} \qquad (5)$$

Assuming that node p is a core node, then p and its local close neighbor set N_p^t form a community C_p^t. If two adjacent nodes are core nodes, most likely they belong to the same community, so community merging is possible.

3.2   Community Evolution Based on Dynamic Contribution

Dynamic networks are time-varying. Some dynamic changes in the network occur over time, which are called increments. The community evolution events occur with these increments. The events studied in this paper are divided into six types, including birth, split, growth, shrink, merge, and death event.

The community membership of a node is given by the core node. The core node-set forms a community structure of the network through a series of community births and merges. Changes in core nodes impact the community and generate community evolution events. To track these changes, a core subgraph is defined.

Definition 8. *Core Subgraph: The core subgraph C_i^t is $CG_i^t(CN_i^t, CE_i^t)$, and the node-set CN_i^t in CG_i^t is composed of core nodes in the community. The edge set CE_i^t in CG_i^t is the relationship between these core nodes. For the core node pairs p and q in CG_i^t, if p and q are local neighbors of each other, they have edge connections. Otherwise, they are not.*

In the core subgraph, the community is connected by the core nodes, and it also changes due to the changes in the number of nodes or the connectivity of nodes. The core node will create a community containing its local close neighbors. Two communities will merge when the two core nodes are locally close to each other, so an edge in the core subgraph of the community represents a community merger that occurred during the formation of this community. Due to the characteristic of the core subgraph, the core subgraph must be a connected graph. Because if the core subgraph is not a connected graph, the various connected components in the graph cannot be divided into the same community through community merger. With the increments increase, the identity label of some nodes may change. The change of the node identity label brings about the change of the core subgraphs of some communities, thus generating community evolution events. For example, in Fig. 5, three nodes p, q, and z are the core nodes of the community C_i^t, and the core subgraph CG_i^t of the C_i^t is a connected graph. At time $t+1$, since the p node is no longer the core node, the community created by q and the community created by z cannot be merged into the same community, so C_i^t is split into C_j^t and C_k^t.

Changes in node identity label will lead to community evolution events. In the process of incremental generation, if a node's neighbor subgraph is affected, its identity label may change, thereby changing the community structure. Therefore, in order to track the community changes, this paper first determines the incremental impact area, that is, the set of nodes that the neighbor subgraph may be affected by the increment. This set is represented by Changed, and then the core subgraph-based community evolution algorithm is used to analyze the impact of the Changed set and update the community structure.

For the three types of increments, the specific process for determining the area of the incremental impact is as follows:

Algorithm 1. Core subgraph-based community evolution algorithm

---

Input: *Changed, Core^t*

 1: **for** node p in *Changed* **do**
 2:     **if** p is in $Core^{t-1}$ **then**
 3:         **if** p in $Core^t$ **then**
 4:             For the nodes that belong to N_p^{t-1} but not N_p^t or the nodes belong to N_p^t but not N_p^{t-1}, re-judge the community belonging (the community shrinks or grows) with the nodes that, and judge whether there are core nodes of other communities in the new local close neighbors (community merger);
 5:         **else**
 6:             **if** the community that p belongs to has only one node **then**
 7:                 Community death;
 8:             **else**
 9:                 Determine whether the core subgraph CG_i^t of the community where p belongs is connected;
10:                 **if** CG_i^t is connected **then**
11:                     Re-judge the community belonging to the original close neighbors of p and p (community shrinks);
12:                 **else**
13:                     The core nodes of each connected component form a new community with their local close neighbors (community split);
14:                 **end if**
15:             **end if**
16:         **end if**
17:     **else**
18:         **if** p in $Core^t$ **then**
19:             Determine whether there are core nodes in the local close neighbors of node p and the community of these core nodes (community growth or community merger or community birth);
20:         **end if**
21:     **end if**
22: **end for**

---

1. **Node increase:** The newly added node is an isolated node at this time, it is not connected to other nodes in the network, so it will not affect other nodes and the existing community structure, so there is no further processing.
2. **Node deletion:** The deletion of a node will affect the neighbor subgraph of his neighbors, the local close neighbor threshold and local minimum clustering threshold of these neighbor nodes may change, so their identity labels may also change, and they will be effect. The deleted node and its neighbors are added to the Changed set and further processed by Algorithm 1.
3. **Edge changes:** In the case where the edge changes, the neighbor subgraphs of the nodes at both ends of the edge and their common neighbor nodes

are affected, so they are added to the Changed set and further processed by Algorithm 1.

It should be noted that when the relationship between the two nodes changes, the most common incremental method needs to re-judgment the community of these two nodes and all their neighbor nodes. However, in the IECD-NS, the change will only affect themselves and their common neighbors. For example, in Fig. 1(b), after the relationship between A and C changes, the neighbor subgraph of node A changes, and the number of neighbors increases, so the local minimum clustering threshold μ_A of A and the local close neighbor threshold ϵ_A are possible change, so it needs to be re-judged whether it is a core node, and C must be re-judged for the same reason. For the common neighbor B of A and C, the change will affect the neighbor subgraph of B, so B should be judged again, and node D is not a common neighbor of nodes A and C, so there is no need to re-evaluate D.

(a)   (b)

Fig. 1. Network change diagram

After determining the affected area of the network, the community subordinates are updated for these nodes using the core subgraph-based community evolution algorithm.

In Algorithm 1, for each node in the affected Changed set, determine whether their identity tags have changed. Figures 2, 3, 4 and 5 shows the community evolution caused by changes in the identity tags of several nodes. In the figure, the red box node is the core node, the local neighbor threshold of the core node is the radius of the circle centered on the core node, and other nodes within the range are the local neighbors of the core node.

There are several types of node identity label transformations:

1. **Maintain the label of the core node:** In this case, the identity label of the node is not changed. For example, in Fig. 2, node p is the core node and belongs to C_i at time $t-1$ and time t, but the node's local close neighbor set may change. Compare the local close neighbor set N_p^{t-1} of the core node p at the previous moment with the current local close neighbor set N_p^t, and deal with the following two cases (line 3–4):

    (a) The original local close neighbor is no longer a local neighbor: in Fig. 2, nodes a and b are both local neighbors of node p at time $t-1$, but are not in the local neighbor set of p at time t, so these two nodes may lose the community membership of C_i^t at time t. For these nodes, determine whether they have other local close neighbors that are the core nodes of the original community. For example, node a is still a local close neighbor of node q at time t, and node q is also the core node belonging to C_i^t, so node a retains the community membership. Because node b is not a local neighbor of other core nodes in the C_i^t, node b loses the community membership of the C_i^t and the C_i^t community shrinks.

(b) There is a new local close neighbor: In Fig. 2, node z and node c are not local close neighbors of p node at time $t-1$, but become local close neighbors of p at time t. For these nodes, determine whether they originally belonged to C_i^{t-1}. For nodes that did not originally belong to C_i^{t-1}, give them C_i^t membership, and for cores that did not originally belong to C_i^{t-1}, merge C_i^t with the community to which the node belongs. For example, node c is a common node, add c into C_i^t and community C_i^t grows. Since node z is a core node and belongs to the community C_j^t, community C_j^t and community C_i^t are merged into C_k^t.

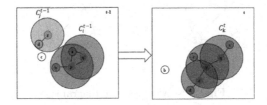

Fig. 2. Community merger diagram

2. **Core nodes become ordinary nodes:** Due to changes in the identity labels of some nodes, the core subgraphs of some communities will be affected. According to the original number of core nodes in the community, there are several possibilities:

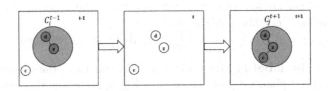

Fig. 3. Community death and community birth diagram

(a) At the last moment there was only one core node in the community: For example, in Fig. 3, node z is the core node of the C_i^{t-1} community and the community has only one core node, so when time t, the z node is no longer the core, the community C_i dies (lines 6–7).

(b) There were multiple core nodes in the community at the previous moment: at this time, the connectivity of the core subgraph of the community at the current moment is determined (line 8–9). As shown in Fig. 4, at time $t-1$, nodes p, q, and z are core nodes of the community C_i^{t-1}. At time t, node q is no longer a core node, but the core subgraph of community C_i^t is still a connected graph, so only node q and node a lose community membership, and community C_i shrinks (lines 10–11). In Fig. 5, at time $t-1$, p, q, and z are the core nodes of the community C_i^{t-1}. At time t, node p is no longer a core node. At this time, the core subgraph of the community C_i^t is not a connected graph, then the core node set of each connected component in CG_i^t forms a new community with their local close neighbors, and the community C_i is split into C_k and C_j (line 12–13).

3. **Ordinary nodes become core nodes:** According to whether there are other core nodes in the local close neighbors of this new core node at the moment, and whether these core nodes belong to the same community, there are the following situations:

   (a) There is no core node in the local close neighbor: For example, in Fig. 3, node z is not a core node at time t, and node z becomes a core node at time $t+1$. Since there is no other core node in the local close neighbor of node z, the node z and its local close neighbors d and c form a new community C_i^t, and community C_i is born.

   (b) There are core nodes in the local close neighbors and these core nodes belong to the same community: For example, in Fig. 4, if time t is regarded as the previous time, $t-1$ is regarded as the current time, because there is only one core node p in the local close neighbors of the new core node q at time $t-1$, and node p to the community C_i^{t-1}. Node q and his local close neighbor a join the C_i^{t-1} community, and the community C_i grows.

   (c) There are core nodes in the local close neighbors and these core nodes do not belong to the same community: For example, in Fig. 5, if time t is regarded as the previous time and time $t-1$ is regarded as the current time, due to there are two core nodes p and z in the local close neighbors of the new core node p, and these two core nodes belong to different communities, merge these communities and form a new community C_i (line 15–16).

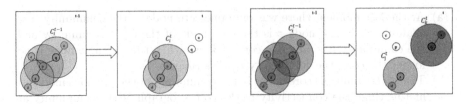

Fig. 4. Community shrink diagram   **Fig. 5.** Community split diagram

4. **Maintain ordinary node identity:** Since ordinary nodes cannot give community membership to other nodes, the community structure will not be affected.

4 Experiment

This paper compares IECD-NS with some other popular community detection methods. In order to prove the accuracy of the algorithm, this paper conducts comparative experiments on static and dynamic networks respectively. To the best of the authors' knowledge, there is currently no canonical way to measure the quality of community evolutionary discovery algorithms. Therefore, in the absence of benchmark results, this paper compares the number of evolutionary events found by IECD-NS and another dynamic evolutionary community discovery method, and the trend of the number of evolutionary events over time.

4.1 Static Real Network

This paper uses five common static real network datasets in social network research. Run IECD-NS and other community discovery algorithms based on these 5 datasets, measured by the Modularity score [19] and the Standard Mutual Information (NMI) [9] score. The static real social networks include: 1) American college football network (NCAA) [3], which has 115 nodes and 602 edges; 2) Dolphin Network (DOLP) [18], an unweighted and undirected network of 62 dolphins; 3) The Polbooks network(POLB), which has 105 nodes; 4) Zachary's Karate Network(KARA) [26] include 34 nodes and 78 edges; 5) A cooperative network [1] with 4 communities (PHYS) including 241 doctors. These five kinds of real networks are widely used in the research of social networks, and each real network has a benchmark community structure. Comparison algorithms include COPRA [4], SHRINK [6] and SLAP [23].

As shown in Fig. 6, IECD-NS obtained higher modularity scores on all experimental datasets compared to other methods, even scoring a modularity score of 1 on DOLP, KARA and POLI; in Fig. 7, IECD-NS has generally higher NMI scores, obtaining optimal NMI scores on three of the datasets, while on the other two datasets the algorithm's scores were not significantly different from those of the optimal algorithm on the other 2 datasets. The experiments show that the proposed algorithm has excellent performance in community discovery for

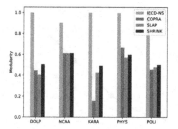 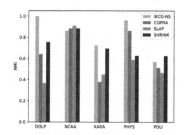

Fig. 6. Modularity score on real network

Fig. 7. NMI score on real network

real networks, and can discover well-structured communities in the network with high accuracy, and the discovered communities have high consistency with the real community segmentation. Taking the KARA network as an example, the proposed IECD-NS algorithm can identify two communities in this network and identify the node representing the administrator and the coach as the core node.

In this paper, the suggested hyperparameter α value is in the range $[0.4, 0.6]$ used. Within this range, not only nodes with larger node degrees, but also adjacent nodes that are closely connected to the core node can be identified.

4.2 Dynamic Real Network Results

A subset of the DBLP dataset, DBLP Co-authorship, consists of 2752 nodes representing authors. The network is a relational network where each edge represents an article published jointly by two authors between 1990 and 2010. This dynamic network is divided into 9-time steps according to time. As the network data grows larger over time, the general incremental algorithm tends to cause a rapid decline in community detection due to error accumulation, however the IECD-NS algorithm performs the opposite.

As shown in Fig. 8, the modularity score increases over time, meaning that the strength of the communities obtained through the algorithm continues to increase and become better in quality. On the T1–T4 time slices, the modularity score of IECD-NS is slightly better than that of ECDR; on the T5–T9 time slices, the scores of IECD-NS and ECDR methods on modularity are almost equal. Compared with ECDR, the proposed algorithm has more stable and superior performance in detecting communities with better structural quality. The increasing performance of the modularity score with increasing time slices also proves that the IECD-NS algorithm can guarantee the performance of the algorithm in large-scale dynamic networks. Figure 9 shows the runtimes of IECD-NS and ECDR at each time slice. As the network size increases, the runtimes of both algorithms increase, but it is clear that the increase in runtime is greater for ECDR and less for IECD-NS, and the runtime of the former is always greater than that of the latter, which indicates that IECD-NS, in large-scale dynamic networks, can guarantee the algorithm efficiency its incremental idea based on the neighborhood subgraph not only guarantees the effectiveness of the algorithm but also improves the efficiency of the algorithm.

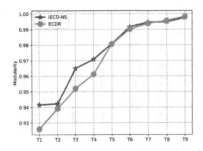
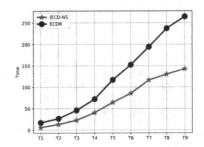

Fig. 8. Modularity score on DBLP   **Fig. 9.** Runtime comparison on DBLP

The evolution of the communities found on the DBLP Co-authorship can be seen in Table 1, which shows that during the initial T1–T4 period, when the network was just being established, there were more evolutionary events in the network, with the highest number of community birth events, and the number of community births in the network was much greater than the number of community deaths, with more communities growing than shrinking. The number of community births is much higher than the number of community deaths, and there are more communities growing than shrinking. In the T3–T4 time period, the number of community Births reached a high of 41, a peak that represents the peak of dynamic community evolution within the network, which gradually shifted to a steady state of growth. During the T4–T6 time period, the number of various evolutionary events in the network tends to decrease, and the state of the network stabilizes. From T7 to T9, the number of evolutionary events decreases significantly, and the number of Shrinking events is greater than the number of Growing events, indicating that the overall community size decreases and the network continues to shrink. From T1 to T9, the DBLP network went through three phases: high growth, stability, and shrinking, which is consistent with the real network development. The low number of Merging and Splitting events in any period indicates that the relationships between communities in the

Table 1. NUMBER OF EVOLVE EVENTS

	Birth	Death	Continuing	Shrinking	Growing	Merging	Splitting
T1–T2	29	11	8	10	15	1	0
T2–T3	25	15	7	11	21	5	1
T3–T4	35	13	4	14	14	4	2
T4–T5	20	13	7	16	12	4	1
T5–T6	11	13	2	8	20	3	1
T6–T7	5	7	5	6	14	1	2
T7–T8	3	5	4	10	10	2	2
T8–T9	6	5	1	12	13	1	1

DBLP network are more stable, which is consistent with the reality that there are fewer connections between different communities and closer relationships between users within communities, and that communities are less likely to merge or split.

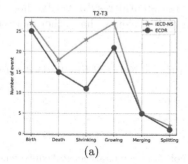 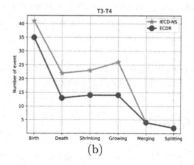

(a)   (b)

Fig. 10. Network change diagram

Although the standard number of community evolution events occurring is not available for comparison, it can be seen in Fig. 10 that the number of community evolution events found by IECD-NS is more similarly distributed across all types of events compared to the number found by the ECDR method, and the community evolution trends found by the two algorithms are nearly identical over the two adjacent time slices (a) and (b), for example, in the former time slice T2–T3, the number of events Shrinking is much smaller than the number of events Growing, while in the latter time slice, the number of events in both categories is almost equal, indicating that the network is moving from a fast-growing state to a stable state, a trend found by both algorithms; the similarity of the results obtained by both algorithms proves that the IECD-NS algorithm is somewhat accurate. In addition to the similarity in distribution, the IECD-NS method finds more events in all categories compared to the ECDR method, especially in the more subtle evolutionary events in the network such as Shrinking and Growing, indicating that the IECD-NS method is more sensitive to evolutionary events and has superior performance in finding more evolutionary events in the network.

5   Conclusion

In this paper, the IECD-NS algorithm is proposed to discover community structure in dynamic networks and track community evolution. Different from most existing methods, the IECD-NS algorithm exploits the neighbor subgraph information of nodes, excavates the relationship between neighbor nodes in the local topology, and discovers the core nodes in the network. In the study of community evolution, the core subgraph of each community is constructed by the features of core nodes. When processing increments, comprehensively consider the types of increments and the types of nodes involved. Due to the special nature of the neighbor subgraph, when the network edge changes, only the common neighbors of the incremental nodes will be affected, and other neighbors are not affected, which further increases the efficiency of processing incremental. The designed incremental processing strategy can track community evolution and identify community evolution events. The experimental results verify that the IECD-NS algorithm achieves better accuracy and efficiency than other methods on some famous datasets.

Acknowledgements. This work was supported by the National Key R&D Program of China (No. 2022YFC3302600).

References

1. Burt, R.S.: Social contagion and innovation: cohesion versus structural equivalence. Am. J. Sociol. **92**(6), 1287–1335 (1987)
2. Chen, Y.C., Zhu, W.Y., Peng, W.C., Lee, W.C., Lee, S.Y.: CIM: community-based influence maximization in social networks. ACM Trans. Intell. Syst. Technol. (TIST) **5**(2), 1–31 (2014)
3. Girvan, M., Newman, M.E.: Community structure in social and biological networks. Proc. Natl. Acad. Sci. **99**(12), 7821–7826 (2002)
4. Gregory, S.: Finding overlapping communities in networks by label propagation. New J. Phys. **12**(10), 103018 (2010)
5. Han, J., Li, W., Zhao, L., Su, Z., Zou, Y., Deng, W.: Community detection in dynamic networks via adaptive label propagation. PLoS ONE **12**(11), e0188655 (2017)
6. Huang, J., Sun, H., Han, J., Feng, B.: Density-based shrinkage for revealing hierarchical and overlapping community structure in networks. Physica A-Stat. Mech. Appl. **390**(11), 2160–2171 (2011)
7. Kanezashi, H., Suzumura, T.: An incremental local-first community detection method for dynamic graphs. In: 2016 IEEE International Conference on Big Data (Big Data), pp. 3318–3325. IEEE (2016)
8. Klein, D.J., Randić, M.: Resistance distance. J. Math. Chem. **12**(1), 81–95 (1993)
9. Lancichinetti, A., Fortunato, S., Kertész, J.: Detecting the overlapping and hierarchical community structure in complex networks. New J. Phys. **11**(3), 033015 (2009)
10. Li, G., Guo, K., Chen, Y., Wu, L., Zhu, D.: A dynamic community detection algorithm based on parallel incremental related vertices. In: 2017 IEEE 2nd International Conference on Big Data Analysis (ICBDA), pp. 779–783. IEEE (2017)
11. Li, W., Li, Y., Liu, W., Wang, C.: An influence maximization method based on crowd emotion under an emotion-based attribute social network. Inf. Process. Manage. **59**(2), 102818 (2022)
12. Li, W., Li, Z., Luvembe, A.M., Yang, C.: Influence maximization algorithm based on gaussian propagation model. Inf. Sci. **568**, 386–402 (2021)
13. Li, W., Ni, L., Wang, J., Wang, C.: Collaborative representation learning for nodes and relations via heterogeneous graph neural network. Knowl.-Based Syst. **255**, 109673 (2022)

14. Li, W., Zhong, K., Wang, J., Chen, D.: A dynamic algorithm based on cohesive entropy for influence maximization in social networks. Expert Syst. Appl. **169**, 114207 (2021)
15. Li, W., Zhou, X., Yang, C., Fan, Y., Wang, Z., Liu, Y.: Multi-objective optimization algorithm based on characteristics fusion of dynamic social networks for community discovery. Inf. Fusion **79**, 110–123 (2022)
16. Li, W., et al.: Evolutionary community discovery in dynamic social networks via resistance distance. Expert Syst. Appl. **171**, 114536 (2021)
17. Liu, W., Suzumura, T., Chen, L., Hu, G.: A generalized incremental bottom-up community detection framework for highly dynamic graphs. In: 2017 IEEE International Conference on Big Data (Big Data), pp. 3342–3351. IEEE (2017)
18. Lusseau, D., Schneider, K., Boisseau, O.J., Haase, P., Slooten, E., Dawson, S.M.: The bottlenose dolphin community of doubtful sound features a large proportion of long-lasting associations. Behav. Ecol. Sociobiol. **54**(4), 396–405 (2003)
19. Newman, M.E.: Fast algorithm for detecting community structure in networks. Phys. Rev. E **69**(6), 066133 (2004)
20. Rossetti, G., Pappalardo, L., Pedreschi, D., Giannotti, F.: Tiles: an online algorithm for community discovery in dynamic social networks. Mach. Learn. **106**(8), 1213–1241 (2017)
21. Wang, Z., Li, Z., Yuan, G., Sun, Y., Rui, X., Xiang, X.: Tracking the evolution of overlapping communities in dynamic social networks. Knowl.-Based Syst. **157**, 81–97 (2018)
22. Wu, L., Zhang, Q., Guo, K., Chen, E., Xu, C.: Dynamic community detection method based on an improved evolutionary matrix. Concurr. Comput. Pract. Experience **33**(8), e5314 (2021)
23. Xie, J., Szymanski, B.K.: Towards linear time overlapping community detection in social networks. In: Tan, P.-N., Chawla, S., Ho, C.K., Bailey, J. (eds.) PAKDD 2012. LNCS (LNAI), vol. 7302, pp. 25–36. Springer, Heidelberg (2012). https://doi.org/10.1007/978-3-642-30220-6_3
24. Xin, Y., Xie, Z.Q., Yang, J.: An adaptive random walk sampling method on dynamic community detection. Expert Syst. Appl. **58**, 10–19 (2016)
25. Xue, C., Wu, S., Zhang, Q., Shao, F.: An incremental group-specific framework based on community detection for cold start recommendation. IEEE Access **7**, 112363–112374 (2019)
26. Zachary, W.W.: An information flow model for conflict and fission in small groups. J. Anthropol. Res. **33**(4), 452–473 (1977)
27. Zhang, C., Zhang, Y., Wu, B.: A parallel community detection algorithm based on incremental clustering in dynamic network. In: 2018 IEEE/ACM International Conference on Advances in Social Networks Analysis and Mining (ASONAM), pp. 946–953. IEEE (2018)
28. Zhuang, D., Chang, M.J., Li, M.: DynaMo: dynamic community detection by incrementally maximizing modularity. IEEE Trans. Knowl. Data Eng. (2019)

Video Rumor Classification Based on Multi-modal Theme and Keyframe Fusion

Jinpeng You[1], Yanghao Lin[1], Dazhen Lin[1(✉)], and Donglin Cao[1,2]

[1] Artificial Intelligence Department, Xiamen University, Xiamen 361005, China
dzlin@xmu.edu.cn
[2] The Key Laboratory of Cognitive Computing and Intelligent Information
Processing of Fujian Education Institutions, Wuyi University,
Wuyishan 354300, China

Abstract. In recent years, short video platforms have become the main
source of online rumors. According to the statistics of Shanghai online
rumor refutation platform in 2021, the number of short video rumors
was about five times that of short video rumors in 2020, which makes
it necessary to detect rumors of short videos. At present, short video
rumor detection has the problem of multi-modal information fusion, the
traditional multi-modal fusion uses deep learning to obtain the underlying features of multi-modality and then aggregate them into cross-modal
features. However, there are distortions of theme and tampering with
key-frame in rumor videos. Therefore, short video rumors need to learn
features from the perspective of theme and key-frame. Aiming at the
problem of multi-modal information fusion of short video rumors, this
paper proposes a short video rumor detection model (TKCM) based on
theme and key-frame. It uses aggregation network to obtain the theme
feature of video, attention network to obtain the key-frame feature, and
fuses multi-modality by modal adjustment mechanism for short video
rumor detection. Experimental results show that the F1 score of the proposed method on the short video rumor dataset is improved by 2%–5%
compared with some state-of-the-art video classification models.

Keywords: Short video rumors detection · Multi-modal fusion ·
Modal adjustment

1 Introduction

With the rapid development of short video platforms such as Tiktok and Kwai in
recent years, short videos are becoming more and more popular with a large audience. According to a report published by QuestMobile, a data analysis website,
as of June 2020, the monthly active users of Tiktok and Kwai reached 513.36
million and 429.75 million respectively. The average user spends 1,569.5 min
on Tiktok and 1,162.6 min on Kwai each month. Everyone can express their
opinions and upload videos on the short video platform anytime and anywhere,
which makes the short video become the front of public opinion. At the same

Y. Sun et al. (Eds.): ChineseCSCW 2022, CCIS 1681, pp. 58–72, 2023.
https://doi.org/10.1007/978-981-99-2356-4_5

time, some people fabricate content, cut video, and combine content to create rumor videos to achieve some undesirable purposes, such as attracting attention, guiding, spreading, etc. For ordinary people, it is difficult to distinguish between rumors and the real situation, which makes some people become the spread of rumors unintentionally. The Shanghai rumor dispelling platform checked online rumors in 2021 and found that the number of fake rumors through short videos was about five times that of short videos in 2020. Statistics from the School of Journalism and Communication at Beijing Normal University show that nearly a fifth of online rumors are now accompanied by short videos. Due to the wide audience, fast spread and strong incitement of short videos, online rumors are easy to cause anxiety and panic among the public, leading to various mass incidents and seriously threatening social security. In the era of rapid development of short video, short video platform has become a hotbed of rumor transmission. Compared with plain text or text, video is more deceptive, and its source and authenticity are difficult to verify, so video rumors are more harmful. Therefore, accurate and timely detection of short video rumors is of great practical significance for maintaining the stability of public opinion on social media platforms, protecting the nation's online discourse power, and ensuring the stable development of social order.

Short video rumor detection can be considered as a sub-task of video classification, but it is different from other video classification tasks. It has the problem of multi-modal information fusion, which brings difficulties to the classification of short video rumors. Classical multi-modal fusion takes more into account multiple modes starting from the low-level features and gradually aggregating into cross-modal features through deep learning. However, in rumor videos, there are means such as theme distortion and key frame tampering. Therefore, we need to obtain rumor features from these two aspects. In this paper, our contributions are as follows:

(1) We propose a multi-modal rumor detection model based on theme and key frame, which detects video rumors from the aspects of theme distortion and key frame tampering. Compared with common video classification models, we have achieved the best performance.

(2) We have collected a small-scale video rumor dataset, and there is no publicly available video rumor dataset at present.

2   Related Work

The research on text and visual information shows that text and picture information are effective in rumor detection task, and combining these two kinds of information to detect rumors can improve the effect of rumor detection. Existing rumor detection methods based on multi-modal information can be divided into three categories.

2.1 Multi-modal Information Fusion

Many researchers use visual feature extractors and text feature extractors to obtain visual and text features respectively, and then combine visual information and text information for rumor detection. Singhal et al. [1] proposed that VGG [2] was used to extract visual information, BERT [3] was used to extract text information, and then the combination of visual and text information was fed into the classifier to classify fake news. Singhal et al. [4] proposes to use VGG to extract visual features and XLNET [5] to extract textual features, and combine them together and input the classifier to classify the rumor task. Liu et al. [6] considering that the rumor picture contains textual information, modeled the text information, the text information in the image and the visual information respectively, and spliced these features together as the final representation of the rumor for inference. However, directly combining visual and textual information is too simple to make full use of multi-modal information, so many scholars have developed some auxiliary tasks to help models better understand multi-modal information. Wang et al. [7] developed an auxiliary task, event discriminator. The event discriminator takes the concatenated multi-modal rumor information as input. This auxiliary task is used to better understand the multi-modal information to perform the rumor detection task. Khattar et al. [8] designed an auxiliary task, namely information reconstruction. The encoder encodes the visual and textual information of the message, and the decoder reconstructs the visual and textual information through the reconstruction task to better combine the multi-modal information.

2.2 Contrast Learning Between Models

It's assumed that if the picture doesn't match the text, then it's a rumor. Based on this assumption, the researchers encoded pictures and text information to calculate how similar they were to each other. If the similarity is high, it means that the textual information matches the visual information and it is true, while otherwise, it is a rumor. Zhou et al. [9] used the fully connected layer to map the extracted text features and visual features in the same vector space, and then compared their similarity. Xue et al. [10]] used pre-trained models to model text and visual information respectively, and then calculated the similarity between the two to determine whether the image and text match.

2.3 Enhance Multi-modal Information

The multi-modal rumors contain both textual and visual information, and these two types of information can complement each other and promote mutual understanding between different model. Based on this, many researchers have proposed that adding information between multiple modalities can help the model better understand the content of rumors and thus better analyze their authenticity. Jin et al. [11] first proposed that inter-modal attention is used to enhance the relationship information between modalities, and inter-modal attention mechanism is used to strengthen inter-modal information to better understand multi-modal information. Zhang et al. [12] proposed to use attention mechanism to obtain visual representation of text information so as to better understand multi-modal information. Wu et al. [13] proposed two-level joint attention of image and text information based on people's habit of reading news, "people tend to look at the text first, then look at the picture, then look at the text, then look at the picture". They modeled the spatial domain and frequency domain information of the image respectively. The two kinds of information are then combined with joint attention to get a better image representation. Qian et al. [14] uses joint attention to supplement visual and textual information, and uses visual information to supplement textual information. Moreover, they noticed that each layer of semantic hierarchical information was useful for fake news detection, so they combined the information of BERT's four layers with the image information. Zhang et al. [15] used multi-head converters to fuse text and visual information for better news representation. In addition, they used supervised contrast learning to learn higher-order features of real news and fake news. They chose theme similar, the same news authenticity as positive samples and chose theme similar, different news authenticity as negative samples. Supervised Contrast learning is used to narrow the distance between positive examples and widen the distance between positive and negative examples, so as to learn the higher-order features of real news and rumor news to better distinguish them.

3   Method

The previous multi-modal fusion mainly considered the gradual aggregation of multiple modalities from the underlying features to the cross-modal features. However, the rumor video contains distortions of the theme and manipulation of key frames, such as a barbecue scene distorted into an explosion scene. Therefore, the multi-modal fusion of short video rumors needs to learn the characteristics of rumors from themes and key frames.

We designed a short video rumor classification model called Theme and Keyframe Classification Model(TKCM), which is shown in Fig. 1. The TKCM model is described in detail from the extraction of modal features, theme features acquisition, key frame features acquisition and modal adjustment fusion mechanism.

3.1   Modal Feature Extraction

In order to obtain the theme feature representation and key-frame representation on the three modalities, it is necessary to obtain the coded representation of text, visual and audio modality first. This paper introduces the extraction methods of three modal features under text, vision and audio.

Textual Modality. The text comes from the title of the video, and the output of the last layer of the pre-trained model BERT is used to obtain the text feature

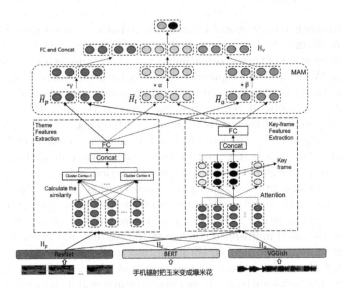

Fig. 1. The short video rumor classification model based on theme and key frames can be divided into four parts in total. It is the feature extraction of each modality, theme feature representation, key frame feature representation and modal adjustment fusion mechanism.

vector corresponding to the context, denoted as H_t.

$$H_t = \{h_{t1}, h_{t2}, ..., h_{tn}\} \tag{1}$$

where $H_t \in R^{tn*768}$, tn is the token length of the text.

Audio Modality. We use the pretrained model VGGish to obtain audio feature vectors. First, the audio was resampled to 16 kHz mono audio, and the spectrum was obtained by short-time Fourier transform with a frame shift of 10 ms using a 25 ms Hann window. Then the spectrum was mapped to the 64 order Mel filter bank to calculate the MEL spectrum, and the $log(Mel - spectrum + 0.01)$ was calculated to obtain stable Mel spectrum. These features are grouped into frames at a time of 0.96 s, with no frame overlap, and each frame contains 64 MEL bands, 10 ms in length, for a total of 96 frames. The output data format of VGGish model is $[NUMs\_frames, 128]$, where $NUMs\_frames$ indicates the frame length which is the audio duration divided by 0.96. Through these operations, the feature representation of the audio is obtained, denoted as H_a.

$$H_a = \{h_{a1}, h_{a2}, ..., h_{an}\} \tag{2}$$

where $H_a \in R^{an*128}$, an is the frame length of the audio.

Visual Modality. The short video is processed by frame extraction, and then the video pre-trained model is used to extract visual features. In order to keep in sync with the audio, a frame is extracted from the video at 0.96 s intervals. Then the corresponding representation of each frame is obtained through the pre-trained Resnet-50 [16] model. The feature vector of a sequence frame in a video is represented as H_p, where $H_p \in R^{pn*1024}$, pn is the number of frames extracted from each video.

$$H_p = \{h_{p1}, h_{p2}, ..., h_{pn}\} \tag{3}$$

3.2 Theme Features and Key-Frame Feature

The multi-modal fusion of short video rumors requires learning the features from the perspective of theme and key-frame. In order to obtain the vector features at the video level, the single frame feature vectors obtained by the pre-trained model of each modality are aggregated to form the overall theme feature. Moreover, the attention mechanism is used to filter the key-frame. In this paper, two aggregation networks are used to complete the experiment, namely NeXtVLAD [17] and AttentionCluster [18].

Theme Features Extraction. We use NeXtVLAD to select the clustering center, and then code visual, text, and audio to get the feature representation of the theme in each modality. The complete structure of NeXtVLAD is shown in Fig. 2, and the simplified structure is shown in the topic feature extraction module in Fig. 1.

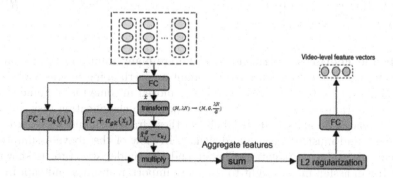

Fig. 2. NeXtVLAD is used to select the cluster center and encode visual, text and audio through three branches to get the theme representation in each modality.

The features of each modality are decomposed into a low-dimensional feature vector using the attention mechanism before aggregation and coding. The NeXtVLAD input has M frames, each frame has N dimensions and G is the size of the group. First, the n-dimensional features of the input vector x are converted to λn dimension through the fully connected layer, denoted by $\dot{x}$, where λ is usually set to 2, which means the dimension of the feature is converted from

(M, N) to (M, 2*N). Then $\dot{x}$ through three branches, the first transforms $\dot{x}$ to $\tilde{x}$, (M, λn) to (M, G, $\frac{\lambda n}{G}$), and then $\tilde{x}$ is subtracted separately with k cluster centers c_k, whose dimension is $\frac{\lambda n}{G}$, that is $\tilde{x}_{ij}^g - c_{kj}$ in Eq. 4. In the second branch, $\dot{x}$ is fed to the fully connected layer and the softmax function, $\alpha_{gk}(\dot{x}_i)$ in Eq. 4, which represent the proportion of the features of group G of frame i at the Kth cluster center c_k. The third branch inputs x to the fully connected layer and then passes through sigmoid function, namely $\alpha_g(\dot{x}_i)$ in Eq. 4, which represent the weight of i-th frame in group G, which is equivalent to the attention weight. Finally, each frame is divided into G feature vector spaces of lower dimensions, and each video frame can be expressed as Eq. 4.

$$v_{ijk}^g = \alpha_g(\dot{x}_i)\alpha_{gk}(\dot{x}_i)(\tilde{x}_{ij}^g - c_{kj}) \tag{4}$$

After obtaining the representation of each video frame, we aggregate the features of multiple images and sum them in the frame dimension and group dimension to get the aggregated feature y_{jk} shown in Eq. 5.

$$y_{jk} = \sum_{i,g} V_{ijk}^g \tag{5}$$

The dimension of the aggregate feature y_{jk} is reduced by a fully connected layer to get the theme feature of the short video. In the experimental part of this paper, we set $\lambda=2$, k=128 and G=8. N represents the dimensions of different modality, N=1024 in visual aggregation, N=768 for text aggregation, N=128 for audio aggregation. Each modality is aggregated by NeXtVLAD, and the theme feature vectors of text, video and vision are denoted as $H_{t-NV} \in R^{1*768}$, $H_{a-NV} \in R^{1*128}$ and $H_{p-NV} \in R^{1*1024}$.

Key-frame Features Extraction. There are many frames in the video, but the information of some frames is redundant or overlapping for the video data processing task, so these frames should be removed in some tasks. Some frames in the video frame sequence are critical to the video classification task, because they are related to classification labels, so these frames should be regarded as key frames and must be given more weight. In view of the above assumptions, this paper introduces Attention Cluster and the model structure is shown in Fig. 3. It can assign more weight to the more important frames and capture the key-frame representation.

Local features are integrated to obtain global features based on attention. The attention output is essentially equivalent to the weighted average, as shown in Eq. 6, v is the global feature derived from the attention unit, and a is the weight vector composed of two fully connected layers, Eq. 7. In the implementation, v is generated by the shift operation as shown in Eq. 8, where α and β are learnable scalars. By adding an independent learnable linear transformation to the output of each attention unit and then performing regularization, each attention unit tends to learn different distribution features, which makes the attention cluster better to learn data from different distributions and improve the representation

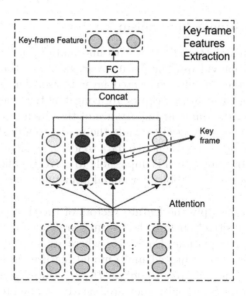

Fig. 3. Key frame feature extraction adopts Attention Cluster model.

of the whole network. Due to the use of attention clusters, the output of each attention unit is combined to obtain multiple global features g, as shown in Eq. 9, where N is the number of clusters.

$$v = aX \tag{6}$$

$$a = softmax(W_2 tanh(W_1 X^T + b_1) + b_2) \tag{7}$$

$$v = \frac{\alpha \cdot X + \beta}{\sqrt{N}\|\alpha \cdot aX + \rho\|_2} \tag{8}$$

$$g = [v_1, v_2, ..., v_N] \tag{9}$$

The global feature is concatenated and the dimension is reduced by the fully connected layer to get the global key frame feature vector. Each modality extracted in the above steps is aggregated through the AttentionCluster network to get the key frame feature vectors of the three modalities, denoted as $H_{t-AC} \in R^{1*768}$, $H_{a-AC} \in R^{1*128}$ and $H_{p-AC} \in R^{1*1024}$. Theme feature vectors and key frame feature vectors from different modalities extracted from the two aggregation networks are concatenated together respectively, shown in Eq. 10–12, to get the video-level feature vectors of each modality.

$$\overline{H}_t = [H_{t-NV}, H_{t-AC}] \quad \overline{H}_t \in R^{1*1536} \tag{10}$$

$$\overline{H}_a = [H_{a-NV}, H_{a-AC}] \quad \overline{H}_a \in R^{1*256} \tag{11}$$

$$\overline{H}_p = [H_{p-NV}, H_{p-AC}] \quad \overline{H}_p \in R^{1*2048} \tag{12}$$

3.3   Modal Adjustment Mechanism

Modalities can complement each other with information, so we use multi-modal fusion to detect rumor videos. The feature vectors of the three modalities are concatenated, and then a fully connected layer is used for linear transformation. In addition, before feature vectors are concatenated, the modal attention is adjusted to reflect the different importance of the three modalities for classification. Attention is usually used to guide the model to adjust the attention of different modalities, but it needs enough data to learn, small amount of data will lead to insufficient training which is impossible to correctly allocate attention to each modality. To solve this problem, a modal adjustment mechanism(MAM) is proposed in this paper.

The MAM is to multiply the feature vectors of the three modalities by the hyperparameter respectively before the features are concatenated, which range is $(0, 1]$, as shown in equations Eq. 13–15, where α, β, and γ are artificially set hyperparameters. The adjusted multi-modal features are linearly changed through the fully connected layer to obtain H_t, H_a, and H_p, and then they are concatenated to obtain H_v. Finally, they are linearly mapped to two-dimensional space for binary classification task, as shown in Eq. 16–21.

$$H_{t-out} = \alpha * \overline{H}_t \tag{13}$$

$$H_{a-out} = \beta * \overline{H}_a \tag{14}$$

$$H_{p-out} = \gamma * \overline{H}_p \tag{15}$$

$$H_t = H_{t-out} W_t \tag{16}$$

The adjusted multi-modal features are linearly changed through the fully connected layer to obtain H_t, H_a, and H_p, and then they are concatenated to obtain H_v. Finally, they are linearly mapped to two-dimensional space for binary classification task, as shown in Eq. 16–21, where W and b are the final linear layer weight and bias. In order to train the model, the minimization CrossEntropy loss function is used, as shown in Eq. 22.

$$H_a = H_{a-out} W_a \tag{17}$$

$$H_p = H_{p-out} W_p \tag{18}$$

$$H_v = [H_t, H_a, H_p] \tag{19}$$

$$logits = W^T H_v + b \tag{20}$$

$$p(y|logits) = softmax(logits) \tag{21}$$

$$L = -\frac{1}{N} \sum_{i=1}^{N} \left[y_i \log p(H_{vi}) + (1 - y_i) \log(1 - p(H_{vi})) \right] \tag{22}$$

The three modalities have different importance in the final rumor detection task. It is assumed that visual features are more worthy of attention in the detection, while the feature values of text and audio vectors are too large, which will lead to the classifier being dominated by text or audio. Although the classifier will learn and give more weight to visual features in the training, small amount of data cannot make the model focus on important modality. Through artificial intervention, it is possible to specify which modality plays a dominant role in the classification and help the model quickly learn feature information from important modalities. This mechanism is proved to be effective in experiment, and a comparative experiment of attention mechanism is set up to verify the effect of modal adjustment mechanism.

4   Experiment

4.1   DataSet

In our survey, there is no publicly available dataset of video rumors. The data used in the experiment is crawled from Douyin and manually labeled by us. There are 584 rumor short videos and 625 non-rumor videos, a total of 1209 data. The data set is divided into training set and test set according to the ratio of 0.8 and 0.2. The details of the division of the data set are shown in Table 1.

Table 1. Short video rumor dataset partitioning.

Rumors dataset	Non-rumor	Rumor	Total
Train set	500	468	968
Test set	125	116	241
Total	256	584	1209

4.2   Implementation Details

In the feature extractor, the dimension of the text feature obtained by BERT is 768, the dimension of the audio feature obtained by VGGish is 128 and the dimension of the image feature obtained by ReNet-50 is 1024. In NeXtVLAD, set λ to 2, k to 128, and G to 8.

$$Accuracy = \frac{1}{n} \sum_{i=1}^{N} (f(x_i) = label_i) \tag{23}$$

$$Precision = \frac{TP}{TP + FP} \tag{24}$$

$$Recall = \frac{TP}{TP + FN} \tag{25}$$

$$F1 = \frac{2 * Precision * Recall}{Precision + Recall} \tag{26}$$

The weights of the modal adjustment mechanism for the three modalities are 1.0 for vision, 0.8 for text and 0.7 for audio. The evaluation metrics used are accuracy, precision of rumors, recall of rumors and F1 of rumors, as shown in Eq. 23–26, where N is the number of samples , $f(x_i)$ is predict labels of sample x_i, $label_i$ is ground label of x_i, TP represents the number of samples with ground labels as rumors and predict labels as rumors, FP represents the number of samples in which the ground label is non-rumor and the predict label is rumor, FN denotes the number of samples in which the ground label is a rumor and the predict label is a non-rumor.

4.3   Modal Combination Analysis

In order to verify the effect of various modalities and their combinations in short video rumor detection, we set up single modality and multi-modal combinations respectively for the experiment. In this experiment, the modal adjustment mechanism is deleted for fairness. Table 2 shows the experimental results.

Table 2. Single-modality and multi-modal results.

Modality	Accuracy	Precision	Recall	F1
Text	69.7%	71.3%	69.9%	70.4%
Vision	72.1%	72.6%	72.8%	73.4%
Audio	68.9%	70.5%	68.8%	69.6%
Text + Vision	**75.9%**	**77.2%**	**76.0%**	**76.6%**
Text + Audio	72.6%	74.0%	72.8%	76.6%
Vision + Audio	74.6%	76.2%	74.4%	75.3%
Text + Vision + Audio	75.5%	76.7%	76.0%	76.3%

Comparing the experimental results of the three single-modality, the accuracy of using visual modality alone is more than two percentage points higher than that of using other modality alone, and it is more than three percentage points higher than that of using audio modal alone. It shows that visual modality plays a more important role in rumor video detection, followed by textual, which indicates the size of the hyperparameter setting for the modal adjustment mechanism. The experimental results of the text modality and its corresponding dual-modality combination show that the performance is improved whether it is integrated into the visual or the audio modality, which indicate that the information contained in the text modality is different from other modalities, and the accuracy of video rumor detection can be enhanced by fusing multi-modality. It is worth paying attention to the results of the three modalities. The best result of the two modalities is higher than the combination of the three in accuracy. It may be that the model does not learn the weights between the modalities well, which indicates that it is necessary to add the modal adjustment mechanism.

4.4 Model Comparison Experiment

Table 3 shows the results of our model and other models, where the best results are in bold. It shows our model outperform the competing methods on the short video rumor dataset, and the accuracy of TKCM is improved by 1.7%–4.6% , which indicate that theme and key frame feature extraction can improve the ability of short video rumor detection task.

Table 3. Results of different models, where VideoLSTM, FSTCN, ActionVLAD and TPN are based on single-modal video classification, while att-RNN, MVT and TKCM are all based on multi-mode.

Model	Accuracy	Precision	Recall	F1
VideoLSTM [19]	73.9%	75.4%	73.6%	74.5%
FSTCN [20]	72.6%	74.4%	72.2%	73.2%
ActionVLAD [21]	75.1%	76.4%	75.2%	75.8%
TPN [22]	75.1%	76.9%	74.4%	75.6%
att-RNN [23]	72.2%	73.8%	72.0%	72.9%
MVT [24]	75.5%	77.0%	75.2%	76.1%
TKCM	**77.2%**	**78.2%**	**77.6%**	**77.9%**

The performance of the multi-modal model is generally higher than that of the single-modality, indicating that multiple modalities are helpful for video rumor detection. Among them, although att-RNN uses both visual and text, its accuracy is low, which may be because it uses LSTM and VGG in feature extraction of each modality, while MVT can obtain advanced features. By comparing them, it can be found that the poor performance of att-RNN on rumor video detection may be caused by the weak feature extraction model and the inability to obtain high-level features of vision and text, which also verifies the importance of modal feature extractor.

4.5 Ablation Experiment

Table 4 shows the experimental results of our model after removing each module, in which the bold part is the best result. It can be seen intuitively that only using theme features or key-frame features can improve the classification performance, and combining them can further improve. Theme extraction and key frame extraction of clustering can mine different information in rumor detection.

In order to explore the performance of the modal adjustment mechanism, we removed it to verify its effectiveness. After removing the modal adjustment mechanism, the accuracy decreases, which shows the three modalities have different importance. The attention mechanism needs enough data to learn. Due to the small amount of data, which cannot allocate enough attention to each

Table 4. Ablation experiment results, AC stands for AttentionCluster, NV stands for NeXtVLAD, MAM stands for modal adjustment mechanism, Attention stands for Attention mechanism, "-" stands for removing this module in the model, and "+" stands for adding this module.

Model	Accuracy	Precision	Recall	F1
TKCM-NV	75.9%	77.2%	76.0%	76.6%
TKCM-AC	75.5%	77.0%	75.2%	76.1%
TKCM-MAM	75.5%	76.7%	76.0%	76.3%
TKCM-MAM+Attention	76.3%	77.9%	76.0%	76.9%
TKCM	**77.2%**	**78.2%**	**77.6%**	**77.9%**

modality. In order to verify this problem, the modal adjustment mechanism is replaced by a layer of self-attention mechanism. The use of the modal adjustment mechanism has a percentage point improvement in F1 score. This artificial hyper-parameter setting method performs better than the attention mechanism in the case of small amount of data.

5   Conclusion

In this paper, we propose a multi-modal fusion model based on theme and key-frame. It can effectively capture the theme and key-frame information of the three modalities in the video, and carry out rumor detection from them. The F1 score of the proposed method on the short video rumor dataset is improved by 2%–5% compared with the commonly used video classification model. The experimental results show that the proposed model performs better on short video rumor dataset than the single-modality and multi-modality models. At the same time, the effect of each module in the model is verified by ablation experiment. In addition, in order to verify the feasibility of the modal adjustment mechanism on a small amount of data, the effectiveness of the modal adjustment mechanism is verified by attention mechanism.

Acknowledgements. This work is supported by the National Natural Science Foundation of China (No. 62076210), the Natural Science Foundation of Xiamen (No. 3502Z20227188) and the Open Project Program of The Key Laboratory of Cognitive Computing and Intelligent Information Processing of Fujian Education Institution-sWuyi University(No.KLCCIIP2020203)

References

1. Singhal, S., Shah, R., Chakraborty, T., et al.: Spotfake: A multi-modal framework for fake news detection. In: 2019 IEEE Fifth International Conference on Multimedia Big Data (BigMM). IEEE, 2019 pp. 39–47 (2019)

2. Kingma, D.P., Welling, M.: Auto-encoding variational bayes. arXiv preprint arXiv:1312.6114 (2013)
3. Devlin, J., Chang, M.W., Lee, K., et al.: Bert: Pre-training of deep bidirectional transformers for language understanding. arXiv preprint arXiv:1810.04805, 2018. Author, F.: Contribution title. In: 9th International Proceedings on Proceedings, pp. 1–2. Publisher, Location (2010)
4. Singhal, S., Kabra, A., Sharma, M., et al.: Spotfake+: A multimodal framework for fake news detection via transfer learning (student abstract). In: Proceedings of the AAAI Conference on Artificial Intelligence, vol. 34(10), 13915–13916 (2020)
5. Yang, Z., Dai, Z., Yang, Y., et al.: Xlnet: Generalized autoregressive pretraining for lan-guage understanding. Adv. Neural Inform. Process. Syst. **32** (2019)
6. Liu, J., Feng, K., Jeff, Z.P., et al.: MSRD: Multi-Modal Web Rumor Detection Method. J. Comput. Res. Develop. **57**(11), 2328 (2020)
7. Wang, Y., Ma, F., Jin, Z., et al.: Eann: Event adversarial neural networks for multi-modal fake news detection. In: Proceedings of the 24th ACM SIGKDD International Conference on Knowledge Discovery and data Mining, pp. 849–857 (2018)
8. Khattar, D., Goud, J.S., Gupta, M., et al.: Mvae: Multimodal variational autoencoder for fake news detection. In: The World Wide Web Conference, pp. 2915–2921 (2019)
9. Zhou, X., Wu, J., Zafarani, R.: SAFE: similarity-aware multi-modal fake news detection. In: Lauw, H.W., Wong, R.C.-W., Ntoulas, A., Lim, E.-P., Ng, S.-K., Pan, S.J. (eds.) PAKDD 2020. LNCS (LNAI), vol. 12085, pp. 354–367. Springer, Cham (2020). https://doi.org/10.1007/978-3-030-47436-2_27
10. Xue, J., Wang, Y., Tian, Y., et al.: Detecting fake news by exploring the consistency of mul-timodal data. Inform. Process. Manage. **58**(5), 102610 (2021)
11. Jin, Z., Cao, J., Guo, H., et al.: Multimodal fusion with recurrent neural networks for rumor detection on microblogs. In: Proceedings of the 25th ACM International Conference on Multimedia, pp. 795–816 (2017)
12. Zhang, H., Fang, Q., Qian, S., et al.: Multi-modal knowledge-aware event memory network for social media rumor detection. In: Proceedings of the 27th ACM International Conference on Multimedia, pp. 1942–1951 (2019)
13. Wu, Y., Zhan, P., Zhang, Y., et al.: Multimodal Fusion with Co-Attention Networks for Fake News Detection. In: Findings of the Association for Computational Linguistics: ACL-IJCNLP 2021, pp. 2560–2569 (2021)
14. Qian, S., Wang, J., Hu, J., et al.: Hierarchical multi-modal contextual attention network for fake news detection. In: Proceedings of the 44th International ACM SIGIR Conference on Research and Development in Information Retrieval, pp. 153–162 (2021)
15. Zhang, W., Gui, L., He, Y.: Supervised Contrastive Learning for Multimodal Unreliable News Detection in COVID-19 Pandemic. In: Proceedings of the 30th ACM International Conference on Information and Knowledge Management, pp. 3637–3641 (2021)
16. He, K., Zhang, X., Ren, S., et al.: Deep residual learning for image recognition. In: Proceedings of the IEEE Conference on Computer Vision and Pattern Recognition, pp. 770–778 (2016)
17. Qi, P., Cao, J., Li, X., et al.: Improving Fake News Detection by Using an Entity-enhanced Framework to Fuse Diverse Multimodal Clues. In: Proceedings of the 29th ACM International Conference on Multimedia, pp. 1212–1220 (2021)
18. Long, X., Gan, C., De Melo, G., et al.: Attention clusters: Purely attention based local fea-ture integration for video classification. In: Proceedings of the IEEE Conference on Computer Vision and Pattern Recognition, pp. 7834–7843 (2018)

19. Li, Z., Gavrilyuk, K., Gavves, E., et al.: Videolstm convolves, attends and flows for action recognition. Comput. Vis. Image Underst. **166**, 41–50 (2018)
20. Sun L, Jia K, Yeung D Y, et al. Human action recognition using factorized spatio-temporal convolutional networks. In: Proceedings of the IEEE International Conference on Computer Vision, pp. 4597–4605 (2015)
21. Girdhar, R., Ramanan, D., Gupta, A., et al.: Actionvlad: Learning spatio-temporal aggregation for action classification. In: Proceedings of the IEEE Conference on Computer Vision and Pattern Recognition, pp. 971–980 (2017)
22. Yang, C., Xu, Y., Shi, J., et al.: Temporal pyramid network for action recognition. In: Proceedings of the IEEE/CVF Conference on Computer Vision and Pattern Recognition, pp. 591–600 (2020)
23. Jin, Z., Cao, J., Guo, H., et al.: Multimodal fusion with recurrent neural networks for rumor detection on microblogs. In: Proceedings of the 25th ACM International Conference on Multimedia, pp. 795–816 (2017)
24. Lv, Z., Lei, T., Liang, X., et al.: A Multi-modal System for Video Semantic Understanding. In: China Conference on Knowledge Graph and Semantic Computing. Springer, Singapore, pp. 34–43 (2021). https://doi.org/10.1007/978-981-19-0713-5_5

Association Rule Guided Web API Complementary Function Recommendation for Mashup Creation: An Explainable Perspective

Pengfei He[1], Wenchao Qi[1], Xiaowei Liu[1], Linlin Liu[2], Dianlong You[1,3], Limin Shen[1,3], and Zhen Chen[1,3(⊠)]

[1] School of Information Science and Engineering, Yanshan University, Qinhuangdao, China
zhenchen@ysu.edu.cn
[2] National Science Libraries, Chinese Academy of Sciences, Beijing, China
[3] Key Laboratory for Computer Virtual Technology and System Integration of Hebei Province, Yanshan University, Qinhuangdao, China

Abstract. As more and more service providers encapsulate and publish their data and services on the internet in the form of Web APIs, the number of Web APIs is ever-increasing. For this reason, Web API recommendation is gaining momentum and has achieved high performance in accuracy. However, few studies paid attention to function recommendation. As an indispensable entity in the mashup-API ecosystem, function is not only the in-facto basis of API taxonomy, but also determines the compatibility and the internal construction pattern of mashup composition. Considering that users adopt multiple function invocations during a development cycle and the number of functions is also increasing, we propose the complementary function recommendation(CFR), a function-to-function problem. To solve the CFR, we regard each mashup as a transaction set for frequent pattern mining and propose an association rule-based complementary function recommendation(ARCFR) system, which provides function recommendation and corresponding probability explanation. Our experiments show that ARCFR can recommend complementary function effectively, and we give two applicable scenarios to demonstrate the practical value of our method in more aspects.

Keywords: Web API · Mashup · Association rule · Complementary function recommendation

1 Introduction

Service Oriented Computing (SOC) has brought great innovation in software engineering and greatly changed the way of software development [17,22].

Supported by National Natural Science Foundation of China No.62102348, 62276226. Natural Science Foundation of Hebei Province F2022203012,F2021203038, Science and Technology Research Project of Hebei University QN2020183, Innovation Capability Improvement Plan Project of Hebei Province 22567626H.

Y. Sun et al. (Eds.): ChineseCSCW 2022, CCIS 1681, pp. 73–83, 2023.
https://doi.org/10.1007/978-981-99-2356-4_6

SOC presents computing resources over the internet in the form of platform-independent Web APIs [21]. Promoted by SOC, mashup has become a promising software development manner which allows software developers to combine existing Web APIs with different functionalities to create value-added web applications in an agile manner [3,10]. Moreover, mashup application has the superiority of short development cycle and strong scalability. Thus, they are easy to be reused when requirements change [11,19].

In practice, Web APIs come from service platforms such as *ProgrammableWeb*. In the repository, an overwhelming number of published Web APIs make it challenging for developers to manually choose appropriate Web APIs to satisfy their requirements [13,20]. Therefore, Web API recommendation for mashup creation is gaining momentum. API recommendation is generally divided into two objectives: one is to recommend Web APIs with better quality of service (QoS); and the other is to recommend Web APIs that better meet functional requirements.

The QoS-based methods recommend Web APIs from the perspective of QoS optimization [2,5]. Existing methods successfully predict missing QoS data to recommend APIs with best QoS. However, the QoS-based approach has two limitations: (1)due to the dynamic nature of the network, QoS is difficult to be measured accurately in real time [8]; (2)QoS is function-independent but function is the indispensable consideration for Web API recommendation.

Requirement-oriented researches [4,6,7,14,18] were done to analyze functional requirements of mashups from their descriptions, then recommend Web APIs based on their semantic compatibility with descriptions. In addition, it is common to directly recommend Web APIs from the entire repository and rank them in a single list. Although they can output meaning recommendation results, there are also two drawbacks: (1)the APIs in the recommendation list may not be compatible; (2)due to the significant long-tail effect and usage sparsity, many APIs are invisible to users.

Generally, all APIs are typically assigned to different categories of the repository according to their functions as shown in Fig. 1(a). And this taxonomy is open and visible to users, so if the compatibility between categories, i.e. function complementarity, is modeled, the coarse-grained relations of all relevant APIs will be well defined. As shown in the Fig. 1(b), suppose hyperlinks of corresponding functional categories are provided for users who have selected a specific API, users can be informed of appropriate types of APIs for their next invocation.

Considering the demand, we propose complementary function recommendation(CFR), a function-to-function recommendation problem. The input of CFR is query function from the selected API, while functions on the output side represent categories where APIs complement the selected ones. In order to implement CFR, we regard mashups as transaction sets and propose an association rule-based complementary function recommendation (ARCFR) system, which not only gives recommendations, but also provides additional additional intuitive probability explanation as shown in Fig. 1(b).

(a) (b)

Fig. 1. 'Mashup', 'Function', 'Web API' on ProgrammableWeb (a) and Toy Example of Complementary Function Recommendation (b)

The main contributions of the paper are four-fold:

(1) This is the first work to cope with the Web API complementary function recommendation (CFR) problem. CFR not only demonstrates the internal construction pattern of mashups, but also the compatibility between different kinds of Web APIs.

(2) We observe two fact that a mashup development always involves multiple function invocations and the number of available functions is increasing. They demonstrates the necessity of complementary function recommendation.

(3) We use association rules to model the complementary relations between functions and propose a rule-based recommendation system, ARCFR. The experiment on real-world dataset shows that ARCFR can effectively recommend complementary functions.

(4) We propose two typical application scenarios of ARCFR: complementary Web API recommendation and Web API bundle recommendation, which show that our system also has practical value in more aspects.

The rest of this paper is organized as follows. Section 2 overviews the related work; Sect. 3 introduces motivations of CFR; Sect. 4 introduces the ARCFR system; Sect. 5 introduces two practical scenarios about ARCFR; and Sect. 6 concludes the paper.

2 Related Work

Recently, a lot of state-of-the-art algorithms have been widely used in API recommendation. e.g., deep learning-based [4,13,23], RL learning-based [16], graph-based [7]. These methods focus on the accuracy and diversity of mashup-API recommendations, which have reached a high level. In this paper, we turn our attention to function recommendation, which will enable mashup developers to have a better experience because of our intuitive and explanatory recommendations.

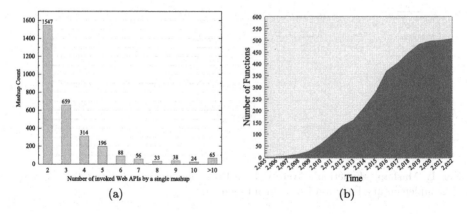

Fig. 2. Users always call multiple APIs to add functions for mashup creation (a), and the number of functions is ever-increasing (b).

3 Motivation

In this section, through data statistics, we demonstrate the motivation of CFR, i.e., the necessity. In addition, CFR is defined.

3.1 Necessity

Generally, mashups are composed of multiple functional modules, so mashup developers always call different kinds of APIs which provided diversify functions. As shown in Fig. 2(a), 1,547 mashups invoked two APIs, which was the most common situation. And function components of mashup can also become relatively complex, maybe with more than 10 functions which are always located in different categories. Consequently, developers need to constantly explore new kinds of APIs to add new functions to their mashup application.

With the expansion of API information, the increase of functions is also overloaded for developers. As shown in Fig. 2(b), from 2005 to 2022, 507 different functions have been provided on the *Programmable Web* and the number is still increasing. Thus, it is necessary and nontrival to help users find the appropriate functions by recommendation system.

3.2 Formulation

Learning from API recommendation systems, CFR can be formalized as formula (1):

$$CFR(A, K) = X \tag{1}$$

A and K are inputs, while A denotes the target function(category in repository) of selected API, K denotes the number of recommended functions, the recommendation system for CFR can predict the complementary function list

Table 1. ARCFR

Target	Top-3 Function Recommendation	Confidence
Music	Video	40.70%
	Social	23.30%
	Photos	16.70%
eCommerce	Search	25.30%
	Mapping	19.30%
	Social	14.80%
Analytics	Social	46.90%
	Mapping	43.80%
	None	None

$X=\{x_k \in X, k \in \{1,2,\ldots,K\}\}$ with respect to A. In the repository, all APIs $a \in x_k$ are functionally complementary to selected API.

4   Methodology

In this section, we first introduce how our rule-based system works. Next, we introduce association rule mining process by Apriori. Then association rules on functional complementarity are analyzed. Finally, we conduct experiments to prove the feasibility of ARCFR on CFR problem.

4.1   Web API Complementary Function Recommendation System

The association rule-based complementary function recommendation system consists of all association rules about functions. As shown in Table 1, provided target function, the system matches all rules triggered by the target at first. Then, all rules triggered are sorted by their $confidence(target \Rightarrow X)$, and the consequent of the *TopK* rules are the functions recommended. E.g., taking Music as input, the diversity degree K is set to 3. *Top3* consequents, [Video, Social, Photos], will be recommended with probability, which means that developers who call Music APIs may need APIs that provide [Video, Social, Photos] with probability of [40.7%, 23.30%, 16.70%].

4.2   Mining Association Rules

Association rule mining is the cornerstone of rule-based recommendation system [15]. The basic motivation is that if some functions co-invoked quite a lot of times, they are likely to complement each other. In this paper, we adopt the most simple and intuitive Apriori algorithm, which was proposed by Agrawal [1].

Apriori is a level-wise algorithm, using the frequent k-itemset to explore frequent $(k+1)$-itemset. First of all, we search in the transaction database to find the set of frequent 1-itemset recorded as L_1. Then, we search for the set of frequent 2-itemset L_2 by L_1 and repeat the process. To find each frequent itemset, we need to scan the database once until no frequent itemset can be found anymore. The relevant concepts and formulas are defined as follows.

Let $\{T = t_1, t_2, \ldots, t_n\}$ be the set of transactions(mashups), and $\{I = i_1, i_2, \ldots, i_n\}$ is a set of attributes called items(functions). Each transaction $t_i(i = 1, 2, \ldots, n)$ corresponds to a subset of $(I\ t_i \subseteq I\ )$. The association rule $A \Rightarrow B$ can be defined as an implication, while $A_i(i = 1, 2, \ldots, n)$ and $B_j(j = 1, 2, \ldots, m)$ be two subsets of I, $A \Rightarrow B$ implies that if the *function* A is applied to build mashups, B would also be invoked $(A \subseteq B, B \subseteq I\ and\ A \cap B = \emptyset)$ with a specific probability.

Association rules mainly involve the following three indicators: *support*, and *confidence*. The *support* of association rule $A \Rightarrow B$ in database T refers to the proportion of mashups involving both A and B in all mashups:

$$\text{Support}(A \Rightarrow B) = P(A \cap B)$$
$$= \frac{|\{A \cap B \subseteq t, t \subseteq T\}|}{|T|} \tag{2}$$

High *support* indicates the high popularity of function A and function B. In particular, the *support*(A) refers to $P(A)$.

The *confidence* of association rule $A \Rightarrow B$ in database T refers to the proportion of mashups involving both A and B to those just containing A:

$$\text{Confidence}\ (A \Rightarrow B) = P(B \mid A)$$
$$= \frac{\text{Support}(A \Rightarrow B)}{\text{Support}(A)} \tag{3}$$

The greater the *confidence*, the stronger the influence of A on B. In our context, *confidence* is the measurement of functional complementarity, hence B with the largest *confidence* would be recommended to A.

Algorithm 1. Frequent itemset generating.

Input: The database of Transaction T, the minimum number of occurrences of items *min-support*.

Output: Frequent itemset L.

1: Initialize the parameters:$k = 1, L = \emptyset$ and $C_1 = \emptyset$;
2: Generate the set of candidate 1-itemset C_1: All the items;
3: Generate the set of frequent 1-itemset L_1: Calculate the *support* of each item in C_1 by formula (2), and add all the items whose *support* $> (min\text{-}support\ /\ |T|)$ into L_1;
4: Generate the set of candidate k-itemset C_2 based on the set of frequent (k-1)-itemset L_1: Link any two different items in L_1;
5: Generate the frequent k-itemset L_k based on the candidate k-itemset C_k: Calculate the *support* of each item in C_k by formula (3), and add all the items whose *support* $> (min\text{-}support\ /\ |T|)$ into L;
6: Return the frequent itemset L.

Table 2. The List of Partial Association Rules

Rule	Antecedent⇒Consequent	Support	Confidence
1	eCommerce,Video⇒Mapping	0.015	0.837
2	Messaging⇒Telephony	0.026	0.460
3	Telephony⇒Messaging	0.026	0.359
4	Music⇒Video	0.021	0.377
5	Music,Video⇒Social	0.007	0.303

Algorithm 1 represents generation process of frequent itemsets. From Step 2 to Step 5 is a recursive process. When no more itemsets can be found, the loop exits. Step 4 is the join step to generate $K+1$ candidate item set. Step 5 is the pruning step. According to the Apriori theorem, if an itemset is not a frequent itemset, its superset cannot be a frequent itemset. The frequent itemset generation is the core process of Apriori.

Algorithm 2 represents the generation of association rules, which are composed of implication expressions of mutually exclusive subsets of frequent itemsets. After the antecedent and consequent of the implication are determined, the *confidence* can be calculated according to formula(3).

Algorithm 2. Association rule generating.

Input: Frequent itemset T, the minimum *confidence* of filtered rules *min-confidence*.
Output: Association rule set R.

1: Initialize $R = \emptyset$;
2: Calculate the *confidence* between the nonempty subsets of each frequent itemset by formula (3);
3: Add all the association rules whose *confidence*>*min-confidence*;
4: Return the set of association rules R.

Accordingly, all association rules on functions are obtained.

4.3   Association Rule Analyses

Through analyses of association rules in Table 2, the characteristics of functional complementarity can be revealed.

(1) *Complementary function chain*

Complementary function chain means that the development process of mashups can be regarded as a continuous extension of the function chain. Observing Rule 4 and Rule 5, when Music is used to build an application, Video is also likely to be called with the probability of 37.7%. Subsequently, when Video and Music are called together, Social will be more complementary to the combination of Music and Video, with the probability of 30.3%. Complementary function chain is critical for ARCFR, which makes each recommendation function not only complementary to the last recommendation function, but also all previous selected ones.

(2) *Asymmetry*

By comparing Rule 2 and Rule 3, the *confidence* of Messaging⇒Telephony is 0.460 but *confidence* of Telephony⇒Messaging is 0.359. Different *confidence* shows that the complementarity is asymmetric. The asymmetry of complementarity between functions can be calculated by *Imbalance Rate(IR)*:

$$IR = \frac{P(B \mid A)}{P(A \mid B)} \tag{4}$$

After calculation by formula(4), the *IR* between Messaging and Telephony is 1.28, which demonstrates that the asymmetrical relation between A and B is not significant.

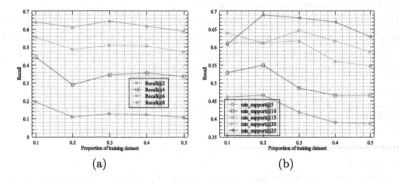

Fig. 3. Recall with different K values (a) and min-support (b).

4.4   Experiments

In order to evaluate the performance of ARCFR, we conduct simulation experiments on real-world dataset. For simplicity, our experiments use all frequent binomial sets as samples (two functions are co-invoked, one is the target function, the other is the recommended function). The dataset is divided into training set and test set in proportion. *Recall* is used to evaluate the performance of the system as Eq. (5). K and min-support are two hyper-parameters of ARCFR. We evaluate the performance of the system with different K and min-support.

$$Recall = \frac{TP}{TP + FN} \tag{5}$$

As shown in Fig. 3(a), if the K value is large, more functions will be recommended to users, which will inevitably improve the *Recall*. When K is set to 8

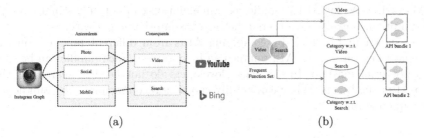

Fig. 4. Complementary Web API recommendation (a) and Web API bundle recommendation (b).

and the test set proportion is set to 30%, the highest *Recall* achieves 64.55%, which means that over half of the recommendations will be useful for users.

In addition, the min-support indicates the reliability of the rule as shown in Fig. 3(b). The higher the minimum support, the higher the reliability of filtered rules. However, a higher min-support will reduce coverage of system, because the number of rules decreases. When the min-support is set to 25 and the test set proportion is set to 20%, *recall* achieves 68.97%.

5   Application Scenarios

In this section, two practical scenarios of CFR are proposed: complementary Web API recommendation and Web API bundle recommendation.

5.1   Typical Application Scenarios

(1) *Complementary Web API recommendation*

Complementary product recommendation (CPR), whose aim is providing product suggestions that are often bought together to serve a joint demand [9], while CFR can be used to conduct complementary API recommendation. In Sect. 2, we draw the conclusion that requirements for cloud APIs are also joint. CFR can provide guidance for complementary API recommendation, because APIs that provide complementary functions are complementary theoretically.

Figure 4(a) shows an actual example: Instagram Graph. First of all, Instagram Graph API provide Photo, Social, and Mobile. Using these functions as inputs, CFR outputs complementary functions, Video and Search. Filtering APIs that provide these complementary functions through other indicators, such as QoS, complementary API recommendation can be obtained.

(2) *Web API bundle recommendation*

Bundling strategy is a form of symbiosis marketing. The appropriate bundling strategy can achieve a desired coordination and mutual promotion of two or more goods with the systemic effect of "1+1>2" [12], such as toothpaste and toothbrushes. As for APIs, bundle recommendation can not only stimulate API consumption, but also give users a better consumption experience.

As shown in Fig. 4(b), by combining APIs from different functions in the frequent function set, the API bundle can be obtained. Each bundle can be seen as a potential mashup. In this way, developers do not need to search for the Web APIs one by one. They can readily choose a recommended API bundle for mashup creation.

6   Conclusion

In this paper, we present the association rule-based complementary function recommendation system to solve the complementary function recommendation in an explainable perspective. To this end, we firstly conduct detailed data analyses on real-world repository, and provide objective facts to illustrate the necessity of complementary function recommendation. Then, we utilize the records of mashups as transaction sets to mine association rules to build our system. Through analyses of association rules, we ascertain the characteristics of functional complementarity, i.e., complementary function chain and asymmetry. And our experiments indicate the effectiveness of the proposed approach. Finally, two typical application scenarios demonstrate that our system also has more practical application value in the Web API ecosystem.

References

1. Agrawal, R., Imieliński, T., Swami, A.: Mining association rules between sets of items in large databases. In: Proceedings of the 1993 ACM SIGMOD International Conference on Management of Data, pp. 207–216 (1993)
2. Ahmed, W., Wu, Y., Zheng, W.: Response time based optimal web service selection. IEEE Trans. Parallel Distrib. Syst. **26**(2), 551–561 (2013)
3. Cao, B., Liu, X.F., Rahman, M.M., Li, B., Liu, J., Tang, M.: Integrated content and network-based service clustering and web apis recommendation for mashup development. IEEE Trans. Serv. Comput. **13**(1), 99–113 (2017)
4. Cao, B., et al.: Web API recommendation via combining graph attention representation and deep factorization machines quality prediction. Concurr. Comput. Pract. Exp. **34**(21), e7069 (2022)
5. Chen, M., Ma, Y.: A hybrid approach to web service recommendation based on qos-aware rating and ranking. arXiv preprint arXiv:1501.04298 (2015)
6. Gao, W., Wu, J.: A novel framework for service set recommendation in mashup creation. In: 2017 IEEE International Conference on Web Services (ICWS), pp. 65–72. IEEE (2017)
7. Gong, W., et al.: Dawar: diversity-aware web apis recommendation for mashup creation based on correlation graph. In: Proceedings of the 45th International ACM SIGIR Conference on Research and Development in Information Retrieval, SIGIR 2022, pp. 395–404. Association for Computing Machinery, New York (2022)
8. Gu, Q., Cao, J., Liu, Y.: CSBR: a compositional semantics-based service bundle recommendation approach for mashup development. IEEE Trans. Serv. Comput. **15**, 3170–3183 (2021)

9. Hao, J., et al.: P-companion: a principled framework for diversified complementary product recommendation. In: Proceedings of the 29th ACM International Conference on Information & Knowledge Management, pp. 2517–2524 (2020)

10. He, Q., et al.: Efficient keyword search for building service-based systems based on dynamic programming. In: Maximilien, M., Vallecillo, A., Wang, J., Oriol, M. (eds.) ICSOC 2017. LNCS, vol. 10601, pp. 462–470. Springer, Cham (2017). https://doi.org/10.1007/978-3-319-69035-3_33

11. Huang, G., Ma, Y., Liu, X., Luo, Y., Lu, X., Blake, M.B.: Model-based automated navigation and composition of complex service mashups. IEEE Trans. Serv. Comput. **8**(3), 494–506 (2014)

12. Liu, Y., Wang, X., Ren, W.: A bundling sales strategy for a two-stage supply chain based on the complementarity elasticity of imperfect complementary products. J. Bus. Ind. Mark. (2020)

13. Ma, Y., Geng, X., Wang, J.: A deep neural network with multiplex interactions for cold-start service recommendation. IEEE Trans. Eng. Manag. **68**(1), 105–119 (2020)

14. Nguyen, M., Yu, J., Bai, Q., Yongchareon, S., Han, Y.: Attentional matrix factorization with document-context awareness and implicit API relationship for service recommendation. In: Proceedings of the Australasian Computer Science Week Multiconference, pp. 1–10 (2020)

15. Sarwar, B., Karypis, G., Konstan, J., Riedl, J.: Item-based collaborative filtering recommendation algorithms. In: Proceedings of the 10th International Conference on World Wide Web, pp. 285–295 (2001)

16. Wan, M., Qiu, Y.: Interactive reinforcement learning-based API recommendation. In: 2022 4th International Conference on Advances in Computer Technology, Information Science and Communications (CTISC), pp. 1–5 (2022)

17. Wei, Y., Blake, M.B.: Service-oriented computing and cloud computing: challenges and opportunities. IEEE Internet Comput. **14**(6), 72–75 (2010)

18. Xia, B., Fan, Y., Tan, W., Huang, K., Zhang, J., Wu, C.: Category-aware API clustering and distributed recommendation for automatic mashup creation. IEEE Trans. Serv. Comput. **8**(5), 674–687 (2014)

19. Xiao, Y., Liu, J., Hu, R., Cao, B., Cao, Y.: DINRec: deep interest network based api recommendation approach for mashup creation. In: Cheng, R., Mamoulis, N., Sun, Y., Huang, X. (eds.) WISE 2020. LNCS, vol. 11881, pp. 179–193. Springer, Cham (2019). https://doi.org/10.1007/978-3-030-34223-4_12

20. Yao, L., Wang, X., Sheng, Q.Z., Benatallah, B., Huang, C.: Mashup recommendation by regularizing matrix factorization with API co-invocations. IEEE Trans. Serv. Comput. **14**(2), 502–515 (2018)

21. Yasmin, J., Tian, Y., Yang, J.: A first look at the deprecation of restful APIs: an empirical study. In: 2020 IEEE International Conference on Software Maintenance and Evolution (ICSME), pp. 151–161. IEEE (2020)

22. Zhang, L.J., Zhang, J., Cai, H.: Services Computing. Springer, New York (2007). https://doi.org/10.1007/978-3-540-38284-3

23. Zhang, Y., Su, J., Chen, S.: A deep recommendation framework for completely new users in mashup creation. In: Gao, H., Wang, X., Iqbal, M., Yin, Y., Yin, J., Gu, N. (eds.) CollaborateCom 2020. LNICST, vol. 349, pp. 550–566. Springer, Cham (2021). https://doi.org/10.1007/978-3-030-67537-0_33

Globally Consistent Vertical Federated Graph Autoencoder for Privacy-Preserving Community Detection

Yutong Fang[1,2,3], Qingqing Huang[1,2,3], Enjie Ye[1,2,3], Wenzhong Guo[1,2,3], Kun Guo[1,2,3(✉)], and Xiaoqi Chen[2]

[1] Fujian Provincial Key Laboratory of Network Computing and Intelligent Information Processing, Fuzhou University, Fuzhou 350108, China
gukn@fzu.edu.cn
[2] College of Computer and Data Science/College of Software, Fuzhou University, Fuzhou 350108, China
[3] Key Laboratory of Spatial Data Mining and Information Sharing, Ministry of Education, Fuzhou 350108, China

Abstract. Community detection is a trendy area in research on complex network analysis and has a wide range of real-world applications, like advertising. As people become increasingly concerned about privacy, protecting participants' privacy in distributed community detection has become a new challenge. When applied to not identically and independently distributed (Non-IID) data, most federated graph algorithms suffer from the weight divergence problem caused by diversified training of local and global models, resulting in accuracy degradation. Furthermore, the privacy protection approaches based on anonymization, such as differential privacy (DP), and cryptography, such as homomorphic encryption (HE), incur accuracy loss and high time consumption, respectively. In this paper, we propose a globally consistent vertical federated graph autoencoder (GCVFGAE) algorithm, which builds a globally consistent model among the coordinator and all participants to solve the Non-IID graph data problem. As well, an attribute blinding strategy based on security aggregation is developed to protect the network privacy of each participant without losing accuracy. Both real-world and artificial networks' experiments show that our algorithm reaches higher accuracy than the existing vertical federated graph neural networks (GNNs) and the simple distributed graph autoencoder without federated learning and detects communities identical to those found by the standard graph autoencoder (GAE).

Keywords: Community detection · Federated learning · Graph neural network · Non-IID data · Privacy-Preserving

1 Introduction

Many complex networks exist in real life, such as social networks among people. Community detection is an essential subject of complex network analysis, which

Y. Sun et al. (Eds.): ChineseCSCW 2022, CCIS 1681, pp. 84–94, 2023.
https://doi.org/10.1007/978-981-99-2356-4_7

aims at mining closely related vertex clusters in complex networks. Community detection algorithms are widely used in many real-world applications such as customer profiling, protein structure discovery, etc. In recent years, privacy protection laws have been enacted in many countries, such as China's Law on Personal Information Protection [4] and the EU's GDPR [5]. Therefore, it is necessary to protect privacy in network data mining tasks such as community detection.

The emergence of the federated learning paradigm offers an effective solution to distributed privacy-preserving data mining [16]. Federated learning requires that local private data should not be exchanged and supports the integration of multiple privacy-preserving techniques. The traditional federated learning for network data mining usually trains a global model simultaneously with multiple local models, which is vulnerable to Non-IID graph data due to weight divergence. We consider that the non-IID attribute value causes the non-IID problem in vertical joint learning, called the attribute non-IID problem for simplicity. Attribute non-IID problems include the problem of non-identically distribution of attributes that each participant has a set of different and independent attribute sets. Additionally, the widely adopted DP or HE based privacy protection techniques in federated learning suffer the problems of accuracy loss or high time consumption [2,13].

In this paper, we propose a globally consistent vertical federated graph autoencoder, namely GCVFGAE, which shares a unified model among the coordinator and all participants to solve the Non-IID data problem under vertical federated learning. The attribute blinding strategy based on security aggregation [1] is employed to protect the intermediate data transferred among the coordinator and participants. The contributions of this paper can be summarized as follows:

1. By sharing a unified model among the coordinator and all participants, GCVFGAE ensures that a globally consistent vertical federated model is trained in the distributed privacy-preserving community detection, therefore achieving higher accuracy compared with the existing vertical federated GNNs and the simple distributed graph autoencoder without federated learning.
2. The attribute blinding strategy ensures that GCVFGAE sustains no accuracy loss in distributed privacy-preserving community detection based on vertical federated learning, that is, it achieves the same accuracy as the standard GAE.
3. We evaluate our algorithm on both real and artificial networks, and the results demonstrate its effectiveness and correctness of GCVFGAE.

2 Related Work

2.1 Privacy-preserving Community Detection

Current privacy-preserving community detection algorithms primarily use anonymization and cryptography techniques to protect network privacy. The method based on anonymization adds noise information to the network so that the attacker can not locate the target vertex according to topology or attribute information [9,14]. Ji et al. [14] proposed a privacy-preserving community detection algorithm using DP. Kamar et al. [9] proposed a fuzzy set-based random anonymization algorithm called PPRA. The methods based on cryptography protect privacy by encrypting the data transmitted between participants. Chu et al. [3] designed a distributed privacy control protocol DPISP based on Shamir secret sharing, which can be used for privacy protection on centralized social networks.

2.2   Federated Learning on Graphs

Existing methods of federated graph learning are categorized as horizontal federated graph learning and vertical federated graph learning. Most approaches [11,15] use a graph neural network (GNN) with some gradient aggregation mechanism in horizontal federated graph learning. In vertical federated graph learning. Zhou et al. [2] designed a framework for vertical federated GNN learning by segmenting the GNNs' computational graph. Meanwhile, DP is used to foreclose information leaking. Ni et al. [13] proposed the framework of a federated graph convolutional networks (GCN) learning. The participants transmitted intermediate results using HE for each iteration of the training process.

3   Preliminaries

3.1   Problem Definition

Assume that n_p participants work together to detect communities within their local networks. n_p represents the number of participants. We denote a local network as $G(V, E, \mathbf{A}, \mathbf{X})$, where $v = \{v_1, v_2, ..., v_n\}$ denotes the set of vertices, E represents the set of edges, $\mathbf{A} \in \mathbb{R}^{n \times n}$ is an adjacency matrix. $\mathbf{A}_{i,j} = 1$ indicates the existence of an edge between v_i and v_j , $\mathbf{X} \in \mathbb{R}^{n \times d}$ denotes an attribute matrix. $\mathbf{X}_{i,k}$ equals to 1 if vertex v_i has k-th attributes, otherwise 0. In the vertical federated learning setting, we assume that each participant has the highest overlap, each participant has the same topology and their adjacency matrix $\mathbf{A_k}$ is the same, which does not belong to private information for all participants. Given networks $G_p = \{G_1, G_2, ..., G_{n_p}\}$, distributed privacy-preserving community detection is the division of vertices on G_p into n_c communities $\{C_1, C_2, ..., C_{n_c}\}$ under the condition that the networks' privacy is not compromised, as defined in [12].

3.2   Standard Graph Autoencoder

In this paper, the algorithm proposed in [8] is used as a baseline algorithm. We call it standard graph autoencoder (SGAE) in the remaining sections to avoid name ambiguity. The procedure of SGAE is as follows:

Stage 1: Forward propagation. Propagate the topology and attributes of a network forward through the autoencoder to calculate the loss function.

Step 1: Encoder. A L_c-layer GCN model is used in the encoder. Caculate vertex embedding vectors according to Eq. (1)

$$\mathbf{Z} = \tilde{\mathbf{A}}\sigma\left(\tilde{\mathbf{A}}\mathbf{X}\mathbf{W}^{(0)}\right)\mathbf{W}^{(1)} = \tilde{\mathbf{A}}\sigma\left(\mathbf{Y}^{(0)}\right)\mathbf{W}^{(1)} \tag{1}$$

where $\tilde{\mathbf{A}} = \mathbf{D}^{-\frac{1}{2}}\mathbf{A}\mathbf{D}^{-\frac{1}{2}}$ is the Laplacian matrix and $\mathbf{Y}^{(0)} = \tilde{\mathbf{A}}\mathbf{X}\mathbf{W}^{(0)}$. $\mathbf{D}$ is the degree matrix. $\mathbf{Z}$ and σ denote the vertex embedding matrix and the activation function, respectively. $\mathbf{W}^{(i)}$ represents the parameter matrix of layer i.

Step 2: Decoder. Use the inner product as a simple decoder to reconstruct the original adjacency matrix $\hat{\mathbf{A}}$ according to Eq. (2).

$$\hat{\mathbf{A}} = \sigma\left(\mathbf{Z}\mathbf{Z}^{\mathrm{T}}\right) \tag{2}$$

Step 3: Loss computation. The goal of SGAE is to make the difference between the original adjacency matrix and the reconstructed adjacency matrix to be minimized. Therefore, the loss function of SGAE is formulated as Eq. (3).

$$L_{GAE} = -\frac{1}{N}\sum_{i,j\in A} s_{i,j}\log s'_{i,j} + (1 - s_{i,j})\log\left(1 - s'_{i,j}\right) \tag{3}$$

where $s_{i,j}$ and $s'_{i,j}$ represent the values of similarity between vertices i and j in the original adjacency matrix $\mathbf{A}$ and the reconstructed adjacency matrix $\hat{\mathbf{A}}$, respectively.

Stage 2:Backward propagation. Propagate the loss backward through the autoencoder to update its parameters by stochastic gradient descending (SGD) according to Eq. (4).

$$\mathbf{W}^{(l)} \leftarrow \mathbf{W}^{(l)} - \eta\nabla l\left(\mathbf{W}^{(l)}\right) \tag{4}$$

where η denotes the learning rate.

4   Globally Consistent Vertical Federated Graph Autoencoder

4.1   Design of GCVFGAE

In order to solve the attribute Non-IID problem in vertical federated graph learning, we propose a globally consistent vertical federated GAE to utilize the attributes of each participant's network for community detection while protecting their privacy. Different from the traditional manner of training global and local models separately, GCVFGAE train a globally consistent model through the collaboration of participants and the coordinator. Specifically, it splits the process of community detection into three stages. The first and second stages are devoted to the forward and backward propagation of GAE, respectively, as shown in Fig. 1. An attribute blinding strategy based on security aggregation is adopted to insure the privacy of the intermediate data exchanged between the coordinator and participants. When applied to community detection, we can use a clustering algorithm to group the embedding vectors of the final hidden layer of GCVFGAE to obtain communities.

Stage 1: Forward Propagation. Each participant cooperates with the coordinator to complete the forward propagation of GAE. To prevent the leakage of each participant's local attributes, each participant P_k first calculates its local first-layer embedding matrix $\mathbf{Y}_{P_k}^{(0)}$ and sends it to the coordinator. Then, the coordinator aggregates all $\mathbf{Y}_{P_k}^{(0)}$s to obain a complete first-layer embedding matrix $\mathbf{H}^{(0)}$. Finally, the loss of GAE is calculated. The stage is composed of five steps.

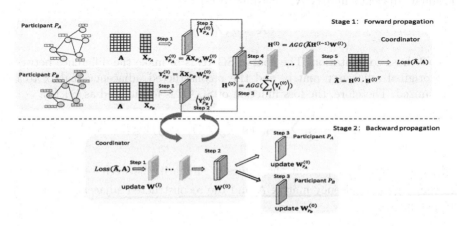

Fig. 1. Framework of GCVFGAE

Step 1: Each participant calculates its local Laplacian matrix $\tilde{\mathbf{A}}$ and attribute matrix $\mathbf{X}_{P_k}$, and then the local first-layer embedding matrix $\mathbf{Y}_{P_k}^{(0)}$ according to Eq. (1).

Step 2: Each participant uses the attribute blinding strategy to compute an encrypted $\left\langle \mathbf{Y}_{P_k}^{(0)} \right\rangle$ and sends it to the coordinator. The attribute blinding strategy guarantees that the ciphertext sum $\sum_k \left\langle \mathbf{Y}_{P_k}^{(0)} \right\rangle$ is equivalent to the plain-text sum $\sum_k \mathbf{Y}_{P_k}^{(0)}$ by adding random mask vectors according to Eq. (5) and canceling out them in summation, where $\mathbf{r}_{k,u}$ is the random vector for participants P_k and P_u. Therefore, the sum obtain by the coordinator is correct.

$$\left\langle \mathbf{Y}_{P_k}^{(0)} \right\rangle = \mathbf{Y}_{P_k}^{(0)} + \sum_{u \neq k} \mathbf{r}_{k,u} \tag{5}$$

Step 3: The coordinator collects all $\mathbf{Y}_{P_k}^{(0)}$s and calculates the complete first-layer embedding matrix $\mathbf{H}^{(0)} = AGG\left(\sum_k \left\langle \mathbf{Y}_{P_k}^{(0)} \right\rangle\right)$.

Step 4: The coordinator continues the remaining $L_c - 1$ rounds of forward propagation by itself until the embedding matrix $\mathbf{H}^{(L_c)}$ is calculated.

Step 5: The loss of GCVFGAE is calculated according to Eqs. (2) and (3).

Stage 2: Backward Propagation. The loss is propagated back to layers 1 to $L_c - 1$ of GCVFGAE on the coordinator side. For the backward propagation of layer 0, the gradients of layer 0 are first sent back to each participant by the coordinator. Second, each participant updates its first-layer local parameters. There are three steps on this stage.

Step 1: The coordinator updates parameter matrix $\mathbf{W}^{(L_c-1)}$ to $\mathbf{W}^{(1)}$ according to Eq. (4).

Step 2: The coordinator split (or decancatenated) the complete first-layer gradient vector $\nabla l\left(\mathbf{W}^{(0)}\right)$ into local first-layer gradients vectors $\nabla l\left(\mathbf{W}_k^{(0)}\right)$s and sends each one to its corresponding participant.

Step 3: Each participant updates its local first-layer parameter matrix $\mathbf{W}_k^{(0)}$ according to Eq. (4).

Stages 1 and 2 are run iteratively until the loss function is converged. If we want to detect communities in the networks, a clustering algorithm can be run by the coordinator to group the final layer's embedding vectors (and their vertices) into communities and sends them back to each participant.

The pseudo-code of GCVFGAE is given in Algorithm 1. Due to page limits, correctness and privacy analysis are available on GitHub [1].

5   Experiments

5.1   Datasets

The performance of GCVFGAE is evaluated using five real-world and two artificial networks. The vertex-cutting-based method [6] is used to split the complete attribute set into 2, 4, 6, 8, and 10 sets of attributes to imitate participants' networks under the vertical federated scenario. In this case, each participant contains only a part of the attributes. Therefore the attribute Non-IID problem emerges naturally.

Cora and Citeseer are real-world networks from LINQS. We select subgraphs from dblp, musae_github (abbreviated as musae), and lastfm_asia (abbreviated as lastfm) networks from SNAP as our dataset.

Artificial Networks. Using the LFR benchmark [10], we create two artificial network groups, D1 and D2. The number of vertices in D1 ranges from 1000 to 5000. D1 is used to evaluate algorithms' accuracy with varying network sizes. The number of vertices in D2 is 5000, and the range of μ is 0.1–0.5. D2 is used to evaluate algorithms with varying degrees of blurry community boundaries because parameter μ determines the mixing degree of communities. The larger the value of μ is, the more difficult for an algorithm to detect communities. The approach proposed in [7] creates vertex attributes for D1 and D2 networks.

---

[1] https://github.com/fytmolly97/GCVFGAE.

Algorithm 1: GCVFGAE

Input: Adjacent matrix $\mathbf{A}$, Laplace adjacency matrix $\tilde{\mathbf{A}}$, Attribute matrix $\mathbf{X}_{P_k}$, Training rounds T

Output: vertex embedding matrix $\mathbf{Z}$

1 **for** j $\leftarrow$ *0 to T* **do**

    // STAGE 1:Forwoard Propagation

    // Participant P_k:

2   Initialize $\mathbf{W}_{P_k}^{(0)}$ randomly;

3    $\mathbf{Y}_{P_k}^{(0)} = \tilde{\mathbf{A}}\mathbf{X}_{P_k}\mathbf{W}_{P_k}^{(0)}$;// Step 1

4    $\left\langle \mathbf{Y}_{P_k}^{(0)} \right\rangle = E(\mathbf{Y}_{P_k}^{(0)})$; // Step 2

5   Send $\langle \mathbf{Y}_{P_k} \rangle$ to the coordinator;

    // Coordinator:

6    $\mathbf{H}^{(0)} = AGG\left(\sum_k \left\langle \mathbf{Y}_{P_k}^{(0)} \right\rangle \right)$;// Step 3

7    $\mathbf{Z} = \sigma\left(\mathbf{W}^{L-1} \cdot \sigma\left(\dots \sigma\left(\mathbf{W} \cdot \mathbf{H}^{(0)} \right) \right) \right)$;// Step 4

8   Reconstruct $\hat{\mathbf{A}}$ according to Eq. (2)// Step 5

9   Calculate loss L_{GAE} according to Eq. (3);

    // STAGE 2:Backward Propagation

    // Coordinator:

10   Upadate $\mathbf{W}^{(l)}$ according to Eq. (4);// Step 1

11   Split $\nabla l\left(\mathbf{W}^{(0)} \right)$ into $\nabla l\left(\mathbf{W}_k^{(0)} \right)$s and send them to its corresponding participant P_k;// Step 2

    // Participant P_k:

12   Update $\mathbf{W}_k^{(0)}$ according to Eq. (4);// Step 3

13 Return $\mathbf{Z}$;

5.2   Baseline Algorithms

We compared GCVFGAE with SGAE, a simple distributed graph autoencoder without federated learning (SDGAE) and VFGNN [2] in the experiments. SGAE can see the complete network and attribute set in embedding vector learning. SDGAE trains a model by each participant itself without their cooperation and is used in the ablation study to reflect the effectiveness of federated learning. VFGNN is used in the accuracy experiment.

5.3   Experimental Settings and Evaluation Metrics

For all algorithms, the learning rate is preset to 0.001. The activation function is chosen from tanhshrink() and tanh(), depending on which brings higher accuracy. The neural network structure of all algorithms is configured to ($|C|$, 256, 256, 256), where C is the number of attributes. We use Kmeans to generate communities according to the embedding vectors learned by the algorithms. To evaluate the communities obtained by clustering, we set the parameter K to the true number of communities per network.

We use Normalized Mutual Information (NMI) and Adjusted Rand Index (ARI) as our evaluation metrics to evaluate these algorithms' accuracy. Due to page limits, the experimental results of all ARI metrics are available on GitHub[1].

5.4 Consistency Experiment

We verify the correctness of GCVFGAE by comparing the accuracy of GCVFGAE with that of SGAE on the same networks. As the Fig. 2 shows, the NMI values of GCVFGAE are the same as that of SGAE on all networks with different participants. Therefore, the experimental results indicate that GCVFGAE's accuracy is identical to SGAE's, that is, it incurs no accuracy loss. Moreover, Fig. 2 demonstrates the attribute blinding strategy employed in GCVFGAE does not affect its correctness while holding the privacy of each participant in good protection.

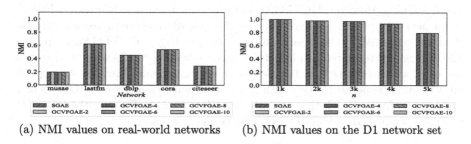

(a) NMI values on real-world networks   (b) NMI values on the D1 network set

Fig. 2. Results of the consistency experiment

5.5 Ablation Experiment

To verify the algorithm's effectiveness, we compare the accuracy of GCVFGAE and SDGAE. As the Fig. 3 shows, on the D2 network with μ=0.5 and Citeseer, the GCVFGAE has a higher NMI value than the SDGAE. Moreover, the accuracy of the SDGAE declined rapidly as the number of participants mounted. On the contrary, GCVFGAE' accuracy is not affected by the number of participants. In vertical federated learning, each participant can only use its local attribute set. Therefore, for traditional vertical graph federated learning methods training multiple local models, the more participants are involved in federated learning, the more unbalanced the attribute sets of their local networks, resulting in a more severe Non-IID problem. In contrast, GCVFGAE learns a globally consistent model with the knowledge of all participants' local networks. Therefore it is not affected by unbalanced attribute sets of the participants.

5.6 Accuracy Experiment

Citeseer and the D2 network are used in the accuracy experiment. Figure 4 depicts the NMI values of GCVFGAE and VFGNN with varying numbers of

---

[1] https://github.com/fytmolly97/GCVFGAE.

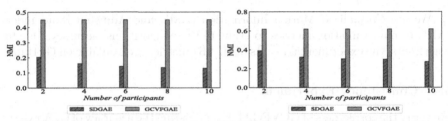

(a) NMI values on citeseer network

(b) NMI values on the D2 network with μ =0.5

Fig. 3. Results of the ablation experiment

participants. As we can observe from the figure, both algorithms' accuracy does not decrease as the number of participants increases, revealing that they can counteract the affection of the attribute Non-IID problem in vertical federated graph learning. However, GCVFGAE performs consistently better than VFGNN in all networks, which is largely due to the globally consistent model learning strategy employed in the algorithm. As shown in Fig. 5, GCVFGAE surpasses VFGNN no matter in real-world networks or artificial networks with varying values of μ, which reflects that the globally consistent model learning strategy in GCVFGAE is superior to the multiple model training strategy in VFGNN when they are confronted with the attribute Non-IID problem. Besides, the lossy DP technique employed in VFGNN also affects its accuracy.

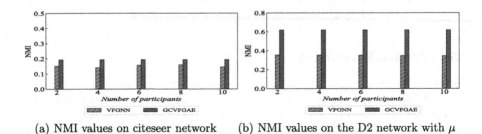

(a) NMI values on citeseer network

(b) NMI values on the D2 network with μ =0.5

Fig. 4. Results of the accurancy experiment on different numbers of participants

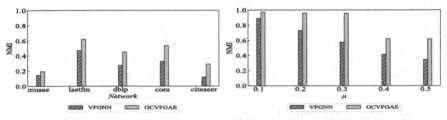

(a) NMI values on real-world networks

(b) NMI values on the D2 network set

Fig. 5. Results of the accurancy experiment

5.7   Running Time Experiment

We conduct running time experiments on GCVFGAE and VFGNN on real-world and artificial networks. As is indicated in Fig. 6, we conduct running time experiments on Cora and the D2 network with $\mu = 0.5$ of different participants. And we conducted a more specific running time experiment with multiple participants. As shown in Fig. 6, VFGNN run much slower than GCVFGAE. As can be seen, the encryption time represents a small proportion of the algorithm's total time.

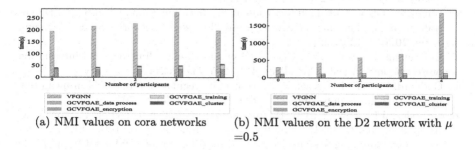

(a) NMI values on cora networks   (b) NMI values on the D2 network with μ =0.5

Fig. 6. Results of the running time experiment

6   Conclusions

We propose a globally consistent vertical federated GAE, namely GCVFGAE, for privacy-preserving community detection. The coordinator and participants jointly construct a globally consistent model to mitigate the attribute Non-IID problem and enhance the accuracy of community detection. The attribute blinding strategy is used to strictly protect the network privacy of each participant without the loss of accuracy under a semi-honest model. The correctness and effectiveness of GCVFGAE are verified by integrated experiments on real networks and artificial networks. Henceforth, we would like to further study the Non-IID problem in network topology in the horizontal federated scenario and develop a federated community detection algorithm based on it.

Acknowledgements. This work was supported by the National Natural Science Foundation of China under Grant No. 62002063 and No. U21A20472, the National Key Research and Development Plan of China under Grant No.2021YFB36-00503, the Fujian Collaborative Innovation Center for Big Data Applications in Governments, the Fujian Industry-Academy Cooperation Project under Grant No. 2017H6008 and No. 2018H6010, the Natural Science Foundation of Fujian Province under Grant No.2020J05112, the Fujian Provincial Department of Education under Grant No.JAT190026, the Major Science and Technology Project of Fujian Province under Grant No.2021HZ022007 and Haixi Government Big Data Application Cooperative Innovation Center.

References

1. Bonawitz, K., et al.: Practical secure aggregation for privacy-preserving machine learning. In: proceedings of the 2017 ACM SIGSAC Conference on Computer and Communications Security, pp. 1175–1191 (2017)
2. Chen, C., et al.: Vertically federated graph neural network for privacy-preserving node classification. In: Raedt, L.D. (ed.) Proceedings of the Thirty-First International Joint Conference on Artificial Intelligence, IJCAI-2022, pp. 1959–1965. International Joint Conferences on Artificial Intelligence Organization (2022). https://doi.org/10.24963/ijcai.2022/272, main Track
3. Chu, S.C., Chen, L., Kumar, S., Kumari, S., Rodrigues, J.J., Chen, C.M.: Decentralized private information sharing protocol on social networks. Secur. Commun. Netw. **2020**, 1–12 (2020)
4. Determann, L., Ruan, Z.J., Gao, T., Tam, J.: China's draft personal information protection law. J. Data Prot. Priv. **4**(3), 235–259 (2021)
5. Goddard, M.: The EU general data protection regulation (GDPR): European regulation that has a global impact. Int. J. Mark. Res. **59**(6), 703 (2017)
6. Gonzalez, J.E., Low, Y., Gu, H., Bickson, D., Guestrin, C.: {PowerGraph}: distributed {Graph-Parallel} computation on natural graphs. In: 10th USENIX Symposium on Operating Systems Design and Implementation (OSDI 2012), pp. 17–30 (2012)
7. Huang, B., Wang, C., Wang, B.: NMLPA: uncovering overlapping communities in attributed networks via a multi-label propagation approach. Sensors **19**(2), 260 (2019)
8. Kipf, T.N., Welling, M.: Variational graph auto-encoders. arXiv preprint arXiv:1611.07308 (2016)
9. Kumar, S., Kumar, P.: Privacy preserving in online social networks using fuzzy rewiring. IEEE Trans. Eng. Manag. **70**, 2071–2079 (2021)
10. Lancichinetti, A., Fortunato, S., Radicchi, F.: Benchmark graphs for testing community detection algorithms. Phys. Rev. E **78**(4), 046110 (2008)
11. Liu, R., Yu, H.: Federated graph neural networks: overview, techniques and challenges (2022)
12. Majeed, A., Lee, S.: Anonymization techniques for privacy preserving data publishing: a comprehensive survey. IEEE Access **9**, 8512–8545 (2020)
13. Ni, X., Xu, X., Lyu, L., Meng, C., Wang, W.: A vertical federated learning framework for graph convolutional network. arXiv preprint arXiv:2106.11593 (2021)
14. Ji, T., Luo, C., Guo, Y., Wang, Q., Yu, L.: Community detection in online social networks: a differentially private and parsimonious approach. IEEE Trans. Comput. Soc. Syst. **7**(1), 151–163 (2020)
15. Xie, H., Ma, J., Xiong, L., Yang, C.: Federated graph classification over non-iid graphs. Adv. Neural Inf. Process. Syst. **34**, 18839–18852 (2021)
16. Yang, Q., Liu, Y., Chen, T., Tong, Y.: Federated machine learning: concept and applications. ACM Trans. Intell. Syst. Technol. (TIST) **10**(2), 1–19 (2019)

Research on User Personality Characteristics Mining Based on Social Media

Yu Zheng, Jun Shen, Ru Jia$^{(\boxtimes)}$, and Ru Li

IT Academy Inner Mongolia University, Hohhot, Inner Mongolia Autonomous Region, China
{csjiaru,csliru}@imu.edu.cn

Abstract. As an important medium for users to share experiences and feelings, social media is the carrier of users' emotions, hobbies and interests, and it has become an important research content to mine user's personality information. Due to the unstructured and sparse characteristics of social texts, it is difficult to grasp the fine-grained word segmentation and contain a large number of noise words in mining user personality characteristics. However, the probability model of traditional language rules has weak generalization ability, and the deep learning model has poor anti-noise performance and poor feature extraction ability. This paper proposes a text analysis model based on attention mechanism, referred to as ATCNN-BiGRU. The model uses the attention mechanism to construct the input feature matrix of the text, solves the interference of noise in the social text, and integrates the double-layer gated unit network to overcome the problem that the fixed-step scanning mechanism in the convolutional neural network affects the extraction of global contextual semantic features. Through the experimental results on datasets in three different domains and different languages, it is found that compared with the existing mainstream text analysis models, the ATCNN-BiGRU proposed in this paper has a significant improvement in the prediction accuracy, especially in the Chinese data set by 2%.

Keywords: Personality Traits · Convolutional Neural Networks · Attention Mechanisms · Layer Gating Units

1 Introduction

Information data has gradually become a necessity for the development of productivity in the Internet era. As of June 2021, mobile Internet users accounted for 99.6% of Chinese Internet users [1]. With the sharp increase in the amount of user interaction data, information overload and inability to accurately obtain demand information, social media is an important medium for users to share their experiences and feelings, and the generated social texts are the carriers of users' emotions, hobbies and interests. Mining user personality information has become an important solution.

Important content in social texts are reviews of related services or products that accumulate a large amount of user personality characteristic information. This data contains information such as users' opinions, emotions and preferences for certain things.

With the help of social text mining user personality feature information, it can further help merchants to familiarize themselves with user preferences, and more quickly expose these products or services that users can demand to places where users can easily contact them.

As the mainstream model of current personality feature extraction and application, deep learning has received extensive attention from researchers [2]. The recommendation system based on deep learning proposed by YouTube improves the online playback time by nearly 1% [3]. The deep learning-based reinforcement learning recommendation model [4] designed and implemented by the Ant Financial team can reduce the need for online training and update the model with feedback results. Relevant technologies for extracting user personality characteristics emerge in an endless stream, but there are still some difficult problems to be solved, such as the interference of noise words in the process of feature extraction, and the ineffectiveness of the extracted feature representation ability. Aiming at such problems, this paper designs a text analysis model ATCNN-BiGRU based on social texts rich in user personality information in social media to mine user personality information more effectively. The main research contents include the following two aspects.

On the one hand, this paper studies the extraction method of user personality features in text information, and proposes a local feature extraction model based on attention mechanism. Aiming at the problem of poor classification effect due to the sparsity of text in the current text feature extraction, the paper introduces an attention mechanism to extract local semantic features and focus on keywords, so as to reduce the influence of noise on the extraction of keyword features. And using the sensitivity of the convolutional neural network model to the language structure, it can effectively improve the performance and efficiency while reducing the feature dimension.

Secondly, through text multi-classification experiments, this paper proposes a global feature extraction model based on bidirectional gated recurrent network, aiming at the problem that the existing models have insufficient ability to extract global semantic features and focus too much on local features during text feature extraction. The model can capture the dependencies between long-distance contextual keywords and consider synchronous learning from the forward and reversed input of the text, so as to fully consider the contextual information of the text and learn the contextual distribution of the sentence. Solve the problem that the existing model lacks consideration of long-distance context keywords due to the sliding convolution characteristics of the convolutional neural network. At the same time, this paper considers and alleviates the problems of model overfitting and excessively large parameters.

2 Related Research

Natural Language Processing (NLP) [5] integrates probabilistic statistics, computer technology, language and literature and other disciplines. With the help of the theoretical support of many disciplines, it converts text content into vector data that can be processed by computers and performs complex formula operations. Computers understand language features and perform NLP tasks. In order to learn the language features in the text and extract the semantic features in the context, scholars at home and abroad have proposed many algorithms and models.

At present, many researchers have mined user feature information and used it in tasks such as text classification and recommendation systems, and achieved good results. In the process of user feature extraction, Geng Lin [6] proposed to establish a text-based sentiment dictionary, using basic sentiment words and online sentiment words to monitor public opinion and analyze sentiment tendency and intensity. However, the dictionary needs to be constructed manually and cannot effectively connect the context of the article and the deep meaning of the article. J Patel [7] proposed to use a context-based latent semantic model to extract user features and opinions as a source of item ratings. The combination of contextual information and comment features simulates the user's rating value for unknown items, which has been shown to have better indicators through experiments. Wang [8] proposed to fuse user social network data, geographic location, and comment text data of user interest points to improve the recommendation accuracy. The topic and topic words are extracted from the text using the latent Dirichlet distribution for the review text information, and the probability model is used to judge the influence probability of social relations. Jin [9] proposed an improved topic model LDA-Phrase for textual information. The word frequency in this model is improved into a sentence frequency model, monolingual words are converted into phrases, and a probability model is constructed using the frequency of phrases. Taking phrases as the basic unit reduces the occurrence probability of words with similar topics, and has higher recommendation quality than the traditional LDA model. Wang H [10] proposed a cross-domain transfer learning method in the absence of sufficient user features, using text embedding methods to transfer from the source domain to the target domain in a semi-supervised manner. And a probability matrix decomposition method is proposed to solve the problem of user personality feature classification, and finally identify user personality features and improve recommendation performance. Perozzi B [11] proposed to use the DeepWalk method to obtain low-dimensional latent vectors as user feature representations. On the basis of the former, Sun [12] and others regarded user comment text as a node and social information mapped in the same vector space, jointly train its distributed representation.

Due to the limitations of hardware development and computing power, before deep learning became the current mainstream model, most natural language processing tasks hovered between language rules and statistical processing models. The increasing demand for improved natural language processing capabilities has accelerated the transition of natural language modeling methods from traditional models to deep learning models. The Google team of Mikolov T [13] and others published a tool called Word2Vec in 2013, which relies on Skip-grams and CBOW methods to establish the vector representation of words. The emergence of the Word2Vec model became the beginning of the use of neural network models for natural language processing. Pan Yuemei [14] proposed to design an intelligent college entrance examination volunteer recommendation system based on machine learning knowledge, with the Word2Vec algorithm as the core, and using the relevant information of the Jiangsu Provincial College Entrance Examination as the data source. Its main research focuses on college entrance examination scores and objective user personal information, but does not consider the impact of user personality characteristics on the recommendation results. Lei C [15] proposed to use Word2Vec to extract semantics to assist LDA topic modeling in the case of similar data distribution to complete transfer learning, and finally alleviate the cold start problem in Web services.

Duan Minmin [16] proposed to use the constructed domain sentiment dictionary to generate sentiment word vectors, which were spliced and fused with traditional word vectors to form an extended word vector containing both semantic information and emotional information, which was used to solve the problem of lack of emotional information in traditional Word2Vec.

Despite its strong universality, Word2Vec cannot solve the problem of polysemy or deep semantic information due to the one-to-one correspondence between words and vectors [15, 17, 18]. Kim Y [19] used the convolutional neural network model for the first time in the text classification task, and the structure diagram used is shown in 1.1. From the data structure, the sentence length n and the word vector dimension d form an n*d matrix. Different from the "pixels" in the image, the convolution kernel processes n complete word vectors at a time and completes a sliding convolution from top to bottom. This process can finally extract the feature vectors of the text, that is, local semantic features.

On the basis of the original model, Niu [20] et al. proposed to use the text representation of LDA for the convolutional neural network model to capture high-order semantic features. The word vector of topic embedding not only contains semantic information, but also can represent the topic of the text. At present, VO Duy-tin [21] et al. proposed a multi-channel convolutional neural network model, which uses word features, location features and part-of-speech features to form different feature combinations to form multiple network input channels, which is more efficient than a single convolutional neural network. High classification results. He [22] et al. proposed the combination of emotion mapping based on emoji and multi-channel convolutional neural network to enhance the ability to capture emotion semantics, and obtained good classification results on multiple different emotion datasets. Although emojis are helpful in sentiment classification, the semantic expressions of emojis for emotions are difficult to be correctly captured in the model, so feature training for emojis is rarely performed in practical applications.

Due to the fixed size of the convolution kernel, there is a problem that only adjacent vocabulary features can be extracted, so that the convolutional neural network has not been able to solve the problem of feature extraction effectiveness and long-range semantic feature extraction in dealing with NLP problems.. Jin [23] proposed that compared with traditional word vector representation, although sentiment embedding can distinguish negative words in contextual semantics, it ignores the changes in word meanings in different contexts. That is, the features of a word will change with the change of context semantics, but will be assigned the same vector representation. Therefore, he proposed to extract emotional information from the corpus based on BiGRU as a semantic training model. Zhang Xiaochuan [24] proposed to use the CNN_BiGRU model to model text semantics and enhance the representation ability of word vectors in order to improve the problem that word vectors cannot effectively distinguish the semantics of polysemy and text order affects semantics.

It can be seen from the existing research that the extraction of user personality characteristics in the comment text is helpful for tasks such as improving the accuracy of text classification and improving the performance of recommendation models. Existing models, whether traditional probability-based topic modeling models, static word vector representation models, or recent deep learning-based semantic models, can extract user personality information from text. However, the sparsity and noise of review texts may limit the accuracy of feature extraction, thereby affecting the accuracy of classification and scoring. Therefore, how to propose and design a more effective user personality feature extraction model according to the characteristics of social text is helpful for optimizing tasks in a wide range of natural language processing fields such as text classification and personalized recommendation.

3   ATCNN-BiGRU Model

At present, in the field of text analysis and feature extraction, convolutional neural network model and RNN model have achieved good results in semantic fine-grained target keyword extraction, but there are still some problems. Convolutional neural networks can effectively extract local semantic features while computing in parallel, but the text has a long-distance contextual keyword dependence, which leads to the problem that global semantic features cannot be effectively extracted. The researchers found that the LSTM model can effectively preserve the long-range contextual semantic features, and can effectively solve the phenomenon of gradient disappearance and gradient explosion in the training process of the unidirectional RNN model. However, it brings a huge amount of parameters, which is nearly 4 times that of the RNN model, and there is a problem that the one-way loop cannot take into account the contextual semantic information. Therefore, the researchers stack the unidirectional GRU with smaller parameters and faster training into a two-layer bidirectional GRU model, namely the BiGRU model with bidirectional gated recurrent network. Input text from both positive and negative directions, so that the model has a stronger ability to perceive front and rear semantics. In order to pay attention to the influence of target keywords and enrich the expression of text emotional features, this paper considers the convolutional neural network ATCNN using the attention mechanism, combined with the bi-directional gated recurrent network BiGRU, to construct a text analysis model ATCNN-BiGRU. The model includes local and global feature extractors, taking into account both local semantics and global semantics, so that the judgment of text personality tendency is more accurate.

3.1   Text Processing

Build an overall dictionary based on all the words that have appeared in the dataset, and use the index order of the words in the dictionary to convert the n texts of user u into an integer matrix $W_u \in \mathbb{R}^{n \times z}$. Then $W_u \in \mathbb{R}^{n \times z}$ is $0 - 1$ encoded using one $-$ hot, and the $0 - 1$ matrix $B_u \in \mathbb{R}^{n \times z \times s}$ is obtained. n represents the number of text sentences of user u, z represents the number of words in the sentence with the largest number of words in the existing sentence text of the user, and s represents the number of words contained in the dictionary. Map $B_u \in \mathbb{R}^{n \times z \times s}$ with the parameter matrix $O_u \in \mathbb{R}^{s \times w}$), the word vector matrix e_u represents the word vector of each word of the user's preference and evaluation text, and the specific expression is as shown in Eq. 1 shown.

$$e_u = B_u * O_u \tag{1}$$

3.2 Feature Noise Reduction and Fusion

Both the multi-channel convolutional neural network and the emotion symbol-based convolutional neural network do not consider the noise reduction of the input text [22, 25]. This summary and the next summary will introduce the text noise reduction integrated with the attention mechanism. Specific steps. In the following chapters, an experimental comparison of the former two models is made to analyze whether the noise reduction method is effective through experiments. Feature extraction is performed on user text and categorical attributes separately using convolutional neural networks. Perform convolution operation on e_u, each convolution kernel $filter_i$ produces a feature sequence result f_i, the specific expression is:

$$f_i = (filter_i \otimes e_u + b_i) * sigmoid(filter_{i+1} \otimes e_u + b_i) \tag{2}$$

The $sigmoid$ function expression is:

$$sigmoid(x) = \frac{1}{1 + e^{-x}} \tag{3}$$

$filter_i$ and $filter_{i+1}$ indicate two convolution kernels with different parameters, $\otimes$ indicates convolution operation, * indicates that the convolution results of two different convolution kernels are multiplied bit by bit, and at the same time The $sigmoid$ function is used to activate a convolution result, and the range of the $sigmoid$ function belongs to (0,1). The features obtained after convolution are filtered using the global max pooling operation, and the filtered feature output is expressed as:

$$F_{new\_u} = \left[f_{new\_1}, f_{new\_2}, \dots, f_{new\_a}\right], f_i \in \mathbb{R}^{n \times 1 \times 1} \tag{4}$$

The hidden vectors h_k and h_i of the category are introduced into the user coding unit E_U, and correspondingly, the implicit vector h_u of the user is also introduced into the category coding unit E_I. The expression for denoising the user text semantic feature F_{new_u} is:

$$a(f_k, h_i) = v_a^{\mathrm{T}} \tanh(W_a h_k + M_a h_i) \tag{5}$$

where $f_k \in \mathbb{R}^a$ represents a single text vector, $h_i \in \mathbb{R}^b$ represents the hidden vector of the category, b is the set hidden vector dimension, $W_a \in \mathbb{R}^{a \times a}$, $v_a \in \mathbb{R}^a$, $M_a \in \mathbb{R}^{a \times b}$ all belong to the weight matrix, and $tanh$ represents the activation function.

3.3 Word Vector Attention Mechanism

The attention mechanism helps the model to focus on more important information during training, similar to focusing on a certain point in the external world with the human eye, thereby improving the computational efficiency of the model. For the use of the attention mechanism in text, such as the sentence "But the staff was so horrible to us.", the adjective "horrible" is used to describe the keyword "staff". Therefore, in this sentence, more attention should be paid to the relationship between "horrible" and "staff", and other words should be regarded as noise or non-key words.

The above example can be converted into a mathematical model, and the keyword t_i word vector is extracted from the text vector matrix $S = \{w_1, w_2, \cdots, t_i, \cdots, w_n\}$, and the attention weight value is obtained by operating on each word, as shown in the following formula 6 shown. Finally, the attention input matrix Ac after each word operation is obtained as the input matrix of the convolutional neural network.

$$A_{ii}^c = \alpha * \frac{\exp(a(f_k, h_i))}{\sum_{k=1}^n \exp(a(f_k, h_i))} \tag{6}$$

α represents a custom parameter, and its role is equivalent to the learning rate parameter during model training, which is used to adjust the degree of influence between different words (Fig. 1).

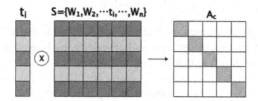

Fig. 1. Word Vector Composition Under Attention Mechanism

3.4 Convolutional Neural Network Module Combined with Attention Mechanism

CNN can reduce the amount of computation while enhancing the anti-noise ability by integrating the attention mechanism, and capture the local semantic features in the comment text, so as to obtain rich semantic information. The following will introduce the proposed model construction method step by step.

The input layer uses the input matrix constructed by the attention mechanism to construct a three-dimensional matrix vector with an image-like RGB three-layer structure, which is used as the input of the model. The multi-channel input form of the convolutional neural network can be fully utilized to perform parallel convolution operations on the input matrix. The first and second feature matrices are the 300-dimensional pretrained word vectors of Word2Vec and Glove [19, 26, 27], and the attention input matrix is generated after the operation of the matrix vector through the attention mechanism, and the third feature matrix is the label vector representation of this paper uses convolution kernels of different sizes for multiple channels, and uses convolution operations on matrix vectors to extract the most important abstract features in text. The convolution operation on the input matrix is shown in Eq. 7 below.

$$c_i = f(w \cdot x_{i:i+h-1} + b) \tag{7}$$

Among them, $w \in R^{h \times m}$ represents the weight of the convolution kernel, $h \times m$ represents the size of the convolution kernel window, the height is h, and the dimension is m. When scanning a convolution kernel, the height is h, and the dimension is When the word matrix of m is used, it will get the eigenvalue b representing the bias value. f represents the activation function. In this paper, the ReLU function is used as the activation function of the convolutional layer. $x_{i:i+h-1}$ represents the word vector matrix from the i th word to the $i + h - 1$ th word in the sentence sequence, and c_i represents the i th eigenvalue obtained by the convolution operation. After the above steps, each text will obtain a feature matrix, as shown in Eq. 8 below.

$$c = [c_1, c_2, \cdots, c_{n-h+1}] \tag{8}$$

In the pooling layer, the convolutional feature maps of different channels are downsampled by setting a fixed step size, and the most important feature C in each channel is extracted, as shown in Eq. 9 below.

$$C = max\{c\} \tag{9}$$

The vectors output from each channel are spliced into a single feature vector, the final result is obtained through softmax, and cross-entropy is used as the loss function for model training. as shown in Eqs. 10 and 11 below.

$$y = \text{softmax}(W_f M_p + b) \tag{10}$$

$$\text{loss} = -\sum_{i=1}^{D} \sum_{j=1}^{C} \hat{y}_i^j \log y_i^j + \lambda \|\theta\|^2 \tag{11}$$

3.5 Overall Model Architecture

In this paper, the text convolution module (ATCNN), is combined with the bidirectional gated unit recurrent network module (BiGRU) to work together in the text classification task. Among them, the paper will describe the parameters of each module in detail, and splicing the feature vectors output by the two models. The overall architecture of the final ATCNN-BiGRU text classification model is shown in Fig. 2.

When the attentional convolutional neural network (ATCNN) extracts local semantic information, the hyperparameters such as the dimension of the word vector, filter size, stride size, etc. have a significant impact on the classification of the convolutional neural network. Therefore, this paper directly conducts experiments using widely accepted hyperparameters. When the input vector is controlled at 300 dimensions, the filter size is set to [3*300, 4*300, 5*300], the number of which is 256, the stride size is set to 1, and the padding is set to 0, the model fits The combined effect is optimal and a better classification result is obtained.

When the bidirectional gating network (BiGRU) extracts global semantic information, it is represented by the word vector of the sentence as the input of the model. The input dimension is the same as the attention convolution network module, both of which are 300 dimensions, and the dropout function is introduced to prevent the model from overfitting caused by over-reliance on a neuron. Then the cat() operation is performed on the outputs of the two hidden layers to obtain the output of the bidirectional gating network.

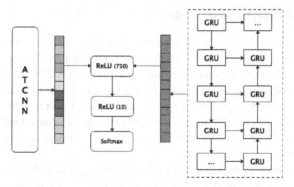

Fig. 2. General Architecture of ATCNN-BiGRU Model

The feature vectors output by the two modules in the merging layer are input into the ATCNN-BiGRU fusion model from two directions respectively. The model uses the cat() method of the Pytorch framework to concatenate and fuse the two modules.

After the feature vectors of each model are passed through the cat function, they are used as input values for the first fully connected layer. Secondly, the Dropout function is used in each fully-connected layer to randomly discard the parameters of neuron training to avoid over-reliance on a neuron to cause overfitting of the model. Finally, the multi-classification results are output through softmax.

4 Experiments

This paper uses the SemEval2017 [28], NLPCC2014 [29], and SanyouEval2019 datasets to randomly divide the training set and the test set according to the ratio of 8:2 for experiments. The performance of the model in this paper is tested through the text classification task, and four indicators are used to measure the performance of the calculation model. See Eq. 12–15. The accuracy rate measures the classification accuracy, and the precision rate and recall rate measure the recall rate and the classification in the precision rate task. Accuracy, the F1 value measures the performance of the model. Five classification models that are most commonly used in text mining tasks and have high accuracy are selected as the baselines of this paper, namely the MNB model [30] (Multinomial Naive Bayes, MNB), the TextCNN model [19], and the BiGRU model [23]], MCCNN model [25], EMCNN model [22].

$$\text{Accuracy} = \frac{TP + TN}{TP + FP + TN + FN} \tag{12}$$

$$\text{Precision}_{micro} = \frac{\sum_{k \in C} TP_k}{\sum_{k \in C} TP_k + FP_k} \tag{13}$$

$$\text{Recall}_{micro} = \frac{\sum_{k \in C} TP_k}{\sum_{k \in C} TP_k + FN_k} \tag{14}$$

$$F1_{micro} = \frac{2 * Precision * Recall}{Precision + Recall} \tag{15}$$

4.1 Analysis of Experimental Results

After comparing with the five models proposed in the previous section, the analysis of the experimental results of text classification found that in the classification tasks of SemEval2017, NLPCC2014 and SanyouEval2019, the ATCNN-BiGRU proposed in this paper is in an advantageous position, and the results are shown in Tables 1, 2, 3 and 4 below. Compared with other multi-channel convolutional neural network models, the increase is between 1% and 2%. In order to verify whether it is the attention mechanism and BiGRU's extraction effect of global features, a comparative experimental analysis will be carried out.

It can be seen from Table 1 that in the Chinese and English multi-classification tasks of each model, the results of the English data set are 1% - 2% higher than that of the Chinese, and the data set cardinality is significantly larger than that of the other two types of Chinese data sets. Higher accuracy.

Table 1. Experimental Results of Accuracy of Different Models

Model	Accuracy		
	SemEval2017	NLPCC2014	SanyouEval2019
MNB	0.7535	0.7280	0.7559
TextCNN	0.7945	0.7634	0.7717
BiGRU	0.8089	0.7885	0.7822
MCCNN	0.8296	0.8154	–
EMCNN	0.8416	0.8255	–
ATCNN-BiGRU	0.8570	0.8397	0.8139

Table 2. Experimental Results of Precision of Different Models

Model	Precision		
	SemEval2017	NLPCC2014	SanyouEval2019
MNB	0.7898	0.6943	0.7692
TextCNN	0.8066	0.6960	0.7712
BiGRU	0.8070	0.7276	0.7809
MCCNN	0.8132	0.7986	–
EMCNN	0.8188	0.8142	–
ATCNN-BiGRU	0.8435	0.8327	0.8186

From the experimental results of the precision rate in Table 2 and the recall rate in Table 3, it can be seen that the model in this paper is better than other models. Especially in SemEval2017, the accuracy rate is 2.5% higher than other multi-channel convolutional

Table 3. Experimental Results of Recall of Different Models

Model	Recall		
	SemEval2017	NLPCC2014	SanyouEval2019
MNB	0.7245	0.6918	0.7355
TextCNN	0.7894	0.7531	0.7609
BiGRU	0.8117	0.7772	0.7754
MCCNN	0.8530	0.7845	–
EMCNN	0.8624	0.7874	–
ATCNN-BiGRU	0.8727	0.8018	0.7953

neural network models, and it also maintains an advantage in the recall rate, indicating that it can maintain a high accuracy regardless of the full and accurate tasks.

Table 4. Experimental Results of F1-sore of Different Models

Model	F1-score		
	SemEval2017	NLPCC2014	SanyouEval2019
MNB	0.7558	0.6931	0.7520
TextCNN	0.7979	0.7234	0.7660
BiGRU	0.8093	0.7516	0.7781
MCCNN	0.8326	0.7915	–
EMCNN	0.8400	0.8006	
ATCNN-BiGRU	0.8579	0.8170	0.8068

Compared with the TextCNN and BiGRU models, the accuracy and F1 value of the model have been significantly improved, with an increase of nearly 4%–6%, indicating that both local and global features will have better performance in text classification tasks. Compared with the best EMCNN model in the three types of data sets, the model ATCNN-BiGRU proposed in this paper is improved by 1%–2% in all four evaluation indicators, indicating that the attention mechanism plays an indispensable role in local feature extraction. The role of CNN, and BiGRU can make up for the shortcomings of CNN in global semantic feature extraction.

4.2 Loss Function Analysis

In this paper, cross-entropy is used as the loss function to quantify the difference between the output of the network and the label, and the network is updated through backpropagation through this difference. The formula is shown in 16. The p in the formula represents the vector representation of the true value, and q is the result after the output of the softmax function.

$$H(p, q) = -\sum_{k=1}^{N}(p_k * logq_k) \tag{16}$$

When comparing the optimal parameters of each model in the SemEval2017 dataset, the change curve of the loss function is shown in Fig. 3. It can be seen from the experimental results that the iteration speed of TextCNN is faster and reaches the optimal state in about 10 iterations, while other models need to pass nearly 20 times to achieve a better fitting state, thanks to the parallel computing capability of CNN. The model ATCNN-BiGRU proposed in this paper achieves convergence in about 30 times, and the loss is lower than other models. And it can be seen that other models have reached the convergence state in about 15 times, and the convergence speed is faster, but there will be obvious overfitting after that. The decline of the model in this paper is relatively stable. Although the time consumption is nearly 10 more iterations than other models, the classification results are better than other models.

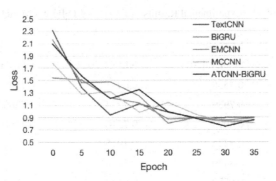

Fig. 3. Loss Function Graph

4.3 Analysis of the Effectiveness of Attention Mechanism

In order to verify whether the attention mechanism and BiGRU play an active role in the model, this paper adopts the experimental comparison of TextCNN, BiGRU, CNN-BiGRU and ATCNN-BiGRU respectively. Among them, TextCNN, BiGRU and CNN-BiGRU replace the attention matrix with the original 300-dimensional word vector and label vector matrix input by the non-attention matrix, and the optimal parameter values are obtained after four experimental iterations. Finally, the experimentally measured accuracy and F1 value indicators are used as validity analysis, as shown in Table 5.

It can be seen that the indicators of the model ATCNN-BiGRU proposed in this paper are significantly better than the model without the attention mechanism, and the highest increase is 1.5%, indicating that the classification accuracy has a significant enhancement effect under the attention mechanism. And compared with the CNN model, the CNN-BiGRU model is 5% higher in accuracy, indicating that BiGRU is indispensable for

Table 5. Experimental Results on the Effectiveness of Attention Mechanism

Model	Accuracy			F1-score		
	SemEval	NLPCC	SanyouEval	SemEval	NLPCC	SanyouEval
TextCNN	0.7945	0.7634	0.7717	0.7979	0.7234	0.7660
BiGRU	0.8089	0.7885	0.7822	0.8093	0.7516	0.7781
CNN-BiGRU	0.8453	0.8241	0.8091	0.8405	0.8156	0.8030
ATCNN-BiGRU	0.8570	0.8397	0.8139	0.8579	0.8170	0.8086

the effectiveness of global feature extraction. Compared with CNN-BiGRU, the index improvement of the model in this paper can reflect that the attention mechanism plays a key role in extracting local features and overcoming text noise in the model. The index F1 value can be reflected in the English data set SemEval2017, which can reflect an improvement of nearly 2%, while in the Chinese data set, the difference is between 0.3% and 0.5%, indicating that the model has more stable performance in the English data set.

5 Summary

At present, most user personality feature mining models focus on different focuses. From the probabilistic model of text topics to the nonlinear model of context semantics, they rarely pay attention to the singularity of features, and rarely consider the effect of text noise on features. The influence of extraction leads to the problem of poor feature representation ability. In order to solve the above problems, this paper proposes to use the attention mechanism to improve the anti-noise ability of local feature extraction, and introduces the semantic features of the global context to improve the model's ability to analyze semantics. The Dropout mechanism is used in the fully connected layer to avoid over-fitting of the model, and the two-part feature connection is completed, and the final experiment obtains more accurate results in the text classification task. Although the model proposed in this paper has a good performance in the classification results, it still has shortcomings such as long training time and incomplete use of comment text information. And short-term personality characteristics, and the vector representation of multi-feature fusion is used as the input of the deep learning model to further improve the performance of the model.

Acknowledgments. This paper is supported by the Inner Mongolia Natural Science Foundation Project (2020MS07018), the Graduate Research Innovation Project of Inner Mongolia University (11200–5223737), the National Natural Science Foundation of China (61862046) and the Inner Mongolia Autonomous Region Scientific and Technological Achievement Transformation Project (CGZH2018124).

References

1. Yang, R., Guo, Y.: Characteristics, problems and psychological analysis of college students' network social behavior. Adv. Psychol. **12**, 777 (2022)

2. Wang, Z.: Research on Recommendation Algorithm Based on Review Text. Inner Mongolia University, Hohhot (2020)
3. Covington, P., Adams, J., Sargin, E.: Deep neural networks for youtube recommendations. In: ACM Conference on Recommender Systems, pp. 191–198. ACM (2016)
4. Chen, X., Li, S., Li, H., et al.: Generative adversarial user model for reinforcement learning based recommendation system. In: International Conference on Machine Learning, pp. 1052–1061. PMLR (2019)
5. Wang, P.: Research on Personalized Recommendation Algorithm Based on User Characteristics. Shandong Normal University, Jinan (2018)
6. Geng, L.: A Weibo Public Opinion Monitoring Model Based on Sentiment Analysis. Northwest Normal University, Lanzhou (2020)
7. Patel, J., Chhinkaniwala, H.: A fusion of aspect and contextual information for rating prediction in recommender system using a latent factor model. Int. J. Web Eng. Technol. **16**(1), 30 (2021)
8. Wang, X., Yuan, J., Qin, F.: Point-of-interest recommendation based on comment text in location social network. Comput. Sci., 251–254 (2017)
9. Xie, J., Zhu, F., Guan, H., et al.: Personalized query recommendation using semantic factor model. China Commun. **18**(08), 169–182 (2021)
10. Wang, H., Zuo, Y., Li, H., et al.: Cross-domain recommendation with user personality. Knowl.-Based Syst. **213**(8), 106664 (2021)
11. Perozzi, B., Al-Rfou, R., Skiena, S.: Deepwalk: online learning of social representations. In: Proceedings of the 20th ACM SIGKDD International Conference on Knowledge Discovery and Data Mining, pp. 701–710 (2014)
12. Sun, X., Guo, J., Ding, X., et al.: A general framework for content-enhanced network representation learning. arXiv preprint arXiv:1610.02906 (2016)
13. Mikolov, T., Chen, K., Corrado, G., et al.: Efficient estimation of word representations in vector space. arXiv preprint arXiv:1301.3781 (2013)
14. Pan, Y.: Intelligent Recommendation System for College Entrance Examination Based on Machine Learning. Nanjing University of Posts and Telecommunications, Nanjing (2019)
15. Lei, C., Dai, H., Yu, Z., et al.: A service recommendation algorithm with the transfer learning based matrix factorization to improve cloud security. Inf. Sci. **513**, 98–111 (2020)
16. Duan, M.: Research on Text Sentiment Analysis Based on Fusion of Dictionary and Word Vector. Xidian University, Xi'an (2019)
17. Ombabi, A.H., Lazzez, O., Ouarda, W., et al.: Deep learning framework based on Word2Vec and CNN for users interests classification. In: Sudan Conference on Computer Science & Information Technology, pp. 1–7 (2017)
18. Wang, Y., Lei, L.: Sentiment Analysis using Word2vec-CNN-BiLSTM Classification. In: 2020 Seventh International Conference on Social Networks Analysis, Management and Security (SNAMS) (2020)
19. Kim, Y.: Convolutional Neural Network for Sentence Classification. University of Waterloo, Waterloo (2015)
20. Niu, X.Y.: CNN text classification based on topic model word vectors. Comput. Modern. **10**, 7 (2019)
21. Vo, D., Zhang, Y.: Target-dependent twitter sentiment classification with rich automatic features. In: Proceedings of Twenty-Fourth International Joint Conference on Artificial Intelligence, Palo Alto, CA:AAAI, pp. 1374–1353 (2015)
22. He, Y.X., Sun, S.T., Niu, F.F., et al.: A deep learning model enhanced with emotion semantics for microblog sentiment analysis. Chin. J. Comput. **40**(4), 773–790 (2017)
23. Wang, J., Zhang, Y., Yu, L.C., et al.: Contextual sentiment embeddings via bi-directional GRU language model. Knowl.-Based Syst. **235**, 107663 (2022)

24. Zhang, X., Lian, X., Dai, X., et al.: CNN_BiGRU text classification model based on part-of-speech features. Comput. Appl. Softw. **38**(11), 155–161 (2021)
25. Eslami, E., Yun, H.B.: Attention-based multi-scale convolutional neural network (A+MCNN) for multi-class classification in road images. Sensors **21**(15), 5137 (2021)
26. Cheng, Y., Yao, L., Zhang, G., et al.: Multi-channel CNN and BiGRU based text sentiment analysis based on attention mechanism]. Computer Research and Development **57**(12), 2583–2595 (2020)
27. Zhang, T., You, F.: Research on short text classification based on TextCNN. J. Phys: Conf. Ser. **1757**(1), 012092 (2021)
28. Tao, Y., Zhang, X., Shi, L., et al.: Research on multi-feature fusion method for sentiment analysis of short texts. Small Microcomput. Syst. **41**(6), 7 (2020)
29. Tao, Y., Zhang, X., Shi, L., et al.: Joint embedding of emoticons and labels based on CNN for microblog sentiment analysis. In: 2019 IEEE Fourth International Conference on Data Science in Cyberspace (DSC). IEEE (2019)
30. Dhola, K., Saradva, M.: A comparative evaluation of traditional machine learning and deep learning classification techniques for sentiment analysis. In: 11th International Conference on Cloud Computing, Data Science & Engineering 2021 (2021)

A Unified Stream and Batch Graph Computing Model for Community Detection

Jinkun Dai[1,2,3], Ling Wu[1,2,3], and Kun Guo[1,2,3(✉)]

[1] Fujian Provincial Key Laboratory of Network Computing and Intelligent Information Processing, Fuzhou University, Fuzhou 350108, China
{wuling1985,gukn}@fzu.edu.cn
[2] College of Computer and Data Science, Fuzhou University, Fuzhou 350108, China
[3] Key Laboratory of Spatial Data Mining and Information Sharing, Ministry of Education, Fuzhou 350108, China

Abstract. An essential challenge in graph data analysis and mining is to simply and effectively deal with large-scale network data that is expanding dynamically. Although batch-based parallel graph computation frameworks have better accuracy, they cannot process incremental data on time and need to be recomputed. To process real-time data, stream processing applications need to be redeveloped, which increases the redundancy of work, and some existing dynamic graph computation schemes are not generalizable. This paper proposes a unified stream and batch graph computing model(USBGM). The model is compatible with both stream and batch graph computing. Graph operators and algorithms developed based on the model can handle stream and batch graph data in a unified manner. The experiments on real-world and artificial networks verified the effectiveness and efficiency of the model.

Keywords: unified stream and batch · graph computing · community detection

1 Introduction

Nowadays, the scale of graph data generated in various fields such as transportation, finance, and social networking is growing fast, so large-scale graph mining and analysis demand is growing. With the development of many big data processing systems, the ability of big data processing in various scenarios is also increasing. These systems are usually divided into two categories from the perspective of data sources, namely batch-based and stream-based processing.

The batch method mainly operates large-scale static data sets and returns the results after completing the calculation. The most typical ones are the MapReduce computing model [1] based on Hadoop and the Spark computing engine [2] based on the DAG computing task scheduling model. Batch datasets are usually limited data collections and are always stored in some persistent storage location. Batch processing is ideal for calculations that require access to all data

Y. Sun et al. (Eds.): ChineseCSCW 2022, CCIS 1681, pp. 110–124, 2023.
https://doi.org/10.1007/978-981-99-2356-4_9

to complete, but this is often time-intensive and, therefore, not suitable for use on occasions that require high processing time. Stream processing frameworks perform computations on data coming into the system at any time; this is a very different way of processing than batch mode, instead of performing operations on the entire data set, stream processing performs operations on each data item that comes in, it can handle an almost unlimited amount of data. However, only one or a small amount of data can be processed at the same time, and only a tiny amount of state is maintained between different records. Stream processing mode is suitable for tasks with real-time processing requirements.

This paper proposes a unified stream and batch graph computing model that can satisfy both stream and batch graph computation in a single development. Stream iteration and real-time update graph model caching mechanism and time decay strategy are used. Finally, we apply the community detection algorithm to the proposed model. The main contributions of this paper are as follows:

(1) The proposed unified stream and batch graph computing model consists of a graph model cache that stores graph and network information and an iterative stream mechanism that updates the graph cache model in real-time. It enables stream and batch processing on large-scale graphs to be completed with a single development. The model can maintain the accuracy of batch processing and the low latency of stream processing.
(2) The introduced time decay strategy in the stream processing can gradually reduce the importance of earlier data objects in the graph according to the degree of time decay and maintain the real-time nature of the model.
(3) The application of graph operators and community detection algorithms based on the proposed unified stream and batch graph computing model can verify the effectiveness and efficiency of the model in real-world and artificial network experiments.

2 Related Work

In this section, we describe the work related to this study of batch and stream large-scale graph computation and unified stream and batch processing.

2.1 Batch Large-Scale Graph Computation

Batch processing is a common solution for most graph-related algorithms and implementations because solving graph problems often requires thinking about the graph as a whole. Pregel [3], first proposed by Google, is a prototype of distributed graph computing, and Pregel is a message-passing batch graph computing engine implemented based on the BSP(Bulk Synchronous Parallel) [4] model. PowerGraph [5], presented by Carnegie Mellon University in 2012 at OSDI, a top conference on computer systems, is a graph computation solution for power-law graphs in real scenarios, which builds on Pregel with a three-stage vertex-centric iterative computation model, Gather-Apply-Scatter, and a point-cut-based graph partitioning. The Spark framework has a batch-based graph computation framework, GraphX, which is mainly based on the same lineage of Resilient Distributed Property Graph RDPG (Resilient Distributed Property Graph); neighboring edge aggregation based on MapReduce idea; and improved Pregel, which collects messages aggregating that vertex by the Master copy of the vertex and then updates the vertex value using the vertex function.

2.2 Stream Large-Scale Graph Computation

Unlike batch graph computation, there is no general graph computing framework in stream processing. Some of the research work is scattered across various research areas related to graphs. Hollocou et al. [6] proposed a linear stream community discovery algorithm in 2017, based on a method that randomly picks an edge in a network to build communities through local changes in the data. Abbas et al. [7] ingest edges or vertices of a graph in the form of online data streams to make partitioning decisions dynamically based on partial knowledge of the graph, but partitioning is costly. Ma et al. [8], on the other hand, proposed a streaming graph neural network model in 2020, capable of handling data that evolves over time and continuously updates node information by capturing sequential information of edges. Community discovery is essentially a similar class of problems to the clustering problem, the labels of data in streaming data change over time, so the phenomenon of concept drift will arise [9], which corresponds to the graph level where the graph structure changes dynamically with time, and to address this phenomenon, Bechini et al. [10,11] successively proposed methods for clustering aspects of coping with streaming data, giving the model the ability to adapt to data changes continuously.

2.3 Unified Stream and Batch Processing

The existing research in the area of unified stream and batch processing is diverse, with many studies proposing different solutions. The designers of the real-time stream computing system Storm proposed the Lambda architecture [12,13] to address the shortcomings of a single computing architecture, which is a theory that combines batch and stream computing frameworks to form a unified computing system. Boykin et al. [14] proposed an extensive data processing system based on the Lambda architecture, which supports Hadoop and Storm hybrid processing. In addition, Fan and Bifet [15] proposed an open-source framework called Oryx [16] based on Lambda architecture, whose goal is to adapt machine learning to Lambda architecture. Pishgoo et al. [17] proposed a stream-batch unified anomaly detection processing approach based on Lambda architecture in 2021, which enables batch processing to provide a base model for stream processing through a unit that combines a stream processing unit with a batch processing unit, but this approach still requires performing a single batch process on all the data. The Kappa architecture [18] is an architectural idea proposed by Jay Kreps, the former chief engineer of LinkedIn, which is based on the Lambda architecture. It is optimized on the basis of Lambda architecture by removing the batch processing layer and storing the data in the data lake, where the data processing is mainly stream processing, and when offline analysis or re-computation is needed, the data from the data lake is retransmitted through the message queue again.

3   Unified Stream and Batch Graph Computing Model

In this section, we describe the framework of the proposed USBGM, and describe the graph cache model and the stream iteration in the model in conjunction with the framework. Finally, we describe the time decay strategy in the update process.

3.1   The Framework of USBGM

We propose a graph computing model that combines stream processing and batch processing to provide solutions to various problems on large-scale graph data. The model takes the arrival events of each edge as the minimum processing granularity. The framework of the model is shown in Fig. 1.

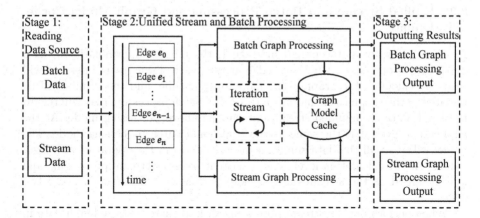

Fig. 1. The Framework of USBGM

Stage 1: Reading Data Source. The model can use bounded batch data as a data source, such as file data; it can also use unbounded streaming data, such as consuming data in the message queue in real-time.

Stage 2: Unified Stream and Batch Processing. Whether it is batch data or streaming data, the model takes one edge as the minimum processing granularity. The changes to the structure of the graph and the characteristics of nodes caused by the arrival of each edge will act on the graph model cache in real-time.

The structure of the graph model cache is divided into a graph information cache part and an algorithm feature cache part. Among them, the graph information cache part includes the nodes themselves in the graph, the information on the relationship between the nodes, and the time information of the arrival of the nodes. The algorithm feature cache part can be designed according to different needs when applied to different graph operators or algorithms.

The model uses an iterative stream that does not set specific iteration termination conditions for the graph operators or algorithms that need to be iterative. Each iteration can update the part of the representation operator or algorithm in the graph model cache. To capture the change of the graph over time, the judgment of time attenuation is introduced in the calculation update, and the old data are attenuated and deleted from the model.

Stage 3: Outputting Results. This stage is a data stream that runs concurrently with the iterative stream, where the contents of the graph model cache are read at a set result output interval, transformed as required, and then the resulting output is performed.

3.2 Unified Stream and Batch Processing and Graph Model Cache Update

In stage 2, for any data entered in stage 1, the minimum granularity of data processing is one edge. After each edge arrives, each downstream operator will read and calculate the graph cache model in real-time, and the results will be updated to the graph cache model on time. The batch processing task will regard the batch data as bounded stream data in the above processing mode. At the application level, it is the same as the traditional batch processing mode. The model will read all the data simultaneously to perform the operators and algorithms. At the calculation level, it is consistent with the stream processing, and it is regarded as the stream data without a time interval between every two edges.

When performing the stream processing task, if there is static batch data in the data source, the batch calculation of this part of data is carried out first, and the batch processing results are cached into the graph model cache as the initialization model. The stream data processing takes the data's generation time as the relevant nodes' processing time and the relationship between nodes. While updating the algorithm model in the graph model cache, it also updates the time information in the node attribute in the cache in real-time.

To support the algorithm that needs iteration, an iterative stream without termination conditions is adopted in the proposed USBGM. Because in the stream processing, we cannot predict the arrival time of the data, and the addition of each new edge will affect the network structure and the results of the iteration. The iterative stream constantly monitors the upstream operator of the calculation model. When there is a new edge, it will immediately join the iterative stream after the processing of the upstream operator to participate in the iteration. In the iteration process, the time attenuation weight of the data is calculated, and the data exceeding the attenuation threshold are eliminated. Decay objects are deleted in both the cache structure and the iterative stream. The iterative stream will update the algorithm model and graph information in the cache in real-time.

3.3   Time Decay Strategy

The time decay strategy acts on the model updating of the stream processing and iterative stream in stage 2. The structure is shown in Fig. 2, and its main task is to capture the dynamic changes in the network structure over time.

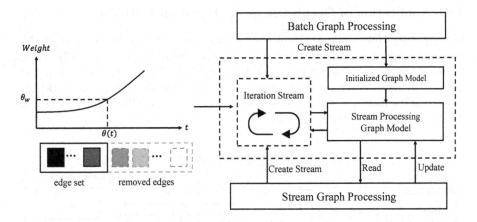

Fig. 2. The Time Decay Strategy

In a continuous stream of incoming data, we can assume that the importance of individual data decreases over time, so the latest data is more important than the older data. In response to this concept, we adopt a strategy of associating a weight with each data object, where the weight is expressed as the decay degree of the edge, which rises as a function of time. The weight calculation method shown by Eq. (1):

$$weight = 2^{\alpha(t-t_0)} \tag{1}$$

Among them, α is an attenuation factor that can be set, and the larger the attenuation factor, the higher the attenuation degree of the earlier data in the stream. By setting an appropriate decay factor, the model can better capture the changes in the network structure over time. In this strategy, the attenuation degree is deleted for objects higher than the attenuation threshold $\theta(w)$. In practical implementation, we can derive the attenuation time interval $\theta(t)$ under a given attenuation factor by formula. When the current time t minus the time t_0 of data arrival is greater than the attenuation time $\theta(t)$, this data will be deleted, the calculation method of $\theta(t)$ is shown in Eq. (2)

$$\theta(t) = t - \frac{log_2\theta_w}{\alpha} \qquad (2)$$

4   Application of the USBGM

This section describes the application of graph operators and community detection algorithms based on USBGM implementation.

4.1   Application of Graph Operators Based on USBGM

We implement four unified stream and batch graph operators based on USBGM: (1) degree operator: calculate the degree of each node in the graph; (2) neighborhood operator: calculate the set of k-th order neighbors for each node in the graph; (3) modularity operator: calculate the modularity of the network; (4) clustering coefficient operator: calculate the clustering coefficient in the graph. The framework is shown in Fig. 3.

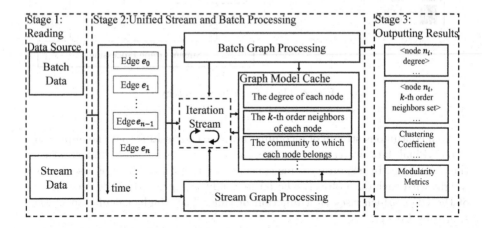

Fig. 3. The framework of graph operator based on USBGM

For batch data, the model is executed in batch mode. In this execution mode, similar to the traditional batch solution, the operator will be executed at one time. For stream processing, the content of the graph model cache structure is the operator content that needs to be calculated, such as node degree, node neighbor set, etc.

Every time a new edge arrives, the model will update the corresponding node information in the cache and synchronize to update the time attribute of the corresponding node. Here, the function of the iterative stream is to poll each node and the time attribute of the node, delete the node that needs to be decayed from the calculation stream, and update the information related to this node in the graph model cache structure in real-time.

4.2 Application of Community Detection Algorithm Based on USBGM

We implemented a label propagation algorithm [19] based on USBGM. The unified stream and batch label propagation algorithm(USBGM-LPA) is to complete community detection on static and dynamic networks. Figure 4 illustrates how the community detection algorithm is specifically implemented based on the framework shown in Fig. 1.

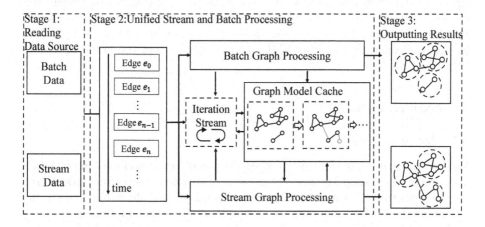

Fig. 4. The framework of community detection algorithm based on USBGM

Stage 1: Reading Data Source. The algorithm's input supports the mixing of multi-source data, including files, distributed file systems, message queues, sockets, etc.

Stage 2: Unified Stream and Batch Processing. The model is executed in batch mode for data that only requires batch processing. In batch processing mode, similar to the traditional batch processing, the model will be executed in one go. When running stream processing, it will first make a judgment whether static data exists, if it does, the algorithm will be executed in batch processing for static data; if it does not exist, it will directly use the arrival of each edge as the update unit of the algorithm model.

Whether batch or stream processing, the model takes the arrival of each edge as the minimum processing granularity. When an edge arrives, the algorithm first initializes the nodes that are not in the cache with their labels randomly, records them as neighboring nodes to each other, and updates the timestamp information of their arrival when the node already exists in the cache. The initialized nodes and their labels will enter the iterative stream. In the label propagation algorithm, iteration is the process of updating node labels. In each iteration round, the node will iterate through the labels carried by its neighboring nodes and select the label with the most labels belonging to the neighboring nodes as its label, and when there is more than one label with the most labels, one of the labels will be randomly selected as its label. While iterating, the time decay strategy is used to eliminate the nodes that have expired to ensure the real-time nature of the model.

Stage 3: Outputting Results. The resulting output and evaluation is a data stream that is performed simultaneously with the iterative stream, where the contents of the graph model cache are read for conversion according to the set result output interval, and the evaluation of the community division is performed by applying operators such as NMI and modularity from the graph operators based on USBGM.

5 Experiments

5.1 Datasets Description

We use five real datasets to verify USBGM-based LPA's accuracy under batch and stream processing. The five real datasets have different sizes and node degree distributions to verify the effectiveness of the implemented algorithm on networks of various sizes. The parameters of each network are shown in Table 1.

To verify the effectiveness of the model stream processing and the time decay strategy, we conduct experiments with artificial datasets S1. To visualize the effect of the time decay strategy, we generate a small-scale artificial network. Dataset S1 has 20 nodes and 34 edges at time t_1, and they form a community; when the time comes to time t_2, 8 nodes and 13 edges will join, and they will form a new community, while 4 edges will decay in the original community; when the time comes to time t_3, 8 edges will join between the two communities, and the true division of the two communities will change accordingly; at time t_4, 3 edges will join and 2 edges will decay, and the true division of the communities will change accordingly. Experiments on this dataset are used to verify the impact of discovering new communities over time and the time-decay strategy on the community partitioning results. The parameters of the network are shown in Table 1.

Table 1. Real-world and Artificial Networks

Networks	Nodes	Edges	Communities
Football	115	616	13
Cora	2708	5278	7
Citeseer	3264	4536	6
Email-Enron	36692	183831	/
Amazon0302	262111	1234877	/
S1	20–28	24–68	1–2

5.2 Baseline Algorithms

We compare USBGM-LPA(Batch) with GraphX-LPA implemented based on GraphX [22], a parallel graph computing framework, and USBGM-LPA(Stream) with Spark Streaming-LPA implemented based on Spark Streaming [23] for accuracy experiments. We also compare USBGM-LPA with and without the time decay strategy to validate the effectiveness of stream processing and the time decay strategy.

5.3 Evaluation Metrics

Normalized Mutual Information (NMI) [20] metric is an objective metric to evaluate the accuracy of a community division compared with the true one, the specific calculation of NMI is defined as follows:

$$NMI(R,F) = \frac{-2\sum_{i=1}^{C_R}\sum_{j=1}^{C_F} N_{ij} log(\frac{N_{ij}S}{N_{i*}N_{*j}})}{\sum_{i=1}^{C_R} N_{i*} log(\frac{N_{i*}}{S}) + \sum_{j=1}^{C_F} N_{*j} log(\frac{N_{*j}}{S})}, \tag{3}$$

where the rows in matrix N denote the real communities and the columns denote the communities obtained by the algorithm. The elements in row i of the matrix are denoted as N_{i*}, the elements in column j are denoted as N_{*j}; the elements in row i of the matrix are denoted as N_{i*}, the elements in column j are denoted as N_{*j}. The elements of the row i of the matrix are denoted as N_{i*}, the elements of the column j are denoted as N_{*j}. N_{ij} denotes the number of nodes in which the real community is the same as the community obtained by the algorithm, S is the number of nodes. C_R denotes the number of real communities and C_F denotes the number of communities obtained by the algorithm.

Newman et al. proposed the modularity Q [21], which has since been widely used to measure the quality of community division where the true community division is not known, and the modularity is calculated as follows:

$$Q = \frac{1}{2m}\sum_{i,j}[A_{ij} - \frac{d_i d_j}{2m}\delta(C_i, C_j)] \tag{4}$$

m is the number of edges in the network, and A_{ij} is the element in the adjacency matrix A, if nodes i, j are connected, then $A_{ij} = 1$, otherwise $A_{ij} = 0$. C_i is the community to which node i belongs, C_j is the community to which node j belongs, $\delta(C_i, C_j) = 1$ when i, j are in the same community and 0 otherwise. d_i represents the degree of node i, $\frac{d_i d_j}{2m}$ denotes the probability of the existence of an edge between node i and node j in a random network.

5.4   Accuracy Experiment

The algorithms involved in the accuracy experiments include the USBGM-LPA(Batch) and GraphX-LPA implemented by GraphX [22], and the USBGM-LPA(Stream) and Spark Streaming-LPA.

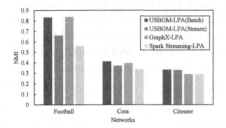
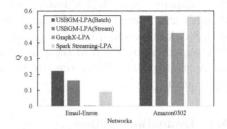

Fig. 5. NMI results on Real-world Networks

Fig. 6. Modularity results on Real-world Networks

Figure 5 shows the NMI metrics for the three network datasets knowing the true community division; from the figure, we can see that the accuracy of USBGM-LPA in batch processing mode is higher than the comparison algorithm on the small-scale dataset, and USBGM-LPA in stream processing mode is not as accurate as GraphX-LPA executed in batch processing on some datasets, but compared to GraphX-LPA also executed in stream processing, but better than the comparison algorithm, which also performs in stream processing. This reflects that USBGM, in the form of a unified stream and batch processing, can perform both stream and batch processing while ensuring the algorithm's accuracy.

Figure 6 shows the modularity metrics for the two datasets without knowing the true community division, from which we can see that USBGM-LPA works better than the other algorithms in both batch and stream processing on the larger dataset. This reflects the effectiveness of USBGM's strategy of using one edge as the minimum processing granularity and streaming iterative update, which can have better results when the traditional batch processing scheme cannot get effective results.

Figure 7 and Fig. 8 show the variation of NMI and modularity metrics over time when the stream processing-based algorithm is run on the datasets football

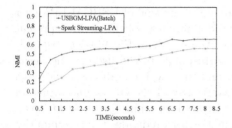

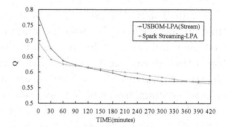

Fig. 7. NMI results over time for the football data set

Fig. 8. Modularity results over time for the Amazon0302 data set

and Amazon0302, from which it can be seen that USBGM-LPA has faster convergence and better algorithmic results on both small and large datasets. The variation of the network represented by the dataset over time can be known in Fig. 8. The stability of the Amazon0302 network community is decreasing. This reflects the better running speed of USBGM and having lower latency for faster changes in the network brought about by changes in the dataset over time.

5.5 Time Decaying Effect Experiment

This part of the experiment will validate the impact of discovering new communities and time decay strategy on community detection results over time with artificial dataset S1.

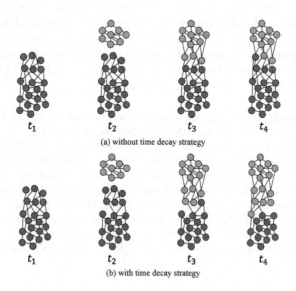

Fig. 9. Evolution of community division over time

Figure 9 show the evolution of the community division of USBGM-LPA over time on the artificial Dataset S1, and the different colors of the nodes represent that they belong to different communities. Among them, Fig. 9(a) corresponds to no time decay strategy, and Fig. 9(b) corresponds to the use of time decay strategy. From time t_1 to time t_2, we can find that both can discover the birth of new communities, which proves the effectiveness of the stream processing of USBGM to capture the change of graph structure. From time t_2 to t_3 and t_3 to t_4, comparing the two graphs, we can find that Fig. 9(b) redivides the communities to which the involved nodes belong due to the time decay strategy that decays the edges between the earlier nodes, making the community division in Fig. 9(b) more consistent with the actual situation at the current time at moments t_3 and t_4, which proves the effectiveness of the time decay strategy in USBGM.

6   Conclusion

This study proposes a unified stream and batch graph computing model(USBGM). USBGM adopts the idea of using one edge as the minimum processing granularity and combines a graph cache structure that can be updated in real-time and an iterative stream mechanism to realize stream processing and batch processing in a unified way, which can obtain an accuracy close to that of batch processing and also take advantage of the low latency of stream processing. In addition, we introduce a time decay strategy that allows the algorithm implemented based on USBGM to reflect the corresponding changes in the network structure over time. We implement the graph operator based on USBGM and apply it to solve the community detection problem. Experimental results on real-world and artificial networks validate the accuracy and low latency of the USBGM and verify that the USBGM can effectively capture changes in the network over time. In the future, we plan to optimize the execution efficiency of the model further and enhance the generalization capability of the model so that the model can be applied to more domains.

Acknowledgments. This work was supported by the National Natural Science Foundation of China under Grant No. 62002063 and No. U21A20472, the National Key Research and Development Plan of China under Grant No.2021YFB3600503, the Fujian Collaborative Innovation Center for Big Data Applications in Governments, the Fujian Industry-Academy Cooperation Project under Grant No. 2017H6008 and No. 2018H6010, the Natural Science Foundation of Fujian Province under Grant No.2020J05112 and No.2020J01420, the Fujian Provincial Department of Education under Grant No. JAT190026, the Major Science and Technology Project of Fujian Province under Grant No.2021HZ022007 and Haixi Government Big Data Application Cooperative Innovation Center and the China Scholarship Council under Grant 202006655008.

References

1. Dean, J., Ghemawat, S.: MapReduce: simplified data processing on large clusters. Commun. ACM **51**(1), 107–113 (2008)
2. Zaharia, M., et al.: Spark: cluster computing with working sets. In: 2nd USENIX Workshop on Hot Topics in Cloud Computing (HotCloud 2010) (2010)
3. Malewicz, G., et al.: Pregel: a system for large-scale graph processing. In: Proceedings of the 2010 ACM SIGMOD International Conference on Management of Data (2010)
4. Gerbessiotis, A.V., Valiant, L.G.: Direct bulk-synchronous parallel algorithms. J. Para. Distrib. Comput. **22**(2), 251–267 (1994)
5. Gonzalez, J.E., et al.: PowerGraph: distributed graph-parallel computation on natural graphs. In: 10th USENIX Symposium on Operating Systems Design and Implementation (OSDI 2012) (2012)
6. Hollocou, A., et al.: A linear streaming algorithm for community detection in very large networks. arXiv preprint arXiv:1703.02955 (2017)
7. Abbas, Z., et al.: Streaming graph partitioning: an experimental study. In: Proceedings of the VLDB Endowment, vol. 11, no. 11, pp. 1590–1603 (2018)
8. Ma, Y., et al.: Streaming graph neural networks. In: Proceedings of the 43rd International ACM SIGIR Conference on Research and Development in Information Retrieval (2020)
9. Gama, J., et al.: A survey on concept drift adaptation. ACM Comput. Surv. (CSUR) **46**(4), 1–37 (2014)
10. Aliperti, A., et al.: A fuzzy density-based clustering algorithm for streaming data. In: 2019 IEEE International Conference on Fuzzy Systems (FUZZ-IEEE). IEEE (2019)
11. Bechini, A., Marcelloni, F., Renda, A.: TSF-DBSCAN: a novel fuzzy density-based approach for clustering unbounded data streams. IEEE Trans. Fuzzy Syst. **30**, 623–637 (2020)
12. Kiran, M., et al.: Lambda architecture for cost-effective batch and speed big data processing. In: 2015 IEEE International Conference on Big Data (Big Data). IEEE (2015)
13. Kroß, J., Brunnert, A., Prehofer, C., Runkler, T.A., Krcmar, H.: Stream processing on demand for lambda architectures. In: Beltrán, M., Knottenbelt, W., Bradley, J. (eds.) EPEW 2015. LNCS, vol. 9272, pp. 243–257. Springer, Cham (2015). https://doi.org/10.1007/978-3-319-23267-6_16
14. Boykin, O., et al.: Summingbird: a framework for integrating batch and online mapreduce computations. In: Proceedings of the VLDB Endowment, vol. 7, no. 13, pp. 1441–1451 (2014)
15. Fan, W., Bifet, A.: Mining big data: current status, and forecast to the future. ACM SIGKDD Explor. Newsle. **14**(2), 1–5 (2013)
16. Oryx2 (2014). http://oryx.io/
17. Pishgoo, B., Azirani, A.A., Raahemi, B.: A hybrid distributed batch-stream processing approach for anomaly detection.". Inf. Sci. **543**, 309–327 (2021)
18. Kreps, J.: Questioning the lambda architecture. Online article 205 (2014)
19. Raghavan, U.N., Albert, R., Kumara, S.: Near linear time algorithm to detect community structures in large-scale networks. Phys. Rev. E **76**(3), 036106 (2007)
20. Danon, L., et al.: Comparing community structure identification. J. Stat. Mech.: Theory Exp. **2005**(09), P09008 (2005)

21. Newman, M.E.J.: Modularity and community structure in networks. Proc. Nat. Acad. Sci. **103**(23), 8577–8582 (2006)
22. Xin, R.S., et al.: Graphx: a resilient distributed graph system on spark. In: First international Workshop on Graph Data Management Experiences and Systems (2013)
23. Zaharia, M., et al.: Apache spark: a unified engine for big data processing. Commun. ACM **59**(11), 56–65 (2016)

A Feature Fusion-Based Service Classification Approach for Collaborative Development

Kun Hu, Aohui Zhou[✉], Ye Wang, Bo Jiang, and Qiao Huang

School of Computer and Information Engineering, Zhejiang Gongshang University, Hangzhou 310018, China
aohuizhou@163.com

Abstract. Collaborative development, as one of the most widely used development models, is very effective at increasing development efficiency and software quality. In collaborative development, developers deploy services on the Internet and provide stable business functionality to the public. However, developers with different levels of development experience and code levels may classify the services into the wrong categories. As a result, reusing these services is impossible due to the confusing service categories, which has a significant impact on developers' development efficiency. Most existing service classification approaches rely on textual information such as Web service descriptions and names, which may not provide enough information to determine their categories when the descriptions and names are too brief or vague. This paper proposes a Service Classification Approach based on Feature Fusion (SCAFF), which combines semantic and structural features. SCAFF first extracts service semantic feature vectors and service structural feature vectors by SimCSE, MixGCF, and LightGCN. Then it combines these two features and finally obtains the service category using two fully connected layers. Compared with TextCNN, LSTM, and ServeNet, SCAFF has higher accuracy on Top-1 accuracy and Top-5 accuracy.

Keywords: Collaborative Development · Service Classification · Feature Fusion · Deep Learning

1 Introduction

In recent years, distributed and cloud computing technologies have become increasingly mature, and collaborative software development work models have gradually replaced centralized software development work models, such as software outsourcing models, structured development models, and software assembly pipelines. Collaborative development provides a collaborative working environment for time-dispersed developers to better complete a temporally separated, spatially distributed, and interdependent project, improving not only work efficiency but also software quality. Among the various collaborative development modes, service-oriented development is currently one of the most popular development models.

© The Author(s), under exclusive license to Springer Nature Singapore Pte Ltd. 2023
Y. Sun et al. (Eds.): ChineseCSCW 2022, CCIS 1681, pp. 125–134, 2023.
https://doi.org/10.1007/978-981-99-2356-4_10

The process of service-oriented development is a complex service developing process in which a large number of services are generated and used. A service is a component that is deployed on the Internet and provides stable business functions to the public. In this paper, both APIs and services are defined as Services. Developers typically search for the category of services they require and then find the services that meet their development requirements under that category. However, developers often have different development experiences and code levels, resulting in the same class of services will be classified under different or incorrect categories. Therefore, when reusing these services, it is difficult for developers to quickly find the right service because of the confusing categories of services. Service classification can help developers automatically classify services and ensure that each service is assigned to the correct category.

There has been a lot of work on service classification, and most of these approaches are based on functional attributes. The main idea of all these approaches is to classify services based on textual information such as service descriptions and service names. However, using textual information alone is often not accurate enough [1]. Many approaches by adding other feature vectors and integrating classifiers have been proposed to improve the overall classification accuracy [2]. With the rapid advancement of deep learning in recent years, many researchers have considered applying deep learning to service classification and have made significant progress, such as LSTM (Long Short-Term Memory) [3], Bi-LSTM (Bi-directional Long Short-Term Memory) [4], Wide&Bi-LSTM [5], and ServeNet [6]. In general, although the above approaches and techniques have improved the accuracy of service classification, they cannot provide enough information for developers to determine its classification when the service description is too brief or vague. Furthermore, most current approaches use semantic and contextual information describing the words in a document or fuse auxiliary information such as tags, but these approaches do not make good use of the relevance of discrete features and cannot deal with the document semantic sparsity problem well. In addition, these approaches rely on information such as text descriptions and labels, without considering the invocation relationship between services. It has been proved that the invocation and other relationships between services can be supplemented with features other than service text descriptions by using service invocation graphs, which improves the accuracy of service category recommendations.

To overcome the problem caused by the insufficient or poor quality of text information in service description documents, this paper proposes a service classification approach based on feature fusion (SCAFF), which uses semantic and structural features to improve the performance of service classification. The contribution of this paper is as follows:

1. This paper proposes SCAFF, a service classification approach for collaborative development that fuses both semantic and structural features. The approach considers both the information contained in the service description text and the service invocation relationship, using SimCSE, MixGCF, and Light-

GCN to extract the service feature vectors and classify the service categories by a feature fusion approach.

2. This paper crawls the real dataset from the programmable[1] web for experiments. The effectiveness of SCAFF is evaluated by comparing it with three baseline approaches.

3. This paper conducts experiments to verify and analyze the different roles played by different types of features in the classification process.

The rest of this paper is structured as follows. Section 2 demonstrates our approach. Section 3 describes the experiments and discusses the experimental results. Section 4 summarizes the paper and discusses our future work.

2   The SCAFF Approach

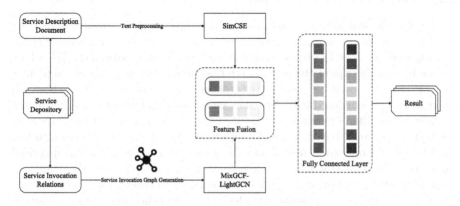

Fig. 1. Framework of the SCAFF

As shown in Fig. 1, the proposed approach SCAFF contains four steps: 1) Generating the service invocation graph. 2) Extracting service features. 3) Feature fusion. 4) Service classification.

This paper defines a service as a component with specific functionality that consists of one or more APIs (also known as service) in SCAFF. It can be defined formally as follows: $s_i = \{d, rs, c\}$, where d denotes the description document of service s_i, $rs = \{s_1, s_2, ..., s_n\}$ is the set of services that have an invocation relationship with s_i, and c_i is the category corresponding to s_i. Each step of SCAFF is described in detail in the following subsections.

---

[1] https://www.programmableweb.com/.

2.1 Service Invocation Graph Generation

A Service Invocation Graph (SIG) is an un-directed and unweighted graph that consists of service nodes and relationship edges in a dataset. The SCAFF first extracts the history of invocations between services and generates an edge r_{ij} if there is an invocation relationship between a service s_i and a service s_j. The SIG can be defined as follows:

$$SIG = \{s, r | s \in S, r \in R\} \tag{1}$$

where s is the service node, r is the invocation relationship between services, and $R = \{r_1, r_2, \ldots, r_n\}$ is the set of invocation edges between services, $S = \{s_1, s_2, \ldots, s_n\}$ is the set of service nodes.

2.2 Service Feature Extraction

In SCAFF, the features of services are divided into semantic features and structural features. For semantic features, traditional approaches often simply splice or sum word vectors to obtain sentence vectors, such as Word2Vec [7], which cannot effectively exploit the implicit relationships between words in a sentence. SCAFF uses the SimCSE model [8] to obtain the semantic features. SimCSE is a contrastive learning framework that generates different embeddings for the same word in different contexts to better capture the features of the sentences. SimCSE is designed based on BERT [9] model, and it can be divided into two models: the unsupervised model and the supervised model. The unsupervised model uses Dropout [10] as noise when constructing samples, and the same sentence is treated as input to the pre-trained encoder in two batches to obtain two different embeddings as positive samples. Then the other sentences are used as negative samples. The supervised model builds upon the research of using natural language inference (NLI) datasets for sentence embeddings [11,12], uses the original tags of the dataset as annotations, and adds annotated sentence pairs to the contrastive learning, to optimize the positive and negative samples in the dataset. The empirical evidence [8] shows that optimization for the training samples and fine-tuning of the model can effectively improve its performance. In comparison with other models, SimCSE can obtain sentence embeddings more accurately. SCAFF inputs the description sentences of each service into the Sim-CSE model to obtain the sentence embeddings as semantic features, and the process can be defined as:

$$e_{desc} = f_{SimCSE}(d_i) \tag{2}$$

where d_i is the description sentence of service i, f_{SimCSE} is the SimCSE model, and e_{desc} is the sentence embeddings obtained by d_i through f_{SimCSE}.

For structural features, this paper uses MixGCF [13] and LightGCN [14] to obtain the embeddings of services on the structure. MixGCF is a general negative sampling tool that can be used to improve the performance of GNN models by adding features from positive samples to negative samples to obtain Hard Negative Samples [13] that are closer to positive samples for training. LightGCN is a simplified GCN network based on the traditional GNN-based recommendation system, which eliminates unnecessary designs such as feature transformation and nonlinear activation compared with traditional GCN networks, and only retains the core component of neighborhood aggregation. By performing linear propagation on the graph, LightGCN can obtain node embeddings and combine the embeddings and weights obtained at its different propagation layers as the final embeddings. The SCAFF uses the SIG as the input of MixGCF and LightGCN to obtain the service node embeddings as structural features, and the process can be defined as:

$$e_{struct} = f_{MixGCF_{LightGCN}}(SIG) \tag{3}$$

where SIG is the service invocation graph, $f_{MixGCF_{LightGCN}}$ is the LightGCN model with MixGCF, and e_{struct} is the structural feature corresponding to service i.

2.3 Feature Fusion

On the feature fusion layer, the SCAFF merges the obtained feature vectors e_{desc} and e_{struct} into one unified feature vector. The SCAFF uses cat as the strategy for merging vectors, and the process can be defined as:

$$e_i = cat\left(e_{desc}, e_{struct}\right) \tag{4}$$

where e_i is the final fusion feature corresponding to service i. After the process, the feature vector corresponding to each service can be obtained.

2.4 Service Classification

On the service classification layer, the SCAFF set up a feed-forward neural network with two fully connected layers. The activation functions of the fully connected layers are $h1$ and $h2$, each fully connected layer is responsible for computing the output obtained from the previous layer and transmitting the result to the next layer. The fully connected layers are defined as follows:

$$o_{h1} = w_1 * e_i + b1 \tag{5}$$

$$o_{h2} = w_2 * o_{h1} + b2 \tag{6}$$

where w_1 and b_1 is the weights and bias factor of the fully connected layer $h1$, and o_{h1} is the output of the fully connected layer $h1$. w_2 and b_2 are the weights and bias factor of the fully connected layer $h2$, and o_{h2} is the output of the fully connected layer $h2$, respectively. Eventually, the fully connected layer $h2$ maps the results onto a dimensional space of Num_{class} (the number of categories contained in the dataset). The SCAFF inverts the probability of each category in the results to obtain the final category recommendation results.

3 Experiments

3.1 Experiment Setup

This paper conducts three independent experiments for each approach (including SCAFF and baseline approaches) to prevent contingency and uses early stopping to avoid overfitting. All experiments were performed on a running GPU GTX3080 device and the source code was implemented based on PyTorch 1.11.0[2]. For the parameters of MixGCF and LightGCN, this paper sets the number of candidates negative to 64, the number of negative in K-pair loss to 1, the learning rate to 1e-4, and the rest parameter to default. For the parameters of SCAFF, this paper sets the Dropout to 0.5 and the learning rate to 1e-6.

3.2 Dataset

Due to the rapid iteration of services, this paper collects a total of 25,353 services from Programmable Web to generate the latest dataset for evaluating the proposed approach. To better utilize the invocation relationship between services, the dataset only retains services that contain invocation relationships for training and evaluation, and removed the stop words from them. The processed dataset contains 3980 services covering 255 categories. This paper randomly divides the dataset into training, validation, and test sets in the ratio of 6:2:2.

3.3 Evaluation Metrics

Top-k accuracy is used to calculate the percentage of correct categories in the k categories with the highest probability in the prediction results. It is widely used for the evaluation of classification models. This paper uses Top-1 accuracy and Top-5 accuracy as the evaluation metrics for the experiments. Top-1 accuracy represents the accuracy obtained by comparing the first category with the highest probability in the classification prediction results with the true category of the sample. Top-1 accuracy is often used to evaluate the effectiveness of binary classification models. Top-5 accuracy indicates the accuracy of the top five categories in the classification prediction results compared to the true category of the sample. Top-5 accuracy is often used to evaluate the effectiveness of multi-classification models. Their calculation can be defined as:

$$Accuracy_{top1} = \frac{Num_{top1\_correct\_samples}}{Num_{samples}} \tag{7}$$

$$Accuracy_{top5} = \frac{Num_{top5\_correct\_samples}}{Num_{samples}} \tag{8}$$

where $Num_{top1\_correct\_samples}$ and $Num_{top5\_correct\_samples}$ denote the sum of the number of correctly predicted samples in the categories with the first and top-5 probability in each sample classification prediction result, respectively. $Num_{samples}$ denotes the total number of samples in the test dataset.

---

[2] https://pytorch.org/.

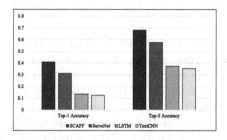 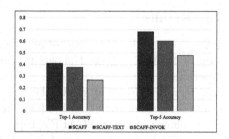

Fig. 2. Results of the Top-1 accuracy, Top-5 accuracy in the comparative experiment.

Fig. 3. Results of the Top-1 accuracy, Top-5 accuracy in the ablation experiment.

3.4   The Comparative Experiment

This paper uses three baseline approaches to evaluate the performance of SCAFF.

1. TextCNN [15]: TextCNN is a neural network model for text classification. It changes the original input layer of the traditional CNN to an embedding layer, so that text can be converted to word vectors and input into the model.
2. LSTM [16]: Long Short Term Memory (LSTM) is a special kind of recurrent neural network (RNN), it is a kind of neural network with the ability to remember long and short term information. The principle is that the gate mechanism is used to control the flow and loss of features, and the gate decides whether to keep or discard the features at the top of the discourse order, thus achieving the ability of long and short-term information memory.
3. ServeNet [17]: ServeNet is a deep neural network for end-to-end service classification that automatically abstracts low-level representations of service names and service descriptions into high-level features and then merges these high-level features into a unified feature for service classification.

3.5   The Ablation Experiment

To further demonstrate the effectiveness of SCAFF, this paper conducts two sets of ablation experiments.

1. SCAFF-TEXT: The SCAFF-TEXT model is based on SCAFF with the service structural features vectors removed. It uses only SimCSE [8] as a semantic features extraction tool for classification after extracting the text embeddings of the service description documents.
2. SCAFF-INVOK: The SCAFF-INVOK model is based on SCAFF by removing the service semantic feature vectors. It only uses MixGCF [13] and Light-GCN [14] as the structural features extraction tool for classification after extracting the feature.

3.6 Results

This paper conducts a series of experiments to evaluate the classification accuracy of SCAFF. Figure 2 shows the experimental results of the comparative experiments compared to the three baseline approaches, i.e. TextCNN, LSTM, and ServeNet. Figure 3 shows the experimental results of the ablation experiments comparing the SCAFF-TEXT and SCAFF-INVOK approaches.

As shown in Fig. 2, SCAFF's Top-1 accuracy and Top-5 accuracy are 9.87% and 10.57% higher than that of ServeNet. Compared with LSTM and TextCNN, the Top-1 accuracy is 27.44% and 28.42% higher, and the Top-5 accuracy is 30.86% and 32.81% higher, respectively. Specifically, ServeNet ranks second because it uses a large-scale pretraining model named Bert in the feature extraction process. However, it performs worse in terms of Top-1 accuracy and Top-5 accuracy than SCAFF as the features are all derived from semantic information. No invocation information between services is considered in ServeNet. LSTM and TextCNN achieved the worst results as the extracted features by these two approaches are sparse. Besides, neither approaches take the invocation relationship between services into account.

As shown in Fig. 3, SCAFF achieved the best results in both Top-1 accuracy and Top-5 accuracy, and its Top-1 accuracy and Top-5 accuracy are 3.29% and 8.05% higher than SCAFF-TEXT, respectively. The results indicate that service invocation relationships extracted by MixGCF and LightGCN play a crucial role in service classification. Compared with SCAFF-INVOK, the Top-1 accuracy of SCAFF is 14.15% higher and the Top-5 accuracy is 20.25% higher, indicating that even though structural features can enhance the classification effect, semantic features still play a major role in the classification process, and both features need to work together to achieve better results.

4   Conclusion and Future Work

This paper proposes a service classification model based on feature fusion SCAFF for collaborative development, by automatically extracting two feature vectors: semantics and structural. The experiments show that the Top-5 accuracy of SCAFF is better than that of ServeNet by 10.57%, 30.86%, and 32.81% higher than that of LSTM and TextCNN respectively.

Although SCAFF has good performance, it still contains limited features, so in future work, we plan to 1) use more advanced methods to extract the features contained in the service and 2) introduce more types of features to better represent the service.

Acknowledgements. This work is supported by the Natural Science Foundation of Zhejiang Province (No. LY21F020011, LY20F020027), and the Key Research and Development Program of Zhejiang Province (No. 2021C01162).

References

1. Platzer, C., Dustdar, S.: A vector space search engine for web services. In: Third European Conference on Web Services (ECOWS 2005), p. 9. IEEE (2005)
2. Katakis, I., Meditskos, G., Tsoumakas, G., Bassiliades, N.: On the combination of textual and semantic descriptions for automated semantic web service classification. In: Iliadis, M., Tsoumakasis, V., Bramer (eds.) IFIP International Conference on Artificial Intelligence Applications and Innovations, pp. 95–104. Springer, Boston (2009). https://doi.org/10.1007/978-1-4419-0221-4_13
3. Shi, M., Liu, J.: Functional and contextual attention-based LSTM for service recommendation in mashup creation. IEEE Trans. Parallel Distrib. Syst. **30**(5), 1077–1090 (2018)
4. Cao, Y., Liu, J., Cao, B., Shi, M., Wen, Y., Peng, Z.: Web services classification with topical attention based Bi-LSTM. In: Wang, X., Gao, H., Iqbal, M., Min, G. (eds.) CollaborateCom 2019. LNICST, vol. 292, pp. 394–407. Springer, Cham (2019). https://doi.org/10.1007/978-3-030-30146-0_27
5. Ye, H., Cao, B., Peng, Z., Chen, T., Wen, Y., Liu, J.: Web service classification based on wide & Bi-LSTM model. IEEE Access **7**, 43697–43706 (2019)
6. Yang, Y., Ke, W., Wang, W., Zhao, Y.: Deep learning for web services classification. In: 2019 IEEE International Conference on Web Services (ICWS), pp. 440–442. IEEE (2019)
7. Mikolov, T., Chen, K., Corrado, G., Dean, J.: Efficient estimation of word representations in vector space. arXiv preprint arXiv:1301.3781 (2013)
8. Gao, T., Yao, X., Chen, D.: SimCSE: simple contrastive learning of sentence embeddings. arXiv preprint arXiv:2104.08821 (2021)
9. Devlin, J., Chang, M.W., Lee, K., Toutanova, K.: BERT: pre-training of deep bidirectional transformers for language understanding. arXiv preprint arXiv:1810.04805 (2018)
10. Srivastava, N., Hinton, G., Krizhevsky, A., Sutskever, I., Salakhutdinov, R.: Dropout: a simple way to prevent neural networks from overfitting. J. Mach. Learn. Res. **15**(1), 1929–1958 (2014)
11. Conneau, A., Kiela, D., Schwenk, H., Barrault, L., Bordes, A.: Supervised learning of universal sentence representations from natural language inference data. arXiv preprint arXiv:1705.02364 (2017)
12. Reimers, N., Gurevych, I.: Sentence-BERT: sentence embeddings using Siamese BERT-networks. arXiv preprint. arXiv:1908.10084 (2019)
13. Huang, T., et al.: MixGCF: an improved training method for graph neural network-based recommender systems. In: Proceedings of the 27th ACM SIGKDD Conference on Knowledge Discovery & Data Mining, pp. 665–674. ACM (2021)
14. He, X., Deng, K., Wang, X., Li, Y., Zhang, Y., Wang, M.: LightGCN: simplifying and powering graph convolution network for recommendation. In: Proceedings of the 43rd International ACM SIGIR Conference on Research and Development in Information Retrieval, pp. 639–648. ACM (2020)
15. Chen, Y.: Convolutional Neural Networks for Sentence Classification. University of Waterloo (2015)

16. Malhotra, P., Vig, L., Shroff, G., Agarwal, P.: Long short term memory networks for anomaly detection in time series. In: 23rd European Symposium on Artificial Neural Networks, Computational Intelligence and Machine Learning, pp. 89–94. IEEE (2015)
17. Yang, Y., et al.: ServeNet: a deep neural network for web services classification. In: 2020 IEEE International Conference on Web Services (ICWS), pp. 168–175. IEEE (2020)

Requirements Classification and Identification Approach for E-Collaboration Systems

Shizhe Song, Bo Jiang, Siyuan Zhou, Ye Wang, and Qiao Huang[✉]

School of Computer and Information Engineering, Zhejiang Gongshang University,
Hangzhou 310018, China
qiaohuang@zjgsu.edu.cn

Abstract. In the background of global economic integration and the pandemic era, e-collaboration systems have become the main tools for people to learn and work. E-collaboration systems in the Internet era face rapid iteration requires, it's important to research how to quickly access the requirements of e-collaboration systems to help developers better update and iterate on them and improve the user experience. As the number of user reviews in the application market is large, covering a wide range, a large number of requirements are contained in it, therefore, this paper starts from two dimensions of functional requirements and non-functional requirements, and proposes 15 requirements categories for the collaboration characteristics and timely characteristics of the e-collaboration system. First crawl the collaboration system user reviews as a dataset, use TextRank ranking algorithm and TextCNN model to classify them, and finally by building a network of co-occurrence relationships between words to feed the users most concerned in a certain classification to the developers. Our method has proven to be excellent in terms of Precision, Recall and F1-measure, and can help developers to obtain requirements from large amount of review data.

Keywords: E-collaboration system · Requirement acquisition · Deep learning · Neural network

1 Introduction

E-collaboration is widely defined as "the high-speed, real-time interaction between people and data through the use of electronic tools, such as shared documents, online meetings, portals and instant messaging, for planning, coordination, decision-making, process integration, efficiency and effectiveness" [1]. With the integration of the world economy and the proposed strategy of a large domestic economic cycle, many companies across regions must rely on e-collaboration systems to create a shared virtual work environment, sharing the same information and environment with colleagues who are unable to complete projects directly, in to break through the limitations of time and space and increase the value of information while making full use of human resources.

With the increasing importance of e-collaboration system in people's production life, its user base and coverage are becoming more and more extensive, and the system

© The Author(s), under exclusive license to Springer Nature Singapore Pte Ltd. 2023
Y. Sun et al. (Eds.): ChineseCSCW 2022, CCIS 1681, pp. 135–146, 2023.
https://doi.org/10.1007/978-981-99-2356-4_11

function evaluation data based on user dimensions also grows, and a large number of explicit or implicit requirements are contained in it [2], but the source group of such data is wide, large, uneven quality and too much noise information, and it's still a difficult problem to fully explore and analyze users' requirements in it to drive system update and iteration to improve user experience.

In the past studies of requirement exploration [3–5], classification is only used to filter data that is not related to requirements and still need manual analysis of specific requirements. More detailed categorization than filtering has been proposed in studies [6–9] to provide developers with clearer and more explicit categories of requirements based on the removal of noisy data, such as Maalej et al. [6] who classified user reviews into four categories: feature requests, bug reports, user experience, and text ratings. However, current work on e-collaboration systems has focused on validation [10] and characteristics modeling [11], and there has been no research on requirements classification and acquisition for such systems, while the traditional requirements classification methods for general systems have shortcomings in completeness, accuracy, and clarity, and the classification results do not help e-collaboration systems to highlight their collaborative nature and real-time performance [12]. Therefore, this paper defines 15 requirement categories for the user review data of the e-collaboration system, which can distinguish functional requirements from non-functional requirements while highlighting the characteristics of collaboration, and can fully explore the explicit and implicit requirements in the user feedback, so as to assist the developers in updating and iterating the system. This method first crawls the user feedback and questions about this collaboration system from the app store, and after data pre-processing to remove the noise data, uses the TextCNN model and TextRank ranking algorithm to classify the requirements and extract keywords respectively, and finally uses the keyword co-occurrence matrix to get the high frequency co-occurrence keywords to give feedback to the developers about the most concerned users under this category specific issues. The study of this problem has important research significance for improving and guaranteeing the quality of e-collaboration system products as well as user experience.

The contribution of this paper is as follows:

1. Requirements knowledge categories for e-collaboration systems are defined and their concepts are explained.
2. The ability to automatically explore requirements from unstructured requirement text helps developers to better update and iterate on e-collaboration systems.
3. Combine TextCNN deep learning model and TextRank ranking algorithm to classification and keyword extraction of user review data, which improves efficiency while ensuring precision, which improves efficiency while ensuring precision.

The rest of this paper is structured as follows. Section 2 demonstrates our approach. Section 3 describes the experiments and discusses the experimental results. Section 4 summarizes the paper and discusses our future work.

2 Method

2.1 Research Framework

The overall research framework of this paper is shown in Fig. 1:

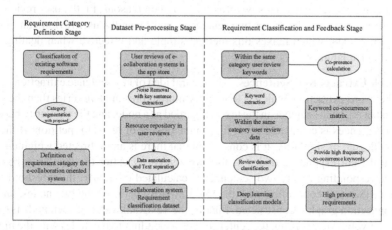

Fig. 1. Approach overview

The first stage is the requirement category definition stage, based on the categories of requirements proposed in previous studies, we have made a more detailed classification of functional and non-functional requirements, taking into account the characteristics of e-collaboration systems, thus, the collaboration system developers can more precisely get the direction of users' requirements. This classification can cover the requirements contained in the user reviews dataset of the e-collaboration system, so it is used as our data annotation strategy.

The second stage is the dataset pre-processing stage. We select the user reviews data under the collaboration software from the APP application market, clean their data, use the noise-removed data to form the user review resource library and to data annotate. Since some redundant content will reduce the characteristic of the text, we use the TextRank ranking algorithm to extract key sentences to simplify the dataset and form a collaboration system requirements review classification dataset.

The third stage is the classification and feedback stage. We choose TextCNN model to train and classify the data after investigation. In order to enable developers to more detailed understanding of the specific needs of users. We extracted keywords from the classified review statements, taking into account the characteristics of user reviews in app stores: they are mainly short reviews and are basically non-structural description language, lacking standardization. We propose to calculate the co-occurrence times of keywords under the same classification by taking a user review as the unit and con-structing the co-occurrence matrix between keywords. In this way, users can get the most concerned about the collaboration system in a certain category, and feedback to the developer.

2.2 Background

TextRank Extracts Keywords. TextRank is a graph-based text processing ranking model proposed by Mihalcea et al. [13], which is improved by the PageRank algorithm launched by Google. It uses adjacent semantic relations between words to build the network, iteratively calculates the Rank value of each node, and then obtains keywords. We chose this model to extract keywords for two main reasons, firstly, user reviews are mainly short texts, mostly one or two sentences, and secondly, user reviews are mostly unstructured texts, which makes this method simple and effective when dealing with non-normative language.

TextRank Extracts Key Sentences. The central idea of key sentence extraction is similar to keyword extraction, which is to identify more representative series than the given text. First of all, each sentence in the text is regarded as a node, and the similarity between the two sentences is calculated according to the degree of lexical repetition. If there is a certain degree of similarity, it is considered that there is an undirected weighted edge between the corresponding nodes of the two sentences. After the similarity between nodes corresponding to any two sentences is calculated circularly, the threshold is set to remove the edge connection with the low similarity between the two nodes, and the node connection graph is constructed. Finally, the TextRank value of each node is calculated iteratively. After sorting, the sentences corresponding to the nodes with the highest TextRank value are taken as key sentences.

2.3 Definition of Requirement Categories for E-Collaboration Systems

The feedback from users for e-collaboration system mainly focuses on two directions, divided into functional and non-functional requirements, and the difference between collaboration system and ordinary software is that users pay more attention to requirements such as collaborative and real-time, so we further subdivide for e-collaboration system based on the previous research on software requirement category classification [14], which is defined as shown in Table 1.

2.4 Dataset Pre-processing

Pre-processing is divided into three steps: noise removal from user reviews of e-collaboration systems, data annotation, and Chinese text segmentation.

Noise Removal. When we deal with user reviews, there are many irrelevant contents and irregular formatting problems due to their arbitrary nature, so before classifying them, we need to perform data cleaning and filter those redundant contents. Noise removal is divided into four steps: 1) Remove special punctuation marks. 2) Remove the content of developers' replies. 3) Remove the deactivation words. 4) Key sentence extraction.

Data Annotation. After pre-processing, we invited five persons from related fields to perform data annotation and consistency check according to the previously defined category settings, and finally the user review data were input into the TextCNN model for classification.

Table 1. Requirement categories and definitions

Requirement Category		Concept Explanation
Functional requirements	Collaborative Function	Users want to add or improve some features that enhance coordination and collaboration ability
	General Function	The requirements to enhance or improve the basic functions of the collaboration system
Non-functional requirements	Real time	Whether the information data received by the user during e-collaboration is instant
	Response time	Time for the collaboration system to respond to the user's request
	Capacity	Collaboration system for its own running capacity and its storage capacity for shared content
	Throughput	Ability of collaboration systems to successfully transfer data per unit time
	Look and feel	User expectations of the operational appearance or interface of the e-collaboration system
	Operability	Operational problems encountered by users when using the collaboration system
	Usability	Whether the features of the collaboration system are easy to use
	Reliability	The ability of the collaboration system to perform the specified functions stably under the specified conditions
	Privacy	No leakage of user privacy to other users when collaborating electronically
	Permission Protection	The feedbacks on collaboration system opening permissions without user's permission
	Security	The ability of the collaboration system to protect user data and the system platform
	Illustrative	User requirements for explanatory notes on the functions or mechanisms of the collaboration system
	Compatibility	The ability to adapt or coordinate the work of collaboration systems in different system environments

Text Segmentation. Since the dataset of this method consists of Chinese text, we use HanLP to separate the sentences into words before performing classification.

2.5 Requirement Analysis and Feedback

Requirement Classification by Using TextCNN Model. TextCNN is a model proposed by Yoon Kim to deal with text classification problem by convolutional neural network [15]. Because of its good classification effect in text classification, especially in the field of short text, we choose the TextCNN model to classify the user review dataset. The model framework is divided into four parts as follows:

Input Embedding Layer. To convert unstructured and non-computable words into structured, computable vectors, we first perform word embedding, using Word2Vec to map each word into a 5-dimensional word vector, just numerizing natural language. As in the example sentence "wish/to/add/virtual/background/function/during/class/" to form an 8 * 5 two-dimensional matrix as input for the convolutional computation of the Convolution layer.

Convolution Layer. Since the data processed by the TextCNN model is 1-dimensional text data with only one dimension of length and high correlation of adjacent words in a sentence, one-dimensional convolution is applied when doing convolution, i.e., the convolution kernel slides in only one direction of the sentence length. The width of the convolution kernel matrix is fixed to the dimension of the word vector d. The height is a hyperparameter. The window sliding step is 1 and its convolution operation is shown in the following equation.

$$o_i = \omega * \alpha[i : i + h - 1], \ i = 1, \ 2, \ \ldots, \ s - h + 1 \tag{1}$$

where ω denotes the convolution kernel matrix with width d and height h, α denotes the matrix obtained after the embedding layer, $\alpha|i : j|$ denotes the matrix α row i to row j, and s denotes the height of matrix α. Then choose different height convolution kernels of 4 and 3 to obtain a richer feature representation, and the activation function is chosen to be sigmoid to finally obtain $s - h + 1$ feature vectors.

Pooling Layer. Since convolution kernels of different heights are used in the convolution layer, the latitude of the feature vectors it obtains is not consistent. To achieve compressing the dimensionality to the same size while retaining the main features, the maximum value of each feature vector is extracted as features by using the 1-Max-pooling pooling function in the pooling layer, and each feature value is stitched together to obtain the final feature vector under that convolution kernel as the input to the fully connected layer.

Fully Connected Layer. The results of pooling the upper layer with the 1-Max-pooling pooling function are stitched together, and the probabilities belonging to each class are obtained using the softmax activation function, and the corresponding e-collaboration system requirement classes are obtained from the obtained probability values.

Requirements Feedback by Using TextRank Algorithm. After we categorize the requirements, we usually summarize the feedback on the categorized requirements in order to give the developers of the collaboration system a more detailed understanding of the requirements that users are the most concerned about in each category (i.e., high priority requirements).

Studies have been conducted mainly by extracting keywords and summarizing them with description templates to give feedback to developers on the requirement content [16]. However, we consider the characteristics of user reviews in app stores: they are mainly short reviews, mostly unstructured descriptive language, and lack of normativity. The review content is diverse and discrete in nature. Therefore, we propose a method for this type of text, firstly, we use TextRank to extract keywords to build a network of co-occurrence relationships between words, and then we use a pair of keywords that appear simultaneously in a single review as a unit to calculate the number of times the keywords appear simultaneously in all reviews under the category, and finally we build it into a keyword co-occurrence matrix to form a combination of popular keywords and feed it to the developers. This allows them to understand user requirements more specifically. For example, in the keyword matrix we built in the reliability requirements, we chose "phone" as an example to present the following view. The vertical coordinate indicates the number of times the keyword "phone" co-occurs with other keywords, and the horizontal coordinate indicates the sequence number of each keyword combination.

Through this method, we can make further refinement of the content under each category that users care about after categorization, and can give specific word feedback to developers about what users care about, instead of just category direction, and we can adapt to the dynamic changes of users' needs, which is helpful for the update and iteration of the e-collaboration system (Fig. 2).

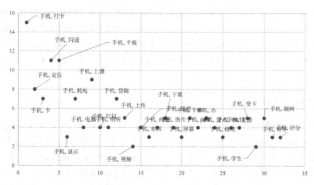

Fig. 2. High frequency words in the co-occurrence matrix of the keyword "phone"

3 Experiments and Effect Analysis

3.1 Comparison Method

For the selection of the classification model, we choose the TextCNN model, and to demonstrate the effectiveness of the method, we use the TextRNN and Transformer classification models as the baseline methods, as discussed below.

TextRNN Model. It is improved based on Recurrent Neural Network (RNN). This model can handle text data of sequence type. When the text sequence information is input, the RNN encodes the text in sequence order. Since RNN has the problem of length dependence and cannot combine the information of whole sentences effectively, we choose its variant - Long Short-Term Memory Network.

Transformer Model. Its structure is based on the Self-Attention mechanism, which was first used in machine translation tasks and later achieved good results in text classification. Unlike the other two models, the Transformer structure does not encode the positional information of the input sequence, so it needs to encode not only the word embedding of the input text, but also the positional information of the words in the text. Some past studies have shown that the information encoding ability of this model is stronger than that of CNN and RNN.

In our data pre-processing stage, we found that the content of some overly long user reviews using TextRank can also express the user's needs after the content is streamlined, because TextRank compares the co-occurrence of words in the statements to determine the weight of the sentences, and we believe that the repeatedly emphasized content has a high probability of being the core needs expressed by the users, so we propose an idea whether the–TextRank summary algorithm can help us enhance the content features of user reviews and remove some useless and distracting information, thus improving the effectiveness of classification. Therefore, for this idea, we construct two datasets based on the same user reviews after noise removal, the first one is the simplified dataset by TextRank algorithm, and the second one is the unsimplified dataset.

3.2 Experiment Setup

Deep Learning Model Setup. This paper implements TextCNN, TextRNN and Transformer deep learning models by using the Pytorch deep learning framework. The generic hyperparameters for the different models are set as follows: The Learning rate is 0.001, the Dropout rate is 0.5, the Batch size is 128, the Pad length is 32, the Epoch is 30, and the optimizer is selected as Adam.In addition to the above general parameters, the sizes of the three convolutional kernels in the TextCNN model are 2, 3, and 4. The number of convolutional kernels is 256, the hidden layer dimension of the RNN in the TextRNN model is 128, and the number of layers is 2. The hidden layer dimension of the Transformer is 1024, the number of encoders is set to 2, and the value of Head is set to 5.

Dataset Setup. Due to the lack of authoritative datasets for user feedback on collaboration systems, most of them currently use self-collected datasets, so we first crawled the user reviews of Ding Talk this collaboration software for the past six months, then invited five professional data annotators to annotate the types of user requirements in user reviews, and then reviewed the annotated content for multiple people, and obtained 4808 user review data. To ensure the validity of the experiment, our dataset was taken as 3600 as the training set, 604 as the test set, and 604 as the validation set for the experiment.

Assessment Metrics. In this paper, we use the metrics of classification task to evaluate the effectiveness of the model, including Precision, Recall and F1-measure, where the Precision is the proportion of the number of requirements correctly classified under the category to the total number of requirements classified under the category. Recall is the proportion of the number of requirements correctly classified under the category to the total number of requirements that should have been classified under the category. F1-measure is a comprehensive performance metric that combines the Precision and Recall and is its reconciliation average.

3.3 Experimental Effects and Analysis

First, the results of comparing the effectiveness of the classification models after the experiments using TextCNN with the other two baseline methods on the complete dataset in this paper are shown in Fig. 3.

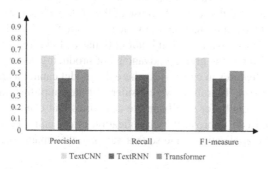

Fig. 3. Comparison of the effectiveness of classification models

Based on the above experimental results, the TextCNN model has the best effectiveness among the three methods, the F1-measure value of the comprehensive evaluation index reaches 0.64, which is 12% higher than that of Transformer model and 18% higher than that of TextRNN model. The Precision and Recall rates are also higher than the other two models. The reason for the above excellent performance of TextCNN stems from the high extraction ability of shallow features of text. In contrast, Transformer's high sensitivity in classifying data imbalance leads to a slightly poor performance.

To verify that simplification of user reviews using TextRank in the data preprocessing stage can enhance the removal of redundant information and improve text features, we conducted a comparison experiment between the simplified dataset using TextRank and the un-simplified dataset, and the results under each category are shown in Fig. 4.

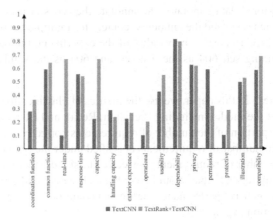

Fig. 4. Comparison of F1-measure for each category after dataset simplification

In the experiment, we found that although the improvement of the simplified weighted index was only about 1.5%, but the average F1-measure index of each of its indexes increased significantly. Among the 15 category of F1-measure indicators after simplification, there are 6 category with more than 10% improvement, 5 category with improvement around 0–10%, and 3 category with a slight decrease of 2%, but they can be regarded as normal fluctuation because of their relatively large sample size. Only the category of permission protection yields negative optimization. Therefore, we find that the simplified dataset with TextRank not only has a slight improvement in overall performance, but also has the greatest advantage of producing a very significant effect of highlighting text features in categories where the model cannot learn effectively due to the small sample size. Therefore, we consider that the simplified data categories are more distinctive, especially for small-sample categories that cannot be learned by the model. This method can improve the classification effect and facilitate the keyword co-occurrence in the application stage so that valuable information can be fed back to users.

4   Conclusion and Future Work

To fully and effectively explore the needs of users for e-collaboration system, it can help developers to update and iterate on it for the purpose of improving people's work and learning efficiency, which has important socio-economic value. There have been many researches on identifying requirements around user reviews of applications, but due to the unique characteristics of e-collaboration systems, stakeholders have more stringent requirements for collaboration and real-time functionality of the system, and past researches have not proposed new requirement categories for this characteristic, and it is easy to ignore the hidden requirements for collaboration and real-time in user reviews, but such requirements are critical for e-collaboration systems. Therefore, this paper proposes 15 requirement knowledge categories from the characteristics of e-collaboration systems, classifies user reviews by using ranking algorithms and deep learning models, and finally also provides feedback to developers on specific requirements under different knowledge categories by constructing co-occurrence relationships between words, which improves the practicality of the method. The experiment proves that the method has good results in the three metrics of Precision, Recall and F1-measure.

In the next work we will consider two optimization ideas: 1) in method selection we will investigate the performance of other deep learning methods on the e-collaboration system user review dataset, such as Bert, TextGCN, and Google's newly introduced neural architecture classification model pQRNN and 2) in experiments we will try to crawl more knowledge information about the e-collaboration system, such as Weibo discussions, Baidu Tieba Q&A, etc., to more fully help developers explore the requirement knowledge.

Acknowledgements. This work is supported by the Natural Science Foundation of Zhejiang Province (No. LY21F020011, LY20F020027), and the Key Research and Development Program of Zhejiang Province (No. 2021C01162).

References

1. Abrantes, C., Mealha, O., Gomes, D., et al.: Human-centric design of unified communications: e-collaboration features. Int. J. e-Collab. (IJeC) **14**(2), 1–18 (2018)
2. Rustam, F., Mehmood, A., Ahmad, M., et al.: Classification of Shopify app user reviews using novel multi text features. IEEE Access **8**, 30234–30244 (2020)
3. Guzman, E., Alkadhi, R., Seyff, N.: An exploratory study of twitter messages about software applications. Requirements Eng. **22**(3), 387–412 (2017)
4. Buchan, J., Bano, M., Zowghi, D., et al.: Semi-automated extraction of new requirements from online reviews for software product evolution. In: 25th Australasian Software Engineering Conference, ASWEC, pp. 31–40. IEEE, Adelaide (2018)
5. Morales-Ramirez, I., Kifetew, F.M., Perini, A.: Speech-acts based analysis for requirements discovery from online discussions. Inf. Syst. **86**, 94–112 (2019)
6. Maalej, W., Kurtanović, Z., Nabil, H., Stanik, C.: On the automatic classification of app reviews. Requirements Eng. **21**(3), 311–331 (2016). https://doi.org/10.1007/s00766-016-0251-9
7. Dhinakaran, V.T., Pulle, R., Ajmeri, N., et al.: App review analysis via active learning: reducing supervision effort without compromising classification accuracy. In: IEEE 26th International Requirements Engineering Conference, RE, pp. 170–181. IEEE, Banff (2018)
8. Chen, Q., Zhang, L., Jiang, J., et al.: Review analysis method based on support vector machine and Latent Dirichlet allocation. J. Softw. **30**(5), 349–362 (2019)
9. Wang, Y., Zheng, L.W., Zhang, Y.Y., et al.: Software requirement mining method for Chinese APP user review data. Comput. Sci. **47**(12), 56–64 (2020)
10. Robra-Bissantz, S.: E-Collaboration: mehr digital ist nicht weniger Mensch. In: Kollmann, T. (ed.) Handbuch Digitale Wirtschaft, pp. 213–239. Springer, Wiesbaden (2020). https://doi.org/10.1007/978-3-658-17291-6_13
11. Wang, Y., Zhao, L.: Eliciting user requirements for e-collaboration systems: a proposal for a multi-perspective modeling approach. Requirements Eng. **24**(2), 205–229 (2017). https://doi.org/10.1007/s00766-017-0285-7

12. Ye, W., Shizhe, S., Bo, J., et al.: Modeling characteristics in the design of E-collaboration systems. Int. J. e-Collaboration (IJeC) **18**(1), 1–17 (2022)
13. Mihalcea, R., Tarau, P.: TextRank: bringing order into text. In: Proceedings of the 2004 Conference on Empirical Methods in Natural Language Processing, ACL, pp. 404–411. ACL, Baecelona (2004)
14. Dias Canedo, E., Cordeiro Mendes, B.: Software requirements classification using machine learning algorithms **22**(9), 1057(2020)
15. Kim, Y.: Convolutional neural networks for sentence classification. In: Proceedings of the 2014 Conference on Empirical Methods in Natural Language Processing, EMNLP, pp. 1746–1751. ACL, Doha (2014)
16. Wang, Y., Zhou, A., Zhou, S., et al.: Requirement acquisition approach for intelligent computing services. J. Comput. Appl., 1–10 (2022)

Community Evolution Tracking Based on Core Node Extension and Edge Variation Discerning

Qifeng Zhuang[1,2,3], Zhiyong Yu[1,2,3], and Kun Guo[1,2,3(✉)]

[1] College of Computer and Data Science, Fuzhou University, Fuzhou 350108, China
{yuzhiyong,gukn}@fzu.edu.cn
[2] Fujian Provincial Key Laboratory of Network Computing and Intelligent Information Processing, Fuzhou 350108, China
[3] Key Laboratory of Spatial Data Mining and Information Sharing, Ministry of Education, Fuzhou 350108, China

Abstract. Communities exist anywhere in various complex networks, and community evolution tracking is one of the most well-liked areas of inquiry in the study of dynamic complex networks. Community evolution tracking has many applications in daily life, such as predicting social network behaviors or analyzing the spread of infectious illnesses. However, the majority of existing evolution tracking algorithms obtain community detection results before matching the community in tracking evolution events, making it difficult to trace the whole evolution of communities because of community matching errors. In addition, the majority of evolution tracking algorithms do not adequately account for the potential scenarios in community evolution, resulting in erroneous detection of evolution events. In this research, a community evolution tracking algorithm based on edge variation discerning and core node extension is proposed. First, we detect communities based on the core node extension strategy, which avoids the problem of community matching errors. Second, we track community evolution based on the edge variation discerning strategy, which fully considers various situations that may occur during the community evolution process. According to the outputs of our experiments, our system can effectively track the evolution of communities in synthetic dynamic networks.

Keywords: Complex network · Dynamic network · Community evolution · Evolution tracking

1 Introduction

Complex networks, such as Twitter, Facebook, and other social networks, are widespread in the real world. The existence of community structure is a fundamental characteristic of complex networks. Nodes within the same community are densely connected, but nodes between communities have few connections [9]. Community detection seeks to find clusters of nodes in networks that are tightly

© The Author(s), under exclusive license to Springer Nature Singapore Pte Ltd. 2023
Y. Sun et al. (Eds.): ChineseCSCW 2022, CCIS 1681, pp. 147–161, 2023.
https://doi.org/10.1007/978-981-99-2356-4_12

related. In reality, dynamic complex networks evolve continuously over time, and the community affiliation of nodes also varies. The objective of dynamic community detection is to identify alterations in the community affiliation of nodes over time. Alterations in the community affiliation of nodes will result in a series of Community evolution events encompassing birth, death, expansion, contraction, merge, and split [2]. Community evolution tracking is a research direction to track how communities evolve in dynamic networks. Community evolution tracking can extract useful information from dynamic networks and help predict social network behaviors or analyze the spread of infectious illnesses.

Existing research on dynamic networks can be broadly divided into three categories: the instant-optimal methods, the temporal trade-off methods, and the cross-time methods [13]. The instant-optimal methods obtain the optimal results of each snapshot's community division using a static algorithm and match the communities between each snapshot to trace the evolution of the community. The cross-time method merges all snapshots in the dynamic network into a single network, which makes it challenging to track the communities' evolution. Particularly, the temporal trade-off methods are the most commonly used because it reduces a significant amount of processing costs by analyzing the network based on the prior snapshot and the present snapshot. But most evolution tracking algorithms obtain community division first and then match the community in tracking evolution events, which makes it difficult to trace the complete evolution of communities due to the community matching errors. And most of the evolution tracking algorithms do not sufficiently consider the possible scenarios in community evolution, resulting in inaccurate detect evolution events.

In this research, we present a method for Community Evolution Cracking based on the Core node extension and Edge variation discerning (CETCE). CETCE starts with calculating the topological potential of all nodes in the initial snapshot network, classifying the nodes according to the definitions, and obtaining the community detection result by using the core node extension approach. Then, CETCE monitors community evolution based on the approach for identifying edge variation, which detects evolution events from the perspective of community evolution. Moreover, we design a new evaluation measure Improved Event Mining Accuracy (IEMA) to measure the performance of community evolution algorithms. The following are the principal contributions of this paper:

1. With the core node extension strategy, CETCE can track the evolution of communities without community matching, which avoids the problem of community matching errors.
2. Based on the edge variation discerning strategy, CETCE considers more various situations that may occur during the community evolution process, e.g. the appearance of two nodes of an edge belonging to the same community may also lead to a community split.
3. Compared to existing metrics for measuring evolution tracking algorithms, IEMA measures the performance of evolution tracking algorithms more comprehensively from the perspective of evolution events.

4. Experiments based on synthetic data suggest that the proposed technique efficiently tracks all types of community evolution events, outperforming current best practices.

2   Related Work

In recent years, a great number of works have been devoted to community detection and evolution traction on dynamic networks, which can be divided into three categories [13], instant-optimal methods, temporal trade-off methods, and cross-time methods.

2.1   Instant-Optimal Methods

The instant-optimal methods are based on the static community detection methods, identifying an optimal community partition for each step. However, the instant-optimal methods are not suitable for tracking community evolution because of the inaccuracy of the community matching. MODEC [14] used common nodes to match each community and obtain the evolutionary relationships of the communities. ICEM [8] tracks community members and considers discontinuous periods. WECEM [12] computes the degree of community overlap and the degree of community members to compare each community, and then identifies various community evolutionary events.

2.2   Temporal Trade-Off Methods

Temporal trade-off approaches make use of the network and communities identified in the preceding stage to identify communities or evolution events in the current one. Therefore, the temporal trade-off methods can accelerate the community detection speed of the current time, but it also leads to error accumulation. QCA [10] identifies communities by the predefined rules of incremental variations. FICET [7] utilizes the subgraph-based incremental technique and derives the core community from the core subgraph, capturing the evolutionary events. DOCET [16] partition the community relies on nodes' evaluation of the peak-valley pattern of the topological potential field. EAS-SAS [17] utilizes the superspreader and superblocker nodes to identify community evolutionary events.

2.3   Cross-Time Methods

The cross-time methods consider all states of the dynamic network, so it does not suffer from error accumulation. The main drawback of the cross-time methods is the inability to track community evolution such as mergers and splits, and the inability to export community evolutionary processes. THRM [6] incorporates two aspects: temporal evolution and multi-scale structure. ESPRA [15] extend the structural perturbation theory to dynamic networks, then capture their evolution. LDA-TCD [3] is a method for learning embedding based on the similarity of users' temporal content.

3   The Proposed Algorithm

3.1   Preliminaries

Definition 1 (Dynamic network). Let $\{G_0, G_1, ..., G_t\}$ represents the dynamic network, where $G_t(V_t, E_t)$ is the snapshot of the dynamic network at time t, V_t is the set of nodes in G_t, E_t is the set of edges in G_t. In addition, for node $v \in V_t$, let $N(v)$ present the neighbors of node v and C_t represents the community set in G_t, while $C_t(v)$ represents the community label of node v in G_t.

Definition 2 (Community evolution events). In the dynamic network finding research (e.g. [5,11]), there is consensus that there are six distinct kinds of community evolution events: BIRTH, DEATH, MERGING, SPLITTING, EXPANSION, and CONTRACTION, we use the all capital form to emphasize that they are constants in the pseudo-code representation of the method. In this paper, let EV_t represent the evolution events at time t detected by the method.

Definition 3 (Topology potential). According to [4], a potential field produced in network space is known as topological potential. Its formula is given as follows:

$$\varphi(v_i) = \sum_{j=1}^{n} (m(v_j) \times e^{(\frac{d_{ij}}{\sigma})^2}) \tag{1}$$

where $\varphi(v_i)$ is the topological potential of node v_i; $m(v_i)$ is the weight of node v_i, used to measure the attribute of the node v_i, we sets $m(v_i) = 1$; d_{ij} is the shortest distance between nodes i and j; σ is the control factor which can be calculated by the potential entropy method [18]. If $d_{ij} > \left\lfloor \frac{3\sigma}{\sqrt{2}} \right\rfloor$, which means if d_{ij} is greater than the greatest integer less than or equal to $\frac{3\sigma}{\sqrt{2}}$, then the topology potential influence between nodes i and j can be neglected, based on the 3σ-rule of the Gaussian function [18].

Definition 4 (Core node). For $v_i \in V_t$, if $\forall v_j \in N(v_i), \varphi(v_j) < \varphi(v_i)$, then node v_i is called a core node. A community is represented by a core node, if the distance between two core nodes is less than $\left\lfloor \frac{3\sigma}{\sqrt{2}} \right\rfloor$, the two communities are merged into one. The merged community's core node is picked as the node with higher topological potential.

Definition 5 (Internal node). For $v_i \in V_t$, if $(1)\exists v_j \in N(v_i), \varphi(v_j) > \varphi(v_i), and \exists v_j \in N(v_i), \varphi(v_j) < \varphi(v_i)$; or $(2) \forall v_j \in N(v_i), \varphi(v_j) > \varphi(v_i)$, and two closest core nodes belong to the same community, then node v_i is called a internal node.

Definition 6 (Overlapping node). For $v_i \in V_t$, if $\forall v_j \in N(v_i), \varphi(v_j) > \varphi(v_i)$, and two closest core nodes belong to the different communities, then node v_i is called a overlapping node.

3.2 Framework of CETCE

The CETCE framework is shown in Fig. 1 and consists of two stages.

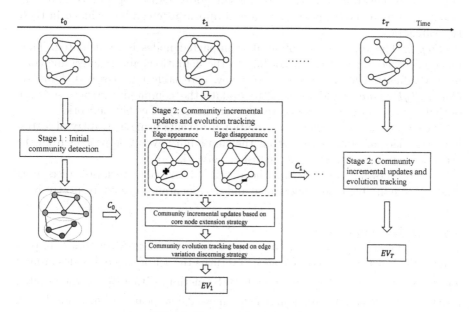

Fig. 1. Framework of CETCE.

Stage 1: Initial Community Detection. In this stage, the initial snapshot network's community detection result is obtained.

Stage 2: Incremental Community Updates and Evolution Tracking. In this stage, we update the current snapshot's structure of the network based on the previous snapshot and track community evolution.

3.3 Initial Community Detection

Initial community detection could be divided into three phases.

Step 1: Given the initial network, we calculate the topological potential of all nodes, then determine the core nodes, overlapping nodes, and internal nodes according to the definitions.

Step 2: Expand the community based on the core node extension strategy. CETCE employs function $CommunityExpand()$ in [16] to update the community structure based on a core node.

Step 3: Output the community detection results for the next snapshot network.

3.4 Incremental Community Updates and Evolution Tracking

The pseudo-code of incremental community updates and evolution track is given in Algorithm 1 and Algorithm 2. The stage of incremental community updates and evolution tracking can be divided into three steps.

Step 1: For the non-initial snapshots of the network, we first obtain the network changes between the previous snapshot and the current snapshot. We only classify network changes into two categories: edge appearance and edge disappearance, as node appearance and disappearance can be included in these two categories.

Step 2: The topological potential of impacted nodes is recalculated. Then redefine the node categories according to the definitions and redetermine community affiliation for these nodes. If a new core node is discovered, Function *ComunityExpand* would be used to update the community structure. Then output the community detection results for the next snapshot network.

Step 3: We detect community evolutionary events using a strategy of distinguishing edge variation, then output the community evolution process from the preview snapshot to the current snapshot network.

In the following, we describe the details of the edge variation discerning strategy in handling edge appearance and disappearance events, respectively.

3.4.1 Edge Appearance

The pseudo-code for processing edge appearance is given in Algorithm 1. In particular, the function $AffectedNodes(e)$ returns the set of affected nodes around an edge e using a Breadth-First Search(BFS) method with $\left\lfloor \frac{3\sigma}{\sqrt{2}} \right\rfloor$ as the affected range. There are two instances in which a new edge appears. As shown in Fig. 2, the new edge is represented by dash lines.

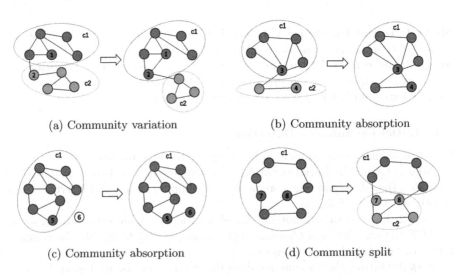

(a) Community variation   (b) Community absorption

(c) Community absorption   (d) Community split

Fig. 2. Cases of the edge variation discerning strategy processing edge appearances

Case 1. **Edge across communities.** When the end nodes of the edge belong to different communities, the community structure may be changed at this moment.

Case 1.1. Community variation: After the incremental community update, if the end nodes belong to the same pre-existing community, which indicates the community variation. As shown in Fig. 2a, node 1 pertains to community c1, and node 2 pertains to community c2. After the appearance of the edge between nodes 1 and 2, two nodes both belong to community c1, and community c2 still exists. In this case, community c1 expands, and community c2 contracts.

Case 1.2. Community absorption: After the incremental community update, if the end nodes belong to the same community, and the community where the end nodes are located at the previous snapshot is dead, which indicates that a community absorption another community. As shown in Fig. 2b, node 3 pertains to community c1, and node 4 pertains to community c2. After the appearance of the edge between nodes 3 and 4, two nodes both belong to community c1, and community c2 disappears. In this case, communities c1 and c2 merge, and community c2 dies.

In particular, if the end node is new, we treat it as a community. As shown in Fig. 2c, node 5 pertains to community c1, and node 6 has no community label. After the appearance of the edge between nodes 5 and 6, two nodes both belong to the community c1. In this case, community c1 expands.

Case 2. **Edge inside a community.** When the end nodes of the new edge belong to the same community, it strengthens the structure of the community, but it may also strengthen the structure of the possible sub-communities, thus splitting the original community into two sub-communities. After the incremental community update, if the end nodes belong to the same community that didn't exist before, which indicates that the community splits and another community birth. As shown in Fig. 2d, nodes 7 and 8 both belong to community c1. After the appearance of the edge between nodes 7 and 8, two nodes both belong to the new community c2. In this case, community c1 splits, and community c2 birth.

3.4.2   Edge Disappearance

The pseudo-code for processing edge disappearance is given in Algorithm 2. There are two cases in which an edge disappears. As demonstrated in Fig. 3, dashed lines depict the disappearing edge.

Case 1. **Edge across communities.** The disappearance of an edge between different communities will enhance the community structure of the two communities. The boundary between the two communities will be clearer too, so we do not deal with this case. As shown in Fig. 3a, node 1 pertains to community c1, and node 2 pertains to community c2. After the disappearance of the edge between nodes 1 and 2, both nodes maintain the former community labels. In this case, no evolutionary event occurs.

Case 2. **Edge inside a community.** After the absence of a community's edge, the community's structure may transform.

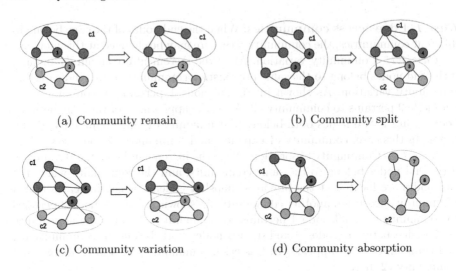

(a) Community remain   (b) Community split

(c) Community variation   (d) Community absorption

Fig. 3. Cases of the edge variation discerning strategy processing edge disappearances

Case 2.1. Community split: After the incremental community update, if the terminal nodes are members of distinct communities, and the community where the end nodes are located at the current snapshot is a new community, which indicates that the community split. As shown in Fig. 3b, nodes 3 and 4 both belong to community c1. After the disappearance of the edge between nodes 3 and 4, node 4 still pertains to community c1, and node 3 pertains to the new community c2. In this case, community c1 splits, and community c2 birth.

Case 2.2. Community variation: After the incremental community update, if the end nodes belong to different pre-existing communities, which indicates the community variation. As shown in Fig. 3c, nodes 5 and 6 both belong to community c1. After the disappearance of the edge between nodes 5 and 6, node 5 still pertains to community c1, and node 6 pertains to the existing community c2. In this case, the community c1 contract, and community c2 expand;

Case 2.3. Community absorption: After the incremental community update, if the end nodes belong to the same community, and the community where the end nodes are located at the previous snapshot is dead, which indicates that a community absorption another community. As shown in Fig. 3d, nodes 7 and 8 both belong to community c1. After the disappearance of the edge between nodes 7 and 8, nodes 7 and 8 both belong to the existing community c2. In this case, community c1 dies and community c2 expands.

Algorithm 1: Edge appearance

Input: $G_{t-1}(V_{t-1}, E_{t-1})$, $G_t(V_t, E_t)$: snapshot network at time $t-1$ and t, respectively; C_{t-1}: the community set at time $t-1$;

Output: C_t: the community set at time t; EV_t: the event set at time t;

1 $C_t \leftarrow C_{t-1}, EV_t \leftarrow \varnothing$

2 **for** $e \in E_t$ **do**

3 | **if** $e \notin E_{t-1}$ **then**

4 | | $V^a \leftarrow GetAffectedNodes(e)$

5 | | **for** $n \in V^a$ **do**

6 | | | recalculate topology potential of n according to equation (1).

7 | | **for** $n \in V^a$ **do**

8 | | | **if** n *is a core node* **then**

9 | | | | $C_t \leftarrow CommunityExpand(G_t, n)$

    | | // Case 1: Edge across communities

    | | // u and v are the end nodes of edge e

10 | | **if** $C_{t-1}(u) \neq C_{t-1}(v)$ *or* $u \notin V_{t-1}$ *or* $v \notin V_{t-1}$ **then**

    | | | // Case 1.1: Community variation

11 | | | **if** $C_t(u) = C_t(v)$ *and* $C_{t-1}(u) \in C_t$ *and* $C_{t-1}(v) \in C_t$ **then**

12 | | | | $EV_t \leftarrow \{CONTRACTION, EXPANSION\}$

    | | | // Case 1.2: Community absorption

13 | | | **if** $C_t(u) = C_t(v)$ *and* $C_{t-1}(u) \notin C_t$ *or* $C_{t-1}(v) \notin C_t$ **then**

14 | | | | $EV_t \leftarrow \{MERGING, DEATH\}$

15 | | | **if** $u \notin V_{t-1}$ *or* $v \notin V_{t-1}$ **then**

16 | | | | **if** $C_t(u) \in C_{t-1}$ **then**

17 | | | | | $EV_t \leftarrow \{EXPANSION\}$

18 | | | | **else**

19 | | | | | $EV_t \leftarrow \{BRITH\}$

20 | | | | **if** $C_t(v) \in C_{t-1}$ **then**

21 | | | | | $EV_t \leftarrow \{EXPANSION\}$

22 | | | | **else**

23 | | | | | $EV_t \leftarrow \{BIRHT\}$

    | | // Case 2: Edge inside a community

24 | | **if** $C_{t-1}(u) = C_{t-1}(v)$ **then**

25 | | | **if** $C_t(u) \notin C_{t-1}$ *or* $C_t(v) \notin C_{t-1}$ **then**

26 | | | | $EV_t \leftarrow \{BIRTH, SPLITTING\}$

27 Return C_t, EV_t;

Algorithm 2: Edge disappearance

Input: $G_{t-1}(V_{t-1}, E_{t-1})$, $G_t(V_t, E_t)$: snapshot network at time $t-1$ and t, respectively; C_{t-1}: the community set at time $t-1$;

Output: C_t: the community set at time t; EV_t: the event set at time t;

1 $C_t \leftarrow C_{t-1}, EV_t \leftarrow \varnothing$

2 **for** $e \in E_{t-1}$ **do**

3   **if** $e \notin E_t$ **then**

        // Case 1: Edge across communities

4   **if** $C_{t-1}(u) \neq C_{t-1}(v)$ **then**

5   Continue;

        // Case 2: Edge inside a community

6   **if** $C_{t-1}(u) = C_{t-1}(v)$ **then**

7              $V^a \leftarrow GetAffectedNodes(e)$

8   **for** $n \in V^a$ **do**

9   recalculate topology potential of n according to equation (1).

10   **for** $n \in V^a$ **do**

11   **if** n *is a core node* **then**

12                     $C_t \leftarrow CommunityExpand(G_t, n)$

        // Case 2.1: Community split

13   **if** $C_t(u) \neq C_t(v)$ *and* $C_t(u) \notin C_{t-1}$ *or* $C_t(v) \notin C_{t-1}$ **then**

14             $EV_t \leftarrow \{SPLITTING, BIRTH\}$

        // Case 2.2: Community variation

15   **if** $C_t(u) \neq C_t(v)$ *and* $C_t(u) \in C_{t-1}$ *and* $C_t(v) \in C_{t-1}$ **then**

16             $EV_t \leftarrow \{EXPANSION, CONTRACTION\}$

        // Case 2.3: Community absorption

17   **if** $C_t(u) = C_t(v)$ *and* $C_t(u) \neq C_{t-1}(u)$ **then**

18   **if** $C_{t-1}(u) \notin C_t$ **then**

19                 $EV_t \leftarrow \{EXPANSION, DEATH\}$

20 Return C_t, EV_t;

3.5   Time Complexity Analysis

Following is an analysis of the time complexity of CETCE. The initial community detection time complexity is $O(n^2)$ [16]. In stage 2, Algorithm 1 updates the community and tracks evolution events in case of edge appearance, $O(an)$ is required to compute the topological potential of the impacted nodes, and a is the number of impacted nodes. If the new core nodes are forming, updating orientation and community requires $O(\langle k \rangle n)$, where k is the mean degrees of all nodes. Thus the time for Algorithm 1 is $O(m_a(a + \langle k \rangle)n)$, where m_a is the number of appearing edges. Similar to Algorithm 1, Algorithm 2 updates the community and tracks evolution events in the event of edge disappearance, so the time complexity is $O(m_d(a + \langle k \rangle)n)$, where m_d is the amount of disappearing edges. In summary, the time complexity of CETCE is $O(n^2 + (m_a + m_d)(a + \langle k \rangle)n)$.

4   Experiments

4.1   Datasets

Using the LFR benchmark generator [5], dynamic synthetic networks are created. The LFR benchmark generator can produce synthetic dynamic network data with base communities and add community evolution events like birth, death, expansion, contraction, merging, and splitting. The parameters are given in Table 1 and the specifics of synthesized dynamic networks are shown in Table 2. The rest parameters are set by default: $s = 5, k = 10, maxk = 15, minc = 10, maxc = 80, muw = 0.2, on = 100, om = 2$.

Table 1. Parameters of synthetic networks

Parameter	Description
N	number of nodes
s	number of time steps to generate
k	average degree
$maxk$	maximum degree
$minc$	minimum for the community size
$maxc$	maximum for the community size
on	number of overlapping nodes
om	number of memberships of the overlapping nodes
E_b	number of community birth events per time step
E_d	number of community death events per time step
E_e	number of community expand events per time step
E_c	number of community contract events per time step
E_m	number of community merge events per time step
E_s	number of community split events per time step

Table 2. Synthetic networks

Network group	Parameter configuration
D1	$N = \{2000, 4000, 6000, 8000\}, E_b = 10, E_d = 10$
D2	$N = \{2000, 4000, 6000, 8000\}, E_e = 10, E_c = 10$
D3	$N = \{2000, 4000, 6000, 8000\}, E_m = 10, E_s = 10$

4.2 Evaluation Metrics

EMA [12] (Event Mining Accuracy) is a metric that evaluates the accuracy of community evolutionary algorithms for detecting evolutionary events. EMA is the ratio of precisely recognized communities to the total number of communities where events are occurring. EMA is described as follows:

$$\text{EMA}(p) = \frac{\sum_{t \in T} \left\{ \left| C_t^p \cap C_t^{p'} \right| \right\}}{\sum_{t \in T} \max \left\{ |C_t^p|, \left| C_t^{p'} \right| \right\}} \tag{2}$$

where $\text{EMA}(p)$ represents the EMA of event p, T is the set of snapshot networks, C_t^p is the set of communities where event p happens at time t detected by the algorithm, $C_t^{p'}$ is the set of true communities where event p happens at time t.

Inspired by EMA, we design IEMA (Improved Event Mining Accuracy) to assess the precision of community evolutionary algorithms for tracking evolutionary events. IEMA overcomes the problem that EMA metrics would have interfered with when the algorithm detects too many community evolutionary events.

Definition 7 (Event Recall). ER (Event Recall) is the ratio of properly recognized communities to the actual number of communities where events are occurring. ER is described as follows:

$$\text{ER}(p) = \frac{\sum_{t \in T} \{ |C_t^p \cap C_t^{p'}| \}}{\sum_{t \in T} |C_t^{p'}|} \tag{3}$$

Definition 8 (Event Precision). EP (Event Precision) is the ratio of properly recognized communities to the number of communities where events have been observed. EP is described as follows:

$$\text{EP}(p) = \frac{\sum_{t \in T} \{ |C_t^p \cap C_t^{p'}| \}}{\sum_{t \in T} |C_t^p|} \tag{4}$$

Definition 9 (Improved Event Mining Accuracy). IEMA (Improved Event Mining Accuracy) is the harmonic mean of ER and EP. IEMA is described as follows:

$$\text{IEMA}(p) = \frac{2 \times \text{ER}(p) \times \text{EP}(p)}{\text{ER}(p) + \text{EP}(p)} \tag{5}$$

4.3 Baseline Algorithms

CETCE is compared to two other community evolution tracking methods. Here are the specifics of the baseline algorithms:

Asur [1]: Asur uses nonoverlapping snapshots of interaction networks to capture and identify evolutionary events based on event-specific behavioral characteristics.

DOCET [16]: DOCET determines the original community structure by analyzing the location of nodes in the peak-valley architecture of the topological potential field. Then, DOCET recognizes events of community evolution based on the change inside the topological potential field.

4.4 Accuracy Experiments

4.4.1 Experimental Results on D1 Network Group

Figure 4 shows the EMA and IEMA results on the $D1$ network group. The $D1$ network group contains only birth and death events. Because both DOCET and CETCE update the community structure based on the node topological potential and core node extension strategy, so the two methods achieve the same accuracy in both EMA and IEMA metrics on the $D1$ network group.

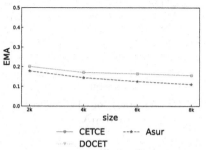
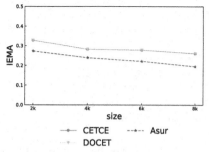

(a) Accuracy of the algorithms measured by EMA

(b) Accuracy of the algorithms measured by IEMA

Fig. 4. Accuracy experiment on $D1$ network group

4.4.2 Experimental Results on D2 Network Group

Figure 5 shows the EMA and IEMA results on the $D2$ network group. The $D2$ network group contains only expand and contract events. The DOCET algorithm relies on community merge or split events to determine community expansion or contraction, resulting in the algorithm's low accuracy in detecting community

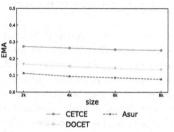
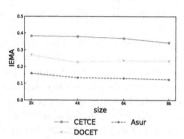

(a) Accuracy of the algorithms measured by EMA

(b) Accuracy of the algorithms measured by IEMA

Fig. 5. Accuracy experiment on $D2$ network group

expansion and contraction events. Compared with Asur and DOCET, CETCE achieves higher accuracy in both EMA and IEMA metrics by judging expansion and contraction events based on the edge variation discerning strategy.

4.4.3 Experimental Results on D3 Network Group

Figure 6 shows the EMA and IEMA results on the $D3$ network group. The $D3$ dataset contains only merge and split events. Compared with DOCET and Asur, CETCE uses the edge variation discerning strategy to detect community merge and split events in dynamic networks and thus achieves higher accuracy in both EMA and IEMA metrics on the D3 network group.

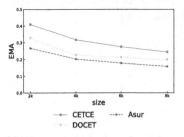
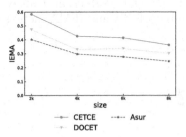

(a) Accuracy of the algorithms measured by EMA

(b) Accuracy of the algorithms measured by IEMA

Fig. 6. Accuracy experiment on $D3$ network group

5   Conclusion

We propose CETCE for tracking community evolution in dynamic networks in this research. First, CETCE divide nodes into three types for community detection based on their topological potential, then use the core node extension strategy to obtain the community detection result. Second, CETCE update community structure and track community evolution according to the edge variation discerning strategy. The results of our experiments indicate that our algorithm can successfully track the evolution of communities in dynamic networks. In the future, we will investigate how to apply CETCE to dynamic attribute networks.

Acknowledgements. This work was supported by the National Natural Science Foundation of China under Grant No. 62002063 and No. U21A20472, the National Key Research and Development Plan of China under Grant No. 2021YFB36 00503, the Fujian Collaborative Innovation Center for Big Data Applications in Governments, the Fujian Industry-Academy Cooperation Project under Grant No. 2017H6008 and No. 2018H6010, the Natural Science Foundation of Fujian Province under Grant No. 2020J05112 and No. 2020J01420, the Fujian Provincial Department of Education under Grant No. JAT190026, the Major Science and Technology Project of Fujian Province under Grant No. 2021HZ022007 and Haixi Government Big Data Application Cooperative Innovation Center.

References

1. Asur, S., Parthasarathy, S., Ucar, D.: An event-based framework for characterizing the evolutionary behavior of interaction graphs. ACM Trans. Knowl. Discov. Data (TKDD) **3**(4), 1–36 (2009)
2. Dakiche, N., Tayeb, F.B.S., Slimani, Y., Benatchba, K.: Tracking community evolution in social networks: a survey. Inf. Process. Manag. **56**(3), 1084–1102 (2019)
3. Fani, H., Jiang, E., Bagheri, E., Al-Obeidat, F., Du, W., Kargar, M.: User community detection via embedding of social network structure and temporal content. Inf. Process. Manag. **57**(2), 102056 (2020)
4. Gan, W.Y., He, N., Li, D.Y., Wang, J.M.: Community discovery method in networks based on topological potential. J. Softw. **20**(8), 2241–2254 (2009)
5. Greene, D., Doyle, D., Cunningham, P.: Tracking the evolution of communities in dynamic social networks. In: 2010 International Conference on Advances in Social Networks Analysis and Mining, pp. 176–183. IEEE (2010)
6. Herlau, T., Mørup, M., Schmidt, M.: Modeling temporal evolution and multiscale structure in networks. In: International Conference on Machine Learning, pp. 960–968. PMLR (2013)
7. Liu, Y., Gao, H., Kang, X., Liu, Q., Wang, R., Qin, Z.: Fast community discovery and its evolution tracking in time-evolving social networks. In: 2015 IEEE International Conference on Data Mining Workshop (ICDMW), pp. 13–20. IEEE (2015)
8. Mohammadmosaferi, K.K., Naderi, H.: Evolution of communities in dynamic social networks: an efficient map-based approach. Expert Syst. Appl. **147**, 113221 (2020)
9. Newman, M.E.J.: Detecting community structure in networks. Eur. Phys. J. B **38**(2), 321–330 (2004). https://doi.org/10.1140/epjb/e2004-00124-y
10. Nguyen, N.P., Dinh, T.N., Xuan, Y., Thai, M.T.: Adaptive algorithms for detecting community structure in dynamic social networks. In: 2011 Proceedings IEEE INFOCOM, pp. 2282–2290. IEEE (2011)
11. Palla, G., Barabási, A.L., Vicsek, T.: Quantifying social group evolution. Nature **446**(7136), 664–667 (2007)
12. Qiao, S., et al.: Dynamic community evolution analysis framework for large-scale complex networks based on strong and weak events. IEEE Trans. Syst. Man Cybern. Syst. **51**(10), 6229–6243 (2020)
13. Rossetti, G., Cazabet, R.: Community discovery in dynamic networks: a survey. ACM Comput. Surv. (CSUR) **51**(2), 1–37 (2018)
14. Takaffoli, M., Sangi, F., Fagnan, J., Zaiane, O.: MODEC-modeling and detecting evolutions of communities. In: Proceedings of the International AAAI Conference on Web and Social Media, vol. 5, pp. 626–629 (2011)
15. Wang, P., Gao, L., Ma, X.: Dynamic community detection based on network structural perturbation and topological similarity. J. Stat. Mech. Theory Exp. **2017**(1), 013401 (2017)
16. Wang, Z., Li, Z., Yuan, G., Sun, Y., Rui, X., Xiang, X.: Tracking the evolution of overlapping communities in dynamic social networks. Knowl. Based Syst. **157**, 81–97 (2018)
17. Xu, Z., Rui, X., He, J., Wang, Z., Hadzibeganovic, T.: Superspreaders and superblockers based community evolution tracking in dynamic social networks. Knowl. Based Syst. **192**, 105377 (2020)
18. Zhi-Xiao, W., Ze-chao, L., Xiao-fang, D., Jin-hui, T.: Overlapping community detection based on node location analysis. Knowl. Based Syst. **105**, 225–235 (2016)

University Knowledge Graph Construction Based on Academic Social Network

Yanzhen Yang[1,2], Jingsong Leng[1,2], Ronghua Lin[1,2], Jianguo Li[1(✉)], and Feiyi Tang[2,3]

[1] South China Normal University, Guangzhou 510631, China
jianguoli@m.scnu.edu.cn
[2] Pazhou Lab, Guangzhou 510330, China
[3] Guangzhou Panyu Polytechnic, Guangzhou 511483, China

Abstract. Knowledge graph is an important knowledge representation method in the era of big data. It has become one of the key technologies of artificial intelligence and has been applied in different fields. However, there are relatively few studies on university knowledge graphs combined with academic social networks. Therefore, in this paper, we combine the academic social network SCHOLAT to complete the construction of the university knowledge graph. We first construct the ontology of the knowledge graph, then extract and fuse knowledge from data that come from different sources, and add the output knowledge to the knowledge graph. The university knowledge graph has 191,089 entities and 1,638,275 relationship pairs after the construction is completed, and we store it in the Neo4j database to provide knowledge reserve for subsequent applications. In addition to the construction, we also conduct an application analysis to study its application in university knowledge graph-based Q&A system.

Keywords: Knowledge graph · Knowledge extraction · Academic social network · SCHOLAT · Question answering

1 Introduction

The Knowledge Graph is a structured knowledge base proposed by Google [1] in 2012. It is an important branch of artificial intelligence technology. The early idea of the Knowledge Graph originated from the vision of Tim Berners-Lee, the father of the World Wide Web. Tim Berners-Lee [2] proposed the idea of The Semantic Web, which is all about modeling and recording the relationships and knowledge in the world through graph structures. Thanks to the development of commonsense understanding and reasoning, many applications such as recommendation systems and question answering have made great progress in research [3].

As intellectual institutions for knowledge creation, recording, and transmission in human society, universities have gathered a large amount of research and teaching data resources. To the best of our knowledge, there are few research works related to the construction of university knowledge graphs combined with academic social networks. There are related works investigating the construction of knowledge graphs based on multi-source encyclopedias [4]. The significance of university knowledge construction includes making full use of university and academic social data, improving the multi-domain reusability of university data and expanding SCHOLAT[1] applications, etc.

In this paper, we construct a university knowledge graph combining data from the academic social network SCHOLAT. There are 191,089 entities and 1,638,275 relationship pairs after the construction is completed. We mainly collect university data from SCHOLAT, China Higher Education Student Information and Career Center (CHSI), and other encyclopedic websites. After the data collection is completed, we use knowledge extraction and knowledge fusion techniques to add them to the university knowledge graph. In addition, we also integrate other academic information in SCHOLAT, such as scholars, teams, and courses, to establish various links with university entities. After the university knowledge graph is constructed, we apply it to various modules of SCHOLAT, such as a university knowledge graph-based Q&A system, which aims to provide Q&A services in the university field for SCHOLAT users or users of other websites. Besides, the university knowledge graph can also provide a knowledge base for other applications of SCHOLAT, such as recommendation systems, intelligent search, and entity links. Combining academic social networks, high quality of knowledge and wide forms of application are the key features of our knowledge graph.

2 Related Work

Although many knowledge graphs have been constructed and applied, such as Wikidata [5], and DBpedia [6], most of these knowledge graphs are open domain-oriented knowledge graphs. Compared with open domain knowledge graphs, domain-specific knowledge graphs are more suitable for domain applications. Many domain-specific knowledge graphs have been built and proved to be more suitable for domain applications, such as Geonames in geographic information, Linked Life Data in the medical domain, and Alibaba's commodity knowledge graph.

So far, although a large number of research works on domain knowledge graph construction have existed, few related works studied the construction and application of university knowledge graphs combined the academic social networks. Liu et al. [7] proposed a scholar website based on the scholar knowledge graph, and Li [8] constructed a scholar knowledge graph for universities incorporating multiple data sources and various university-related applications. However, none of these studies combined academic social networks to construct a knowledge graph. Combining academic social networks would have the following advantages: 1) It reinforces the academic nature and facilitates academic research. Academic social networks contain rich academic resources, such as

---

[1] https://www.scholat.com.

papers, patents, and projects, which are mostly the research results of universities. Some academic resources are the cooperative results of multiple universities, which makes universities produce academic connections. 2) It introduces high-quality information about the user community and allows for more connections between university entities through the social network. The audience groups of the academic social network are generally researchers, teachers, students, and other people associated with universities. Therefore, we use techniques such as ontology construction, knowledge extraction, and graph database to construct a university knowledge graph based on the academic network SCHOLAT, and integrate data from other university information websites.

Knowledge extraction is the most fundamental and critical step in knowledge graph construction, which includes three parts: entity extraction, relationship extraction, and attribute extraction. Since entity attributes can be regarded as the nominative relationship between attribute values and entities, attribute extraction is usually converted to relational extraction. Named Entity Recognition (NER) is the task of entity extraction. Early NER used rule-based and dictionary-based methods. With the development of machine learning, many researchers started to use some machine learning methods in NER, such as Hidden Markov Model(HMM) [9], Support Vector Machine(SVM) [10], and Conditional Random Field (CRF) [11]. CRF is one of the most effective methods. With the rapid development of deep learning, many related research works have proposed to use of neural networks to accomplish the NER task. Lample et al. [12] proposed a neural network model LSTM-CRF combining Long Short-Term Memory Networks (LSTM) and CRF. Zheng et al. [13] made further improvements to LSTM and proposed a Lattice-LSTM to fuse lexical information. Li et al. [14] proposed a Flat-Lattice Transformer(FLAT) model to introduce lexical information by designing a clever positional encoding structure to fuse Lattice structures based on Transformer. Compared with entity recognition, relationship extraction is more complex. An effective approach for relation extraction is to use neural network models for text classification to perform the relation extraction task. Zeng et al. [15] proposed a relationship extraction model by improving TextCNN. Wu et al. [16] modified the BERT input form to accomplish the relationship extraction task. Miwa et al. [17] proposed using bidirectional LTSM and syntactic dependency tree to do an end-to-end model of relation extraction.

3   Construction of University Knowledge Graph

There are two ways to build a knowledge graph, which are top-down and bottom-up. The bottom-up approach is suitable for building open domain knowledge graphs and certain industry domain knowledge graphs with complex data and business. The top-down approach is suitable for building domain-specific knowledge graphs. We use a top-down approach to build our university knowledge graph.

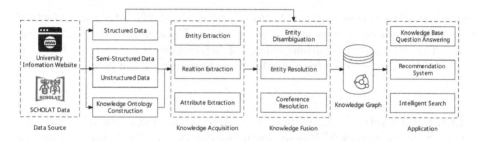

Fig. 1. Overview of university knowledge graph construction.

An overview of the construction of the university knowledge graph is shown in Fig. 1. We obtain university data and academic social network data through the SCHOLAT and university information websites and construct the knowledge graph ontology. Then we extract and fuse knowledge from the data according to the criteria and rules of the ontology to form our knowledge graph. We store the constructed knowledge graph in the Neo4j database to provide a knowledge base for various applications.

3.1 Ontology Construction

The construction of a domain knowledge graph requires a standardized knowledge graph standard, which serves as a guideline for knowledge extraction, storage, updating, and sharing. An ontology is a way to describe a knowledge mapping standard, which is an explicit description of a shared concept schema for adding semantics to a semantic network and describing relationships among concepts. There are many knowledge graphs ontology building tools, such as Protégé[2] and NeOn Toolkit[3]. We choose Protégé as the ontology-building tool. The specific build process is as follows.

Firstly, we create various university knowledge graph classes such as university class, scholar class, and team class. Secondly, we create relationships between classes. We create the relationship "WORK AT", where a scholar will have information about his workplace, and his workplace and university can be related to each other, which means the scholar has the relationship of working in a university. Similarly, we also create other relationships, to make as many entities in the knowledge graph as possible related. We use the strictly defined and constructed ontology to store and manage the knowledge.

3.2 Knowledge Extraction

Knowledge extraction is an integral and critical part of building a knowledge graph. Knowledge extraction consists of three parts, including entity extraction,

---

[2] https://protege.stanford.edu.
[3] http://neon-toolkit.org/wiki/Main_Page.html.

relationship extraction and attribute extraction. Generally, attribute extraction can be transformed into relationship extraction. Through knowledge extraction and data integration, multiple sources of heterogeneous data are unified into standard structured data for the subsequent knowledge graph construction process.

Entity Extraction. As an important step in knowledge graph information extraction, the task of NER is to identify entities in the text that have a specific meaning, such as people, places, and organizations. The structure of Chinese sentences is different from that of English, and extracting entities requires word separation, so Chinese NER is more challenging. The lattice structure has been shown to make good use of Chinese word information and maintain excellent parallel optimization capabilities. Because most of the unstructured data sources of the university knowledge graph are Chinese texts, we use the Chinese-oriented FLAT model for the NER task.

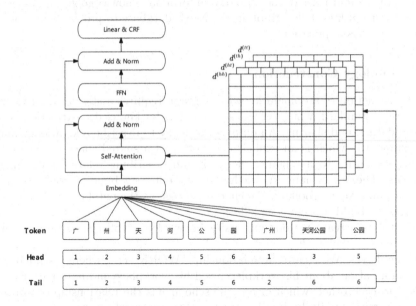

Fig. 2. The structure of FLAT model.

The model structure of FLAT is shown in Fig. 2. This model obtains a Lattice structure based on a vocabulary and then expands it into a plane. The flat-lattice structure consists of spans of different lengths, and this method models the relationship between the encoded spans by a dense vector to contain more detailed information between the spans. The model calculates four relative distances with the span head position and tail position information and obtains the final relative position encoding by simple non-linear variation. Where p_d is calculated in the same way as in Vaswani et al. [18]. The self-attention is calculated using a variant of the original method [19]. The detailed calculation process is shown as the following formulas:

$$R_{ij} = \text{ReLU}(W_r(\mathbf{p}_{d_{ij}^{(hh)}} \oplus \mathbf{p}_{d_{ij}^{(th)}} \oplus \mathbf{p}_{d_{ij}^{(ht)}} \oplus \mathbf{p}_{d_{ij}^{(tt)}})) \tag{1}$$

$$\mathbf{p}_d^{(2n)} = \sin\left(d/10000^{2n/d_{model}}\right) \tag{2}$$

$$\mathbf{p}_d^{(2n+1)} = \cos\left(d/10000^{2n/d_{model}}\right) \tag{3}$$

$$\begin{aligned}\mathbf{A}_{i,j}^* = \mathbf{W}_q^\top \mathbf{W}_{k,E} \mathbf{E}_{x_i}^\top \mathbf{E}_{x_j} + \mathbf{W}_q^\top \mathbf{W}_{k,R} \mathbf{E}_{x_i}^\top \mathbf{R}_{ij} \\ + \mathbf{u}^\top \mathbf{W}_{k,E} \mathbf{E}_{x_j} + \mathbf{v}^\top \mathbf{W}_{k,R} \mathbf{R}_{ij}\end{aligned} \tag{4}$$

where $\mathbf{W}_r, \mathbf{W}_q, \mathbf{W}_{k,R}, \mathbf{W}_{k,E} \in \mathbb{R}^{d_{model} \times d_{head}}$ and $\mathbf{u}, \mathbf{v} \in \mathbb{R}^{d_{head}}$ are learnable parameters and $\oplus$ denotes the concatenation operator. The obtained A^* is permuted to A in the transformer head calculation formula, and then subsequent calculations are performed in the same way as vanilla transformer. After FLAT, the character representations are output and connected to the CRF for entity recognition to obtain the final recognition results. After training, the model achieves 94% entity recognition accuracy on the test dataset. The entity recognition model can directly input sentences or long text and return recognition label results for entities including persons, universities, organizations, etc. These entities identified from unstructured text data can be generated into triples by the relationship extraction technique, and then processed using the knowledge fusion technique to add to the university knowledge graph.

Relationship Extraction. A relationship is defined as some kind of connection between two or more entities. The task of relationship extraction is to identify some semantic relationship between entities. For example, "Peking University is a public research university in Beijing, China. The university is funded by the Ministry of Education". In this sentence, we want to identify the semantic relationship between "Peking University" and the city of "Beijing", and the relationship between "Peking University" and the "Ministry of Education" of the People's Republic of China, which is a difficult task for the machine.

Since it is time consuming to train a model that can handle all relationship types, we focus on only a small number of relationship categories, such as "LOCATED IN", "FOUNDED IN", and "MANAGED BY". We train a pipeline model BiLSTM-Attention to extract relationships from the entities extracted in the previous subsection to obtain knowledge triples. Then we add the triples to our university knowledge graph by the knowledge fusion technique.

3.3   Knowledge Graph Storage

Similar to traditional data, knowledge requires databases for storage and management. The RDF graph model and the property graph model are the two most dominant graph models for knowledge graphs [20]. Since traditional relational databases cannot effectively adapt to the graph data model of knowledge graphs, the field of knowledge graph storage has formed the Triple Store and the Graph Database. The Triple Store is used for storing RDF graphs, and the Graph Database is used for storing property graphs.

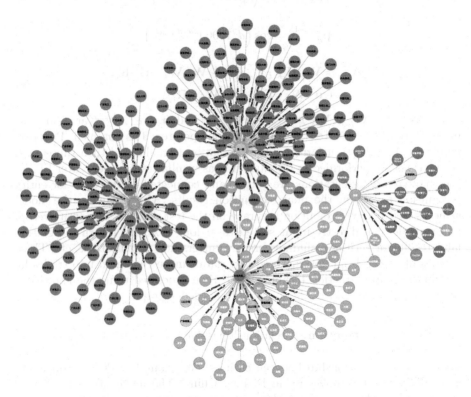

Fig. 3. University knowledge graph stored in Neo4j.

Compared with the Triple Store, native graph databases have various advantages such as high query performance, high flexibility in graph design, and rich community ecology. Neo4j is the most popular native graph database. Neo4j has the advantages of a graph data storage optimization mechanism and efficient indexing mechanism, more suitable for social networks, intelligent recommendations, and other fields.

Considering the above factors, we decide to use the Neo4j database to store the university knowledge graph. Our graph data are of three types: structured, semi-structured, and unstructured. The structured data has a clear entity classification and entity relationships, so we use tool libraries such as py2neo and pymysql to import the data directly into the Neo4j database. For semi-structured and unstructured data, we use entity extraction and relationship extraction techniques to get triples, and then use knowledge fusion techniques to add them to the university knowledge graph and store them in the Neo4j database. The visualization effect of the university knowledge graph is shown in Fig. 3.

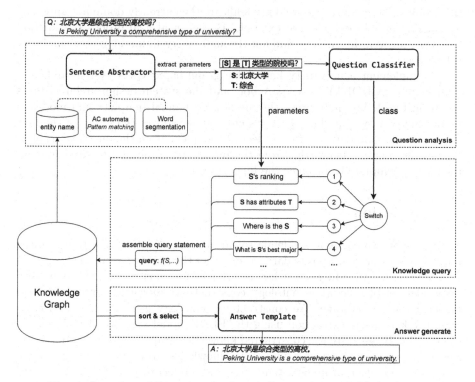

Fig. 4. Overview of the university knowledge graph-based Q&A system.

4 Application Analysis of the University Knowledge Graph

An effective means to verify the value of the knowledge graph is to apply the knowledge graph to applications. SCHOLAT has rich academic social network data and university information. We use this data information to build a university knowledge graph and apply it to various functional modules of SCHOLAT, such as a university knowledge graph-based Q&A system. The task of KQBA is to find or reason out the answer corresponding to a question based on the knowledge graph. KBQA faces the challenges of multiple semantic relations, semantic structure matching computation, and sparse knowledge graphs.

Semantic-based parsing or ranking is a common approach for KBQA. The goal of semantic parsing-based approaches is to find the best [question, semantic query] pair rather than a simple answer entity. Related studies include the lexicon-grammar-based semantic parsing approach proposed by Berant [21], the semantic graph-based question parsing approach proposed by Reddy [22], and the neural network semantic parsing approach based on the encoder-decoder model of the ATTENTION mechanism proposed by Jia et al. [23]. Ranking-based methods directly rank candidate entities without a formal formulation of the problem. Deep learning-based methods are the currently dominant approach for ranking-based methods. For example, Bordes et al. [24] proposed a method to return answers by scoring ranking through entity link and vector similarity calculation.

We implement a university knowledge graph-based Q&A system and integrate it into SCHOLAT as a Q&A bot, and the system design architecture is shown in Fig. 4. We mainly use the method of manual template and model to build the Q&A system. The Q&A system first recognizes the intent of the user input question and extracts the subject of the query from the question. Then it queries the relevant knowledge from the university graph and finally combines the answer template to produce the final answer.

5   Conclusion

In this paper, we combine academic social network SCHOLAT data and other university information website data to construct the university knowledge graph. In addition, we introduce some key techniques for constructing the university knowledge graph, including ontology construction, knowledge extraction, and knowledge graph storage. We construct the ontology using protégé and complete the knowledge extraction using the FLAT model and BiLSTM-Attention model. Finally, we store the constructed knowledge graph in the Neo4j database. Besides, we also implement a university knowledge graph-based Q&A system using a combination of manual templates and models to provide Q&A services in the university domain.

The university knowledge graph is currently rich in entities and relationships, but there is still room for improvement. Our next step is to work on the expansion of the scale of the university knowledge graph and the improvement of knowledge reasoning. The university knowledge graph includes not only university information but also rich academic social information, which is the advantage of the university knowledge graph. In the future, we will develop more applications based on the university graph and SCHOLAT, such as university recommendations and intelligent search.

Acknowledgment. This work was supported in part by the National Natural Science Foundation of China under Grant U1811263.

References

1. Singha, A.: Official Google blog: introducing the knowledge graph: things not strings. Google Blog (2012)
2. Bizer, C., Heath, T., Berners-Lee, T.: Linked data: the story so far. In: Semantic Services, Interoperability and Web Applications: Emerging Concepts, pp. 205–227. IGI Global (2011)
3. Ji, S., Pan, S., Cambria, E., et al.: A survey on knowledge graphs: representation, acquisition, and applications. IEEE Trans. Neural Netw. Learn. Syst. **33**(2), 494–514 (2021)
4. Wu, T., Wang, H., Li, C., et al.: Knowledge graph construction from multiple online encyclopedias. World Wide Web **23**(5), 2671–2698 (2020)
5. Vrandečić, D., Krötzsch, M.: Wikidata: a free collaborative knowledgebase. Commun. ACM **57**(10), 78–85 (2014)
6. Bizer, C., Lehmann, J., Kobilarov, G., et al.: DBpedia-a crystallization point for the web of data. J. Web Semantics **7**(3), 154–165 (2009)
7. Liu, J., Ren, J., Zheng, W., et al.: Web of scholars: a scholar knowledge graph. In: Proceedings of the 43rd International ACM SIGIR Conference on Research and Development in Information Retrieval, pp. 2153–2156 (2020)
8. Li, M.-N.: Research on university academic knowledge graph construction and its application based on multi-source data (2020). https://doi.org/10.27463/d.cnki.gzgyu.2020.001267
9. Rabiner, L.R.: A tutorial on hidden Markov models and selected applications in speed recognition. Proc. IEEE **77**(2), 257–286 (1989)
10. Asahara, M., Matsumoto, Y.: Japanese named entity extraction with redundant morphological analysis. In: Proceedings of the 2003 Conference of the North American Chapter of the Association for Computational Linguistics on Human Language Technology, Edmonton, Canada, pp. 8–15 (2003)
11. Lafferty, J.D., Mccallum, A., Pereira, F.C.N.: Conditional random fields: probabilistic models for segmenting and labeling sequence data. In: Proceedings of the Eighteenth International Conference on Machine Learning, San Francisco, CA, United States, pp. 282–289 (2001)
12. Lample, G., Ballesteros, M., Subramanian, S., et al.: Neural architectures for named entity recognition. In: Proceedings of the 2016 Conference of the North American Chapter of the Association for Computational Linguistics: Human Language Technologies, San Diego, California, USA, pp. 260–270 (2016)
13. Zhang, Y., Yang, J.: Chinese NER using lattice LSTM. In: Proceedings of the 56th Annual Meeting of the Association for Computational Linguistics, Melbourne, Australia, USA, pp. 1554–1564 (2018)
14. Li, X., Yan, H., Qiu, X., et al.: FLAT: Chinese NER using flat-lattice transformer. In: Proceedings of the 58th Annual Meeting of the Association for Computational Linguistics, Seattle, Washington, USA, pp. 6836–6842 (2020)
15. Zeng, D., Liu, K., Lai, S., et al.: Relation classification via convolutional deep neural network. In: Proceedings of COLING 2014, The 25th International Conference on Computational Linguistics: Technical Papers, pp. 2335–2344 (2014)
16. Wu, S., He, Y.: Enriching pre-trained language model with entity information for relation classification. In: Proceedings of the 28th ACM International Conference on Information and Knowledge Management, pp. 2361–2364 (2019)
17. Miwa, M., Bansal, M.: End-to-end relation extraction using LSTMs on sequences and tree structures. In: Proceedings of the 54th Annual Meeting of the Association for Computational Linguistics (Volume 1: Long Papers) (2016)

18. Vaswani, A., Shazeer, N., Parmar, N., et al.: Attention is all you need. In: Advances in Neural Information Processing Systems, vol. 30 (2017)
19. Dai, Z., Yang, Z., Yang, Y., et al.: Transformer-XL: attentive language models beyond a fixed-length context. arXiv preprint arXiv:1901.02860 (2019)
20. Wang, X., Zou, L., Wang, C.K., et al.: Research on knowledge graph data management: a survey. J. Softw. **30**(7), 2140 (2019)
21. Berant, J., Chou, A.K., Frostig, R., et al.: Semantic parsing on freebase from question answer pairs. In: Conference on Empirical Methods in Natural Language Processing, pp. 1533–1544 (2013)
22. Reddy, S., Lapata, M., Steedman, M.: Large-scale semantic parsing without question-answer pairs. Trans. Assoc. Comput. Linguist. **2**, 377–392 (2014)
23. Jia, R., Liang, P.: Data recombination for neural semantic parsing. In: Meeting of the Association for Computational Linguistics, pp. 12–22 (2016)
24. Bordes, A., Weston, J., Usunier, N.: Open question answering with weakly supervised embedding models. In: Calders, T., Esposito, F., Hüllermeier, E., Meo, R. (eds.) ECML PKDD 2014. LNCS (LNAI), vol. 8724, pp. 165–180. Springer, Heidelberg (2014). https://doi.org/10.1007/978-3-662-44848-9_11

Country-Level Collaboration Patterns of Social Computing Scholars

Jingcan Chen, Yuting Shao, Qingyuan Gong, and Yang Chen[✉]

School of Computer Science, Fudan University, Shanghai, China
{chenjc19,ytshao20,gongqingyuan,chenyang}@fudan.edu.cn

Abstract. *Social Computing* has been attracting scholars from different disciplines and countries. To study the collaboration preference in this field of research, we construct a global collaboration network of social computing scholars with 2387 publications from 1999 to 2021 from five representative social computing journals. We define the concept of *Established Country, Developing Country* and *Ordinary Country* according to the tendency of paper publication of each country. Two new indices, *Attract Index* and *Group-wise Attract Index* are introduced to study the collaboration preferences. Overall, Established Countries are preferred in the collaboration with all kinds of countries. Results of negative binomial regression show that collaboration with Established Countries brings better academic influence of the research outcome.

Keywords: Social Network Analysis · Social Computing · Country Collaboration · Bibliographic Analysis · Negative Binomial Regression

1 Introduction

The concept of *social computing* was originally proposed by Schuler [22] and rapidly extended to a series of technologies that are used to extract the patterns of interactive behaviors [19]. For instance, social network analysis (SNA) [23] empowers researchers to transform the complex interactions on social media into networks [6]. As a globally prevailing field, social computing requires collaboration between scholars from different institutes and countries [27]. Country-level collaboration has been shown beneficial to scholars. International collaboration brings higher academic impact [17]. For governments, collaboration supporting policy needs to make sure the intellectual property is shared with critical and valuable partner countries. The study of the country-level collaboration patterns may assist scholars to determine where to conduct oversea research activity and help policy makers decide which kinds of collaboration to support [17].

One of the effective methods to research collaboration is SNA (detailed in Sect. 3.2), which is based on graph theory [11] and is used to depict the topological properties of a collaboration network. However, it is not profound enough to extract collaboration patterns and explain why such collaboration occurs. Thus, on the country-level, we propose *Attract Index*, and *Group-wise Attract*

© The Author(s), under exclusive license to Springer Nature Singapore Pte Ltd. 2023
Y. Sun et al. (Eds.): ChineseCSCW 2022, CCIS 1681, pp. 173–181, 2023.
https://doi.org/10.1007/978-981-99-2356-4_14

Index (detailed in Sect. 4) to explore collaboration preferences and then employ regression models to explain the preferences (detailed in Sect. 5).

The country-level collaboration in the field of social computing is rarely explored. In this paper, we explore the country collaboration preferences. Key contributions of this research are summarized as follows:

- We originally define *Established Country, Developing Country* and *Ordinary Countries* to classify the countries, *Attract Index* and *Group-wise Attract Index* to measure the importance of one country (group) to another.
- We apply both SNA method and regression models to analyze the correlation between citation count and collaboration between countries, providing insights on why the collaboration patterns form.

The rest of the paper is organized as follows. Section 2 introduces related work. Section 3 describes the dataset and introduces main methods. Section 4 presents the country collaboration patterns and preferences. Section 5 explains the preferences by regression analysis. Section 6 concludes this paper and proposes some prospective future work.

2   Related Work

2.1   Country-Level Co-authorship Collaboration Network

Scholar-level co-authorship networks were thoroughly studied by previous works [5,7,14]. However, for the country-level co-authorship collaboration, previous researches only focused on the basic properties of collaboration or on a specific pattern or a specific country in the collaboration. Yu et al. [30] researched the network in the field of analytic hierarchy process (AHP). Han et al. [10] revealed the primary collaboration pattern in library and information science (LIS) from the country-level. Zhang et al. [31] put forward novel measures to quantify China's emerging role in the global scientific research network. Liu et al. [16] defined collaboration patterns based on the nationality and order of the authors and compared the citation impact of different contribution patterns.

2.2   Country-Level Collaboration Preference

Few studies concentrated on the collaboration preference in recent years. Dating back to 2006, Schubert et al. [21] proposed novel indices to quantify co-authorship preference, cross-citation preference and cross-reference preference, based on the collaboration matrices. They focused on every pair of the selected countries, giving a precise preference value of each pair. Results revealed that geopolitical location and cultural relations shape such preferences. However, nowadays the cultural barriers are collapsing due to the rapid globalization and are less impeding international collaborations. Thus, collaboration preferences need up-to-date researches. This work was the first to study the clustering phenomenon in pair-wise country collaboration. To the best of our knowledge, few of previous work attended to a certain group of countries to examine the collaboration preference and few were in the field of social computing.

3   Data and Methods

3.1   Data Collection and Collaboration Network Construction

Bibliographic data of publications from five representative journals in the field of social computing are collected, including *Social Networks (SocNets)* starting from 1999, published by Elsevier, *Social Network Analysis and Mining (SNAM)* from 2011 by Springer, *IEEE Transactions on Computational Social Systems (TCSS)* from 2014 by IEEE, *ACM Transactions on Social Computing (TSC)* from 2018 by ACM and *Journal of Social Computing (JSC)* from 2020 by IEEE. The publication numbers are 926, 809, 553, 69, 30, respectively, 2387 in total. These journals cover most of the leading publishers. We fetch the meta data of each publication from the official websites and the citation count of each publication from Google Scholar based on the publication title.

There are existing academic databases developed by researchers, e.g. MAG [24], AceMap [25] and AMiner [26]. However, MAG no longer provides service and AceMap does not provide raw bibliographical data. The data from AMiner does not contain SNAM and JSC. Bibliographic information for major computer science publications is openly provided by DBLP and the five selected journals are all available there. Therefore, we choose DBLP as our data source.

To construct the country co-authorship collaboration network (country network for short), (1) the scholars from the same country are coalesced into a country node. The country of a scholar is where the scholar's affiliation belongs to. We only consider the first affiliation of each author. (2) The co-authorship between scholars from different countries will be an edge between two country nodes in the country network. The number of such co-authorships is the edge weight. Self-loops are not considered in the country network. In total, there are 66 nodes and 245 edges in the country network.

3.2   Methods

Social Network Analysis (SNA) and Metrics. SNA has been widely employed in diverse areas, such as social media [28] and public infrastructure [20]. Several metrics are used in SNA. *Degree centrality* is the number of edges connected to a node. *Closeness centrality* represents how close a node is to other nodes on average. *Clustering coefficient* represents the extent to which the neighbors of a node are connected to each other.

Structural hole is a concept originally developed by Burt [3]. It is a hole between nodes that are not directly connected in a network, and a node occupying the structural hole is called a *structural hole spanner* [15]. *Constraint* is a commonly used measure of structural hole spanners. The smaller constraint, the higher ability of a node to acquire information from different communities.

Negative Binomial Regression. In Sect. 5, we adopt negative binomial regression model [12] to study the correlation between collaboration preferences and academic influence. Negative binomial regression model is based on negative binomial distribution [12]. Usually, the negative binomial regression model is used when the dependent variable is non-negative integer and over-dispersed. It is widely adopted in different areas [29], for instance, medicine and public health [13,18] and transportation [4].

4   Country Collaboration Preference

In this section, we first classify the countries and propose several measures to delve into the collaboration preference of each country type.

4.1   Different Types of Countries in The Collaboration Network

We classify the 64 countries in our dataset into several groups defined as follows:

Definition 1. *A country is an **Established Country** if its number of publications reaches k_{est} before $Year_{est}$. A country is a **Developing Country** if its number of papers reaches k_{dev} before $Year_{dev}$ and it is not an established country. A country is an **Ordinary Country** if it is neither an Established Country nor a Developing Country.*

An Established Country has an influence in an early year, based on its number of publications, while a Developing Country gains academic influence in this field later. We set $Year_{est}$ as 2014 and $Year_{dev}$ as 2018, which are the begin years of TCSS and TSC respectively. It is flexible to choose $Year_{est}$ and $Year_{dev}$, and more experiments are left for future work. The k_{est} here is set to 25, and k_{dev} is set to 15. Based on the definitions above, Table 1 shows the detailed classification.

Table 1. Three types of countries/regions

Established Countries	Developing Countries	Ordinary Countries
Australia, Canada, UK, Netherlands, USA	China (including Hong Kong, Macao and Taiwan), France, Germany, India, Ireland, Italy, Japan, Singapore, Slovenia, Spain, Sweden, Switzerland	All other countries

4.2   Attract Index and Group-wise Attract Index

In order to learn the collaboration preference among different types of countries, we propose *Attract Index* and *Group-wise Attract Index*, defined as follows:

Definition 2. *Let i and j denote two countries, C_{ij} is the number of pairs of collaborated scholars from the two countries, equal to the sum of weights of all edges between i and j in the country network. D_i denotes the times of international collaboration of country i, equal to the sum of weights of all edges incident to i. **Attract Index** is formulated as follows:*

$$Attr_{ij} = \frac{C_{ij}}{D_i}. \tag{1}$$

*For two country sets A and B, **Group-wise Attract Index** is the mean of the Attract Index of all country pairs (i, j), where i is any country in set A and j in set B. Formally,*

$$GAttrI_{AB} = \frac{\sum_{i \in A} \sum_{j \in B} Attr_{ij}}{|A||B|}. \tag{2}$$

Briefly, *Attract Index* between country i and country j measures the extent to which country i prefers country j. *Group-wise Attract Index* reflects the preference of group A to group B.

Attract Index is inspired by *Affinity Index*, first proposed by Zitt et al. [32], to measure the importance of one country to another. The denominator of *Affinity Index* is the number of internationally co-authored publications of j, i.e. D_j.

4.3   Collaboration Preferences of Different Types of Countries

Let A denote one of the three types of countries and let B denote one of Developing Countries and Established Countries, generating 6 pairs of (A, B). We compute the $GAttrI_{AB}$ for each pair of (A, B). The results are listed in Table 2. The "Ratio" column is the quotient of Established column to Developing column.

Table 2. $GAttrI_{AB}$ for each (A, B) pair

Set A	Set B		
	Established	Developing	Ratio
Established	0.088	0.038	2.32
Developing	0.106	0.028	3.79
Ordinary	0.068	0.015	4.53

For Established Countries, Developing Countries and Ordinary Countries (as Set A), the Established Countries are more preferred in collaboration than Developing Countries, with the ratios all greater than 1. However, Ordinary Countries, prefer Established Countries much more than other two types, with a ratio of 4.53. Obviously, Established Countries take a pivotal part in the collaboration network, and less developed countries are more willing to collaborate with Established Countries than the countries of their own types.

5   Academic Influence of the Collaboration Preference

5.1   Hypothesis

In Sect. 4, we observe the preference for Established Countries. We name it *experience preference*. We hypothesize that the advantage of such preference is the high academic influence.

We now consider each pair of authors co-authoring a paper. The citation count for this collaboration is the citation count of the co-authored publication. Based on the types of countries (Established, Developing or Ordinary), the collaborations are classified. We count the number of each type of collaboration and compute the average citation count of each type. (type, citation count) pairs are then drawn in a box plot, Fig. 1. From the box plot, est-*(any) outnumbers other types in median, 75th percentile as well as outliers. Established Countries are considered the most experienced in social computing. We denote the six types of collaboration by number 1 to number 6. 1 denotes the "est-est" collaboration and 6 denotes the "ord-ord" collaboration. The smaller the number, the more experienced the collaboration. Based on the observations above, we hypothesize:

Hypothesis. Collaboration Citation Count tends to be higher in a more experienced collaboration.

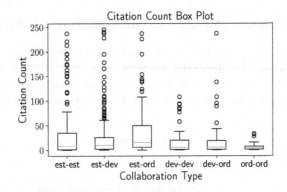

Fig. 1. Box Plot of Citation Count to Collaboration Type

5.2   Model Results

We apply regression analysis to verify the hypothesis above. In our regression model, a sample is a pair of countries. The dependent variable is the average citation count of this pair of countries (named Collaboration Citation Count, CCC for short), which is the average citation count of all author collaboration pairs between a pair of countries. The collaboration type (CT for short) is the explanatory variable. Besides, we choose four representative network indices in SNA as controlled variables: degree centrality, closeness centrality, constraint and clustering coefficient. As each sample is a pair of countries, we take the average indices of the two countries as the independent variables. We adopt the negative binomial regression model to analyze the correlations between CCC and the independent variables above. CCC is non-negative integer and the mean of CCC is 4.14 while the standard variance is 22.74, apparently greater than the mean. It indicates that dependent variable CCC is over-dispersed, meeting the requirement of the negative binomial regression model. Table 3 shows the regression results.

Table 3. Analytical results of CCC negative binomial models

Variable	Model 1	Model 2
Intercept	18.04323***	18.82661***
1. *Degree*	0.68871***	0.61559***
2. *Closeness*	−45.15597***	−43.32034***
3. *Constraint*	−8.90331***	−9.00776***
4. *Clustering*	0.60701	0.62925
5. *CT*		−0.25651*

Signif. : ***$p < 0.001$, **$p < 0.01$, *$p < 0.05$, .$p < 0.1$

From the results of model 1, and model 2, CT has a negative influence on CCC, with the p-value less than 0.05. It indicates that a more experienced collaboration type increases the CCC. It supports *Hypothesis* that experienced collaboration brings higher academic influence. In the country collaboration network, Established Countries tend to possess more intelligent scholars, better academic environment and more support from country policies, with abundant academic input, investment, experience. Thus, the more experienced collaboration type implies a higher citation count.

6   Conclusions and Future Work

In this paper, we explore the patterns of country-level collaboration in the field of social computing. We classify countries into *Established Countries, Developing Countries* and *Ordinary Countries. Attract Index* and *Group-wise Attract Index* are calculated and it is found that all types countries prefer to collaborate with Established Countries. Results of negative binomial regression models show that there is a correlation between the citation count and the collaboration type, which might serve as a motivation for the scholars to have such a preference.

In the future, we will use machine learning methods to explore more factors that influence the citation count [1,2,8]. Key countries in social computing, such as structural hole spanners, can be detected by machine learning [9]. The keywords of each publication can also be further used to characterize the trend of research directions in social computing.

References

1. Abrishami, A., Aliakbary, S.: Predicting citation counts based on deep neural network learning techniques. J. Informetrics **13**(2), 485–499 (2019)
2. Beranová, L., Joachimiak, M.P., Kliegr, T., Rabby, G., Sklenák, V.: Why was this cited? Explainable machine learning applied to COVID-19 research literature. Scientometrics pp. 1–37 (2022)
3. Burt, R.S.: The social structure of competition. Netw. Knowl. Econ. **13**, 57–91 (2003)
4. Chang, L.Y.: Analysis of freeway accident frequencies: negative binomial regression versus artificial neural network. Saf. Sci. **43**(8), 541–557 (2005)
5. Chen, Y., Ding, C., Hu, J., Chen, R., Hui, P., Fu, X.: Building and analyzing a global co-authorship network using google scholar data. In: Proceedings of the 26th International Conference on World Wide Web Companion, pp. 1219–1224 (2017)
6. Chen, Y., Hu, J., Xiao, Y., Li, X., Hui, P.: Understanding the user behavior of Foursquare: a data-driven study on a global scale. IEEE Trans. Comput. Soc. Syst. **7**(4), 1019–1032 (2020)
7. Gao, M., Chen, Y., Gong, Q., Wang, X., Hui, P.: Understanding scholar social networks: taking scholat as an example. In: CCF Conference on Computer Supported Cooperative Work and Social Computing, pp. 326–339. Springer (2021) https://doi.org/10.1007/978-981-19-4549-6_25
8. Ghasemian, F., Zamanifar, K., Ghasem-Aqaee, N., Contractor, N.: Toward a better scientific collaboration success prediction model through the feature space expansion. Scientometrics **108**(2), 777–801 (2016). https://doi.org/10.1007/s11192-016-1999-x
9. Gong, Q., Zhang, J., Wang, X., Chen, Y.: Identifying structural hole spanners in online social networks using machine learning. In: Proceedings of the ACM SIGCOMM 2019 Conference Posters and Demos, pp. 93–95 (2019)
10. Han, P., Shi, J., Li, X., Wang, D., Shen, S., Su, X.: International collaboration in LIS: global trends and networks at the country and institution level. Scientometrics **98**(1), 53–72 (2014)
11. Haythornthwaite, C.: Social network analysis: an approach and technique for the study of information exchange. Libr. Inf. Sci. Res. **18**(4), 323–342 (1996)
12. Hilbe, J.M.: Negative Binomial Regression. Cambridge University Press, Cambridge (2011)
13. Iqbal, W., Tang, Y.M., Chau, K.Y., Irfan, M., Mohsin, M.: Nexus between air pollution and NCOV-2019 in china: application of negative binomial regression analysis. Process Saf. Environ. Prot. **150**, 557–565 (2021)
14. Kumar, S.: Co-authorship networks: a review of the literature. Aslib J. Inf. Manage. **67**(1), 55–73 (2015)
15. Lin, Z., Zhang, Y., Gong, Q., Chen, Y., Oksanen, A., Ding, A.Y.: Structural hole theory in social network analysis: a review. IEEE Trans. Comput. Soc. Syst. **9**(3), 724–739 (2022)
16. Liu, H.-I., Huang, M.-H.: Research contribution pattern analysis of multinational authorship papers. Scientometrics **127**(4), 1783–1800 (2022). https://doi.org/10.1007/s11192-022-04277-x
17. Ortega, J.L., Aguillo, I.F.: Institutional and country collaboration in an online service of scientific profiles: Google scholar citations. J. Informetrics **7**(2), 394–403 (2013)

18. Oztig, L.I., Askin, O.E.: Human mobility and coronavirus disease 2019 (COVID-19): a negative binomial regression analysis. Public Health **185**, 364–367 (2020)
19. Parameswaran, M., Whinston, A.B.: Social computing: an overview. Commun. Assoc. Inf. Syst. **19**(1), 37 (2007)
20. Prabhakar, N., Anbarasi, L.J.: Exploration of the global air transport network using social network analysis. Soc. Netw. Anal. Min. **11**(1), 1–12 (2021). https://doi.org/10.1007/s13278-021-00735-1
21. Schubert, A., Glänzel, W.: Cross-national preference in co-authorship, references and citations. Scientometrics **69**(2), 409–428 (2006)
22. Schuler, D.: Social computing. Commun. ACM **37**(1), 28–29 (1994)
23. Scott, J.: Social network analysis. Sociology **22**(1), 109–127 (1988)
24. Sinha, A., et al.: An overview of microsoft academic service (MAS) and applications. In: Proceedings of the 24th International Conference on World Wide Web, pp. 243–246 (2015)
25. Tan, Z., Liu, C., Mao, Y., Guo, Y., Shen, J., Wang, X.: AceMap: a novel approach towards displaying relationship among academic literatures. In: Proceedings of the 25th International Conference on World Wide Web Companion, pp. 437–442 (2016)
26. Tang, J., Zhang, J., Yao, L., Li, J., Zhang, L., Su, Z.: ArnetMiner: extraction and mining of academic social networks. In: Proceedings of the 14th ACM SIGKDD International Conference on Knowledge Discovery and Data Mining, pp. 990–998 (2008)
27. Wang, T., Zhang, Q., Liu, Z., Liu, W., Wen, D.: On social computing research collaboration patterns: a social network perspective. Front. Comput. Sci. **6**(1), 122–130 (2012)
28. Weber, D., Nasim, M., Mitchell, L., Falzon, L.: Exploring the effect of streamed social media data variations on social network analysis. Soc. Netw. Anal. Min. **11**(1), 1–38 (2021). https://doi.org/10.1007/s13278-021-00770-y
29. Yang, S., Berdine, G.: The negative binomial regression. Southwest Respir. Crit. Care Chronicles **3**(10), 50–54 (2015)
30. Yu, D., Kou, G., Xu, Z., Shi, S.: Analysis of collaboration evolution in AHP research: 1982–2018. Int. J. Inf. Technol. Decis. Making **20**(01), 7–36 (2021)
31. Zhang, Z., Rollins, J.E., Lipitakis, E.: China's emerging centrality in the contemporary international scientific collaboration network. Scientometrics **116**(2), 1075–1091 (2018)
32. Zitt, M., Bassecoulard, E., Okubo, Y.: Shadows of the past in international cooperation: collaboration profiles of the top five producers of science. Scientometrics **47**(3), 627–657 (2000)

An Intelligent Mobile System for Monitoring Relapse of Depression

Wenyi Yin, Chenghao Yu, Pianran Wu, Wenxuan Jiang, Youzhe Liu, Tianqi Ren, and Weihui Dai[✉]

School of Management, Fudan University, Shanghai 200433, China
{18307100087,18307100049,18307100128,17307100116,18307100052, 18307100006,whdai}@fudan.edu.cn

Abstract. Depression is a common psychological disorder with high relapse rate in modern society. Due to weak self-perception and fear of public bias, most relapse patients fail to receive timely treatment. Aiming to provide a self-monitoring means in home environment and daily life, this paper studied the machine learning and natural language processing technologies for extracting the patient's acoustic features and semantic features from the designed speech diagnostic test, and proposed an improved CNN-LSTM learning model suitable for the monitoring, which can combine acoustic features, semantic features, weather and environmental information as well as the patient's personalized features for achieving ideal results. On this basis, an intelligent mobile system is designed for daily monitoring on the relapse of depression.

Keywords: Depression Disorder · Relapse Monitoring · Machine Learning · Daily Environment · Mobile System

1 Introduction

Depression is a psychological disorder characterized by an extensive and persistent low mood, led by low self-assurance along with loss of interest in enjoyable activities [1]. Globally, more than 264 million people of all ages suffer from this disease [2]. Different from usual mood fluctuations and short-lived emotional responses to challenges in everyday life, long-lasting clinical depression could cause huge negative effects on individuals, families, and society if not found and treated timely.

The diagnosis of major depressive disorder (MDD) requires a distinct change of mood, characterized by sadness or irritability and accompanied by at least several psychological and physiological changes [3]. Due to its heterogeneity and complexity of pathogenesis, current depression diagnosis is limited by assessment methods that rely mostly on patient's self-reports and clinical judgments [4], risking a range of subjective biases and causing inaccurate assessment [5]. Moreover, in recovered depressed patients, the thinking activated by dysphoria will show similarities to the thinking patterns that previously occurred in episode [6]. Therefore, prediction and monitoring of relapse of

© The Author(s), under exclusive license to Springer Nature Singapore Pte Ltd. 2023
Y. Sun et al. (Eds.): ChineseCSCW 2022, CCIS 1681, pp. 182–193, 2023.
https://doi.org/10.1007/978-981-99-2356-4_15

depression is available and especially significant for timely intervention. However, different from the very first diagnosis, the monitoring of depression relapse should consider the individual differences of patients and the dynamic changes of the disease.

Intelligent detection of depression has made significant gains in recent years. Cohn et al. analyzed prosodic and facial expression elements using two machine learning classifiers: support vector machine (SVM) and logistic regression [7]. They achieved the accuracy of 79–88% for identification of depression from facial expressions, and the accuracy of 79% from prosodic features. Jiang et al. noticed the gender differences in identifications. They examined the discriminative abilities of three classifiers for detection of depression: SVM (Support Vector Machine), GMM (Gaussian Mixture Model), and KNN (K-Nearest Neighbor), and showed that SVM achieved the best results with the accuracy of 80.30% for males, and 75.96%for females [8].

This study focuses on the improvement of both accuracy and convenience in detection of the trend of diagnosed patients' relapse of depression. Different from previous restudy that mainly emphasized on depression detection, the study extends efforts to improving the quality of follow-up clinical intervention, providing patients and their families with dynamic monitoring and early warning mobile system for relapse of depression based on the real situation.

2 Literature Review

2.1 Acoustic Detection

Early studies have proved that minor changes in psychology could cause significant changes in acoustic features including intensity, loudness, zero-crossing rate, voice onset time, second formant transition, prosody, power spectral density, grammar, etc. [8]. Current researches further verify that patients who meet the criteria of major depressive disorder have inactive responses to emotional stimuli of different valences. Patients lack prosody changes in speech than normal people and respond more actively to negative facial and vocal expressions, and the second dimension of MFCC could be used as a useful biomarker to detect the major depressive disorder [9].

In the deep learning of acoustic detection, Ma et al. introduced a learning method for audio-based depression classification [10], which extracted MFCCs features of audio as the input of the model, and used a two-layer convolutional neural network (CNN), a layer long and short-term memory networks (LSTM) and two fully connected layers (FC) to predict whether audio subjects are depressed. Lang et al. made improvements based on the characteristics of the local binary model (LBP) [11]. They designed a robustly extended local binary model (MRELBP), and used a deep convolutional neural network (DCNN) to predict depression assessment scores. Chao et al. extracted the features of audio and video, fused them into signs of abnormal behavior, and used long-and short-term memory recurrent neural networks (LSTM-RNN) for depression scale prediction from video [12].

Furthermore, some researchers studied the impacts of language types and culture differences on the acoustic features of MDD. Alghowinem et al. tested two different languages of English and German in the United States, Germany, and Australia. It was found that language type does not significantly affect the quality of speech detection results [13]. They pointed out that spontaneous language's accuracy of sound classification is higher than that of text reading, which indicates that unstructured questions could work better in prediction than structured questions [14].

2.2 Semantic Analysis

Depression relapse is not only manifested in its acoustic features of languages, but also may be closely related to the semantic contents and semantic emotions. However, this is still an issue that has not been studied deeply, which differs from the pure acoustic feature analysis, but has relations with the wording, syntax and habitual expression of different languages and different individuals. The semantic analysis of natural language processing (NLP) have mainly experienced three development stages: from statistical methods to shallow machine learning, and now turning to deep learning.

In shallow machine learning, Paltoglou et al. built an SVM classification model and used the TF-IDF algorithm for sentiment analysis [15]. Experiments show that this method improves the effect of text classification effectively. Wang et al. proposed a very short text classification model based on sentiment tendency and SVM, and proved its high classification accuracy [16]. In deep learning, the CNN model proposed by Kim [17] in 2014 solved the shortcomings of similar encoding of antonyms in the same context, and achieved high accuracy in sentence-level text classification. Wang proposed a new CNN algorithm based on a dual-channel structure and attention mechanism, which achieved an accuracy rate of more than 90% in short text classification [18].

In the semantic analysis and affective computation, it is usually necessary to construct a sentiment library, which is a set of words that are formed by sentiment vocabulary, and has significant meanings for subjective sentiment mining and analysis. For example, SentiWordNet is a well-known English sentiment library, which classifies vocabulary to three tendencies based on WordNet: neural, negative, and positive; and HowNet Sentiment Dictionary is a Chinese vocabulary for sentiment analysis which contains more than 17000 entries based on HowNet Knowledge Base. Nevertheless, there is no sentiment library suitable for semantic analysis of patients with depression so far, and its construction method remains to be studied.

3 Data Collection and Preprocessing

3.1 Data Collection

Different from existing studies that mainly focus on the detection and diagnosis of depression, this study aims to explore its relapse monitoring, and therefore collected the data from 38 patients and 30 healthy people through a standard three-month clinical investigation with the diagnostic assessments of every two weeks. The HAMD17 (Hamilton Depression Scale with 17 items) Scale was used for professional assessment of depressive degree changes, which includes 17 items with 5 points for each. The scale classifies depression in 4 levels according to the total assessment scores: 0–7 no depression, 8–17 mild depression, 18–24 moderate depression, 25- severe depression. Usually, the scores of 18 or more are regarded as the diagnosis standard of relapse.

In every investigation, the speeches of subjects were recorded in audio files for data preprocessing and machine learning, which were structured by the tasks: text reading, picture description, counting numbers and answering questions, as following example:

1. Text reading: read aloud the given texts such as "North wind and sun".
2. Picture description: each participant is required to describe three pictures of positive, medium, and negative.
3. Counting number: counting from 1 to 20.
4. Answering seven questions:
(1) Could you talk about your favorite entertainment activities?
(2) Could you please talk about any jobs that will make you feel difficult to complete and want to avoid or escape?
(3) Please describe your mood changes during the past week and events or people related to these mood changes as much detailed as possible.

In the investigation, each of the 10 speeches, including 3 speeches of text reading, picture description, counting numbers and 7 speeches of answering questions, were collected as a record respectively, and obtained total 4760 records. Numerous cases show that the factors such as climate changes, family conflicts, work and income pressures, etc. have also impacts on the relapse of depression. For example, Cobb et al. have proved that the prevalence of major depression and sad mood showed seasonal variation, with peaks in the summer and fall [19]. Therefore, the study set the related questions and took the descriptive information of the subjects' speeches into the analysis.

3.2 Acoustic Data Preprocessing

In order to conduct the feature extraction effectively, the valid audio data of each subject's speech was first segmented into a group of audio clips with the same length of 6 s for each clip corresponding to time series. Thereafter, this study utilized OpenSmile software tools [20] to exact a 32*12 feature data matrix from each sample, including short-term energy, short-term zero-crossing rate, formant, and MFCCs (Mel Frequency Cepstrum Coefficients) [21], etc. Those parameters have been shown in previous studies to be significantly associated with the acoustic changes in speeches of depression patients.

In real life, different individuals have different volume and tone characteristics, and this personalization features can lead to decline of depression recognition accuracy rate. Therefore, the parameters' data not only contain depression-related features, but also incorporate the speaker's personality characteristics. It can weaken the generalization ability of the model. In order to solve this problem, the study used the MADN (Multiscale Audio Delta Normalization) algorithm [22] to normalize the features of different scales. Those features are based on audio difference reflecting the audio change information, not easily affected by the personalized characteristics, and therefore improve the learning accuracy.

3.3 Semantic Text Preprocessing

Semantic features can reflect the interests, concerns, emotions, living environment, and daily activities of the patients with great significance for the diagnosis of disease situation changes. Semantic analysis involves the analysis of the semantic vocabulary and the above information in the speeches, which needs to convert the speeches into text first, and then adopts the NLP technology to fulfill the analysis.

The study used Xunfei voice transliteration API to convert the Chinese voice of the subjects' speeches into texts. Unlike the obvious delimiters between words in English, Chinese sentences are required to be segmented into a series of words. As people's spoken language is more casual than written ones, text conversion might not be so precise, and sentences might not strictly abide by traditional grammar and format, the "noise" is so huge that denoising is required. In doing so, the study used a word segmentation tool Jieba to obtain the segmented words and filter the "noise" to form the text corpus for semantic dictionary construction and machine learning.

3.4 Semantic Dictionary Construction

The semantic features of speeches are very important for depression analysis, but the existing dictionaries are mainly used for sentiment analysis and affective computation of usual natural languages, and there is no such a semantic dictionary suitable for depression analysis. Based on the speech corpus collected from patients, this study extracted the meaningful feature vocabulary, and constructed a special semantic dictionary suitable for the monitoring and diagnosis of depression relapse.

Firstly, the study selected the basic words manually according to their significance for diagnosis including the descriptive keywords about interests, concerns, emotions, living environment, and daily activities, and produced a seed set; Secondly, the candidate words reflecting the language behavior habits of the subjects were derived from the corpus produced by the semantic text processing. Thirdly, the combination of SO-PMI (Semantic Orientation Using Pointwise Mutual Information) and SO-WV (Sentiment Orientation from Word Vector) algorithms were used to measure the relationship between words, and expand the dictionary with new vocabulary. Finally, the skip-gram model of word2vec tool was employed to generate the semantic word vectors for the semantic feature extraction from the subjects' speeches.

4 Machine Learning

4.1 Learning Model

The subjects' speeches include acoustic features and semantic features, which need to be learned and combined with their personalized features such as ID number, gender, age, and historical diagnostic results, etc. for the analysis and monitoring of depression relapse. Therefore, this study designed an improved CNN-LSTM learning model to perform the process, as shown in Fig. 1.

In the above model, the acoustic features are learned by a typical CNN-LSTM model with two convolutional layers, one max polling layer, one flatten layer, one LSTM layer and the full connected layer, but the semantic features and the subjects' personalized features are combined into the full connected layer, and finally output the assessment results of diagnosis by the Softmax classification vector of HAMD17 scores or its different levels.

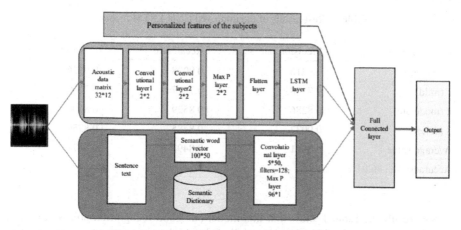

Fig. 1. The improved CNN-LSTM learning model.

In acoustic feature learning, each speech is first extracted by OpenSmile tools to form a 32*12 acoustic data matrix. Thereafter, the two-dimensional matrix data are convoluted and pooled to obtain deep features, and then imported into the LSTM layer to extract long term dependence information. Finally, the fully connected layer at the end of the network encodes long-term changes on the timeline. In semantic feature learning, each speech is first converted into a sentence text, and then produce a semantic word vector based on the constructed semantic dictionary, which contains up to 100 semantic words, and each word has 50 dimensions. Thereafter, the data of semantic word vector are convoluted by 128 filters with the size of 5*50 for each filter. Finally, the output feature maps are pooled and sent to the full connected layer. Besides, because the feature extraction of the CNN-LSTM model has time-dependent characteristics, the collected data must be input according to the time series for machine learning.

4.2 Learning Results

In the learning process, the scores of HAMD17 Scale assessed by clinicians in each investigation are taken as the annotations of the corresponding samples for training. Because the output of the full connected layer is a Softmax vector of the score distribution in HAMD17 Scale, so it needs to be first processed by weighting each vector component with the corresponding score, and then calculate out the weighted sum as the final assessment score. Finally, the assessment score is divided into the four intervals: 0 to 7, 8 to 17, 18 to 24, and above 24, labelled as 0, 1, 2, 3 respectively, which represent normal, mild, moderate, and severe. The intervals of 2 and 3 indicate the state of relapse.

This study uses 21737 samples of audio clips for acoustic feature learning, and 4760 sentence texts for semantic feature learning, which have been obtained from the data preprocessing and produced 476 units of data groups with annotations. Among which, 70% annotated data (333 units) are randomly extracted out as the training set, while the remaining 30% annotated data (143 units) are used as the test set. Table 1 shows the test results of the improved CNN-LSTM model after being trained.

Table 1. Test results of the improved CNN-LSTM model.

Depressive level	Precision rate	Recall rate	f1-score
0 (normal)	0.9216	0.9038	0.9126
1 (mild)	0.7308	0.7917	0.7600
2 (moderate)	0.8286	0.8529	0.8406
3 (severe)	0.9032	0.8485	0.8750
Average value	0.8461	0.8492	0.8471
Accuracy rate: 86.01%			

The results in Table 1 show that this model has good recognition ability, and can reach the accuracy rate of 86.01%. Especially, it has high precision rates and recall rates with excellent f1-scores for the levels of 0, 2 and 3. The confusion matrix of 143 test units is shown in Fig. 2. It shows that only 5 units are misidentified between the levels of 0–2 and 3–4 with a very high accuracy rate of 99.97% if only considering those two classifications, which is very suitable for relapse monitoring.

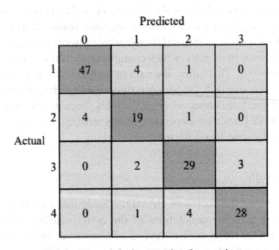

Fig. 2. The confusion matrix of test units.

5 System Design

5.1 System Architecture

The system is designed to provide relapse monitoring for patients who have been diagnosed with depression at home and in daily working and living environment. It also can be used for the detection of new patients. In order to facilitate the utilization, the client

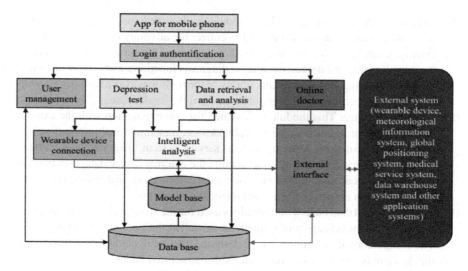

Fig. 3. App system architecture.

of the system is designed as an APP for mobile phones with its architecture as shown in Fig. 3.

The system can perform the user's entry, depression test and intelligent monitoring, connection of external wearable device such as special voice acquisition equipment, EEG device, etc., as well as contacting with online doctors and connecting with external systems, which includes the following modules:

(1) Login authentification. This module is responsible for user authentication and secure access. Through the user's ID, it can retrieve the relevant historical data, and provides the basis for depression monitoring and analysis.

(2) User management. This module is designed for user's information management and maintenance, including the information about age, gender, occupation, location, living and working environment, etc. The user can also input some information about recent activities, concerns, interests and mood changes for assisting in diagnosis.

(3) Depression test. This module is used to present the materials to be read, and the questions to be answered according to the test method designed by this study, perform the test process, and make a brief diagnostic report. It can call the wearable device connection module to collect the relevant data from external devices during the test process, and call the intelligent analysis module to fulfill the machine learning and intelligent analysis.

(4) Data retrieval and analysis. This module is applied to historical data retrieval, detailed result display, and visualized analysis. It can call the intelligent analysis module to complete the related computation and analysis tasks.

(5) Online doctor. This module can provide the access to external doctors for obtaining professional consultation and medical service. It is also used as the call for help in case of emergency.

(6) Wearable device connection. This module is designed for calling the external wearable device in case that it is used to collect the auxiliary data synchronously.

(7) Intelligent analysis. This module is the key module of the system, which can fulfill machine learning and depression relapse diagnosis functions, and is embedded with the API for calling the dynamic link library of the tools to perform feature parameter extraction, speech-to-text conversion, etc., from the model base.

(8) External interface. This module is designed for communication with the external device and systems, such as the wearable device, meteorological information system, global positioning system, medical service system, data warehouse system and other application systems. It can acquire the external device data, user position information, local weather and environmental information, and realize the access and output with external services and application systems.

(9) Model base and data base. This module is used for the storage of the computational procedures of models and tool's functions, as well as the storage of the system data. The computational procedures are all designed into the dynamic link libraries, and the data can be stored as unstructured files or structured tables.

5.2 System Operation

The system provides an APP operation interface, as shown in Fig. 4. Through the interface, the user can enter the following four modules: user management, depression test, data retrieval and analysis, and online doctor, and perform the corresponding operations, while the other modules mainly provide functional support for the above modules and cannot be directly operated by the user.

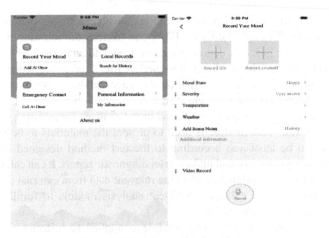

Fig. 4. The APP operation interface.

As an example, this study gives the operation procedure's design of its depression test module, which mainly includes the following steps:

Step 1: Test preparation and parameter setting.

When the user starts the module, the system will display the user's basic information, and asks whether to automatically collect the positing information, local weather information, and environmental information from the external systems. If not, the user needs to enter the relevant parameters manually. Besides, if the test process requires synchronous collection of data from the external wearable device, the user also needs to input the device type and required parameters. In the end of this step, the system will remind the user of the matters needing attention in the test process, and waiting for the user's preparation.

Step 2: Task presentation and speech collection.

After the user completes the preparation, the system will enter the test interface, which will present the four structured test tasks designed by this study: text reading, picture description, counting numbers and answering questions. The above test materials and questions are selected from a topic library based on the user's historical data. For the same user, the test materials and questions may vary according to the monitoring requirements for the user. The system will automatically collect the user's speech information during each test task, check the validity, and store it in the data base after numbering.

Step 3: Data processing and intelligent analysis.

When all test tasks have been performed completely, this module will call the intelligent analysis module to process the collected data, generate the input dataset of the improved CNN-LSTM learning model proposed by this study, and obtain the output result of that model. It will thereafter make the analysis and diagnosis of relapse based on the model's output and the user's historical data.

Step 4: Result output and disease trend prediction.

In the final step of this module's operation, the system will output the results and conduct a disease trend prediction by comparing with the user's historical status based on a regression analysis model. Finally, all the result and indicator data will be stored in the data base, and a brief report will be shown to the user. Meanwhile, the system will also notify the user that the historical data retrieval, detailed result display, and visualized analysis are available by the data retrieval and analysis module.

6   Summary and Discussion

Depression has a high relapse rate, but most patients didn't see the doctor for receiving timely treatment due to their weak self-perception and fear of public bias. This study aims to provide a new means for self-monitoring of relapse in home environment and daily life. It designed a speech diagnostic test, and studied the machine learning and natural language processing technologies for extracting the patient's acoustic features and semantic features based on the collected data of 38 patients and 30 healthy people through a standard three-month clinical investigation.

On this basis, the study proposed an improved CNN-LSTM learning model which can combine acoustic features, semantic features, weather and environmental information as well as the patient's personalized features for the leaning. Test results showed that it can reach the accuracy rate of 86.01% for the four-level recognition of HAMD17 Scale, and a very high accuracy rate of 99.97% for distinguishing whether the disease is relapsing.

Furthermore, the study designed an intelligent mobile APP system for relapse monitoring at home or in daily working and living environment, which can perform the speech test and machine learning based on the proposed CNN-LSTM model, as well as connecting with external device or systems, and contacting with online doctors for help. It provides comprehensive references for the development of depression relapse monitoring system.

There are also some limitations in this study. Only a total of 68 subjects participated in the three-month clinical investigation, so it is difficult to fully grasp an extensive personalized features and the long-term evolution situations of the disease, which may also affect the computational accuracy of the semantic dictionary due to the limited collected corpus. Besides, considering the computational efficiency and the possibility of deploying some programs on the mobile phone client, the proposed CNN-LSTM model adopts a relatively simple structure, and its optimal structure needs to be further explored. Nevertheless, this study provides a new technical approach and heuristic scheme for solving the difficult problem of depression relapse monitoring in daily environment.

Acknowledgements. This work was supported by Project of Ministry of Education of China (No.18YJA630019, 19JZD010), National Natural Science Foundation of China (No. 71971066), and Undergraduate Program of Fudan University (No.202011, No.202010). Wenyi Yin, Chenghao Yu, Pianran Wu are the joint first authors, and Weihui Dai is the corresponding author of this paper.

References

1. Boniwell, I.: Positive psychology in a nutshell: A balanced introduction to the science of optimal functioning. Personal Well-Being Centre (2008)
2. Lépine, J.P., Briley, M.: The increasing burden of depression. Neuropsychiatr. Dis. Treat. 7(1), 3–7 (2011)
3. Belmaker, R.H., Agam, G.: Major depressive disorder. N. Engl. J. Med. **358**(1), 55–68 (2008)
4. Lyness, J.M., Bruce, M.L., Koenig, H.G., et al.: Depression and medical illness in late life: report of a symposium. J. Am. Geriatr. Soc. **44**(2), 198–203 (1996)
5. Angst, J., Azorin, J.M., Bowden, C.L., et al.: Prevalence and characteristics of undiagnosed bipolar disorders in patients with a major depressive episode: the BRIDGE study. Arch. Gen. Psychiatry **68**(8), 791–799 (2011)
6. Teasdale, J.D., Segal, Z.V., Williams, J.M.G., et al.: Prevention of relapse/recurrence in major depression by mindfulness-based cognitive therapy. J. Consult. Clin. Psychol. **68**(4), 615–623 (2000)
7. Cohn, J.F., Kruez, T.S., Matthews, I, et al.: Detecting depression from facial actions and vocal prosody. In: Proceedings of the 3rd International Conference on Affective Computing and Intelligent Interaction and Workshops, Amsterdam, pp. 1–7 (2009)
8. Jiang, H., Hu, B., Liu, Z., et al.: Investigation of different speech types and emotions for detecting depression using different classifiers. Speech Commun. **90**, 39–46 (2017)
9. Taguchi, T., Tachikawa, H., Nemoto, K., et al.: Major depressive disorder discrimination using vocal acoustic features. J. Affect. Disord. **225**, 214–220 (2018)
10. Ma, X., Yang, H., Chen, Q., et al.: DepAudioNet: An efficient deep model for audio based depression classification. In: Proceedings of the 6th International Workshop on Audio/Visual Emotion Challenge, New York, pp. 35–42 (2016)

11. Lang, H., Cui, C.: Automated depression analysis using convolutional neural networks from speech. J. Biomed. Inform. **83**, 103–111 (2018)
12. Chao, L., Tao, J., Yang, M., Li, Y.: Multi task sequence learning for depression scale prediction from video. In: Proceedings of the International Conference on Affective Computing and Intelligent Interaction. Lisbon, pp. 526–531 (2015)
13. Alghowinem, S., Goecke, R., Epps, J., et al.: Cross-cultural depression recognition from vocal biomarkers. In: Proceedings of the 17th Annual Conference of the International Speech Communication Association, San Francisco, pp. 1943–1947 (2016)
14. Alghowinem, S., Goecke, R., Wagner, M., et al.: Detecting depression: A comparison between spontaneous and read speech. In: Proceedings of the 2013 IEEE International Conference on Acoustics, Speech and Signal Processing, New York, pp. 7547–7551 (2013)
15. Paltoglou, G., Thelwall, M.: A study of information retrieval weighting schemes for sentiment analysis. In: Proceedings of the 48th Annual Meeting of the Association for Computational Linguistics, Uppsala, pp. 1386–1395 (2010)
16. Wang, H.Q, W., Yang, W.: A hybrid very short text classification model based on sentiment orientation and SVM. Science and Technology Bulletin, **34**(8), 149–154 (2018)
17. Kim, Y.: Convolutional Neural Networks for Sentence Classification, arXiv preprint, 1746–1751 (2014)
18. Wang, R.: Research on Short Text Representation and Classification Based on Convolutional Neural Network, Shandong Normal University (2018)
19. Cobb, B.S., Coryell, W.H., Cavanaugh, J., et al.: Seasonal variation of depressive symptoms in unipolar major depressive disorder. Compr. Psychiatry **52**, 1891–1899 (2014)
20. Eyben, F., Wllmer, M., Schuller, B.: Opensmile: the munich versatile and fast open-source audio feature extractor. In: Proceedings of the 18th ACM International Conference on Multimedia, pp. 1459–1462 (2010)
21. Beritelli, F. Grasso, R.: A pattern recognition system for environmental sound classification based on MFCCs and neural networks. In: Proceedings of 2008 International Conference on Signal Processing and Communication Systems, pp. 1–4 (2008)
22. Li, J.M., Fu, X.Y.: Audio depression recognition based on deep learning. Comput. Appl. Softw. **36**(9), 161–167 (2019)

Fine-Grained Sentiment Analysis of Online-Offline Danmaku Based on CNN and Attention

Yan Tang and Hongyu Zhang[✉]

College of Computer and Information, Hohai University, Nanjing, China
{tangyan,hongyu.zhang}@hhu.edu.cn

Abstract. Sending danmaku is a popular way of social communication and It provides a direct way for users to express their opinions and sentiments. However, the classification of the sentiment intents of danmaku is not a trivial task. In this study, we propose a new approach to depict the relationship between the users' sentiment and contents of online videos and offline events by analyzing the sentiment of Danmaku. Firstly, we specify the classification of the danmaku intents by considering the characteristics of danmaku and the association between the intents and the sentiments. Secondly, we get the sentiment intensity of danmaku through the sentiment classifier constructed based on the long short-term memory network (LSTM). Thirdly, the sentiment embedding of danmaku encoded by the sentiment classier is used to improve the performance of the intent classifier constructed based on convolution neural network (CNN). The sentiment embedding is injected into the intent classifier through the self-attention mechanism. The experiment results show that the accuracy of this model is higher than four recent baseline models. Finally, we compute the overall sentiment curves of danmaku and specific intents to achieve the fine-grained sentiment analysis for online videos and offline events.

Keywords: Danmaku · Sentiment Analysis · Sentiment Embedding · Convolutional Neural Network · Self-attention

1 Introduction

Danmaku is a new way of social interaction and online commentary that is popular in Asia since 2010 [11] (see Fig. 1). Users can view the comments sent by other users while watching the video. This will not only enrich the video watching and interaction experiences but also fully stimulate the users to provide their viewpoints when watching the videos. Meanwhile, in addition to the online video danmaku, there are also danmaku in the offline social events. However, most of the papers in the field of sentiment analysis now focus on traditional reviews or articles, and there is a lack of relevant research on Danmaku sentiment analysis

Y. Sun et al. (Eds.): ChineseCSCW 2022, CCIS 1681, pp. 194–206, 2023.
https://doi.org/10.1007/978-981-99-2356-4_16

supported by both online streaming and offline social events data [8,15]. This paper aims to conduct sentiment analysis based on Danmaku with fine-grained sentiment analysis for both online and offline activities.

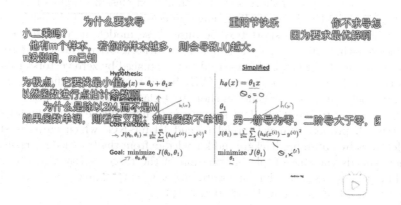

Fig. 1. An example of online video Danmaku.

In this paper, we analyze the sentiment tendency of a video content through the sentiment intensity of all danmaku in the same time interval. Further, we analyze the sentiment intensity of different intents of users to achieve fine-grained analysis. To improve the accuracy of the classifier used to distinguish the intents of danmaku, we divide the classification task into two subtasks and construct two models. The first task is the danmaku sentiment classification and the second task is the classification of danmaku intents. Through the first classification subtask, we can obtain the sentiment intensity and the sentiment embedding of each danmaku which will be used in the second subtask. Through the second classification subtask, we can obtain the intent of each danmaku. We can draw the sentiment curves of these videos or activities according to the result of above two subtasks. Based on these curves, we analyze the user's sentiment tendency in depth. The main contributions of this work are summarized as follows:

- We propose a model of intent classification of danmaku designed to capture the characteristics of short text danmaku that contains sentiment intents. The result of the method is better than four baseline models.
- We design an analytical method for users' sentiments to produce the sentiments intensity curves of videos or events with the proposed intent classification model.
- We analyze the users' sentiment tendency in a fine-grained way with the sentiment curves and conduct several empirical studies using the real world datasets.

2   Related Work

2.1   Short Text Classification

Danmaku is a new type of short text. The short text classification task is always a challenging problem in natural language processing. The LSTM-based models are not adequate for the short text because these models need to set a fixed sequence length, while the length of short text varies relatively large, as a result, many positions of word embeddings need to be replaced by zero vectors. To solve this problem, Kim et at. proposed a CNN based sentence classification model which has achieved decent results in short text classification [6].

Another way to overcome data sparsity is to introduce external knowledge. Zhong et al. propose a novel model named BERT-KG, which enriches short text features by obtaining background knowledge from the knowledge graph and further embeds the three-tuple information of the target entity into a BERT-based model and fuses the dynamic word vector with the knowledge of the short text to form a feature vector for short text [14].

2.2   Sentiment Analysis

Nasukawa [7] first proposed the term of sentiment analysis. At present, sentiment analysis is applied in many fields. Wu [13] et al. propose a stock price prediction method that incorporates multiple data sources and the investor sentiment. Bermingham and others take Twitter's tweets as independent variables, and the voting results are independent variables. They build a linear regression model to predict the election results.

At present, most of the research papers on bullet screen are analyzed from the perspectives of literature and culture. Most of the papers in the field of sentiment analysis focus on the traditional comments or articles and lack of relevant research on video Danmaku sentiment analysis supported by data. This paper will conduct sentiment analysis based on Danmaku, a new way of comment.

3   Proposed Method

In order to realize the intents classification of danmaku which can express emotions of users and provides the corresponding emotion intensity, we designed the classification standard and the corresponding classifier to get the intents of danmaku and the corresponding emotion intensity. And the basic structure of the classifier is proposed by us in [2], we redesign the model and change the experimental settings to classify the danmaku and obtain the sentiment intensity from the model at the same time. We also propose a method to draw the sentiment curves with different intents. The overall processes of our method is shown in Fig. 2.

We first propose the intents classification criteria to utilize the abundant sentiment information in danmaku. Then we train a sentiment classifier based

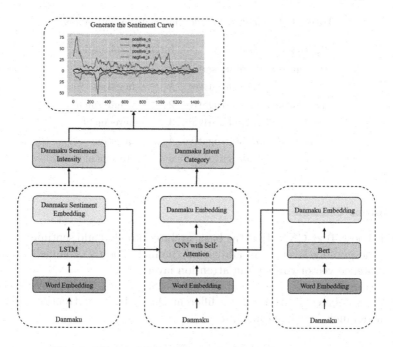

Fig. 2. The overall flow chart of our proposed method.

on LSTM to get the sentiment intensity and danmaku sentiment embedding. The sentiment embedding will introduced to the intent classifier based on CNN through self-attention mechanism to realize the intent classification. In order to further improve the accuracy of model, we introduce the sentence embedding obtained from Bert into CNN. Finally, we obtain the sentiment curves of every intents to complete the fine-grained sentiment analysis.

3.1 Classification Criteria of Danmaku

A short sentence can be divided into positive sentiment, negative sentiment and neutral sentiment; it can also be divided into statement and question in language type. And the three kinds of emotions and the two kinds of sentence types can finally form the six kinds of users' intent. See Table 1 for the specific classification criteria.

3.2 Sentiment Classifier

With good performance of LSTM in short text classification ([4,10]), we input the danmaku and obtains its sentiment embedding via LSTM for sentiment classification. After the model training, we can not only get the sentiment category of the danmaku, but also take the sentiment embedding in softmax layer as the sentiment intensity of the danmaku.

Table 1. Danmaku classification criteria and labels

Sentiment	Language	Intent	Explanation
0: negative	0: interrogative	0	doubt
	1: declarative	1	negation
1: positive	0: interrogative	2	wonderment
	1: declarative	3	agreement
2: neutral	0: interrogative	4	question
	1: declarative	5	statement

3.3   Intent Classifier

We still choose Text-CNN [1] as the basic architecture and add sentiment embedding to the pooling layer as an additional channel. The two channels are fused into a sentence vector through an attention layer.

The two-channel sentence embedding is $(S_{initial}, S_{sentiment})$. We need to pay varying degrees of attention to different channels. The attention operation between channels is defined in Eq. 1:

$$S = (S_{initial} \oplus S_{sentiment}) \tag{1}$$

In equation (1), $\oplus$ is the concatenation operation, and it can concatenate two sentences' embedding into a single embedding S corresponding to the sentence embedding of one Danmaku. The definition of the Danmaku embedding e_i can be generalized as equation (2), where $K = 2$:

$$e_i = tanh(W_i * S + b_i), i \in [1, K] \tag{2}$$

Then, the weight of the i-th sentence embedding is denoted as α_i,

$$\alpha_i = \frac{exp(e_i)}{\sum_{i=1}^{K} exp(e_k)} \tag{3}$$

By summing the different sentence embedding according to their weights, the Danmaku intent embedding S_{intent} is defined as:

$$S_{intent} = \sum_{i=1}^{K} \alpha_i * S_i \tag{4}$$

where S_i is the i-th sentence embedding.

In order to improve the accuracy of model, we use *bert-as-service* (https://bert-as-service.readthedocs.io/), which is a simple and quick method that can map a variable-length sentence to a fixed length vector by using a pre-trained BERT model. After the BERT encoder, we obtain a feature matrix $B_{embedding}$ and the final embedding $S_{embedding}$ is defined in (5).

$$S_{embedding} = (S_{intent} \oplus B_{embedding}) \tag{5}$$

Finally, we will get the classification result of the six intents of danmaku.

3.4 Visualization of Sentiment Intensity

In order to describe the user's emotion and intention in a fine-grained way, in addition to the overall sentiment curves, we take advantage of the intent categories of danmaku to draw the sentiment curves of every intent. Dividing danmaku into different categories for sentiment analysis is conducive to a deeper understanding of the sentiment response of users to the contents of videos or activities.

We can get a sentiment intensity in [0, 1] through the sentiment classifier. Then, we take a time window w, with the sliding step s of the window, and take the sum of the sentiment intensity of all the danmaku of the time window as the sentiment intensity of a step of a video or activity episode. Considering the de-duplicating process of danmaku in the date preprocessing, we add all intensity of danmaku in the same episode because the number of danmaku also reflects the intensity of sentiment of users.

4 Experiment

4.1 Dataset

The data of online video Danmaku is crawled from bilibili.com. Videos belongs to four different types. The offline Danmaku is collected through Usee [9], which is Danmaku of two parties. The detailed information of dataset is shown in Table 2

Table 2. The information of dataset

	Title	Type
Online	Your name	Anime
	Introduction to Python	Education
	Can we Eat the Chip On the Ground?	Science
	Dead stranded	Game Commentory
Offline	Party of the School of Computer	——
	Party of the School of Science	——

4.2 Model Comparison

To evaluate our model, we conduct experiments on three baseline models and make a comparative analysis.

Baseline Models

- LSTM model [5]: This model based on LSTM. It is a basic classifier consisting of two LSTM layers.
- LSTM-ATT model [12]: This model is constructed by adding an attention layer after the first layer of the LSTM model.
- Text-CNN model [6]: This model is a classical model of short text classification.
- BERT based model [3]: This model is a pre-training language model based on bidirectional transformer.

Results. The introduction of sentiment embedding and attention mechanism really improves the performance of the classifier in the Danmaku dataset. We use accuracy as the evaluating indicator. The results are shown in Fig. 3.

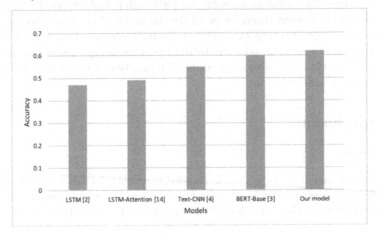

Fig. 3. The accuracy of the intent classification of models used in experiments.

4.3 The Generation of Sentiment Curves

We take a time window w, with the sliding step s of the window. Many settings have been tried to generate better curves for the fine-grained analysis of danmaku and we take different w and s for different videos and acitvities. For example, 'Can we Eat the Chip On the Ground?', its video time is relatively short and plot conversion is frequent, so we choose $w = 10 seconds$ and $s = 2 seconds$. For 'Your Name', a 100 min animation, we take $w = 30$ and $s = 5$.

5   Sentiment Analysis

We first conducted a survey on the usage habits of Danmaku users. 325 Danmaku users completed the survey. Most of them will actively use the Danmaku function, and 69.34% of users said that the emotion of watching videos will be affected by Danmaku. They said that when watching a funny video, watching Danmaku will make the video more funny. When watching the sad video, Danmaku will also make their emotions lower. It can be seen that Danmaku promotes the effective circulation between the user's acceptance information and feedback information.

The results of the questionnaire confirm the feasibility of sentiment analysis through Danmaku, we will start from this, based on Danmaku analysis of social network users' emotions, construct event heat model, realize sentiment visualization, and combine original video, user emotion and video The content is interpreted in depth. More specifically, quantitative analysis is as follows.

5.1 Online Danmaku

Analysis of the Overall Sentiment. We collected Danmaku of the online video and mapped the sentiment intensity curve of the corresponding video. We learned that the beginning of the video user's check-in behavior more. Positive emotions also occur at the end of the video because the users expresses gratitude emotions. In general, the sentiment tendency of video is mainly positive emotion, the overall sentiment trend and positive emotion trend are similar.

We have selected games, science, animation, education and other video danmaku analysis. The sentiment intensity curve is shown in Fig. 4

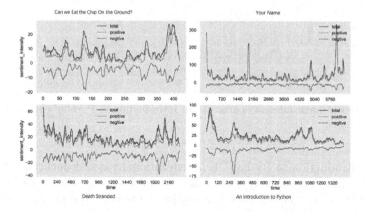

Fig. 4. The sentiment intensity curve of online Danmaku.

'Your Name' is the anime video we study. At the beginning of the video and towards the end of the video, the user's sentiment tendency peaks. Users have seen the same type of movie "Son of the Weather" and then revisited the film, so the video begins with some 'Just Watched the Weather Son', "One Again" and other danmaku content. Before the end of the video, the content of the danmaku is mostly 'leave footprints', 'thank you', 'meaning is not finished' and so on. We can see that the user's sentiment tendencies tend to focus on positive emotions at the beginning and end, especially at the end of the video to express gratitude and hospitality. The sentiment intensity of this anime movie is the same as that of most of the videos described in the previous section.

Analysis of the Intents' Sentiment Trend. We draw the sentiment curve corresponding to six user intents to achieve fine-grained sentiment analysis. We observe that the fluctuation of the questioning curve (netural-q) in 'An Introduction to Python' is obviously larger than others. The sentiment trend is shown in Fig. 5.

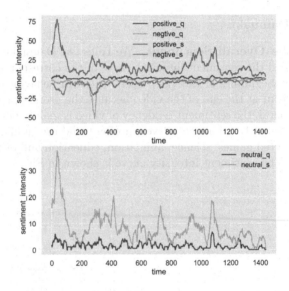

Fig. 5. The sentiment intensity curve of 'An Introduction to Python' corresponding to different intents.

"An Introduction to Python" is an educational video. Educational video is less interesting than other types of video, so until the end, the user's sentiment fluctuations are not large, there is no spike at the end. The negative emotions of educational videos are reflected in questions about what to learn. When the user does not understand the knowledge of the teacher, it will raise questions, and these questions reflect users' uncertainty about the knowledge points in the video.

5.2 Offline Danmaku

Analysis of the Overall Sentiment. Offline, we used USee, a Danmaku social system, to collect the offline Danmaku. The difference between party with USee and traditional evening party is that the audience can't have good interaction, the program can only be enjoyed by the audience and Danmaku provides a platform for the user to entertain the public, so that the audience can enjoy the stage program while being able to be used by other users. The release of content entertainment has increased the fun of the event.

Through the processing of Danmaku, Danmaku's emotions displayed at the two parties are positive. In addition, there will be a small climax at the end of the party, and users will send Danmaku to express their feelings about the programs in the events as shown in Fig. 6.

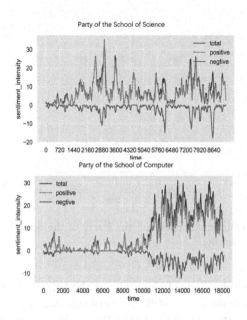

Fig. 6. The sentiment intensity curve of offline Danmaku.

Compared with 'the Party of the School of Computer Science' event, Danmaku of 'the Party of the School of Science' has a greater range and amplitude of emotions. Comparing the data of the two graduation parties, Danmaku's content reflects the quality of the program to a certain extent. At 2880 s seconds, Danmaku's positive emotions reached its peak. It can be seen that the effect of the School of Science is more exciting than that of the School of Literature. At 8640 s seconds, the negative emotions reached their peak, and the disappointing sentiment spread throughout the audience. The users sent Danmaku responses to interact with each other, and we can leverage the Danmaku to extract and analyze users' sentiment trend throughout the offline event.

Analysis of the Intents' Sentiment Curve. The experiment defined six kinds of Danmaku intents from three sentiment polarities and two Danmaku language types. It can be seen from the offline experiment that most of the Danmaku language types in the party are declarative sentences and the proportion of interrogative sentences is small; And the majority of descriptive sentences contain positive emotions. The curve is shown in Fig. 7.

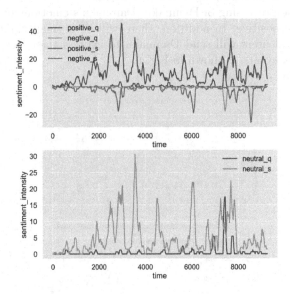

Fig. 7. The sentiment intensity curve of 'the Party of the School of Computer' corresponding to different intents.

By analyzing the emotions of Danmaku at the School of Science, you can see that the positive statements are still the overwhelming majority, and the climax corresponds to the beginning of the party, the finale program and the end of the party. These three moments are the most active and exciting moments for the users, respectively.

6   Conclusion

Nowadays, Danmaku has become one of main attraction for users to watch online video and attend offline events. This paper proposes a fine-grained intent classification model. Through this model, we can not only get the overall sentiment intensity of Danmaku, but also get the sentiment intensity with different fine-grained intents. We draw the sentiment intensity curve of Danmaku with the change of time and analyze the curve with user generated Danmaku content while watching online videos and attending offline events. The fine-grained sentiment curve can also reflect the audiences' intents in different segments. This study can be further studied to explore more relations between Danmaku and online videos and offline events.

References

1. Cha, J., Lee, J.: Extracting topic related keywords by backtracking CNN based text classifier. In: 2018 Joint 10th International Conference on Soft Computing and Intelligent Systems (SCIS) and 19th International Symposium on Advanced Intelligent Systems (ISIS), Toyama, Japan, December 5–8, 2018. pp. 93–96 (2018). https://doi.org/10.1109/SCIS-ISIS.2018.00026
2. Chen, Z., Tang, Y., Zhang, Z., Zhang, C., Wang, L.: Sentiment-aware short text classification based on convolutional neural network and attention. In: 31st IEEE International Conference on Tools with Artificial Intelligence, ICTAI 2019, Portland, OR, USA, November 4–6, pp. 1172–1179 (2019). https://doi.org/10.1109/ICTAI.2019.00162
3. Devlin, J., Chang, M., Lee, K., Toutanova, K.: BERT: pre-training of deep bidirectional transformers for language understanding. CoRR abs/1810.04805 (2018). http://arxiv.org/abs/1810.04805
4. Gan, C., Feng, Q., Zhang, Z.: Scalable multi-channel dilated cnn-bilstm model with attention mechanism for chinese textual sentiment analysis. Future Generation Computer Systems, vol. 118, pp. 297–309 (2021). https://doi.org/10.1016/j.future.2021.01.024 https://www.sciencedirect.com/science/article/pii/S0167739X21000340
5. Graves, A., Fernández, S., Schmidhuber, J.: Bidirectional LSTM networks for improved phoneme classification and recognition. In: Artificial Neural Networks: Formal Models and Their Applications - ICANN 2005, 15th International Conference, Warsaw, Poland, September, pp. 11–15, 2005, Proceedings, Part II, pp. 799–804 (2005). https://doi.org/10.1007/11550907_126.
6. Kim, Y.: Convolutional neural networks for sentence classification. In: Proceedings of the 2014 Conference on Empirical Methods in Natural Language Processing, EMNLP 2014(October), pp. 25–29, 2014. Doha, Qatar, A meeting of SIGDAT, a Special Interest Group of the ACL, pp. 1746–1751 (2014). https://www.aclweb.org/anthology/D14-1181/
7. Nasukawa, T., Yi, J.: Sentiment analysis: capturing favorability using natural language processing. In: Proceedings of the 2nd International Conference on Knowledge Capture (K-CAP 2003), October 23–25, 2003, Sanibel Island, FL, USA, pp. 70–77 (2003). https://doi.org/10.1145/945645.945658
8. Obiedat, R., et al.: Sentiment analysis of customers 'reviews using a hybrid evolutionary svm-based approach in an imbalanced data distribution. IEEE Access 10, 22260–22273 (2022). https://doi.org/10.1109/ACCESS.2022.3149482
9. Sun, Y., Li, J., Zhen, Y., Tang, Y., Hu, Q., He, L.: Usee: An online-offline hybrid danmaku social system. In: 22nd IEEE International Conference on Computer Supported Cooperative Work in Design, CSCWD 2018, Nanjing, China, May 9–11, 2018, pp. 253–258 (2018). https://doi.org/10.1109/CSCWD.2018.8465286
10. Tan, K.L., Lee, C.P., Anbananthen, K.S.M., Lim, K.M.: Roberta-lstm: a hybrid model for sentiment analysis with transformer and recurrent neural network. IEEE Access 10, 21517–21525 (2022). https://doi.org/10.1109/ACCESS.2022.3152828
11. Tang, Y.,et al.: Is danmaku an effective way for promoting event based social network? In: Proceedings of the 2017 ACM Conference on Computer Supported Cooperative Work and Social Computing, CSCW 2017, Portland, OR, USA, February 25 - March 1, 2017, Companion Volume, pp. 319–322 (2017), http://dl.acm.org/citation.cfm?id=3026347

12. Wang, Y., Huang, M., Zhu, X., Zhao, L.: Attention-based LSTM for aspect-level sentiment classification. In: Proceedings of the 2016 Conference on Empirical Methods in Natural Language Processing, EMNLP 2016, Austin, Texas, USA, November 1–4(2016), pp. 606–615, 2016. https://www.aclweb.org/anthology/D16-1058/
13. Wu, S., Liu, Y., Zou, Z., Weng, T.H.: S_i_lstm: stock price prediction based on multiple data sources and sentiment analysis. Connection Science **34**(1), 44–62 (2022). https://doi.org/10.1080/09540091.2021.1940101
14. Zhong, Y., Zhang, Z., Zhang, W., Zhu, J.: Bert-kg: a short text classification model based on knowledge graph and deep semantics. In: Wang, L., Feng, Y., Hong, Y., He, R. (eds.) Natural Lang. Process. Chinese Comput., pp. 721–733. Springer International Publishing, Cham (2021)
15. Zhu, Q., Jiang, X., Ye, R.: Sentiment analysis of review text based on bigru-attention and hybrid cnn. IEEE Access **9**, 149077–149088 (2021). https://doi.org/10.1109/ACCESS.2021.3118537

Ramp Merging of Connected Vehicle With Virtual Platooning Control

Yijia Guo[1], Wenhao Wang[1], Wang Chen[2], Chaozhe Han[1], and Yanjun Shi[1(✉)]

[1] School of Mechanical Engineering, Dalian University of Technology, Dalian 116024, China
{guoyijia,wangwenhao,hcz0613}@mail.dlut.edu.cm, syj@dlut.edu.cn
[2] China North Vehicle Research Institute, Beijing 100072, China

Abstract. Because the number of lanes in the expressway ramp area is reduced, and the ramp vehicles need to change lanes to join the main road, resulting in the merge area is prone to stop and congestion, which is the bottleneck area affecting the road capacity. Intelligent connected vehicles with strong detection and perception and network interaction ability can effectively cooperate with traffic participants, to achieve effective regulation of traffic flow. This paper mainly constructs the scenario of ramp merging of intelligent networked vehicles. The ramp area is divided into the pre-merge area, speed adjustment area, and import area, and the optimization mechanism based on the event trigger is applied. Based on the ramp scenario above, the virtual formation merging control method is applied in this paper. Finally, SUMO, a traffic simulation controller, is used to construct the ramp scenario, and the virtual formation-based merging method is verified in the full CAV scenario. Simulation results show that the proposed method can effectively reduce vehicle traffic delay and improve road throughput.

Keywords: Intelligent connected vehicle · Ramp confluence · Virtual formation

1 Introduce

The development of China's logistics industry highly depends on the construction of high-speed roads and the innovation of transport vehicles. The development of high-level smart roads and advanced automatic driving technology will greatly promote the development of related industries. With the introduction of China's transportation power policy [1], more and more researchers begin to pay attention to relevant studies on intelligent transportation. Among them, the research and development of intelligent connected vehicles are particularly important.

In the full CAV scenario, there are two kinds of ramp merging methods which are based on rules and based on optimization. The rule-based merging methods mainly include the following: Awal, Tanveer et al. [2] studied the strategy of vehicle flow merging based on a right-rotation rule, optimized the overall time of vehicle merging, and improved the performance of energy consumption, road capacity, and average speed at the cost of slightly increasing the traveling time of vehicles on the main road. Lv Lingling [3] studied the merging method based on auxiliary vehicles. Through a reasonable

Y. Sun et al. (Eds.): ChineseCSCW 2022, CCIS 1681, pp. 207–216, 2023.
https://doi.org/10.1007/978-981-99-2356-4_17

selection of auxiliary vehicles, the on-ramp vehicles can safely merge into the main road and eliminate the stop-and-go wave in the crowded traffic flow. Optimization methods are also studied by numerous scholars: Pei, Huaxin et al. [4] apply dynamic programming to solve the calculation of optimal pass order, and obtain the global optimal pass order by defining state space, state transition conditions, and evaluation function under the time complexity of two. Haigen Min et al. [5] proposed the passing time allocation of multiple vehicles based on complete information static game, and selected its strategy by calculating the mixed strategy Nash equilibrium of a single-vehicle. Aiming at total fuel consumption and total travel time, the Pontryagin minimization principle is applied to obtain the vehicle trajectory.

Based on the vehicle-road cooperative system, this paper studies the intelligent network vehicle-road combined traffic flow, adopt the movement of virtual formation of vehicles to merge ramp traffic flow, and verifies the proposed cooperation method with vehicle-road simulation software.

2   Ramp Merging Algorithm Based on the Virtual Formation

2.1   Combined Zoning and Model Assumptions

According to the characteristics of the ramp area, this paper divides the ramp area into three parts, namely, the premerger area, the speed adjustment area, and the import area, as shown in Fig. 1. The function of the pre-merge area is to plan the merging sequence of vehicles in the area. The main road is $[\gamma_0, \gamma_1]$ area, and the ramp is $[\gamma'_0, \gamma'_1]$ area. The area $[\gamma_1, \gamma_2]$ is the speed adjustment area, where vehicles will perform the merge sequence and form a safe merge spacing; Ramp vehicles will change lanes and merge at the entry zone of $[\gamma_2, \gamma_3]$. Both the pre-merging zone and the speed adjusting zone belong to the merging zone, and the CAV movement in the merging zone is completely controlled by the ramp merging system. After the import zone, the control of CAV will be gradually transferred to the vehicle itself until the vehicle exits the import zone. Based on this scenario, this paper makes the following assumptions:

(1) The main lane and ramp are single-lane, and vehicles are prohibited to overtake and change lanes except for the inflow zone;
(2) The speed range of vehicles in the main lane is 80–100 km /h;
(3) The speed range of on-ramp vehicles is 60–80 km/h;
(4) The vehicle speed adjustment in the speed adjustment zone, so that the speed difference of the driver ramp is reduced;
(5) Ramp vehicles change lanes in the import area, and merge with the main road vehicles;
(6) At any time, only one vehicle on the ramp and the main lane passes through the merging point, and vehicles before and after the merging point need to keep a safe distance;
(7) In this paper, the lateral movement model is not considered in the confluence area, that is, the lane-changing model is not considered, and lane changing is prohibited for vehicles on the main ramp in this area. In the merging area, time is allocated for vehicles to pass through the merging area to create enough lane change clearance for vehicles. Vehicles are free to change lanes after entering the intake zone.

(8) Due to the rapid development of Internet of vehicles technology, packet loss rate and delay in the process of information transmission have decreased significantly. Therefore, communication delay and packet loss will not be considered in this paper.

2.2 Optimization of Traffic Order in the Pre-merge Area

The purpose of solving the passage order is to arrange the time for the vehicles on the main ramp to pass through the speed adjustment zone, ensure the safe spacing of vehicles, and improve the traffic density and speed as much as possible. Therefore, this paper considers modeling it as an optimization problem, to minimize the time for all vehicles to pass through the speed adjustment zone. When defining the objective function, this paper will first define the expected arrival time of the vehicle, as shown in Formula (1) and (2).

$$
t_{min}^{main} = \frac{v_{max}^{main} - v_i}{a_{max}} + \frac{L_{all} - x_{cur} - \frac{v_{max}^{main^2} - v_i^2}{2a_{max}}}{v_{max}} \tag{1}
$$

$$
t_{min}^{ramp} = \frac{v_{max}^{ramp} - v_i}{a_{max}} + \frac{L_{ramp} - x_{cur} - \frac{v_{max}^{ramp^2} - v_i^2}{2a_{max}}}{v_{max}^{ramp}}
$$

$$
+ \frac{v_{max}^{main} - v_{max}^{ramp}}{a_{max}} + \frac{L_{main} - \frac{v_{max}^{main^2} - v_{max}^{ramp^2}}{2a_{max}}}{v_{max}^{main}} \tag{2}
$$

x_{cur} is the current length of the vehicle through the pre-consolidation area, L_{all} is the length of $[\gamma_0, \gamma_2]$, The vehicle first passes through maximum acceleration to reach the maximum speed limit v_{max}^{main}, Maximum ramp speed v_{max}^{ramp}, And maintain the ramp speed limit after entering the speed adjustment zone.

(1) Velocity and acceleration constraints

The operation of the vehicle in any area must comply with the road speed limit and its acceleration and deceleration capacity. This constraint is reflected in time, namely, the time t_{min} when the vehicle passes through the corresponding area at the highest speed mode and the time t_{max} when the vehicle passes through the area at the lowest speed shown in the formula. The constraints obtained are shown in Formula (3) and (4).

$$
t_{max}^{main} = \frac{v_i - v_{min}^{main}}{d_{max}} + \frac{L_{all} - x_{cur} - \frac{v_i^2 - v_{min}^{main^2}}{2a_{max}}}{v_{min}^{main}} \tag{3}
$$

$$
t_{max}^{ramp} = \frac{v_i - v_{min}^{ramp}}{d_{max}} + \frac{L_{all} - x_{cur} - \frac{v_i^2 - v_{min}^{ramp^2}}{2a_{max}}}{v_{min}^{ramp}} \tag{4}
$$

$$
t_{access}^i \leq t_{max}^i, \quad i = 0, \ldots, k
$$

$$
t_{max}^i \leq t_{access}^i, \quad i = 0, \ldots, k
$$

(2) Constraint of safe workshop distance

In the case of safety factors, the safe time interval $t_{gap}^1 = 1s$ considered in literature [5] is adopted in this paper, and the safe workshop distance constraint shown in Formula (5) is obtained.

$$t_{access}^i - t_{access}^{i-1} \geq t_{gap}^1, i = 0, \ldots, k \tag{5}$$

(3) Constraints on safe lane change

Vehicles in different lanes need to maintain a safe longitudinal workshop distance. Therefore, this paper considers the safe lane change time interval as $t_{gap}^2 = 1.5\,s$, , and obtains the lane change constraint as shown in (6).

$$t_{access}^n - t_{access}^m \geq t_{gap}^2, n = 0, \ldots, Nm = 0, \ldots, M \tag{6}$$

Based on the continuous decision variable t_{access}, a Boolean decision variable $Order_{ij}$ is added in this paper, which will represent the sequence of vehicles entering the import area. At the same time, this paper applies big-M method to obtain the mixed-integer linear programming model as shown in Formulas (7)–(13):

$$\min \sum_{i=0}^{k} t_{access}^i - t_{min}^i \cdot i = 0, \ldots, k \tag{7}$$

$$s.t.$$

$$t_{access}^i \leq t_{max}^i, i = 0, \ldots, k \tag{8}$$

$$t_{min}^i \leq t_{access}^i, i = 0, \ldots, k \tag{9}$$

$$t_{access}^i - t_{access}^{i-1} \geq t_{gap}^1 \tag{10}$$

$$t_{access}^n - t_{access}^m + M \cdot Order_{nm} \geq t_{gap}^2 \tag{11}$$

$$t_{access}^m - t_{access}^n + M \cdot (1 - Order_{nm}) \geq t_{gap}^2 \tag{12}$$

$$Order_{nm} = \begin{cases} 0, t_{access}^n > t_{access}^m \\ 1, \; else \end{cases} \tag{13}$$

The passing Order of vehicles can be obtained by judging the Boolean value of $Order_{ij}$.

2.3 Merging Method of Virtual Formation in the Inbound Area

After the adjustment of the speed adjustment area, safe space and time-space between vehicles will be formed. At the front end of the intake zone, ramp traffic will merge into the main lane. This paper applies the import method based on virtual formation, as shown in Fig. 1. The ramp merging system maps the ramp vehicle to the main lane when the vehicle enters the inflow area and assigns its following relation according to the position relation. According to the mapping relation between vehicles and the relative distance, it can effectively control the speed of the vehicle.

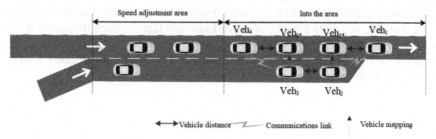

Fig. 1. Virtual formation method schematic

3 Simulation and Analysis of Ramp Confluence

3.1 Ramp Confluence Simulation Scenario Construction

This paper adopts SUMO [6] to construct a two-lane ramp convergence scenario. SUMO is an open-source micro traffic simulation software that enables detailed modeling of traffic elements, including traffic networks, vehicles, detectors, and more.

SUMO simulation of ramp confluence scenarios requires the following files: road network data (*.net. Xml files), traffic data (*.rou. Xml files), detector data (*.add. Xml), and simulation configuration files (*.sumocfg files).Traffic Control Interface (Traci) is an important Interface for SUMO to be coupled with external software. The Traci uses the TCP protocol on the server and client to provide external software with access to the SUMO. Traci provides data access to traffic participants. For example, the status of vehicles and detectors in the current simulation step can be read by ID. Traci also supports asynchronous control of the state of the traffic actor described above. In this paper, asynchronous simulation control is carried out with SUMO through the Traci library in Python.

4 Simulation Results and Analysis of All CAV Scenarios

This section first verifies the ramp merging method based on virtual formation in the full CAV scenario and compares it with the unregulated scenario to verify the effectiveness of the algorithm. The traffic density of the whole CAV scenario is unified: 1600 cars/h in the main lane and 800 cars/h in the ramp. The step size of the simulation is set as 0.01s and the simulation ends at 200 s. In the non-control scenario, this paper uses the detector and Traci interface to track the data of each vehicle.

In the unregulated experiment, the passage delay of vehicles is calculated first, that is, the actual arrival time of vehicles minus the shortest time of vehicles arriving at the arrival point. Due to the failure of on-ramp traffic arrival time regulation in the acceleration lane, there is a lack of appropriate merging time when the on-ramp traffic enters the main lane, and vehicles need to slow down at the end of the acceleration lane to wait for the opportunity. At the same time, in the process of ramping vehicles into, because of turning and waiting for lane changing factors such as time, the import rate is low, causing traffic generation, causing subsequent main vehicle deceleration to form a safe distance, triggered a merge area blockage, and that the more frequently it back, make the main passage of the vehicle delay increase gradually, as shown in Fig. 2. With the accumulation of time, frequent acceleration and deceleration can easily lead to a decrease in regional average speed.

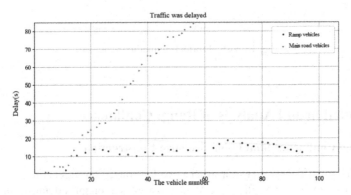

Fig. 2. Traffic delay for vehicles in the combined area

In the control scenario, the simulation will enable the merging method based on virtual formation to allocate appropriate passing time for all vehicles. Due to the safe arrival time difference of each vehicle, the huge delay difference of the main ramp in the unregulated scene can be improved. In the simulation, 106 vehicles passed in 200 s with an average delay of 3.16 s, including 70 vehicles on the main road with an average delay of 3.55 s and 37 vehicles on the ramp with an average delay of 2.41 s. Compared with the unregulated scenario, both main lane and on-ramp vehicles are significantly reduced, and the delay does not superimpose backward, as shown in Fig. 3.

At the same time, the average speed of vehicles in each sub-area increased significantly, especially the average speed of the main lane merging area and main lane speed adjustment area. In the speed adjustment zone, vehicles will speed first. In this zone, vehicles on the main road realize smooth speed change through the Hamiltonian function, so their average speed curve is the most stable. When the vehicle reaches the inflow zone, the speed has been adjusted to 25 m/s, which improves the overall speed of

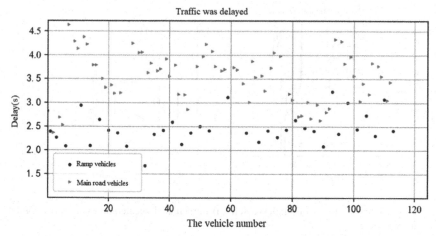

Fig. 3. Traffic delay at the regulated main ramp

the region. Therefore, the intersection of the average speed in the inflow zone is more consistent with the speed without adjustment.

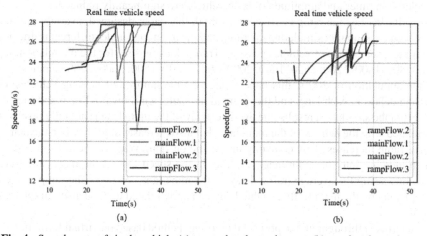

Fig. 4. Speed curve of single-vehicle (a) unregulated speed curve, (b) regulated speed curve

Figure 4(a) shows the real-time speed curves of Rampflow.2, Main flow.1, Main-flow.2, and RampFlow.3 without adjustment. It can be found that the last three vehicles decelerate first and then increase near the inflow area, especially rampflow.3 of ramp vehicles has a large range. Figure 4(b) shows the speed curve after speed adjustment. The on-ramp vehicle first reaches the road speed limit of 22.22 m/s in the pre-merge area, and the Hamiltonian function is applied to accelerate smoothly in the speed adjustment area, and the speed is 25 m/s when reaching the exit of the speed adjustment area. After that, ramp flow ramp vehicle enters the inflow area and enters the lane, leading to the deceleration of ramp flow1 rampflow.2 and rampflow.3 of main lane vehicles, but their

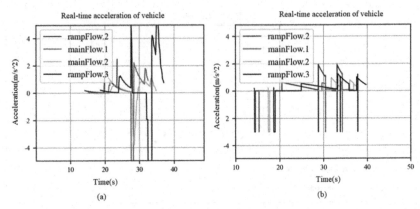

Fig. 5. Acceleration curves of single-vehicle (a) unregulated acceleration curve, (b) regulated acceleration curve

deceleration amplitude is significantly reduced. This means that the ramp merging algorithm proposed in this paper can effectively coordinate traffic flow and optimize vehicle trajectory. Figure 5(b) shows the acceleration curves of the above four vehicles after regulation. Compared with Fig. 5(a) in the non-regulation scenario, the acceleration and deceleration times and amplitude of each vehicle are significantly reduced.

To further test the ramp confluence method, this paper designed a variety of traffic flow scenarios, mainly simulating the ramp and the main road under different traffic densities and proportions of vehicles passing. Traffic density is set for the main lane-ramp: 1600–800, 1600–1200, 1600–1600, 2000–1000, 2000–1500, 2000–2000 vehicles/hour. In the simulation of 200 s, this paper compares the number of passing vehicles and passing delays in each lane, and the simulation results are shown in Fig. 6 and Fig. 7.

From the simulation results, the average delay of the main lane is not only positively correlated with the density of the main lane, but also increases slightly when the density of the ramp increases. This is mainly due to the on-ramp vehicles' need to slow down when merging into the main lane, resulting in the speed loss of the main lane traffic flow, increasing the average traffic delay of the main lane vehicles. The ramp traffic is not affected by the main traffic, so the delay is mainly related to the density of the ramp traffic.

In terms of throughput, the proposed merging method based on virtual formation has an optimization bottleneck. When the traffic density is 1600–1200, the on-ramp vehicles passing through is about 1.5 times that in the 1600–800 scenario, and the capacity of vehicles passing through the main road is not affected. With the further increase of ramp traffic flow, the number of ramp vehicles is still improved, but the capacity of the main road vehicles is affected, from 69 to 55, which is to reach the optimization bottleneck. The main reason for this phenomenon is that the merging zone will be reduced from two

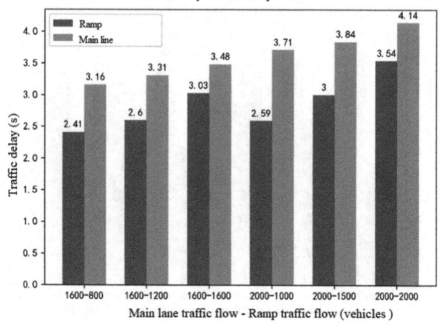

Fig. 6. Multi-vehicle flow density Vehicle passage delay in each lane

lanes to a single lane. Although the arrival sequence of vehicles is optimized in this paper, it is still required to keep an interval of 1s between vehicles in the same lane and 1.5 s between vehicles in different lanes, which will limit the passing capacity of the merging zone. According to the experimental data, when the total vehicle density exceeds 2800 vehicles/h, the optimization bottleneck will be reached, and the total number of vehicles passing at this time is about 119. Even in the simulation group with a higher traffic flow of 2000 vehicles/h on the main road, the total number of vehicles passing through does not change significantly, and the total number is about 120. When the traffic density exceeds the optimization bottleneck, the ramp merging algorithm based on virtual formation can still allocate the passage time for vehicles to ensure that vehicles can pass through the inflow area as soon as possible.

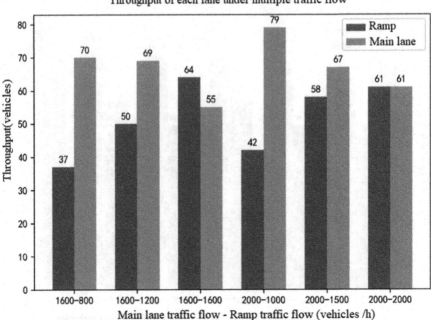

Fig. 7. Vehicle throughput in each lane with multiple traffic flow

Acknowledgement. This work was funded by China National Key Research and Development Program, grant number: NO.2018YFE0197700.

References

1. LNCS Homepage. http://www.gov.cn/zhengce/2019-09/19/content_5431432.htm, Accessed 19 Sept 2019
2. Awalt, T., Kulik, L., Ramamohanrao K.: Optimal traffic merging strategy for communication- and sensor-enabled vehicles: IEEE (2013)
3. Lv, L.: Research on confluence control method and Simulation of off-ramp in Vehicle network (2019)
4. Pei, H., Feng, S., Zhang, Y., et al.: A cooperative driving strategy for merging at on-ramps based on dynamic programming. IEEE Trans. Veh. Technol. **68**(12), 11646–11656 (2019)
5. Min, H., Fang, Y., Wu, X., et al.: On-ramp merging strategy for connected and automated vehicles based on complete information static game. J. Traffic Transport. Eng. (English Edition) **8**(4), 582–595 (2021)

Community Detection Based
on Enhancing Graph Autoencoder
with Node Structural Role

Ling Wu[1,2(✉)], Jinlong Yang[1,2], and Kun Guo[1,2,3]

[1] College of Computer and Data Science, Fuzhou University, Fuzhou 350108, China
{wuling1985,gukn}@fzu.edu.cn
[2] Fujian Key Laboratory of Network Computing and Intelligent Information,
Processing (Fuzhou University), Fuzhou 350108, China
[3] Key Laboratory of Spatial Data Mining and Information Sharing,
Ministry of Education, Fuzhou 350108, China

Abstract. The representation learning approach aims to obtain a low-dimensional representation of nodes and accomplish community detection by clustering. Adjacency matrix is the most common form of network representation, but it only represents the direct connection relationship of network nodes and lacks more useful topological information. Existing approaches, such as jaccard coefficient for topology extraction, are still limited to neighborhoods, and the available information is not rich enough. In addition, roles, another vital idea, lack a more profound application to network topology. This paper proposes a novel community detection algorithm based on enhancing graph autoencoder with node structural role (CDESR). On the one hand, the structural role we designed effectively specifies the importance of nodes in the network. Based on this idea, a new strategy for computing node topological relations is proposed for their information extraction. On the other hand, the enhancement matrix constructed using the extracted rich information efficiently optimizes the graph autoencoder to obtain a high-quality representation. The experimental results on real-world and synthetic networks verify the effectiveness of our algorithm.

Keywords: representing learning · community detection · structural role · graph autoencoder

1 Introduction

People, things, and objects in the real world are interconnected to form various complex networks, such as social networks, transportation networks, and co-authorship networks. Network nodes represent the entity, and edges represent their connection. The network can be viewed as consisting of many groups. They are tightly connected internally, while their connections are sparse; such a group is also known as a community [1]. Role [2] is another critical point of the network,

Y. Sun et al. (Eds.): ChineseCSCW 2022, CCIS 1681, pp. 217–231, 2023.
https://doi.org/10.1007/978-981-99-2356-4_18

which indicates the similarity of the connection structure of different nodes. As shown in Fig. 1, the nodes in the dashed box belong to the same community, while nodes of the same color have the same role.

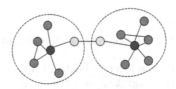

Fig. 1. An example of community and role

As the network structure becomes more complex, traditional community detection algorithms perform poorly, while traditional high-dimensional sparse data storage is not conducive to scaling to subsequent data mining tasks. Therefore, representation learning [3] has become an essential technical means. Network representation learning, also known as graph embedding, aims to map large-scale, high dimensional sparse networks into low-dimensional space and represent nodes with low dimensional and dense vectors to preserve the original network structural features as much as possible. The existing algorithms for network representation learning applied to community detection can be divided into three categories: the random walk-based [4,5], the matrix decomposition-based [6,7], and deep learning-based [8–11] methods. The deep learning-based method uses deep learning techniques to extract the network's high-dimensional nonlinear characteristics to learn the network's low-dimensional representation. Among deep learning-based methods, graph autoencoders are widely used. Although existing works have been quite successful, they still face some challenges. The sparsity of the adjacency matrix leads to poorly learned node representations. Despite the use of e.g. jaccard coefficient [12], the extraction of topological representations stays in the direct neighborhood. In addition, the idea of roles is not deeply extended to the mining of network topological information.

In this paper, we propose a community detection algorithm based on enhancing graph autoencoder with node structural role(CDESR) to solve the above problem. First, we design different structural roles to distinguish different connectivity patterns of nodes. Second, a node topological information extraction strategy is proposed to enrich the available representations in combination with the structural role. Third, we construct an enhancement matrix for the network to optimize the graph autoencoder for embedding learning. Finally, we feed them to K-Means to discover community structure. Our contributions can be summarized as follows.

1. The topological relationship extraction strategy based on structural roles can accurately capture the profound similarity between nodes and enrich the available information.

2. The enhancement matrix can effectively optimize the learning of graph autoencoder, improving network embedding quality.
3. We evaluate CDESR on several synthetic and real-world networks. Experimental results demonstrate that the proposed algorithm outperforms the compared algorithms in community detection.

2 Related Work

Label Propagation Algorithm(LPA) [13] is one of the classic community detection algorithms. Its core idea is to use the label with the most frequent occurrences of neighbor nodes as its label in the iterative process. When done, the labels of nodes in the same community tend to be the same. LPA is easy to implement, but the results are unstable and have poor robustness. Representation learning for community detection can be divided into the following three categories: random walk-based method, matrix decomposition-based method and deep learning-based method.

Random Walk-Based Method is inspired by Word2vec [14], a word vector training model in natural language processing. DeepWalk [4] captures the neighborhood structure features by random walks on the graph to obtain a node corpus. It is then fed into the Skip-Gram [14] model to maximize the probability of neighborhood nodes appearing around the target node to learn node embeddings. Node2vec [5] adds two parameters, p and q, to control walking, allowing richer structural information. The main challenge in this category is that the topology may not be fully captured due to randomness.

Matrix Decomposition-Based Method is to use techniques such as eigenvalue decomposition for feature extraction and dimensionality reduction to obtain the network representation matrix. GraRep [6] represents the node topology relations in the range of order k separately and then combines them to get the final representation. M-NMF [7] preserves community structure features for the network representation matrix by utilizing modularity constraints in the matrix decomposition process. The main challenge in this category is scalability because matrix decomposition is time-consuming.

Deep Learning-Based Method extracts network features by building deep nonlinear neural network models to learn high-quality embeddings. Among them, autoencoders are widely used. SDNE [9] uses a deep autoencoder combined with first-order and second-order structural similarity trained jointly to capture information about the nodes locally and globally to learn the node representation. Due to graph convolutional networks (GCN) [15], the graph autoencoder (GAE) [10] proposed by Kipf naturally exploits topological and attribute information. ARGA [11] proposed an adversarial regularization scheme to force potential vectors to match a priori distributions and learn robust representations with graph autoencoder. The main challenge in this category is the existence of overfitting problems.

3   CDESR Algorithm

The framework of CDESR is illustrated in Fig. 2. It consists of three main parts. First, we design the corresponding roles according to the structural connection pattern of the nodes to clarify their importance in the network. Second, we develop a strategy for extracting topological information between nodes based on roles. Specifically, we use label-based similarity calculation and region-center-based similarity calculation to reinforce similarity jointly. Third, we construct an enhancement matrix for the network and combine it with a graph autoencoder to obtain an optimized embedding. Finally, we use K-Means to get the community divisions.

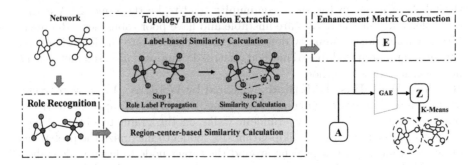

Fig. 2. Framework of CDESR

3.1   Preliminaries

In this section, we describe the definition of the designed roles and the associated judgments.

Definition 1 (Centrality). Suppose S_i is a sub-network formed by node i and its neighbors. The centrality of node i in S_i is defined as Eq.(1).

$$Ce_i = \frac{d_i}{\sum_{j \in S_i} d_j}, \tag{1}$$

where d_i, the degree of node i, reflects the connection of edges. For all edges of S_i, the more edges connecting node i with its neighbors occupy, the more central the status of node i become. Ce_i takes values in the range of $(0,0.5]$, and the larger the value, the more central the node is.

Definition 2 (Region). Suppose S_i is a sub-network formed by node i and its neighbors. If Re_i as defined below exceeds 1, we call S_i a region.

$$Re_i = \frac{|S_i|}{round(\sqrt{num}/2)}, \tag{2}$$

where round(*) denotes the rounded value, and num is the total number of network nodes. $round(\sqrt{num}/2)$ is the critical value of the region in different networks.

Definition 3 (Region-center Role). Suppose S_i is a sub-network formed by i and its neighbors. When S_i is a region and node i sufficient centrality, node i is defined as region-center role. In this paper, we set a threshold to filter the nodes with low centrality.

Definition 4 (Region-bridging Role). When a node connects more than one region-center, the node is defined as region-bridging role. It is at the boundary of multiple regions and plays a linking role in the network.

Definition 5 (Ordinary Role). A node that is neither region-center nor region-bridging is defined as ordinary role.

3.2 Node Structure Role Recognition

In real life, there is a phenomenon that both A and B are captains and play an essential role in team decision-making. Even though A and B belong to two teams, their roles at work are the same. There is a similar situation in the network; in terms of node structural connection, different patterns make the node have distinct influences and play different roles, which is crucial for network analysis. According to the definition given in the previous subsection, we judge centrality and region for a node, recognizing its role. We regard nodes corresponding to the three roles as region-center nodes, region-bridging nodes, and ordinary nodes, respectively, and they are next utilized.

3.3 Topology Information Extraction

In this section, we propose a topology information extraction strategy containing label-based similarity and region-center-based similarity calculation.

Label-Based Similarity Calculation. Traditional methods expresse the similarity of nodes by measuring the neighborhood and suffer from a local limitation. We apply label propagation(LP) to break this limitation and make the transmission of topological similarity effectively scalable. It includes the following two steps.

Step 1: Role Label Propagation. The traditional LP is to randomize the nodes to determine their order, but this ignores the influence and importance of the nodes in the network, making some unimportant nodes affect some important nodes, i.e., the "random backflow" situation. We use structural roles to improve LP and apply it more effectively.

The region-center node is at the center of the region, with significant influence, and the label is easy to spread here. The region-bridging node is at the junction of multiple regions, and frequent label changes are expected. The ordinary node has a weak influence, and the labels are susceptible to change by outside forces. Therefore, according to the impact and role of different roles, the node update order is re-established as follows:

Region-center Node > Region-center Neighbor Node > Ordinary Node > Region-Bridging Node

The above is a fundamental order. And for ordinary nodes, our algorithm particularly considers the internal order between them.

Definition 6 (Intimacy Score). The intimacy score measures the sum of the similarity of a node to all region-center nodes.

$$Ins(i) = \sum_{k=1}^{K} \frac{|N_i \cap N_k|}{|N_i \cup N_k|}, \tag{3}$$

where N_i is the set of node i's neighbors and N_k is the set of the kth region-center node's neighbors. Obviously, the closer a person is to essential people, the more likely they will influence him. So when an ordinary node is close to the region-center node in the network, it should have higher priority than other ordinary nodes. We eventually formed a fixed order of nodes and updated the labels uniformly according to this order during LP.

Step 2: Similarity Calculation. The LP determines the division result purely by one label during the final label selection, resulting in a heavy dependence on the label for accuracy and insufficient robustness. To improve robustness, We record multiple different labels that appear at a node during the iteration to form a label set. By considering the consistency of the label sets, the label-based similarity is proposed to express the similarity between nodes.

Definition 7 (Label-based Similarity). Label-based similarity is calculated in Eq. (4).

$$LS(i, j) = \frac{|L_i \cap L_j|}{\sqrt{|L_i| * |L_j|}}, \tag{4}$$

where L_* is the set of the node's all different labels. This steps beyond the local neighborhood and uses label propagation to extend the similarity comparison, enriching the topological information. Moreover, the label-based similarity expresses the topology more stably than traditional single-label selection.

Region-Center-Based Similarity Calculation. In many fields, qualitative analysis is an excellent statistical method that, unlike quantitative analysis, which requires accurate measurements, gives a relative result by comparison. Inspired by this, a new approach is proposed to relatively measuring the similarity between nodes.

Since the region-center node plays a vital role in the network, it is natural to consider it a third-party reference coordinate for measuring the proximity of two nodes. Assume that the network contains k region-center nodes. For node i, its cosine similarity to the k region-center nodes is computed and ordered to form two sequences, $slt(i)$ and $clt(i)$. $slt(i)$ denotes an ordered sequence of cosine similarity of length k, and $clt(i)$ is a sequence of the corresponding region-center nodes. clt shows the similarity between a node and each region-center node.

Definition 8 (Region-center-based Similarity). region-center-based similarity measures the similarity of two nodes in space relatively, as in Eq.(5).

$$RS(i,j) = \sum_{m=1}^{k} xnor\left(clt(i)_m, clt(j)_m\right) * \left(\frac{1}{k} + \frac{slt(i)_m + slt(j)_m}{2}\right), \quad (5)$$

where $slt(i)_m$ denotes the mth element of $slt(i)$, i.e., the cosine similarity value, and $clt(i)_m$ represents the mth element of $clt(i)$, i.e., a region-center node. $xnor$ denotes the "same or" operation: same is 1, different is 0.

We consider that if two nodes in the network are relatively close to each other, their similar relationship with region-center nodes should also be the same. This similarity is converted into a relative proximity measure by comparing the number of co-occurrence of region-center nodes in $clt(i)$ and $clt(j)$. The node pairs (a,b) and (a,c) have the same number of co-occurrence, but the co-occurring region-center nodes are not the same. To further differentiate, our algorithm also considers the similarity of nodes to the region-center node based on co-occurrence counts. This refined calculation then better measure the spatial similarity between nodes and enhance topological information.

3.4   Enhancement Matrix Construction

The network enhancement matrix E is defined by fusing label-based similarity calculation and region-center-based similarity calculation to extract the rich topological information between all node pairs. E is a matrix of size $n \times n$, n is the total number of nodes, and the calculation of any element e_{ij} in the matrix is shown in Eq.(6).

$$e_{ij} = \alpha * LS(i,j) + (1 - \alpha) * RS(i,j), \quad (6)$$

α is used to adjust the weight of two calculation methods.

3.5   Community Detection

The E matrix contains an enhanced expression of the network topology information. We combines graph autoencoder for representation learning with E to preserve the structure potential features for node embedding. It is encoded using graph convolutional network, see Eq.(7).

$$Z = GCN(X, A) = \tilde{A}\sigma\left(\tilde{A}XW_0\right)W_1, \quad (7)$$

where $\tilde{A} = D^{-\frac{1}{2}}AD^{-\frac{1}{2}}$, D is the diagonal node degree matrix of A, W_0 and W_1 are the weights to be trained, and σ is the ReLu activation function. A is the adjacency matrix, X is the attribute matrix but is represented as an identity matrix in the attributeless network and does not contain any valid topological information; here, E from above is used instead, and the new encoding is given in Eq.(8):

$$Z = GCN(E, A) = \tilde{A}\sigma\left(\tilde{A}EW_0\right)W_1, \tag{8}$$

We uses reconstructed cross-entropy as the loss function, calculated in Eq.(9).

$$L = -\frac{1}{N}\sum y\log\hat{y} + (1-y)\log(1-\hat{y}), \tag{9}$$

where y represents the value of an element in the adjacency matrix A and $\hat{y}$ represents the value of the corresponding element in the reconstructed adjacency matrix $\hat{A}$, the closer the reconstructed graph is to the original graph, the smaller the loss.

4   Experiments

To verify the performance of the CDESR algorithm, we conduct experiments on synthetic and real-world networks.

4.1   Datasets

Synthetic Networks. The synthetic networks are generated using the currently popular tool LFR [16]. Networks generated by LFR are close to the natural distribution and contain known community structures. By adjusting the parameters, LFR generates two network groups. The parameters of LFR are given in Table 1 and the details of synthetic networks are shown in Table 2.

Table 1. Parameters of LFR

Parameter	Description
N	number of nodes
k	average degree
kmax	maximum degree
cmin	minimum community size
cmax	maximum community size
μ	mixing parameter

Table 2. Synthetic networks

Network	Configuration
D1	N=100~3000, k=20, kmax=50, cmin=10, cmax=100, μ=0.2

Real-World Networks. The real-world networks include two social networks Karate and Dolphin, the match relationship network Football, the political book network Polbooks, and the email network Email-Eu. The descriptions of real-world networks are present in Table 3.

Table 3. Real-World networks

dataset	nodes	edges	communities
Karate	34	78	2
Dolphin	62	159	2
Football	115	613	12
Polbooks	105	441	3
Email-EU	1005	25571	42

4.2   Baseline Algorithms

In experiments, seven algorithms were selected as baselines for comparison. LPA and Louvain are traditional community detection algorithms. DeepWalk, SDNE, NetMF [17], ARGA and SDCN [18] are representation learning algorithms.

1. LPA: The algorithm is a semi-supervised method, and it uses the label information of labeled nodes to predict the label information of unlabeled nodes.
2. Louvain: The algorithm is based on multilevel optimization, aiming to maximize the entire network's modularity.
3. DeepWalk: The algorithm uses random walks to generate a sequence of nodes and then feeds them into the Skip-Gram model to train the node representation.
4. SDNE: The algorithm uses an autoencoder structure to optimize both 1st and 2nd order similarity, and the vector representations learned are able to preserve both local and global structures.
5. NetMF: The algorithm proves the theoretical connection between DeepWalk and implicit matrix decomposition then improves the matrix for representation learning.
6. ARGA: The adversarial restriction is added to the GAE such that the generated node representations match a prior Gaussian distribution.
7. SDCN: The algorithm combines the advantages of autoencoder and GCN and integrates structural information into deep clustering.

4.3   Evaluation Metrics

Normalized Mutual Information(NMI) [19] and Modularity [20] are adopted as evaluation in experiments.

Normalized Mutual Information(NMI) measures the quality of community detection by calculating the difference between divided communities and real communities. The closer the NMI value is to 1, the more effective the algorithm is.

$$NMI = \frac{-2\sum_{i=1}^{C_A}\sum_{j=1}^{C_B} H_{ij} \log\left(\frac{H_{ij} \times N}{H_{i\cdot} \times H_{\cdot j}}\right)}{\sum_{i=1}^{C_A} H_{i\cdot} \log\left(\frac{H_{i\cdot}}{N}\right) + \sum_{j=1}^{C_B} H_{\cdot j} \log\left(\frac{H_{\cdot j}}{N}\right)}, \tag{10}$$

A and B are the real community division and the algorithmic community division, respectively, and C_A and C_B represent the number of communities. H is a mixing matrix, $H_{i\cdot}$ is the sum of the elements of the ith row, and $H_{\cdot j}$ is the sum of the elements of the jth column. H_{ij} represents the number of nodes in the same community under both divisions, and N is the total number of nodes.

Modularity is a metric that evaluates the quality of the segmentation structure; a higher value of Modularity indicates a tighter internal structure of the segmented community. The Modularity equation is as below.

$$Q = \frac{1}{2m} \sum_{uv} \left(A_{uv} - \frac{d_u d_v}{2m}\right) \delta\left(C_u, C_v\right), \tag{11}$$

where m denotes the total number of edges in the network, A is the adjacency matrix, d_* is the node degree, C_u and C_v denote the community belonging to nodes u and v, respectively, and $\delta\left(C_u, C_v\right)$ denotes the probability that nodes u and v belong to the same community.

4.4 Parameter Settings

For CDESR, the maximum number of iterations for label propagation is set to 200, other parameters are determined by parameter experiments. For baseline algorithms, we use the default parameter settings shown in their paper.

4.5 Parameter Experiment

The CDESR algorithm includes three parameters: t, α, and d. In this section we will specify them and conduct experiments to explore their effects.

parameter t. The parameter t acts as a threshold to control the screening of the centrality of nodes, and Fig. 3 shows the experimental results.

As shown in Fig. 3, when $t < 0.3$, the restriction of centrality is weak, resulting in unimportant nodes becoming the region-centers and reducing the accuracy. When $t > 0.3$, the limitation of centrality is gradually strengthened, and valuable region-centers are filtered, leading to the algorithm's poor performance. Therefore, we set t at 0.3 in the remaining experiments.

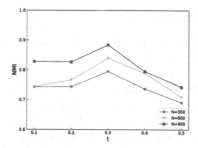

Fig. 3. NMI values with varying values of t.

parameter α. The enhancement matrix takes into account label-based similarity and region-center-based similarity. In Eq.(6), the value of parameter α controls the weight of two calculations. To find the best effect of α, we analyze the variation of *NMI*, and the results are shown in Fig. 4.

In Fig. 4, the *NMI* value steadily increase to reach the peak and then slowly decrease, indicating that the fusion of label-based similarity and region-center-based similarity achieves the best results when α equals 0.55, and the extracted topological information is best presented. Therefore, the parameter α is equal to 0.55 in the subsequent experiments.

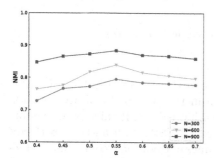

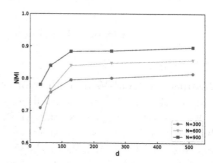

Fig. 4. NMI values with varying values of α.

Fig. 5. NMI values with varying values of d.

parameter d. The network representation learning uses low-dimensional vectors to represent nodes, so the effect of vector dimension cannot be ignored. The experiment is carried out on network with different d, and the change of *NMI* is shown in Fig. 5.

In Fig. 5, when d is less than 128, the *NMI* value show a significant increase with the enlargement of the vector dimension, as this alleviates the loss of node features. When d exceeds 128, the metric rises slightly and slowly until it eventually plateaus approximately. In summary, 128-dimension would be able to retain the original information well. Therefore, in the subsequent experiments, the dimension d equals 128.

4.6 Accuracy Experiment

We compared the accuracy of CDESR with baseline algorithms on the synthetic and real-world networks, and the results are presented in Fig. 6 and Table 4.

Results on Synthetic Networks. Figure 6 shows the NMI and Q results of the algorithms on the synthetic networks. As shown in Fig 6, CDESR achieves the highest accuracy value compared to all baseline algorithms. It is because CDESR incorporates roles to highlight critical nodes in the network. In addition, our proposed two similarity calculations can effectively enhance the extraction of topological information between nodes. Based on such a strategy, the constructed enhancement matrix usefully improves the quality of the learned embeddings.

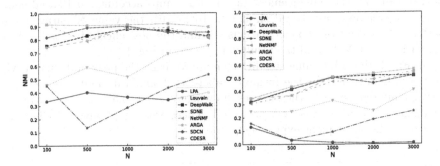

Fig. 6. NMI and Q results on synthetic networks

Results on Real-World Networks. As can be seen from Table 4, CDESR achieves the highest values in all evaluation metrics except Email-Eu network. In Karate, CDESR, SDCN, and ARGA all achieve an NMI value of 1, dividing the communities precisely as they actually are. CDESR significantly outperforms Louvain and LPA, which shows the shortcomings of traditional community detection algorithms in coping with complex networks. Although CDESR is not as accurate as the SDCN algorithm in Email-Eu networks, it also produces better results than other baseline algorithms, proving that the enhancement matrix effectively enhances the extraction of topological information and facilitates community detection.

4.7 Ablation Study

In this section, we evaluate the effectiveness of the proposed strategy. The label-based similarity calculation is abbreviated as LSC, and the region-center-based similarity calculation is abbreviated as RSC. As in Fig. 7, '-' represents removing a particular calculation from CDESR. CDESR-RSC achieves reasonable results, while CDESR-LSC consistently deteriorates performance. CDESR performs the best, with an average gain of 12% in *NMI*. This is because community detection

Table 4. NMI and Q results on real-world networks

dataset	metric	LPA	Louvain	DeepWalk	SDNE	NetMF	ARGA	SDCN	CDESR
Karate	NMI	0.6201	0.6319	0.7307	0.5852	0.5115	**1.0000**	**1.0000**	**1.0000**
	Q	0.2918	0.2633	0.3450	0.1722	0.2673	**0.3733**	**0.3733**	**0.3733**
Dophin	NMI	0.7005	0.5014	0.8141	0.5438	**0.8888**	0.6146	**0.8888**	**0.8888**
	Q	0.2586	0.2031	0.3547	0.2867	0.3487	0.3707	**0.3787**	**0.3787**
Football	NMI	0.6733	0.8885	0.8916	0.7003	0.9181	0.8295	0.9224	**0.9245**
	Q	0.4937	0.5044	0.5689	0.3315	0.5469	0.5069	0.5819	**0.5881**
Polbooks	NMI	0.5286	0.5385	0.5783	0.3492	0.5359	0.5044	0.4294	**0.5950**
	Q	0.4252	0.2872	0.5000	0.2020	0.4815	0.5062	0.4646	**0.5153**
Email-EU	NMI	0.2021	0.2504	0.3531	0.3920	0.1166	0.3719	**0.4164**	0.4031
	Q	0.0630	0.0412	0.0670	0.0766	0.0461	0.0682	**0.0888**	0.0836

is essentially graph clustering, where the similarity has a dominant effect on clustering. Therefore, the experimental results validate the effectiveness of the combination of LSC and RSC.

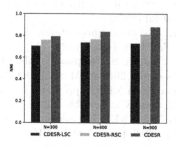

Fig. 7. Ablation study

5   Conclusion

This study proposes community detection algorithm based on enhancing graph autoencoder with node structural role. CDESR can recognize the roles of network nodes to clarify their importance. Also, based on role, it creatively develops two similarity calculations and effectively fuses them for topological information extraction to enrich the available representations. Furthermore, the enhancement matrix we construct can enhance the quality of network embedding. Theoretical analysis and experiments show that our proposed algorithm can effectively improve the accuracy of community detection. In the future, we plan to extend CDESR to dynamic networks to improve its practicality.

Acknowledgement. This work was supported in part by the National Natural Science Foundation of China under Grant 62002063, in part by the Fujian Natural Science Funds under Grant 2020J05112, in part by the Funds of Fujian Provincial Department of Education under Grant JAT190026, and in part by the Fuzhou University under Grant 510872/GXRC-20016, the National Natural Science Foundation of China under Grant No. 62002063 and No. U21A20472, in part by the National Key Research and Development Plan of China under Grant No. 2021YFB3600503, in part by the Fujian Collaborative Innovation Center for Big Data Applications in Governments, in part by the Fujian Industry-Academy Cooperation Project under Grant No. 2018H6010, in part by the Natural Science Foundation of Fujian Province under Grant No. 2020J05112, in part by the Fujian Provincial Department of Education under Grant No. JAT190026, in part by the Major Science and Technology Project of Fujian Province under Grant No.2021HZ022007 and Haixi Government Big Data Application Cooperative Innovation Center and the China Scholarship Council under Grant 202006655008.

References

1. Girvan, M., Newman, M.E.: Community structure in social and biological networks. Proc. Natl. Acad. Sci. **99**(12), 7821–7826 (2002)
2. Lorrain, F., White, H.C.: Structural equivalence of individuals in social networks. J. Math. Sociol. **1**(1), 49–80 (1971)
3. Mohan, A., Pramod, K.: Network representation learning: Models, methods and applications. SN Appl. Sci. **1**(9), 1–23 (2019)
4. Perozzi, B., Al-Rfou, R., Skiena, S.: Deepwalk: Online learning of social representations. In: Proceedings of the 20th ACM SIGKDD International Conference on Knowledge Discovery and Data Mining, pp. 701–710 (2014)
5. Grover, A., Leskovec, J.: node2vec: Scalable feature learning for networks. In: Proceedings of the 22nd ACM SIGKDD International Conference on Knowledge Discovery and Data Mining, 2016, pp. 855–864 (2016)
6. Cao, S., Lu, W., Xu, Q.: Grarep: Learning graph representations with global structural information," In: Proceedings of the 24th ACM International on Conference on Information and Knowledge Management, 2015, pp. 891–900 (2015)
7. Wang, X., Cui, P., Wang, J., Pei, J., Zhu, W., Yang, S.: Community preserving network embedding. In: Thirty-First AAAI Conference on Artificial Intelligence (2017)
8. Cao, S., Lu, W., Xu, Q.: Deep neural networks for learning graph representations. In: Proceedings of the AAAI Conference on Artificial Intelligence, vol. 30, no. 1 (2016)
9. Wang, D., Cui, P., Zhu, W.: Structural deep network embedding. In: Proceedings of the 22nd ACM SIGKDD International Conference on Knowledge Discovery and Data Mining, 2016, pp. 1225–1234 (2016)
10. Kipf, T.N., Welling, M.: Variational graph auto-encoders. arXiv preprint arXiv:1611.07308 (2016)
11. Pan, S., Hu, R., Long, G., Jiang, J., Yao, L., Zhang, C.: Adversarially regularized graph autoencoder for graph embedding. In: Proceedings of the 32th International Joint Conference on Artificial Intelligence, 2018, pp. 2609–2615 (2018)
12. Jaccard, P.: Étude comparative de la distribution florale dans une portion des alpes et des jura. Bull. Soc. Vaudoise Sci. Nat. **37**, 547–579 (1901)
13. Raghavan, U.N., Albert, R., Kumara, S.: Near linear time algorithm to detect community structures in large-scale networks. Phys. Rev. E **76**(3), 036106 (2007)

14. Mikolov, T., Chen, K., Corrado, G., Dean, J.: Efficient estimation of word representations in vector space. arXiv preprint arXiv:1301.3781, (2013)
15. Kipf, T.N., Welling, M.: Semi-supervised classification with graph convolutional networks. arXiv preprint arXiv:1609.02907 (2016)
16. Lancichinetti, A., Fortunato, S., Radicchi, F.: Benchmark graphs for testing community detection algorithms. Phys. Rev. E **78**(4), 046110 (2008)
17. Qiu, J., Dong, Y., Ma, H., Li, J., Wang, K., Tang, T.: Network embedding as matrix factorization: Unifying deepwalk, line, pte, and node2vec. In: Proceedings of the eleventh ACM international conference on web search and data mining, 2018, pp. 459–467 (2018)
18. Bo, D., Wang, X., Shi, C., Zhu, M., Lu, E., Cui, P.: Structural deep clustering network. In: Proceedings of The Web Conference, 2020, pp. 1400–1410 (2020)
19. Danon, L., Diaz-Guilera, A., Duch, J., Arenas, A.: Comparing community structure identification. J. Stat. Mech: Theory Exp. **2005**(09), P09008 (2005)
20. Newman, M.E.: Modularity and community structure in networks. Proc. Natl. Acad. Sci. **103**(23), 8577–8582 (2006)

Representation of Chinese-Vietnamese Bilingual News Topics Based on Heterogeneous Graph

Zhilei He[1,2], Enchang Zhu[1,2], Zhengtao Yu[1,2], Shengxiang Gao[1,2(✉)], Yuxin Huang[1,2], and Linjie Xia[1,2]

[1] Kunming University of Science and Technology, Kunming 650504, China
gaoshengxiang.yn@foxmail.com
[2] Key Laboratory of Artificial Intelligence in Yunnan Province, Kunming 650504, China

Abstract. The Chinese-Vietnamese bilingual news topic representations are generated from Chinese-Vietnamese bilingual news texts describing the same topic into concise Chinese sentences that can correctly describe the topic. However, there is a semantic gap between Chinese and Vietnamese, and the association relationship between multiple documents in multiple languages is complicated, which makes it challenging to generate concise and correct topic representations. In this paper, we propose a cross-language topic representation method based on heterogeneous graphs. The method first uses a heterogeneous graph containing sentences and entity nodes to represent bilingual Chinese-Vietnamese news texts and effectively models the complex association relationships between multiple texts in multiple languages through graph attention networks (GAT). The topic encoder is then used to encode topic words into cues for topic representation generation, and the decoder side constraints are incorporated to generate the correct topic representation. The experimental results show that the proposed method improves the ROUGE value by up to 3.5 compared with the baseline method.

Keywords: Chinese-Vietnamese Bilingual · Heterogeneous graph · topic representation · Cross-language · GAT

1 Introduction

In the context of "the Belt and Road", China and Vietnam are exchanging more and more closely, and there are more and more news topics of common interest between the two countries. The timely understanding of the news topics of common interest and the main contents of the two countries is of great value in promoting the exchange and cooperation between China and Vietnam. In order to cope with information overload, topic discovery technology [1,2] is used to organize the news by topic and help readers to get relevant information quickly. However, from the reader's perspective, organizing news texts by topic clusters

Y. Sun et al. (Eds.): ChineseCSCW 2022, CCIS 1681, pp. 232–244, 2023.
https://doi.org/10.1007/978-981-99-2356-4_19

only, there is a problem with multiple news headlines and texts with two language descriptions under one topic, and it is impossible to understand the general content of these topics in a short time. Therefore, topics need to be presented to readers in a concise form. For example, "Strictly implement all epidemic prevention and control measures," The reader can understand that the news text mainly describes the epidemic prevention and control measures through this topic. This allows readers to quickly understand these news texts and get the main content of the news quickly, which reduces time and energy consumption and facilitates analysis of the news by public opinion workers.

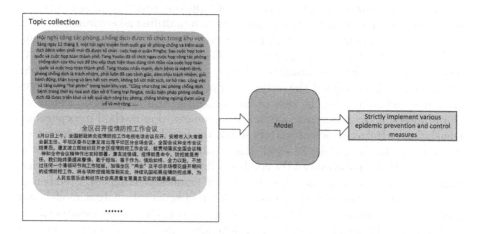

Fig. 1. Topic presentation task of Chinese Vietnamese Bilingual News

In this paper, as shown in Fig. 1, we study how to automatically generate concise and correct Chinese topic representation for multiple Chinese and Vietnamese news texts under each topic. There are few studies on topic representation at home and abroad, and the traditional method uses keywords to represent topics in a monolingual environment [3]. The difficulty of this method is how to find keywords that contain key information and can be quickly understood by readers. For example, Zheng et al. [4] proposed to extract the 5W1H (when, where, who, what, whom, how) six-tuple feature of news text to represent the topic; Liu Tong [5] proposed to calculate the index of essential words in the text by constructing a word co-occurrence relationship network, to mine the topic keywords of the text. However, the method of keyword representation of topics has certain limitations, and the different order of keywords may lead to different semantics. Therefore, some scholars propose to use temporal information [6] and citation information [7] to smooth the connection between keywords. For example, Han [8] et al. proposed a concept bagging approach to represent documents by characterizing text as vector clusters on word2vec and using the frequency of clusters; other scholars proposed using extractive methods to represent documents, e.g., Weiyu Wang [9] et al. proposed an extractive topic representation method to extract common information from the headings of document sets and then fuse them to generate a short topic representation. Some scholars also use deep learning methods to represent texts, e.g., Jiang et al. [10] proposed a potential topic text representation model, which obtains a representation of text by measuring the distance between texts; Li et al. [11] proposed a neural network-based comment representation model, which classifies each sentence into a combination of text representations by calculating its weight.

Due to language differences, monolingual topic representation tasks cannot be directly applied to cross-lingual topic representation tasks. The topic representation task is similar to the topic summarization [12] task in that the cross-language summarization task is a process of inputting source language text and outputting a summary in the target language in a multilingual environment. The cross-language summarization task is more complex than the monolingual summarization task. It is challenging to solve the problem of linguistic variability and, at the same time to complete the text summarization task. For example, Ayana et al. [13] simulated the output of a pre-trained translation or title generation model to achieve the task of cross-language title generation; Zhu et al. [14] proposed a cross-language automatic summarization method incorporating translation patterns, which effectively solved the problems of large model capacity and long training time; Li et al. [15] combined multiple documents on the same topic, then pre-processed the combined documents by word separation, and finally used hLDA topic modeling to extract summary sentences; Steinberger et al. [16]built a sentence matrix based on a latent semantic analysis model, and selected some sentences as summaries by using singular value decomposition; Litvak et al. [17]proposed a language independent multilingual sentence extraction (Muse) algorithm based on the optimization of multiple sentence ranking methods using genetic algorithms; Conroy et al. [18] proposed three methods to assign weights to sentences using non-negative matrix decomposition, LSA, and LDA, and weighted the weights of the three methods to extract topic summaries; Abdelkrime et al. [19] used the fuzzy clustering algorithm to cluster the sentences according to the topic, score each sentence according to the degree of the topic covered by the sentence, and select the sentence with the highest score to construct the topic summary.

Although the above methods can effectively solve the task of monolingual multi-text topic representation, in the task of this paper, there are complex association relationships between multi-lingual multi-texts. The existing topic generation models are difficult to effectively model the association relationships between multi-lingual texts, resulting in deviations between the generated topic representation and the original text description of the topic. Therefore, this paper proposes a multi-lingual topic representation method that models the complex linguistic relationships between multi-lingual multi-texts through heterogeneous graphs and incorporates topic knowledge. The method first uses a heterogeneous graph containing sentences and entity nodes to characterize Chinese and Vietnamese bilingual news texts and effectively models the complex association relationships between multi-lingual multi-texts through GAT. Then the topic words are encoded into clues for topic representation generation by a topic encoder, which is incorporated into the decoder-side constraint to generate the correct topic representation. The experimental results show that the proposed approach of the text is effective.

2   Methodology

The model is illustrated in Fig. 2. Here, we denote the number of words in the source language and the target language by V_s and V_t , respectively. Given multiple documents in different languages $D = (d_1, d_2, ..., d_n)$, d_i represents a sentence. First, we extract the subject word $T = \{t_1, t_2, ..., t_3\}$ from D, and t_i represents each subject word $(T \subseteq V_s)$. Then, entity $E = (e_1, e_2, ..., e_n)$ and sentence $S = (s_1, s_2, ..., s_n)$ are extracted from D, e_i and s_i represent each entity and each sentence, respectively. Construct a heterogeneous graph $G = (V, E)$ with the obtained entities and sentences, where V is composed of e_i and s_i.Input the obtained T into the topic encoder and the obtained G into the graph encoder.Finally, the topic $S = \{w_1, w_2, ..., w_n\}$ is generated by the decoder,represents each topic word $(S \subseteq V_t)$.

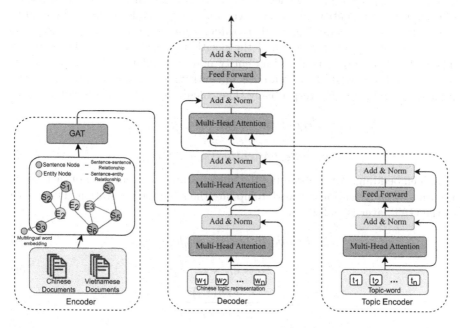

Fig. 2. Topic representation model of Chinese and Vietnamese news based on heterogeneous graph

2.1   Encoder

Construction of Graph. This section describes how to build heterogeneous diagrams based on paragraphs and entities. Given a source document cluster D, we first divide it into smaller semantic units sentences S and entities E. Then construct the heterogeneous graph $G = (V, E)$, where V includes the sentence node V_s and the entity cluster node V_e. E represents an undirected edge between nodes. There is no undirected edge between the entity node and the entity node. However, there is an undirected edge between the entity and the paragraph and between the paragraph. We linked paragraphs and entities in different languages through the bilingual dictionary built by previous work. The sentence contains the entity if there is an edge between s_i and e_i. The weight of the edge is the number of times the sentence contains the entity. If there is an edge between s_i and s_i, there is a common entity between the two edges, and the weight of the edge is the number of entity repetitions. We delete vertices with a weight of 0 to reduce the impact of noise or useless sentences.

Graph Encoder. Vertex embedding: as described above, the vertex is represented by the entity $E = \{e_1, e_2, ..., e_n\}$ and by the word sequence $S = \{\omega_1, \omega_2, ..., \omega_n\}$ make up sentences.In order to capture the position information of each word in an entity and a sentence, a position encoder needs to be used to obtain the position code. The final embedded representation of a sentence node is the sum of the word vector and the position of each word in the sentence. The embedded representation of an entity node is similar to that of a sentence node. Then the embedding of sentence and entity nodes is encoded to obtain the hidden states $\widetilde{h}_s$ and $\widetilde{h}_e$, respectively. The calculation method is as follows:

$$\widetilde{h}_s = SelfAttention \left(\|_{t=1}^t \left(\omega_i + PE \left(\omega_i \right) \right) \right) \tag{1}$$

$$\widetilde{h}_e = SelfAttention \left(s_i + PE \left(s_i \right) \right) \tag{2}$$

Graph embedding: After obtaining the hidden state representation of each node, use the Graph Attention Network to update the node representation. The design of the GAT layer is as follows:

$$z_{ij} = LeakyReLU \left(W_a \left[W_q h; W_k h_j \right] \right) \tag{3}$$

$$\widetilde{z}_{ij} = \widetilde{e}_{ij} \times z_{ij} \tag{4}$$

$$\alpha_{ij} = \frac{exp \left(\widetilde{z}_{ij} \right)}{\sum_{l \in N_i} exp \left(\widetilde{z}_{il} \right)} \tag{5}$$

$$\widetilde{u}_i = \sigma \left(\sum_{j \in N_i} \alpha_{ij} W_v h_j \right) \tag{6}$$

W_a, W_q, W_k, W_v denote the trainable weight matrix, σ represents sigmoid activation function, $\widetilde{e}_{ij}$ represents the weight of the edge. Following Wang et al.

[20] iteratively update the node representation by discretizing real values into integers to follow the weights of the updated scalar edges $\tilde{e}_{ij}$ and then learn the embedding of these integers. The weights are mapped to the multidimensional embedding space $\tilde{e}_{ij} \in R^{de}$. Thus, the information contained in the value needs to be learned through a different embedding matrix.

Combining the GAT with a multi-headed attention mechanism, plus a residual connection to avoid gradient disappearance after multiple iterations:

$$\tilde{h}_i = \tilde{h}_i + \tilde{u}_i \tag{7}$$

The node representation is then iteratively updated using the GAT layer above and the position feedforward layer. Each iteration contains a sentence-to-sentence and a sentence-to-entity update procedure. After t iterations, $\tilde{H}_p$ is connected to each corresponding input representation vector to obtain the output $\tilde{H}_{pw}$ of the graph encoder.

Topic Encoder. Although the graphical encoder already captures the global article structure and sentence semantics, some important information is still omitted because vertices cannot represent different word meanings in a sentence. Therefore, we use Transformer's encoder as a topic encoder to capture the key topics in sentences. The Chinese and Vietnamese bilingual topics obtained from the above study are input to the pre-trained language model and mapped to the same semantic space, and then these key topics are stitched together as the input to the topic encoder. After encoding these topics, the resulting hidden vectors are fed into a multi-headed attention layer as q, k, and v:

$$MultiHead(Q, K, V) = [head_i; ...; head_h]W^O \tag{8}$$

$$head_i = Attention\left(QW_i^Q, KW_i^K, VW_i^V\right) \tag{9}$$

$$Attention\left(QW_i^Q, KW_i^K, VW_i^V\right) = softmax\left(\frac{\left(QW_i^Q\right)\left(KW_i^K\right)^T}{\sqrt{d_k}}\right)\left(VW_i^V\right) \tag{10}$$

$$Q = K = V = \|_{i=1}^n (c_i) \tag{11}$$

where W^O, W_i^Q, W_i^K, and W_i^V are learnable matrices, $\sqrt{d_k}$ is the dimension of the key value, and h is the number of heads. The results of multi-head attention are passed through the last layers of the topic encoder shown in Fig. 2 to obtain the output z_i^C of the topic encoder.

2.2 Decoder

This decoder has the same structure as the topic encoder in the previous section, except that two additional multi-head attention layers are added to perform multi-head attention on the outputs of the graph encoder and the cue encoder.

Considering that some of the words in the generated topics are directly translated from the topic words, we use the Naive strategy proposed by Zhu et al. [21] to obtain the translation probabilities P_{trans} to decide which words are directly translated. The translation probabilities $P_{trans} \in [0, 1]$ are computed from the decoder hidden state H_{dec} through dynamic gates as follows:

$$P_{trans} = \sigma \left(W_2 \left(W_1 H_{dec} + b_1 \right) + b_2 \right) \tag{12}$$

where b_1 and b_2 are learnable offset vectors and W_1 and W_2 are learnable parameter matrices, σ Is the sigmoid activation function.

3   Experimental Results and Analysis

3.1   Evaluation Metric

This chapter conducts an experimental evaluation and comparative analysis of the Chinese-Vietnamese bilingual news topic representation model based on heterogeneous graphs. It mainly includes the selection and calculation of evaluation indicators and the experimental analysis of different parameter models. By reviewing domestic and foreign topic generation-related literature, we basically refer to the evaluation criteria of text abstract extraction for topic generation tasks, that is, the ROUGE (Recall-Oriented Understudy for Gistin Evaluation) [22] evaluation index is used. ROUGE is an automatic extraction task for evaluating text abstracts. And a set of indicators for machine translation tasks, mainly by comparing the text generated by the model with the standard text to compare the similarity of the two texts. The mathematical formula for ROUGE is as follows:

$$ROUGE - N = \frac{\sum_{s \in \{RefSum\}} \sum_{n-gram \in s} count_{match} \left(n - gram \right)}{\sum_{s \in \{RefSum\}} \sum_{n-gram \in s} count \left(n - gram \right)} \tag{13}$$

In the formula, n represents the length of $N - Gram$, and $Count_{match}(n - gram)$ is the number of $N - Gram$ contained in the generated topic representation and the labeled topic representation together. By using the ROUGE formula, we can find that the scoring system is mainly related to the recall rate of topics. In this thesis, the accuracy of the automated topic model is evaluated by considering the similarity from ROUGE-1, ROUGE-2, and ROUGE-3.

3.2   Datasets

In this paper, ten topics of Chinese and Vietnamese news, such as "epidemic prevention and control", "nuclear pollution", "China's anti-corruption" and "Civil Code" were crawled through the web crawler technology as the data set of the Chinese and Vietnamese news topic discovery experiment. Among them, 7664 news texts were crawled from Chinese news websites, and 3116 news texts were crawled from Vietnamese news websites. The specific distribution is shown in

Table 1. In order to verify the effectiveness of our method, this paper will use the Google translation engine to translate the Vietnamese extracted into Chinese. The texts with high translation errors are filtered by manual screening based on the translation.

Table 1. Chinese Vietnamese cross language news topic representation task dataset

News Topic	Chinese News Articles	Vietnamese News Articles
Epidemic prevention and control	1093	529
Nuclear pollution	532	143
Civil code	1097	283
The Belt and Road Initiative	972	498
Racial problem	482	277
War on terror	587	239
Anti corruption in China	865	244
Food Safety	753	368
2020 US general election	544	367
Explosion in Lebanese capital	423	168

3.3   Baseline Model

The topic representation task in this chapter is a generative method. To verify the effectiveness of this method, the following models are set in the same data set for comparison:

(1) STM-seq2seq [23]: The method first constructs a bilingual feature space with the help of a Chinese-Vietnamese bilingual dictionary and uses LSTM neural networks in both the encoder and decoder. A vector representation based on time series is obtained at the encoder side, and the sequence is extracted from the vector at the decoder side. It is often used as a baseline method in text generation tasks.

(2) NCLS [24]: The approach proposes to improve the end-to-end model (NCLS) for achieving cross-language summarization using the transform model, which is enhanced by jointly training the tasks MT and MS. Cross-language summarization is achieved by aligning different languages under the semantic space through an attention mechanism.

(3) hLDA [25]: The method extracts features from hLDA modeling for sentence scoring and selects sentences with high scoring results to generate summaries. First, the documents are modeled using the hLDA algorithm, and from the hLDA modeling results, a new feature is proposed that can reflect the semantic information to some extent. Then, this new feature is combined with other different features for sentence scoring. Based on the results of sentence scoring, candidate summary sentences are extracted from the documents to generate summaries.

(4) MT-GAT: This method first translates the Vietnamese text into Chinese through the Google translation tool and then uses the method of this paper to construct a heterogeneous map for calculation.

3.4 Comparative Experimental Analysis

In this study, the heterogeneous graph-based bilingual Chinese and Vietnamese news topic representation model is compared with the four models introduced in the previous section on a self-constructed dataset, and the results are shown in Table 2.

Table 2. Topic representation comparison experiment

Way	ROUGE-1	ROUGE-2	ROUGE-3
LSTM-Seq2seq	23.4	16.6	11.3
NCLS	25.6	17.5	13.4
hLDA	26.2	19.8	15.8
MT-GAT	24.5	17.6	12.6
ours	**29.7**	**21.8**	**17.6**

The experimental results in Table 2 show that the heterogeneous map-based topic representation model for Chinese-Vietnamese bilingual news outperforms the other four methods in all three indexes, which indicates that the method in this paper can effectively generate the correct topic representation. Among them, the ROUGE value of this paper is improved by 3.5 on average compared with the traditional hLDA model, which indicates that it is difficult for the Chinese-Vietnamese bilingual dictionary to map two languages into the same semantic space under the low-resource scenario. the performance of the MT-GAT method is weaker, and it can be seen that the accuracy of machine translation has a more significant impact on the model.

3.5 Ablation Experiment

The topic representation model of Chinese Vietnamese Bilingual News Based on a heterogeneous graph generates concise sentences that can describe the topic correctly from the Chinese Vietnamese bilingual news texts that describe the same topic. In this method, the association between texts is modeled by heterogeneous graphs, encode topic words into clues generated by topic representation through topic encoder, and integrate into decoder-side constraints to generate the correct topic representation. Three ablation experiments were designed to verify the effectiveness of the heterogeneous graph and topic word coder in the topic generation task. Wherein Transformer means to change the heterogeneous graph coding into Transformer coding at the encoder stage; GCN indicates that the heterogeneous graph in the encoder stage is replaced by a graph convolutional network; W/OTE indicates that it is not integrated into the theme encoder. The experimental results are shown in Table 3.

Table 3. Ablation experiment results

Way	ROUGE-1	ROUGE-2	ROUGE-3
Transformer	22.3	16.4	11.5
GCN	26.6	18.6	15.3
W/OTE	24.7	16.0	12.7
ours	**29.7**	**21.8**	**17.6**

Table 3 shows that both the construction of the heterogram and the incorporation of the topic encoder have an impact on the model performance in the Chinese-Vietnamese bilingual news topic representation model proposed in this chapter. The reason is that the heterogram can effectively model the complex association relationship between multiple languages and multiple texts, while the topic encoder plays a certain constraining role in the model. The experimental results showed that the three ROUGE values decreased by an average of 5.25, 4.3, and 4.2 after replacing the heterogeneous map. In contrast, the ROUGE values of the model effect decreased by 5, 5.8 and 4.9 after not incorporating the topic encoder. It can be seen that the effect of both on the model is close, with the topic encoder having a slightly more significant effect on the model.

3.6   Case Analysis

Table 4 shows the samples generated by the Chinese-Vietnamese bilingual news topic representation model based on heterogeneous graphs. The topic number is only used as serial number identification, with no special meaning, and the sample generation process is shown in Fig. 1. From this, we can see that the model can basically generate concise and concise topic representations for news texts describing the same topic. However, there are still some inaccurate descriptions; for example, topic two should be "food safety", but the generated example is "genetically modified food causing controversy", which is easily misunderstood. This is due in large part to the small size of the dataset used to train the model in this paper, which leads to weak model generalization.

Table 4. Examples of generation results of Chinese Vietnamese Bilingual News Topic

Topic Number	Generate Topic Representation
0	Explosion in Lebanese capital
1	The US election was a complete success
2	Controversy over genetically modified food
3	Anti corruption in China
4	War on terror
5	Alleviation of racial problems in the United States
6	Implement the Belt and Road
7	Promulgation of civil code
8	Nuclear waste water discharge in Japan
9	Epidemic prevention and control in various places

4   Conclusions and Future Work

This paper first introduces the background and significance of bilingual Chinese and Vietnamese news topic representation research and briefly describes the task of topic representation under multilingual and multi-text. Then, we propose a heterogeneous graph-based bilingual Chinese and Vietnamese news topic representation model to generate concise and concise topic representations for multilingual and multi-text under the same topic and introduce the principles and framework of the model in detail. Comparative experiments are conducted with existing methods on a self-built news topic dataset, and the experiments show that the method in this paper outperforms the comparative model, and the results of topic generation are demonstrated.

For the problems in this paper, including the experiments are limited by the size of the dataset, resulting in a weak generalization of the model. And the constructed dataset is limited by the quality of the translation model, which is not accurate enough in the translation process, and the possibility of reducing the complexity of the model has not been carefully studied. The next work will consider incorporating multilingual external knowledge to solve the low resource problem.

Acknowledgements. The research work described in this paper has been supported by the National Natural Science Foundation of China (U21B2027, 61972186, 62266028), Yunnan provincial major science and technology special plan projects (202002AD080001, 202103AA080015, 202202AD080003), Yunnan High and New Technology Industry Project (201606). We thank the three anonymous reviewers for their insightful comments and suggestions.

References

1. Yang, S., Tang, Y.: News topic detection based on capsule semantic graph. J. Big Data Mining Anal. **5**(2), 98–109 (2022). https://doi.org/10.26599/BDMA.2021.9020023

2. Zheng X.: A Topic Detection Method Based on Word-attention Networks. J. J. Data Inform. Sci.**6**(04), 139–163(2021). https://doi.org/10.2478/JDIS-2021-0032

3. Li, J.: A comparative study of keyword extraction algorithms for english texts. J. Intell. Syst. **30**(1), 808–815 (2021). https://doi.org/10.1515/jisys-2021-0040

4. Zheng, L., Jin, P., Zhao, J., Yue, L.: A Fine-Grained Approach for Extracting Events on Microblogs. In: International Conference on Database and Expert Systems Applications. Springer International Publishing (2014)

5. Liutong.: Algorithm research of text key word extraction based on complex networks. J. Appl. Res. Comput. **33**(2), 5 (2016). https://doi.org/10.3969/j.issn.1001-3695.2016.02.010

6. Myronenko A., Song X., MÁ Carreiraperpiñán.: Advances In Neural Information Processing Systems (2007)

7. Kataria, S.S., Mitra, P., Caragea, C., Giles, C.L.: Context sensitive topic models for author influence in document networks. IJCAI 2011, In: Proceedings of the 22nd International Joint Conference on Artificial Intelligence, Barcelona, Catalonia, Spain, July 16–22, 2011. AAAI Press (2011)

8. Kim, H.K., et al.: Bag-of-concepts: Comprehending document representation through clustering words in distributed representation. J. Neurocomput. **29**, 336–352 (2017) . https://doi.org/10.1016/j.neucom.2017.05.046

9. Wang, W., Shi, C., Yu, Xi., et al.: An extractive topic brief representation generation method to event. J. Shandong Univ. (Natural Science), **56**(5), 11 (2021)

10. Jiang, B., Li, Z., Chen, H., et al.: Latent Topic Text Representation Learning on Statistical Manifolds. J. IEEE Trans. Neural Netw. Learning Syst. **29**, 1–12(2018). https://doi.org/10.1109/TNNLS.2018.2808332

11. Li, L., Qin, B., Ren, W., et al.: Document Representation and Feature Combination for Deceptive Spam Review Detection. J. Neurocomput. **254**(sep.6):33–41(2017). https://doi.org/10.1016/j.neucom.2016.10.080

12. Silvana, C., Alfio, F., Stefano, M.: Topic Summary Views for Exploration of Large Scholarly Datasets. J. Journal on Data Semantics, **7**(3), 155–170 (2018)

13. Ayana, Shen, S.Q., Chen, Y., Yang, C., Liu, Z.Y., Sun, M.S: Zero-shot cross-lingual neural headline generation. IEEE/ACM Trans. Audio, Speech, Lang. Process. PP(99), 1–1(2018). https://doi.org/10.1109/TASLP.2018.2842432

14. Zhu, J., Zhou, Y., Zhang, J., Zong, C.: Attend, Translate and Summarize: An Efficient Method for Neural Cross-Lingual Summarization. In: Meeting of the Association for Computational Linguistics, Association for Computational Linguistics (2020)

15. Lei, L., Wei, H., Jia, Y., Yu, L., Wan, S.: CIST System Report for ACL MultiLing 2013 - Track 1: Multilingual Multi-document Summarization. In: Proceedings of the MultiLing 2013 Workshop on Multilingual Multi-document Summarization (2013)

16. Steinberger, J.: The UWB Summariser at Multiling-2013. Proceedings of the MultiLing 2013 Workshop on Multilingual Multi-document Summarization (2013)

17. Litvak, M., Last, M.: Multilingual Single-Document Summarization with MUSE. In: Proceedings of the MultiLing 2013 Workshop on Multilingual Multi-document Summarization (2013)

18. Conroy, J., Davis, S.T., Kubina, J., Liu, Y.K., O'Leary, D.P., Schlesinger, J.D.: Multilingual Summarization: Dimensionality Reduction and a Step Towards Optimal Term Coverage. In: Proceedings of the MultiLing 2013 Workshop on Multilingual Multi-document Summarization. Association for Computational Linguistics (2013)
19. Abdelkrime, A., Eddine, Z.D., Walid, H.K.: AllSummarizer system at MultiLing 2015: Multilingual single and multi-document summarization. In: Annual Meeting of the Special Interest Group on Discourse and Dialogue (SIGDIAL)(2015)
20. Wang, D., Liu, P., Zheng, Y., Qiu, X., Huang, X.: Heterogeneous Graph Neural Networks for Extractive Document Summarization. In: Proceedings of the 58th Annual Meeting of the Association for Computational Linguistics (2020)
21. Zhu, J., Zhou, Y., Zhang, J., Zong, C.: Attend, Translate and Summarize: An Efficient Method for Neural Cross-Lingual Summarization. In: Meeting of the Association for Computational Linguistics, Association for Computational Linguistics (2020)
22. Lin, C. Y.: ROUGE: A Package for Automatic Evaluation of summaries. In: Proceedings of the Workshop on Text Summarization Branches Out (WAS 2004)(2004)
23. Sutskever, I., Vinyals, O., Le, Q.V.: Sequence to Sequence Learning with Neural Networks. MIT Press, NIPS (2014)
24. Zhu, J., Wang, Q., Wang, Y., Zhou, Y., Zhang, J., Wang, S., et al.: Ncls: neural cross-lingual summarization (2019). https://doi.org/10.18653/v1/D19-1302
25. Huang, T., Lei, L., Zhang, Y.: Multilingual Multi-document Summarization with Enhanced hLDA Features. J. Springer International Publishing (2016)

Convolutional Self-attention Network for Sequential Recommendation

Yichong Hu[1,2], Liantao Lan[1(✉)], Ronghua Lin[1,2], Chengzhe Yuan[2,3], and Yong Tang[1,2]

[1] South China Normal University, Guangdong, Guangzhou 510631, China
lanlt@m.scnu.edu.cn
[2] Pazhou Lab, Guangdong, Guangzhou 510330, China
[3] School of Electronics and Information, Guangdong Polytechnic Normal University, Guangdong, Guangzhou 510665, China

Abstract. Sequential recommendation has important applications in many fields that need to predict users' intentions from their historical behavior. Modeling for sequential recommendation is a challenging problem. In particular, Bert4Rec uses deep bidirectional self-attention to model, which solves the limitations of one-way modeling from left to right. However, it can still be optimized in terms of short-term feature extraction of users' behavior sequences and enhancing the distinguishability between recommended items. To address these limitations, we propose a sequential recommendation model called TR-BERT4Rec-CNN, based on the Bert4Rec. To fully extract the features of users' behavior sequences, we design a convolutional layer to extract the local dependencies for the hidden dimension of input data and extract the potential relationships for the sequence dimension of input data. To enhance the discriminability of items, we use a triplet loss to fine-tune our model. We conduct experiments on the Scholat-courses and the MovieLens datasets. Experiments show that our model outperforms the methods commonly used in recent years.

Keywords: Sequential Recommendation · Bert4Rec · Convolutional Layer · Triplet Loss · SCHOLAT

1 Introduction

Techniques involving sequential recommendation systems have emerged in an endless stream in both industry [1,2] and academia [3,4]. The goal of general recommendation systems is to focus on long-term user behavior patterns. In contrast, sequential recommendation systems focus on predicting users' short-term preferences by using the behavior sequences as "context". Since users' behavior is dynamic and evolving, users' subsequent behavior is influenced by historical behavior. For example, if a user has recently taken a computer-related course on MOOC, the user will likely take a course in the computer field in the future.

Due to the infinite potential value of sequential recommendation in the future, it has attracted many researchers. Researchers have proposed various sequential

Y. Sun et al. (Eds.): ChineseCSCW 2022, CCIS 1681, pp. 245–256, 2023.
https://doi.org/10.1007/978-981-99-2356-4_20

recommendation algorithms. [5] based on Markov chains, predicting the user's next interaction through the historical behavior, successfully describe short-term item recommendations but are challenging to model complex relationships. The methods [6,7] based on RNNs try to mine all previous behaviors with hidden states, which is used to predict the next behavior. However, they require vast amounts of data for training on dense datasets. In addition, Caser [8] used Convolutional Neural Network(CNN) and Latent Factor model(LFM) to obtain short-term behavioral patterns of users, which paid more attention to short-term behavior patterns compared to the user's general preferences. But it was essentially one-way modeling, only considering information in one direction. Recently, a new model, Transformer, has achieved excellent results in multiple domains. Thus some researchers have used the self-attention mechanism for sequential recommendation[9,10]. Bert4Rec [11] used deep bidirectional self-attention to model, which solves the limitation of one-way modeling from left to right. Compared with the Caser model, the processing of the initial input sequences is slightly insufficient.

Inspired by these models, we consider combining the advantages of Caser and Bert4Rec, using the self-attention mechanism and CNN for modeling. On the other hand, we optimize the recommendation performance by increasing the discriminability between recommended items. So we use a fine-tuning technique based on triplet loss [12] and a behavioral sequence feature extraction technique to improve the model's performance.

In this paper, our main contributions are as follows.

First, vertical and horizontal convolutional filters are applied to the input sequence to capture short-term behavioral relationships in sequences.

Second, we introduce the triplet loss function technique for fine-tuning, which enhances the distinguishability between items in the model, resulting in better model performance.

2   Related Work

2.1   General Recommendation

Early recommendation systems are typically modeled based on Collaborative Filtering (CF [13]), focusing on using users' historical long-term preferences to predict their preferences. Matrix Factorization (MF) mined potential information to represent users' preferences and attributes and estimates similarity by the inner product of user and item vectors. Based on Item Similarity Models (ISM [14]) is another branch, where PALAM [15] model uses a two-margin ranking loss and an adaptive margin to learn the relationship between items, and shortens the distance between similar users and items. Recently, deep learning has been applied to the recommendation, and various new technologies have emerged, NCF [16] learned user-item interactions via Multilayer Perceptron, CDAE [17] used implicit feedback data to model users' preferences to make top-N recommendations.

2.2 Sequential Recommendation

Sequential recommendation attempts to understand and model continuous user behavior, user-item interactions, and changes in user preferences and item popularity over time. Early sequential recommendations relied on Markov chains [5], which can capture sequential patterns from historical user interactions but are challenging to model complex relationships in behavior sequences. Caser [8] used Convolutional Neural Network to model behavior sequences, and then [33] further improved it by increasing the reception area through an expanded convolutional network. The above two methods can tap into the recent behavior patterns of users through their behavior. On the other hand, sequential recommendation models based on Recurrent Neural Network is more suitable for dealing with long sequence data. GRU4Rec [18] is a session-based model that models click sequences through gated recurrent units (GRU[19]), which can mine long-term relationships of sequences and improve Top-N recommendation performance. Recently, the self-attention mechanism gets achieved outstanding results in several fields, such as text classification [20,21] and machine translation [22], and has also been applied to sequential recommendation systems. SASRec [23] is nearly ten times faster in sequential recommendation compared to earlier RNN approaches, mainly due to the attention mechanism. But it is still one-way modeling, which can only extract sequence information from left to right. Recently, Bert4Rec [11] used a deep bidirectional self-attention network to process behavior sequences, addressing the limitations of one-way modeling. Recently, comparative learning has also made some progress in sequential recommendation. Cl4srec [24] proposes to extract the self-supervisory signal from the original data by using the comparative learning framework and use data augmentation methods to construct comparative learning tasks.

3 Model Design and Architecture

3.1 Problem Formulation

In sequential recommendation, given a set of m items and n users, the next item of interest to the user is predicted by the sequence of any length generated by the interaction between the users and the items in a certain period.

$$s_i = (v_{i1}, v_{i2}, \ldots, v_{iT}), 1 \leq i \leq n \tag{1}$$

where v_{iT} represents the index of the T_{th} interaction of user i with the items. The s_i with length T represents the length of the interaction sequence between user i and the T items, and the sequence is arranged in time order. The length of the interaction sequences may be different for different users. To keep the length of interaction sequences as T, we can add padding to the sequences with a fixed flag.

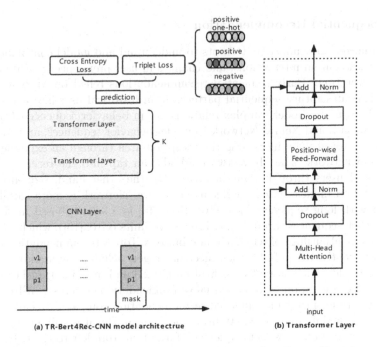

(a) TR-Bert4Rec-CNN model architectrue   (b) Transformer Layer

Fig. 1. TR-Bert4Rec-CNN model architecture, including CNN layer, Transformer layer and loss function module.

3.2   Model Architecture

In this paper, we propose a sequential recommendation model called TR-Bert4Rec-CNN, based on Bert4Rec. As shown in Fig. 1a, the TR-Bert4Rec-CNN contains three modules: CNN layer, Transformer layers, and loss function module. We design a convolution layer, roughly divided into two parts. Firstly, we perform a conv1d convolution operation in the direction of the sequence dimension of the input data, set the size of the convolution filter to an appropriate size according to different datasets, and set the strides to 1 to ensure that the output dimension is consistent with the input data dimension. Then we perform the same conv1d convolution in the direction of the hidden dimension of the input data to ensure that the output dimension is consistent with the input dimension. We propose such a convolutional layer to focus on capturing the local dependencies of the input sequences and mining the potential short-term relationships. Bert4Rec only uses the cross-entropy loss to optimize the model. Although it does get stable output, to enhance the discriminability between recommended items, the model is further fine-tuned by introducing triplet loss after training the model with the cross-entropy loss. As shown in Fig. 1b, the Transformer layer contains multiple sub-layer structures.

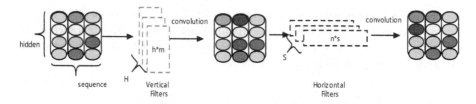

Fig. 2. CNN Layer

3.3 Convolutional Layer

We leverage the success of CNN in extracting local features from images and natural language processing [25] domains. Our method draws on the idea of CNN and uses convolution filters to extract local features of input behavior sequences, capturing short-term behavior patterns. As shown in Fig. 2, we perform two convolution operations. Firstly, the "vertical filter" captures short-term patterns between behavioral sequences. This filter is represented by $h * m$ matrices, where h represents the hidden dimension of the sequence, m represents kernel size, and H in the figure represents the number of convolutions filters. Secondly, the "horizontal filter" is able to capture the local dependencies of the hidden dimension in the sequence. This filter is represented by $n * s$ matrices, where s represents the sequence dimension of the input data, n represents kernel size, and S represents the number of convolution filters.

3.4 Transformer Layer

As shown in Fig. 1b, a Multi-Head Attention sub-layer and a Position-wise Feed-Forward sub-layer are the main structures of the Transformer layer. The Multi-Head Attention network [26] can combine the feature information learned from different head parts, and the complex structure of the network can capture the entire user's behavioral interaction. In fact, learning by stacking self-attention layers can achieve better results. However, as the number of layers of the network increases, the training process becomes increasingly difficult. We use the residual connection [27] network to alleviate the vanishing gradient. In addition, the output of the sub-layer will have dropout applied and then normalized to it. The Position-wise Feed-Forward layer [26] acts separately on the output vectors of the attention layer at each position. It is able to impart nonlinearities and interactions between different dimensions to the model.

3.5 Fine-Tuning Technique Based on Triplet Loss

As in Fig. 1b, use triplet loss to further optimize the model, so that there is a more obvious distinction between items, and the model has a better recommendation effect. In particular, we do not use triplet loss for model training at the beginning of the model training, but use triplet loss to further optimize the model after training with the cross-entropy loss.

The embedding is represented by $f(x) \in \mathbb{R}^d$. Items x are embedded in a d-dimensional space. We hope that the distance between the item x_i^a (anchor) of a specific target and all other items x_i^p of the same target is closer than that of any items x_i^n (negative) of any other target.

$$\sum_i^N \left[\|f(x_i^a) - f(x_i^p)\|_2^2 - \|f(x_i^a) - f(x_i^n)\|_2^2 + \alpha \right]_+ \tag{2}$$

where α is a hyperparameter representing the margin between positive and negative pairs.

For triplet loss to be used in our model, we need to make changes to Eq. 2 to fit our model.

$$L = \sum_i^N \left[\|target(x_i^p) - f(x_i^p)\|_2^2 - \|target(x_i^p) - f(x_i^n)\|_2^2 + \alpha \right]_+ \tag{3}$$

where $target(x_i^p)$ represents the one-hot code for x_i^p.

4   Experiments and Result

4.1   Dataset Description

Two datasets, MovieLens (MovieLens 1 m) and Scholat-courses, are used to evaluate our models. The MovieLens dataset contains up to 6,040 users, 3,420 movie data, and 9,996,111 user interactions, which is a benchmark dataset for evaluating sequential recommendations. The Scholat-courses dataset consists of data from SCHOLAT+ student course selections, which contain 1,796 students, 720 courses, and 30,192 user interactions. According to the user's interaction records, these interaction records are sorted according to their timestamp to construct the user's interaction sequences. The dataset follows the common strategy [16], and the length of our users' interaction sequences is at least 7.

4.2   Dataset Preparation

Before model training, we need to process the dataset. Divide the dataset into a training set, a validation set and a test set. To guarantee data leakage in the validation set, the training data needs to appear before the validation set. Therefore, the test set is composed of the last item of the sequence, the validation set is composed of the penultimate item of the sequence, and the other parts are made as the training set. To avoid heavy computation, we follow the common strategy [16] to choose 100 negative items based on the popularity of each user. Our task becomes ranking the real item with these 100 negative items.

4.3   Evaluation Metrics

We evaluate the performance of the model using the following evaluation metrics, including Hit Rate (HR), Mean Reciprocal Rank (MRR), and Normalized Discounted Cumulative Gain (NDCG).

$$HR = \frac{1}{N} \sum_{i=1}^{N} hits(i) \tag{4}$$

where N denotes the length of the recommended sequences and $hits(i)$ denotes whether the item of interest to the user is hit at the i_{th} position of the recommendation sequences.

$$NDCG = \frac{1}{N} \sum_{i=1}^{N} \frac{1}{\log_2 (p_i + 1)} \tag{5}$$

where p_i indicates whether the i_{th} position of the recommendation sequence is for the user's real access value. If yes, the value of p_i is i, otherwise, $p_i \to \infty$.

$$MRR = \frac{1}{N} \sum_{i=1}^{N} \frac{1}{p_i} \tag{6}$$

The meaning of p_i is the same as in Eq. 5, where Eq. 5 and Eq. 6 are concerned with finding these items in a more prominent position for the user, emphasizing "sequential".

4.4   Comparative Methods and Implementation Details

To verify the feasibility of our method, we use the following methods for verification.

- Caser [8]: Modeling with CNN in horizontal and vertical directions respectively.
- Bert4Rec [11]: The deep bi-directional self-attention network is used to deal with the complex relationship between sequences, addressing the limitations of one-way modeling.

We implement TR-Bert4Rec-CNN with PaddlePaddle. All parameters in the model are initialized with a normal distribution, and the range is [-0.05, 0.05]. Based on the Adam [24] function training model, we set the learning rate of 1e-4, $\beta_1 = 0.9$, $\beta_2 = 0.999$, and ℓ_2 weight decay of 0.01. Furthermore, we set the value of Transformer layers $K=2$ and the head value $h=4$, the sequence length of MovieLens is N=200, and the sequence length of Scholat-courses is N=50. The hidden dimension of input data is H=128. The "vertical filter" is represented by $h * m$ matrices, where the value of h is equal to H, and M = 3. The "horizontal filter" is represented by $n * s$ matrices, where the value of s is equal to N, and n = 3. All models are trained from scratch on NVIDIA Tesla V100 GPU without pre-training.

4.5 Experimental Setup

We conduct a total of three sets of experiments. The first group of experiments is an overall performance comparison: our method is compared with other methods. The second group of experiments is to explore whether the model is affected by the value of the margin of the triplet loss. The third group of experiments is ablation experiments to verify the effect of the CNN layer and triplet loss.

Table 1. Performance comparison of different models for predicting the next interactive item. Bold values represent the best.

Datasets	Metric	Caser	Bert4Rec	TR-Bert4Rec-CNN
MovieLens	HR@1	0.2064	0.2821	**0.3001**
	HR@5	0.5223	0.5705	**0.5886**
	HR@10	0.6547	0.6857	**0.6982**
	NDCG@5	0.3778	0.4340	**0.4534**
	NDCG@10	0.4324	0.4713	**0.4889**
	MRR	0.3515	0.4160	**0.4345**
Scholat-courses	HR@1	0.4153	0.5311	**0.5472**
	HR@5	0.6541	0.7983	**0.8140**
	HR@10	0.7916	0.8511	**0.8528**
	NDCG@5	0.5823	0.6665	**0.6927**
	NDCG@10	0.6138	0.6839	**0.7054**
	MRR	0.5717	0.6437	**0.6612**

4.6 Overall Performance Comparison

The experiment aims to compare the overall performance of TR-Bert4Rec-CNN with other models. Comparison experiments are performed on two datasets using three models Caser, Bert4Rec, and TR-Bert4Rec-CNN. We remove the NDCG@1 performance metric in the experiment since NDCG@1 and HR@1 are equal. To ensure fairness, we use the best parameters for all experiments. As shown in Table 1, the highest performing value in each row is highlighted in boldface. Experiments show that our proposed TR-Bert4-CNN model performs best. The scores on the Scholat-courses dataset are generally higher than the MovieLens dataset, mainly due to the strong backward and forward logic of students' course selection sequences on the Scholat-courses dataset. Our model introduces a triplet loss with a margin hyperparameter. The effect of this hyperparameter on the model is unknown, so we set up an experiment to verify the effect of the margin on the model.

4.7 Impact of Margin of Triplet Loss

To investigate the influence of the value of the margin of the triplet loss function on the model, we experiment on the Scholat-courses dataset for different margins.

In Eq. 2, the margin of triplet loss is denoted as α. We record the final results of the model with different parameters by continuously changing the value of α in triplet while controlling the model as a whole to be unchanged. As shown in Fig. 3, the performance of the model is affected by different α. When the α is 0.5, the evaluation metric of the model is the best. When the α is too large, the model's performance will degrade. From the results, our recommendation is to set the α to 0.5.

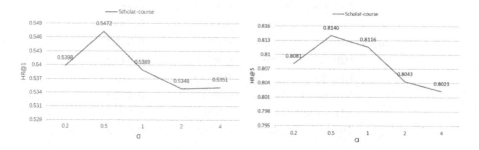

Fig. 3. Values of HR@1 and HR@5 in Scholat-course with different margins.

4.8   Ablation Study

We set up an ablation experiment to investigate the effectiveness of various modules in the model, which includes exploring the effect of the introduced CNN layer and the effect of the introduced triplet loss.

The Effect of Convolutional Layer. The experiment aims to explore the effect of convolutional layers in our model. Comparing the original Bert4Rec and Bert4Rec-CNN on MovieLens and Scholat-course datasets. As shown in Table 2, the Bert4Rec-CNN outperforms Bert4Rec in overall performance on both datasets, proving that the CNN module can indeed optimize the recommendation performance of the model.

The Effect of Triplet Loss. The purpose of the experiment is to explore the effect of triplet loss in our model. As shown in Table 2, we compare the Bert4Rec-CNN and TR-Bert4Rec-CNN on MovieLens and Scholat-course datasets. For the convenience of observation, Fig. 4 shows the experimental results of Bert4Rec, Bert4Rec-CNN, and TR-Bert4Rec-CNN using HR@5 indicators. We find that the TR-Bert4Rec-CNN outperforms the model Bert4Rec-CNN in several metrics in both datasets. Although in the case of the HR@10 indicator of the Scholat-course dataset, it appears to be slightly lower than the Bert4Rec-CNN, in most cases, it can improve the model's performance. Overall, the triplet loss function we introduced improves the evaluation metrics, demonstrating the effectiveness of the triplet loss.

Table 2. Performance comparison of Bert4Rec, Bert4Rec-CNN and TR-Bert4Rec-CNN.

Datasets	Metric	Bert4Rec	Bert4Rec-CNN	TR-Bert4Rec-CNN
ML-1m	HR@1	0.2821	0.2912	**0.3001**
	HR@5	0.5705	0.5758	**0.5886**
	HR@10	0.6857	0.6909	**0.6982**
	NDCG@5	0.4340	0.4407	**0.4534**
	NDCG@10	0.4713	0.4781	**0.4889**
	MRR	0.4160	0.4233	**0.4345**
Scholat-courses	HR@1	0.5311	0.5342	**0.5472**
	HR@5	0.7983	0.8056	**0.8140**
	HR@10	0.8511	**0.8539**	0.8528
	NDCG@5	0.6665	0.6886	**0.6927**
	NDCG@10	0.6839	0.7004	**0.7054**
	MRR	0.6437	0.6597	**0.6612**

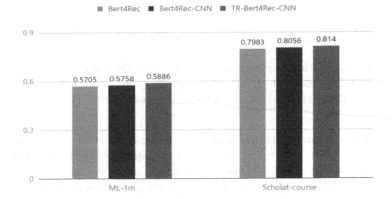

Fig. 4. Comparison(HR@5) of three models on two datasets: our models can improve the performance compared to the original Bert4Rec.

5   Conclusion

In this paper, we design a TR-Bert4Rec-CNN model based on Bert4Rec. The convolutional layers used by this model sequentially extract horizontal and vertical features from the input sequence, capturing the local dependencies of the behavior sequences. Furthermore, the triplet loss is used to optimize the model to make the recommended items more discriminative, which leads to better recommendation performance of the model. Experiments show that our model overall outperforms other models in MovieLens and Scholat-course datasets. In the future, one direction is to use model ensemble methods and knowledge distillation methods to further optimize models for online deployment. Another valuable direction is that we will investigate the integration of rich item features (e.g., user personal information, the course content) for modeling.

Acknowledgment. This work was supported in part by the National Natural Science Foundation of China under Grant U1811263.

References

1. Lv, F., et al.: Sdm: Sequential deep matching model for online large-scale recommender system. In: Proceedings of the 28th ACM International Conference on Information and Knowledge Management, pp. 2635–2643 (2019)
2. Pi, Q., Bian, W., Zhou, G., Zhu, X., Gai, K.: Practice on long sequential user behavior modeling for click-through rate prediction. In: Proceedings of the 25th ACM SIGKDD International Conference on Knowledge Discovery & Data Mining, pp. 2671–2679 (2019)
3. Guo, X., Shi, C., Liu, C.: Intention modeling from ordered and unordered facets for sequential recommendation. In: Proceedings of The Web Conference 2020, pp. 1127–1137 (2020)
4. Yu, Z., Lian, J., Mahmoody, A., Liu, G., Xie, X.: Adaptive user modeling with long and short-term preferences for personalized recommendation. In: IJCAI, pp. 4213–4219 (2019)
5. Rendle, S., Freudenthaler, C., Schmidt-Thieme, L.: Factorizing personalized markov chains for next-basket recommendation. In: Proceedings of the 19th international conference on World wide web, pp. 811–820 (2010)
6. Hochreiter, S., Schmidhuber, J.: Long short-term memory. Neural Comput. **9**(8), 1735–1780 (1997)
7. Li, J., Ren, P., Chen, Z., Ren, Z., Lian, T., Ma, J.: Neural attentive session-based recommendation. In: Proceedings of the 2017 ACM on Conference on Information and Knowledge Management, pp. 1419–1428 (2017)
8. Tang, J., Wang, K.: Personalized top-n sequential recommendation via convolutional sequence embedding. In: Proceedings of the Eleventh ACM International Conference on Web Search and data mining, pp. 565–573 (2018)
9. Li, J., Wang, Y., McAuley, J.: Time interval aware self-attention for sequential recommendation. In: Proceedings of the 13th International Conference on Web Search and Data Mining, pp. 322–330 (2020)
10. Wu, L., Li, S., Hsieh, C.-O., Sharpnack, J.: Sse-pt: Sequential recommendation via personalized transformer. In: Fourteenth ACM Conference on Recommender Systems, pp. 328–337 (2020)
11. Sun, Fei.: Bert4rec: Sequential recommendation with bidirectional encoder representations from transformer. In: Proceedings of the 28th ACM International Conference on Information and Knowledge Management, pp. 1441–1450 (2019)
12. Schroff, F., Kalenichenko, D., Philbin, J.: Facenet: A unified embedding for face recognition and clustering. In Proceedings of the IEEE Conference on Computer Vision and Pattern Recognition, pp. 815–823 (2015)
13. Koren, Y., Bell, R.: Advances in collaborative filtering. In: Recommender systems Handbook, pp. 77–118 (2015)

14. Kabbur, S., Ning, X., Karypis, G.: Fism: factored item similarity models for top-n recommender systems. In: Proceedings of the 19th ACM SIGKDD International Conference on Knowledge Discovery and data mining, pp. 659–667 (2013)

15. Ma, C., Ma, L., Zhang, Y., Tang, R., Liu, X., Coates, M.: Probabilistic metric learning with adaptive margin for top-k recommendation. In: Proceedings of the 26th ACM SIGKDD International Conference on Knowledge Discovery & Data Mining, pp. 1036–1044 (2020)

16. He, X., Liao, L., Zhang, H., Nie, L., Hu, X., Chua, T.-S.: Neural collaborative filtering. In Proceedings of the 26th International Conference on World Wide Web, pp. 173–182 (2017)

17. Wu, Y., DuBois, C., Zheng, A.X., Ester, M.: Collaborative denoising auto-encoders for top-n recommender systems. In: Proceedings of the ninth ACM International Conference on Web Search and Data Mining, pp. 153–162 (2016)

18. Hidasi, B., Karatzoglou, A.: Recurrent neural networks with top-k gains for session-based recommendations. In: Proceedings of the 27th ACM International Conference on Information and Knowledge Management, pp. 843–852 (2018)

19. Cho, K.: Learning phrase representations using rnn encoder-decoder for statistical machine translation. In: Empirical Methods in Natural Language Processing (2014)

20. Changshun, D., Huang, L.: Text classification research with attention-based recurrent neural networks. Int. J. Comput. Commun. Control 13(1), 50–61 (2018)

21. Lin, R., Fu, C., Mao, C., Wei, J., Li, J.: Academic news text classification model based on attention mechanism and rcnn. In: CCF Conference on Computer Supported Cooperative Work and Social Computing, pp. 507–516 (2018)

22. Yang, J., Wang, M., Zhou, H., Zhao, C., Zhang, W., Yong, Yu., Li, L.: Towards making the most of bert in neural machine translation. In Proceedings of the AAAI Conference on Artificial Intelligence, vol. 34, pp. 9378–9385 (2020)

23. Kang, W.-C., McAuley, J.: Self-attentive sequential recommendation. In: 2018 IEEE International Conference on Data Mining (ICDM), pp. 197–206. IEEE (2018)

24. Xie, X., et al.: Contrastive learning for sequential recommendation. In: 2022 IEEE 38th International Conference on Data Engineering (ICDE), pp. 1259–1273. IEEE (2022)

25. Quamer, W., Jain, P.K., Rai, A., Saravanan, V., Pamula, R., Kumar, C.: Sacnn: self-attentive convolutional neural network model for natural language inference. Trans. Asian Low-Resour. Lang. Inf. Process. 20(3), 1–16 (2021)

26. Devlin, J., Chang, M.-W., Lee, K., Toutanova, K.: Bert: Pre-training of deep bidirectional transformers for language understanding. arXiv preprint arXiv:1810.04805 (2018)

27. He, K., Zhang, X., Ren, S., Sun, J.: Deep residual learning for image recognition. In: Proceedings of the IEEE Conference on Computer Vision And Pattern Recognition, pp. 770–778 (2016)

Towards Using Local Process Mining to Analyse Learning Behavior Pattern

Sipeng Ouyang[1], Yiping Wen[1(✉)], Jianxun Liu[1], and Lianyong Qi[2]

[1] Hunan Key Laboratory for Service Computing and Novel Software Technology, Hunan University of Science and Technology, Xiangtan 411201, China
ypwen81@gmail.com
[2] Qufu Normal University, Qufu 273165, China

Abstract. Learning behavior is the key factor to promote the occurrence of effective learning. Analyzing learning behavior pattern is helpful to understand the common learning behavior of different types of learners. This paper introduces the application of traditional process mining methods such as Sequence Miner, Heuristics Miner and Inductive Miner in the area of learning behavior analysis. The shortcomings of these methods are also analyzed. To overcome their shortcomings, a method of local process mining-based learning behavior pattern analysis is proposed in this paper. Comparative experiments based on real data sets are performed to verify its effectiveness.

Keywords: Local process mining · Learning behavior · Behavior pattern

1 Introduction

Process mining (PM) is to extract new insights from event log [1], and educational process mining (EPM) refers to its application in the field of education. EPM usually mine learning behavior through the analysis of event log to build process model base on process discover [2], it combines data analysis, modeling and insights of the educational process, bridging the gap between educational data mining and educational science [3]. Learning behavior is the key factor to promote the occurrence of effective learning. Analyzing learning behavior pattern (LP) is helpful to understand the common learning behavior of different types of learners. Martinez et al. [11] applied sequence mining method to process the behavior data of students solving problems on interactive desktops, and obtained the frequent behavior sequences of students as their learning behavior patterns. On the one hand, these patterns can only describe the sequential relationship between activities, not the complex relationship such as parallelism between activities. On the other hand, traditional process mining algorithms such as heuristics miner (HM) and inductive miner (IM) are widely used in learning behavior data analysis to automatically extract learning process models. Although these learning process models can describe complex relationships such as parallelism, they can't explicitly express common learning behavior patterns, and manually extracting learning behavior patterns from process models is time-consuming and error-prone.

Y. Sun et al. (Eds.): ChineseCSCW 2022, CCIS 1681, pp. 257–265, 2023.
https://doi.org/10.1007/978-981-99-2356-4_21

In recent years, some process mining algorithms have emerged that can extract frequent sub-processes from process models, *w-find* [12], local process mining (LPM) [13] and WoMine algorithm [14] are three representative algorithms. Inspired by this, this paper tries to apply this kind of algorithm to mine learning behavior patterns, that is, to extract frequent sub-processes which contain the parallelism and other complex relationships between activities from the historical data.

The main contributions of this paper include:

(1) This paper analyzes the shortcomings of two kinds of traditional process mining algorithms in analysis of learning behavior pattern.
(2) This paper applies the Local Process Mining in the field of education for the first time, proposes a method of local process mining-based learning behavior pattern analysis.

2 Preliminaries

Definition 1 (Event log). An *event* e consists of *activity, ID, timestamp* and some attributes related to the occurrence of the event. A *trace* is a sequence $\sigma = <e_1, e_2,...,e_n>$, each trace corresponds to an execution of a process. An *event log* L is a set of traces, $L = \{\sigma_1, \sigma_2,...,\sigma_m\}$.

Definition 2 (Petri net. [1]). A Petri net is a triple $N = (P, T, F)$ where:

- P is a finite set of places;
- T is a finate set of trasition;
- F(flow relation) is the set of directed arcs, $F \subseteq (P \times T) \cup (T \times P)$.

Definition 3 (Learning Behavior Pattern). Let $N = (P, T, F)$ be a Petri net as a process model. A connected sub-model represented by the Petri net $P = (P', T', F')$ is a *pattern* of N if and only if:

- $P' \subseteq P, T' \subseteq T, F' \subseteq F$;
- The frequency of P $F_P \geq F_s$, F_s is a value set by user.

The patterns obtained by the process model which mined by learning behavior event log is the *learning behavior patterns*.

3 Analyse Learning Behavior Pattern by Local Process Mining

3.1 LBPA Method

Local process mining can be positioned between process mining and sequence mining, it can mine behavior patterns containing complex relationships such as sequence, parallelism, selection, and looping like traditional process mining [13]. Process mining focuses on the all process model from the beginning to the end. Sequence pattern mining only considers frequent sequences containing sequential relationships as behavior patterns, and doesn't consider other relationships between activities. The behavior patterns obtained by local process mining is a subset of the whole process model, which also contains sequence, parallelism, selection, and looping relationships. The steps of the method of local process mining-based learning behavior pattern analysis(LBPA) are shown in Algorithm 1.

In the LBPA method, the first step is to obtain the set Activity = $\{a_1, a_2, a_3,...,a_n\}$, $a_n \in e$, Activity contains all the unique activities in the event log.

Algorithm 1. Learning behavior pattern analysis method based on Local Process Mining

Input: The event log of learning behavior $L = \{\sigma_1,\sigma_2...,\sigma_m\}$, the maximum number of activities M, the minimum frequency threshold of the learning behavior pattern F_s and the maximum number of iterations

max_iteration

Output: *SM*: a set of Learning behavior pattern

1. $Activity$ = extractActivitySet (L)

2. $CM = \{LP_1, LP_2, ..., LP_n\}$, $SM = \{\}$; $i = 0$

3. While($i \geq max\_iteration$)

4. $i = i + 1$

5.   For each LP in CM

6. $SCM = \{\}$

7.   If ($M_{LP} < M$) and ($F_{LP} > F_s$)

8. SCM = add_to_SCM (LP)

9.   If ($SCM = \{\}$) Break

10. CM = expand_Learning_Pattern (SCM)

11. $SM = SM \cup SCM$

12. SM = deleteIncluded (SM)

13. SM = processTree_to_PetriNet (SM)

14. Return SM

The second step is to construct a candidate set of learning behavior pattern (LP) CM = $\{LP_1, LP_2, LP_3,..., LP_n\}$ according to the Activity. LP_i is a process tree, which is used to represent a learning behavior pattern. The LP_i in the initial CM is constructed from a_i.

Steps 5–11 are to select the learning behavior patterns that meet the set conditions from CM. After adding them to the SM, expand each LP in the SCM. Then go to step 5 to select the LP that meet the set conditions and add them into SM. The loop stops when the SCM is empty or when the maximum number of iterations max_iteration is reached. The 10th step is to expand LP and use the expanded the LP in SCM as a new CM, and delete the unexpanded LP. The expansion of LP is to search the learning activities from log that have sequence, parallelism, and looping relationships with learning activities contained in the current *LP* and its frequency of occurrence meets the minimum frequency requirement, then add it to the *LP*.

The 12th step is to delete the *LP* contained by other *LP* in the *SM* to avoid the redundancy of the *LP* in the *SM*. Finally, in order to make the result easy to understand, the 15th step converts the process tree into the form of Petri net.

3.2 Application Analysis

The commonly used traditional process mining methods can be divided into two categories: 1)heuristics miner (HM) [6–9]; 2) inductive miner (IM) [5, 10–12]. This paper will apply these two process mining methods to compare with LBPA base on real data set.

The data set selected in this paper comes from the log data of 46 undergraduates learning Digital Circuit course on the learning platform of a university. The data set contains a total of 5385 behavior records, involving 8 types of learning activities. Data attributes include student ID, learning activity name, time stamp, and number of mouse and keyboard operations. Since the names of the learning activities stored in the logs are difficult to understand, to increase the readability of the model, the learning activities need to be coded first, as shown in Table 1.

Table 1. Coding scheme of learning activities

Learning activity	Code	Interpretation of Learning Activities
Task analysis	Read	Read the exercise questions and requirements
Do the task	Exercise	Do a simulation exercise
Discuss or write reports	Editor	Use text editor
Results test	Test	Test simulation results
Adjust the parameters	Adjust	Adjust simulation parameters
View Study Materials	Study	Take relevant courses
Managing Learning Materials	Manage	Upload or download learning materials
Other activity	Other	It may be doing activities unrelated to the course

Heuristics Miner. This paper uses ProM to obtain direct follow graph(DFG), dependency graph and C-net based on HM, as shown in Fig. 1.

In Fig. 1(a), the dependency graph only supports the analysis of the dependencies between learning activities, and cannot obtain the learning behavior patterns. In Fig. 1(b), the connection between the two edges in the figure indicates that the two learning activities have parallelism relationship. Therefore, C-net only supports the analysis of the sequence, parallelism and looping relationships between learning activities. In Fig. 1(c), the direct follow graph only supports the analysis of the follow frequency.

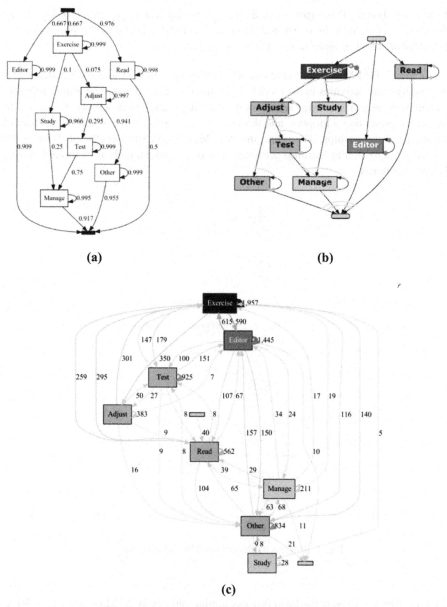

(a)   **(b)**

(c)

Fig. 1. Process model obtained by heuristics miner

In short, the three process models obtained by the HM algorithm can interpret learning behaviors from different perspectives. Although the model can be simplified by setting thresholds, it is still impossible to directly obtain the learning behavior patterns.

Inductive Miner. This paper uses the Inductive visual Miner plug-in in ProM to realize the application of the inductive miner. The process model obtained by this plug-in named IvM Model, which is more intuitive than the process tree.

In Fig. 2, IvM Model can represent all learning behaviors. There are 8 nodes representing learning activities in the model, 7 of which have an edge representing a looping, and another node has an edge representing skipping the learning activity in addition to an edge representing a looping, and the learning activities are presented in the form of parallelism relationships. Therefore, the IvM Model only supports the analysis of the overall participation in learning activities, and is still not suitable for mining learning behavior patterns.

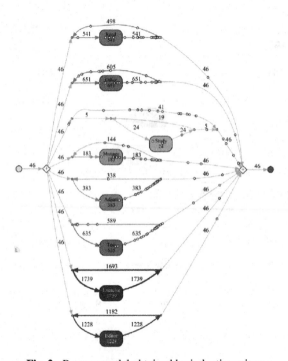

Fig. 2. Process model obtained by inductive miner

LBPA. This paper uses the local process mining plug-in in ProM to apply the LBPA. After deleting behavior patterns related to unknown activities such as Blank and Other, several of learning behavior patterns are shown in Fig. 3. The behavior patterns are represented by Petri Net, and the black rectangles in the figure represent invisible tasks.

As can be seen from Fig. 3, the first learning behavior pattern of the students in this course is: first read the analysis task (Read), and then download the learning materials (Manage) from the learning management software or directly enter the task to adjusting the parameter settings tasks required (Adjust), the second learning behavior

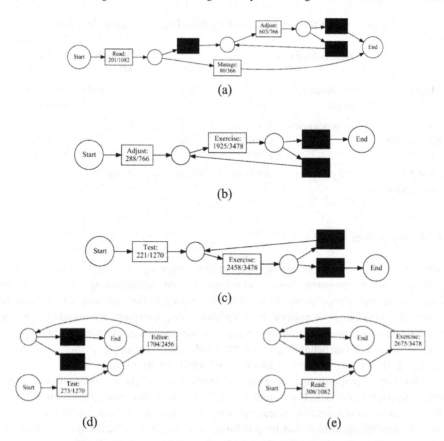

Fig. 3. Process model representing learning behavior patterns

pattern is: after adjusting the parameters (Adjust), Exercise is continuously performed, the third learning behavior pattern is: after the result test (Test), Exercise is continuously performed, the fourth learning behavior pattern is: after performing the result test (Test) and then using the text editor (Editor) continuously, it is possible to seek help, the fifth learning behavior pattern is: after the reading analysis task (Read), Exercise is continuously performed.

The above five learning behavior patterns are also reflected in the direct following graph obtained by the HM algorithm, but the direct following graph only presents the direct following relationship. Therefore, compared with the traditional process mining algorithm, the LBPA can analyze the learning behavior patterns in the learning behavior data without manual analysis.

The comparison of these methods is shown in Table 2.

Table 2. Characteristics analysis of traditional process mining algorithms

	Heuristics Miner			Inductive Miner	LBPA
Model	Dependency graph	C-net	DFG	IVM model	Local process model
Support relationship	Dependencies	Sequence parallelism looping	Frequency sequence	Frequency	Sequence parallelism looping
Model representation	All process	All process	All Process	All process	Sub-process

4 Conclusion

Although there are process mining and sequence mining to mine learning behavior patterns in existing research, these two methods still have shortcomings. Process mining focus on the entire process model from the beginning to the end, and it is difficult to analyse learning behavior patterns by traditional process mining. The sequence mining can only obtain sequences that only represent the sequence relationship, and cannot obtain the real learning behavior pattern. The LBPA method can obtain a more convincing result, which contains sequence, parallelism, looping relationships.

This paper compares the application characteristics of three process mining algorithms through real cases. It is found that different process mining algorithm supports different analysis perspective of learning behavior data, therefore, in the future, several process mining algorithms can be combined, and applied in the analysis of learning behavior data, so that the results obtained by these process mining algorithms can complement each other and the learning data can be understood from multiple perspectives. In practical applications, it is not limited to these several process mining algorithms, multiple process mining algorithms can be combined and applied according to requirements. The idea of this combined application process mining algorithm can provide a reference for subsequent research work on educational process mining.

Acknowledgement. This work was supported by the Natural Science Foundation of China (No. 62177014), National Key R&D Program of China (No. 2020YFB1707600), and Research Foundation of Hunan Provincial Education Department of China(No. 20B222).

References

1. Van Der Aalst, W.: Process mining: data science in action, 2nd edn. Springer, Heidelberg (2016). https://doi.org/10.1007/978-3-662-49851-4
2. Cairns, A.H., Gueni, B., Fhima, M., Cairns, A., David, S., Khelifa, N.: Process mining in the education domain. Int. J. Adv. Intell. Syst. **8**(1), 219–232 (2015)
3. Bogarín, A., Cerezo, R., Romero, C.: Discovering learning processes using inductive miner: A case study with learning management systems (LMSs). Psicothema **30**(3), 322–329 (2018)

4. Juhaňák, L., Zounek, J., Rohlíková, L.: Using process mining to analyze students' quiz-taking behavior patterns in a learning management system. Comput. Hum. Behav. **92**, 496–506 (2019)
5. Engelmann, K., Bannert, M.: Analyzing temporal data for understanding the learning process induced by metacognitive prompts. Learning and Instruction, 101205 (2021)
6. Ariouat, H., Cairns, A.H., Barkaoui, K., Akoka, J., Khelifa, N.: A two-step clustering approach for improving educational process model discovery. In: 2016 iEEE 25th International Conference on Enabling Technologies: Infrastructure for Collaborative Enterprises, pp. 38–43 (2016)
7. Bogarín, A., Romero, C., Cerezo, R., Sánchez-Santillán, M.: Clustering for improving educational process mining. In: Proceedings of the Fourth International Conference on Learning Analytics and Knowledge, pp. 11–15 (2014)
8. Cerezo, R., Bogarín, A., Esteban, M., Romero, C.: Process mining for self-regulated learning assessment in e-learning. J. Comput. High. Educ. **32**(1), 74–88 (2019). https://doi.org/10.1007/s12528-019-09225-y
9. AlQaheri, H., Panda, M.: An education process mining framework: unveiling meaningful information for understanding students' learning behavior and improving teaching quality. Information **13**(1), 29 (2022)
10. Okoye, K., Nganji, J.T., Hosseini, S.: Learning analytics for educational innovation: A systematic mapping study of early indicators and success factors. Int. J. Comput. Inf, Syst. Indust. Manag. Appli. **12**, 138–154 (2020)
11. Martinez, R., Yacef, K., Kay, J., Al-Qaraghuli, A., Kharrufa, A.: Analysing frequent sequential patterns of collaborative learning activity around an interactive tabletop. In: Educational Data Mining 2011, pp. 111–120 (2011)
12. Greco, G., Guzzo, A., Manco, G., Pontieri, L., Saccà, D.: Mining constrained graphs: The case of workflow systems. In: Constraint-Based Mining and Inductive Databases, pp. 155–171. Springer, Heidelberg (2006)
13. Tax, N., Sidorova, N., Haakma, R., van der Aalst, W.M.: Mining local process models. J. Innovat. Digital Ecosyst. **3**(2), 183–196 (2016)
14. Chapela, D., Mucientes, M., Lama, M.: Mining frequent patterns in process models. Inf. Sci. **472**, 235–257 (2019)
15. Weijters, A.J.M.M., van Der Aalst, W.M., De Medeiros, A.A.: Process mining with the heuristics miner-algorithm. Technische Universiteit Eindhoven, Tech. Rep. WP, 166 (July 2017), 1–34 (2006)
16. Leemans, S.J., Fahland, D., Van Der Aalst, W.M.: Discovering block-structured process models from event logs-a constructive approach. In: International Conference on Applications and Theory of Petri nets and Concurrency, pp. 311–329. (2013). https://doi.org/10.1007/978-3-642-38697-8_17
17. Prasetyo, H. N., Sarno, R., Budiraharjo, R., Sungkono, K.R.: The effect of duration heteroscedasticity to the bottleneck in business process discovered by inductive miner algorithm. In: 2021 IEEE Asia Pacific Conference on Wireless and Mobile (APWiMob), pp. 52–58 (2021)

Collaborative Mechanisms, Models, Approaches, Algorithms and Systems

Memory-Effective Parallel Mining of Incremental Frequent Itemsets Based on Multi-scale

Linqing Wang, Yaling Xun$^{(\boxtimes)}$, Jifu Zhang, and Huimin Bi

Taiyuan University of Science and Technology (TYUST),
Taiyuan 030024, Shanxi, China
xunyl55@126.com

Abstract. Frequent Itemset Mining (FIM), as an effective means of discovering related information or knowledge, has high time and space complexity. However, in the era of big data, data shows distributed characteristics and dynamic growth, which brings greater challenges to frequent itemsets mining. Considering that the data in the practical application field usually involves different concept hierarchies and granularity, the multi-scale concept is introduced into the incremental mining process of frequent itemsets to avoid the huge overhead of rescanning the dataset and adjusting the tree structure in the maintenance process. Simultaneously, in order to effectively deal with large-scale and massive data, a memory-effective parallel incremental FIM algorithm is proposed based on Spark parallel computing platform, which can ensure the load balance of the node calculation as much as possible by estimating the load of each group. And in the RDD caching strategy of the parallel algorithm, factors such as RDD access frequency and cost are comprehensively considered to reduce the memory occupancy rate and the recalculation of RDDs with high computational cost. Extensive experimental results verify that the memory-effective parallel algorithm has good scalability and high efficiency.

Keywords: Frequent itemsets mining · Incremental data mining · Spark · RDD caching strategy · Load balance

1 Introduction

Association rule mining, as a main research field of data mining, can find the relationship and correlation between transactions in a large amount of data. Frequent itemset mining (FIM), as a key step of association rule discovery, has high temporal and spatial complexity, so it has attracted extensive attention in the field of data mining and various practical application fields.

Nowadays, the rapid development of the Internet of Things and mobile technology has made the dataset constantly updated and rapidly expanded, and the performance of FIM has been severely challenged. On the one hand, continuously

© The Author(s), under exclusive license to Springer Nature Singapore Pte Ltd. 2023
Y. Sun et al. (Eds.): ChineseCSCW 2022, CCIS 1681, pp. 269–283, 2023.
https://doi.org/10.1007/978-981-99-2356-4_22

updated data will change the pattern distribution of the original database. Therefore, effective incremental FIM mining will help to extract the latest valuable information from dynamic datasets. On the other hand, the excessive amount of data renders traditional stand-alone computing power incapable of meeting users' high-performance resource requirements. Therefore, the effective integration of distributed computing and incremental mining technology has become a research hotspot [3, 20, 22].

This study combines the multi-scale theory to accelerate the update process of frequent itemsets. It uses the correlation between different scales to realize indirect pattern mining, which largely avoids the rescanning of the dataset and the continuous adjustment of the tree structure. At the same time, in order to break through the limitations of single-machine resources for big data processing, a distributed solution based on the in-memory computing platform–Spark was developed. The solution uses effective load balancing and caching strategies to further accelerate the incremental update of frequent itemsets.

The main contributions of this study are summarized as follows:

- The multi-scale theory with hierarchical concept is introduced into our incremental FIM algorithm. The final frequent itemsets are directly updated based on the relationship among datasets of different scales, instead of re-scanning the updated datasets and adjusting the tree structure to re-execute the mining process.
- The Spark platform is adopted to accelerate frequent itemsets mining with high spatiotemporal complexity and continuous iteration. In the proposed parallelization scheme, the concept hierarchical characteristics of multi-scale are used to complete the balanced grouping to balance the calculation amount of each computing node.
- In order to make full use of memory to improve cluster efficiency, a low cost double execution replacement policy (LCDERP) is proposed, which comprehensively considers the number of reliances and the cost of generation during the RDDs conversion process.
- Extensive experimental results on real-world and synthetic datasets demonstrate that the proposed parallel incremental algorithm based on Spark cluster is efficient and scalable.

2   Related Work

2.1   Parallel Incremental FIM

Faced with the rapid expansion of the current data volume, the algorithms under a single machine are slightly inferior in terms of operating efficiency and scalability.

Aiming at the dilemma of parallel frequent itemsets mining for dynamic datasets, Xu et al. proposed an incremental balanced parallel algorithm PFUP [17], which uses overlapping data partitions to effectively improve the data parallelism among the computing nodes. In order to fully and effectively utilize the computing power of the cluster node processors, parallel algorithms of shared-memory multithreads have been studied to improve algorithm throughput [4]. The era of big data has given birth to new advanced computing platforms, which have been effectively and widely used. Sun et al. proposed a new FCFP-Tree structure (i.e., Full Compression Frequent Pattern Tree) and an effective tree structure adjustment strategy to speed up update of frequent itemsets based on MapReduce computing platform [14]. However, FCFP-Tree maintains the information of all itemsets, resulting in high space overhead. Recently, a new incremental conditional pattern tree (ICP-tree) was developed, which retrieves the corresponding mining results from the original dataset, and then efficiently mines the final frequent itemsets from the newly added dataset and the ICP-tree based on them [15]. The focus of this research is on how to avoid duplicating scans of the original dataset as much as possible. But it still follows the traditional tree structure. A novel parallel FIM algorithm MapReduce-based (MR-PARIMIEG) was proposed, which used information entropy and genetic algorithm [10].

Spark, as an emerging platform of big data processing framework, inherits the advantages of Hadoop [2]. And its powerful processing capabilities based on memory computing have attracted widespread attention. A hybrid frequent itemset mining (HFIM) algorithm is proposed based on Spark, which takes advantage of the vertical layout of the dataset to cope with complex iterative scans [13]. Experiments have verified that this vertical structure layout makes it more efficient. Yu et al. gave an incremental solution based on the classic Apriori on the Spark platform, which tries to reuse the calculation results of the original dataset to update the frequent itemsets, thereby avoiding a large number of redundant calculations [21]. A distributed frequent itemset mining method SWEclat is proposed for massive flow data on Spark [16], which utilizes sliding windows to deal with streaming data.

2.2 Spark Caching Mechanism

Spark is a framework based on memory computing, so the performance of the overall Spark framework directly depends on the effective use of memory resources. So, its development team has been continuously optimizing the Spark memory management module. For example, the UnifiedMemoryManager (unified memory management) memory management model was added in Spark 1.6 version [1].

In order to adapt to various practical applications, Li et al. proposed a distributed file system (i.e., Tachyon) [8], which is located between the computing layer and the storage layer and can be simply understood as a Cache system. Tachyon achieves better operating efficiency through more detailed storage hierarchy division. However, when the system's memory resources are insufficient, LRU (Least Recently Used) is still used for cache replacement. Jiang et al. proposed a method of compressing datasets cached in memory, so that memory resources can be fully utilized [6]. However, in the actual data processing process, both compression and decompression operations will be accompanied by a large consumption of CPU resources, which will affect the efficiency of application execution. Koliopoulos et al. proposed a mechanism for the Spark framework to automatically determine the cache level [7]. The mechanism is designed based on the ratio of storage memory size to disk size. However, when the ratio is below a certain threshold, the mechanism does not choose to cache data in memory, although there is still a small amount of free space in memory. Inagaki et al. gave an adaptive data caching strategy to alleviate frequent I/O operations that interact between memory and disk [5]. Xu et al. designed and developed Dagon, a middleware that exploits the complexity and heterogeneity of DAGs to jointly perform task scheduling and cache management [18]. Dagon makes full use of data dependencies to avoid significant cache misses and performance degradation. Seongsoo Park et al. developed a cost model based on multiple representative inputs and an execution flow analysis scheme based on DAG scheduling to select the most dominant candidates among intermediate results to cache [12]. In the subsequent execution process, the best cache selection will be automatically completed.

In summary, the research on Spark's memory caching mechanism is still in its infancy. Existing weight-based cache replacement algorithms often involve the following defects: inaccurate weight calculations, incomplete considerations, and insufficient measurement methods, which profoundly affect the hit rate of the cache and the efficiency of job execution.

3 Incremental Frequent Itemsets Mining Based on Multi-scale

3.1 Related Definitions of Multi-scale

As an objective phenomenon, multi-scale can reflect the internal structure and essential characteristics of data objects from different perspectives and aspects. Broadly speaking, the scale is the unit or measurement of the research object. When investigating the data from a certain level or perspective, the data objects will cover a specific set of attributes involving the level. And, the collection of the attribute set usually have a conceptual hierarchy structure with a clear partial order relationships [11]. The analysis based on multi-scale theory is to divide the dataset according to the conceptual hierarchy to obtain the conclusion corresponding to the dataset of this scale, and then derive and convert the conclusion to the dataset of other scales. For incremental frequent itemset mining, scale conversion can avoid repeated scanning and recursive mining of the database. To effectively cope with incremental FIM mining of dynamic and massive data, multi-scale theory is introduced into this study. The concepts involved are given as follows.

Definition 1. *Lower scale (upper scale).*
    H_i and H_j are two conceptual hierarchies in the datasets. If $H_i < H_j$ ($H_i < H_j$), the dataset divided by H_i is the lower scale (upper scale) compared to the dataset divided by H_j

In the above definition, the concept of upper and lower scale is relative. Generally speaking, the lower scale corresponds to a lower conceptual hierarchy and smaller granularity, as well as involving a more specific data. The upper scale divides the conceptual hierarchy into a higher level and has a large granularity, and contains a larger range of data.

Definition 2. benchmark-scale [19]. *In the lower scale divided by the concept H_i, the sub-dataset in the lower scale dataset is the reference scale dataset, then the dataset corresponding to H_i is the benchmark-scale, denoted as BS.*

Definition 3. Target Scale [19]. *When studying an object, the upper scale dataset of the the BS dataset divided by concept H_j is taken as the target scale dataset, and its corresponding H_i is taken as the target scale, denoted as TS.*

Because of the relationship among datasets on different scales, it is possible to achieve the indirect mining to obtain the frequent itemsets on another scale based on the result on one scale, and to update the result according to the relationship among different scale datasets in the process of data maintenance, so as to reduce the data processing overhead and improve the mining efficiency.

3.2 The Process of Incremental Frequent Itemsets Mining Based on Multi-scale

Incremental mining of frequent itemsets involves two cases: frequent items are transformed into infrequent items, or infrequent items are transformed into frequent items after the dataset is updated. For the second case, the original dataset needs to be rescanned in order to get the new frequency information of the item. Simultaneously, the tree structure is also completely disrupted and needs to be reconstructed again. Thereby, the cost of incremental mining will increase dramatically. Incremental frequent itemsets mining integrating with multi-scale theory can quickly update frequent patterns based on the relationship among the newly added dataset and benchmark-scale (BS) dataset. In this process, the newly added dataset is regarded as a new benchmark-scale dataset. Thus, the global frequent patterns corresponding to the upper-scale (TS) can be directly derived by using lower-scale (BS) frequent patterns. In this way, repeated scanning of the original database and complicated tree structure adjustment costs are avoided.

In the initial mining stage, the original dataset is divided into different benchmark-scale datasets according to the concept hierarchy, and the frequent pattern tree (Fp-tree) is used to mine the local frequent itemsets corresponding to each benchmark-scale dataset. Then these local frequent itemsets are merged into global frequent candidate itemsets, which are saved in the candidate itemsets information table (marked as can_info in Fig. 1). A similarity matrix is constructed by calculating the similarity between benchmark-scale datasets. Here, the calculation of similarity adopts Jaccard similarity. If FI_i and FI_j respectively indicate the frequent itemsets corresponding to the BS dataset i and j, then the similarity between them is: $S_{ij} = \dfrac{FI_i \cap FI_j}{FI_i \cup FI_j}$.

In the process of scaling up, if a certain itemset count is missing, that is, it is judged as an infrequent item during local frequent itemsets mining. Jaccard similarity is used as the weight coefficient to estimate the approximate frequency value of some itemsets with missing frequency counts to reduce the impact on the accuracy of scaling up (See [19] for details). When the missing supports of these itemsets are filled, the global frequent itemsets will be obtained.

When the dataset is updated, the classic Fp-tree is still used to generate the frequent itemsets corresponding to the newly added dataset. Then the *can_info* is updated according to the frequent itemsets similarity between each benchmark-scale dataset and the newly added dataset to get the final patterns. The entire processing flow is shown in Fig. 1.

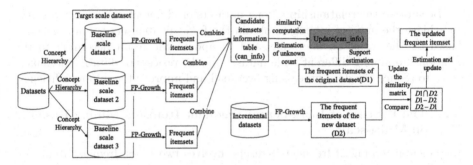

Fig. 1. Overview of incremental itemsets mining based on multi-scale (Color figure online)

In the mining process in Fig. 1, the update of the candidate itemsets information table (marked blue in Fig. 1) will inevitably cause estimation errors due to the use of similarity estimation to estimate some missing frequency counts.

4   Multi-scale Incremental Frequent Itemsets Mining Based on Spark

When all RDDs can be accommodated in memory, Spark can show the best performance. However, in many practical situations, the memory is insufficient for large data collections. Many existing parallel FIM algorithms only focus on the parallelization algorithm itself without considering the caching strategy. Therefore, we designed a low-cost double execution replacement policy (called LCDERP) to reduce the memory occupancy rate and high-cost RDD recalculation.

4.1   Introduction to Parallel Algorithms

Apache Spark uses the memory calculation scheme based on RDDs to alleviate the consumption of Hadoop disk operations, that is, the I/O cost is greatly reduced. Relying on the advantages of the Spark cluster, a novel parallel incremental frequent itemsets mining algorithm on Spark is given. The specific steps are as follows:

Step 1: TextFile is used to read the dataset from HDFS, and the BS dataset is converted into RDD, which is recorded as TransactionRDD and stored in memory.

Step 2: Divide TransactionRDD into different partitions according to the benchmark-scale. In the proposed multi-scale frequent itemset mining process, the dataset is divided into different benchmark-scale datasets according to the concept hierarchy, so we adopt the partition strategy based on the concept hierarchy of muti-scale. The number of partitions is determined by the number of benchmark-scale datasets, that is, each partition corresponds to a benchmark-scale dataset.

Step 3: Fp-Growth is applied to each partition to obtain all frequent itemsets of the corresponding BS dataset, which is denoted as BSDSFrequentItemRDD.

Step 4: The mining results of different partitions are combined to obtain the candidate itemsets of target scale can_list ($<$ M, itemsets, I, count, sum $>$), denoted as CandidataItemRDD.

Step 5: Calculate the similarity between frequent itemsets of each BS to estimate and update the can_list of each missing itemsets.

Step 6: Filter frequent itemsets based on min_sup and store frequent itemsets in FI_list (<itemset, count>), denoted as TSFrequentItemRDD.

Step 7: Convert the newly added BS datasets to RDDs and divide them into corresponding partitions.

Step 8: The Fp-Growth is applied to generate frequent itemsets of each partitions. Then, the similarity among the frequent itemsets of the new data and the initial frequent itemsets corresponding to the BS datasets are calculated, and can_list is updated.

Step 9: According to the updated sum value in the can_list, the frequent itemsets of the target scale meeting the minimum support constraint are filtered out.

4.2   The RDD Conversion Process of Parallel FPMSIM Algorithm

Figure 2 shows the RDD conversion diagram of the parallel incremental FIM algorithm based on Spark. In this process, stage 0 and stage 1 involve the RDD conversion process of frequent itemset mining of original data, and stage 2 corresponds to the RDD conversion process of incremental mining. Stage 0 transforms datasets into RDDs through TextFile and divides them into different partitions based on concept hierarchical grouping strategies, then Fp-Growth is applied to separately generate itemsets of different partitions. Stage 1 combines the results of different partitions (BS datasets) to obtain a candidate set of information (CandidataItemRDD) using "union" operator and estimates unknown counts of missing itemsets based on similarity. The frequent itemsets (TSFrequentItemRDD) of the original dataset (TS dataset) are filtered by the "filter" operator. Stage 2 first converts the new added dataset into RDDs and divides them into

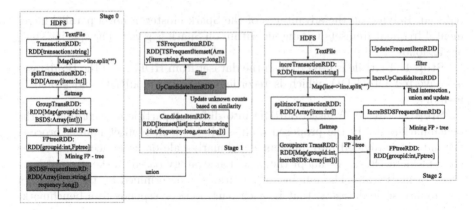

Fig. 2. RDD conversion process

different partitions, and get the frequent itemsets of each partition. Then, the updated candidate itemsets IncreUpCandidataItemRDD are obtained by comparing with the corresponding original BS dataset. Finally, the updated frequent itemset (UpdateFrequentItemRDD) was filtered out.

In the above process, some RDDs need to be reused, such as upcandidateitemRDD and BSDSFrequentitemRDD marked in blue in Fig. 2. When the dataset is updated, the former needs to be updated, and the latter needs to be compared with the frequent itemsets of the newly added dataset. Moreover, they are generated by various benchmark-scale datasets, and the generation cost is relatively high. Caching them can avoid recalculations caused by the release of intermediate results due to insufficient memory during subsequent calculations. In order to avoid the additional computational overhead caused by the release of expensive RDDs, we propose a low cost double execution replacement policy LCDERP. We will delete the RDD with a cost value of 0, and sort the remaining RDDs in ascending order based on the cost value. When the memory is insufficient, the low-cost RDD is first eliminated.

5   Low Cost Double Execution Replacement Policy (LCDERP)

As a basic data abstraction in spark, the RDD operator constructs the relationship among them, and the entire calculation process forms a DAG composed of RDDs and their relationships. Partition is the basic unit of RDD, and each partition will be processed by a computing task. All partitions can be recalculated through lineage backtracking. If a node loses connection or the partition that a task depends on is missing, recalculation is necessary. However, large-scale iterative calculations are resource intensive, so it is meaningful to design reasonable caching strategies for intermediate results or RDDs that are known to be reused.

The proposed caching strategy comprehensively takes into account the number of reliances and the cost of generation. RDD cost is determined as follows: cost=N*T, where N represents the number of times a certain RDD is relied on, and T indicates the time required for generating the RDD.

Algorithm 1 describes the pseudo code of LCDERP algorithm, in which the time consumption is mainly the calculation of N[] and C[], and the corresponding storage or elimination of RDD according to the relationship between the memory resources required by RDD and the remaining memory resources. As can be seen from the algorithm pseudocode, the time complexity of the cache policy is O(n).

Algorithm 1. LCDERP Policy

1: **Input:**Select a small part of the data to test(first execution). Obtain the number of items that each RDD is dependent N[] and the generation time T[]
2: **Output:** Updated c[] and RDD
3: C[] ← N[] * T[] // Calculate the cost of each RDD,and sort it
4: Test all data // Second execution
5: **if** RDD is used
6:   Update N and C corresponding to the RDD
7:   **if** RDD With N=0
8:     delete the RDD
9:     **if** out of memory
10:      Update RDD and c[] // According to the sorting result of C[], RDD with small generation value is eliminated and c[] is updated.
11:     **else break**
12:   **else** go to step 8
13: **else** go to step 6
14: **return** C[] and RDD

---

6   Experimental Results and Analysis

6.1   Experimental Setup

In this experiment, three VMS were created on VMware Workstation as Spark cluster, and we implemented the proposed algorithm and comparison algorithms in Python. To verify the performance of the proposed algorithm, we compare our parallel FIM algorithm (labelled FPMSIM) with the PFP (Parallelization Fp-Growth) and EFUFP [9]. The experimental datasets use T10I4D100K, T40I10D100K and retail datasets, as shown in Table 1. When implementing scale division, datasets T10I4D100K and T40I10D100K are divided into equal scales of a specific size, while retail is divided into different scales according to its own conceptual hierarchy.

Table 1. Datasets

Datasets	Average length	Count	Size(MB)
T10I4D100K	10	500000	11M
T40I10D100K	40	500000	16M
retail	11	500000	13M

6.2 Experimental Results and Analysis

Impact of Low Cost Double Execution Replacement Policy (LCDERP). In order to verify the effect of our caching strategy LCDERP, this set of experiment is carried out on T10I4D100K, T40I10D100K and retail. The memory size of each node was set to 2G, the support corresponding to the three datasets was set to 1%, 2% and 5%, and the steps of incremental data were 100K, 100K, and 80K, respectively.

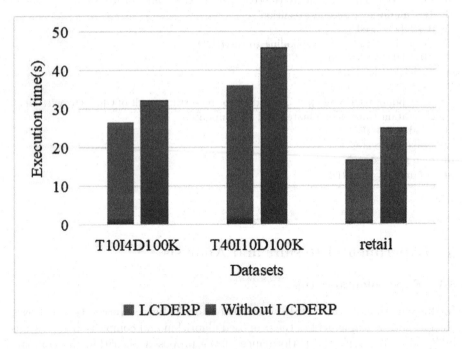

Fig. 3. Impact of LCDERP

Figure 3 compares the execution time of the parallel algorithm with and without the LCDERP strategy on the three datasets. It can be clearly seen that the execution time of the parallel FPMSIM algorithm using LCDERP is less on any dataset than that without it, which indicates that LCDERP plays a role in the process of algorithm execution. Because the high-cost RDD is effectively cached when memory is low to avoid the overhead of RDD recalculation. Obviously, compared with the results on the dataset T10I4D100K and the results on the other two datasets, the effect of the caching strategy is not so obvious. This is because T10I4D100K is sparse and relatively few frequent itemsets are mined, thus the caching strategy cannot significantly improve the performance of the algorithm.

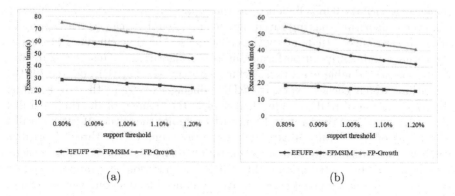

(a)   (b)

Fig. 4. Impact of Support threshold on the efficiency

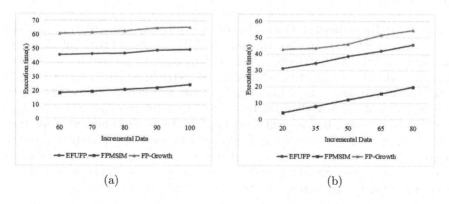

(a)   (b)

Fig. 5. Impact of incremental data on the efficiency

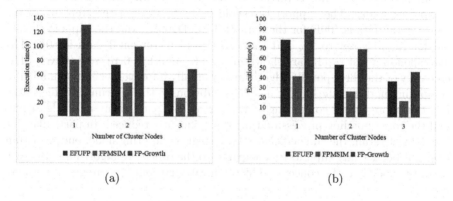

(a)   (b)

Fig. 6. Impact of cluster computing nodes

Impact of Support Threshold. T10I4D100K and retail datasets were used in this set of experiments. The support threshold ranges for datasets T10I4D100K and retail were respectively set to 0.8% to 1.2% and 1% to 3%, and the sizes of the incremental datasets were set to 100,000 and 80,000. Figure 4(a) depicts the trend of FPMSIM, Fp-Growth and EFUFP parallel algorithms when support changes on T10I4D100K. Obviously, as the support increases, the time efficiency of all three algorithms has improved significantly, mainly because greater support means fewer itemsets that satisfy the constraints. The time efficiency of the our algorithm significantly outperforms the other algorithms. This is mainly due to the low-cost double execution caching strategy (LCDERP) adopted by the algorithm, which caches expensive RDDs during execution, thereby avoiding the recalculation of RDDs. Figure 4(b) depicts the changes of the three parallel algorithms on the dataset retail. Figure 4(b) exhibits the effects of three parallel algorithms on the retail dataset. The execution time of the three algorithms behaves a declining trend, and our algorithm is relatively superior to the others. In addition to the contribution of LCDERP, the partitioning strategy based on the Concept hierarchies enables a relatively balanced load among various nodes. However, on the dataset T10I4D100K, the grouping (division) strategy adopts a sequential division manner, which does not follow the essential characteristics of the research object.

Impact of Incremental Data. In this group of experiments, three parallel algorithms (FPMSIM, Fp-Growth, and EFUFP) were tested with the change of incremental data. T10I4D100K and retail datasets were selected for the experimental evaluation, support thresholds are respectively set to 1.1% and 2%, and the incremental data ranges from 60K to 100K and 20K to 80K, respectively. Figure 5(a) and Fig. 5(b) show the time efficiency of the three parallel algorithms on the two datasets. It is evident from Fig. 5 that the algorithm execution time shows an upward trend as the incremental data increases, mainly due to the increase in the number of items that fit the minimum support as the amount of data increases. Similarly, our parallel algorithm behaves a higher time efficiency than the other two algorithms in the dataset T10I4D100K or retail.

Impact of Cluster Computing Nodes. In this experiment, the performance of our parallel algorithm is further verified by changing the number of cluster computing nodes. The support threshold is set to 1% and the step size of the incremental data is 100K for the dataset T10I4D100K. And the support threshold for Retail is set to 2% and the step size of incremental data is 80K. The corresponding test results are shown in Fig. 6(a) and Fig. 6(b), respectively. The efficiency of the three parallel algorithms gradually improves when the number of computing nodes in the cluster increases. Obviously, this is primarily due to the fact that more cluster computing nodes increase the parallelism of the algorithm, and the corresponding processing time is significantly reduced. In particular, for the dataset retail, the time efficiency on a single computing node, our algorithm does not behave any superiority compared to the other two algorithms. Because when the node is 1, the conceptual hierarchical partitioning strategy cannot play its role.

Speedup. This section employs the speedup ratio to further verify our parallel schema. Figure 7 shows the speedup performance of these three algorithms in T10I4D100K. It can be seen from Fig. 7 that the speedup ratio of the three algorithms shows an upward trend when the number of nodes in the cluster increases. This change is attributed to the reason that the more cluster nodes, the more resources that can perform tasks. Obviously, the parallel scheme can effectively improve the mining efficiency. In particular, the speedup ratio of the FPMSIM parallel algorithm is higher than the other two algorithms, which is mainly because the proposed algorithm uses a the low-cost double execution caching strategy (LCDERP) in the RDD conversion process to make full use of memory resources.

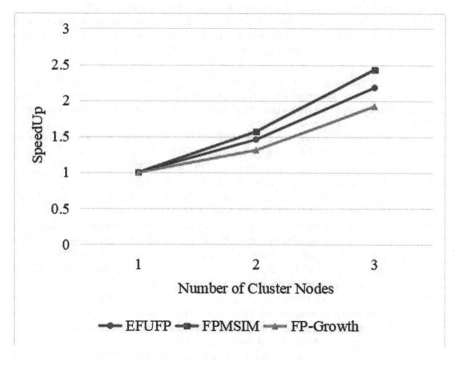

Fig. 7. SpeedUp

7 Conclusion and Future Work

In this study, we developed the Spark-based a multi-scale incremental mining algorithm, which aims at the limitations of incremental mining algorithms based on Apriori and Fp-Growth, such as iteratively scanning the database, constantly adjusting the tree structure. To solve the challenges of insufficient memory, a low cost double execution replacement policy (LCDERP) is designed, which only considers the number of RDDs dependencies and RDDs generation overhead. Therefore, a universal and efficient cache strategy on Spark should be a research focus for us.

Acknowledgments. This work is supported by the National Natural Science Foundation of P.R. China (No. 62272336, U1931209), Graduate student scientific research innovation projects of Shanxi Province, China (No. 2022Y699).

References

1. Dessokey, M., Saif, S.M., Salem, S., Saad, E., Eldeeb, H.: Memory management approaches in apache spark: a review. In: Proceedings of the International Conference on Advanced Intelligent Systems and Informatics **2020** (2020)
2. Enders, T., Martin, D., Sehgal, G., Schüritz, R.: Igniting the spark: overcoming organizational change resistance to advance innovation adoption - the case of data-driven services, pp. 217–230 (Jan 2020). https://doi.org/10.1007/978-3-030-38724-2_16
3. Huynh, V.Q.P., Küng, J., Dang, T.: A parallel incremental frequent itemsets mining IFIN+: improvement and extensive evaluation: special issue on data and security engineering, pp. 78–106 (Jan 2019). https://doi.org/10.1007/978-3-662-58808-6_4
4. Huynh, V., Küng, J., Jger, M., Dang, T.K.: IFIN+: a parallel incremental frequent itemsets mining in shared-memory environment. In: International Conference on Future Data and Security Engineering, pp. 121–138 (2017)
5. Inagaki, H., Fujii, T., Kawashima, R., Matsuo, H.: Adaptive control of apache spark's data caching mechanism based on workload characteristics, pp. 64–69 (Aug 2018). https://doi.org/10.1109/W-FiCloud.2018.00016
6. Jiang, Z., Chen, H., Zhou, H., Wu, J.: An elastic data persisting solution with high performance for spark. In: 2015 IEEE International Conference on Smart City/SocialCom/SustainCom (SmartCity), pp. 656–661. IEEE Computer Society, Los Alamitos, CA, USA (Dec 2015). https://doi.org/10.1109/SmartCity.2015.144, https://doi.ieeecomputersociety.org/10.1109/SmartCity.2015.144
7. Koliopoulos, A.K., Yiapanis, P., Tekiner, F., Nenadic, G., Keane, J.: Towards automatic memory tuning for in-memory big data analytics in clusters. In: 2016 IEEE International Congress on Big Data (BigData Congress), pp. 353–356 (2016). https://doi.org/10.1109/BigDataCongress.2016.56
8. Li, H., Ghodsi, A., Zaharia, M., Baldeschwieler, E., Shenker, S., Stoica, I.: Tachyon: memory throughput I/O for cluster computing frameworks. In: Proceedings of the 27th IEEE Conference on SYSTEM-ON-CHIP. Las Vegas, NV, pp. 1–15. IEEE (2014)
9. Lv, D.T., Fu, B., Sun, X., Qiu, H., Liu, X.: Efficient fast updated frequent pattern tree algorithm and its parallel implementation. In: 2017 2nd International Conference on Image, Vision and Computing (ICIVC), pp. 970–974. IEEE (2017)
10. Mao, Y., Deng, Q., Chen, Z.: Parallel association rules incremental mining algorithm based on information entropy and genetic algorithm. J. Commun. **42**(5), 122–136 (2021)
11. Mengmeng, L., Shuliang, Z., Yuhui, H., Donghai, S., Xiaochao, L., Min, C.: Research on multi-scale data mining method. Res. Multi-Scale Data Min. Method **27**(12), 3030–3050 (2016)

12. Park, S., Jeong, M., Han, H.: CCA: cost-capacity-aware caching for in-memory data analytics frameworks. Sensors **21**, 2321 (2021). https://doi.org/10.3390/s21072321
13. Sethi, K.K., Ramesh, D.: HFIM: a spark-based hybrid frequent itemset mining algorithm for big data processing. J. Supercomputing **73**(8), 3652–3668 (2017). https://doi.org/10.1007/s11227-017-1963-4
14. Sun, J., Xun, Y., Zhang, J., Li, J.: Incremental frequent itemsets mining with FCFP tree. IEEE Access **PP**(99), 136511–136524 (2019)
15. Thurachon, W., Kreesuradej, W.: Incremental association rule mining with a fast incremental updating frequent pattern growth algorithm. IEEE Access **PP**(99), 55726–55741 (2021)
16. Xiao, W., Hu, J.: SWEclat: a frequent itemset mining algorithm over streaming data using Spark Streaming. J. Supercomputing **76**(10), 7619–7634 (2020). https://doi.org/10.1007/s11227-020-03190-5
17. Xu, L., Zhang, Y.: A novel parallel algorithm for frequent itemset mining of incremental dataset. In: International Conference on Information Science and Control Engineering, pp. 41–44 (2015)
18. Xu, Y., Liu, L., Ding, Z.: Dag-aware joint task scheduling and cache management in spark clusters, pp. 378–387 (May 2020). https://doi.org/10.1109/IPDPS47924.2020.00047
19. Xun, Y., Cui, X., Zhang, J., Yin, Q.: Incremental frequent itemsets mining based on frequent pattern tree and multi-scale. Expert Syst. Appl. **163**, 113805 (2020). https://doi.org/10.1016/j.eswa.2020.113805
20. Youssef, N., Abd elkader, H., Abdelwahab, A.: Enhanced parallel mining algorithm for frequent sequential rules. Ain Shams Eng. J. **13**(2), 1–11 (2021). https://doi.org/10.1016/j.asej.2021.05.019
21. Yu, M., Zuo, C., Yuan, Y., Yang, Y.: An incremental algorithm for frequent itemset mining on spark, pp. 276–280 (03 2017). https://doi.org/10.1109/ICBDA.2017.8078823
22. Zhao, Y., Huang, F., Wang, S., Yu, K., Zhang, C.: Incremental temporal frequent pattern mining based on spark streaming. In: 2020 12th International Conference on Intelligent Human-Machine Systems and Cybernetics (IHMSC). vol. 2, pp. 22–27 (2020). https://doi.org/10.1109/IHMSC49165.2020.10084

An AST-Based Collaborative Discussion Tool for the MOOC Environment

Xinyue Yu[1,2] and Tun Lu[1,2(✉)]

[1] School of Computer Science, Fudan University, Shanghai, China
{xyyu18,lutun}@fudan.edu.cn
[2] Shanghai Key Laboratory of Data Science, Fudan University, Shanghai, China

Abstract. Online study becomes increasingly popular. Most existing massive open online course (MOOC) platforms provide a Community Question Answering (cQA) area where learners can seek for information, however, these cQA areas inevitably meet the following problems, such as low participation rate, insufficient contents and poor topic quality. Other online-learning websites equipped with the bullet screen achieve high interactivity by presenting history comments, but users who are watching the same course video with different progress cannot truly interact with each other. Therefore, it's necessary to design a collaborative discussion tool which takes the advantages of both collaborative editing and the bullet screen. The present collaborative editing schemes focus on supporting instant interaction and reducing conflicts between real users while there is only one learner online is often the practical case in the MOOC environment. In this paper, we propose a simulated interaction solution which is adapted for the MOOC environment and based on the Address Space Transformation (AST) scheme to promote online study experience. Firstly, four interaction modes which simulate the collaboration between historical and real users are concluded according to applicable scenarios. Secondly, we propose a simulated interaction approach based on the AST scheme. Finally, taking the edX platform as an example, we implement a collaborative editing tool by using the approach mentioned above.

Keywords: MOOC Learning · Simulate Interaction Mode · Collaborative Editing · Address Space Transformation

1 Introduction

The combination of Internet and education makes high-quality study resources truly open to all people. There are two mainstream approaches to get lessons online: the first one is to attend the massive open online courses (MOOCs) such as Coursera, edX and Udacity; the second one is to search in the video websites such as Bilibili and YouTube. Despite that MOOC is more formal and is supported by universities, its studying atmosphere is less active than those video websites with bullet screen. One study [1] showed that the not-so-intuitive interface in the MOOC platform negatively influences learners' study experience. Another study [2] proposed a quality assessment method to the answers in the educational cQA platforms, which indicates the importance of providing high

Y. Sun et al. (Eds.): ChineseCSCW 2022, CCIS 1681, pp. 284–294, 2023.
https://doi.org/10.1007/978-981-99-2356-4_23

quality content. Influenced by the number of users and the quality of topics, the contents presented in the discussion area are not rich enough and questioner's posts are often neglected. So, users can not get timely responses which to some extent reduces the willingness and enthusiasm of learners and accounts for the low class-completion rate in MOOC studying. Unlike MOOC platforms separate the video page and the discussion area, video websites with the bullet screen provide instant interaction and make the communication between historical learners and current learners possible, but users have to seek for answers among the quick flow comments. The bullet screen is suitable for the gradual, individualized and repetitive study process. It catches the point that learners may come to the same or similar confusions in their own study process, so it tries to synchronize users' questions by attaching the video time to the comments.

To address the problems mentioned above and combine the characteristic of bullet screen with group editing techniques, a collaborative approach which can not only support real-time online interaction but also make full use of historical content to simulate the interaction between historical users and real users is needed in the MOOC environment to inspire users and give full play to group wisdom. The major contributions of our work are presented below:

1. The interaction modes between historical users and real users are summarized according to the applicable scenarios, including reading supplementary mode, cumulative discussion mode, guidance mode and replay mode.
2. We apply the AST scheme to the MOOC environment by explaining the data model, the operation model and the consistency model of the replay mode. In order to validate the feasibility of our approach, we implement it in the edX platform.

The rest of this paper is organized as follows. Section 2 presents the related work on collaborative editing. Section 3 summarizes four collaboration modes between historical users and real users and in Sect. 4 we propose a simulated interaction approach based on the AST scheme. Section 5 describes our implementation and presents the results. In Sect. 6, we make a conclusion and discuss the future work.

2   Related Work

Collaborative editors have been widely applied by either using an algorithm to maintain consistency or determining the order of operation events to avoid conflicts. Among the consensus algorithms, the Operation Transformation (OT) [3, 4] scheme and the Address Space Transformation (AST) [5] scheme both focus on the CCI (Causality-preservation, Convergence, Intention-preservation) model.

OT algorithms have been evolved for decades. Existing OT researches have covered from one dimensional to 3D collaborative design tool [6], have expanded its data structure from linear document to HTML DOM [7], wikis [8], XML [9] and have been used into various situations, such as multimedia collaborative environments [10] and mobile environment [11]. However, as Joseph Gentle wrote "There's a million algorithms with different trade-offs", implementing the OT algorithms is difficult.

The contribution of the AST scheme is that it proposes a mark and retrace based approach to record deleted characters and changes the address space of the operation rather than the operation itself, thus directly finds the location where the operation is executed. Since its first work in 2005 [5], the AST-based techniques have been used into several fields, such as the mobile commenting [12], heterogeneous cloud service [13], web2.0 [14] and so on. It has also evolved from plain-text collaboration to string-wise editing [15].

Due to the unique learning process under the MOOC environment, the requirement of communicating with those have had the same confusions emerges. Although there exist attempts to build interactive classrooms by embedding bullet screen messages into the lecture [16], it cannot provide a collaborative area where learners can modify other's opinions and improve the quality of discussion. Students have been using Google Docs for collaborative editing when they are in a multi-site learning environment [17], but the Google Docs is an integrated application which cannot relate the documents with online course videos. To our knowledge, there is no suitable method that offers a resolution of conflicts between historical users and current users. This paper will focus on the simulated interaction between historical users and real users while still follows the CCI model among real users. The detailed simulated collaboration modes, approaches and the implementation will be shown in the remainder of this paper.

3 Simulated Collaboration Modes

3.1 Reading Supplementary Mode

Reading supplementary mode is the practical application case of collaborative editing schemes. In this mode, all users who share the same document build their own local replica with the historical contents, but cannot acquire the detailed operation execution process of the historical users. For beginners who have no clear concept of the course and for those try to consult historical discussion contents to find information, reading supplementary mode is quite useful. With modification and supplement, the quality and quantity of questions and answers are both improved. However, this mode is not suitable for the MOOC environment because it doesn't conform to the gradually rising learning curve and makes the users unable to know the operation process of the historical users.

3.2 Cumulative Discussion Mode

Cumulative discussion mode provides a blank co-edit area for the editorial team in each time period, and attaches the results of each round of discussion to the historical document to form a new edit version. Once the message the user typed is similar to the historical content, the virtual user generates new operations to present the related discussion process. The cumulative discussion mode enables users to start a new discussion process under the inspiration of ideas in the historical records. The challenge of realizing this mode is that in order to convert the real user from passively receiving historical contents to actively triggering the presentation of historical operations, we need to combine operation intentions with the semantics of the knowledge.

3.3 Guidance Mode

Guidance mode means that the questions raised by real users are directly answered by using the history record. After receiving the input from the actual user, the virtual user will go through five steps: semantic analysis, similarity calculation, information retrieval, answer extraction and generation operation. Yet, the process of information retrieval and answer extraction requires the analysis of natural language and it's hard to measure the accuracy of the answer since the preserved answers may not cover all questions.

3.4 Replay Mode

Replay mode aims to completely reproduce the process of historical discussion when users are watching the course video. The bullet screen relates each message with the its post time and then pops it automatically at that time as long as other users reach the same point. Such method connects topics with the video time by taking advantages of users' learning habits rather than analyzing the semantic knowledge and successfully strikes a chord in learners. However, only users at the same time point of the video can actually interact with each other, otherwise the messages they see are the historical records. The replay mode groups the users and makes it possible to communicate between users with different progress in the course video.

In the replay mode, we first add the post time to each atomic operation and record it by the order of the receive time in the server. A virtual user reproduces the history operations whenever there is a learner reaches the time point. Then, we define the co-editing group as the collection of the learners in the same round which begins from the entrance of the first user and ends with quit of the last user. A heartbeat check is set to tell the server each user's progress in the video and keep the connection between the server and clients. The history operations executed by the virtual user can show the thinking and discussion process of historical users and the real users can constantly supplement it which finally create a new version of records. From the perspective of real users, it looks like there are multiple learners editing collaboratively. The replay mode simulates the interaction between real users and historical users. The challenge to realize this mode is to resolve the conflicts between current operations and history operations, for that the executed position of history operations needs to be adjusted in the new document.

4 An AST-Based Approach for the Replay Mode

4.1 Data Model

Most discussion areas in MOOC platforms are independent of course videos and structured as a tree with questions and answers. In order to spare users from switching pages to post questions, we utilize the sidebar to provide a new discussion area and model the document as a liner structure consists of character nodes. Define each character node CN = {character, effectiveness, position, video time, List < logs >}, where CN.character represents the content of the operation, CN.effectiveness represents the visibility of the character and CN.position reveals the executed location in the liner document. Each character node also contains a related video time and multiple action records. Define Logs = {operation type, operation executor, executed state vector}.

We also adopt the Browser-Server model and let users create their own replica by synchronizing with the server's. The server contains two layers: the first one is responsible for managing the co-editing groups which is identified by the video identifier; the second layer is the group manager who supervises the operations each member does and hands out operation messages to all members. A virtual user is registered in the server in the same way as the real users. In the replay mode, the discussion version is updated continuously by storing operation records each round.

4.2   Consistency Model

The collaborative editing discussion area based on the AST scheme maintains the requirements of the CCI model. Causality-preservation is to ensure that two dependent operations are executed in a consistent sequence on all sites, that is, if the operation OP_A causal order precedes the operation OP_B, then the operation OP_A precedes the operation OP_B on all sites. Convergence refers that the structure of the character nodes under the participation of the virtual user remains the same. Intention-preservation has the following two meanings in the replay mode. Firstly, for an operation O, if the operation is a local operation of a real user, then its performance on remote sites and on the virtual site is the same. If the operation is generated by a virtual user, then real users can correctly receive the remote operation and perform it on their local copy. Secondly, for two operations with concurrent relationships, the execution effect of the operation does not interfere with each other. Intention-preservation ensures that the effect of the remote operation execution is consistent with the local execution, regardless of the concurrent execution of independent operations, the transmission of operation messages and the operation producer.

4.3   Operation Model

Atomic Operation. There are two kinds of users in the collaborative editing discussion area under the MOOC learning environment: real users and a virtual user. All users' granularity of operation is character and their atomic operations are insert character node "Insert(CN)" and delete character node "Delete(CN)". For real users, their operations are detected by the event of key press and key down. Once the key press or key down event happens, we figure out the actual character through the key code and record the current video time. Then the message with the format "operation type + character + position + video time" is sent to the server. For the virtual user, its operation is generated from the history records. A heartbeat check will start after the establishment of the connection between the browser and the server, and every 60 s it sends a message to the server to inform the current video time. The heartbeat check will be reset if the threshold time goes out or the user triggers a new operation. So, if the server receives a heartbeat message, then it's the time to pop the history records whose posted time is earlier than the current video time, because users have not typed for a short time and the possibilities of conflicts can be reduced.

State Vector Timestamp. In the MOOC environment, users enter and exit the discussion area unpredictably, so it's not suitable to predetermine the dimension of the state vector. Creating a vector with big dimensions will cause the waste of space while the situation of high concurrency cannot be handled with small vectors. Therefore, we adopt a timestamp with dynamically changing dimensions to record the address space when the operation occurs. We set a variable to count the cumulative number of people entering the discussion area in a certain period. When a new learner joins in the discussion, the dimension of the state timestamp for each site synchronously grows but it does not shrink when sites exit. Each dimension of the status timestamp SV is expressed as $< N_J, C_J >$, where N_J represents the number of site J and C_J represents the number of operations at site J. The number of operations executed at site J in the timestamp of site I is $C_J = SV_I[N_J]$.

Partial Order and Full Order. The dimension of the status timestamp of each site is equal and increases synchronously. If there are two timestamps with different dimensions, it means that one operation happens before a new user comes in and the other one is the opposite case. We follow the definition of partial order and full order in the AST scheme, and adjust them to adapt to the dynamically increasing dimensions.

The partial-order relation is used to determine the causality of two operations. For operation OP_A and operation OP_B, the operation OP_A causal order precedes the operation OP_B ($OP_A \rightarrow OP_B$) if and only if any of the following conditions are met:

1. Operations occur on the same site ($N_A = N_B$):

   $\forall N_K \in SV_A \cap SV_B : SV_A[N_K] \leq SV_B[N_K], SV_A[N_A] < SV_B[N_B]$
   If the dimension of SV_A is bigger than the one of SV_B, then:
   $\forall N_K \in (SV_A - SV_B) : SV_A[N_K] = 0$

2. Operations occur on different sites ($N_A \neq N_B$):

   $\forall N_K \in (SV_A \cap SV_B - N_A - N_B) : SV_A[N_K] \leq SV_B[N_K],$
   $SV_A[N_A] = SV_B[N_A], SV_A[N_B] < SV_B[N_B]$
   If the dimension of SV_A is bigger than the one of SV_B, then:
   $\forall N_K \in (SV_A - SV_B) : SV_A[N_K] = 0$

3. $\exists OP_C : OP_A \rightarrow OP_C, OP_A \rightarrow OP_C$

Full-order relations are used to rank two concurrent atomic operations. We follow the definition in the AST scheme and determine the relationship through calculating the sum of the state vector timestamp and considering the number of the operation site which is assigned by the server. For operation OP_A and operation OP_B, $TOrder(OP_A) < TOrder(OP_B)$, if and only if any of the following conditions are met:

1. $sum(SV_A) < sum(SV_B), where\ sum(SV_A) = \sum_K SV_A[N_K]$
2. $sum(SV_A) = sum(SV_B), N_A < N_B$

Operation Process. The replay mode in the MOOC environment not only supports the collaboration among real users, but also realizes the simulated interaction between real users and the virtual user. The virtual user also maintains a replica and the status timestamp. When the heartbeat arrives, it first checks if there are history operations ready to popup and then executes the operation on its local copy, finally the server broadcasts the message to all real users. Since the virtual user works in the same way as the real users, it is possible to generate conflicts when both the real user and the virtual user is operating.

We consider the situation below. The history records are ordered by the latest round of discussion and we get a linear document. The document contains the following content and the first sentence is posted by history user A around video time t1 while the second sentence is posted by history user B around video time t2.

Why is processing a sorted array faster than processing an unsorted array?
You are a victim of branch prediction fail.

Because of the heartbeat check arrives every 60 s or longer, it is possible that there is a real user C answers or edits the first sentence before the sentence of user B wrote is popped. Then the address space is different from the one when the second sentence is generated in the history. In order to deal with the situation, we set a variable *lastSV* to describe the virtual user's status timestamp regardless of the executed operations of real users. If the virtual user is ready to operate on its local copy, it first retraces to the address space with the variable *lastSV* and then operates normally, finally retraces to the current timestamp. To make it clearer, we use the state vector to explain the process described above. Suppose that there are two real users E and F in this round of discussion, then the state vectors are " $< E{:}a,\ F{:}b,\ V{:}c >$ " and $lastSV = \ < E{:}0,\ F{:}0,\ V{:}c >$. Before virtual user V executes, user E and F edit the document collaboratively and the state vectors are updated to " $< E{:}a+x,\ F{:}b+y,\ V{:}c >$ ". For the virtual user V, it stores the current status timestamp as $currentSV = \ " < E{:}a+x,\ F{:}b+y,\ V{:}c >$ ", and retraces to the address space of *lastSV* to do the operations and return to the *currentSV*. Function 1 presents the control process of virtual user's operation. Function 2 shows the actions when the server receives a heartbeat check and triggers the virtual user to operate. Each round we record the details of the operations which will later be used in the next round group editing. For those operations retrieved from the history records, we update the operation's position by calculating its current effective index in the document.

Function 1 Control-Algorithm (Doc*s*, *O*, *lastSV*), virtual user executes *O* on Doc*s* with the last status timestamp *lastSV*

1:    *currentSV = getState()*

2:    Retrace(Doc*s*, *lastSV*)

3:    Execute the history operation O

4:    Attach the operation with its timestamp to the character node

5:    *SVs[R] = SVs[R] + 1*

6:    Retrace(Doc*s*, *currentSV*)

Function 2 onMessage (message, username, video time), server receives the heartbeat check and triggers the virtual user to operate

---

1:    **if** the message is a heartbeat check **then**

2:        **while** history records != null && opTime < videoTime **do**

3:            *virtual user* runs Control-Algorithm(Doc*s*, *O*, *lastSV*)

4:            *server* broadcasts to other users

5:            *server* marks the current effective position of *O* as *curIndex*

6:            *server* updates historical operation's position with *curIndex*

7:        **end while**

8:    **end if**

---

5 Implementation and Evaluation

The collaborative discussion area is implemented as a plugin of Chrome DevTools in the sidebar, so it's convenient to type in messages when watching the course videos. The plugin handles the events happened on the text area and periodically sends heartbeat checks or user's operations to inform the server. The server provides the AST-based controller to ensure the consistency for users' operations. The plugin interface can be seen in Fig. 1.

Average synchronize time in Fig. 2 was measured to evaluate the responsiveness in multi-sites environment. The synchronize time consists of the local execution time and the remote execution time in other sites' replica. We started the threads consecutively and let them generate operations incessantly to create a concurrent situation by using JMeter. When the number of running threads reached the test size, we let the threads operate for 100 times and calculated the average synchronize time. During the experiment, we observed that the synchronize time increased when a new thread entered and after seconds it dropped and stabilized to a certain range. The Browser-Server structure may account for the positive correlation between the total execution time and the thread size.

We also measured the average synchronize time with different historical records size to figure out whether the size of executed history records has an impact on users' execution. As is shown in Fig. 3, with the increase of the size of historical records, local execution time stays at zero while virtual user's execution time grows. It's explainable that the virtual user takes longer to transform its address space with a larger document.

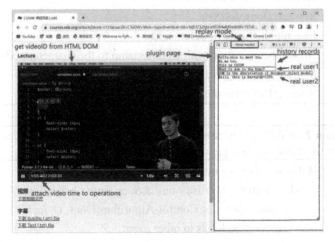

Fig. 1. The plugin interface

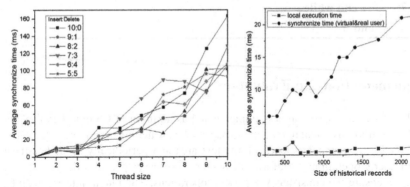

Fig. 2. Average synchronize time for different thread size

Fig. 3. Average synchronize time for different historical records size

6   Conclusion and Future Work

This work is a preliminary attempt to apply the AST scheme to the MOOC environment. In this paper, we give four kinds of collaboration modes between historical users and real users to provide learners with new studying experience in the MOOC environment. We propose a simulated interaction approach of a typical collaboration mode based on the AST scheme by expatiating the data structure, operation process and its consistency model. The simulated interaction approach aims to support learners in collaborating with those who have the same or similar questions, no matter they are actually online or have already exit.

There still exist many challenges and problems which are deserved to be studied in the future. On one hand, taking the semantic knowledge of history contents into consideration through deep learning methods or natural language process can be helpful in better arousing students' interest. On the other hand, the granularity of operations in the simulated approach is character-wise which causes a frequent transformation of address space, so we consider to adopt string-wise operations or use other document structure in the future work.

Acknowledgements. This work was supported by the National Natural Science Foundation of China (NSFC) under Grant No. 62172106.

References

1. Min, L., Jinas, K., Emily, M.: Examining learners' perspective of taking a MOOC: reasons, excitement, and perception of usefulness. Educ. Media Int. **52**, 1–18 (2015). https://doi.org/10.1080/09523987.2015.1053289
2. Le, L.T., Shah, C., Choi, E.: Evaluating the quality of educational answers in community question-answering. In: 2016 IEEE/ACM Joint Conference on Digital Libraries (JCDL), pp. 129–138. (2016)
3. Sun, C., Zhang, Y., Jia, X., Yang, Y.: A generic operation transformation scheme for consistency maintenance in real-time cooperative editing systems. In: Proceedings of the International ACM SIGGROUP Conference on Supporting Group Work: The Integration Challenge (GROUP 1997), pp. 425–434 (1997)
4. David, S., Steven, X., Sun, C., David, C.: Operational transformation for collaborative word processing. In: Proceedings of the 2004 ACM Conference on Computer Supported Cooperative Work (2004)
5. Gu, N., Yang, J., Zhang, Q.: Consistency maintenance based on the mark & retrace technique in groupware systems. In: Proceedings of the 2005 International ACM SIGGROUP Conference on Supporting Group Work (GROUP 2005), pp. 264–273 (2005)
6. Agustina, N., Sun, C.: Dependency-conflict detection in real-time collaborative 3D design systems. In: Proceedings of the 2013 Conference on Computer Supported Cooperative Work, ACM (2013), pp. 715–728 (2013)
7. Gadea, C., Ionescu, B., Ionescu, D.: New algorithms and methods for collaborative co-editing using HTML DOM synchronization. In: 2018 IEEE 4th International Conference on Collaboration and Internet Computing (CIC), 2018, pp. 217–226 (2018). https://doi.org/10.1109/CIC.2018.00038
8. Ignat, C.-L., Andŕe, L., Oster, G.: Enhancing rich content wikis with real-time collaboration. In: Concurrency and Computation:Practice and Experience (2017)
9. Puttaswamy, K.P., Marshall, C.C., Ramasubramanian, V., Stuedi, P., Terry, D.B., Wobber, T.: Docx2Go: collaborative editing of fidelity reduced documents on mobile devices. In: Proceedings of the 8thInternational Conference on Mobile Systems, Applications, and Services - MobiSys 2010, ACM Press, San Francisco, CA, USA; 2010, pp. 345–356 (2010)
10. Ionescu, B., Gadea, C., Solomon, B., Trifan, M., Ionescu, D., Stoicu-Tivadar, V.: A chat-centric collaborative environment for web-based real-time collaboration. In: 2015 IEEE 10th Jubilee International Symposium on Applied Computational Intelligence and Informatics, 2015, pp. 105–110 (2015). https://doi.org/10.1109/SACI.2015.7208180

11. Lv, X., Yuan, J., He, F., Cheng, Y., Cai, W.: Cloud-based lightweight collaborative editing algorithm for mobile devices. In: 2021 IEEE 24th International Conference on Computer Supported Cooperative Work in Design (CSCWD), 2021, pp. 250–255 (2021). https://doi.org/10.1109/CSCWD49262.2021.9437719

12. Xia, H., Lu, T., Shao, B., Li, G., Ding, X., Gu, N.: A partial replication approach for anywhere anytime mobile commenting. In: Proceedings of the 17th ACM Conference on Computer Supported Cooperative Work & Social Computing (CSCW 2014), pp. 530–541 (2014). https://doi.org/10.1145/2531602.2531609

13. Xia, H., Lu, T., Shao, B., Ding, X., Gu, N.: Hermes: on collaboration across heterogeneous collaborative editing services in the cloud. In: Proceedings of the 2014 IEEE 18th International Conference on Computer Supported Cooperative Work in Design (CSCWD), pp. 655–660 (2014). https://doi.org/10.1109/CSCWD.2014.6846922

14. Yang, J., Wang, H., Gu, N., et al.: Lock-free consistency control for web2.0 applications. In: Proceedings of the 17th International Conference on World Wide Web, Beijing, China, pp. 725–734 (2008)

15. Zhang, J., Lu, T., Xia, H., Shao, B., Gu, N.: ASTS: a string-wise address space transformation algorithm for real-time collaborative editing. In: 2017 IEEE 21st International Conference on Computer Supported Cooperative Work in Design (CSCWD), pp. 162–167 (2017)

16. Yang, R., Zhou, C., Huang, M., Wen, H., Liang, H.-N.: Design of an Interactive Classroom with bullet screen function in university teaching. In: 2021 9th International Conference on Information and Education Technology (ICIET), 2021, pp. 47–51 (2021). https://doi.org/10.1109/ICIET51873.2021.9419627

17. Liu, M., et al.: Exploration of best practices to support active learning in a synchronous multi-site learning environment. In: T. Bastiaens (edn.), Proceedings of World Conference on E-Learning, pp. 1190–1199. New Orleans, LA, USA: Association for the Advancement of Computing in Education (AACE) (2014)

DQN-Based Comprehensive Consumption Minimization on Calculation Offloading in Mobile Edge Computing

Kai Ding[1], Wenan Tan[1,2(✉)], Zhejun Liang[1], and Jin Liu[1]

[1] Nanjing University of Aeronautics and Astronautics, Nanjing 211106, China
wtan@foxmail.com
[2] Shanghai Polytechnic University, Shanghai 201209, China

Abstract. When Internet of Things (IoT) devices similar to sensors collect and analyze information outdoors, they often encounter insufficient energy or information cannot be analyzed in time. To make sensor devices work more continuously and efficiently, we apply Mobile Edge Computing (MEC) to Multi-Sensor Domain Exploration (MSDE) scenarios. The computation offloading strategy is selected by capturing the devices' battery level, assigning the offload rate of tasks, and observing the latency of each job. Committed to achieving this idea, we describe the offloading process as a Markov Decision Process (MDP), introduce action and state spaces, and propose an efficient offloading strategy based on the DQN. Simulation results verify the effectiveness and practicability of the proposed algorithm.

Keywords: IoT devices · mobile edge computing · Markov Decision Process · Deep Q Networks

1 Introduction

As one of the most promising technologies in the 5G era, IoT has opened up a bridge between the physical world and the information world to enrich human life [1,7] by analyzing and processing various external heterogeneous information. However, IoT devices such as sensors and wearables have computational bottlenecks due to memory, computing, and energy constraints. Therefore, this paper sinks Mobile Edge Computing (MEC) network into the IoT system. By macro-allocating the task proportion of IoT devices, offloading tasks to base stations, wireless access points, or even efficient smartphones within the radio access range of IoT devices, we can alleviate the dilemma of insufficient computing power or limited resources of IoT devices. In addition, computation offloading can also reduce the computing delay of the device and even effectively guarantee the security of IoT devices [10,11]. As one of the critical technologies in

This paper is supported by the National Natural Science Foundation of China (61672022, U1904186), Shanghai Second Polytechnic University Key Discipline Electronic Information Special Master Program Project (XXKZD1604).

MEC, computation offloading is being widely developed and applied with the increase of human needs and the rise of various emerging technologies. Zuo et al. deployed edge mobile computing into the IoT network to support blockchain technology and described the user's current selection strategy. An alternate optimization algorithm is proposed for temporal user selection, ensuring users' utility maximization in untrusted MEC-assisted mobile networks [13]. Liu et al. decoupled the computation offloading problem into the problems on radio resource and computational resource allocation, as well as further decomposed the radio resource allocation problem into the issues about sub-channel allocation and power allocation. They solve each sub-problem separately by applying matching and sequential convex programming algorithms and knapsack algorithms to improve the energy efficiency of MEC-enabled IoT networks [5]. Diao et al. proposed a scheduling-based algorithm in the NOMA MEC network supporting D2D communication to reduce the cost of edge computing servers through D2D communication and jointly optimize computing resources, transmit power, and channel allocation to minimize system costs [3]. In order to deal with the multi-edge application deployment problem (MEAD) in the EMC environment, Zhao et al. proposed a heuristic algorithm named DPG-D&C, which maximized the overall quality of service for program users with minimal deployment cost [12].

This paper attempts to minimize the comprehensive cost of device clusters, which can be defined as a linear combination of total latency and total energy consumption. We propose a system model for multi-sensor domain exploration. The tasks of the sensor devices can be partially offloaded to the edge server through the wireless channel. In addition, this paper needs to satisfy two subtasks. One is to ensure that the remaining energy of the sensor devices must be sufficient to execute calculation offloading strategy. The other is to guarantee that the delay of each task must be less than the corresponding threshold. Because the task size, computing power, and channel quality are time-varying in the natural environment, this will inevitably turn into a dynamic offloading problem. This paper defines the offloading process as MDP, and both the action and the state space are described. We designed an offloading strategy based on DQN to offload part of the task to the edge server. Finally, the simulation results effectively prove the efficiency and practicability of the DQN offloading strategy. The main contributions of this study are summarized as follows.

- This paper is committed to the more durable and efficient work of sensor devices and uses the comprehensive function of delay and energy consumption as the optimization objective function. We can adjust the parameters according to the current devices cluster's specific situation to lead weight tends to be more concerned in the present time.
- This paper deeply analyzes the time-varying process of the offloading process. We formulate state space, action space, and reward function reasonably and applicably to perfectly integrate the offloading process with the MDP.
- This paper uses the advanced DQN algorithm to optimize the objective function proposed in this paper and verifies the practicability and efficiency of the algorithm from multiple levels

2   System Model for MSDE

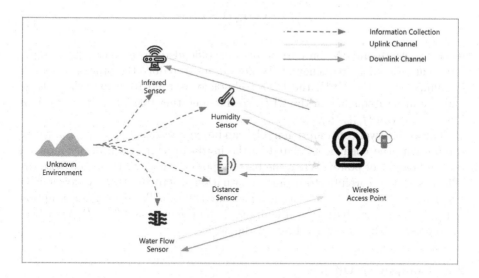

Fig. 1. System Model for MSDE

Sensor devices are often used to detect an unknown area. At this time, sensor devices often need to collect, analyze, and process surrounding information to ensure the validity of the information and the device's security. However, the problem of limited energy and computing power of the sensor device often occurs in the information collection. For this reason, we need to use the MEC network for task offloading to relieve the pressure of the sensor device.

As shown in Fig. 1,We build a multi-sensor MEC network, which includes a device cluster consisting of M sensor devices and a wireless access point, including a MEC server. Each device generates one task in each time slot, and the mission of each device is to analyze and process the collected information. Due to device energy and computing power constraints, these tasks could be transmitted to wireless access points over wireless channels. The device task can be denoted as $Q_m = \{I_m, C_m, T_m^d, B_m\}$, where $1 \leq m \leq M$. I_m represents the size of the task that the device m needs to complete, C_m represents the complexity of the task, T_m^d represents the acceptable delay for each task and B_m represents the remaining power of the device m.

2.1 Local Computing

The time required for each task Q_m can be expressed as follows.

$$T_m^l = \frac{C_m I_m (1 - x_m)}{f_m} \tag{1}$$

where x_m represents the proportion of tasks offloaded to the server [2], and f_m represents the CPU frequency of the device m. To reduce the processing power consumption of the CPU, the DVS technology is used to reduce the voltage and operating frequency of the CPU, so the operating frequency of the CPU is limited between $[f_{min}, f_{max}]$.

The local power consumption model can be expressed as $E_m^l = k f_m^3 T_m$. where k represents the coefficient related to the hardware chip. Each device stores a certain amount of power. When the battery power is low, we need to choose the offload strategy carefully to avoid the situation where the battery power is 0. The battery power of each device is represented as B_m. The energy consumption of the task that the battery can maintain is represented as $E_m^b = B_m V_m$ where V_m represents the working voltage of the device.

2.2 Computing Offload

When the task is decided to be partly offloaded to the edge server, it needs to send and receive the job through the wireless channel. This paper adopts the frequency division duplex mode, and the uplink and downlink channels are flat Rayleigh fading channels.

The path loss between the sensor device and the wireless access point can be modelled as d^{-v} Where d represents the direct distance from the device to the wireless access point, and v represents the path loss coefficient. We assume that the channel bandwidth is W, the fading coefficient of the uplink and downlink channels is expressed as h, and the interfering noise in the channel can be expressed as N. The channel transmission rate can be defined as follows.

$$R = W \log_2\left(\frac{1 + (pd^{-v}|h|^2}{N}\right) \tag{2}$$

Assuming that α represents the channel transmission cost coefficient, the transmission time in the channel can be expressed as follows.

$$T_m^u = \frac{\alpha I_m x_m}{W \log_2\left(\frac{1 + (pd^{-v}|h|^2}{N}\right)} \tag{3}$$

Meanwhile, the energy consumption of the sensor device m for sending tasks can be expressed as follows.

$$E_m^u = \beta P_m^u T_m^u \tag{4}$$

Among them, β represents the power amplifier efficiency coefficient, and P_m^u represents the transmission power of the uplink channel. In addition, when the task is offloaded to the edge server for computation, the computation time of the MEC server can be expressed as follows.

$$T_{mec} = \frac{C_m I_m x_m}{f} \tag{5}$$

2.3   Latency and Energy Consumption

The delay can be expressed as follows when tasks are partially offloaded to the MEC server for processing.

$$T_m^{all} = \max\{T_m^l, T_{mec} + T_m^u + t_m^d\} \tag{6}$$

Among them, T_m^u and T_m^d represent the transmission time of the uplink and downlink channels, respectively.

In addition, when the processing time transmitted to the MEC server is greater than the processing time locally, the sensor device will generate a waiting time T_w. At the same time, static energy consumption will be generated. The total energy consumption of this task can be expressed as follows [8].

$$E_m^{all} = E_m^l + \beta P_m^u T_m^u + \beta P_m^d T_m^d + P_w T_w \tag{7}$$

3   Problem Formulation

For the comprehensive utilization of the sensor devices, this paper establishes a combining consumption function of delay and energy consumption as the objective function [4].

$$\min_{x_m, f_m} \sum_{m=1}^{M} (\lambda T_m^{all} + (1 - \lambda) E_m^{all}) \tag{8}$$

$$
\begin{aligned}
s.t. \quad & C1: \quad T_m^{all} \leq T_m^d \\
& C2: \quad E_m^{all} \leq E_m^b \\
& C3: \quad 0 \leq x_m \leq 1 \\
& C4: \quad f_{min} \leq f_m \leq f_{max}
\end{aligned}
$$

The combining consumption function established in this paper has a significant advantage in practicability. We can adjust the linear proportion according to the current situation so that the weight tends to the side that is more concerned at the moment. When $\lambda = 0$ or $\lambda = 1$, it means minimizing energy consumption or minimizing delay.

Among them, C1 represents the delay constraint, C2 means that the total energy consumption cannot be greater than the overhead supported by the remaining battery, C3 represents the value range of the offloading rate and C4 represents the value range of the CPU frequency of the sensor device.

4 DQN-Based Offloading Strategy

4.1 MDP Process

During the dynamic computing offloading process, the state of the sensor device at the next moment only depends on the current action and state. Therefore, the offloading process can be defined as an MDP.

Action and state spaces play essential roles in describing the MDP process. When the time slot is $t = 1, 2 \ldots \infty$, this paper defines the state space as $S = \{s_t | s_t = [X_t, F_t]\}$, where $X_t = \{x_t^1, x_t^2 \ldots x_t^M\}, F_t = \{f_t^1, f_t^2 \ldots f_t^M\}$ are the offloading rate and the local CPU frequency at time t, respectively. The action space can be defined as $A = \{a_t | a_t = [\Delta x_t, \Delta f_t, flag, m] \, 1 \leq m \leq M\}$. For a given action a_t at time t, there are:

$$x_{t+1}^i / f_t^i = \begin{cases} x_{t+1}^i / f_t^i + \Delta x_t / \Delta f_t, & if \quad i = m, flag = 1 \\ x_{t+1}^i / f_t^i - \Delta x_t / \Delta f_t, & if \quad i = m, flag = 0 \\ x_{t+1}^i / f_t^i, & if \quad i \neq m \end{cases} \quad (9)$$

Here $\Delta x_t, \Delta f_t$ are fine-tuning parameters of offloading rate and CPU frequency. The $flag$ is a flag bit. When the $flag = 1$, the offloading rate and CPU frequency develop positively, and when the $flag = 0$, it grows in an adverse order. m represents the execution object of the current action.

When an action is selected in any state, the reward function will be evaluated according to the delay, battery power, and the comprehensive cost at the next moment, and the corresponding reward will be given. The specific reward function can be expressed as follows.

$$R_t = \begin{cases} -\gamma_1, & if \quad \forall E_m^t \geq E_m^b \\ -\gamma_2, & if \quad \forall T_m^t \geq T_m^d \\ -\gamma_3, & if \quad U^t \geq U^{t-1} \\ \gamma_3, & if \quad U^t < U^{t-1} \end{cases} \quad (10)$$

where $\gamma_1, \gamma_2, \gamma_3$ are three positive numbers, and $\gamma_1 > \gamma_2 > \gamma_3$. When the energy consumption of any device in time slot t is greater than the energy consumption supported by its battery or the delay is greater than the delay that the device can accept, the rewards are negative, which is not acceptable. What's more, we focus on the change of the comprehensive cost. if the cost value decreases, the immediate reward is γ_3. Otherwise, it is $-\gamma_3$.

The more action lagger, the less reward brings. We can focus on the average reward and try to find the best offloading policy.

4.2 DQN Algorithm

The environment at a certain moment can obtain the corresponding reward by selecting the action and then judging the pros and cons of the action. In the traditional Q Learning algorithm, the function of the Q table is to record the value of the corresponding state-action pair. However, due to the time-varying environment, the dimensions of its corresponding state and action are immeasurable. Therefore, the traditional Q-table is no longer applicable, and the alternative method is to use a neural network to approximate the Q-function. The Q value at a specific time can be expressed as follows [6].

$$Q(s_t, a_t) = R_t + \xi \max_{a_{t+1}} Q(s_{t+1}, a_{t+1}) \tag{11}$$

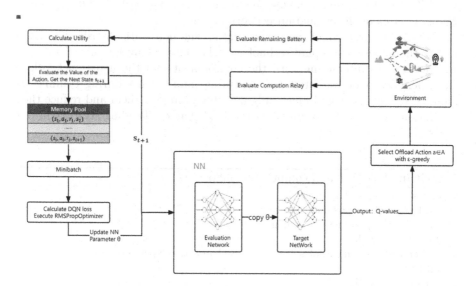

Fig. 2. DQN Algorithm Framework Diagram

As shown in Fig. 2, the neural network of DQN consists of an evaluation network and a target network. After a few rounds, the target network that lags behind the evaluation network will copy the parameters θ of the evaluation network. We use the current state of the environment as the input of the evaluation network and $Q(s_t, a_t|\theta_t)$ as the output of the evaluation network. The current environment acquires the action through the ϵ-greedy strategy and enters the state of the next moment. We evaluate the device battery power and computing delay of the environment and finally calculate the combined cost at this time. We use the reward function to assess the value of this action and store this experimental sample in the experience pool. Next, a set of mini-batches are selected from the experience pool to calculate the loss of the neural network and then update the evaluation network parameter θ. Finally, the state at the next moment and the updated parameter θ are passed into the neural network to enter the next round of iteration.

DQN contains two neural networks: the evaluation network and the other is the target network. The structure of the target network is consistent with the evaluation network, and the parameters of the evaluation network are copied every several iterations. Then we can maintain the differentiation of the two networks over time. We can calculate the loss function using the Q-value difference between the evaluation network and the target network and update the parameters θ of the neural network through the RMSprop optimizer. The loss function of DQN can be expressed as follows.

$$L_t = E\left[(TargetQ - Q\left(s_t, a_t | \theta_t\right))^2\right] \tag{12}$$

where $TargetQ$ represents the Q-value of the target network, and θ_t represents the parameters of the evaluation network at time t.

To solve the problem of sample correlation and non-static distribution, DQN adopts the experience replay technology. The data replay is realized by storing the samples interacting with the environment and the neural network in the experience pool and randomly capturing mini-batches during training for training. Independent and identically distributed among them and reduce their correlation. Algorithm 1 summarizes the DQN-based offloading strategy in this paper.

Algorithm 1. DQN-based computation offloading scheme

Input: $s_1 \leftarrow \{X_1, F_1\}$.
Output: optimal deployment strategy s
 1: Initialize the parameter θ of neural networks
 2: **for** $i = 1$ to I **do**
 3:     Deposit random samples $\{s_i, a_i, r_i, s_{i+1}\}$ into the experience pool
 4: **end for**
 5: **for** $t = 1$ to T **do**
 6:     The current state s_t selects the action a_t with ϵ-greedy through the NN
 7:     Carry out a_t and observe the battery level and latency of each device
 8:     Calculate the reward r_t for the action a_t
 9:     The environment reaches the next state s_{t+1}
10:     $experience\ pool \leftarrow \{s_t, a_t, r_t, s_{t+1}\} \cup experience\ pool$
11:     get minibatch from experience pool
12:     Execute RMSPropOptimizer to L_t
13:     Update parameters of target network
14:     $s_t \leftarrow s_{t+1}$
15: **end for**
16: **return** s

---

5   Experimental Simulation

To verify the effectiveness and practicability of the algorithm, we designed some simulation experiments and some variables to simulate the natural environment. The devices are randomly distributed within 200 m of the server. The CPU frequency of the device is between $4 * 10^8$ and $6 * 10^8$. The frequency of the edge server is $4 * 10^9$. The device's remaining power is maintained between $0mAh$ and $100mAh$, and the working voltage is $3.7V$. The transmit power of the device is held between $0.1W$ and $0.2W$. The channel bandwidth is $10MHz$, and the channel noise is $-174dBm/Hz$ [9].

In addition, the neural network model of this paper is shown in the Table 1. This paper chooses to use RMSProp Optimizer as the optimizer. The size of the experience pool is 1000, the mini-batch size is 32, the parameter θ of the target network is updated every 200-time slots, and the default linear parameter λ is 0.8.

Table 1. NN Structure.

Layer	FC1	FC2	OutPut
Input Size	num(State)	50	30
Structure	num(State) * 50	50 * 30	30 * num(Action)
Activation	ReLU	ReLu	
Output Size	50	30	num(Action)

When the input task size is $1M \sim 10M$, the number of devices is 10, 20, 30, 40, 50, and the number of iterations is 16,000, the performance of the DQN-based offloading scheme is shown in Fig. 3 and Fig. 4. Figure 3 is the comprehensive consumption effect diagram, and Fig. 4 is the energy consumption effect diagram. When the number of devices is small, the algorithm can quickly converge. When the task of the device gradually increases, the global search performance of the algorithm is not suitable due to the small action step size. However, it still shows the phenomenon of rapid convergence. After continuous iteration, the comprehensive cost is 21, 50, 78, 118, and 145, respectively. The minimum energy loss is 45J, 132J, 230J, 321J, and 455J.

Next, when the number of devices is $10 \sim 50$ and the task size is $1M \sim 10M$. This paper compares the proposed algorithm with complete local computation, all MEC offloading, random offloading, and particle swarm offloading schemes at $\lambda = 0$ and $\lambda = 1$, respectively. $\lambda = 0$, the comprehensive cost of the combination can be regarded as the energy cost. When $\lambda = 1$, the comprehensive cost can be considered the delay cost.

It can be seen from Fig. 5 and Fig. 6 that if all tasks are executed locally, the device will consume a lot of energy. As such, local execution is highly undesirable. Suppose all tasks are executed on the MEC server. Although the device does not need to drink too much power, the rate will be reduced since many jobs are transmitted over unlimited channels. The delay will be seriously affected, and eventually, the tasks will not be completed on time. So this is also not advisable. The performance of the random algorithm is also not very good due to its instability. Although the particle swarm algorithm has a good convergence performance in the early stage, it is still not comparable to the DQN-based offloading strategy with the increase of equipment. When the number of devices is 50, the latency of the remaining algorithms is 8.75, 3.5, 2.5, and 1.5 times that of the proposed algorithms in this paper. Combining the comprehensive cost of the linear combination of the two cases, only the DQN-based offloading method proposed in this paper can achieve a perfect performance.

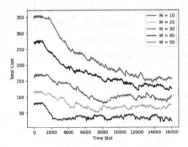

Fig. 3. Comprehensive Consumption

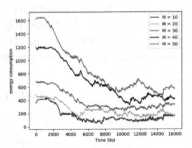

Fig. 4. Energy Consumption

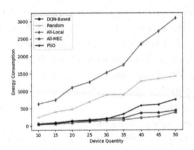

Fig. 5. Energy Consumption

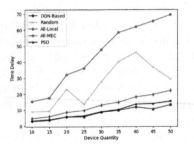

Fig. 6. Time Delay

6   Summary and Outlook

Mobile edge computing comprehensively considers energy consumption and latency a desirable approach, especially in clusters of sensor devices with insufficient energy. In this paper, we formulate a rational optimization objective function and deeply analyze the offloading process's time-varying process. Finally, we propose a DQN-based computing offloading strategy for sensor devices, which can ensure the adequacy of energy and stable efficiency of sensor devices when collecting, analyzing, and processing unknown environment information. Simulation experiments verify the feasibility of the algorithm. In future investigations, we will continue implementing reinforcement learning-based offloading schemes and consider the combination with heuristics.

References

1. Ali, B., Gregory, M.A., Li, S.: Multi-access edge computing architecture, data security and privacy: a review. IEEE Access **9**, 18706–18721 (2021). https://doi.org/10.1109/ACCESS.2021.3053233
2. Bi, S., Zhang, Y.J.: Computation rate maximization for wireless powered mobile-edge computing with binary computation offloading. IEEE Trans. Wirel. Commun. **17**(6), 4177–4190 (2018). https://doi.org/10.1109/TWC.2018.2821664
3. Diao, X., Zheng, J., Wu, Y., Cai, Y.: Joint computing resource, power, and channel allocations for D2D-assisted and NOMA-based mobile edge computing. IEEE Access **7**, 9243–9257 (2019). https://doi.org/10.1109/ACCESS.2018.2890559
4. Li, C., et al.: Dynamic offloading for multiuser muti-CAP MEC networks: a deep reinforcement learning approach. IEEE Trans. Veh. Technol. **70**(3), 2922–2927 (2021). https://doi.org/10.1109/TVT.2021.3058995
5. Liu, B., Liu, C., Peng, M.: Resource allocation for energy-efficient MEC in NOMA-enabled massive IoT networks. IEEE J. Sel. Areas Commun. **39**(4), 1015–1027 (2021). https://doi.org/10.1109/JSAC.2020.3018809
6. Min, M., Xiao, L., Chen, Y., Cheng, P., Wu, D., Zhuang, W.: Learning-based computation offloading for IoT devices with energy harvesting. IEEE Trans. Veh. Technol. **68**(2), 1930–1941 (2019). https://doi.org/10.1109/TVT.2018.2890685
7. Ranaweera, P., Jurcut, A.D., Liyanage, M.: Survey on multi-access edge computing security and privacy. IEEE Commun. Surv. Tutorials **23**(2), 1078–1124 (2021). https://doi.org/10.1109/COMST.2021.3062546
8. Tan, W., Ding, K., Zhang, X., Liang, Z., Liu, J.: Minimizing terminal energy consumption of task offloading via resource allocation in mobile edge computing. In: 2022 IEEE 25th International Conference on Computer Supported Cooperative Work in Design (CSCWD), pp. 683–688 (2022). https://doi.org/10.1109/CSCWD54268.2022.9776100
9. Wang, Y., Sheng, M., Wang, X., Wang, L., Li, J.: Mobile-edge computing: partial computation offloading using dynamic voltage scaling. IEEE Trans. Commun. **64**(10), 4268–4282 (2016). https://doi.org/10.1109/TCOMM.2016.2599530
10. Xu, X., et al.: A computation offloading method over big data for IoT-enabled cloud-edge computing. Future Gener. Comput. Syst. **95**, 522–533 (2019)
11. Zhao, L., et al.: Joint coverage-reliability for budgeted edge application deployment in mobile edge computing environment. IEEE Trans. Parallel Distrib. Syst. **33**(12), 3760–3771 (2022). https://doi.org/10.1109/TPDS.2022.3166163
12. Zhao, L., et al.: Joint shareability and interference for multiple edge application deployment in mobile-edge computing environment. IEEE Internet Things J. **9**(3), 1762–1774 (2022). https://doi.org/10.1109/JIOT.2021.3088493
13. Zuo, Y., Jin, S., Zhang, S.: Computation offloading in untrusted MEC-aided mobile blockchain IoT systems. IEEE Trans. Wirel. Commun. **20**(12), 8333–8347 (2021). https://doi.org/10.1109/TWC.2021.3091861

Stochastic Task Offloading Problems for Edge Computing

Kexin Ding[1], Zhi Zhong[1], and Jie Zhu[1,2(✉)]

[1] Nanjing University of Posts and Telecommunications, Nanjing 210003, China
zhujie@njupt.edu.cn
[2] Institute of Computing Technology, Academy of Sciences, State Key Laboratory Chinese of Computer Architecture, Beijing 100864, China

Abstract. The edge-cloud computing is extensively deployed to provide convenient computing. A stochastic task offloading problem in edge-cloud environment is considered. For the problem under study, a greedy simulated annealing heuristic algorithm based online offloading framework (SAOF) is proposed. In consideration of the stochastic arrival of independent tasks and the heterogeneity of resources, SAOF offloads tasks to cloud servers or edge servers dynamically. During the offloading process, each server preemptively schedules the uncompleted tasks according to the latency-sensitivity of the task. The optimization objective is to minimize the total weighted response time. Experiments are delicately designed on the testing instances with various settings. SAOF is compared with the baseline algorithm. Experimental results indicate that SAOF can more effectively reduce the total weighted response time of all tasks.

Keywords: Edge-cloud computing · Task offloading · Heuristic algorithm · Stochastic task scheduling

1 Introduction

In the past decade, cloud computing has grown quickly and been used extensively. Given their unrestricted and scalable computing capabilities, cloud computing can provide highly available and dependable services. However, it is impossible to process massive data in the distant cloud platforms given the rapid expansion of digital data generated by various data gathering devices dispersed globally. Since remote clouds are typically located far from end users, the users would experience significant communication delay. Long delay is typically unsatisfactory, especially for users with high demand on latency, even though the cloud resources can greatly boost computation-intensive users. Considering the balance between high performance and low latency, a new paradigm of the edge-cloud computing is derived.

Massive intelligent and affordable edge servers are set up at the edge of the network in edge computing environments. The service efficiency could be greatly increased by offloading tasks to cloud/edge servers which are either closer to end devices or more powerful on computing. How to assign tasks to servers effectively under different limitations is crucial in edge-cloud computing. Effective task scheduling algorithms can offload tasks to the optimal locations while taking into account the necessary computing durations and transmission delays. Edge-cloud projects such as Azure IoT Edge [1], Google Cloud IoT Edge [2] and AWS IoT Greengrass [3] offload the data-intensive tasks such as the machine learning tasks to a number of edge devices, allowing for real-time processing of data collected by extensive sensors. There are a large number of researches devoted to the problem of task offloading in edge-cloud systems. Chen et al. [4] study a dependency-aware offloading problem under device budget constraints, where both the mode of edge-cloud cooperation and edge-edge cooperation are considered. With the aim of minimizing overall delay and energy cost, Chen et al. [5] jointly investigate the problems of task offloading & transmission power allocation in edge-cloud environments. The problem of security task offloading based on the IoT-Edge-Cloud system is developed in a few studies.

In the paper, the problem of dynamic task offloading under the edge-cloud environments is explored with the objective of minimizing the total weighted response time. There are two main problems considered: (1) arranging stochastic arrival tasks to the optimal servers efficiently take account of heterogeneous resources and transmission latency; (2) computing the execution priorities of tasks on each computing instance and assigning the required resources to tasks.

It is proved that the problem of static task offloading is NP-hard [6], therefore it stands to reason that the problem of dynamic task offloading under investigation is NP-hard. The problem under consideration faces several significant challenges. Generally, the resources on the edge devices and the cloud servers are heterogenous on the computing capability. The transmission latency and cost of edge resources are low, but the efficiency is also low. The efficiency of cloud resources is high, but the cost and transmission latency are also high. It is challenging to strike a balance between time and cost.

The existing researches mostly assume that the information of tasks to offload are known or that the arrival distribution of tasks is given. With the given static information of all tasks, effective offline offloading algorithms could be applied [5, 7]. However, the arrival distribution of tasks could change dramatically along with time. These offline algorithms may not be applicable for dynamic ones. As a result, an efficient dynamic offloading policy is critical to be developed.

The following is a summary of the main contributions in this paper: (1) The problem under study is formulated as a mixed integrate programming model with the goal of minimize the total weighted response time. A unique weight is assigned to each task. The weight represents the latency-sensitivity of a task. (2) An online task offloading algorithm is developed based on the resource availability. The framework offload and schedule tasks dynamically and periodically. The management of each resource is in the form of time slots and updated periodically. (3) The new arrival tasks are separated into groups based on the weights. The arrange order and servers of these tasks to offload are determined by performing a greedy simulated annealing heuristic algorithm on each group. A highest residual density first heuristic rule is applied during the offloading process to sequence tasks on each instance. (4) The data set of Google Cluster [8] are used to evaluate the performance of the developed algorithm. The results of the experiments indicate that the proposal is more effective and the tasks with higher weights could typically gain faster response times compared with the baseline.

2   Related Work

In cloud computing platform, increasingly mobile devices could take advantage of the plentiful computing resources of remote cloud data centers. The cloud computing can significantly extend the computing abilities for mobile devices. It is essential to implement efficient task scheduling on the cloud, which has been widely studied. Xiong et al. [9] design a two-stage task scheduling mathematical model for cloud data center and consider the multi-processor task scheduling. They propose a genetic algorithm based on Johnson-rule to minimize the makespan. Guo et al. [10] develop a task scheduling method in consideration of the deadline in multiple clouds. The random operators are used in genetic method and the discrete particle swarm is optimized. The goal is to minimize the total cost of transmission, calculation and execution. Most of the problems in these works ignore the transmission time. However, in practical scenarios, the data are transferred to the remote cloud centers and then the computation results are returned, which inevitably lead to long transmission times. The transmission times may significantly reduce the effectiveness of the scheduling schemes, especially for latency-sensitive and data-intensive tasks.

The edge-cloud computing is a solution to the limitations of cloud computing mentioned above. The edge servers with less computing power are deployed at network edge and close to the mobile devices. It can satisfy the user's demands while data can be processed without being transmitted to the remote cloud and significantly reduce the transmission delay [11]. Massive research works are concerning on the system architecture of edge-cloud computing. Jonathan et al. [12] develop a distributed edge-cloud framework named Nebula, which has a lightweight infrastructure. Nebula takes into account the location-aware data, voluntary storage and computing resources. The recovery, computation placement and replication methods are adopted. Pan et al. [13] explore the management of network, computing offload, data and resources in edge-cloud. They discuss the emerging enabling technologies the application scenarios of edge-cloud systems.

In edge-cloud systems, the effective task offloading strategy is an emerging research work. On the basis of the dependency between tasks, the research can be divided into the offloading for tasks with dependencies (which is normally known as DAG task offloading) and tasks without dependencies (i.e., independent task offloading). For the offloading problems of tasks with dependencies, Chen et al. [4] consider the constraints of device budget and task dependency in mobile edge computing. The offloading problem is divided into two NP-hard sub-problems, under the mode of both the edge-edge and edge-cloud collaborations and the mode of edge-cloud collaboration. Two efficient greedy algorithms are designed for these sub-problems respectively to minimize the completion time. Sahni et al. [14] consider a dependency-aware task scheduling problem take account of network flow adjustment and different task placement. A multistage greedy adjustment algorithm is proposed to optimize the completion time. The problem scenarios of these works are mostly static. For the offloading problems of tasks without dependencies, Meng et al. [15] propose an online task scheduling and dispatching algorithm take account of the computing resources and networking management. The goal is to maximize the number of tasks completed before the deadline. Kuang et al. [16] consider partial offloading and resource assignment problem with the objective of reduce the energy consumption and execution delay. An iterative two-level alternation algorithm is proposed under the constraint of transmission power.

In addition, on the basis of the real-time characteristics of the problem scenario, the research on task offloading in edge-cloud environments can be divided into dynamic and static problems. For the dynamic task offloading problems, Ding et al. [17] develop a dynamic coalition formation policy to decrease the user cost. The status of tasks and servers change continuously during execution in consideration of the parallel processing. Bi et al. [18] explore the optimal task offloading policy with the goal of improve the system utility. An incremental greedy algorithm based on gradient method is proposed, considering the fairness and throughput. Wu et al. [19] consider the blockchain-edge-cloud scenario and propose an efficient dynamic offloading algorithm to select computing placement adaptively. The objective is to optimize the response time and energy cost. For the static task offloading problems, Chen et al. [5] develop a two-level alternation algorithm under the constraint of power allocation. They make use of the Deep Q-Network and sequential quadratic programming method to reduce the sum system cost. Naouri et al. [7] propose a three-layer offloading model and a greedy task graph partition offloading algorithm. The goal is to minimize the processing delay and communication cost.

The problems of dynamic task offloading in edge-cloud environments are more universal and actual. The work of [20] consider the problem of online task dispatching and scheduling in edge-cloud computing. The tasks are generated at random time without regard to the release distribution between tasks. An online algorithm is proposed in consideration of transmission delays to minimize the sum of weighted response times. The investigation in [20] is used as the baseline for this paper.

3 Problem Description

Newly tasks arrive in the system randomly in the problem under study. Assuming that the system begins at time zero. Let t represents a scheduling period and the system offloads tasks periodically. During the time interval $[(q - 1) \times t, q \times t]$, i.e., the qth scheduling period, a set of n_q tasks $\mathbb{T}_q = \{T_{1,q}, T_{2,q}, \cdots T_{n_q,q}\}$ arrive in the system. These tasks are independent to each other. $T_{i,q}$ is the ith task in $\mathbb{T}_q$.

For a task $T_{i,q}$, it can be represented as $< \alpha_{i,q}, \beta_{i,q}, p_{i,q}(I), d_{i,q}^{\uparrow}(I), d_{i,q}^{\downarrow}(I) >$. Where $\alpha_{i,q}$ is the arrival time satisfying $\alpha_{i,q} \in [(q - 1) \times t, q \times t]$. $\beta_{i,q}$ is a static property of $T_{i,q}$. It represents the weight of $T_{i,q}$. A larger value of the weight indicates the higher latency-sensitivity, emergency or the VIP level of $T_{i,q}$. Supposing that the weights range from the value 1 to M and higher values imply higher priorities of the tasks. $p_{i,q}(I)$, $d_{i,q}^{\uparrow}(I)$ and $d_{i,q}^{\downarrow}(I)$ depend on the computing instance I. $p_{i,q}(I)$ is the processing time of $T_{i,q}$ on instance I. $d_{i,q}^{\uparrow}(I)$ is the time upload the data of $T_{i,q}$ to I. $d_{i,q}^{\downarrow}(I)$ is the time download the computation result of $T_{i,q}$ from I. During the execution, the tasks cannot be transferred to other servers in order to avoid the transfer cost. However, the tasks can be preempted or interrupted.

The computing instances of edge servers are defined as a set $\mathbb{E} = \{I_1^e, I_2^e, \cdots, I_K^e\}$ and the computing instances of cloud servers are defined as a set $\mathbb{C} = \{I_1^c, I_2^c, \cdots, I_J^c\}$. The computing instances are isolated computing units such as the virtual machines or containers. All the computing instances are heterogeneous and without regard to multi-tenancy. Each instance is single-threaded and could execute at most one task at a time. These instances have different data transmission bandwidths and different computing power. In general, the edge servers result in smaller transmission delays than cloud servers, the cloud servers have stronger computing power than edge servers.

For the assignment $a_{i,q}$ of $T_{i,q}$, it can be described as $< I_{i,q}, f_{i,q}^\uparrow, e_{i,q}^\uparrow, f_{i,q}^\downarrow, e_{i,q}^\downarrow, F_{i,q}, E_{i,q}, w_{i,q}, r_{i,q} >$. $I_{i,q}$ is the computing instance arranged for $T_{i,q}$ and $I_{i,q} \in \mathbb{C} \cup \mathbb{E}$. $f_{i,q}^\uparrow$ and $e_{i,q}^\uparrow$ are the times that $T_{i,q}$ begin and end the upload to $I_{i,q}$ respectively. $f_{i,q}^\downarrow$ and $e_{i,q}^\downarrow$ are the times that $T_{i,q}$ begin and end the download from $I_{i,q}$ respectively. $F_{i,q}$ and $E_{i,q}$ are the times that $T_{i,q}$ begin and end the calculation on $I_{i,q}$ respectively. If the task is interrupted, $F_{i,q}$ and $E_{i,q}$ may be not single value. The calculation interval of $T_{i,q}$ can be denoted as $[f_{i,q,h}, e_{i,q,h}] (f_{i,q,h} \in F_{i,q}, e_{i,q,h} \in E_{i,q})$. $w_{i,q}$ represents the total waiting time that $T_{i,q}$ is interrupted when executing, defined as Eq. (1). $r_{i,q}$ represents the response time of $T_{i,q}$, which is the time interval from $T_{i,q}$ arrive in system to the result of $T_{i,q}$ download end time, defined as Eq. (2).

$$w_{i,q} = \max\{e_{i,q,h} | e_{i,q,h} \in E_{i,q}\} - \min\{f_{i,q,h} | f_{i,q,h} \in F_{i,q}\} - p_{i,q}(I_{i,q}) \qquad (1)$$

$$r_{i,q} = e_{i,q}^\downarrow - \alpha_{i,q} \qquad (2)$$

In the time $[0, Q \times t]$, S_Q is the set of schedule arrangements for all tasks. Along with the continuous arrival of new tasks, some old tasks that are not completed may be preempted by the newly arrived tasks. S_Q is updated constantly over time. The constraints of S_Q are as follows.

$$\max\left\{f_{i,q,h}, f_{i',q',h'} | I_{i,q} = I_{i',q'}\right\} \geq \min\left\{e_{i,q,h}, e_{i',q',h'} | I_{i,q} = I_{i',q'}\right\} \qquad (3)$$

$$f_{i,q}^\uparrow \geq \alpha_{i,q} \qquad (4)$$

$$f_{i,q} \geq e_{i,q}^\uparrow \qquad (5)$$

$$f_{i,q}^\downarrow \geq e_{i,q} \qquad (6)$$

$$e_{i,q}^\uparrow = f_{i,q}^\uparrow + l_{i,q}^\uparrow(I_{i,q}) \qquad (7)$$

$$e_{i,q}^\downarrow = f_{i,q}^\downarrow + l_{i,q}^\downarrow(I_{i,q}) \qquad (8)$$

$$p_{i,q}(I_{i,q}) = \sum_{e_{i,q,h} \in E_{i,q}, f_{i,q,h} \in F_{i,q}} (e_{i,q,h} - f_{i,q,h}) \qquad (9)$$

$$\forall f_{i,q,h} \in F_{i,q}, \forall e_{i,q,h} \in E_{i,q}, I_{i,q} \in \mathbb{C} \cup \mathbb{E}$$

$$i = 1, \cdots, n_q, q = 1, \cdots, Q$$

Constraint (3) means that the tasks do not overlap in execution time on each computing instance. Constraint (4) indicates that each task cannot begin until its arrival. Constraint (5) indicates each computing instance cannot calculate the task until the transmission of the task data is completed. Constraint (6) means that the task must finish the processing on the computing instance before returning the calculation result. Equations (7), (8) define the end uploading and end downloading times respectively. Constraint (9) means that each task must have sufficient processing time.

The goal is to gain the optimal scheduling assignments with minimizing total weighted response times $W(S_Q)$. $W(S_Q)$ defined as Eq. (10).

$$W(S_Q) = \sum_{q=1}^{Q} \sum_{i=1}^{n_q} \left(\beta_{i,q} \times r_{i,q} \right) \tag{10}$$

4 Proposed Methods

4.1 Simulated Annealing Based Online Offloading Framework

In this paper, aiming at the problem of stochastic task offloading problem in edge-cloud computing, a greedy simulated annealing heuristic algorithm (SA) based online offloading framework (SAOF) is developed. At the very beginning of time zero, S_Q is empty. It is updated periodically at time $\epsilon = t, 2t, \cdots Q \times t$. The randomly arriving tasks are arranged by period and the execution of all the tasks is monitored at each time period. The resource availabilities of all the servers are also managed and updated. Newly tasks that arrive within the time window $[\epsilon - t, \epsilon]$ are collected for scheduling. The collected tasks are divided into M task sets in a non-increasing order based on their weights. A SA algorithm is applied to each task sets to achieve the arrangements of tasks. The essence is to ensure that tasks with a higher weight get a faster response.

SAOF is described as Algorithm 1.

Algorithm 1: SAOF.

```
1. S_Q ← Ø;
2. for q = 1 to Q
```

> Monitoring the states of tasks and resource availa-
> bilities;
> Collecting new tasks $T_{1,q}, T_{2,q}, \cdots T_{n_q,q}$ to be offloaded;
> Dividing tasks into M groups $G_1, G_2, \cdots, G_M$ based on
> their weights;
> for $m = M$ to 1
> > Executing SA procedure for G_m to achieve arrange-
> > ments of tasks in G_m;
> > $S_Q \leftarrow S_Q \cup \{a_{i,q} | T_{i,q} \in G_m\};$

```
3. return S_Q.
```

4.2 Simulated Annealing Based Algorithm

The greedy simulated annealing (SA) algorithm is a crucial procedure of SAOF. For tasks with same weight that to be scheduled, the task sequence π_0 is created stochastically as the initial solution at the start of the iteration. The ARR algorithm is performed on each group to gain the arrangements of tasks. The optimal task arrange sequence π^* is obtained and the optimal total weighted response time W^* is recorded. The neighborhood of π_0 is generated from the generating function $\mathbb{N}$. New neighborhoods can be generated by swapping any two tasks in the sequence. The new solution is received using the commonly used Metropolis criterion: if the objective function difference $\Delta < 0$, the new solution is received; otherwise the new solution is received with probability P, which is calculated as shown in Eq. (11).

$$P = \frac{1}{1 + e^{-\frac{\Delta}{\lambda}}} \tag{11}$$

where λ is the control parameter that gradually decreases as the algorithm runs. The cooling mechanism during annealing is set to $\lambda_{s+1} = \lambda_s \times r(0 < r < 1)$ to maintain a balance between the computational rate and the attainment of the low energy state. The greedy simulated annealing is applied to the neighborhoods of π^* iteratively until meet the termination conditions. Thus, it is possible to jump out of the local optimum with a certain probability while ensuring convergence. There are three termination conditions: (1) the solution can be improved in the current iteration; (2) the calculation time of the iteration exceeds the preset value. The calculation time for generating the offloading solution for the next time interval cannot exceed t/M. Otherwise, the new tasks of the next time interval cannot be offloaded in time; (3) λ is lower than the lower limit λ_{min}. The search is stopped if λ drops to λ_{min}. During the iterative process, the best schedule S^* and the best task sequence π^* are continuously updated.

SA is described as Algorithm 2.

Algorithm 2: SA(G_m).

1. Constructing initial task sequence $\pi_0 = \left(T_1, T_2, \cdots T_{n_g}\right), T_i \in$ G_m;
2. $S^* \leftarrow ARR(\pi_0)$;
3. $W^* \leftarrow W(S_0)$;
4. $\pi^* \leftarrow \pi_0$;
5. Constructing neighborhood $\Pi = N(\pi^*)$;
6. while (Termination conditions are not met)
       for $\forall \pi \in \Pi$ do
           $S \leftarrow ARR(\pi)$;
           $W \leftarrow W(S)$;
           $\Delta \leftarrow W - W^*$;
           if $\Delta < 0$ then $S^* \leftarrow S$; $W^* \leftarrow W$; $\pi^* \leftarrow \pi$;
           else
               $P \leftarrow 1/\left(1 + e^{-\frac{\Delta}{\lambda}}\right)$;
               if $P > random(0,1)$ then $S^* \leftarrow S$; $W^* \leftarrow W$; $\pi^* \leftarrow \pi$;
           $\lambda = \lambda \times r$;
           $\Pi \in N(\pi^*)$;
7. return S^*.

4.3 ARR

For a given sequence π, the ARR algorithm is to obtain the arrangements of tasks. In ARR, the OFFLOADING algorithm is executed for each task in π to determine the arrangements of tasks.

ARR is described as Algorithm 3.

Algorithm 3: ARR(π).

```
1. S ← ∅;
2. W ← W(S_Q);
3. for i = 1 to n_g do
       a_i ← OFFLOADING(T_i, W);
       Offloading T_i to I_i;
       S ← S ∪ {a_i};
4. return S.
```

4.4 OFFLOADING

For a given task T, OFFLOADING algorithm is applied to compute the optimal computing instance and determine the executing order of the given task on the optimal computing instance. W records the current objective value, T will be offloaded to the computing instance that bring the minimal increment for W. Let a_{best} records the best arrangement of T and Δ_{min} denote the minimal increment for W. Assume that a_{best} is empty and Δ_{min} is infinite at the start of the OFFLOADING algorithm.

a_{best} is computed through the followed procedures: At the current time ϵ, the data of T will upload to instance I at time ϵ'. The task T^* being processed at time ϵ' is obtained. The residual densities of T^* and T are computed. Let $R\left(I, \epsilon'\right)$ represents the residual density of T on I at time ϵ' and $p(I, \epsilon')$ represents the residual processing time of T on I at time ϵ'. $R\left(I, \epsilon'\right)$ is computed by Eq. (12).

$$R\left(I, \epsilon'\right) = \beta/p(I, \epsilon') \tag{12}$$

β is the weight of T. The residual density of T^* is defined similarly. The residual densities of T^* and T are compared. T will preempt T^* if T has a higher residual density. The calculation of T is begin at time ϵ' and T^* is moved to the waiting queue $\mathbb{Q}$. If T has a lower residual density, T is moved to $\mathbb{Q}$. The residual densities of tasks in $\mathbb{Q}$ are calculated and the tasks are sorted in non-increasing order based on residual densities. The arrangements of all tasks (including T, T^* and waiting tasks in $\mathbb{Q}$) on I are obtained. The state of T at time ϵ' determines the arrangement a of T. If T preempts T^* at time ϵ', the calculation begin time of T is ϵ'. Otherwise, the calculation begin time of T depends on the executing order of T in $\mathbb{Q}$. The increment of W for task T on each instance is computed, Δ_{min} and a_{best} are updated if the obtained increment value is smaller. The objective value W' is constantly updated during the iteration.

OFFLOADING is described as Algorithm 4.

Algorithm 4: OFFLOADING(T, W).

```
1. a_best ← NULL;
2. Δ_min ← +∞;
3. for ∀I ∈ C ∪ E do
       ε' = ε + d↑(I);
       Obtaining T* under processing status on I at time ε';
       Computing R* of T* at time ε';
       Computing R of T at time ε';
       if R > R* then
         T preempt T* at time ε';
         Begin the calculation of T at time ε';
         Moving T* to Q;
       else
         Moving T to Q;
       Computing the residual densities of tasks in Q at
       time ε';
       Sorting tasks in Q in non-increasing order based on
       residual densities;
       Obtaining the arrangements of all tasks on I;
       Computing the updated W';
       Δ ← W' − W;
       if Δ < Δ_min then
         Δ_min ← Δ;
         a_best ← a;
4. return a_best.
```

5 Experimental Evaluation

The proposed SAOF algorithm is compared to the baseline algorithm in [20]. Both algorithms are compiled by Eclipse JDK11.0.8 and run on a 1.5 GHz、16G RAM PC. The average relative percentage deviation (ARPD) is used to examine the algorithms. ARPD is defined as follows:

$$ARPD = \frac{W^{ALG} - W^{best}}{W^{best}} \times 100\% \tag{13}$$

where W^{best} represents the optimal objective value achieved by all the algorithms and ALG ∈ {SAOF, OnDisc}.

The main parameters are set as follows: the task processing times on edge servers, the task arrival times and the task weights are set based on the Google cluster [8] data set. A scheduling period size t is set to 1s. The weight $\beta_{i,q}$ of $T_{i,q}$ is chosen at random between 1 and 11. On the cloud servers, the processing time of $T_{i,q}$ is set to $\theta_p \times p_{i,q}(I)(I \in \mathbb{E})$, where θ_p follows the uniform distribution $U(0.60, 0.80)$. The downloading delay $d_{i,q}^{\downarrow}(I)(I \in \mathbb{C})$ and uploading delay $d_{i,q}^{\uparrow}(I)(I \in \mathbb{C})$ to/from the cloud servers follows the uniform distribution $U(0.2, 0.4)$. The downloading delay $d_{i,q}^{\downarrow}(I)(I \in \mathbb{E})$ and uploading delay $d_{i,q}^{\uparrow}(I)(I \in \mathbb{E})$ to/from the edge servers follows the uniform distribution $U(0.01, 0.03)$. The number of cloud servers J is set to 2, 4 and edge servers K is set as 10, 15, 20, 25, and 30. The overall number of tasks $N = \sum_{q=1}^{Q} n_q$ is set as 100, 200, 500, 800, 1000, where Q is randomly set to 5, 10, 20 and 50. In particular, in the SAOF algorithm, the control parameter λ is initially set to 100, the lower limit λ_{min} is set to 10^{-8} and the rate of descent r is set to 0.98.

There are $5 \times 2 \times 5 = 50(N \in \{100, 200, 500, 800, 1000\}, J \in \{2, 4\}, K \in \{10, 15, 20, 25, 30\})$ various instance parameter combinations. 5 instances are randomly created for each combination. On these instances, SAOF algorithm and OnDisc algorithm are tested. As a result, there are $50 \times 5 \times 2 = 500$ experimental results. Table 1 and Fig. 1 are the experimental results for all instance parameter combinations of the algorithms.

Table 1 shows that the average ARPD for SAOF (0.000%) is better compared with OnDisc (5.446%) on all instances. The reasons may be lie in that when massive tasks arrive simultaneously, OnDisc arranges tasks in random order and lacks of efficient task arrangement sequence. The interactions between instance parameters and algorithms are depicted in Fig. 1. It shows that SAOF performs better than OnDisc algorithm and has statistical differences. SAOF is more stable under the change of instance parameters.

The simulation results indicate that SAOF is more suitable and efficient for solving the problem under investigation.

Table 1. Average Relative Percentage Deviation of Algorithms/%

Param	Value	ARPD(%)	
		OnDisc	SAOF
N	100	3.362	0.000
	200	4.906	0.000
	500	6.784	0.000
	800	6.211	0.000
	1000	5.985	0.000
J	2	5.248	0.000
	4	5.636	0.000
K	10	2.985	0.000
	15	4.118	0.000
	20	5.226	0.000
	25	6.631	0.000
	30	8.264	0.000
Avg		5.446	0.000

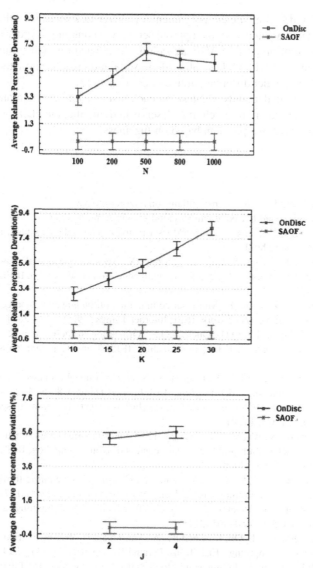

Fig. 1. Interactions between instance parameters and the compared algorithms with 95.0% Tukey HSD intervals

6   Conclusion

In this paper, a stochastic task offloading problem in edge-cloud environments has been studied with the optimization objective of minimizing the total weighted response time. A greedy simulated annealing heuristic algorithm (SA) based online offloading framework (SAOF) has been developed. SAOF is composed of SA, ARR and OFFLOADING algorithms: SA is applied to achieve the optimal task arrangement for the new arrival tasks. ARR is used to compute the assignment for a given task sequence. OFFLOADING is used to offload a given task to the optimal server and compute its order of execution. The performance of proposed SAOF algorithm is evaluated through simulation experiments and compared with OnDisc algorithm. Simulation results show that SAOF has better performance under different parameter combinations.

In the problem under study, the task on each instance has a certain and given processing time. In the future research, it is deserve studying the non-clairvoyant resource model and task offloading problem based on fuzziness.

References

1. Azure, M.: Azure IoT edge. https://github.com/Azure/iotedge
2. Google. Google cloud IoT edge. https://cloud.google.com/iot-edge/
3. Amazon. AWS IoT greengrass. https://docs.aws.amazon.com/zhcn/greengrass/latest/develo perguide/what-is-gg.html
4. Chen, L., Wu, J., Zhang, J., Dai, H.-N., Long, X., Yao, M.: Dependency-aware computation offloading for mobile edge computing with edge-cloud cooperation. IEEE Trans. Cloud Comput. 1–1 (2020)
5. Chen, Q., Kuang, Z., Zhao, L.: Multiuser computation offloading and resource allocation for cloud edge heterogeneous network. IEEE Internet Things J. 9(5), 3799–3811 (2022)
6. Dinh, T.Q., Tang, J., La, Q.D., Quek, T.Q.S.: Offloading in mobile edge computing: task allocation and computational frequency scaling. IEEE Trans. Commun. 65(8), 3571–3584 (2017)
7. Naouri, A., Wu, H., Nouri, N.A., Dhelim, S., Ning, H.: A novel framework for mobile-edge computing by optimizing task offloading. IEEE Internet Things J. 8(16), 13065–13076 (2021)
8. Reiss, C., Wilkes, J., Hellerstein, J.L.: Google cluster-usage traces: format+ schema. Google Inc., White Paper. vol. 1 (2011)
9. Xiong, Y., Huang, S., Wu, M., She, J., Jiang, K.: A Johnson's-rule based genetic algorithm for two-stage-task scheduling problem in data-centers of cloud computing. IEEE Trans. Cloud Comput. 7(3), 597–610 (2019)
10. Guo, W., Lin, B., Chen, G., Chen, Y., Liang, F.: Cost-driven scheduling for deadline-based workflow across multiple clouds. IEEE Trans. Netw. Serv. Manage. 15(4), 1571–1585 (2018)
11. Abbas, N., Zhang, Y., Taherkordi, A., Skeie, T.: Mobile edge computing: a survey. IEEE Internet Things J. 5(1), 450–465 (2018)
12. Jonathan, A., Ryden, M., Oh, K., Chandra, A., Weissman, J.: Nebula: distributed edge cloud for data intensive computing. IEEE Trans. Parallel Distrib. Syst. 28(11), 3229–3242 (2017)
13. Pan, J., McElhannon, J.: Future edge cloud and edge computing for Internet of Things applications. IEEE Internet Things J. 5(1), 439–449 (2018)
14. Sahni, Y., Cao, J., Yang, L.: Data-aware task allocation for achieving low latency in collaborative edge computing. IEEE Internet Things J. 6(2), 3512–3524 (2019)
15. Meng, J., Tan, H., Li, X.-Y., Han, Z., Li, B.: Online deadline-aware task dispatching and scheduling in edge computing. IEEE Trans. Parallel Distrib. Syst. 31(6), 1270–1286 (2020)
16. Kuang, Z., Li, L., Gao, J., Zhao, L., Liu, A.: Partial offloading scheduling and power allocation for mobile edge computing systems. IEEE Internet Things J. 6(4), 6774–6785 (2019)
17. Ding, S., Lin, D.: Dynamic task allocation for cost-efficient edgecloud computing. In: 2020 IEEE International Conference on Services Computing (SCC), pp. 218–225 (2020)
18. Bi, R., Liu, Q., Ren, J., Tan, G.: Utility aware offloading for mobile-edge computing. Tsinghua Sci. Technol. 26(2), 239–250 (2021)

19. Wu, H., Wolter, K., Jiao, P., Deng, Y., Zhao, Y., Xu, M.: EEDTO: an energy-efficient dynamic task offloading algorithm for blockchain-enabled IoT-edge-cloud orchestrated computing. IEEE Internet Things J. **8**(4), 2163–2176 (2021)
20. Tan, H., Han, Z., Li, X.-Y., Lau, F.C.: Online job dispatching and scheduling in edge-clouds. In: IEEE INFOCOM 2017 – IEEE Conference on Computer Communications, pp. 1–9 (2017)

Container-Driven Scheduling Strategy for Scientific Workflows in Multi-vCPU Environments

Peng Xiang, Bing Lin$^{(\boxtimes)}$, Hongjie Yu, and Dui Liu

College of Physics and Energy, Fujian Normal University, Fuzhou 350118, China
WheelLX@163.com, duiliu@fjnu.edu.cn

Abstract. In a distributed resource environment, container technology highly facilitates the deployment and execution of scientific workflow tasks. However, existing scientific workflow scheduling studies barely consider the multi-channel programming of computational resources, which makes it hard to simultaneously achieve effective container sharing and optimize task parallelism and resource utilization. In this paper, we propose a segmented workflow scheduling strategy based on container technology in multi-vCPU devices environment. It reduces the solution space size of the heuristic algorithm through a segmented scheduling approach. And it uses an adaptive discrete particle swarm optimization algorithm with genetic operators (ADPSOGA) to optimize the average completion time of each workflow under the constraint of device rental cost. In addition, we propose a dynamic scaling scheme between containers and devices to reuse containers and solve the problems related to resource contention when tasks are parallel in a device. Experimental results indicate that ADPSOGA outperforms other similar heuristics algorithms, and the segmented scheduling approach significantly improves the optimization-seeking efficiency of the algorithm.

Keywords: Scientific Workflow Scheduling · Container · vCPUs · Particle Swarm Optimization

1 Introduction

Scientific workflow is a common model widely used to describe scientific computing problems in fields such as bioinformatics, astronomy, and physics. With the increasing complexity of scientific computing systems, the data-intensive, communication-intensive and computing-intensive characteristics of scientific workflow are intensifying [3], which requires high-performance computing (HPC) resources or distributed computing resources to assure the normal operation of the system. These distributed resources can be clustered servers, dispersed computers, virtual machines providing leased services in the cloud, and IoT devices in edge environments, etc. For convenience, we will call these distributed resources collectively "devices" in the following.

Y. Sun et al. (Eds.): ChineseCSCW 2022, CCIS 1681, pp. 320–334, 2023.
https://doi.org/10.1007/978-981-99-2356-4_26

Container technology is a lightweight virtualization solution, which can provide a packaging mechanism for workflow tasks in distributed system design and development [6]. In addition, through OS-level virtualization, multiple containers can coexist and run in isolation on the same machine, thus improving resource utilization [5]. Unlike virtual machines that perform hardware virtualization, containers are lightweight and they only bundle application dependencies when reusing the underlying operating system [2]. Based on container technology, this paper studies the scheduling problem of scientific workflow in multi-vCPU devices environment.

Due to the high complexity of scientific workflows, existing task scheduling methods often address the task assignment problem using heuristic algorithms; however, they are easily trapped in local optima [11]. Therefore, these algorithms need to be improved to overcome this drawback. Meanwhile, most existing workflow scheduling algorithms are only applicable to single-channel batch processing systems, where tasks in a device are assumed to be executed only serially [3,4,7–10]. But the computational resources of a device are usually sufficient to support the parallel or concurrent execution of tasks. If the device executes tasks in a serial manner, some of the device's computational resources will be idle, which will reduce the resource utilization. Thus, we should consider the parallelism or concurrency of tasks in the device. Meanwhile, concurrently executed tasks in a single device may compete with each other for computational resources, leading to task timeouts and subsequently affecting the completion time of the workflow. Therefore, the resource contention between concurrent tasks must be considered when scheduling scientific workflows on multi-vCPU devices. In order to ensure the smooth execution of each task, the computational resources allocated to the task need to be adaptively adjusted, and the process of dynamically increasing or decreasing is called "dynamic scaling". With the adoption of container technology, the new container layer brings new challenges to the dynamic scaling of computational resources.

In response to these challenges, the major contributions of this work are summarized below:

1) A segmented scheduling approach is proposed to reduce the solution space size by splitting the overall workflow and invoking the heuristic algorithm for solution in stages, which greatly improves the optimization seeking efficiency and effectiveness of the overall strategy.
2) ADPSOGO is proposed. The crossover operator and mutation operator of the genetic algorithm are introduced in the particle update, and the adaptive inertia weights are used to balance the local search and global search, which avoid the premature local convergence of particles and improve the global search performance.
3) A container scaling scheme is designed to achieve container reuse by dynamically generating and starting and stopping containers in the device, so that containers can be deployed rationally.

2   Model and Problem Definition

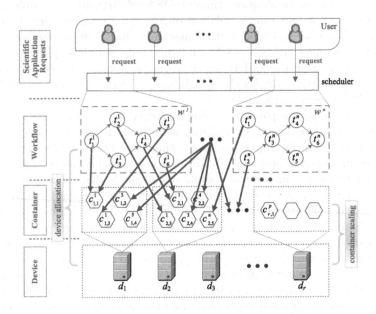

Fig. 1. Architecture of container-based workflow scheduling system.

The system model is shown as Fig. 1. Multiple scientific application requests are sent to the scheduler, and each application request corresponds to a set of computational tasks with priority constraints. The scheduling manager converts each application request into the corresponding workflow, and then assigns the workflow tasks to the appropriate device and the corresponding type of container for execution according to the scheduling scheme. The focus of this paper is on "device allocation" and "container scaling", that is, deciding which device and which resource configuration of containers to run each task on, and how to deploy container instances in a given device. The objective is to optimize the workflow completion time under the limited device resources and budget constraints.

2.1   Workflow Model

Multiple users submit scientific application requests at the same time, and the corresponding set of generated workflows is defined as $W = \{w^1, w^2, ..., w^n\}$. As shown in the workflow layer in Fig. 1, each workflow is represented as a directed acyclic graph $G^q = \langle V^q, E^q \rangle$. Where $V^q = \{t_1^q, t_2^q, ..., t_m^q\}$ denotes the set of m tasks contained in the q-th workflow, and $E^q = \{e_{1,2}^q, e_{1,3}^q, ..., e_{i,j}^q\}$ denotes the data dependencies between the tasks in the q-th workflow.

Each data dependency edge $e_{i,j}^q = (t_i^q, t_j^q)$ indicates the existence of a data dependency relationship between task t_i^q and task t_j^q, where task t_i^q is the direct predecessor node of task t_j^q and task t_j^q is the direct successor node of task t_i^q. In the workflow scheduling process, the data dependencies between tasks determine the order of their execution. In the workflow graph, a task without direct predecessor is called an enter-task t_{enter}^q, and similarly, a task without direct successors is called an exit-task t_{exit}^q.

Each workflow w^q is preassigned an execution budget δ_{w^q} before execution, and a scheduling scheme is said to be a feasible solution when it can execute and complete all workflows under the total budget constraint δ_{total}.

2.2   Resource Model

The distributed multi-vCPU resource environment has multiple types of devices, each with a specific resource configuration $r_i = <\eta_i, \alpha_i, \beta_i, \gamma_i>$, where η_i is the number of available instances in the corresponding type of device, α_i is the number of vCPUs owned by the corresponding type of device, β_i is the single vCPU computational performance in the corresponding type of device, and γ_i is the unit price of the billing cycle in the corresponding type of device.

Each device can run multiple container instances simultaneously while satisfying its computational resources, and each container instance has its corresponding type and resource occupation level. The container type determines the tasks that can be run in that container, i.e., the tasks of each workflow can only be run in the container instance of its corresponding type, while the container resource occupancy level indicates the amount of computational resources allocated to the container instance when it is running.

In this paper, the resource occupancy of a container is divided into μ levels, and when the resource occupancy level is i, it means that the container occupies i/μ vCPU resources. We assume that each task is a single-threaded task and the tasks in the container are executed serially, then the maximum computational resources that can be occupied by 1 container in a multi-vCPU device is 1 vCPU resource.

2.3   Problem Definition

The research content of this paper is a multi-workflow scheduling optimization problem based on container, and its purpose is to optimize the workflow completion time under limited device resource conditions and budget constraints.

We define a scheduling solution as $S = (Re, Map, T_{total}, C_{total})$. Where $Re = \{d_1, d_2, ..., d_r\}$ denotes a set of device resources need to be used and $d_i = \{c_1, c_2, ..., c_s\}$ denotes the list of containers generated by the i-th device. $Map = \{(t_i^q, c_{j,k}, R_c(t_i^q, c_{j,k}), AST(t_i^q)) | t_i^q \in V^q, c_{j,k} \in d_j, d_j \in Re\}$ denotes the mapping relationship of devices and containers corresponding to each task in n workflows. Where t_i^q is the i-th task of the q-th workflow, d_j is the j-th device in the device resource R_e, $c_{j,k}$ is the k-th container in the device d_j container. $R_c(t_i^q, c_{j,k})$ denotes the resource level that task t_i^q can occupy when it is assigned to container $c_{j,k}$. And $AST(t_i^q)$ denotes the actual start time of task t_i^q. $T_{total} = \{T_{total}^1, T_{total}^2, ..., T_{total}^n\}$ contains the completion time of each workflow. C_{total} is the rental cost of devices required to complete all workflows.

After a mapping solution Map is generated, the lease start time $UST(d_j)$ and the lease end time $UET(d_j)$ corresponding to each device can be obtained, and thus, the individual workflow completion time T_{total}^q and the total cost C_{total} of all workflows can be calculated as following equations.

$$T_{total}^q = \max_{t_i^p \in V_{exit}^q} \{AFT(t_i^q)\} \tag{1}$$

$$C_{total} = \sum_{i=1}^{|Re|} \left\lceil \frac{UET(d_i) - UST(d_i)}{\theta} \right\rceil * \gamma_{R_d(d_i)} \tag{2}$$

where V_{exit}^q is the set of all exit-tasks for the q-th workflow, θ is the unit time interval, and $\gamma_{R_d(d_i)}$ is the unit time rental price for the corresponding type of device.

Based on the above definition, the multi-workflow scheduling problem based on container technology with the budget constraint can be finally expressed formally as Eq. (3):

$$\min \sum_{q=1}^{|W|} T_{total}^q \tag{3}$$

$$\text{s.t. } c_{total} \leq \delta_{total}$$

3   Container-Based Segmented Workflow Scheduling Strategy

The container-based segmented workflow scheduling strategy consists of four main parts, which are generation of task scheduling sequence table, segmented scheduling approach, modified heuristic algorithm ADPSOGA, and container scaling scheme. First, the individual workflows are merged as a whole to generate a schedule sequence table for all tasks. Then the merged workflow is split into multiple sub-workflows. The modified heuristic is called step by step to find the best solution for each sub-workflow scheduling problem, and the proposed container scaling scheme is applied in the process. Finally, the optimal scheduling solutions for each sub-workflow are merged to the final scheduling solution.

3.1   Generation of Task Scheduling Sequence Table

We adopt a post-merge scheduling approach for multi-workflow scheduling, so that tasks of different workflows can share the same device resources and improve device resource utilization.

To schedule the merged multiple workflows, we need to consider the task scheduling order of each workflow. We calculate the critical path of each workflow individually once beforehand, and use $LST(t_i^q)$ to denote the latest start time of task t_i^q in the q-th workflow, which is the latest start moment of task t_i^q under the premise that the completion time of the q-th workflow is guaranteed to be minimal. In the classical algorithm HEFT [12], $rank_u$ denotes the critical path length of a task to the exit-task and is used to prioritize the individual tasks of the workflow. And the meaning of $LST\,(t_i^q)$ is similar to $rank_u$, so we sort all the tasks by $LST\,(t_i^q)$ in ascending order to generate a scheduling sequence table.

The smaller $LST\,(t_i^q)$ is, the earlier the task t_i^q is scheduled. The scheduling sequence table in ascending order of $LST\,(t_i^q)$ provides the topological order of tasks, while also ensuring priority constraint relationships between tasks.

3.2 Segmented Scheduling Approach

Since the solution space of the heuristic algorithm grows exponentially with the number of tasks involved in scheduling, the solution efficiency of the heuristic algorithm will be seriously affected when the number of tasks involved in scheduling is large. To reduce the solution space of the algorithm, this paper proposes a segmented scheduling method: first, the scheduling sequence table is split by the splitting granularity (i.e., a fixed number of tasks) to generate a set $W_{sub} = \{w_{sub_1}, w_{sub_2}, w_{sub_3}, \ldots\}$; secondly, the sub-workflows in W_{sub} are scheduled sequentially based on the improved heuristic algorithm in this paper; finally, all the sub-workflow scheduling schemes are combined to generate the overall scheduling scheme. It is worth noting that after the current sub-workflow completes scheduling, the resource pool Re of its best solution will be used as the initial resource pool of the next sub-workflow.

To determine the fitness of a scheme in the segmented scheduling process, this paper introduces the cumulative budget $CC\,(w_{sub_i})$ corresponding to the current sub-workflow, which represents the tolerable usage cost of the equipment required to schedule w_{sub_1} to w_{sub_i}, defined as shown in Eq. (4).

$$CC\,(w_{sub_i}) = \begin{cases} \dfrac{ET_{sum}\left(w_{sub_i}\right)}{ET_{sum}(w_{all})} * \delta_{total} & i = 1 \\ CC\left(w_{sub_{i-1}}\right) + \dfrac{ET_{sum}\left(w_{sub_i}\right)}{ET_{sum}(w_{all})} * \delta_{total} & i > 1 \end{cases} \tag{4}$$

where ET_{sum} is the sum of the estimated execution times of all tasks in a workflow

$$ET_{sum}\,(w^q) = \sum_{t \in V^q} ET_t \tag{5}$$

3.3 Modified Heuristic Algorithm ADPSOGA

We propose an adaptive discrete particle swarm optimization with genetic algorithm (ADPSOGA) to search for the position of each task assigned in the workflow. The algorithm introduces the crossover operator and mutation operator of genetic algorithm in particle updating, which enables the particles to explore new regions and thus obtain better global search ability. For the individual cognitive factor and social cognitive factor, the crossover operator of the genetic algorithm is introduced to update each particle to achieve the learning process toward the better particle. In addition, we combine the inertia weight factor with the mutation operator of the genetic algorithm to better balance local search and global search.

Particle Encoding. PSO is typically used to solve continuous problems [13], however workflow scheduling is a discrete problem that requires a new problem encoding strategy. We adopt the nested approach of "device instances, container resources" to encode the task assignment. In the particle swarm algorithm, a particle represents a scheduling solution. At the t-th iteration, the position X_i^t of the i-th particle is shown in the following equation.

$$X_i^t = \left(x_{i,1}^t, x_{i,2}^t, \ldots, x_{i,n}^t\right) \tag{6}$$

$$x_{i,k}^t = (I, r_c) \tag{7}$$

where each node $x_{i,k}^t (k=1,2,\ldots,n)$ is nested into 2 subdivisions, indicating the k-th task assigned to the I-th device instance and the amount of resources occupied by the task when it runs as r_c, respectively.

A particle encoding with 8 subtasks as shown in Fig. 2. Suppose there are 5 types of rentable devices and the number of instances provided by each type of device is 4,2,3,5,3, and the maximum container resource occupation level μ is 4. Therefore, I takes values from 1 to 17 and r_c takes values from 1 to 4. In Fig. 2, the task t_1 is assigned to the 8th device instance, and the corresponding container resource occupation is 3/4 vCPU.

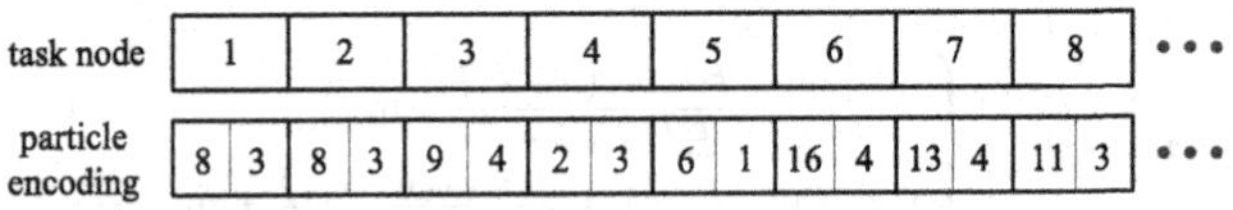

task node	1		2		3		4		5		6		7		8		•••
particle encoding	8	3	8	3	9	4	2	3	6	1	16	4	13	4	11	3	•••

Fig. 2. Particle encoding.

Particle Update. In the traditional PSO particle update strategy, three important parameters are involved in the particle swarm update in the traditional PSO: inertia weight factor, individual cognitive factor and social cognitive factor. In order to overcome the defect that the traditional PSO is prone to fall into local optimum, ADPSOGA introduces mutation and crossover operations of genetic algorithm to improve the corresponding part, as shown in Eq. (8).

$$X_i^t = c_2 \oplus C_g \left(c_1 \oplus C_p \left(w \otimes M \left(X_i^{t-1}\right), pBest_i^{t-1}\right), gBest^{t-1}\right) \tag{8}$$

where w is the inertial weight factor, c_1 and c_2 are the cognitive factors, $M(\ )$ denotes the mutation operation, and $C_p(\ )$ denotes crossover operation with its individual historical optimal particle $pBest_i^{t-1}$, and $C_g(\ )$ denotes crossover operation with the global historical optimal particle $gBest^{t-1}$.

We combine the inertia weight factor part of Eq. (8) with the idea of variation in the genetic algorithm, which is updated as shown in Eq. (9).

$$A_i^t = w \otimes M\left(X_i^{t-1}\right) \tag{9}$$

where, the inertia weight factor w here represents the variation strength of the particle, and when this value is larger, the number of variation operations of the particle in each iteration is higher.

For one mutation operation, a node in the particle will be selected randomly and its quantile value will be changed irregularly, and the new values must all be within the corresponding range of taken values. A mutation operation for the particle encoded in Fig. 2 is shown in Fig. 3, where a node p1 of the particle is randomly selected and the value at position p1 is updated from (2,3) to a random value (11,4).

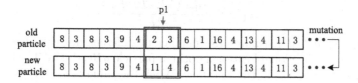

Fig. 3. Particle mutation operation.

We combine the individual cognitive part and social cognitive part with the idea of crossover in the genetic algorithm, and the updated results are shown in Eq. (10) and Eq. (11), respectively.

$$B_i^t = c_1 \oplus C_p\left(A_i^t, pBest^{t-1}\right) = \begin{cases} C_p\left(A_i^t, pBest^{t-1}\right) & r_1 \le c_1 \\ A_i^t & r_1 > c_1 \end{cases} \tag{10}$$

$$C_i^t = c_2 \oplus C_g\left(B_i^t, gBest^{t-1}\right) = \begin{cases} C_g\left(B_i^t, pBest^{t-1}\right) & r_2 \le c_2 \\ B_i^t & r_2 > c_2 \end{cases} \tag{11}$$

where r_1 and r_2 are random numbers from 0 to 1, c_1 and c_2 are the individual cognitive and social cognitive factors, respectively, representing the crossover probabilities with the individual historical optimal particle and with the global historical optimal particle, respectively.

After the mutation operation, a random number r_1 (or r_2) from 0 to 1 is generated, and if it is less than or equal to the crossover probability c_1 (or c_2), the crossover operation is executed: 2 crossover positions (i.e., p2 and p3) are randomly selected and the value between the particle p2 and p3 positions is replaced with the value of $pBest$ (or $gBest$) in that interval, as shown in Fig. 4.

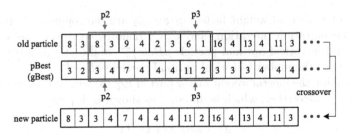

Fig. 4. Particle crossover operation.

Parameter Update. In the classical PSO algorithm, the inertia weight factor w changes only with respect to the number of iterations, which is not well suited to the nonlinear and complex multivariable nature of the actual problem. Therefore, we construct an inertia weight factor adjustment strategy that adaptively adjusts according to the current particle's fitness. The strategy adjusts the inertia weight factor based on the difference degree $d(X_i^t)$ between the current particles and the global historical optimal particles, and $d(X_i^t)$ as shown in Eq. (12).

$$d\left(X_i^t\right) = \frac{div\left(X_i^t, gBest^t\right)}{2T} \tag{12}$$

where $div\left(X_i^t, gBest^t\right)$ denotes the number of different divisions between the particle X_i^t and the global historical optimal particle $gBest^t$, and T is the size of the number of subtasks in the workflow. When the value of $div\left(X_i^t\right)$ is small, it means that the difference degree between X_i^t and $gBest^t$ is small, and the value of w should be reduced to make the particle mutation intensity weaker so as to ensure that the particles can search better in a small area for finding the optimal solution. Otherwise, the value of w should be increased to make the search space of the particle larger in order to find the optimized solution space faster. The new inertia weight factor w we define is calculated as shown in Eq. (13).

$$w = w_{\max} - (w_{\max} - w_{\min}) * \exp\left(\frac{d\left(X_i^{t-1}\right)}{d\left(X_i^{t-1}\right) - 1.01}\right) \tag{13}$$

The 2 cognitive factors c_1 or c_2 of ADPSOGA are set by the classical linear increasing or decreasing strategy [1].

3.4   Container Scaling Scheme

Algorithm 1 provides a container scaling scheme to maintain the list of already generated containers in the device. Its purpose is to achieve dynamic scaling between containers and multi-vCPU devices. And the process is to select an old container or generate a new container in the specified device to run the task according to the current resource situation, and update the properties of the relevant devices and containers.

For a task, the amount of resources remaining in the assigned device is calculated in advance before selecting the old container or generating a new container. If the remaining resources are insufficient, it is necessary to wait for the currently running container to finish executing the task and then release the corresponding resources until the remaining resources meet the required amount of resources for the task, as expressed in lines 6 to 13 of Algorithm 1. And lines 14 to 22 in Algorithm 1 are the process of selecting specific container instances, which aims to keep the task running as early as possible while considering container reuse.

Algorithm 1. Container Selection

Input: the task t, assigned device d , the list of corresponding type containers c_list, the amount of resources required c_R
Output: the selected container c
1: **if** d is close **then**
2:      start d
3:      $UST(d) = \max\left(EST(t) - T_{dboot} - T_{pull} - T_{cboot}, 0\right)$;
4:      $EFreeT(d) = UST(d) + T_{dboot}$
5: **end if**
6: **if** $c\_R > R(d)$ **then**
7:      $c\_R = R(d)$
8: **end if**
9: **while** getRemaining_$R(d) < c\_R$ **do**
10:      $c = $ getEarliestFreeContainer(d)
11:      stop c
12:      $EFreeT(d) = EFreeT(c)$
13: **end while**
14: $c = $ getEarliestFreeContainerInCList(c_list)
15: **if** $(c$ exist$)$ **and** $((EFreeT(c) <= EST(t))$ **or** $(EFreeT(c) < EFreeT(d)+T_cboot))$ **then**
16:      $EFreeT(c) = \max(EFreeT(c), EFreeT(d))$
17: **else**
18:      creatContainer$(d,$ type$(t))$
19:      ST$(c) = max($ EFreeT(d) , EST(t) $)$
20:      $EFreeT(c) = ST(c) + T_cboot$
21:      $c\_list = c\_list + c$
22: **end if**
23: $R_c(c) = c\_R$
24: start c
25: return c

---

4   Experiments and Analysis

4.1   Experimental Setup

In the experiments, we set up five different types of devices and the data transfer rate between devices is defined as 100 Mbps. The relevant settings are shown in

Table 1, and the pricing will be converted to USD per second in the experiments due to the short completion time of some workflows.

Table 1. Equipment resource settings.

type	number of instances	number of vCPU	computing performance of single vCPU	price
1	4	2	1.0	0.102 USD per hour
2	5	4	0.9	0.184 USD per hour
3	3	8	0.8	0.338 USD per hour
4	4	16	0.9	0.716 USD per hour
5	2	32	0.88	1.332 USD per hour

To evaluate our scheduling strategy, we perform simulation experiments with the workflow data from scientific applications. Some related work was done by Bharathi et al. [1], who investigated the structure of five real-world workflows from different scientific fields. These include Montage for astronomy, CyberShake for earthquake science, Epigenomics for biology, LIGO for gravitational physics, and SIPHT for biology, and these workflows have different structural characteristics. In addition, they have developed a workflow generator to construct workflows. The constructed workflows are stored in XML files with four different number of tasks for each scientific workflow: small (with 30 tasks), medium (with 50 tasks), large (with 100 tasks) and very large (with 1000 tasks). The experiments will use these files as input for the relevant tests.

4.2 Segmented Scheduling Effectiveness Verification

To compare the difference in effectiveness between segmented scheduling and non-segmented scheduling, we use ADPSOGA to solve for Montage and Cyber-Shake workflows with different multiplicative budget constraints, respectively, for 20 times each experiment, and the experimental results are shown in Fig. 5.

The success rate in Fig. 5 indicates the probability of the algorithm finding a feasible solution, and the completion time is the average completion time of the workflow for 20 experiments with different multiplicative budget constraints.

From Fig. 5, it can be observed that segmented scheduling significantly outperforms non-segmented scheduling. In the experiment, the non-segmented scheduling is set to perform 1000 iterations, while the segmented scheduling is 100 iterations, but the success rate and the workflow average completion time of the segmented scheduling are significantly better than the non-segmented scheduling under the same budget constraint. For example, in Fig. 5c and Fig. 5d, when the budget constraint is 2.5 times, Montage has a 100% success rate in segmented scheduling with an average workflow completion time of 203.38 s,

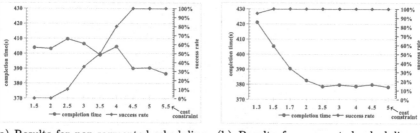

(a) Results for non-segmented scheduling of CyberShake (1000 iterations)

(b) Results for segmented scheduling of CyberShake(100 iterations)

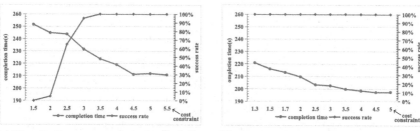

(c) Results for non-segmented scheduling of Montage(1000 iterations)

(d) Results for segmented scheduling of Montage(100 iterations)

Fig. 5. Completion time and success rate of ADPSOGA for scheduling CyberShake, Montage with different multiplier budget constraints.

while non-segmented scheduling has a 65% success rate with an average workflow completion time of 243.91 s. Meanwhile, we found that it takes 4.5 times the budget constraint to find a feasible solution with 100% probability for 1000 iterations of non-segmented scheduling, while it takes only 1.5 times the budget constraint to find a feasible solution with 100% probability for 100 iterations of non-segmented scheduling. We also found that it takes more than 4.5 times the budget constraint to find a feasible solution with 100% probability for 1000 iterations of non-segmented scheduling, while it takes only 1.5 times the budget constraint to find a feasible solution with 100% probability for 100 iterations of segmented scheduling.

Intuitively, it seems that directly splitting workflows will lose some global information and lead to unsatisfactory scheduling results at the end. However, the experimental results reveal that segmented scheduling after splitting the workflow gives better results. The optimization is particularly effective in the case of a large number of tasks, due to the fact that splitting workflow reduces the solution space, resulting in a significant improvement in the algorithm's optimization-seeking capability and a reduction in the number of required iterations.

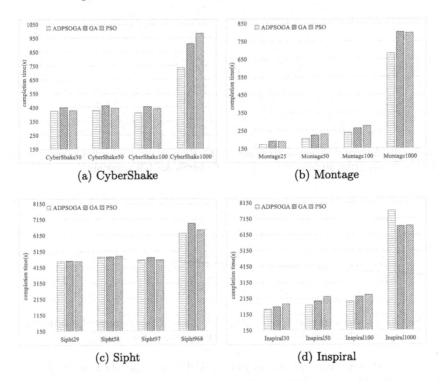

Fig. 6. Completion times for various types of workflows and different number of tasks with different algorithms.

4.3 Comparison of Algorithms

To compare the performance of the modified heuristic algorithms in this paper, we applied segmented scheduling as well as container scaling schemes to conduct relevant experiments using ADPSOGA, classical PSO algorithm and GA algorithm (roulette selection), respectively. We conducted 20 experiments for different number of tasks and types of workflows under 1.5 times budget constraint (the split granularity was set to 10 and the iteration number of sub-workflows was set to 100) to calculate the average completion time of various workflows under different algorithms, and the experimental results are shown in Fig. 6.

From the experiments of the four workflows in Fig. 6, we can notice that the completion time of each workflow does not increase proportionally with the number of tasks. That is because as the number of tasks increases, it mainly increases the parallelism of tasks, while the theoretical earliest completion time of workflows does not increase much. Therefore, the experimental results also show that the segmented scheduling approach and the container scaling scheme proposed in this paper can well adapt to the impact of increasing task parallelism. In Fig. 6c, we found that the results of the three algorithms are similar for the Sipht workflow when the number of tasks is less than 100. This is because there is a very obvious critical path in the Sipht workflow structure and the execution time of the tasks on the non-critical path is very short, so the three algorithms can easily find the solution that can make the completion time of this workflow close to its optimal earliest completion time. In Fig. 6d, we observe that the proposed algorithm in this paper does not outperform the results of other algorithms when scheduling an Inspiral workflow containing 1000 tasks. The preliminary analysis is that the Inspiral workflow has a special structure and the tasks are hierarchically very obvious. When there are too many tasks in each layer, the segmented scheduling makes the lack of dependency information in the front and back layers serious, resulting in the inability to effectively use the dependency relationships between workflow tasks for optimization search.

From the overall view of Fig. 6, the proposed ADPSOGA performs well in terms of workflow scheduling for various types and number of tasks, while classical PSO and GA have their own advantages and disadvantages, but both perform worse than ADPSOGA overall. This is because ADPSOGA is designed with adaptively updated inertia weights and introduces a cross-variance mechanism from genetic algorithm, which enhances the ability to search the solution space and improves convergence, enabling ADPSOGA to find a better solution with fewer iterations.

5   Conclusion

To address the workflow scheduling problem of scientific applications in a distributed multi-vCPU device environment and to optimize the workflow completion time under limited resource conditions and budget constraints, this paper proposes a scheduling strategy based on container technology and taking into account task parallelism/concurrency in the device. In the strategy, a container scaling scheme is developed for the problem of dynamic deployment of containers in multi-vCPU devices, and the ADPSOGA algorithm and a segmented scheduling approach are proposed to schedule the tasks. Experimental results show that ADPSOGA converges faster and performs better search than classical heuristics, and the introduction of the segmented scheduling approach has considerably improved the overall scheduling strategy. The experimental results also illustrate that the heuristic algorithm commonly suffers from a large solution space when solving discrete optimization problems, which critically affects their solution efficiency, and that problem can be solved effectively by using segmented scheduling.

Acknowledgements. This work is partly supported by the Natural Science Foundation of China under Grant No. 62072108, the University-Industry Cooperation of Fujian Province under Grant No. 2022H6024.

References

1. Bharathi, S., Chervenak, A., Deelman, E., Mehta, G., Su, M., Vahi, K.: Characterization of scientific workflows. In: 2008 Third Workshop on Workflows in Support of Large-Scale Science, pp. 1–10. https://doi.org/10.1109/WORKS.2008.4723958

2. Dua, R., Raja, A.R., Kakadia, D.: Virtualization vs containerization to support paas. In: 2014 IEEE International Conference on Cloud Engineering, pp. 610–614. https://doi.org/10.1109/IC2E.2014.41

3. Gao, Y., Zhang, S., Zhou, J.: A hybrid algorithm for multi-objective scientific workflow scheduling in IAAS cloud. IEEE Access **7**, 125783–125795 (2019). https://doi.org/10.1109/ACCESS.2019.2939294

4. Liu, L., Zhang, M., Buyya, R., Fan, Q.: Deadline-constrained coevolutionary genetic algorithm for scientific workflow scheduling in cloud computing. Concurr. Comput. Pract. Exp. **29**(5), e3942 (2017). https://doi.org/10.1002/cpe.3942

5. Nardelli, M., Hochreiner, C., Schulte, S.: Elastic provisioning of virtual machines for container deployment. In: Proceedings of the 8th ACM/SPEC on International Conference on Performance Engineering Companion, pp. 5–10. Association for Computing Machinery (2017). https://doi.org/10.1145/3053600.3053602

6. Pahl, C.: Containerization and the paas cloud. IEEE Cloud Comput. **2**(3), 24–31 (2015). https://doi.org/10.1109/MCC.2015.51

7. Pang, S., Li, W., He, H., Shan, Z., Wang, X.: An eda-ga hybrid algorithm for multi-objective task scheduling in cloud computing. IEEE Access **7**, 146379–146389 (2019). https://doi.org/10.1109/ACCESS.2019.2946216

8. Rajasekar, P., Palanichamy, Y.: Scheduling multiple scientific workflows using containers on IaaS cloud. J. Ambient Intell. Human. Comput. **12**(7), 7621–7636 (2020). https://doi.org/10.1007/s12652-020-02483-0

9. Rodriguez, M.A., Buyya, R.: Deadline based resource provisioning and scheduling algorithm for scientific workflows on clouds. IEEE Trans. Cloud Comput. **2**(2), 222–235 (2014). https://doi.org/10.1109/TCC.2014.2314655

10. Taghinezhad-Niar, A., Pashazadeh, S., Taheri, J.: Workflow scheduling of scientific workflows under simultaneous deadline and budget constraints. Cluster Comput. **24**(4), 3449–3467 (2021). https://doi.org/10.1007/s10586-021-03314-3

11. Tan, B., Ma, H., Mei, Y.: A group genetic algorithm for resource allocation in container-based clouds. In: Paquete, L., Zarges, C. (eds.) EvoCOP 2020. LNCS, vol. 12102, pp. 180–196. Springer, Cham (2020). https://doi.org/10.1007/978-3-030-43680-3_12

12. Topcuoglu, H., Hariri, S., Min-You, W.: Performance-effective and low-complexity task scheduling for heterogeneous computing. IEEE Trans. Parallel Distrib. Syst. **13**(3), 260–274 (2002). https://doi.org/10.1109/71.993206

13. Wu, Z., Ni, Z., Gu, L., Liu, X.: A revised discrete particle swarm optimization for cloud workflow scheduling. In: 2010 International Conference on Computational Intelligence and Security, pp. 184–188 (2010). https://doi.org/10.1109/CIS.2010.46

A Segmented Path Heuristic Recovery Algorithm for WSNs Based on Mobile Sink

Nie Wenmei⬡, Song Xiaoxia^(✉)⬡, Li Yong⬡, and Zhang Xulong⬡

School of Computer and Network Engineering, Shanxi Datong University,
Datong, China
sxxly2002@163.com

Abstract. Mobile sink can effectively solve hot issues in wireless sensor networks (WSNs), but its mobility will lead to changes in network topology and unreliable transmission links. By analyzing various efficient energy-saving and fault-tolerant routing methods, a dynamic segmented path heuristic recovery algorithm for WSNs based on mobile sink is proposed. The data transmission path is divided into anterior segment path and posterior segment path, and the whale optimization algorithm is used to recover the posterior segment path. The fitness function of the posterior segment path recovery is constructed, considering the residual energy, node distance, node energy consumption and delay. The performance of the proposed algorithm is evaluated and the whale heuristic algorithm is used to efficiently recover the posterior segment path in different dimensions. Analysis and simulation experiments show that the segmented path recovery method can effectively save path energy consumption and delay, and the whale recovery algorithm is simple and effective.

Keywords: dynamic segmented path · path recovery · heuristic algorithm · woa

1 Introduction

Recently, WSNs has been widely used in medical, scientific, military and life fields, such as agricultural monitoring, environmental monitoring, field biological tracking, security, smart home and so on. WSNs are composed of low-power, low-cost and energy-constrained sensors, which are randomly deployed in specific areas to perceive the environment, process the sensing information, and provide wireless communication between the source and the target. Once deployed, the sensor will use its own energy to run, so how to provide an energy-efficient, reliable, and extended network lifetime wireless sensor is the key issue we consider. The traditional wireless sensor network adopts static deployment [1–3].

Supported by Supported by Shanxi Provine Natural Science fund project (201901D111311), Key R&D projects in Datong city(2020023),and Datong University project(2019k5).

When the data collection area is large, this method is inefficient, and the sensor-aware data are transmitted to the sink through multi-hop mode, which causes the nodes around the sink to run out of energy quickly, forming hot issues and funnel effect [4].

To prolong the network lifetime of WSNs and reduce the forwarding of sensing data around sink nodes, the famous WSNs routing protocol Low-Energy Adaptive Clustering Hierarchy (LEACH) is proposed [5]. Therefore, clustering method can effectively alleviate the forwarding data pressure of sink node, but it cannot completely solve the funnel effect. To address the hot issues and funnel effect, mobile sink is used in the monitoring area of WSNs. It not only avoids the hot issues and funnel effect but also greatly reduces the occurrence of data delay and data loss.However, the mobility of mobile sink may cause to changes of network topology and unreliable transmission links. For example, the sink may not be able to contact a certain cluster head node during movement, which is fatal for WSNs because the failure of the cluster head node means that a large amount of sensor node data will not be collected. Recently years, fault-tolerant mechanism has make a research hotspot in the fields of mobile WSNs [6]. Energy saving and fault-tolerant are the two major challenges in the development of large-scale WSNs [7].

In view of the above problems, we propose an energy-saving and reliable segmented routing recovery algorithm for mobile WSNs based on whale optimization algorithm(WOA). In each cluster, when the mobile sink is disconnected from the cluster node, the node containing the transmission task, sufficient node energy and less node hops is searched according to the information contained in the transmission node in the previous information transmission path as a new cluster node to establish a new connection with the mobile sink node. After the new clustering node is formed, the previous information transmission path is divided into anterior segment path and posterior segment path. The anterior segment path refers to the transmission path from the source node to the segmentation node, which no longer needs to be updated. The posterior segment path refers to the transmission path from the segmentation node to the new clustering node. Considering the node residual energy, the distance between nodes, the energy consumption and delay of the node, the fitness model of path is established, and WOA is used to reconstruct the posterior path.

The major contributions of this paper are as follows:

(1) A segmented path heuristic recovery algorithm for WSNs based on mobile sink is proposed.
(2) The data transmission path is divided into anterior segment path and posterior segment path, and the posterior segment path is reconstructed by the whale optimization algorithm.
(3) The fitness function of the posterior segment path recovery is constructed, considering the residual energy, node distance, node energy consumption and delay.
(4) The proposed algorithm is analyzed and evaluated from the perspectives of energy consumption, delay, and path recovery.

2   Related Work

At present, various efficient and energy-saving fault-tolerance routing methods have been posed and implemented in the article. There are three main fault-tolerant routing methods for WSNs: link retransmission, error-correcting code mechanism and multi-path method. Here, we mainly discuss the related research of multi-path algorithm. In [8–11], mainly elaborated the clustering-related multi-path algorithms in WSNs. Using fault-tolerant target tracking protocol based on clustering to track and monitor moving objects, compared with LEACH, energy consumption is reduced by 25% [8]. A position-aware and fault-tolerant WSNs clustering protocol is designed, which is energy-saving and reliable, and reduces end-to-end data transmission delay [9]. In [10], a distributed energy-saving and fault-tolerant algorithm is proposed for WSN, which selects the next hop cluster head in an energy-saving way and restores the connection with neighbor nodes when the cluster head fails. In [11], an energy-optimized clustering routing algorithm based on multi-path is proposed. The algorithm is based on fuzzy rule algorithm. Many researchers have designed fault-tolerance schemes. A trust-based fault-tolerant data aggregation framework is designed to reduce the impact of error data [12]. In [13], an efficient fault tolerant multipath routing scheme is designed for WSNs. A distributed fault-tolerant topology control algorithm is proposed, which assigns the transmission range to each sensor, so that each sensor has at least K paths with disjoint vertices to the super node, and minimizes the total energy consumption [14].

Mobile sink can effectively solve the energy black hole and effectively balance node energy consumption. In [15], an intelligent agent-based routing protocol is proposed, which reduced the cost of mobile sink. Based on the generated graph, a heuristic mobile aggregation path planning algorithm is given to find the shortest path of obstacle avoidance. In [16], researchers proved that the path planning is NP-complete problem, and proposed an effective reliable data collection path planning (EARTH) algorithm, this method can find a shorter path to collect sensing data without losing packets.

Based on the enlightenment of nature, natural element heuristic optimization algorithms are increasingly used in WSNs. In [17], genetic algorithm as an effective clustering and routing algorithm is used for WSNs. In [18], the particle swarm optimization algorithm was applied to select cluster heads, thereby reducing the energy consumption of wireless sensor networks. A mobile aggregation clustering algorithm based on PSO is proposed in [19], node position and residual energy are the major parameters for selecting cluster heads. In [20], an improved ant colony algorithm considering cluster head distance is proposed. The mobile sink finds the optimal trajectory to communicate with the cluster head. The simulation shows that the proposed algorithm can significantly improve the performance of WSNs compared with other routing algorithms. For static aggregation and multi-hop routing, In [21], In order to improve the efficiency of data collection, researchers proposed enhanced clustering approach based on ant colony for multiple mobile sinks. Researchers entered a special mobile sink, mobile data transmission node (MDT), which collects the data of sensor nodes by accessing each sensor node and sends it to the base station [22]. A path optimization method for mobile sink in WSNs based on artificial bee colony algorithm is proposed in [23]. In [24], in order to reduce the data loss, effectively control the network overhead and maximize the performance of heterogeneous sensor networks, a clustering routing algorithm for heterogeneous WSNs based on the wolf swarm algorithm was proposed. In [25], a natural heuristic optimization algorithm, whale optimization algorithm, is proposed. The WOA is tested by 29 mathematical optimization problems and 6 structural design problems. The results show that the WOA algorithm has strong competitiveness compared with the existing metaheuristic algorithms and traditional algorithms. Researchers proposed an effective WOA-based cluster head selection algorithm. [26].

A large number of literatures show that WSNs data collection using clustering and mobile sink can effectively improve data collection, balance energy consumption and prolong network lifetime. However, the collection strategy of mobile sink is relatively complex and challenging. It is very important to design a reliable and energy-saving adaptive recovery path.

3   Network Model and Proposed Algorithm

The innovation of the algorithm in this paper is to extend network lifetime, balance node energy consumption, and enhance data collection reliability. The dynamic path reconstruction is carried out on the network routing failure problem that the cluster head cannot be connected with the mobile sink in data collection.

3.1   Network Model

WSNs adopts a hierarchical clustering structure. The mobile sink wireless sensor network model is shown in Fig. 1. WSNs is composed of low-level layer and high-level layer. The low-level layer is composed of all sensor nodes in the monitoring environment, which is to be in charge of collecting all data in the region of interest. The high-level layer is composed of the nodes that meet the cluster head selection function, which is to be in charge of collecting cluster member node data. For the purpose of prolonging the network lifetime and achievement the load balance of sensor nodes, the cluster head selection fully considers the factors such as the node residual energy, the number of adjacent nodes and nodes. The cluster member nodes transmit data to the cluster head in a multi-hop manner.

In the network structure based on hierarchical clustering, cluster head nodes consume more energy than cluster member nodes. In order to better save energy and prolong the network lifetime, we use mobile sink to collect cluster head node data. The mobility of mobile sink will produce the dynamics change of the network structure, resulting in the failure of the original link. In order to provide a reliable and efficient sink collection link, we propose a dynamic segmented path heuristic recovery.

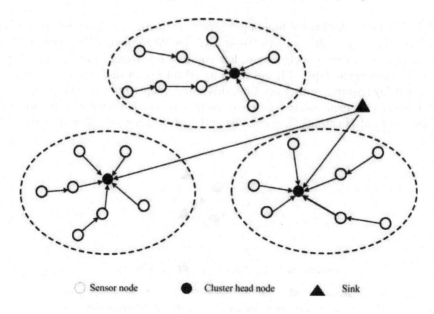

Fig. 1. Mobile sink wireless sensor network model.

3.2   Dynamic Segmented Path Heuristic Recovery

This paper adopts the dynamic segmented path recovery model shown in Fig. 2. In order to describe simply, Fig. 2 only shows the failure and recovery of a single path in the cluster. In the process of collecting cluster head data by mobile sink, once it is found that a cluster head node cannot be contacted, in order to ensure the accurate and complete collection of data, a suitable new alternative cluster head must be found. It is necessary to find a node with sufficient energy and fewer hops as a new cluster head node to establish a new connection with the mobile sink node. In order to save energy consumption and shorten the delay, after formation of the new cluster head node, the previous information transmission path is divided into anterior segment path and posterior segment path. The anterior segment path refers to the previous transmission path from the source node to the segmentation node, which no longer needs to be updated. Posterior segment path refers to the transmission path from the segmentation node to the new cluster head node. It is necessary to establish a connection through the path optimization algorithm to segment the historical path. The WOA is used to reconstruct the posterior segment path. The residual energy consumption, energy consumption, distance between and delay of nodes are comprehensively considered. The fitness model of the path is established to reconstruct posterior segment path. According to the historical information of the historical path, it is easy to find the segmentation node. The recovery problem of dynamic path is mainly the reconstruction of the posterior segment path, so this section focuses on the reconstruction of the posterior segment path. The heuristic algorithm can effectively convert the multi-objective problem into the single-objective problem solving through the fitness function, thereby reducing the difficulty of solving the problem. Through comparative study, the WOA heuristic algorithm has the advantages of simple algorithm, low complexity, strong local search ability, and fast convergence speed. It has a strong advantage in the path recovery with certain delay requirements. Therefore, this paper adopted to the WOA to recover the posterior segment path. The recovery process needs to consider population coding and initialization, fitness model and specific algorithm flow design.

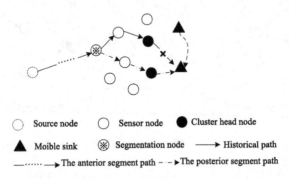

Fig. 2. Dynamic segmented path recovery model.

3.2.1   Population Coding and Initialization

The posterior segment path reconstruction needs to select the optimal path from sink to the segmentation node according to various factors. The optimal path problem first needs to determine the encoding method. Considering that the data does not pass through all the nodes in the middle in the transmission process from the segmentation node to the sink, it is difficult to reconstruct the path by using the traditional decimal coding. Binary coding has the characteristics of simple, easy to encode and decode, so it adopts the encoding method as shown in formula 1.

$$M_k^i = \begin{cases} 0, \\ 1. \end{cases} \tag{1}$$

M_k^i represents the value of the ith node in the kth path of M path, 1 means the i node on the path, 0 means the i node is not on the path.

With binary encoding, the whale population can be initialized as matrix 2.

$$pop_{woa} = \begin{bmatrix} X_{1,1} & X_{1,2} & \cdots & X_{1,N-1} & X_{1,N} \\ X_{2,1} & X_{2,2} & \cdots & X_{2,N-1} & X_{2,N} \\ \vdots & \vdots & \ddots & \vdots & \vdots \\ X_{M,1} & X_{M,1} & \cdots & X_{M,N-1} & X_{M,N} \end{bmatrix} \quad X_{M,N} \in \{0,1\}. \tag{2}$$

M is the quantity of whales, N is the quantity of sensors, initialize the first column and the last column are 1, others position is random initialized value.

3.2.2   Fitness Model

WSNs routing model can be represented by an undirected weight graph $G =<V, E >$,V means all nodes, E means the connection between path nodes, each E represents the direct path between two adjacent nodes. Assuming that the segmentation node is X and the destination node is S, the optimal recovery path is the path $Q(X, S)$,whose nodes are determined by the fitness function of the path optimization algorithm. The fitness function satisfied by path is fully considered the residual energy Re, distance D, node energy consumption e and delay factor L of the path.

Firstly, the residual energy $Re(Q_k(X, S))$of any path k from X to S is calculated by Formula 3. The optimal path probability $p \propto Re$, so the larger the value of $Re(Q_k(X, S))$is, the greater the probability of being selected as the optimal path is.

$$Re(Q_k(X, S)) = \sum_{V_k^i \in Q_k} Re\left(V_k^i\right). \tag{3}$$

In addition, path distance is also an important factor in optimal path selection. The distance $D(Q_k(X, S))$ of any path k from X to S is expressed as formula 4, because the communication energy consumption between nodes is directly proportional to the square of the distance between nodes, the optimal path probability $p \propto \frac{1}{D}$.

$$D(Q_k(X, S)) = \sum_{E_k^i \in Q_k} D\left(E_k^i\right). \tag{4}$$

Considering another factor path energy consumption e, any path k from X to S energy consumption $e(Q_k(X, S))$ is expressed as formula 5, the optimal path probability $p \propto \frac{1}{e}$.

$$e(Q_k(X, S)) = \sum_{V_k^i \in Q_k} e\left(V_k^i\right) + \sum_{E_k^i \in Q_k} e\left(E_k^i\right). \tag{5}$$

The delay $L(Q_k(X, S))$ of any path k from X to S is expressed as formula 6, the optimal path probability $p \propto \frac{1}{L}$.

$$L(Q_k(X, S)) = \sum_{e \in EQ} L\left(V_k^i\right) + \sum_{n \in VQ} L\left(E_k^i\right). \tag{6}$$

In order to reconstruct an optimal path, the multi-objective function model obtained after fully considering the above multiple factors. it is shown in Formula 7.

$$\begin{cases} \max Re(Q_k(X, S)) = \sum_{V_k^i \in Q_k} Re\left(V_k^i\right), \\ \min D(Q_k(X, S)) = \sum_{E_k^i \in Q_k} D\left(E_k^i\right), \\ \min e(Q_k(X, S)) = \sum_{V_k^i \in Q_k} e\left(V_k^i\right) + \sum_{E_k^i \in Q_k} e\left(E_k^i\right), \\ \min L(Q_k(X, S)) = \sum_{e \in EQ} L\left(V_k^i\right) + \sum_{n \in VQ} L\left(E_k^i\right), \\ s.t. \quad \sum_{V_k^i \in Q_k} e\left(V_k^i\right) + \sum_{E_k^i \in Q_k} e\left(E_k^i\right) \le e, \\ s.t. \quad \sum_{e \in EQ} L\left(V_k^i\right) + \sum_{n \in VQ} L\left(E_k^i\right) \le L_{lim}. \end{cases} \tag{7}$$

It is difficult to solve the multi-objective function. Therefore, considering the above factors, namely the constraint conditions, the multi-objective function is converted into the fitness function of the heuristic algorithm, and the fitness function fitness of the heuristic algorithm is constructed as Formula 8.

$$fitness = \max \left(w_1 \cdot Re(Q_k(X, S)) + \frac{w_2}{D(Q_k(X, S))} + \frac{w_3}{e(Q_k(X, S))} + \frac{w_4}{L(Q_k(X, S))} \right). \quad (8)$$

where $w_1 + w_2 + w_3 + w_4 = 1$. In the actual solution process, each function value needs to be normalized.

3.2.3   Dynamic Segmented Path Heuristic Recovery Algorithm

For save energy consumption and shorten the delay, after formation of the new cluster head node, the previous information transmission path is divided into anterior segment path and posterior segment path. The posterior segment path refers to the transmission path from the segmentation node to the new cluster head node, which needs to be obtained by path optimization algorithm to establish a connection. WOA is used to update the posterior segment path ,and the fitness model of the path is established by comprehensively considering the remaining energy consumption, distance, energy consumption and delay of the path. Dynamic path optimization algorithm 1 pseudocode as Table 1.

Table 1. Pseudocode of Dynamic Path Optimization Algorithm

Algorithm 1:
Input: node set
Output:optimal path
Step 1: Determine the segmentation node;
Step 2: To mobile sink as the destination node, the node from the segmentation node to sink is used as the possible node set of the path;
Step 3: Compute the fitness value of per node in the node set, and sort according to the fitness value;
step4: Using whale algorithm to find the best path.

WOA is used to reconstruct the posterior segment path. WOA is based on the foraging behavior of the humpback whale. The mathematical expression is as follows

$$D = |C \cdot P^* (t) - P(t)|, \quad (9)$$

$$P(t + 1) = P^*(t) - B \cdot D. \quad (10)$$

where t is the current iteration number, $P(t)$ is the humpback whale coordinate vector, $P(t+1)$ is the coordinate vector after the next reiteration, $P^*(t)$ represents the best coordinate vector currently obtained, D is the distance between the current position and the best position of the humpback whale.

B and C are coefficients, they are respectively expressed as follows:

$$B = 2a \cdot r - a. \tag{11}$$

$$C = 2r. \tag{12}$$

where the initial value of a is 2, which decreases linearly to 0 with iteration time, r is a random vector in range $[0, 1]$.

In the whale algorithm, different search methods are selected according to the size of coefficient vector B. When $|B| > 1$, the whales swam toward random individuals for food. P_{rand} is a random individual coordinate, and the mathematical expression is as follows:

$$P(t+1) = P_{rand}(t) - B \cdot D. \tag{13}$$

When $|B| < 1$, the whale herd surrounds predators and attacking prey, i.e., the whale shrinks the prey enclosure while spiraling up close to the prey. The mathematical expression is as follows:

$$P(t+1) = P^*(t) - D \cdot e^{bl} \cdot \cos(2\pi l). \tag{14}$$

where b is a constant defining the spiral shape, l is a random number uniformly distributed in $[-1, 1]$.

Because the contraction mechanism and spiral position update are synchronous behavior, the position update of whale is carried out with the same probability. The mathematical formula is as follows:

$$P(t+1) = \begin{cases} P^*(t) - B \cdot D, & prob \le 0.5 \\ P^*(t) - D \cdot e^{bl} \cdot \cos(2\pi l). & prob \ge 0.5 \end{cases} \tag{15}$$

The pseudo-code of algorithm 2 for the posterior segment path recovery based on WOA is shown in Table 2.

Table 2. Pseudo-code of the posterior segment path Recovery Algorithm Based on Whale Optimization Algorithm

Algorithm 2:
Input: node set V
Output:optimal path P^*
Step 1: Initialization parameters. Let all nodes from the segmentation node to sink be node set V, the total number of sensor nodes is N, the total number of whale population is M, randomly generate whale position, determine the initial iteration number is 1, the maximum iteration number Tmax .
Step 2: Regularization formula 8, calculate the whale individual fitness value and sort. The maximum value is selected as the current best whale P^*.
Step 3: Entering the main iteration cycle
while($t \leq Tmax$)
For each whale
Update parameters a, B, C, l, prob
IF($prob \leq 0.5$)
IF($|B| < 1$)
$D = |CP^*(t) - P(t)|$
$P(t+1) = P^*(t) - BD$
ELSE IF($|B| >= 1$)
Select a random whale P_{rand}
$P(t+1) = P_{rand} - BD$
ELSE IF($prob >= 0.5$)
$D = |P^*(t) - P(t)|$
$P(t+1) = P^*(t) - De^{bl}cos(2\pi l)$
Endfor
Calculate fitness for each whale
Update P^*if there is an optimal location value
$t = t + 1$
endwhile
step4: Output optimal path P^*

Table 3. Experimental parameter table

Parameter	Value
Node number	50,100
Sensor radius	20m
Initial energy	0.5J
E_{elec}	50nJ/bit
E_{fs}	10pJ/bit/m^2
E_{mp}	0.0013pJ/bit/m^4
$SearchAgents_{no}$	30
$Max_i ter$	100

4   Experimental Simulation and Result Analysis

To verify the feasibility and effectiveness of the method, it is simulated in matlab. Three experiments are mainly used to verify the feasibility and effectiveness of the segmented path recovery method and the performance advantages of the multi-factor path recovery algorithm. The main experimental parameters are shown in Table 3.

4.1   Feasibility of Segmentation Path Recovery Method

To verify the feasibility of the segmented path algorithm, a clustering network of WSNs is simulated. randomly deploy 50 nodes in a $50 * 50$ square area. Using the traditional method, an initial node and an endpoint are randomly selected to generate an optimal path, and the endpoint is arbitrarily changed to generate an alternative path. It is found that most of the initial path and the alternative path will overlap in the anterior segment path. As shown in Fig. 3(a), the blue solid line denotes the initial path, the red dotted line represents alternative path after the change of the target node. If the initial node is 15, and the ending points are 3, 38, 18, 7 and 47, respectively, the optimal paths are $15 \rightarrow 29 \rightarrow 10 \rightarrow 11 \rightarrow 3, 15 \rightarrow 29 \rightarrow 10 \rightarrow 11 \rightarrow 3 \rightarrow 38, 15 \rightarrow 29 \rightarrow 10 \rightarrow 11 \rightarrow 14 \rightarrow 20 \rightarrow 17, 15 \rightarrow 29 \rightarrow 10 \rightarrow 4 \rightarrow 7, 15 \rightarrow 29 \rightarrow 10 \rightarrow 11 \rightarrow 3 \rightarrow 47$. It can be seen that there are $15 \rightarrow 29 \rightarrow 10$ nodes in all the five paths. Therefore, when the sink cannot contact the original cluster head node in the process of data collection, the path can be segmented in the process of path reconstruction, which can be divided into the anterior segment path overlapped with the initial path and the posterior segment path not overlapped. Only the posterior segment path is reconstructed, which can avoid the repeated construction of the path and the repeated transmission of data, so as to save delay and energy consumption.

4.2   Energy Consumption Analysis of Segmented Path Algorithm

To verify the effectiveness of the path segmentation method, the energy consumption of path is analyzed. A initial node is randomly selected in the network

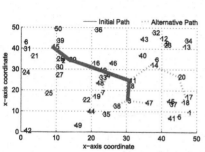

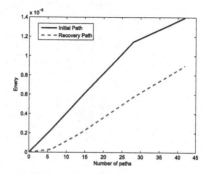

(a) Path diagram in a cluster of WSNs.   (b) Energy consumption comparison diagram.

Fig. 3. Feasibility and energy consumption analysis (Color figure online).

environment of Fig. 3(a). The energy consumption simulation analysis of all possible paths is carried out when transmitting 1 bit data. The energy consumption diagram of Fig. 3(b) is obtained. The blue solid line is energy consumption of the initial path, The red dotted line is energy consumption after using segmentation method. The segmented path reconstruction method can greatly reduce the energy consumption of path transmission.

4.3   Delay Analysis of Path Recovery Algorithm

To further testify the effectiveness of the study method, 5, 10, 15 and 700 paths are selected from the environment set in Fig. 3(a) to analyze the delay. It is found that the number of hops can be reduced from 77% to 60.4%. Assuming that the number of routing hops sent is used as the evaluation index of delay, the delay can be expressed as follows:

$$Delay = i * Delay_{hop} + Delay_{any}. \tag{16}$$

where i is the quantity of path nodes, $Delay_{hop}$ is the per node transmission delay, and $Delay_{any}$ is the transmission delay of MAC layer and queue, which is the fixed value. By formula 13, it can be seen that the delay is proportional to nodes quantity on the path, which is proportional to quantity of hops on the path.

Through the analysis of 700 paths obtained from Fig. 3(a), the delay analysis diagram shown in Fig. 4 is obtained, indicating that the path is into anterior segment path and posterior segment path, and only the reconstruction of the posterior segment path can effectively save about 60% of the delay.

4.4   Effectiveness Analysis of WOA Reconstruction Algorithm

In the reconstruction process of the posterior segment path, in order to be closer to the actual situation, a clustering network of WSNs is simulated. In a $100 * 100$ square area,100 nodes are randomly deployed. the four-dimensional factors of node residual energy, distance between nodes, node energy consumption and

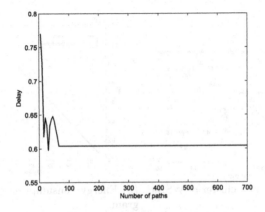

Fig. 4. Delay analysis diagram.

delay are comprehensively considered to determine the optimal posterior segment path. The consideration of multi-dimensional factors makes the problem a multi-objective optimization problem, which is difficult to solve. Therefore, the heuristic whale optimization algorithm is used . To verify the effectiveness of WOA and the influence of multi-dimensional factors on the algorithm results, it is compared from one-dimensional, two-dimensional, three-dimensional and four-dimensional perspectives. The main environment for this experiment is set in Table 3.

In the experimental process, the weight of each factor is set as residual energy$w_1 = 0.4$, distance $w_2 = 0.3$, energy consumption $w_3 = 0.2$, delay $w_4 = 0.1$, maximum iteration number 300.

Figure 5(a) is the relationship between the quantity of iterations of the posterior segment path recovery algorithm and the fitness function under various dimensions. Figure 5(b) is the relationship between the quantity of iterations and the convergence curve in the posterior segment path recovery process. From the actual simulation results of Fig. 5(a) and Fig. 5(b), it can be concluded that the convergence can be obtained after about 5 iterations. Figure 5(a) shows that the more factors are considered, the smaller the fitness function value is. Figure 5(b) shows that the more factors are considered, the faster the convergence rate is.

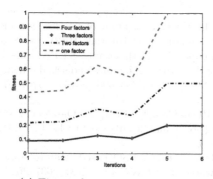

(a) Fitness for various dimensions.

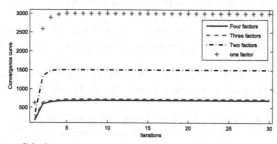

(b) Convergence curves for various dimensions.

Fig. 5. Fitness and convergence curves for various dimensions.

5   Conclusion

Considering the use of mobile sink for data collection in WSNs, due to the mobility of sink, it is easy to cause the interruption of data link. In this paper, we analyze that the nodes are easy to overlap in the process of reconstruction path. In order to save energy consumption and reduce delay, the recovery path is divided into anterior segment and posterior segment path, and the WOA heuristic optimization algorithm is used to reconstruct the posterior segment path, so as to save energy consumption of path transmission, improve path recovery delay, and improve reliability of WSNs data collection.

In this paper, we mainly analyze and study the feasibility, energy consumption and delay of the recovery of the posterior segment path of WSNs. We hope that we can further study the hybrid network and consider more aspects of comparative studies, such as network size and reliability.

Acknowledgements. This work was supported by Shanxi Provine Natural Science fund project (20190-1D111311), Key R & D projects in Datong city(2020023), and Datong University project(2019k5).

References

1. Deif, D.S., Gadallah, Y.: Classification of wireless sensor networks deployment techniques. IEEE Commun. Surv. Tutorials **16**(2), 834–855 (2014)
2. Krishnan, M., Rajagopal, V., Rathinasamy, S.: Performance evaluation of sensor deployment using optimization techniques and scheduling approach for K-coverage in WSNs. Wireless Netw. **24**(3), 683–693 (2016). https://doi.org/10.1007/s11276-016-1361-5
3. Almobaideen, W., Hushaidan, K., Sleit, A., Qatawneh, M.: A cluster-based approach for supporting qos in mobile adhoc networks. Int. J. Digital Content Technol. Appl. **5**(1), 1–9 (2011)
4. Azharuddin, M., Jana, P.K.: A PSO based fault tolerant routing algorithm for wireless sensor networks. Wireless Netw. **22**(8), 2637–2647 (2016)
5. Kallapur, P.V., Geetha, V.: Research challenges in using mobile agents for data aggregation in wireless sensor networks with dynamic deadlines. Int. J. Comput. Appl. **30**(5), 34–38 (2011)
6. Wang, J. Cao, S. Ji, et al.: Energy-efficient clusterbased dynamic routes adjustment approach for wireless sensor networks with mobile sinks. J. Supercomput., **73**(7), 3277–3290 (2017)
7. Sara, G., Kalaiarasi, R., Pari, N., Sridharan, D.: Energy efficient clustering and routing in mobile wireless sensor network. Int. J. Wirel. Mobile Netw. **2**(4), 106–114 (2010)
8. Bhatti, S., Xu, J., Memon, M.: Clustering and fault tolerance for target tracking using wireless sensor networks. IET in Wireless Sensor Syst., **1**(2), 66–73 (2011)
9. Karim, L., Nasser, N.: Reliable location-aware routing protocol for mobile wireless sensor network. IET Commun. **6**(14), 2149–2158 (2012)
10. Azharuddin, M., Jana, P.K.: A distributed algorithm for energy efficient and fault tolerant routing in wireless sensor networks. Wireless Netw. **21**, 251–267 (2015)

11. Jiyao, T., Liu, G.: Energy-optimized clustering routing algorithm based on multi-factors in WSN. Comput. Eng., **46**(1), 179–186(2020)
12. Sun, Y., Luo, H., Das, S.K.: A trust-based framework for fault-tolerant data aggregation in wireless multimedia sensor networks. IEEE Trans. Dependable Secure Comput. **9**(6), 785–797 (2012)
13. Chanak, P., Banerjee, I., Rahaman, H.: Distributed Multipath Fault Tolerance Routing Scheme for Wireless Sensor Networks. In: Third International Conference on Advanced Computing and Communication Technologies (ACCT), pp. 241–247 (2013)
14. Bagci, I. Korpeoglu, Yazlcl, A.: A distributed fault-tolerant topology control algorithm for heterogeneous wireless sensor networks. IEEE Trans. Parallel Distributed Syst. **26**(4), 914–923(2015)
15. Hur, K., Kim, J.W., Eom, D.S.: An intelligent agent-based routing structure for mobile sinks in WSNs. IEEE Trans. Consum. Electron. **56**(4), 2310–2316 (2010)
16. Wang, Y.-C., Chen, K.-C.: Efficient path planning for a mobile sink to reliably gather data from sensors with diverse sensing rates and limited buffers. IEEE Trans. **18** (2019) 1527–1540. https://doi.org/10.1109/TMC.2018.2863293
17. Gupta, S.K., Prasantam, K.J.: Energy efficient clustering and routing algorithms for wireless sensor networks: GA based approach. Wireless Pers. Commun. **83**(3), 2403–2423 (2015)
18. Rao, P.C.S., Jana, P.K., Banka, H.: A particle swarm optimization based energy efficient cluster head selection algorithm for wireless sensor networks. Wireless Netw. **23**(7), 2005–2020 (2016). https://doi.org/10.1007/s11276-016-1270-7
19. Wang, J., Cao, Y., Li, B., Kim, H., Lee, S.: Particle swarm optimization based clustering algorithm with mobile sink for WSNs. Futur. Gener. Comput. Syst. **76**, 452–457 (2017). https://doi.org/10.1016/j.future.2016.08.004
20. Wang, J., Cao, J., Sherratt, R.S., Park, J.H.: An improved ant colony optimization-based approach with mobile sink for wireless sensor networks. J. Supercomput. **74**, 6633–6645 (2018). https://doi.org/10.1007/s11227-017-2115-6
21. Krishnan, M., Yun, S., Jung, Y.M.: Enhanced clustering and ACO-based multiple mobile sinks for efficiency improvement of wireless sensor networks. Comput. Netw. **160**, 33–40 (2019).https://doi.org/10.1016/j.comnet.2019.05.019
22. Yogarajan, G., Revathi, T.: Nature inspired discrete firefly algorithm for optimal mobile data gathering in wireless sensor networks. Wirel. Netw. **24**, 2993–3007 (2018). https://doi.org/10.1007/s11276-017-1517-y
23. Lu, Y., Sun, N., Pan, X.: Mobile sink-based path optimization strategy in wireless sensor networks using artificial bee colony algorithm. IEEE Access. **7**, 11668–11678 (2019).https://doi.org/10.1109/ACCESS.2018.2885534
24. Xiu-wu, Y.U., Hao, Y.U., Yong, L., Ren-rong, X.: A clustering routing algorithm based on wolf pack algorithm for heterogeneous wireless sensor networks. Comput. Networks. 167 (2020).https://doi.org/10.1016/j.comnet.2019.106994
25. Mirjalili, S., Lewis, A.: The whale optimization algorithm. Int. J. Adv. Eng. Softw. **95**(5), 51–67 (2016)
26. Jadhav, A.R., Shankar, T.: Whale Optimization Based Energy-Efficient Cluster Head Selection Algorithm for Wireless Sensor Networks. ArXiv, abs/1711.09389 (2017)

TRindex: Distributed Double-Layer Road Network Trajectory Index

Weiqi Chen, Na Tang$^{(\boxtimes)}$, Jingjing Li, and Yong Tang

College of Computer Science, South China Normal University, Guangzhou, China
tangna@scnu.edu.cn

Abstract. With the wide application of mobile device positioning technology, the scale of traffic trajectory data generated is becoming larger and larger. How to store this massive data is a hot research topic in recent years. At present, most stand-alone road network trajectory indexes process large-scale spatio-temporal data with low efficiency, and most distributed indexes either support few query methods or have low efficiency. Therefore, this paper proposes a distributed double-layer trajectory data indexing technology (TRindex). The index adopts a global-local two-layer structure. First, the global index is divided into upper and lower layers. The upper layer is the time shards based on the time attributes of massive trajectory data, and the lower layer is the STR partition built for each time shard. Next, a two-layer local index is constructed for each STR partition. The upper-level time index is constructed based on the linear order partition algorithm, and the lower-level R^*-tree index is constructed based on the spatial attributes of the data in the partition; Secondly, the hot data cache scheduling algorithm and Redis are used to reduce the disk query overhead; In addition, to support the trajectory query method of moving objects, HBase is used to store trajectory data; At the same time, to ensure the load balance of nodes, the pre-partition strategy and consistent hash algorithm are adopted; Finally, the incremental update of the index is realized. The index's performance is evaluated by designing relevant experiments, and its efficiency and feasibility are verified by comparing it with the existing related work.

Keywords: Road network trajectory index · Linear order partition · Distributed index

1 Introduction

With the wide application of GPS and other positioning technologies, more and more mobile data can be gathered from various moving objects, which can be applied to fields such as traffic monitoring and epidemic monitoring. These data often have both temporal and spatial attributes, and temporal features are usually described by timestamp or time interval (period). Moreover, spatial features are usually described by approximate geometric figures such as minimum circumscribed rectangle MBR [1].

The rapid development of mobile device positioning technology makes the scale of road network trajectory data larger and larger. Therefore, how to store massive data is

Y. Sun et al. (Eds.): ChineseCSCW 2022, CCIS 1681, pp. 350–364, 2023.
https://doi.org/10.1007/978-981-99-2356-4_28

a hot research topic in recent years. It is necessary to build a specific index to improve query efficiency.

Therefore, this paper proposes a distributed two-layer road network trajectory index technology (TRindex) for the historical data. The underlying database of TRindex is HBase, and the cache database is Redis. It adopts a global-local two-layer structure, in which the global index and the local index are divided into upper and lower layers. The construction process is as follows: First, time shards are performed on the massive trajectory data, and then STR partitions are performed on the data in each time shard. Secondly, a two-layer local index is constructed for each STR partition, the upper layer is the temporal index constructed based on the linear order partition algorithm, and the lower layer is the spatial index R*-tree. Finally, the query algorithm and update algorithm of the TRindex are discussed.

The contributions of this paper are as follows:

- The global index adopts time shard of different granularity and the STR partition method; the local index indexes time first, then indexes space, and uses the linear order partition algorithm to filter the data;
- Use a pre-partitioning strategy and consistent hashing algorithm to balance data distribution; Batch loading technology is used to build a local spatial index, which speeds up index construction.
- Combined with hot data scheduling algorithm, the Redis database is introduced as the memory cache hotspot data, and the latest STR partition is cached in the memory to reduce the disk overhead.
- Use Hadoop to realize efficient distributed queries; In addition, HBase is used as the underlying database, and various query methods are designed for the index structure.

The other parts of this paper are as follows. Section 2 summarizes related work in the corresponding areas. Section 3 describes the structure of TRindex in detail. Section 4 discusses the query and update algorithm of TRindex. Section 5 evaluates the performance of TRindex in comparison with other indexes. Section 6 concludes the full text.

2 Related Work

After decades of development of trajectory indexing technology, these indicators can be divided into three categories: past location information, current location information and future location information [2]. This paper mainly studies the road network trajectory index based on past location information, thus it focuses on the related work in this area. In recent years, many spatio-temporal data management systems and trajectory indexes have been proposed, which can be divided into two categories: stand-alone and distributed.

One of the most classic stand-alone indexes is the R-tree. The 3DR-tree [3] extends the 2DR-tree and takes the time attribute as the common dimension, which can query data efficiently. In addition, some indexes improved the R-tree, including MR-tree [4], HR-tree [5], and MV3R-tree [6], which integrate the idea of multi-version B-tree and have high time range query efficiency. Also, to support trajectory query, some indexes including SETI [7] and SEB-tree [8], are for moving objects with unlimited movement. Their main idea is to grid the spatial attributes of data and then use R-tree to index the trajectory data of each grid. Moreover, for moving objects on the road network, several indexes have emerged, such as FNR-tree [9] and MON-tree [10]. Among them, FNR-tree [9] is a two-layer structure of road network trajectory index, the upper layer uses 2DR-tree to index the road network, and the lower layer uses 1DR-tree to index moving objects. Furthermore, MON-tree [10] improves based on FNR-tree, adding a Hash structure to store leaf node data.

Traditional stand-alone indexes are no longer suitable for massive data scenarios. Along with the wide application of distributed architecture, the research on the distributed index has made good progress.

Among distributed indexes, MD-HBase [11], GeoMesa [12], and JUST [13] are all created based on a NoSQL database. They all use the spatial filling curve to encode multidimensional data and are easy to construct. Also, some indexes are built on Hadoop frameworks, for example, SpatialHadoop [14] and ST-Hadoop [15]. SpatialHadoop supports spatial data and ST-Hadoop supports spatio-temporal data. Additionally, both SpatialHadoop and ST-Hadoop partition the data first, and then build the index for the data in the partition. However, these systems may face efficiency issues due to the high disk overhead of Hadoop processing jobs. Besides that, there are a number of Spark-based indexes, like GeoSpark [16] and Beast [17]. GeoSpark uses Spark to construct RDDs for spatial data, and then spatially partitions the RDDs; Beast integrates multiple open source components to support multiple file formats. Furthermore, it supports R*-Grove, STR, Grid, and KD-tree for data partitioning, and uses R*-tree to index each partition. Nevertheless, these Spark-based systems store data in memory, which can result in prohibitive storage costs.

The above distributed spatio-temporal index is suitable for trajectory data in unlimited cases. At present, some researchers have proposed a batch of distributed road network trajectory indexes, like DSI [18], STCode-tree [19], HadoopTrajectory [20], TrajMesa [21] and Dragoon [22]. To be more exact, DSI simply divides the space into nonoverlapping horizontal or vertical strips, which are allocated to child nodes; STCode-tree is based on HBase and uses spatial filling curve STCode to encode data; HadoopTrajectory extends the core layer of Hadoop, enabling Hadoop to support spatio-temporal data. What is more, its global index can be selected from grid index or 3DR-tree, and HadoopTrajectory allows to build of indexes with the granularity of moving objects or trajectories. Moreover, TrajMesa is a NoSQL-based distributed trajectory management system that supports queries of different types of data. And it uses two indexes, both based on a variant of the Z-curve technique, to generate keys for storage in HBase. In addition, Dragoon is a hybrid trajectory management system built on Spark, which supports historical and online trajectories. Since RDDs in Spark are immutable after construction, any update will create a new RDD. Therefore, Dragoon proposes a mutable RDD model for this problem. However, these indexes either support few query methods, or traverse all child nodes resulting in low query efficiency, or face the situation of high storage cost, or do not consider the problem that the Z-curve may produce mutations.

3 TRindex Model

Each trajectory segment is Tr_i, and Γ also represents the time interval set and the quasi-ordered set.

3.1 Linear Order Partition

Definition 1. Time shard (TS): starting from epoch time 1970–01-01 00:00:00, the time attribute of the data is divided according to a fixed period to obtain time shards. Additionally, so as to meet different query requirements, the fixed period can be set to hours, days, weeks, months, and years.

Definition 2. Linear order: when there is a pseudo-order [23] relationship that satisfies reflexivity and transitivity, and furthermore, the pseudo-order relationship satisfies the linear order condition at the same time, it is called pseudo-linear order, referred to as linear order.

- $Tr_i \leq Tr_j (0 \leq i \leq n, 0 \leq j \leq n) \Leftrightarrow Tr_i \subseteq Tr_j$
- $Tr_i \leq Tr_j (0 \leq i \leq n, 0 \leq j \leq n) \Leftrightarrow Sta(Tr_i) < Sta(Tr_j) \vee (Sta(Tr_i) = Sta(Tr_j) \wedge End(Tr_i) \leq End(Tr_j))$
- $\forall Tr_i, Tr_j, Tr_k \in \Gamma, Tr_i \leq Tr_j \wedge Tr_j \leq Tr_k \Leftrightarrow Tr_i \leq Tr_k$

The above formula can verify that "$\leq$" is a linear order relationship on Γ that satisfies reflexivity and transitivity.

Definition 3. Linear order branch (LOB): LOB is a set of time intervals of trajectory segments, that is $LOB = \{TI_0, \ldots, TI_j\}$. And the start point of LOB, is called the maximum element, denoted as $\max(LOB)$. Moreover, the end point is called the minimum element, denoted as $\min(LOB)$.

Definition 4. Linear order partition (LOP): is defined as the set of non-intersecting LOB, that is, $LOP = \{LOB_0, \ldots, LOB_i, \ldots, LOB_j\} \wedge LOB_i \cap LOB_j = \emptyset$.

3.2 TRindex Structure

Definition 5. TRindex memory-disk model: is a global-local two-layer index structure. The index file and trajectory data are stored in the disk. On the other hand, the hot data of local index and the latest STR partition are cached in the memory. The memory-disk distribution diagram is shown in the figure (see Fig. 1).

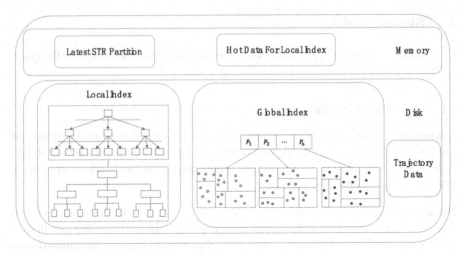

Fig. 1. Memory-disk distribution diagram

Definition 6. Global index: a double-layer structure composed of time shards and STR partitions. The upper structure is time shard, and the lower layer uses the STR method (Sort-Tile-Recursive) to partition the data in the shards [24]. In order to improve query efficiency, the latest STR partition will be stored in memory. In addition, the old partition will be flushed to the disk when the partition expires.(see Fig. 2).

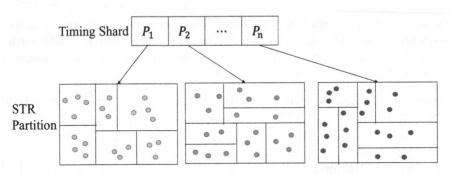

Fig. 2. Schematic diagram of the global index structure

Algorithm 1 Building the global index

Import: trajectory dataset: $\Gamma =< trj_1, trj_2, \ldots, trj_n >$, Time shard period: *period* ;
Export: global index = (TS: Time Shard Collection, R : STR partition collection);
Period(Time) represents the corresponding period of extraction;
1. **for** $n = 1 : |\Gamma|$ **do**
2. $code = Period(Sta(Trj_n))$; $TS_{code}.add(Trj_n)$;
3. **end for**
4. **for** $i = 0 : |TS|$ **do**
5. $R_1 = \varnothing$;Randomly select $0.01 \times |TS_i|$ trajectory data to generate multiple STR partition; $R_1.add(STR)$;
6.   **for** $j = 0 : |R_1|$ **do**
7.   **for** $k = 0 : |TS_i|$ **do**
8.   **if** MBR(Trj_k) $\in$ STR_j **then** $STR_j.add(Trj_k)$;
9.   **end if**
10.   **end for**
11. $R.add(STR_j)$;
12.   **end for**
13. **end for**

The second step of Algorithm 1 uses Hadoop to classify the data, thus the time complexity is $O(n)$. And then traverses the entire time shard set, so the time complexity is $O(n^3)$. Therefore, the total time complexity of Algorithm 1 is $O(n^3)$.

Definition 8. Local index: is a two-layer structure composed of a temporal index module Tindex and a spatial index module Sindex(see Fig. 3).

(1) Tindex: a tree structure with three levels of nodes:

- *LOP* Level: save each *LOP* node in the partition;
- *LOB* Level: saves the root node $r_i = (\max(P\Gamma \max), \min(P\Gamma \min))$ of each *LOB* in *LOP*, where $P\Gamma$ max is the set of $\max(LOB_i)$, and $P\Gamma$ min is the set of $\min(LOB_i)$.
- Leaf Level: saves several *LOB* corresponding to the root node-set.

(2) Sindex: consists of multiple R*-trees, each R*-tree corresponds to a STR partition. So as to speed up the construction and reduce the overlapping area of MBR, a recursive grid sorting algorithm (Sort-Tile-Recursive, STR) is used to construct R*-tree.

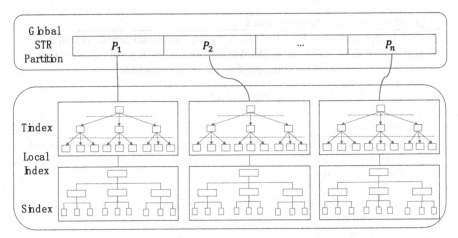

Fig. 3. Schematic diagram of the local index structure

Algorithm 2 Building the local index

Import: STR partition collection $R = < STR_1, STR_2, \ldots, STR_n >$
Export: local index = (LOP, R*-tree set T)

1. Γ represents the temporal interval, $Time(Trj_p)$ represents the time attribute of the trajectory; $Tail(LOB_k)$ represents the last trajectory time interval of LOB_k;
2. **for** $n = 0 : |R|$ **do**
3. $\Gamma = \varnothing$;
4. **for** $p = 0 : |STR_n|$ **do**
5. $t_p = Time(Trj_p)$; $\Gamma.add(t_p)$;
6. **end for**
7. First sort Γ according to "$\leq$";
  $i = i+1$; $i = 0, k = 0, j = 1$; $LOB_k = \varnothing$, $LOB_k.add(t_i)$;
8. **if** $i \leq |\Gamma|$ **then**
9.   **if** $Sta(t_i) == Sta(Tail(LOB_k))$ && $End(t_i) \leq End(Tail(LOB_k))$ **then**
10. $LOB_k.add(t_i)$, $i = i+1$; **goto** step 8;
11.   **end if**
12.   **if** $\exists t_i \in \Gamma$ && $Sta(t_i) == (Sta(Tail(LOB_k)) + j)$ &&
   $End(t_i) == End(Tail(LOB_k))$ **then**
13. $LOB_k.add(t_i)$, $i = i+1$; **goto** step 9;
14.   **else** $j = j+1$;
15.   **end if**
16.   **if** $(Sta(Tail(LOB_k)) + j) == End(Tail(LOB_k))$ **then**
17. $LOP.add(LOB_k)$, $k = k+1$, $LOB_k = \varnothing$, $j = 1$; **goto** step 9;
18.   **end if**
19. **end if**
20. build R*-tree; $T.add(R*-tree)$;
21. **end for**

The seventh step of Algorithm 2 uses the quick sort algorithm, so the time complexity is $O(n \log n)$. And then traverses the entire temporal interval set Γ and uses the recursive grid sorting algorithm to construct the R*-tree, thus the time complexity is $O(n^2)$. Therefore, the total time complexity of Algorithm 2 is $O(n^2)$.

3.3 Data Cache

HBase is used to store massive trajectory data, and HDFS is used to store index files. On the other hand, Redis is used to cache hot data so as to reduce disk I/O overhead and index query overhead.

For the purpose of separating hot and cold data, a hot data cache scheduling algorithm similar to the LRU algorithm is adopted: the recently accessed data is most likely to be repeatedly accessed in the future. The algorithm periodically counts the accessed heat of the data, sorts when the heat reaches the threshold, and selects the top K records to be cached in memory [25]. Calculated as follows:

$$T(t_n) = \alpha \times \frac{visitCount}{countPeriod} + e^{-\alpha \times (t_n - t_{n-1})} \times T(t_{n-1}) \tag{1}$$

Among them, $\alpha(0 \leq \alpha \leq 1)$ is the set temperature attenuation coefficient, $T(t_n)$ is the heat of the data at time t_n, $countPeriod$ is the heat calculation cycle, $visitCount$ is the number of times the data is accessed in the calculation cycle, and $T(t_{n-1})$ is the heat of the data at time t_{n-1}. The historical popularity of the data decays at the speed of an exponential function. After many calculations, the impact of the early popularity of the data on the current popularity value gradually decreases.

3.4 Load Balancing

In order to distribute the massive data evenly on HBase and avoid data writing hotspots, a pre-partitioning strategy is adopted. First, the table is initially partitioned, and then the formula used by HBase is as follows:

$$rowKey = MD5(ID_{last}) + ID + Rid + timestamp \tag{2}$$

Among them, ID_{last} represents the last digit of the moving object identifier, $MD5(ID_{last})$ represents the last digit of the moving object identifier encoded in MD5 mode, Rid represents the road segment identifier. Moreover, using the MD5 method to calculate the last digit of the ID. Since the result is 0–15, 16 regions are created in HBase, which effectively avoids the problem of write hotspots.

The memory part of the TRindex system is deployed on the Redis cluster. To evenly distribute read and write requests, a consistent hash algorithm with virtual nodes is used to map requests to the corresponding Redis server.

4   TRindex Index Operation

This section will discuss the query and update algorithms for TRindex.

4.1   The Query of TRindex

The query is mainly divided into three query methods: Spatio-temporal query, K-nearest neighbor query, and Moving object trajectory query.

Spatio-Temporal Region Query
See Algorithm 3 for details.

Algorithm 3   Spatio-temporal region query

Import: Time query range: Q_{time}, Spatial query range: $Q_{spatial}$
Export: Collection of spatio-temporal points: $P_{spatiotemporal}$

1. Global index query. Find the partition satisfying Q_{time} in the time-series partition set, and then select the partition conforming to $Q_{spatial}$ from the corresponding STR partition.
2. Local index query. Find the LOB matching the Q_{time} in the LOB set corresponding to the STR partition, and then binary search in the LOB to obtain the temporal point set. This algorithm is the work of predecessors[26], so it is not described in detail. Search the R*-tree set corresponding to the LOB set obtained in the previous step to obtain the spatial point set conforming to $Q_{spatial}$.
3. Integrate temporal query and spatial query. By finding the intersection of the ID corresponding to the temporal point set and the spatial point set, the spatio-temporal point set $P_{spatiotemporal}$ is obtained.

K-Nearest Neighbor Query
The K-nearest neighbor query method is carried out based on the Spatio-temporal region query, see Algorithm 4 for details.

Algorithm 4   K-nearest neighbor query

Import: Time query range: Q_{time}, Spatial point: $P_{spatial}$, Query range: $Range = 1$;
Export: Collection of spatio-temporal points: $P_{spatiotemporal}$;

1. Global index query. Same as step 1 of algorithm 3.
2. Local index query. Integrate $P_{spatial}$ and $Range$ into $Q_{spatial}$; Next, it is the same as step 2 of algorithm 3.
3. Integrate temporal query and spatial query. After obtaining the spatio-temporal point set $P_{spatiotemporal}$, if the number of points is greater than or equal to K, the first k results will be returned after sorting. Otherwise, the previous step will be returned, and the $Range$ will be expanded to the square of the $Range$.

Moving Object Trajectory Query
Since HBase is used as the underlying database for storing massive trajectory data, the

primary key query operation of HBase can be directly used to search for the trajectory corresponding to the specified ID.

4.2 The Update of TRindex

The update operation of the index supports the minimum time granularity, which is the fixed period set during time sharding. See Algorithm 5 for details.

Algorithm 5   The update of TRindex

Import: Time range: Q_{time} ;

Export: TRindex

1. Global index update. Update the time shard specified in the global index.
2. Local index update. Locate the local index and update the corresponding Tindex and Sindex. If the corresponding index file is in the disk, update the index file; otherwise, update the index file in Redis.
3. HBase update. Update the trajectory points in the underlying database HBase in batches.

---

5 Performance Evaluation

The road network dataset comes from Guangzhou city, and the trajectory dataset is generated by the moving object generator implemented by Thomas Brinkhoff [27]. The experimental environment is a cluster with three servers. In addition, the reason why MD-HBase and 3DR-tree are used as comparison objects is that they have high spatio-temporal query efficiency.

5.1 TRindex Construction

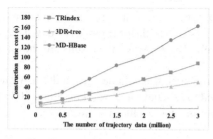

Fig. 4. Time cost of index building

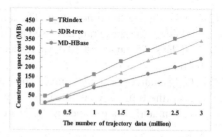

Fig. 5. Space cost of index building

The amount of experimental data goes up from 100 thousand to 3 million. Two cases are discussed: the time cost(see Fig. 4) and space cost(see Fig. 5) of building the index. We can see from the Fig. 4 that MD-HBase takes more time. This is because MD-HBase needs to perform Z encoding on each data one by one. As the amount of data continues to climb, the number of bits taken by Z encoding also increases. In addition, it is manifest from the Fig. 5 that MD-HBase has the least space overhead because both the index and source data of MD-HBase are stored in the HBase.

5.2 TRindex Query

Spatio-temporal region query can be divided into three cases: spatio-temporal range changes at the same time, only change the time range and only change the spatial range.

(1) Spatio-temporal range changes at the same time: The number of experimental data rises from 100 thousand to 3 million. Two cases are discussed: the spatio-temporal query range is 1 (see Fig. 6) and the spatio-temporal query range is 10 (see Fig. 7). It can be observed that the time query overhead of the three indexes grows with the increase of the amount of data, and TRindex is the best. The reason for the poor performance of the comparative index is that with the rise of data volume and the expansion of the query range, MD-HBase needs to span multiple region servers, while 3DR-tree is getting bigger and bigger, which leads to the continuous increase in the time overhead of the tree from disk cache to memory.

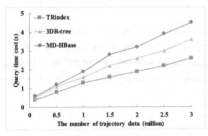 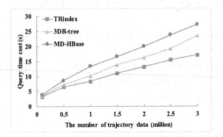

Fig. 6. The spatio-temporal query range is 1   **Fig. 7.** The spatio-temporal query range is 10

(2) Only change the time range: The amount of experimental data is 1.5 million. In addition, the space range is fixed at 10 km as well as the time range is 1 day, 5 days, 10 days, 15 days, and 20 days, respectively. The experimental results are shown in Fig. 8.

(3) Only change the spatial range: The experimental data volume is 1.5 million. Moreover, the time range is fixed to 1 day, and the spatial range is 1 km, 5 km, 10 km, 15 km, and 20 km respectively. The experimental results are shown in Fig. 9.

It can be seen from Fig. 8 and Fig. 9 that the time cost of the three indexes rises with the expansion of space and time range, and finally tends to be stable. Compared with the other two indexes, TRindex has better performance. This is because, with the expansion of the query range, MD-HBase needs to traverse multiple region servers to find all qualified values. On the other hand, 3DR-tree may need to traverse the entire tree because it simply combines the spatial and temporal dimensions.

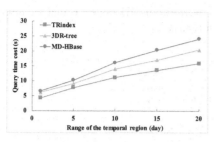

Fig. 8. The time range changes

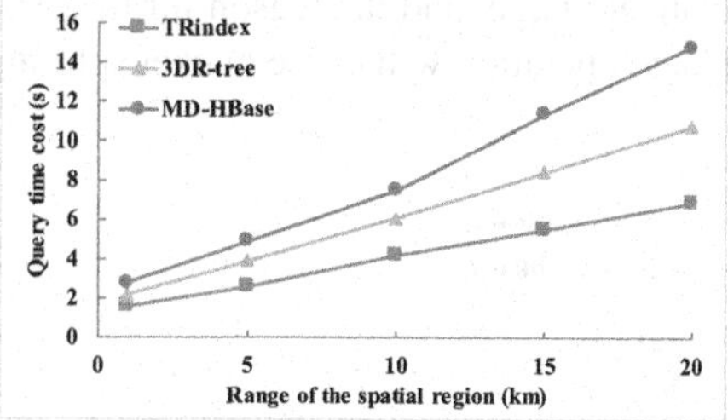

Fig. 9. The space range changes

(4) K-nearest neighbor query: Query can be divided into two cases: fixed k-value and unfixed k-value. The data volume in Fig. 10 ranges from 100 thousand to 3 million, and the fixed data volume in Fig. 11 is 1.5 million, both with a time range of 1 day. According to the Fig. 10, when the fixed k value is 5, the performance of the TRindex is best as the amount of data ascends. Moreover, Fig. 11 shows that with the rise of the value of k, the time cost of the query of the three indexes goes up gradually. The primary reason is that as the value of k rises, the client in MD-HBase will communicate with the region server frequently, resulting in high I/O overhead, and 3DR-tree needs to traverse the child nodes multiple times.

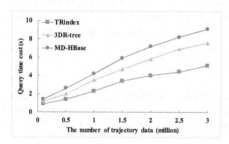

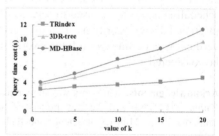

Fig. 10. Query with fixed k value

Fig. 11. Query with different k value

(5) Moving object trajectory query: The experimental data volume is 1.5 million. In addition, MD-HBase does not support moving object trajectory query. The experimental results are shown in Fig. 12. As can be seen from the figure, the query cost of TRindex is much smaller than the transformed 3DR-tree, because TRindex relies on the query function of the underlying database HBase.

5.3 TRindex Insert

The amount of experimental data is 1.5 million, and the number of newly inserted trajectory points is from 10 thousand to 100 thousand. The experimental results are shown in Fig. 13. As is shown in the figure, the insertion and update cost of the TRindex is smaller than the other two indexes. This is because the I/O overhead of 3DR-tree is relatively large, and the reason for the largest overhead of MD-HBase is that the insert update operation will cause bucket splitting in HBase.

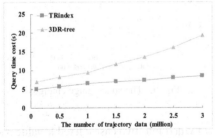

Fig. 12. Moving object trajectory query   **Fig. 13.** Insert update

6 Conclusion

In this paper, a distributed two-layer road network trajectory index TRindex is proposed based on historical data. TRindex adopts a global-local structure. To improve query efficiency, the global index uses time shard and STR partition to quickly locate eligible data. The local index is further searched using the linear order partition algorithm and the R*-tree. To ensure node load balancing, the pre-partitioning method and consistent hashing algorithm are used; in order to reduce the cost of index query, the hot data cache scheduling algorithm is used to separate the hot and cold index data. Then, the query, insert and delete algorithms are introduced in turn. Finally, the efficiency of TRindex is verified by experiments. In future work, support for other types of trajectory data will be considered.

Acknowledgments. This work was supported by National Natural Science Foundation of China (Grant U1811263) and the Key Project of Science and Technology Innovation 2030 which supported by the Ministry of Science and Technology of China (Grant No. 2018AAA0101300).

References

1. Tang, Y., Ye, X., Tang, N.: Temporal information processing technology and its application, 1 edn. Springer, Heidelberg (2011). https://doi.org/10.1007/978-3-642-14959-7
2. Tang, N., Zhu, Z.H., Li, J.J., Tang, Y., Ye, X.P.: Temporal-spatial phase point moving object data indexing: PM-tree. Chin. J. Comput. **44**(03), 579–593 (2021)
3. Theodoridis, Y., Vazirgiannis, M., Sellis, T.: Spatio-temporal indexing for large multimedia applications. In: Proceedings of the Third IEEE International Conference on Multimedia Computing and Systems, pp. 441–448 (1996)
4. Nascimento, M.A., Silva, J.R.: Towards historical R-trees. In: Proceedings of the 1998 ACM Symposium on Applied Computing, pp. 235–240 (1998)
5. Tao, Y., Papadias, D.: Efficient historical R-trees. In: Proceedings Thirteenth International Conference on Scientific and Statistical Database Management (SSDBM 2001), pp. 223–232 (2001)

6. Tao, Y., Papadias, D.: The mv3r-tree: a spatio-temporal access method for timestamp and interval queries. In: Proceedings of Very Large Data Bases Conference (VLDB), pp. 11–14 (2001)

7. Chakka, V.P., Everspaugh, A., Patel, J.M.: Indexing large trajectory data sets with SETI. In: CIDR, p. 76 (2003)

8. Song, Z., Roussopoulos, N.: SEB-tree: an approach to index continuously moving objects. In: International Conference on Mobile Data Management, pp. 340–344 (2003)

9. Frentzos, E.: Indexing objects moving on fixed networks. In: International Symposium on Spatial and Temporal Databases, pp. 289–305 (2003)

10. De Almeida, V.T., Güting, R.H.: Indexing the trajectories of moving objects in networks. GeoInformatica **9**(1), 33–60 (2005)

11. Nishimura, S., Das, S., Agrawal, D., El Abbadi, A.: MD-HBase: a scalable multi-dimensional data infrastructure for location aware services. In: 2011 IEEE 12th International Conference on Mobile Data Management, pp. 7–16 (2011)

12. Fox, A., Eichelberger, C., Hughes, J., Lyon, S.: Spatio-temporal indexing in non-relational distributed databases. In: 2013 IEEE International Conference on Big Data, pp. 291–299 (2013)

13. Li, R., et al.: Just: Jd urban spatio-temporal data engine. In: 2020 IEEE 36th International Conference on Data Engineering (ICDE), pp. 1558–1569 (2020)

14. Eldawy, A., Mokbel, M.F.: Spatialhadoop: a mapreduce framework for spatial data. In: 2015 IEEE 31st international Conference on Data Engineering, pp. 1352–1363 (2015)

15. Alarabi, L., Mokbel, M.F., Musleh, M.: St-hadoop: a mapreduce framework for spatio-temporal data. GeoInformatica **22**(4), 785–813 (2018)

16. Yu, J., Wu, J., Sarwat, M.: Geospark: a cluster computing framework for processing large-scale spatial data. In: Proceedings of the 23rd SIGSPATIAL International Conference on Advances in Geographic Information Systems, pp. 1–4 (2015)

17. Eldawy, A., Hristidis, V., Ghosh, S.: Beast: scalable exploratory analytics on spatio-temporal data. In: Proceedings of the 30th ACM International Conference on Information & Knowledge Management, pp. 3796–3807 (2021)

18. Yu, Z., Liu, Y., Yu, X., Pu, K.Q.: Scalable distributed processing of K nearest neighbor queries over moving objects. IEEE Trans. Knowl. Data Eng. **27**(5), 1383–1396 (2014)

19. Van Le, H., Takasu, A.: A scalable spatio-temporal data storage for intelligent transportation systems based on hbase. In: 2015 IEEE 18th International Conference on Intelligent Transportation Systems, pp. 2733–2738 (2015)

20. Bakli, M., Sakr, M., Soliman, T.H.A.: HadoopTrajectory: a Hadoop spatiotemporal data processing extension. J. Geogr. Syst. **21**(2), 211–235 (2019). https://doi.org/10.1007/s10109-019-00292-4

21. Li, R., He, H., Wang, R.: Trajmesa: A distributed nosql storage engine for big trajectory data. In: 2020 IEEE 36th International Conference on Data Engineering (ICDE), pp: 2002–2005 (2020)

22. Fang, Z., Chen, L., Gao, Y., Pan, L., Jensen, C.S.: Dragoon: a hybrid and efficient big trajectory management system for offline and online analytics. VLDB J. **30**(2), 287–310 (2021). https://doi.org/10.1007/s00778-021-00652-x

23. Tang, N., Ye, X.P., Tang, Y., Peng, P., Du, M.Y.: Temporal XML index based on temporal partial-order relationship. J. Softw. **27**(9), 2290–2302 (2016)

24. Leutenegger, S.T., Lopez, M.A., Edgington, J.: STR: A simple and efficient algorithm for R-tree packing. In: Proceedings 13th International Conference on Data engineering, pp. 497–506 (1997)

25. Ge, W., et al.: HiBase: a hierarchical indexing mechanism and system for efficient HBase query. Chin. J. Comput. **39**(1), 140–153 (2016)

26. Yang, Z.X., Tang, N., Tang, Y., Pan, M.M., Li, D.D., Ye, X.P.: Temporal index and query based on timing partition. Journal of Software **31**(11), 3519–3539 (2020)
27. Brinkhoff, T.:Generating network-based moving objects. In: Proceedings. 12th International Conference on Scientific and Statistica Database Management, pp. 253–255 (2000)

Sleep Scheduling for Enhancing the Lifetime of Three-Dimensional Heterogeneous Wireless Sensor Networks

Haoyang Zhou and Jingjing Li[✉]

College of Computer Science, South China Normal University, Guangzhou, China
lijingjing@scnu.edu.cn

Abstract. How to provide reliable coverage for a field of interest (FOI) and prolong network lifetime is a critical issue in three-dimensional (3D) Wireless Sensor Networks (WSNs). In practical applications, sensors may not have the same energy consumption model, which profoundly influences the network lifetime. In this paper, we address the problem of maximizing the network lifetime while satisfying k-coverage of the 3D FOI by determining redundant sensors. We assume different sensors have different sensing and communication range, and energy consumption models. We propose a method to find the redundant sensors and their neighbors based on the border effect and probability sensing model and develop a distributed sleep scheduling algorithm. Through simulations, the results show that the proposed algorithm outperforms the other existing approach, providing a longer lifetime and higher average coverage ratio by using few communication messages.

Keywords: k-coverage · probabilistic sensing model · border effects · heterogeneous energy consumption · 3D WSNs

1 Introduction

Wireless Sensor Networks(WSNs) are composed of many sensors with limited energy, simple computation ability, and little storage. Sensors can collect date from surrounding environment and transmit information.

Coverage problem is critical in WSNs. It is usually classified into point coverage, area coverage, and barrier coverage [1]. Dense sensors ensure high coverage, but this leads to the increased energy consumption of the network. Therefore, it is necessary to schedule a some sensor nodes to be active to perform covering while the rest of the sensors switch to sleep for saving energy [2, 3].

The major of previous studies focus on solving the problems in two-dimensional (2D) WSNs, which are the sensors deployed in a plane. However, in the natural environment, the fields to be monitored are three dimensions (3D) [4–6]. Thus, we need to design a novel algorithm. This paper develops a distributed sleep scheduling algorithm with k-coverage to enhance the network lifetime in 3D heterogeneous WSNs. We assume that the sensing radius, communication radius and energy consumption model of different

© The Author(s), under exclusive license to Springer Nature Singapore Pte Ltd. 2023
Y. Sun et al. (Eds.): ChineseCSCW 2022, CCIS 1681, pp. 365–375, 2023.
https://doi.org/10.1007/978-981-99-2356-4_29

sensors are different. We propose an estimation method to find all the combinations that make the sensor itself redundant according to the number of different types. The sensors get neighbors' information through simple control messages in the scheduling. Then, according to the estimation method, each sensor determines whether it goes to sleep.

The main contributions of this paper are as follows:

1. We fully consider the actual energy consumption attribute in 3D heterogeneous WSNs and use a quadratic model.
2. We propose a redundant sensor estimation method based on the border effects and probabilistic sensing model.
3. A distributed sleep scheduling algorithm is proposed to schedule sensors to enhance network lifetime while satisfying k-coverage of the field without knowing localization information.
4. We develop simulations to show the efficiency of the proposed algorithm.

The rest of this paper is organized as follows: Sect. 2 reviews the related works on k-coverage of 3D FOI. Section 3 introduces the system model and problem definition. Section 4 proposes a method to estimate the redundant sensor based on the border effect and probability sensing model. Section 5 proposes a distributed sleep scheduling algorithm. Section 6 presents the simulation results of the proposed algorithm. The paper is concluded in Sect. 7.

2   Related Work

To ensure the k-coverage and enhance the network lifetime, a standard way is to control the number of nodes working based on location information. In [7], the algorithm divided the FOI into small blocks based on Voronoi tessellation, Kelvin's conjecture, and Kepler's conjecture. It ensured k-coverage by maintaining the k-coverage of each small block. In [8], Sakib et al. used the existing single covering integer linear programming (ILP) formulas on k-coverage. In [9], the authors proposed a new method based on the imperialist competition algorithm (ICA). The standard ICA increases the possibility of colony migration from weak to strong. In [10], the authors proposed a new geometrical shape called Sixsoid, which can better cover the 3D FOI. Paper [11] applied Helly's theorem to solve the k-coverage and data collection problem and proposed a global framework.

In [12–14], the authors proposed a method based on probability rather than location information to determine whether the sensors are redundant. In [12], based on the probability that two different types of sensors cover an event, the proposed algorithm deduced the probability that k types of sensors cover an event. In [13], Luiz Filipe et al. first considered the probability of that 1-coverage event and then extended it to k-coverage. In [14], Hari et al. derived heterogeneous k-coverage from homogeneous k-coverage. These papers did not consider the heterogeneous energy consumption of different sensors. However, considering the heterogeneous consumption models help to achieve a more accurate and realistic calculation of the energy consumption to enable a better sensor selection.

In summary, the previous studies on k-coverage have the following limitations:

1. Position information of sensors is required. In [7–11], sensors need to know their own or neighbor position information, which will bring significant restrictions to the practical application due to the additional energy consumption of GPS, and the accuracy of positioning will also impact the performance of the WSNs.
2. At present, most algorithms are to enhance the WSNs' lifetime by reducing the number of working nodes. However, when considering the heterogeneous energy consumption of different sensors, extending the lifetime while meeting the k-coverage requirements becomes more complex.

To overcome the above limitations, we propose a distributed sleep scheduling algorithm for heterogeneous WSNs. The algorithm allows the network to cover FOI with a more energy-efficient combination of sensors under heterogeneous sensing energy consumption.

3 System Model and Problem Definition

This section introduces a system model consisting of a network, a probability spherical sensing, and an energy consumption model. Then we define the sleep scheduling problem.

3.1 System Model

Network Model. We assume that T types of N static nodes are deployed randomly in a 3-Dimension FOI. The shape of FOI is a cuboid that Λ denotes. Each sensor has different sensing ranges and communication ranges according to type. Let N_t denote the number of type-t sensors, where $t \in \{1, 2, 3, \ldots, T\}$, thereby the totality of sensors in the network is $N = \sum_1^T N_t$. If sensers are the same type, they have the same identical sensing and communicating radius.

Probability Spherical Sensing Model. We assume that the sensing radius of a sensor s_i is a regular sphere centered at the location of s_i with the sensing radius of r_i, labeled a sensing sphere. Since sensor detections are uncertain and its sensing ability depends on the distance between the itself and the event interested, the sensing model should be expressed in probabilistic terms [2]. If an event E locates at the point q within the sensing radius r_i of sensor s_i, a sensor s_i perceives the event E with the probability $P(s_i, E)$ that is calculated as:

$$P(s_i, E) = f(d) = \begin{cases} e^{-\lambda d(s_i, q)}, & d(s_i, q) \le r \\ 0, & d(s_i, q) > r_i \end{cases} \tag{1}$$

where the parameter λ is a physical properties constant of the sensor, $d(s_i, q)$ is the distance from the event E to the sensor node s_i.

Energy Consumption Model. Our model assumes that each sensor has two states: ACTIVE and SLEEP. In the ACTIVE state, the sensor's sensing and communication modules are turned on to monitor the environment and communicate with neighbors.

Moreover, in the SLEEP state, all the modules are turned off. Thus, the sensor consumes energy in the ACTIVE state, including energy consumption for sensing, transmitting, and receiving. We consider that different sensors have different energy consumption models. The sensing, transmit and receiving energy consumption is as follow.

$$ES_i = \mu r_i^2 \tag{2}$$

$$ET_i = E_{elec}k + E_{fs}kd^2 \tag{3}$$

$$ER_i = E_{elec}k. \tag{4}$$

where μ is the physical properties constant of sensors, E_{elec} is the energy dissipated when sensor transmits or receives 1 bit data and E_{elec} is the free space fading energy.

3.2 Problem Definition

Definition 1 (Round). The sensor periodically is in the ACTIVE state, and each such period is defined as an around.

Definition 2 (Network Lifetime). The lifetime L_T of 3D WSNs is divided into c rounds $R_1, R_2, \ldots, R_c$, and the duration L_R of each round is identical. The network lifetime is the sum of the duration of rounds.

$$L_T = cL_R. \tag{5}$$

The problem in this paper is defined as follows:

Given there are 3D heterogeneous WSNs with N sensors belong to T different types. The sensors are deployed in the FOI Λ densely and randomly. Assume all sensors have the same initial energy E_{init} and different energy consumption model. $r_i \neq r_j$ and $c_i \neq c_j$ if s_i and s_j are not the same type. The objective is to maximize the network lifetime L_T, satisfying the sensors in each round can k-cover the FOI with ratio p_c.

4   Redundant Sensor Estimation Method

This section proposes a method to estimate the redundant sensor based on the analysis of redundancy proposed in [12]. Paper [12] only considers the Boolean sensing model [2], which is not realistic in practical applications. Therefore, we consider the probability sensing model and border effective [15]. For a point $q \in R(s_i, r_i)$, where $R(s_i, r_i)$ denotes the sensing region of s_i, let $X_j(q)$, $Y_{j,m}(q)$, and $Z_k(q)$ denote that a neighbor s_j covers q, m type-j neighbors cover q exactly and at least k neighbors of any type cover q. The probabilities of $X_j(q)$, $Y_{j,m}(q)$, and $Z_k(q)$ are given by

$$P\big(X_j(q)\big) = \frac{V_{R(q,r_j) \cap R(s_i,\min(r_i+r_j,c_j))}}{V_{R(s_i,\min(r_i+r_j,c_j))}} \tag{6}$$

$$P(Y_{j,m}(q)) = C_m^n \left(\frac{n_j V_{R(q,r_j) \cap R(s_i,\min(r_i+r_j,c_j))}}{n V_{R(s_i,\min(r_i+r_j,c_j))}} \right)^m \times \left(1 - \frac{n_j V_{R(q,r_j) \cap R(s_i,\min(r_i+r_j,c_j))}}{n V_{R(s_i,\min(r_i+r_j,c_j))}} \right)^{n-m} \quad (7)$$

$$P(Z_k(q)) = 1 - \sum_{\substack{l_1, l_2, \ldots, l_t \in [0, k-1] \\ 0 \le l_1 + l_2 + \ldots + l_t \le k-1}} \prod_{j=1}^t P(Y_{j,l_j}(q)) \quad (8)$$

where $R(q, r_j)$ denotes the sensing region of s_i, $V_{R(q,r_j)}$ denotes its volume. The expected volume of s_i, which is denoted as $v_{i,k}$ that can be obtained by integrating $P(Z_k(q))$ on $R(s_i, r_i)$.

$$v_{i,k} = \iiint_{R(s_i,r_i)} P(Z_k(q)) dV. \quad (9)$$

If the required k-coverage rate is ω_k, and the following inequality (10) is true [12].

$$v_{i,k} \ge \omega_k V_{R(s_i,r_i)} \quad (10)$$

where $V_{R(s_i,r_i)}$ denotes the volume of $R(s_i, r_i)$. Then sensor s_i is redundant for k-coverage.

When the sensor's position is near the border, the $v_{i,k}$ will be overestimated because partial sensing region will be outside the FOI border. According to [15], the effective sensing volume considered with the probability sensing model can be obtain by integrating $f(d)$ on the $R(s_i, r_i')$. $R(s_i, r_i')$ is calculated as

$$V_{R(s_i,r_i')} = \int_0^{r_i'} \int_0^\pi \int_0^{2\pi} f(\delta)(\delta \sin\phi d\theta)(\delta d\phi) d\delta \quad (11)$$

where r_i' is given by

$$r_i' = \left(\frac{1}{V_\Lambda} \left(1.41 r_i^6 + 0.99 r_i^3 V_\Lambda - 0.43 r_i^5 (1 + w + h) - 0.37 r_i^4 (lh + lw + hw) \right) \right)^{\frac{1}{3}} \quad (12)$$

and l, w, h is the length, width and height of the FOI, respectively. The effective sensing radius r_i'' could be obtained by

$$r''_i = \sqrt[3]{\frac{3 V_{R(s_i,r'_i)}}{4\pi}}. \quad (13)$$

By substituting (13) in (6), (7), (8) and (9), we get the final probabilities of $X_j(q)$, $Y_{j,m}(q)$, and $Z_k(q)$.

5 A Distributed Sleep Scheduling Algorithm

This section develops a distributed sleep scheduling algorithm based on the protocol proposed in [12]. Because of consideration of heterogeneity of energy consumption, we propose a novel strategy to schedule the nodes.

Before deployment, according to Eq. (10), a sink node calculates a table named redundancy table $\Pi = \{\pi_1, \pi_2, \ldots, \pi_L\}$, $\pi_i = \{n_1, n_2, \ldots, n_t\}$ [12] for each sensor. As shown in Table 1, it is a redundancy table stored in a type-1 node for 2-coverage. The column names are the names of types. The values are the number of neighbors corresponding to the type names. Each row records the amount of each type of neighbors that make a sensor redundance for FOI k-coverage [12]. For example, the first row in Table 1 is 1, 17, which means if the sensor has greater or equal 1 type-1 neighbors or more and 17 type-2 neighbors or more, the sensor is redundant.

Table 1. Redundancy table

type-1	type-2
1	17
5	16
9	15

Algorithm 1 REDUNDANT SENSOR ESTIMATION

1   **Input:** $\Gamma = \{\gamma_1, \gamma_2, \ldots\}, \gamma_i = \{ID, Type\}$,
             $\Pi = \{\pi_1, \pi_2, \ldots, \pi_L\}, \pi_i = \{n_1, n_2, \ldots, n_t\}$
2   **Output:** $is\_redundant$
3   Set $nei_1, nei_2, \ldots, nei_t$ as 0
4   **for each** $\gamma_i \epsilon \Gamma$ **do**
5    $nei_t = nei_t + 1;$
6   **for** $l \rightarrow 1\, to\, L$ **do**
7   **if** $\exists_{i=1}^{t} n_i < n_i\, in\, \pi_l$ **then**
8      $is\_redundant = false;$
9   **else**
10     $is\_redundant = true;$
11   **break;**
12   **return** $is\_redundant;$

The lifetime of 3D WSNs is divided into rounds. Each sensor is in an ACTIVE state for a short time slot at the beginning of each round. Each slot is further divided into T mini sub-slots. Each sub-slot corresponds to a type of sensors that is in the order of descending sensing radius. The different sensors can broadcast a HELLO message in their corresponding sub-slot while all the sensors listen to the channel for any HELLO message(s) from its neighboring node(s) in the sub-slot. The HELLO message contains the sensor's ID and type, i.e., $\Gamma_H = \{ID, TYPE\}$. On reception of the HELLO message, the surrounding sensors update their neighbor tables. If the sensor receives the HELLO message from the sensor with a smaller sensing radius, it checks whether itself is redundant according to the redundant sensor estimation (shown in Algorithm 1). If the sensor is redundant, it will broadcast a SLEEP message with its ID and set its state as SLEEP.

Otherwise, the sensor will keep in an ACTIVE state. After receiving the SLEEP message, the sensors delete the information of the sending sensor in their neighbor tables. The type of sensors at the last slot does not send a SLEEP message.

Algorithm 2 SLEEP SCHEDULING ALGORITHM

---

1   **Input:** $\Gamma, \Pi, type_{self}, type_{sender}, timer_{transit}, timer_{sleep};$
2   **Output:** $state_{self};$
3   Set $state_{self}$ as ACTIVE;
4   **if** $self_{state}$ is ACTIVE **then**
5   Set $timer_{transit} \rightarrow (T - self_{type}) \times$ transit time;
6   **if** $timer_{transit}$ expires **then**
7   **if** sensor is redundant **then**
8   Set $state_{self}$ as SLEEP;
9   **else** broadcast a HELLO message;
13   **if** receives a HELLO message **then**
14   Append sender's <ID, TYPE> in Γ;
15   **if** $type_{self} > type_{sender}$ **then**
16   **if** sensor is redundant **then**
17   Set $state_{self}$ as SLEEP;
18   Broadcast a SLEEP message;
22   **if** receives a SLEEP message **then**
23   remove sender's <ID, TYPE> from the Γ;
26   **if** $state_{self}$ is SLEEP **then**
27   Set $timer_{sleep}$ as sleep time;
29   **if** $timer_{sleep}$ expires **then**
30   Set $state_{self}$ as ACTIVE;
32   **return** $state_{self};$

To prevent communication interference of sensors, each sensor has a *random_time* $\in$ [*random_min, random_max*]. If the sensor is redundant during the broadcasting delay, it will not send a HELLO message. We call the above process as Discovery Stage. This Stage focuses on discovering the neighbors and the redundant sensors. The sensor decides its state. It will stay in the ACTIVE state or switch to the SLEEP state until the next round. Algorithm 2 describes the pseudo-code of the distributed sleep scheduling algorithm.

6   Simulation Results

We implemented the algorithms using the NS-3 simulator. The sensors in the network have two different types, whose sensing radius and communicating radius are $\omega_k = 0.9$, $r_1 = 10$ m, $r_2 = 15$ m, $c_1 = 28$ m, $c_2 = 30$ m respectively, and the corresponding energy consumption is $ET_1 = 0.018$ J/bit, $ET_2 = 0.02$ J/bit, $ER = 0.01$ J/bit, $ES_1 = 14$ J, $ES_2 = 31.5$ J. The initial energy of sensor is $E_{init} = 56$ J. The deployment positions of sensors are generated by the uniform distribution Random Number Generator

(RNG) in the NS-3 simulator. For evaluating the k-coverage, we randomly put 100 sampling points in the FOI, and the k-coverage rate of these sampling points in each round represents that of the FOI. The average k-coverage is given by $\alpha_k = \sum_{i=1}^{c} p_i/c$, where p_i denotes the ratio of k-coverage round i, c is the number of rounds.

6.1 Comparison Results

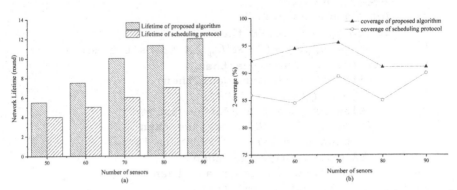

Fig. 1. Comparison of the network lifetime (a) and average k-coverage ratio of the proposed algorithm with the scheduling protocol (b), the volume of FOI is 27000 m^3.

In the first experiment, we compare the network lifetime and 2-coverage ratio computed by our algorithm and scheduling protocol when we vary the amount of nodes deployed in the 3D FOI with the size of 27000 m^3. It can be seen in Fig. 1(a) that the network lifetime produced by both algorithms is proportional to the quantity of sensors. When increasing the quantity of sensors, the network lifetime produced by the proposed algorithm increases at a higher rate than that produced by the scheduling protocol. In addition, the proposed algorithm has a more extended network lifetime and higher average coverage ratio than the scheduling protocol, as shown in Fig. 1(a) and Fig. 1(b).

From Fig. 2, we can also observe that the scheduling protocol's coverage rate is higher than that of the proposed algorithm in the first 5 rounds. This phenomenon is because the energy of type-2 sensors is used up, leading to the uneven distribution of the residual sensors. Our algorithm tries to minimize the totality consumption of energy instead of the quantity of active nodes. This simulation results justify the contribution of this paper can significantly contribute to enhance the network lifetime and coverage ratio.

In the second experiment, we compare the quantity of control messages sent by the proposed algorithm and scheduling protocol. We measure the quantity of control messages when the size of FOI varies between 10^3 m^3 to 50^3 m^3 with an increment of 10 m in length, width and height of the FOI respectively, and the quantity of sensors is 90. We use three different ratios of the quantity of sensors of type-1 and type-2(N1 & N2; 1:1, 1:2, 2:1).

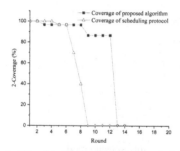

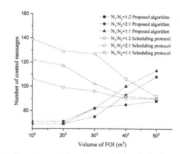

Fig. 2. The distribution of each round of network coverage of the scheduling protocol and the proposed algorithm in a simulation.

Fig. 3. Comparison of the number of control message sent in a round scheduled by the proposed algorithm with the scheduling protocol, $N = 90$

Figure 3 shows that in the proposed algorithm, the quantity of control messages sent by sensors increases as the size of FOI increases. By contrast, in the scheduling protocol, the quantity of control messages decreases with the increased size of FOI because of the different sending message mechanisms of the algorithms. In the scheduling protocol, all the sensors must send a HELLO message once in each round, and the sensor that needs to enter the SLEEP state will send a SLEEP message. Therefore, in each round of the scheduling protocol, $N + N_{sleep}$ control messages are sent, where N_{sleep} denotes the quantity of SLEEP messages. The quantity of messages will increase as the deployment density increases.

However, in our algorithm, the redundant sensors do not need to send **HELLO** messages. Thereby the quantity of control messages is calculated as $N + N_{sleep}$. When the size of FOI becomes more extensive, more sensors are needed to be active, resulting in more **HELLO** messages being sent. Furthermore, in Fig. 7. we can observe that, from $V_\Lambda = 10^3$ to $V_\Lambda = 40^3$, the quantity of control messages sent by the proposed algorithm is smaller than the scheduling protocol. Especially when the deployment is in the ratio of 2:1, the quantity of messages sent by our algorithm is always smaller than that sent by scheduling protocol because type-1 sensors at the last slot do not need to send SLEEP messages. Hence, when the quantity of sensors is constant, more type-1 sensors mean fewer messages.

6.2 Impact of Border Effects and Probabilistic Sensing Model

We study the impact of border effects and the probabilistic sensing model on the network lifetime and coverage ratio. We consider 90 sensors deployed in the FOI, and we vary the size of FOI between 303 and 603. For better comparison, we modify the proposed algorithm. We remove border effects from consideration and use the Boolean sensing model instead of the probabilistic one. Here, the modified algorithm is called the original algorithm. Figure 4 compares the original and proposed algorithm's network lifetime and average k-coverage ratio. As we can see, the 2-coverage ratio of the proposed algorithm is greater than that of the original algorithm in Fig. 4(b).

Meanwhile, the lifetime of the original algorithm is slightly longer than that of the proposed algorithm in Fig. 4(a). The reason is as follows. While considering border

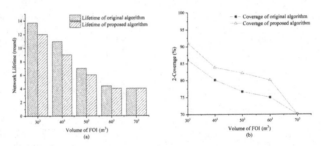

Fig. 4. The impact of the border effects and probability sensing model, $N = 90$.

effects and the probabilistic sensing model, the effective sensing radius of the sensor is smaller than the ideal sensing radius of the original algorithm. Therefore, according to formula (9), the coverage volume of the sensor calculated by the original algorithm will be greater, resulting in errors in estimating redundant sensors. A sensor that should be in an ACTIVE state may change to a SLEEP state due to false estimation, which leads to insufficient active sensors in the network to provide a high coverage ratio. Under this scenario, the coverage ratio obtained by the original algorithm is much lower without considering border effects. Therefore, the simulation results verify that the border effects and probabilistic sensing model should be considered while scheduling sensors to satisfy k-coverage.

7   Conclusion

To extend the lifetime of 3D heterogeneous WSNs while satisfying the quality of k-coverage, we design a redundant sensor estimation method based on the border effects and probabilistic sensing model and propose a novel distributed algorithm to schedule the state of sensors. Our algorithm does not need to know the positions of sensors. In order to make calculation of the energy consumption more accurate and realistic, we use the heterogeneous energy consumption model. Instead of covering the FOI with the amount of working sensors as few as possible, for the energy efficiency of the network, we try to select the sensor with the minimum energy consumption to cover the FOI. The simulation results show the efficiency of our algorithm in terms of the network lifetime, the quantity of control messages, and the k-coverage ratio.

Acknowledgement. This work was supported by the Key Project of Science and Technology Innovation 2030 supported by the Ministry of Science and Technology of China (Grant No. 2018AAA0101300).

References

1. He, S., et al.: Efficient fault-tolerant information barrier coverage in internet of things. IEEE Trans. Wirel. Commun. **20**, 7963–7976 (2021)
2. Elhabyan, R., Shi, W., St-Hilaire, M.: Coverage protocols for wireless sensor networks: Review and future directions. J. Commun. Netw. **21**(1), 45–60 (2019)

3. Ahn, N., Park, S.: An optimization algorithm for the maximum lifetime coverage problems in wireless sensor network. Manag. Sci. Finan. Eng. **17**, 39–62 (2011)

4. Donta, P.K., Rao, B.S.P., Amgoth, T., Annavarapu, C.S.R., Swain, S.: Data collection and path determination strategies for mobile sink in 3D WSNs. IEEE Sensors J. **20**(4), 2224–2233 (2020)

5. Puccinelli, D., Haenggi, M.: Wireless sensor networks: applications and challenges of ubiquitous sensing. IEEE Circuits Syst. Mag. **5**(3), 19–31 (2005)

6. Gungor, V.C., Hancke, G.P.: Industrial wireless sensor networks: challenges, design principles, and technical approaches. IEEE Trans. Industr. Electron. **56**(10), 4258–4265 (2009)

7. Nazrul Alam, S.M., Haas, Z.J.: Coverage and connectivity in three-dimensional networks with random node deployment. Ad Hoc Netw. **34**, 157–169 (2015). ISSN 1570–8705

8. Malek, S.M.B., Sadik, M.M., Rahman, A.: On balanced k-coverage in visual sensor networks. J. Netw. Comput. Appl. **72**, 72–86 (2016). ISSN 1084–8045

9. Barkhoda, W., Sheikhi, H.: Immigrant imperialist competitive algorithm to solve the multi-constraint node placement problem in target-based wireless sensor networks. Ad Hoc Netw. **106**, 102183 (2020). ISSN 1570–8705

10. Pal, M., Medhi, N.: Sixsoid: a new paradigm for k-coverage in 3D wireless sensor networks. In: 2015 International Conference on Computing, Communication and Security (ICCCS), pp. 1–5 (2015)

11. Ammari, H.M.: A unified framework for k-coverage and data collection in heterogeneous wireless sensor networks. J. Parallel Distrib. Comput. **89**, 37–49 (2016). ISSN 0743–7315

12. Gupta, H.P., Rao, S.V., Venkatesh, T.: Sleep scheduling protocol for k-coverage of three-dimensional heterogeneous WSNs. IEEE Trans. Veh. Technol. **65**(10), 8423–8431 (2016)

13. Vieira, L.F.M., Almiron, M.G., Loureiro, A.A.F.: Link probability, node degree and coverage in three-dimensional networks. Ad Hoc Netw. **37**(2), 153–159 (2016). ISSN 1570–8705

14. Gupta, H.P., Rao, S.V., Venkatesh, T.: Analysis of stochastic coverage and connectivity in three-dimensional heterogeneous directional wireless sensor networks. Perv. Mob. Comput. **29**, 38–56 (2016). ISSN 1574–1192

15. Gupta, H.P., Venkatesh, T., Rao, S.V., Dutta, T., Iyer, R.R.: Analysis of coverage under border effects in three-dimensional mobile sensor networks. IEEE Trans. Mob. Comput. **16**(9), 2436–2449 (2017)

16. Wang, J., Medidi, S.: Energy efficient coverage with variable sensing radii in wireless sensor networks. In: Third IEEE International Conference on Wireless and Mobile Computing, Networking and Communications (WiMob 2007), p. 61 (2007)

CoSBERT: A Cosine-Based Siamese BERT-Networks Using for Semantic Textual Similarity

Wenguang Yu[1,2], Yu Weng[1], Ronghua Lin[1,2], and Yong Tang[1,2(✉)]

[1] South China Normal University, Guangzhou 510631, China
ytang@m.scnu.edu.cn
[2] Pazhou Lab, Guangzhou 510330, China

Abstract. By mining rich semantic information from large-scale unlabeled texts and incorporating it into pre-trained models, BERT and RoBERTa have achieved impressive performance on many natural language processing tasks. However, these pre-trained models rely on fine-tuning for specific tasks, and it is very difficult to use native BERT or RoBERTa for the task of Semantic Textual Similarity (STS).

In this paper, we present CoSBERT, a cosine-based siamese BERT-Networks modified from the pre-trained BERT or RoBERT models to derive meaningfully semantic embeddings. Its main feature is to optimize the cosine-similarity between the semantic embeddings of input texts in training stage. And it also improves the efficiency and accuracy for the computation of STS tasks in prediction stage. Experiments on multiple STS tasks prove that CoSBERT performs well and its effectiveness is verified. In addition, by deploying CoSBERT into the SCHOLAT user recommendation system, the efficiency and accuracy of the system has been improved.

Keywords: Semantic Textual Similarity · Siamese Networks · BERT · SCHOLAT

1 Introduction

Semantic Textual Similarity (STS) [1] is an important basic problem in natural language processing [2]. Many tasks in natural language processing can be abstracted as matching tasks using semantic textual similarity, such as information retrieval [3], machine translation [4], automatic question answering [5], etc. Among them, information retrieval can be related to the matching of query and document, machine translation can be related to the matching between two languages, and automatic question answering can be related to the matching of question and answer. In this paper, our research task is to figure the semantic textual similarity between user profile texts, and use it as one of the weights of the SCHOLAT user recommendation system.

The most popular approach for semantic textual similarity is based on deep learning, because the models based on deep neural networks have a powerful

Y. Sun et al. (Eds.): ChineseCSCW 2022, CCIS 1681, pp. 376–389, 2023.
https://doi.org/10.1007/978-981-99-2356-4_30

representation of textual semantics. Through these models, we can convert the text into embeddings that contain rich semantic information. After that, we can get the semantic textual similarity between texts by calculating the cosine-similarity of these semantic embeddings. At present, a simple and direct way to obtain the semantic embeddings is using BERT model [6]. This is done by feeding texts into BERT model, and take the first token of the model output as the embedding of the whole text. However, due to the limitations of the MLM (Mask Language Model) and NSP (Next Sentence Prediction) pretraining tasks in the BERT model, native BERT model cannot get the deep semantic information well. To address the limitations of BERT, Facebook's proposed InferSent [7] considered extracting semantic embeddings as a supervised task, where the model was trained on a Natural Language Inference (NLI) [8] dataset and subsequently used as a feature extractor to obtain semantic embeddings. Soon after, Sentence-BERT (SBERT) [9] proposed to use siamese BERT-Networks to learn the representation of sentence embeddings, which further affirmed InferSent's effectiveness on BERT.

However, when we actually applied the models listed above, whether using InferSent or Sentence-BERT, we faced different problems in fine-tuning models for specific tasks. The reason for these problems may be the inconsistency in the training and inference phases, making it difficult to find which adjustments in the training process will positively help the prediction results. In order to address the above problems, we propose CoSBERT, which is a cosine-based siamese BERT-Networks.

The main contributions of this paper are as follows: (1) We propose CoS-BERT that can be consistent in the training and inference phases to improve the efficiency and accuracy for the computation of STS tasks. (2) We propose a loss function to optimize the cosine-similarity of sentence pairs , which is CoS-BERT's biggest difference from other networks. (3) We evaluate the CoSBERT on multiple datasets. Experiments show that CoSBERT performs well, and its effectiveness has been verified. (4) We have deployed the CoSBERT into the SCHOLAT user recommendation system. Through the practical application of the model, its performance is stable with good user feedback.

2   Related Work

2.1   Semantic Textual Similarity

In recent years, deep neural networks have been widely used in constructing models to solve the STS tasks, and also have achieved some important progress. Generally speaking, these neural network models dealing with the tasks mainly have two kinds: Interaction-based [11] model and Representation-based [12] model. The way of Interaction-based model is concatenating two texts into a single text. Through the text, the model's deep neural networks can construct an interaction matrix by text interaction. Finally, the softmax classifier is used to process the interaction matrix and output the similarity. In contrast, Representation-based model encodes the two texts into two dense embeddings in the same space by the encoders. Then, these two embeddings can be calculated by different distance calculation methods such as cosine distance, Euclidean distance, Manhattan distance, etc. Finally the calculated result is used as the semantic textual similarity.

Typically, Interaction-based model usually performs better because it enables two texts to be deeply compared, but its obvious disadvantage is less efficient in retrieval scenarios. On the contrary, Representation-based model can compute and cache the semantic embeddings in advance, which makes it more efficient. However, its interaction level between texts is not deep enough to identify the semantics, resulting in a less accuracy. According to the demand for ensuring the efficiency of the model's actual application in the SCHOLAT user recommendation system, we choose the Representation-based model as main research in this paper.

2.2 Related Models

We first introduce the traditional semantic textual neural model DSSM. Its training is to map two sentences into a semantic space of same dimensions and maximize the cosine similarity between the semantic vectors of sentences. Finally, the implicit semantic model is obtained to compute the semantic textual similarity between sentences. However, DSSM cannot extract the information of context and word order in the corpus, resulting in the failure to recall semantically related content in many scenarios.

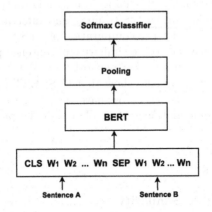

Fig. 1. BERT architecture for STS task.

After 2018, the BERT model has brought huge changes in the NLP field. BERT is a pre-trained model based on Transformer [13]. Since BERT came out, it has performed well in many natural language processing tasks. This is precisely because BERT can mine rich semantic information in large-scale unlabeled texts and get contextual semantic embeddings through Transformer encoders. With the semantic embeddings, we can compute the similarity for specific downstream tasks. However, the disadvantage of the native BERT model is that it cannot get the corresponding embeddings independently for the two input texts, which makes it not suitable for the STS tasks.

As shown in Fig. 1, the approach of the native Bert about semantic textual similarity is to convert the task into binary classification task. The two input texts are spliced into a sequence (segmented by the special token [SEP] in the middle). Then, the sequence is encoded into hidden state vectors by 12-layer (base-model) or 24-layer (large-model) Transformer modules. Finally, the pooling-layer averages the hidden state vectors or takes the [CLS] token (the first position of the vectors) as semantic embedding of the text. With the embeddings, the similarity is computed by softmax classifier.

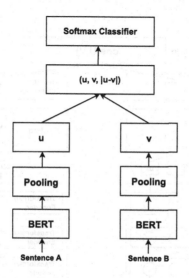

Fig. 2. SBERT architecture with classification objective function

However, Reimers et al. [9] pointed out in their experiments that the results produced by native BERT were not ideal (at least when dealing with semantic retrieval and clustering problems), even worse than the averaging Glove [14] embeddings. In order to make Bert better extract semantic information, they proposed the following networks shown in Fig. 2. SBERT used the structure of Siamese BERT-Networks. Besides, they experimented with three pooling strategies (CLS-Pooling, Avg-Pooling, Mean-Pooling), which further compressed the hidden state vectors output by Bert to get embedding u and v representing 2 sentences respectively. For the STS tasks, u and v are spliced into $(u, v, |u - v|)$, then plugged into a fully connected network. Finally, the softmax classifier outputs the result as semantic textual similarity. And the cross-entropy is set as loss function. In the inference phase, SBERT directly calculates the cosine-similarity of two semantic embeddings. Although this shortens the inference time, it leads to inconsistency between training and inference, which makes it difficult for model fine-tuning.

To address the inconsistency between training and inference phases, we propose the CoSBERT that follows the structure of siamese BERT-Networks. Unlike the traditional neural networks training from random initialization, we directly use the pre-trained BERT or RoBERTa [15] models. With the pre-trained models, we can fine-tune them to optimize the cosine-similarity in the training phase to make the training process consistent with inference stage. In the end, we can get a model that is suitable for the STS tasks.

3   Model

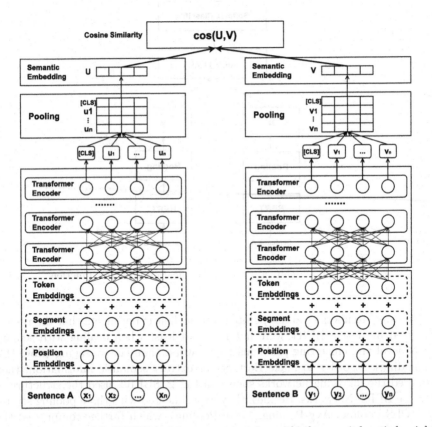

Fig. 3. Overview of CoSBERT architecture at training and inference, it has tied weights with the siamese network structure.

In this paper, we use siamese BERT-Networks as the structure of CoSBERT to update the weight parameters of the networks. Through the siamese networks, the model can effectively identify the difference between two sentences to be matched and complete the accurate calculation of the similarity between sentences. Meanwhile, with the pre-trained BERT or RoBERTa models, which have been trained with large-scale texts, it can greatly reduce the time for training by the way of fine-tuning them for specific tasks.

3.1   CoSBERT

The overview of CoSBERT architecture at training and inference is shown in Fig. 3. The input sentence A and B are serialized by the BERT Tokenizer to get the Position Embeddings, Segment Embeddings and Token Embeddings of the sentences. All the embeddings will then be fed into the Transformer Encoders based on Self-Attention. After encoding, the hidden state vectors $([CLS], u_1, ..., u_n)$ and $([CLS], v_1, ..., v_n)$ are obtained. However, the dimensions of two output vectors are not always the same. And it is difficult to calculate the cosine-similarity between vectors of different dimensions. Therefore, it is necessary to further process the hidden state vectors by pooling operation to generate semantic embeddings U and V with the same dimensions. Among the strategies of pooling operation, we mainly study three different kinds for comparison:

CLS Strategy : It takes the first position of the hidden state vectors as the semantic embedding for the whole sentence.

FLA (First Last Average) Strategy : It takes the average of the first position and last position of the hidden state vectors as the semantic embedding for the whole sentence.

MEAN Strategy : It takes the average of each hidden state vector as the semantic embedding for the whole sentence.

For the semantic embeddings U and V obtained above, we can calculate the cosine-similarity between them as shown in Eq. (1).

$$\cos(U, V) = \frac{U \cdot V}{\|U\|\|V\|} = \frac{\sum_{i=1}^{n} U_i \times V_i}{\sqrt{\sum_{i=1}^{n} (U_i)^2} \times \sqrt{\sum_{i=1}^{n} (V_i)^2}} \tag{1}$$

3.2   Loss Function

We propose a new loss function to optimize the cosine-similarity $\cos(U, V)$ in the training phase, which is the CoSBERT's biggest difference from other networks. The purpose of this loss function is to make the positive sample pairs achieve the highest possible cosine-similarity, and the negative sample pairs get the lowest possible cosine-similarity.

Specifically as follows, denote Ω_{pos} as the set of all positive sample pairs, and Ω_{neg} as the set of all negative sample pairs. For any pair of positive samples $(i, j) \in \Omega_{pos}$, and any pair of negative samples $(k, l) \in \Omega_{neg}$, we hope both of them will satisfy the condition shown in Eq. (2).

$$\cos(U_i, V_j) > \cos(U_k, V_l) \tag{2}$$

In a nutshell, we try to guarantee that the similarity of the positive sample pairs is higher than the similarity of the negative sample pairs as much as possible. With this condition satisfied, there is no need to consider the specific value about how high is it. It only depends on the relative order of the positive and negative sample pairs. An effective solution for dealing with such optimization requirements was introduced in Circle Loss [16], which could be called the unified loss function shown in Eq. (3).

$$\mathcal{L}_{\text{uni}} = \log \left[1 + \sum_{p \in \Omega pos, n \in \Omega neg} e^{(\lambda(s_n - s_p) + m)} \right] \tag{3}$$

In Eq. (3), it has used a symmetric optimized form of $(s_n - s_p)$. Under the premise that the similarity s_n and s_p are all positive numbers, only the smallest $(s_n - s_p)$, can we achieve the goal of maximizing s_p and minimizing s_n. This optimization strategy allows the model to flexibly update its weights based on the similarity calculation during the training phase. Corresponding to this paper, the cosine-similarity is used as the similarity measure.

And m is a margin used to control the interval of the classification boundary, so that there is a certain degree of separation between s_p and s_n. In general, It is only considered in Metric Learning [17]. In Representation Learning, if m is not set to 0, a fuzzy boundary will be generated in the embedding space, which will have a great impact on the separability of the embedding space. So m can be ignored in our loss function.

As for λ, it is a scaling factor set to 20 as default. In that way, the unified loss function is transformed into the following.

$$\mathcal{L}_{\text{cos}} = \log \left(1 + \sum_{(i,j) \in \Omega_{pos}, (k,l) \in \Omega_{neg}} e^{\lambda(\cos(U_k, V_l) - \cos(U_i, V_j))} \right) \tag{4}$$

After the above transformation, we can get a new loss function shown in Eq. (4). Its goal is to optimize the cosine-similarity between sentence pairs, which is the core of CoSBERT.

3.3   Training Details

Through a large number of training, we have found the main parameter settings during the training of CoSBERT shown in Table 1. It can maximize our GPU memory utilization, better match the size of the datasets and speed up the convergence of the training.

Besides, in order to slow down the model overfitting, 10% of the training data is used as a warmup, and the training is performed until the model converges.

Table 1. The parameter settings during training.

Parametar	value
Batchsize	64
Epoch	10
Learning-rate	$2e-5$
Weight decay	0.01
Optimizer	AdamW

The default pooling strategy is MEAN. The computer graphics card for the training is NVIDIA TESLA V100 32G and the running environment is Python 3.8, PyTorch 1.11 and CUDA 10.2.

4 Experiment

4.1 Datasets and Metrics

The datasets used for the experiments are as follows.

Chinese-STS-B [18] (The Semantic Textual Similarity Benchmark). This is a collection of sentence pairs extracted from news titles, video titles, image titles, and natural language inference data, each pair is manually labeled for the task of semantic textual similarity.

LCQMC [19] (A Large-scale Chinese Question Matching Corpus) from Harbin Institute of Technology (Shenzhen), this dataset is constructed by extracting user questions from different domains of Baidu Knows. It is a semantic matching dataset of Chinese questions in Baidu Knows.

BQ [20] (the Bank Question corpus). A Chinese corpus for sentence semantic equivalence identification (SSEI), contains 120, 000 question pairs from 1-year online bank custom service logs.

PAWSX [21] (Paraphrase Adversaries from Word Scrambling). This dataset contains 23, 659 human translated PAWS evaluation pairs and 296, 406 machine translated training pairs in six typologically distinct languages: French, Spanish, German, Chinese, Japanese, and Korean. All translated pairs are sourced from examples in PAWS-Wiki.

SCHOLAT. This dataset is constructed by extracting the profile text information from SCHOLAT users. We pair the profile texts of users who follow each other as positive samples of the dataset. Besides, random sampling is used to pair profile texts of unrelated users as negative samples of the dataset. After the operations of de-duplication, cleaning and manual labeling on the data, a dataset that meets the requirements of the STS task is obtained (Table 2).

The datasets listed above are all supervised tasks, and the structure of the data is (sentence A, sentence B, label). The label indicates whether the two sentences are similar. Denote U, V as the semantic embeddings of sentence A and sentence B. Through the distance between the label of sentence pair and cosine-similarity of U, V, we can get:

Table 2. Details about the amount, task, language, domain of all the datasets

Dataset	Train	Eval	Test	Task	Language	Domain
STS-B	5.2k	1.4k	1.3k	sentence similarity	Chinese	misc.
LCQMC	**238k**	8.8k	**12.5k**	sentence similarity	Chinese	Baidu Knows
BQ	100k	**10k**	10k	paraphrase	Chinese	Bank
PAWSX	49.4k	2k	2k	paraphrase	Multilingual	Wikipedia
SCHOLAT	22.1k	2.7k	2.7k	sentence similarity	Chinese	Academic Social

$$d_i = label(A, B) - \cos(U, V) \qquad (5)$$

$$\rho = 1 - \frac{n \sum_{i \in n} d_i^2}{n(n^2 - 1)} \qquad (6)$$

For the Eq. (5) and Eq. (6), d_i is the distance between label and cos-similarity of each sentence pair in the dataset, and n is the total amount of dataset. The Spearman's rank correlation [31] $\rho \times 100$ is used as the experimental metrics. Spearman's rank correlation only depends on the relative order of the cosine-similarity and the labels, which is suitable for evaluating the model performance on the STS tasks. Like other correlation coefficients, this coefficient varies between -1 and +1, with 0 indicating no correlation. A larger coefficient means a greater correlation.

4.2 Pre-trained Models

The pre-trained models used in the experiment are all composed of 12 layers of Transformers, including 12 Attention Heads, and the dimensions of hidden state vectors are 768. The features are as follows:

BERT-base-Chinese (referred as BERT-base later), released by Google AI team in 2018, is the most common Chinese BERT pre-trained model based on Chinese Wikipedia related corpus.

Chinese-MacBERT-base [22] (referred as MacBERT-base later), is an improved BERT with novel MLM (Mask Language Model) as correction pre-training task, which mitigates the discrepancy of pre-training and fine-tuning. Besides, WWM (Whole Word Masking) and N-gram masking were also introduced in the pre-training of model.

Chinese-RoBERTa-wwm-ext [23] (referred as RoBERTa-wwm-ext later), it is a natural combination of RoBERTa and BERT with the advantages both of them. This model is not an original RoBERTa model, but a BERT model trained in a similar way to RoBERTa, namely RoBERTa-like BERT. The WWM strategy is also used for masking (but dynamic masking is not used). Besides, NSP (Next Sentence Prediction) has been simply canceled in the pre-training phase of this model.

4.3 Evaluation

Table 3. The results are only trained with the Train of the datasets and evaluated on the Test. The metrics use the Spearman rank correlation ($\rho \times 100$) based on a 10-fold cross-validation.

Arch	Pre-trained Model	BQ	LCQMC	PAWSX	STS-B	SCHOLAT	Avg.
BERT	BERT-base	59.70	74.30	37.06	72.78	40.74	56.91
	MacBERT-base	60.84	73.40	40.56	74.61	45.14	58.91
	RoBERTa-wwm-ext	58.24	72.91	39.92	74.85	43.40	57.86
SBERT	BERT-base	66.25	75.17	52.48	63.3	64.71	64.38
	MacBERT-base	64.96	75.55	56.6	64.69	65.07	65.43
	RoBERTa-wwm-ext	65.71	75.72	55.59	67.15	64.92	65.82
CoSBERT	BERT-base	71.71	78.94	57.9	80.01	72.48	72.21
	MacBERT-base	**73.16**	79.36	61.54	80.33	72.14	73.30
	RoBERTa-wwm-ext	72.35	**79.59**	**61.83**	**80.45**	**72.8**	**73.42**

In this experiment, we evaluate the performance of CoSBERT and compare it with other networks. The pre-trained models were fine-tuned on the Train part of each dataset, and the performance is evaluated corresponding to the Test part of the dataset, without external data. After fine-tuning different pre-trained models according to different methods, the experiment results are shown in Table 3.

The experimental results show that by comparing the performance of different pre-trained models on different datasets, CoSBERT has a more obvious improvement on all tasks, and the average improvement of native training is close to 8%, achieving the highest average score. It can be seen that it is greatly effective about the method of directly optimizing the cosine-similarity values between sentence pairs in the training phase. And it also confirms that CoSBERT is usable for the task of semantic textual similarity.

In order to further analyze whether the performance of CoSBERT is improved on different datasets when only trained on a single dataset, we selected the SCHOLAT dataset for training, which is closer to the downstream application system. And we evaluated the performance of the models in the Test part of each dataset. The results are shown in Table 4.

The experimental results show that all the models in the whole process have low scores on PAWSX. Because the negative samples of PAWSX are almost with the same words but different semantics, which makes it require deeper interaction to be better identified. Therefore, the inherent shortcomings about deep interaction of the Representation-based model lead to poor performance on this task. However, except for the PAWSX, CoSBERT achieves the highest scores on other tasks, which further indicates that it is effective for the downstream tasks.

Table 4. The results are only trained with the Train of SCHOLAT dataset and evaluated on each Test of all datasets. The metrics use the Spearman rank correlation ($\rho \times 100$) based on a 10-fold cross-validation.

Arch	Pre-trained Model	BQ	LCQMC	PAWSX	STS-B	SCHOLAT	Avg.
BERT	BERT-base	24.74	27.31	10.11	47.41	40.74	30.06
	MacBERT-base	29.58	28.72	10.58	50.14	45.14	32.83
	RoBERTa-wwm-ext	25.33	31.16	10.88	43.40	43.40	30.83
SBERT	BERT-base	26.31	50.57	12.36	46.80	64.71	40.15
	MacBERT-base	26.70	57.05	**13.40**	59.76	65.08	44.40
	RoBERTa-wwm-ext	31.13	64.84	12.73	62.58	62.93	46.84
CoSBERT	BERT-base	30.02	60.19	11.70	61.48	72.49	47.17
	MacBERT-base	**32.34**	59.83	12.65	63.81	72.15	48.15
	RoBERTa-wwm-ext	32.18	**67.43**	12.59	**67.48**	**72.89**	**50.51**

4.4   Ablation Study

In previous experiments, we have demonstrated the excellent performance of CoSBERT. In this section, we mainly evaluate the impact of the pooling strategies (CLS, FLA, MEAN) mentioned earlier in this paper. In order to better understand which pooling strategy is more suitable for the task of semantic textual similarity. In the ablation experiments, we fine-tune different pretrained models according to CoSBERT, and evaluate the impact of different pooling strategies on each dataset. The experimental results are shown in Table 5.

Table 5. The pre-trained models in this experiment were all fine-tuned according to the architecture of CoSBERT. The results are only trained with the Train of the datasets and evaluated on the Test. The metrics use the Spearman rank correlation ($\rho \times 100$) based on a 10-fold cross-validation.

pooling	Pre-trained Model	BQ	LCQMC	PAWSX	STS-B	SCHOLAT	Avg.
CLS	BERT-base	71.88	78.16	60.29	71.51	78.05	71.97
	MacBERT-base	72.22	79.40	61.64	71.72	78.66	72.72
	RoBERTa-wwm-ext	72.06	79.44	61.52	71.97	78.86	72.77
FLA	BERT-base	72.40	78.93	55.38	71.88	79.67	71.65
	MacBERT-base	72.04	78.52	60.13	71.61	79.25	72.31
	RoBERTa-wwm-ext	71.80	78.53	59.34	72.38	79.68	72.34
MEAN	BERT-base	71.71	78.94	57.90	80.01	72.48	72.21
	MacBERT-base	**73.16**	79.36	61.54	80.33	72.14	73.30
	RoBERTa-wwm-ext	72.35	**79.59**	**61.83**	**80.45**	**72.88**	**73.42**

It can be seen from the experimental results that the performance of different pooling strategies does not differ much. The gap between the maximum value and the minimum value is only 1.77%. It shows that the pooling strategy has a small impact. Looking further, the FLA strategy performs worse than MEAN or CLS strategy, and MEAN strategy achieves highest score. Therefore, we choose MEAN as the default pooling strategy of CoSBERT.

5 Conclusion

In this paper, we propose CoSBERT that can be consistent in the training and inference phases, which can optimize the cosine-similarity between sentence pairs and easier to fine-tune for the downstream tasks. Experiments on multiple datasets show that our model performs well and has improved the accuracy for the computation of STS tasks.

At present, we have deployed our model into the SCHOLAT user recommendation system to calculate the semantic similarity of the user's profiles and use it as one of the weights for recommending users. Through the practical application of the model, its performance is stable with good user feedback.

Meanwhile, the model in this paper will be improved around two aspects in the future. The first one is the depth of the model. When there are a large number of texts with the same words but different semantics, or when deep matching of texts is required, the performance is often poor. The second is the breadth of the model, which can be applied to more STS tasks through transfer learning to improve the applicability of the model.

Acknowledgment. This work was supported in part by the National Natural Science Foundation of China under Grant U1811263.

References

1. Majumder, G., Pakray, P., Gelbukh, A., et al.: Semantic textual similarity methods, tools, and applications: a survey. Computación y Sistemas **20**(4), 647–665 (2016)
2. Chowdhary, K.R.: Natural language processing. Fund. Artif. Intell., 603–649 (2020)
3. Li, H., Xu, J.: Semantic matching in search. Found. Trends Inf. Retr. **7**(5), 343–469 (2014)
4. Chen, M.X., Firat, O., Bapna, A., et al.: The best of both worlds: combining recent advances in neural machine translation. arXiv preprint arXiv:1804.09849 (2018)
5. Demszky, D., Guu, K., Liang, P.: Transforming question answering datasets into natural language inference datasets. arXiv preprint arXiv:1809.02922 (2018)
6. Devlin, J., Chang, M.W., Lee, K., et al.: Bert: pre-training of deep bidirectional transformers for language understanding. arXiv preprint arXiv:1810.04805 (2018)
7. Conneau, A., Kiela, D., Schwenk, H., et al.: Supervised learning of universal sentence representations from natural language inference data. arXiv preprint arXiv:1705.02364 (2017)
8. Bowman, S.R., Angeli, G., Potts, C., et al.: A large annotated corpus for learning natural language inference. arXiv preprint arXiv:1508.05326 (2015)
9. Reimers, N., Gurevych, I.: Sentence-bert: sentence embeddings using siamese bert-networks. arXiv preprint arXiv:1908.10084 (2019)

10. Chicco, D.: Siamese neural networks: an overview. Artif. Neural Netw., 73–94 (2021)
11. Wan, S., Lan, Y., Guo, J., et al.: A deep architecture for semantic matching with multiple positional sentence representations. In: Proceedings of the AAAI Conference on Artificial Intelligence, vol. 30, no. 1 (2016)
12. Chang, W.C., Yu, F.X., Chang, Y.W., et al.: Pre-training tasks for embedding-based large-scale retrieval. arXiv preprint arXiv:2002.03932 (2020)
13. Vaswani, A., Shazeer, N., Parmar, N., et al.: Attention is all you need. Adv. Neural Inf. Process. Syst. **30**, 1–11 (2017)
14. Pennington, J., Socher, R., Manning, C.D.: Glove: global vectors for word representation. In: Proceedings of the 2014 Conference on Empirical Methods in Natural Language Processing (EMNLP), pp. 1532–1543 (2014)
15. Liu, Y., Ott, M., Goyal, N., et al.: Roberta: a robustly optimized bert pretraining approach. arXiv preprint arXiv:1907.11692 (2019)
16. Sun, Y., Cheng, C., Zhang, Y., et al.: Circle loss: a unified perspective of pair similarity optimization. In: Proceedings of the IEEE/CVF Conference on Computer Vision and Pattern Recognition, pp. 6398–6407 (2020)
17. Wang, X., Han, X., Huang, W., et al.: Multi-similarity loss with general pair weighting for deep metric learning. In: Proceedings of the IEEE/CVF Conference on Computer Vision and Pattern Recognition, pp. 5022–5030 (2019)
18. Agirre, E., Banea, C., Cardie, C., et al.: Semeval-2015 task 2: semantic textual similarity, english, spanish and pilot on interpretability. In: Proceedings of the 9th International Workshop on Semantic Evaluation (SemEval 2015), pp. 252–263 (2015)
19. Liu, X., Chen, Q., Deng, C., et al.: Lcqmc: a large-scale Chinese question matching corpus. In: Proceedings of the 27th International Conference on Computational Linguistics, pp. 1952–1962 (2018)
20. Chen, J., Chen, Q., Liu, X., et al.: The BQ corpus: a large-scale domain-specific Chinese corpus for sentence semantic equivalence identification. In: Proceedings of the 2018 Conference on Empirical Methods in Natural Language Processing, pp. 4946–4951 (2018)
21. Yang, Y., Zhang, Y., Tar, C., et al.: PAWS-X: a cross-lingual adversarial dataset for paraphrase identification. arXiv preprint arXiv:1908.11828 (2019)
22. Cui, Y., Che, W., Liu, T., et al.: Revisiting pre-trained models for Chinese natural language processing. arXiv preprint arXiv:2004.13922 (2020)
23. Cui, Y., Che, W., Liu, T., et al.: Pre-training with whole word masking for Chinese bert. IEEE/ACM Trans. Audio Speech Lang. Process. **29**, 3504–3514 (2021)
24. Bentivogli, L., Clark, P., Dagan, I., et al.: The fifth PASCAL recognizing textual entailment challenge. In: TAC (2009)
25. Choi, H., Kim, J., Joe, S., et al.: Evaluation of BERT and ALBERT sentence embedding performance on downstream NLP tasks. In: 2020 25th International Conference on Pattern Recognition (ICPR), pp. 5482–5487. IEEE (2021)
26. Hinton, G., Vinyals, O., Dean, J.: Distilling the knowledge in a neural network, vol. 2, no. 7. arXiv preprint arXiv:1503.02531 (2015)
27. Khattab, O., Zaharia, M.: Colbert: efficient and effective passage search via contextualized late interaction over bert. In: Proceedings of the 43rd International ACM SIGIR Conference on Research and Development in Information Retrieval, pp. 39–48 (2020)
28. Tang, R., Lu, Y., Liu, L., et al.: Distilling task-specific knowledge from bert into simple neural networks. arXiv preprint arXiv:1903.12136 (2019)

29. Myers, L., Sirois, M.J.: Spearman correlation coefficients, differences between. Encycl. Stat. Sci. **12** (2004)
30. Gao, T., Yao, X., Chen, D.: Simcse: simple contrastive learning of sentence embeddings. arXiv preprint arXiv:2104.08821 (2021)
31. Su, J., Cao, J., Liu, W., et al.: Whitening sentence representations for better semantics and faster retrieval. arXiv preprint arXiv:2103.15316 (2021)

Towards Heterogeneous Federated Learning

Yue Huang[1], Yonghui Xu[2,3], Lanju Kong[1,4], Qingzhong Li[1,4(✉)],
and Lizhen Cui[1,2]

[1] College of Software, Shandong University, Jinan 250101, China
{klj,lqz,clz}@sdu.edu.cn
[2] Joint SDU-NTU Centre for Artificial Intelligence Research (C-FAIR),
Shandong University, Jinan 250101, China
[3] China-Singapore International Joint Research Institute, Guangzhou 510663, China
[4] Dareway Software Co., Ltd., Jinan 250200, China

Abstract. Federated Learning (FL), a novel distributed machine learning framework, made it possible to model collaboratively without risking participants' privacy. All components of FL, including devices, networks, data, and models, are heterogeneous because of the dispersed feature. These heterogeneity issues impeded FL's performance. HFL (Heterogeneous Federated Learning) offers a viable solution to these issues.

HFL has become an emerging research topic. We have conducted detailed research into the unique characteristics and challenges of HFL in the paper. And summaries methods of HFL at different levels. We reviewed the evaluation methods for HFL and provided an outlook on the future direction of HFL by analyzing the strengths and limits of the existing study.

Keywords: Heterogeneous · Federated Learning

1 Introduction

In classical machine learning, the model's efficiency and accuracy are rely heavily on the computational power and training data of a small number of servers. High quality and vast amounts of data, on the other hand, are becoming more challenging to acquire as data security and privacy concerns have grown. Data fragmentation is a severe problem in the healthcare and financial industries, leads to data isolation. Data isolation resulted in the model being trained without enough access to each participant's data, preventing the model's performance from improving.

McMahan et al. presented Federated Learning (FL [46] as a solution to the challenge above. Collaborative learning is another term for federal learning. FL made it possible for the owners of various data sources to become clients (or trainers), with each client training a local model before working on a global model. FL has carefully developed the method of transmitting information amongst customers to ensure that no one participant may guess the private data of the other

Y. Sun et al. (Eds.): ChineseCSCW 2022, CCIS 1681, pp. 390–404, 2023.
https://doi.org/10.1007/978-981-99-2356-4_31

participants, providing the participants' privacy and data security. Because of FL's advantages in privacy protection [43], it is now widely employed in personalized recommendations, the Internet of Things, and clinical disease diagnosis. FL is facing numerous challenges. Critical is the heterogeneity problem that occurs in all aspects of the learning process. These problems include: (1) The problem of differences in the storage, computing and communication capabilities of clients; (2) The problem of differences in the network environment in which clients are located; (3) The problem of Non-Idependently and Identically Distributed (Non-IID) problem for client's local data; (4) The problem of different models required by clients according to their application scenarios.

The device configurations (e.g., different edge devices and network conditions) of various clients in practice are different, and this heterogeneity problem is called system heterogeneity [33]. System heterogeneity tends to lead to significant variations in overhead when the same training task is conducted. While high-performance devices complete the training, other devices are affected by their GPU, network conditions, Etc., and take longer or complete the training, which leads to reduced performance of the global model [2]. To deal with these "slower" devices, the server often chooses to wait or ignore them [15]. System heterogeneity seriously slows the speed of convergence and reduces the model's accuracy [61]. And summarise methods of HFL at different levels.

FL also suffers from non-systematic heterogeneity, such as data and model heterogeneity. Typically in order to aggregate models, client's model structure and servers must be the same. However, models are also crucial for privacy in some fields, such as insurance or finance. LiYiying et al. [38] tried to support a heterogeneous model of FL. However, his method requires a public dataset in the server, which consists of a part of each private dataset or existing dataset [19]. Obtaining part of the local private dataset from the client may violate participants' privacy. There may also be statistical heterogeneity in the datasets, with clients having different amounts of data from various local distributions.

In response to these heterogeneity problems, we provide a comprehensive survey of research efforts in HFL, in this paper. We propose a multi-level taxonomy of HFL. The taxonomy is divided according to the reasons why FL heterogeneity problems occur. Their solutions are analyzed to help the reader understand the impact this heterogeneity brings to FL. We summarize commonly used performance evaluation methods and suggest future directions for the HFL framework.

2   Preliminaries

2.1   Definition

Before diving into the investigation, it is necessary to define Heterogeneous Federated Learning. In [31], HFL's definition is a Federated Learning paradigm with per client having a private dataset and a uniquely designed model. Clients convert the relevant parameters into a standard format when communicating and collaborating. The server collects these parameters and aggregates them. In this paper, we extend the definition of HFL as follows.

Definition 1 (Heterogeneous Federated Learning, HFL). *A federated learning paradigm that can be targeted to deal with heterogeneous problems. These heterogeneous problems typically exist due to clients' differences in devices, networks, data, models, Etc.*

2.2 Analysis

Device Heterogeneity. In a natural federation setting, clients have significantly different device configurations (e.g., GPU, CPU, software, and network conditions). It leads to significant variation in device overhead (e.g., compute time and resources) to accomplish the same task, further reducing performance in a global model.

Network Heterogeneity. Different clients have different communication resources, such as transmission rates. The performance of these protocols suffers severe reductions owing to their inability to accommodate the speed of the existing network and the fluctuations in network quality over time [13]. Uneven network resources can also eventually lead to the performance reduction of a global model.

Data Heterogeneity. The most common data heterogeneity is the statistical heterogeneity of data, i.e., not fully independent and identically distributed (non-i.i.d.). As a result, it is not easy to generalize the global model to all clients [42].

Model Heterogeneity. When participants collaborate without sharing private data, they may be reluctant to share the details of their models, possibly due to privacy and intellectual property concerns. The problem of heterogeneity between the models of the clients arises at this point, and traditional FL algorithms all require centralized control over the design of local models [31].

3   The Proposed Heterogeneous FL Taxonomy

Based on the extended definition of HFL in Sect. 2.2, we propose a classification of HFL based on where the type of heterogeneity problem occurs. This taxonomy can classify HFL into four types, where heterogeneous device and heterogeneous network belong to system heterogeneity. Heterogeneous data and heterogeneous model belong to non-system heterogeneity.

We analyzed 30 methods of HFL, as shown in Table 1. These methods are classified into the four types mentioned above depending on the treatment of the heterogeneous problem. Table 1 summarizes the methods and the datasets used in the experiments. It is worth noting that we have divided them according to methods rather than the effect produced. For example, FedMD [31] uses knowledge distillation to deal with model heterogeneity and therefore classifies it as heterogeneous model FL. Also, knowledge distillation indirectly compresses the communication overhead and can address network heterogeneity, but we do not classify FedMD as a heterogeneous network FL.

Table 1. Application of Heterogeneous FL

Category	Ref.	name	Adjustment of training	Clients selection	Compression parameters/gradients	Reducing communication rounds	Asynchronous (Semi-asynchronous)	Local model correction	Global model optimisation	Knowledge distillation	Update/Clustering optimisation	MNIST [28]	FEMNIST[9]	CIFAR-10[27]	CIFAR100[27]	Sentiment140[16]	Synthetic[49]	CelebA[40]	Shakespeare[48]	UCI-HAR[3]	ImageNet[56]	other
Heterogeneous Device	[33]	FedSAE	✓									✓	✓			✓	✓					
Heterogeneous Device	[58]	CFL-HC	✓	✓																		①
Heterogeneous Device	[1]	Distributed Learning System	✓																			②
Heterogeneous Device	[13]	HeteroSAg	✓	✓								✓		✓								
Heterogeneous Device	[51]	FedBalancer		✓													✓		✓	✓	✓	③
Heterogeneous Device	[10]	HELCFL		✓													✓					
Heterogeneous Network	[65]	FL Framework for Heterogeneous Devices of IoT			✓																✓	
Heterogeneous Network	[34]	Communication Compression Approach			✓							✓		✓								
Heterogeneous Network	[37]	Federated DNNs Framework			✓								✓	✓								
Heterogeneous Network	[30]	FedMask			✓								✓	✓						✓	✓	
Heterogeneous Network	[42]	FedSkel			✓					✓		✓	✓	✓	✓							
Heterogeneous Network	[63]	FedSeq				✓								✓	✓							
Heterogeneous Network	[19]	FedHe					✓		✓			✓		✓								
Heterogeneous Network	[44]	FedSA					✓					✓		✓								
Heterogeneous Network	[17]	DISCO					✓					✓		✓								
Heterogeneous Network	[15]	FedSeC		✓			✓					✓	✓	✓								
Heterogeneous Data	[59]	FedNova						✓						✓		✓						
Heterogeneous Data	[23]	SCAFFOLD						✓					✓									
Heterogeneous Data	[36]	FedProx						✓				✓	✓	✓	✓							
Heterogeneous Data	[50]	CReFF							✓					✓	✓						✓	
Heterogeneous Data	[6]	CoFED							✓					✓	✓						✓	④
Heterogeneous Model	[31]	FedMD								✓		✓	✓	✓	✓							
Heterogeneous Model	[53]	Fed2KD								✓		✓	✓									⑤
Heterogeneous Model	[8]	Fed-ET								✓				✓	✓	✓						
Heterogeneous Model	[41]	Heterogeneous Model Fusion FL Mechanism									✓	✓										⑥
Heterogeneous Model	[38]	FedH2L									✓	✓										⑦
Heterogeneous Model	[54]	FedProto									✓	✓	✓	✓								
Heterogeneous Model	[22]	FairBest+ FairAvg+ FairAccRatio+ FairAccDiff									✓							✓				⑧
Heterogeneous Model	[68]	TFL-CNN									✓	✓	✓									⑨
Heterogeneous Model	[12]	FedGroup									✓	✓	✓			✓	✓					

① original or coded datasets [58]. ②Heartbeat [21], Seizure [52]. ③Reddit [4]. ④ Chars74K [11], Adult [26]. ⑤FashionMNIST [60]. ⑥Caltech101 [25]. ⑦PACS [32],Office-Home [57]. ⑧UTK [67], FairFace [24]. ⑨BelgiumTSC [55].

3.1 Federal Learning Strategies with Heterogeneous Device

In practice, differences of device configurations (e.g., GPU, CPU, software, and network conditions) will create device heterogeneity. High-performance devices can perform their tasks quickly, while other devices are poorly trained and can only do part of the training work, resulting in reduced global model performance. If these "slower" devices are ignored, the aggregation of the model is severely slowed down, reducing the model's accuracy. The most common methods for device heterogeneity are adjustment of training tasks and clients selection. Their core idea is to assign appropriate training tasks to edge devices with different computational capabilities to optimize global efficiency. **Training Tasks Adjustment.** Adapting training tasks by analyzing information from individual clients can mitigate performance degradation due to device heterogeneity. However, measuring clients' training capability while ensuring privacy is a significant challenge.

FedSAE [33] automatically adjusts the training tasks of devices and actively selects participants to mitigate performance degradation. FedSAE adaptively selects participants by using complete information about the device's historical training tasks to predict the affordable training workload of each device. CFL-HC [58] designs a two-step optimization scheme to find the optimal training deadline for each optimal deadline training round and the optimal computational task size assigned to each computing device. Distributed learning system [1] proposes an efficient user allocation and resource allocation scheme for horizontal FL. This system allows massive amounts of data generated by IoT devices to train deep learning models while effectively addressing challenges and demands posed by data privacy and resource-constrained environments. HeteroSAg [13] allows the use of heterogeneous quantization to perform secure aggregation while allowing users to scale their quantization to their communication resources.

Clients Selection. Somewhat different from the adjustment of training tasks, client selection provides better protection for user's privacy. In order not to reduce the aggregation speed and accuracy of the model, client selection needs to select more clients with a high contribution. Also, client selection is often used in conjunction with adjustment of training tasks to solve device heterogeneity problems such as CFL-HC [58] and HeteroSAg [13].

FedBalancer [51] can actively select clients' training samples, and its sample selection strategy prioritizes more 'informative' data while respecting clients' privacy and computational power. Client selection strategy improve FL performance and reduce training latency. HELCFL [10] introduces a method for determining device operation frequency to reduce the training energy cost by analyzing and exploiting the idle time in FL training.

3.2   Federal Learning Strategies with Heterogeneous Network

FL imposes a vast communication and computational burden on the participating devices due to periodic global synchronization and continuous local training. This is even more pronounced in heterogeneous network FL. The server must wait for the slowest client in synchronous FL, and the heterogeneous network configuration problem can lead to significant latencies. Common approaches to deal with network heterogeneity are compression parameters/gradients, reducing communication rounds, and asynchronous (semi-asynchronous) training.

Compression Parameters/Gradients. The significant communication costs associated with the FL algorithm prevent the use of federal data to train large-scale models. The use of compressed parameters/gradients, therefore, reduces communication costs and solves the problem of network heterogeneity.

FL Framework for Heterogeneous Devices of IoT [65] compresses the global model into a local model while using the gradient of the local model to update the global model. Communication Compression Approach [34] designs a compression control scheme that balances local computation and wireless communication from a long-term learning perspective in terms of energy consumption. The algorithm adapts to the computational and communication environments of FL participants by carefully selecting compression parameters. Federated DNNs Framework [37] replaces each fully-connected (FC) layer with two low-rank projection matrices to compress the DNNs (deep neural networks) model. It builds a global error function to recover the output of the compressed DNNs model. A communication efficient federation optimization algorithm is also designed to reduce the communication overhead further. FedMask [30] uses a personalized, structured sparse DNN (deep neural network) on clients, thereby substantially reducing communication and computational costs while reducing the energy consumption of edge devices. FedSkel [42] enables federated learning for efficient computation and efficient communication on edge devices by updating only the essential parts of the model.

Reducing Communication Rounds. The increased communication costs associated with network heterogeneity are a significant constraint on the efficiency of federation learning. Similar to compressing parameters/gradients, increasing the convergence speed of the server's global model, i.e., reducing communication rounds, can similarly reduce the communication cost and address the problem of network heterogeneity.

FedSeq [63] improves the final performance and convergence speed of the algorithm by giving a fixed budget for the number of communication rounds.

Asynchronous (Semi-asynchronous) Training. Synchronous interaction is simple enough to guarantee a serial computing model but is difficult to implement due to different devices. Heterogeneous devices have a high level of unreliability. The aggregation server waits for updated local gradients, and these may be offline due to device heterogeneity, severely reducing learning efficiency [61]. Asynchronous strategies can reduce the problem of unstable environments, especially in public storage systems [35].

FedHe [19] uses a knowledge distillation-like approach to the training process asynchronously, significantly reducing the communication overhead. FedSA [44] proposes a semi-asynchronous federation learning mechanism in which the parameter server aggregates a certain number of local models according to the order of arrival of each round of models. DISCO [17] proposes a heterogeneous-aware dynamic scheduling approach to minimize global loss functions considering dropouts and limited device energy. DISCO can make intelligent decisions about the set and order of scheduled devices in each round of communication. FedSeC [15] proposes a new differential private federation learning framework and employs an update-based optimization of relative-staleness and semi-asynchronous optimization method for fast aggregation in heterogeneous networks.

3.3   Federal Learning Strategies with Heterogeneous Data

The non-i.i.d data from clients mainly causes the problem of data heterogeneity. How to mitigate the adverse effects of non-i.i.d. is still an open question. Non-i.i.d. containing distributional skews are commonly label distribution skew, feature distribution skew, and quantity skew [29]. Label distribution skew has the most significant impact on the accuracy of the FL algorithm. The processing for non-i.i.d. can be divided into two main types, local model correction and global model optimisation.

Local Model Correction. The skewed distribution of client data due to non-i.i.d. can eventually lead to a "drift" of the model on clients. Therefore, limiting or correcting local models by introducing specific global parameters is one way to address heterogeneous data.

FedNova [59] introduces a regularisation term based on locally trained local steps to limit the impact on the global model. A general framework is provided to analyze the convergence of Federated Optimisation algorithms with heterogeneous local training progress. The analysis is performed for both smooth non-convex and strongly convex settings and can be generalized to the case of partial client participation. FedNova is a normalized averaging method that removes factual inconsistencies while maintaining fast error convergence. SCAFFOLD [23] uses controls variables (variance reduction) to correct for 'client-side drift' in its local updates. SCAFFOLD proves that the algorithm is convergent while using rigorous mathematical theory. SCAFFOLD introduces server and local client control variables in its implementation, which are used to estimate the direction of the server model update and the direction of the local client model-used to estimate the update direction of the server model and update the direction of each client. The difference between these two update directions is then used to approximate the local training bias, i.e., drift is introduced to correct the model update direction during local training. FedProx [36] is an improved version of the FedAvg [46]. FedProx introduces a proximal term, i.e., $\min_w h_k(w; w^t) = F_k(w) + \frac{\mu}{2} \|w - w^t\|^2$, which suppresses local model divergence during local optimization and limits parameter differences.

Global Model Optimisation. As corresponding to the restricting local model, the global model can also be optimized on the server to solve the problem of data heterogeneity. Unlike model aggregation optimizing on the heterogeneous model, it is more about optimizing the global model by obtaining more information while maintaining privacy.

CReFF [50] demonstrates that biased classifiers constitute a significant contributor to poor global model performance. Classifiers retrained by CReFF on federated features can yield comparable performance to classifiers retrained on actual data without revealing local data information and class distribution. In each round, the CReFF client sends an updated local model and natural feature gradients to the server and sends a global model that will be aggregated and retrained to the client. CoFED [6] proposes an efficient communication FL scheme based on pseudo-labeled unlabeled data such as collaborative training. CoFED introduces pseudo-labeling so that each client pseudo-labels its dataset and votes for each class of pseudo-labeled datasets with high confidence on the server. Finally, the client trains on the local and pseudo-labeled datasets.

3.4   Federal Learning Strategies with Heterogeneous Model

The existing FL framework can only be used for isomorphic models, i.e., models with the same configuration, ignoring user preferences and the various attributes of their devices. The most commonly used methods to deal with model heterogeneity are knowledge distillation and update/Clustering optimization.

Knowledge Distillation. Knowledge distillation [31] is a class of model compression and acceleration techniques developed in recent years. Its main idea lies in using the predicted logits of the student network to learn the output logits of the teacher network, thus guiding the student network training, which can learn knowledge of similarities between classes that are not predicted by themselves. Knowledge distillation aims to compress and improve models by transferring knowledge from deep networks to smaller networks. Knowledge distillation optimizes federated learning through model compression and acceleration techniques, reducing model heterogeneity while ensuring efficient and real-time model transfer.

FedMD [31] uses migration learning and knowledge distillation to develop a generic framework that allows each client to have not only its private data but also a uniquely designed model. fed2KD [53] proposes a new FL framework based on bi-directional knowledge distillation. Knowledge exchange between global and local models is achieved by extracting information into a mini-model with a uniform configuration. Fed2KD use a conditional variational autoencoder (CVAE) to generate a public dataset. And the dataset will be used as a proxy dataset for distillation. Fed-ET [8] trains small models (of different architectures) on the client and is used to train a larger model on the server. Fed-ET employs a weighted consensus distillation scheme that effectively extracts reliable knowledge from the ensemble through diversity regularisation consensus while exploiting the diversity within the set to improve generalization.

Update/Clustering Optimisation. Unlike the heterogeneous data, where more data information needs to be collected for global model updates, the update strategy is directly optimized at the heterogeneous model, again correcting for the effects of local model 'drift'. The client gradient updating is affected by client data heterogeneity and diverges too much, making the aggregated global models far from the global optimum.

In Heterogeneous Model Fusion FL Mechanism [41] each node trains learning models of different sizes according to its computational power. After receiving the trained gradients from each node, the Parameter Server (PS) of the mechanism corrects the received gradients with a repetition matrix. According to the mapping matrix, the mechanism updates the region corresponding to the global model. At the end of all update operations, the PS assigns the compressed model to the corresponding node. FedH2L [38] proposes a new optimization strategy to find gradient updates that do not conflict between local and global update cues. Also, FedH2L introduces heterogeneous models across nodes, robust decentralized learning, and privacy-preserving parameter/gradient-free communication. FedProto [54] communicates with abstract class prototypes rather than gradients. FedProto aggregates the local prototypes collected from different clients and then sends the global prototype to all clients to standardize the training of the local model. Training for each client aims to minimize the classification error of the local data while keeping the resulting local prototypes close enough to the corresponding global prototypes. Kanaparthy et al. [22] investigated how fair classification can be achieved in federation learning (FL) with heterogeneous data. Four aggregation techniques, FairBest, FairAvg, FairAccRatio, and FairAccDiff, were proposed. TFL-CNN [68] proposed a two-layer federated learning model, including a new multilayer heterogeneous model selection, aggregation scheme and a distributed learning mechanism based on context-awareness. FedGroup [12] based on client similarity between optimization directions to group training and construct a new data-driven distance metric to improve the efficiency of the client-side clustering process. FedGroup can be improved by dividing the joint optimization into multiple sub-optimization groups and is used in conjunction with FL optimizer FedProx.

4   Heterogeneous Federal Learning Evaluation Methods

To assess the effectiveness of the HFL method, we next carry out a theoretical analysis and experimental evaluation of the evaluation method for HFL.

4.1   Theoretical Analysis of HFL

The theoretical analysis of HFL evaluation methods can similarly be divided into systematic and non-systematic evaluation methods. The former addresses the issue of system heterogeneity, which is generally due to differences in client devices and network communication. Therefore, when evaluating systemic HFL methods, it is necessary to make the GPU, network, and other conditions differ between clients. For example, [15, 17, 33, 34, 37, 42, 65], these works generally require the performance of the model to be evaluated in the presence of differences or limitations in client devices or communication networks. The former addresses the non-systematic heterogeneity problem, which is generally focused on data and models. Traditional FL evaluation methods can be used when evaluating non-systematic HFL methods.

4.2   Experimental Evaluation Metrics

Experimental evaluation helps to test a given verifiable FL method in a simulated or actual misbehaving environment to study its effectiveness in a complex environment. The following evaluation metrics are commonly used to quantify the effectiveness of these methods.

Model Performance and Communication Overhead. Model performance and communication overhead are vital evaluation metrics for HFL. The ultimate goal of processing heterogeneous problems is to obtain a better model. Training data is usually allocated randomly so that each client has the same number of data samples to study the performance of the FL model. Model accuracy, time overhead, and memory overhead are standard metrics used to assess model performance. Some processing is also performed to ensure heterogeneity. For example, to ensure heterogeneity, the original distribution of the data is simulated [22].

Resistance to Attacks. Due to the distributed nature of HFL, defending against such adversarial attacks becomes a more challenging problem due to local data unavailability and resource heterogeneity. A poisoned local model is pushed to the server separately for each round of the attacker. At the same time, the same setup of attacks is usually followed for a fair comparison and ensures that at least one attacker participates in model aggregation in each round [18]. By resisting attacks, one can thereby ensure the robustness of the system and improves the performance of the learning task [7].

Customer Contribution. Credit allocation and reward mechanisms are crucial for the motivation of current, and potential participants in FL. Therefore the ability to calculate customer contributions is also an important metric for evaluating incentives to HFL. FedCav [64] proposes a contribution-aware model aggregation algorithm that can calculate customer contributions containing fine-grained heterogeneous data.

Privacy Protection. Privacy protection is an essential metric for evaluating HFLs. Experimental evaluations of privacy protection are typically validated using security analysis and simulated attacks. For example, the secret-sharing protocol, HFTL [14], proves the security of its protocol by confirming that the underlying algorithm's secret sharing scheme is secure. pbfl [45] is evaluated using Gaussian attacks to demonstrate that the algorithm's previous Byzantine Robust Federated Learning algorithm is more secure compared to its predecessor.

5   Promising Future Research Directions

Our survey clearly shows that HFL research is beginning to attention. However, many issues remain to be resolved to make this technology capable of meeting the challenges in practical applications. For heterogeneous problems to be better dealt with in future FL systems, we look at the following future research directions.

Incentive Design. The quality of the FL algorithm is closely related to the quality of the incentives [39]. As data heterogeneity often generates, the quality and quantity of data used for training vary across clients. While FL ensures that data remains local, clients need to provide their resources such as computational power, data samples, communication costs, etc. These factors may cause clients to be reluctant to participate in FL [20] without compensation. Especially in HFL, clients often do not have access to high-quality, high-volume data. It is, therefore, necessary to use incentives that maximize the overall benefits, ensuring that individual interests are not compromised, and promoting participation by more customers with high-quality data.

Prevent Participants from Cheating. A participant may fraudulently claim the number of training data points it can contribute to the model to gain more by reporting the test results of the linguistic model. In addition, these dishonest participants could claim rewards by using old results with corresponding correct proofs from the previous FL period. This behaviour is difficult to detect as we cannot detect any participant in the dataset. In particular, model and data heterogeneity lead to the inability to detect cheating by heterogeneous participants using conventional validation methods [66].

Reliable and Efficient Communication Mechanisms. Comparing participants' intermediate training results in models with extensive physical distances takes time. Excessive data transferring delays impair the efficiency of computing resource use because parties must wait for intermediate findings before beginning or conducting training on their end. At each iteration, FL, on the other hand, incurs high communication costs by sending the necessary parameter modifications to the service segment to the user side. In particular, for deep learning models with thousands of parameters, the size can be in the range of GB [1].

Enhanced Privacy Protection. Clients often only provide gradients to the server rather than raw data, protecting participants' personal information. Recent research has shown that sharing gradients is insufficiently secure for participants. For example, [47] demonstrated that a hostile participant might infer the presence of specific data points in other people's training data (e.g., membership inference). The primary approach for improved FL privacy protection during training is secure multi-party computation (SMC) [62]. However, the solutions are vulnerable to system heterogeneity. SMC based on homomorphic encryption and secret sharing consumes a lot of computational and communication resources [5]. In the presence of heterogeneity issues, they lead to a reduction in FL. Therefore, HFL employing an SMC protocol enhanced privacy protection is an important issue that needs to be addressed.

Acknowledgments. This paper is partly supported by the National Research and Development Plan under Grant No. 2021YFF0704102, the National Social Science Fund under Grant No. 20BJY131, the major Science and Technology Innovation of Shandong Province under Grant Nos. 2021CXGC010108, the China-Singapore International Joint Research Project under Grant No. 206-A021002, the Industrial Experts Program of Spring City, the Fundamental Research Funds of Shandong University.

References

1. Abdellatif, A.A., et al.: Communication-efficient hierarchical federated learning for IoT heterogeneous systems with imbalanced data. Fut. Gener. Comput. Syst. **128**, 406–419 (2022)
2. Abdelmoniem, A.M., Ho, C.Y., Papageorgiou, P., Canini, M.: Empirical analysis of federated learning in heterogeneous environments. In: Proceedings of the 2nd European Workshop on Machine Learning and Systems, pp. 1–9 (2022)
3. Anguita, D., Ghio, A., Oneto, L., Parra Perez, X., Reyes Ortiz, J.L.: A public domain dataset for human activity recognition using smartphones. In: Proceedings of the 21th International European Symposium on Artificial Neural Networks, Computational Intelligence and Machine Learning, pp. 437–442 (2013)
4. Baumgartner, J., Zannettou, S., Keegan, B., Squire, M., Blackburn, J.: The pushshift reddit dataset. In: Proceedings of the International AAAI Conference on Web and Social Media, vol. 14, pp. 830–839 (2020)
5. Bonawitz, K., et al.: Practical secure aggregation for privacy-preserving machine learning. In: proceedings of the 2017 ACM SIGSAC Conference on Computer and Communications Security, pp. 1175–1191 (2017)
6. Cao, X., Li, Z., Yu, H., Sun, G.: COFED: cross-silo heterogeneous federated multi-task learning via co-training. arXiv preprint arXiv:2202.08603 (2022)
7. Chen, L.Y., Chiu, T.C., Pang, A.C., Cheng, L.C.: Fedequal: defending model poisoning attacks in heterogeneous federated learning. In: 2021 IEEE Global Communications Conference (GLOBECOM), pp. 1–6. IEEE (2021)
8. Cho, Y.J., Manoel, A., Joshi, G., Sim, R., Dimitriadis, D.: Heterogeneous ensemble knowledge transfer for training large models in federated learning. arXiv preprint arXiv:2204.12703 (2022)
9. Cohen, G., Afshar, S., Tapson, J., van Schaik, A.: Emnist: extending mnist to handwritten letters. In: 2017 International Joint Conference on Neural Networks (IJCNN), pp. 2921–2926 (2017). https://doi.org/10.1109/IJCNN.2017.7966217
10. Cui, Y., Cao, K., Zhou, J., Wei, T.: HELCFL: high-efficiency and low-cost federated learning in heterogeneous mobile-edge computing. In: 2022 Design, Automation & Test in Europe Conference & Exhibition (DATE), pp. 1227–1232. IEEE (2022)
11. De Campos, T.E., Babu, B.R., Varma, M.: Character recognition in natural images. VISAPP **7**(2), 2 (2009)
12. Duan, M., et al.: Fedgroup: efficient federated learning via decomposed similarity-based clustering. In: 2021 IEEE International Conference on Parallel & Distributed Processing with Applications, pp. 228–237. IEEE (2021)
13. Elkordy, A.R., Avestimehr, A.S.: Heterosag: secure aggregation with heterogeneous quantization in federated learning. IEEE Trans. Commun. **70**(4), 2372–2386 (2022)

14. Gao, D., Liu, Y., Huang, A., Ju, C., Yu, H., Yang, Q.: Privacy-preserving heterogeneous federated transfer learning. In: 2019 IEEE International Conference on Big Data (Big Data), pp. 2552–2559. IEEE (2019)

15. Gao, Z., Duan, Y., Yang, Y., Rui, L., Zhao, C.: Fedsec: a robust differential private federated learning framework in heterogeneous networks. In: 2022 IEEE Wireless Communications and Networking Conference (WCNC), pp. 1868–1873 (2022). https://doi.org/10.1109/WCNC51071.2022.9771929

16. Go, A., Bhayani, R., Huang, L.: Twitter sentiment classification using distant supervision. Processing **150** (2009)

17. Guo, K., Chen, Z., Yang, H.H., Quek, T.Q.: Dynamic scheduling for heterogeneous federated learning in private 5g edge networks. IEEE J. Sel. Topics Signal Process. **16**, 26–40 (2021)

18. Guo, Y., Wang, Q., Ji, T., Wang, X., Li, P.: Resisting distributed backdoor attacks in federated learning: a dynamic norm clipping approach. In: 2021 IEEE International Conference on Big Data (Big Data), pp. 1172–1182. IEEE (2021)

19. Hin, C.Y., Edith, N.: Fedhe: heterogeneous models and communication-efficient federated learning. arXiv preprint arXiv:2110.09910 (2021)

20. Hu, M., Wu, D., Zhou, Y., Chen, X., Chen, M.: Incentive-aware autonomous client participation in federated learning. IEEE Trans. Parallel Distrib. Syst. **33**(10), 2612–2627 (2022)

21. Kachuee, M., Fazeli, S., Sarrafzadeh, M.: ECG heartbeat classification: a deep transferable representation. In: 2018 IEEE International Conference on Healthcare Informatics (ICHI), pp. 443–444. IEEE (2018)

22. Kanaparthy, S., Padala, M., Damle, S., Gujar, S.: Fair federated learning for heterogeneous face data. arXiv preprint arXiv:2109.02351 (2021)

23. Karimireddy, S.P., Kale, S., Mohri, M., Reddi, S., Stich, S., Suresh, A.T.: Scaffold: stochastic controlled averaging for federated learning. In: International Conference on Machine Learning, pp. 5132–5143. PMLR (2020)

24. Karkkainen, K., Joo, J.: Fairface: face attribute dataset for balanced race, gender, and age for bias measurement and mitigation. In: Proceedings of the IEEE/CVF Winter Conference on Applications of Computer Vision, pp. 1548–1558 (2021)

25. Kinnunen, T., Kamarainen, J.K., Lensu, L., Lankinen, J., Käviäinen, H.: Making visual object categorization more challenging: randomized caltech-101 data set. In: 2010 20th International Conference on Pattern Recognition, pp. 476–479. IEEE (2010)

26. Kohavi, R.: Scaling up the accuracy of naive-bayes classifiers: a decision-tree hybrid. In: KDD, vol. 96, pp. 202–207 (1996)

27. Krizhevsky, A., Hinton, G., et al.: Learning multiple layers of features from tiny images. University of Toronto (2009)

28. LeCun, Y., Bottou, L., Bengio, Y., Haffner, P.: Gradient-based learning applied to document recognition. Proc. IEEE **86**(11), 2278–2324 (1998)

29. Li, A., Set al.: Lotteryfl: personalized and communication-efficient federated learning with lottery ticket hypothesis on non-iid datasets. arXiv preprint arXiv:2008.03371 (2020)

30. Li, A., Sun, J., Zeng, X., Zhang, M., Li, H., Chen, Y.: Fedmask: joint computation and communication-efficient personalized federated learning via heterogeneous masking. In: Proceedings of the 19th ACM Conference on Embedded Networked Sensor Systems, pp. 42–55 (2021)

31. Li, D., Wang, J.: FEDMD: heterogenous federated learning via model distillation. arXiv preprint arXiv:1910.03581 (2019)

32. Li, D., Yang, Y., Song, Y.Z., Hospedales, T.M.: Deeper, broader and artier domain generalization. In: Proceedings of the IEEE International Conference on Computer Vision, pp. 5542–5550 (2017)
33. Li, L., et al.: Fedsae: a novel self-adaptive federated learning framework in heterogeneous systems. In: 2021 International Joint Conference on Neural Networks (IJCNN) (2021)
34. Li, L., Shi, D., Hou, R., Li, H., Pan, M., Han, Z.: To talk or to work: flexible communication compression for energy efficient federated learning over heterogeneous mobile edge devices. In: IEEE INFOCOM 2021-IEEE Conference on Computer Communications, pp. 1–10. IEEE (2021)
35. Li, T., Sahu, A.K., Talwalkar, A., Smith, V.: Federated learning: challenges, methods, and future directions. IEEE Signal Process. Maga. **37**(3), 50–60 (2020)
36. Li, T., Sahu, A.K., Zaheer, M., Sanjabi, M., Talwalkar, A., Smith, V.: Federated optimization in heterogeneous networks. Proc. Mach. Learn. Syst. **2**, 429–450 (2020)
37. Li, X., Li, Y., Li, S., Zhou, Y., Chen, C., Zheng, Z.: A unified federated DNNs framework for heterogeneous mobile devices. IEEE Internet Things J. **9**(3), 1737–1748 (2021)
38. Li, Y., Zhou, W., Wang, H., Mi, H., Hospedales, T.M.: Fedh2l: federated learning with model and statistical heterogeneity. arXiv preprint arXiv:2101.11296 (2021)
39. Liu, Y., Zhang, L., Ge, N., Li, G.: A systematic literature review on federated learning: from a model quality perspective. arXiv preprint arXiv:2012.01973 (2020)
40. Liu, Z., Luo, P., Wang, X., Tang, X.: Deep learning face attributes in the wild. In: Proceedings of the IEEE International Conference on Computer Vision, pp. 3730–3738 (2015)
41. Lu, X., Liao, Y., Liu, C., Lio, P., Hui, P.: Heterogeneous model fusion federated learning mechanism based on model mapping. IEEE Internet Things J. **9**, 6058–6068 (2021)
42. Luo, J., Yang, J., Ye, X., Guo, X., Zhao, W.: Fedskel: efficient federated learning on heterogeneous systems with skeleton gradients update. In: Proceedings of the 30th ACM International Conference on Information & Knowledge Management, pp. 3283–3287 (2021)
43. Ma, C., et al.: On safeguarding privacy and security in the framework of federated learning. IEEE Netw. **34**(4), 242–248 (2020)
44. Ma, Q., Xu, Y., Xu, H., Jiang, Z., Huang, L., Huang, H.: FEDSA: a semi-asynchronous federated learning mechanism in heterogeneous edge computing. IEEE J. Sel. Areas Commun. **39**(12), 3654–3672 (2021)
45. Ma, X., Zhou, Y., Wang, L., Miao, M.: Privacy-preserving byzantine-robust federated learning. Comput. Stand. Interfaces **80**, 103561 (2022)
46. McMahan, B., Moore, E., Ramage, D., Hampson, S., y Arcas, B.A.: Communication-efficient learning of deep networks from decentralized data. In: Artificial Intelligence and Statistics, pp. 1273–1282. PMLR (2017)
47. Melis, L., Song, C., De Cristofaro, E., Shmatikov, V.: Exploiting unintended feature leakage in collaborative learning. In: 2019 IEEE Symposium on Security and Privacy (SP), pp. 691–706 (2019). https://doi.org/10.1109/SP.2019.00029
48. Shakespeare, W.: The Complete Works of William Shakespeare. Race Point Publishing (2014)
49. Shamir, O., Srebro, N., Zhang, T.: Communication-efficient distributed optimization using an approximate newton-type method. In: International Conference on Machine Learning, pp. 1000–1008. PMLR (2014)

50. Shang, X., Lu, Y., Huang, G., Wang, H.: Federated learning on heterogeneous and long-tailed data via classifier re-training with federated features. arXiv preprint arXiv:2204.13399 (2022)

51. Shin, J., Li, Y., Liu, Y., Lee, S.J.: Sample selection with deadline control for efficient federated learning on heterogeneous clients. arXiv preprint arXiv:2201.01601 (2022)

52. Stevenson, N.J., Tapani, K., Lauronen, L., Vanhatalo, S.: A dataset of neonatal EEG recordings with seizure annotations. Sci. Data **6**(1), 1–8 (2019)

53. Sun, C., Jiang, T., Zonouz, S., Pompili, D.: Fed2kd: heterogeneous federated learning for pandemic risk assessment via two-way knowledge distillation. In: 2022 17th Wireless On-Demand Network Systems and Services Conference (WONS), pp. 1–8. IEEE (2022)

54. Tan, Y., et al.: Fedproto: federated prototype learning across heterogeneous clients. In: AAAI Conference on Artificial Intelligence, vol. 1 (2022)

55. Timofte, R., Zimmermann, K., Van Gool, L.: Multi-view traffic sign detection, recognition, and 3d localisation. Mach. Vision Appl. **25**(3), 633–647 (2014)

56. Van Oord, A., Kalchbrenner, N., Kavukcuoglu, K.: Pixel recurrent neural networks. In: International Conference on Machine Learning, pp. 1747–1756. PMLR (2016)

57. Venkateswara, H., Eusebio, J., Chakraborty, S., Panchanathan, S.: Deep hashing network for unsupervised domain adaptation. In: Proceedings of the IEEE Conference on Computer Vision and Pattern Recognition, pp. 5018–5027 (2017)

58. Wang, D., et al.: CFL-HC: a coded federated learning framework for heterogeneous computing scenarios. In: 2021 IEEE Global Communications Conference (GLOBECOM), pp. 1–6. IEEE (2021)

59. Wang, J., Liu, Q., Liang, H., Joshi, G., Poor, H.V.: A novel framework for the analysis and design of heterogeneous federated learning. IEEE Trans. Signal Process. **69**, 5234–5249 (2021)

60. Xiao, H., Rasul, K., Vollgraf, R.: Fashion-mnist: a novel image dataset for benchmarking machine learning algorithms. arXiv preprint arXiv:1708.07747 (2017)

61. Xu, C., Qu, Y., Xiang, Y., Gao, L.: Asynchronous federated learning on heterogeneous devices: a survey. arXiv preprint arXiv:2109.04269 (2021)

62. Xu, G., Li, H., Liu, S., Yang, K., Lin, X.: Verifynet: secure and verifiable federated learning. IEEE Trans. Inf. For. Secur. **15**, 911–926 (2019)

63. Zaccone, R., Rizzardi, A., Caldarola, D., Ciccone, M., Caputo, B.: Speeding up heterogeneous federated learning with sequentially trained superclients. arXiv preprint arXiv:2201.10899 (2022)

64. Zeng, H., Zhou, T., Guo, Y., Cai, Z., Liu, F.: Fedcav: contribution-aware model aggregation on distributed heterogeneous data in federated learning. In: 50th International Conference on Parallel Processing, pp. 1–10 (2021)

65. Zhang, H., Kim, J.: Towards a federated learning framework for heterogeneous devices of internet of things. arXiv preprint arXiv:2105.14675 (2021)

66. Zhang, X., Li, F., Zhang, Z., Li, Q., Wang, C., Wu, J.: Enabling execution assurance of federated learning at untrusted participants. In: IEEE INFOCOM 2020-IEEE Conference on Computer Communications, pp. 1877–1886. IEEE (2020)

67. Zhang, Z., Song, Y., Qi, H.: Age progression/regression by conditional adversarial autoencoder. In: Proceedings of the IEEE Conference on Computer Vision and Pattern Recognition, pp. 5810–5818 (2017)

68. Zhou, X., et al.: Two-layer federated learning with heterogeneous model aggregation for 6G supported internet of vehicles. IEEE Trans. Veh. Technol. **70**(6), 5308–5317 (2021)

A Graph-Based Efficient Service Composition Method for Computer Aided Engineering (CAE)

Zhuo Tian, Changyou Zhang[(⊠)], and Jiaojiao Xiao

Institute of Software, Chinese Academy of Sciences, Beijing, China
changyou@iscas.ac.cn

Abstract. Complex CAE (Computer Aided Engineering) logic in the network can be implemented by combining existing services, but the network environment changes dynamically, and different service instances of the same function have different performances. In this paper, we propose a graph-based efficient service composition method. Using the service discovery method based on the shortest path in the graph, a calculation method of service matching degree is proposed in service selection, which solves the problem of partial matching of service relationships and the dynamics of service instances. Experiments show that the improved algorithm reduces the running time and improves the search efficiency on a dataset for the same size.

Keywords: CAE · Web Service · Dynamic Composition · Graph

1 Introduction

With the wide application of service-oriented architecture and the continuous development of service technology, service-oriented computing has become the current development trend in the field of CAE [1]. Service computing puts forward the concepts of service quality, software as a service, etc., and leads to service management related issues such as service interaction, service composition, and service recommendation [1]. Then, how to effectively combine various services distributed on the Internet and realize the close integration and collaboration between services has become a research hotspot in industry and academia. It is under this background that service composition is proposed and has become a key research direction in the field of distributed computing and software engineering [2].

At present, most service composition strategies only consider the static characteristics of services [3], such as service response time, throughput and other service quality information, but do not consider the operating characteristics of service instances under the microservice architecture. Therefore, the default service path may not be the current optimal path [4]. How to monitor and manage the real-time processing capabilities of microservices and dynamically update microservice paths to achieve efficient application execution efficiency is a hot research topic today. At present, some dynamic adaptive algorithms [5–7] can select suitable candidate services to create the optimal service path, and can dynamically update the service path according to the change of service status

© The Author(s), under exclusive license to Springer Nature Singapore Pte Ltd. 2023
Y. Sun et al. (Eds.): ChineseCSCW 2022, CCIS 1681, pp. 405–410, 2023.
https://doi.org/10.1007/978-981-99-2356-4_32

[8]. However, according to the different service granularity of the microservice platform, the same task may have different processing efficiency under different granular service spaces.

In order to cope with the dynamic service management and composition in the microservice system [9, 10], this paper proposes an effective service management mechanism and service composition method, which effectively improves the service reuse rate in the microservice platform and improves the search efficiency of service composition.

2 N-WSPR Algorithm

The algorithm divides the process of searching for a solution that satisfies the request in the existing service graph database into three stages: service discovery, service selection, and service ranking. These three stages will be described in detail below.

2.1 Service Discovery

In the service file library of a large-scale system, if the service file is directly read and recorded, it will take a long time to process the data. Therefore, this algorithm uses the service graph database created in the previous chapter to directly read the service data on the service graph database during the service discovery phase. In the service discovery phase, the current service graph database is traversed for the first time, and after the services related to the request are filtered out, the service is selected based on the matching degree.

Algorithm 1: Service Discovery

Input: r^i, r^o, service graph data

Output: PD_{ws}

    $s = r^i; C = \emptyset;$

    Initialize $d_{r^i}(p);$

    while $\neg(s \supseteq r^o)$ **do**

        $curWS = \{w | w \in \Omega(s), w \notin C\}$

        for w **in** $curWS$

            $d(w) = 0$

            for p' **in** w^i

                $d(w) = max\left(d(w), d_{r^i}(p')\right)$

            end for

            for p **in** w^o

                if $d_{r^i}(p) = +\infty$ **or** $d_{r^i}(p) > d(w) + c(w)$

                    $d_{r^i}(p) = d(w) + c(w); PD_{ws}(p) = w;$

                end if

            end for

            $s = s \cup w^o$

        end for

        $C = C \cup curWS$

    end

The basic idea of the service discovery phase is: take the acquired parameter set as the current state s, search along the services that can be called in the current state s, and obtain more parameters to join the state s. In this search process, the prefix service w of each parameter p is calculated according to the shortest path algorithm idea of the directed graph. The prefix service w of the parameter p means: p is one of the output parameters of the service w, that is, $p \in w^o$. The obtained prefix service set is the filtered service set.

The pseudo code of the algorithm in the service discovery phase is shown in Algorithm 1. The input parameters of the algorithm are the initial parameter set r^i and the target parameter set r^o of the request r, and the graph data of the service. The output parameter PD_{ws} of the algorithm refers to the optimal prefix (Predecessor) service set of all relevant parameters in the service dependency graph.

2.2 Service Selection

The service selection stage is to perform a reverse search on the state space of the service planning graph, that is, start the search from the target parameter r^o. Using the $d_{r^i}(p)$ and PD_{ws} obtained in the service discovery phase as a prerequisite guide, find the service set with the highest matching degree. In the reverse search process, the classic regression search algorithm is used, and the second round of selection is performed on the related services obtained in the previous step.

The basic idea of the service selection stage is to evaluate the matching degree of related services in the regression search process, and to select the service with high matching degree to proceed to the next stage of service ranking. The search process at this stage will start from the target parameter r^o to find the prefix service, that is, to find the service that can achieve this goal as the goal.

The service matching degree (Matching Degree) calculation formula proposed in this stage is as follows:

$$MD(w) = \frac{|w^o \cap Goal|}{|w^o \cup Goal|} - \frac{|(w^o - Goal) \cup (Goal - w^o)|}{|w^o \cup Goal|}$$

2.3 Service Ordering

Service ordering refers to ordering the optimal service set selected in the previous stage into the final service combination sequence. In this stage, the search will be started from the known parameter r^i of the request, and the services in the service result set $wsSet$ obtained in the first two steps will be sorted, and the final service combination sequence will be obtained.

The algorithm sets the initial state s to the requested known parameter r^i. Starting from the initial state, when the services in the $wsSet$ have not been sorted, the traversal continues. Search for services that are also in $wsSet$ in the service set $\Omega(s)$ that can be called in the current state s, and output this service. After that, update the current state s, add the generation parameter w^o of the service w output in the previous step to the state, and remove this service from the $wsSet$. Repeat this process until all the services in the $wsSet$ are output. Output services according to the forward search order, then a set of orderly optimal service output sequences can be obtained.

2.4 Analysis of Algorithms

This section will analyze the algorithm complexity of the three stages of the N-WSPR algorithm, and provide a theoretical basis for the analysis of the results of subsequent experiments.

The time complexity in the service discovery phase is $O(|W|^2|P|)$, where $|W|$ refers to the number of Web services, and the maximum length of the service composition sequence is $|W|$. Therefore, there are at most $|W|$ cycles in each round of traversal in the service matching phase. The time complexity of the service matching phase is $O(|W|^2 log|P|)$, because there are at most $|W|$ iterations in the service matching phase, and in each iteration, the maximum time in the step of calculating the matching degree between the service and the target The complexity is $O(|W|log|P|)$. The time complexity of the service composition sequence generation stage is $O(W)$, because the service composition sequence generation stage has at most $|W|$ iterations.

3 Experiments

3.1 Operating Environment

This article will verify the performance of the service composition algorithm in a simulated data set of Web services. The experimental platform is a PC with GPU like accelerator. In this study, a cluster is used with the SIMT accelerator made in China. The cluster includes many nodes each containing 1 CPU and 4 accelerators. The CPU has four NUMA nodes, each NUMA node has 8 X86 based processors. The accelerator adopts a GPU-like architecture consisting of a 16 GB HBM2 device memory and many compute units, with peak FP64 performance of 7.0TFLOPS.

3.2 Comparison of the Running Time of Different Algorithms

Because in the simulation data set, the request file is randomly generated, so this article does 10 tests on each data set, and finally takes the average running time and the number of service results as the comparison result. Among them, the running time refers to the running time from the start of the algorithm to the finding of a combined solution. In this paper, experiments are carried out under the Scale-free model of the public service network dataset and the Small-world model of the workflow service network dataset.

3.3 The Influence of the Number of Services on the Running Time of the Algorithm

During the experiment, we found that the running time of the algorithm is not all related to the size of the Web service library, but also to the size of the search space of the algorithm. Therefore, this paper designs an experiment to detect the relationship between the number of services and the running time in the final combined result. Given the network model and scale of the Web service library, test different requests, record the service combination result and running time, and compare the trends of the two.

Figure 1 plots the relationship between the number of Web services and the running time in the combined results of 20 requests tested under the Scale-free model when the number of Web services is 1000. It can be seen from the figure that when the number of combined services is larger, the running time will be larger. And from the perspective of the changing trends of the two, they are basically the same.

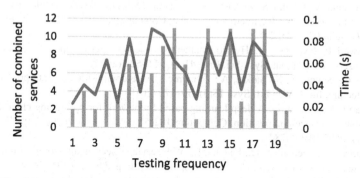

Fig. 1. Relationship between number of composite services and running time

3.4 Analysis of the Results

It can be seen from the above two experimental results that in the same scale of data, the running time of the algorithm under the Small-world model and the number of combined services are significantly higher than those of the Scale-free model. This is because the Small-world model serves as a workflow service network. There are more associations between services, and there are more services in the result of the called service combination. Therefore, more search time will be spent in service discovery and service matching.

4 Conclusion

This paper proposes a set of graph-based service composition method N-WSPR for the problem of how to perform service composition in large-scale service data, which improves the existing classic service composition algorithm WSPR, and adds the QoS attributes of the service to it. The service matching style of this system is more suitable. First, it introduces the three steps of the algorithm-service discovery, service selection, and service ranking. Then, the three steps are described in detail and the complexity of the algorithm is analyzed. Finally, the experimental plan design and experimental results analysis are carried out on the Web service simulation data set.

Acknowledgments. This work was supported by National Key Research and Development Project—CAE cloud service platform based on open architecture (2020YFB1709503). This work was supported by the GHfund A (202202014484).

References

1. Khan, H.M., Chua, F., Yap, T.T.V.: ReSQoV: a scalable resource allocation model for qos-satisfied cloud services. Future Internet **14**(5), 131 (2022)
2. Viriyasitavat, W., Bi, Z.: Service selection and workflow composition in modern business processes. J. Ind. Inf. Integr. **17**, 100126 (2020)
3. Hayyolalam, V., Otoum, S., Özkasap, Ö.: Dynamic QoS/QoE-aware reliable service composition framework for edge intelligence. Clust. Comput. **25**, 1–19 (2022). https://doi.org/10.1007/s10586-022-03572-9
4. Rajeswari, P., Jayashree, K.: Hybrid metaheuristics web service composition model for QoS aware services. Comput. Syst. Sci. Eng. **41**(2), 511–524 (2022)
5. Khan, G., Sengupta, S., Sarkar, A.: Dynamic service composition in enterprise cloud bus architecture. Int. J. Web Inf. Syst. **15**(5), 50–576 (2019)
6. Haytamy, S., Omara, F.: A deep learning based framework for optimizing cloud consumer QoS-based service composition. Computing **102**(5), 1117–1137 (2020). https://doi.org/10.1007/s00607-019-00784-7
7. Yasmina, R.Z., Fethallah, H., Fadoua, L.: Web service selection and composition based on uncertain quality of service. Concurr. Comput. Pract. Exp. **34**(1), e6531 (2022)
8. Barakat, L., Miles, S., Luck, M.: Adaptive composition in dynamic service environments. Fut. Gener. Comput. Syst. **80**, 215–228 (2018)
9. Elmaghraoui, H., Benhlima, L., Chiadmi, D.: Automatic dynamic web service composition using AND/OR directed graphs. Int. J. Web Serv. Res. **16**(3), 29–43 (2019)
10. Hidri, W., M'tir, R.H., Saoud, N.B.B.: A semantic driven approach for efficient cloud service composition. In: EMCIS, pp. 229–243. Springer, Heidelebrg (2021). https://doi.org/10.1007/978-3-030-95947-0_16

Privacy-Preserving Federated Learning Framework in Knowledge Concept Recommendation

Yangjie Qin[1], Jia Zhu[2], and Jin Huang[1(✉)]

[1] South China Normal University, Guangzhou, China
jinhuang@m.scnu.edu.cn
[2] Zhejiang Normal University, Zhejiang, China

Abstract. Online education has become a new growth point, providing a massive worldwide learning opportunity for college students and workers. The recommendation system is provided to help users choose suitable courses wisely to satisfy their learning needs better. However, the traditional recommendation methods are more inclined to recommend a series of courses to users and ignore the user's interest in knowledge concepts, and conventional centralized training algorithms risk data leakage. In this paper, we propose a federated framework FedAttn that can train model using decentralized data and aggregate gradient using an attention-based method. Additionally, we conduct experiments utilizing real-world datasets to validate that our approach can achieve a decent result and effectively protect user privacy.

Keywords: online education · federated learning · recommendation framework

1 Introduction

Depending on the rapid development of online education, higher education is no longer unreachable to ordinary people. There are still a lot of problems in online education. For example, the overall course completion rate is low, and the homework completion rate is low. A recommendation system is applied to help them find suitable learning knowledge concepts to satisfy the learning needs better and address the above problems. Unlike traditional recommendation, which directly recommends courses, recommending knowledge concepts can conduct a learning path in users' interest in a higher dimension. We can better understand and capture users' interests from the knowledge concept angle to conduct a suitable learning path. Traditional recommendation limits the recommendation performance because of the sparsity of user-item relationships and the cold start problem. To overcome the above restrictions, researchers turn to feature-rich situations in which users' and items' properties are employed to compensate for the sparsity and increase recommendation performance [15].

In online education, there is an abundance of side information, multiple entity types, and corresponding relations. Leveraging these heterogeneous relations can provide rich side information and improve the performance of recommendation as follows. Graph-based recommendation algorithms can meet the needs of these heterogeneous relationships in entity representation learning. User's interests connect their historical record

© The Author(s), under exclusive license to Springer Nature Singapore Pte Ltd. 2023
Y. Sun et al. (Eds.): ChineseCSCW 2022, CCIS 1681, pp. 411–421, 2023.
https://doi.org/10.1007/978-981-99-2356-4_33

with these historical relationships, thereby bringing explainability to a recommendation. Users' interests can be appropriately broadened, and the number of suggested knowledge concepts can be increased.

Firstly, processing this massive, heterogeneous, and trivial data needs a lot of computing power. Secondly, the communication cost of data transmission is unimaginable. Last but not least, users care about their privacy-sensitive data. Governors even set up policies like GDPR to prevent information leakage. Considered with the above problems, federated learning (FL) is applied to solve the problem of data leakage and meet legal regulations. Since Google [11] proposed this method in recent years, distributed learning has taken a step further. Learning a high-performance, centralized model from decentralized data ensures data security and reduces computing requirements.

Motivated by FL algorithms, we propose FedAttn, a privacy-preserving federated framework for GNN-based recommendation that exploits high-order user-course interaction information. Compared with the centralized learning framework, it consists of the server and client parts. In the client part, user data is reserved locally. There is a graph neural network (GNN) and embedding models. Each client calculates the gradients of models and embedding based on the user-course graph conducted from local interaction data, then uploads them to the server, which is in charge of aggregating gradients and distributing global models for local update. As for the server, we calculate each client's contribution by aggregating gradients across an attention-based mechanism. In addition, to better protect user data, we employ local differential privacy to encrypt client-server communication. A series of experiments were conducted on a real-world dataset. The results demonstrate that our method is capable of achieving an outstanding performance in knowledge concept recommendation. Our contribution can be summed up as follows:

– We propose a framework that protects privacy while training an accurate knowledge concept recommendation model using the user's enrolled record history and interaction with courses.
– We propose an approach that can aggregate model gradients dynamically by an attention-based mechanism, protecting the data from leakage in the meantime.
– Experiments are conducted using a real-world dataset. The simulation results indicated that our framework is effective. Extensive analysis demonstrates that our strategy can produce comparable outcomes to the current approach.

2   Related Work

Recently, Graph Neural Network [8, 14] has become popular in deep learning. Some researcheres [5, 19] have utilized the strength of GNN for recommendation. In order to alleviate sparsity and cold start problems in classic recommendation methods [9, 13], Wang et al. [16] proposed their framework which edge information is incorporated into the graph embedding framework to increase the attributes of goods, such as brand, price, etc. The EGES is obtained by weighting different pieces of side information. On existing deep learning recommendation model [7] basis, GNN embedding method helps to archieve more. NGCF [17] explicitly models the higher-order connection between user and item to improve embedding. However, NGCF is obtained by standard GCN, Light-GCN [6] have made a further improvement, which adapts a simple weighted sum aggregator, and abandons the use of feature transformation and nonlinear activation. In the same time, researcheres have applied different recommendation methods in education. Gong et al. [4] proposed ACKRec to recommend knowledge concepts in heterogeneous information graphs. To deal with the sparse problem, the authors try to build a multientity heterogeneous graph. The main processing of ACKRec is designing the different meta paths to guide the propagation of students' interests. Besides, Li et al. [10] proposed HFGN to recommend outfits across unified modeling of users, items, and outfits with a heterogeneous graph network. Aside from the importance of edge information in deep learning models, privacy breaches are the greatest drawback for users. Federated learning is a machine learning paradigm in which a high-performance centralized model is trained using distributed data from multiple clients. Besides, differential privacy [2] is usually utilized in privacy-preserving recommendation systems. The framework of federated learning has been applied to personalized recommendations. For example, Chai et al. [3] proposed the FedMF framework, which protects item embedding by a homomorphic encryption method. Ammad et al. [1] proposed FCF framework which applied traditional collaborative filtering in federated learning. Wu et al. [18] proposed FedGNN to take advantage of high-order user-item interactions derived from decentralized data. Furthermore, recommendations in federated learning are applied in real-world scenarios [12,20] . In contrast, our contribution to this work is the flexible and adaptable modeling of edge information. Futhermore, our framework demonstrates how the default architecture of federated learning is optimal for user privacy protection in recommendation.

3   Methodology

In this section, we first present the definitions of our task, and then introduce the framework of our Fig. 1 method.

3.1   Problem Formulation

The objective is to calculate the user's interest score and then recommend the top N list of knowledge concepts given a target user and corresponding interactive data. This task is similar to rating predictions. Denote $U = \{u_1, u_2, ..., u_m\}$ and $C = \{c_1, c_2, ..., c_n\}$ as the set of users and knowledge concepts, where m is the number of users and n is the number of knowledge concepts, and denote U_i is the user set of client i. Given interactive data of a user u, a prediction function f is learned, and used to generate a recommend list of knowledge concepts C, such that $f : u \rightarrow \{c_i | c_i \in C, i < N\}$ [4].

3.2   Recommendation in Client

Our framework consists of two components: the client and the server. In each client, we configure the recommendation model, and in the server, we configure the parameter generator.

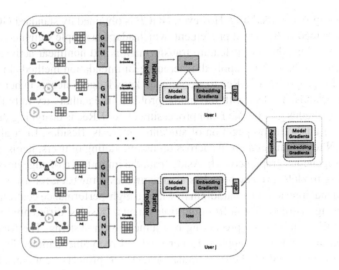

Fig. 1. The federated framework of our FedAttn approach.

Each client builds user and knowledge concepts embedding and GNN models with their subgraph and uploads training gradients to a centralized server. The central server is applied for managing the model learning process for multiple user clients by aggregating and transmitting gradients received from multiple user clients. After that, we'll examine their operation in detail. In this section, we first introduce the client part.

To protect user information from leaking, we set up our models and the courses to enroll records of users in local clients. First of all, there would be a feature extraction, which conducts low-dimensional representations of the entities by using data collected from online education. In this instance, we embed users and knowledge concepts by extracting content information as a content feature, analyzing various relationships between various types of entities, and producing concept features.

We model our online data as a heterogeneous information network $G = \{V, E\}$, which consists of an object set V and a edge set E. And we use this network to represent users, knowledge concepts, and the heterogeneous relationships between them. Since then, we first introduce two related concepts, neighboring users and neighboring knowledge concepts. Using the data of users online learning rolling records, there will be a user-click-knowledge matrix A, where its element $a_{i,j} \in 0, 1$ implies that a user i clicked a knowledge concept j during his learning activities. We denote the neighboring users $A^U = A \cdot A^T$, where A^T is the transpose of the matrix A. For instance, if two distinct users enrolled in similar courses corresponding to the same knowledge concepts, we bring an edge between two users [4]. And we denote the neighboring knowledge A^C concepts in a similar way. Using above relations we conduct two new networks G^U and G^C.

Then we conduct each client subgraph $G_i = \{V_i, E_i\}$, which consists the subset of object V_i and the subset of edge E_i. And we construct above meta-paths from client subgraph, and denote them as G_i^U and G_i^C. For the whole system, we assume

$V = V_1 \cup \ldots \cup V_p$, where p is the number of clients. To simulate the scenario with the greatest number of missing links, we assume that no data owners share overlapping nodes, namely $V_r \cap V_t = \phi$, for $\forall r, t \in [p]$ and $r \neq t$.

To protect the privacy of the user, each client stores its interactions locally, and the origin data never leaves the client. Any client C_r cannot directly retrieve $\epsilon \in V_t$ from another client C_t. Therefore, for an edge, it might exist a reality between C_r and C_t, but is not stored anywhere in the whole system.

Next, we employ a graph neural network to model the interactions between nodes on the local first-order subgraph using these embeddings. In our framework, we employ two distinct GNN networks: graph convolution network (GCN) and graph attention network (GAT). The GNN model outputs the concealed user and knowledge concept representations, which denoted as e_i^u, e_i^k. In GCN mode, we employ a multilayer graph neural network with the following propagation rule for each layer:

$$h^{l+1} = \sigma(Ph^l W^l) \tag{1}$$

where σ is denoted as ReLU function, P is a adjusted adjacency matrix, h^l is the l-layer representation of the entity and W^l is the shared trainable weight matrix for all the entities at l-layer. In GAT mode, we use one-head attention and adapt another graph neural network with a propagation rule shown below:

$$h^i = \sigma(\sum_{j \in \aleph_i} \alpha_{ij} W h_j) \tag{2}$$

where $\alpha_{ij} = softmax_j(e_{ij})$ is an normalized attention coefficient computed by the attention mechanism, $\aleph_i$ is the set of node i neighbours and h^i is the representation of node i.

Since then, we have obtained the representation of users and knowledge concepts using graph neural network. On the basis of their embedding, a rating predictor module is utilized to predict the ratings provided by the user and his interacted knowledge concepts. We adapt a method based on extended matrix factorization to recommend knowledge to users. Each client's training rating $r_{ui,k}$ is determined by the users clicking times on knowledge concepts. The following defines the rating of a user on a knowledge concept in each client:

$$\hat{r}_{ui,k} = x_{ui}^T y_k + bias \tag{3}$$

where $x_{ui} \in R^{D \times m_i}$ represents users' latent factors and $y_k \in R^{D \times n}$ represents concepts' latent factors. D is the number of latent factors. $Bias$ is a trainable tuning parameter. And m_i is the number of people in client i, n is the number of knowledge concepts. To compute the loss function, these predicted ratings are compared to the existing ratings locally stored on each client, and we define the loss function of our recommendation as follows:

$$L = min \frac{1}{m_i \times n} \sum_{u_i=1}^{m_i} \sum_{k=1}^{n} (r_{ui,k} - \hat{r}_{ui,k})^2 + L_2 \tag{4}$$

where $L_2 = \lambda(\|x_{ui}\|_2 + \|y_k\|_2 + \|bias\|_2)$ is a regularization term to this loss function. We then optimize the local minimum of the loss function using the AdamW algorithm.

3.3   Federated Setting in Server

Here's our framework's server. This section shows how the server coordinates clients and computes global gradients to update model and parameters. The server awakens a set number of clients each round to calculate gradients and send them. The server's aggregator combines local gradients to update global model parameters. Then, the server broadcasts the new model parameters to the next round of participants. Denote the parameter set in the j-th epoch as $\ominus_j = \ominus_{j-1} - \beta g_j$, where β is the learning rate and g_i is the aggregation gradient in epoch j. This procedure will be carried out iteratively until the model converges.

If we upload the GNN model and gradients for item embedding directly, there may be privacy concerns. First, the leakage of the GNN embedding model and rating predictor gradient may reveal real-world information because the gradient encodes user preferences and knowledge concepts. Second, the server can recover the entire user-item interaction history based on non-zero item embedding gradients. Thirdly, an attacker can contaminate model training by sending similar requests to upload fabricated data. To address the aforementioned issues, we apply a local differential privacy method to encrypt each client's gradient, the formula is presents as follows:

$$g_i = g_i + Laplace(0, \delta) \tag{5}$$

where δ is the strength of Laplacian noise, and the protected gradient g_i is the origin gradient in client i.

To address this issue that existing methods overlook the connection among participant clients, we present our attention-based gradient aggregation method, which aims to improve the presentation of subgraphs while maintaining privacy. Before the server aggregates each epoch gradient, it will take each participant gradient to calculate the parameters first. There would be an evaluation data set on the server. We repeat the rating prediction in this using their embedding model and calculate the weights that aggregate the gradient from each client. We present attention formula as follows:

$$\alpha_i = \frac{exp(\sigma(\eta e_i))}{\sum_{j \in C} exp(\sigma(\eta e_j))} \tag{6}$$

where e_i is the embedding of client i, η presents a attention vector and σ presents a nonlinear gating function.

From Algorithm 1, concluding our federated recommendation framework FedAttn in the following steps:

- Step 1: Clients download a model from the central server, which serves as the global shared model;
- Step 2: Clients commence training recommendation models using local data;
- Step 3: Enhancing the model by learning participant data and uploading gradient to a central server;
- Step 4: The procedure is repeated until convergence occurs.

Algorithm 1: FedAttn

Data: The private dataset of users, Participants p
Result: Our Knowledge concept recommendation model

1 **Procedure** Server-Update;
2 **foreach** *epoch m in global epoch G* **do**
3   **Procedure** Local-Update;
4   **while** *Local convergence is not true* **do**
5   Check global model first;
6   **foreach** *client i in participant Clients p* **do**
7              $e_i^u \leftarrow GNN(user)$;
8              $e_i^k \leftarrow GNN(knowledgeconcept)$;
9   **end**
10   Rating prediction;
11   Upload local model gradient to central server after LDP encryption;
12   **end**
13   Collecting gradients g_i from participant clients p;
14   Using G_i to conduct embedding model calculating embedding e_i;
15   Calculate each client attention weights α_i with their embedding e_i by Eq.6;
16   Aggregating Global Gradients $G_m = \sum_{u_i=1}^{p} \alpha_i g_i$;
17   Calculate the parameters by G_m;
18   Broadcast global model;
19 **end**

---

4 Experiment

4.1 Dataset and Experiment Setting

We use a real-world dataset [4] to conduct a series of experiments. The data was collected between January 1, 2018 and March 31, 2018. This dataset comprises 2,136 users, 937 knowledge concepts, and multiple types of corresponding relationships. Each instance in the training set or test set represents the click behavior history of a user. In order to evaluate the performance of the recommendation, we generated 100 prediction scores for each of the 99 randomly selected negative instances that were paired with each positive example. To simulate the actual situation of federated learning, we use a method that divides the data set into multiple shares. Each share contains a predetermined amount of data and proceeds in both IID and non-IID circumstances. In addition, we assume that eleven clients will collect this information. And the additional data would be stored as an evaluation data set on the server.

In our experiments, we employ GAT and GCN as GNN models and MF as the rating predictor. GNN has learned 256-dimensional and 64-dimensional user and knowledge concept embeddings and their hidden representations, respectively. 5000 local training epochs have occurred. There are 178 users within each client. There are thirty latent factors. In our experiments, we employed a metric known as root-mean-square error.

The Hit Ratio of topK items (HR@K), Normalized Discounted Cumulative Gain of topK items (NDCG@K), mean reciprocal rank (MRR), and the area under the curve of the receiver operating characteristic (ROC) are used to evaluate our experiments.

4.2 Detailed Analysis

Evaluation of Different Global Epoch. In this part, we investigate how the choice of global epoch affects the performance of FedAttn and compare it to FedAvg. More global epoch We conduct experiments with different numbers of global epoch (e.g., 10, 20, 30, 40) and find that 30 provides the best performance.

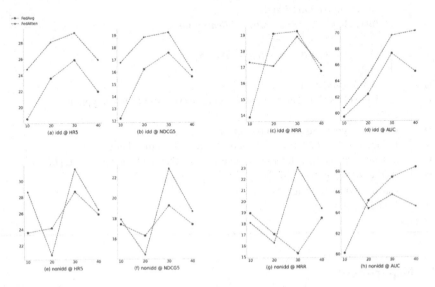

Fig. 2. Performance of different number of global epoch with GCN.

We investigate how GCN layers affect model performance. As shown in Fig. 2, it is evident that the model's performance varies as the number of global epochs increases or decreases. As shown in Fig. 3, we also investigate how GAT layers affect the performance of the model.

In addition, we can observe that GCN's performance is superior to GAT's, despite the fact that the performance increase is not readily apparent. This is likely due to the fact that modeling the high-order interactions between users and knowledge concepts can enhance the learning of user and knowledge concept representations, thereby increasing the precision of recommendation. Their comparison reveals a number of findings. First, compared with the different number of global epochs, GAT performance is more smooth, which indicates that the training is successful. In the case of IID data, there was a big fluctuation in FedAvg performance. And in the situation of non-IID data, there was a big fluctuation in FedAttn performance. Second, based on GCN and GAT, FedAttn slightly outperforms FedAvg. This may be because attention-based aggregation can model the significance of interactions between nodes more effectively, which is advantageous for user and knowledge concept modeling. Differently, FedAvg makes it difficult to compute the client weights due to the absence of subgraph relationships.

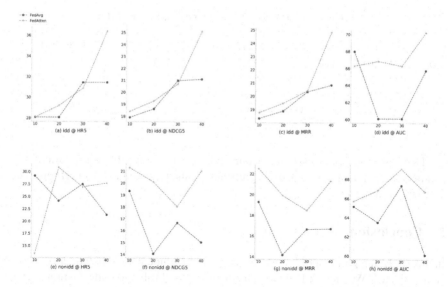

Fig. 3. Performance of different number of global epoch with GAT.

If a federated framework wishes to achieve a high level of performance in graph structure, it appears that a situation distinct from centralized training must be taken into consideration.

Table 1. Performance of different process with FedAvg.

		HR@1	HR@5	HR@10	HR@20	NDCG@5	NDCG@10	NDCG@20	MMR	AUC
IID	GCN	9.55	29.21	38.2	53.93	17.24	22.06	26.01	19.23	67.66
	GAT	10.11	31.46	39.89	51.12	20.98	23.7	26.52	20.34	60.11
nonIID	GCN	10.3	28.66	34.27	49.07	19.26	18.1	21.11	15.29	65.42
	GAT	6.18	27.53	38.2	50	16.67	20.05	24.12	16.62	67.35

Evaluation Between IID and NonIID Data. Identifying explicit and implicit coupling patterns embedded in mixed heterogeneous data from single/multiple sources is one of the most fundamental problems of learning from big data. The connection and heterogeneity of nonIID attributes are central to big data and the majority of real-world applications, as the data is nonIID. In this part of the experiments, we analyze how non-IID and IID data perfrom in FedAttn, and make a comparison with FedAvg as well. The result is shown in Table 1 and Table 2.

We validate both the efficacy of incorporating high-order information into user-concept graphs and the generalizability of our methodology. The GAT result of FedAvg in the IID situation is worse than the result in non-IID. Compared with the result of FedAttn, we find that FedAttn's performance is more stable no matter the IID or non-IID situation. Besides, FedAttn has a better performance in GAT.

Table 2. Performance of different process with FedAttn.

		HR@1	HR@5	HR@10	HR@20	NDCG@5	NDCG@10	NDCG@20	MMR	AUC
IID	GCN	10.67	25.84	39.33	60.11	19.57	21.92	27.2	18.9	69.42
	GAT	11.24	30.9	39.89	55.06	20.7	23.52	27.35	20.41	66.29
nonIID	GCN	12.92	31.46	41.57	53.93	22.87	26.36	29.21	23.04	67.73
	GAT	8.43	26.97	37.64	54.49	18.04	21.47	24.57	18.46	69.1

This research demonstrates that our approach is compatible with various GNN architectures. In addition, FedAttn significantly enhances the model's performance on a variety of indicators.

5   Conclusion

In this study, the problem of knowledge concept recommendation in federated learning is investigated. We present FedAttn, an attention-based subgraph information aggregation method that incorporates client gradients naturally. The advantage of our framework over existing methods, such as FedGNN, is the ability to extract the connections between subgraphs using the attention mechanism in gradients generation. We model the online education data with GNN to make more natural and intuitive use of context-rich information. With the assistance of attention-based aggregation, we are able to outperform FedAvg. The promising experimental results demonstrate that the proposed method is effective.

Future research will concentrate on expanding the scope of application. In federated learning, we will recommend learning paths based on the recommendation of knowledge concepts and improve performance in various ways.

References

1. Ammad-Ud-Din, M., et al.: Federated collaborative filtering for privacy-preserving personalized recommendation system. arXiv preprint arXiv:1901.09888 (2019)
2. Balu, R., Furon, T.: Differentially private matrix factorization using sketching techniques. In: Proceedings of the 4th ACM Workshop on Information Hiding and Multimedia Security, pp. 57–62 (2016)
3. Chai, D., Wang, L., Chen, K., Yang, Q.: Secure federated matrix factorization. IEEE Intell. Syst. **36**, 11–20 (2020)
4. Gong, J., et al.: Attentional graph convolutional networks for knowledge concept recommendation in moocs in a heterogeneous view. In: Proceedings of the 43rd International ACM SIGIR Conference on Research and Development in Information Retrieval, pp. 79–88 (2020)
5. Hamilton, W.L., Ying, R., Leskovec, J.: Inductive representation learning on large graphs. In: Proceedings of the 31st International Conference on Neural Information Processing Systems, pp. 1025–1035 (2017)
6. He, X., Deng, K., Wang, X., Li, Y., Zhang, Y., Wang, M.: Lightgcn: simplifying and powering graph convolution network for recommendation. In: Proceedings of the 43rd International ACM SIGIR conference on research and development in Information Retrieval, pp. 639–648 (2020)

7. He, X., Liao, L., Zhang, H., Nie, L., Hu, X., Chua, T.S.: Neural collaborative filtering. In: Proceedings of the 26th International Conference on World Wide Web, pp. 173–182 (2017)
8. Kipf, T.N., Welling, M.: Semi-supervised classification with graph convolutional networks. arXiv preprint arXiv:1609.02907 (2016)
9. Koren, Y., Bell, R., Volinsky, C.: Matrix factorization techniques for recommender systems. Computer **42**(8), 30–37 (2009)
10. Li, X., Wang, X., He, X., Chen, L., Xiao, J., Chua, T.S.: Hierarchical fashion graph network for personalized outfit recommendation. In: Proceedings of the 43rd International ACM SIGIR Conference on Research and Development in Information Retrieval, pp. 159–168 (2020)
11. McMahan, B., Moore, E., Ramage, D., Hampson, S., Arcas, B.A.: Communication-efficient learning of deep networks from decentralized data. In: Artificial intelligence and statistics, pp. 1273–1282. PMLR (2017)
12. Qi, T., Wu, F., Wu, C., Huang, Y., Xie, X.: Privacy-preserving news recommendation model learning. arXiv preprint arXiv:2003.09592 (2020)
13. Su, X., Khoshgoftaar, T.M.: A survey of collaborative filtering techniques. In: Advances in Artificial Intelligence, vol. 2009 (2009)
14. Veličković, P., Cucurull, G., Casanova, A., Romero, A., Lio, P., Bengio, Y.: Graph attention networks. arXiv preprint arXiv:1710.10903 (2017)
15. Wang, H., Zhao, M., Xie, X., Li, W., Guo, M.: Knowledge graph convolutional networks for recommender systems. corr abs/1904.12575 (2019). arXiv preprint arXiv:1904.12575
16. Wang, J., Huang, P., Zhao, H., Zhang, Z., Zhao, B., Lee, D.L.: Billion-scale commodity embedding for e-commerce recommendation in alibaba. In: Proceedings of the 24th ACM SIGKDD International Conference on Knowledge Discovery & Data Mining, pp. 839–848 (2018)
17. Wang, X., He, X., Wang, M., Feng, F., Chua, T.S.: Neural graph collaborative filtering. In: Proceedings of the 42nd International ACM SIGIR Conference on Research and Development in Information Retrieval, pp. 165–174 (2019)
18. Wu, C., Wu, F., Cao, Y., Huang, Y., Xie, X.: Fedgnn: federated graph neural network for privacy-preserving recommendation. arXiv preprint arXiv:2102.04925 (2021)
19. Ying, R., He, R., Chen, K., Eksombatchai, P., Hamilton, W.L., Leskovec, J.: Graph convolutional neural networks for web-scale recommender systems. In: Proceedings of the 24th ACM SIGKDD International Conference on Knowledge Discovery & Data Mining, pp. 974–983 (2018)
20. Zhao, S., Bharati, R., Borcea, C., Chen, Y.: Privacy-aware federated learning for page recommendation. In: 2020 IEEE International Conference on Big Data (Big Data), pp. 1071–1080. IEEE (2020)

RCPM: A Rule-Based Configurable Process Mining Method

Yang Gu[1], Yingrui Feng[1], Heng Huang[2], Yu Tian[3], and Jian Cao[1(✉)]

[1] Department of Computer Science and Engineering, Shanghai Jiao Tong University,
Shanghai, China
{gu_yang,cao-jian}@sjtu.edu.cn
[2] NeZha Smart Port and Shipping Technology (Shanghai) Co., Ltd., Shanghai, China
huangheng@nuzarsurf.com
[3] Shanghai International Port (Group) Co., Ltd., Shanghai, China

Abstract. Due to rapidly changing business environments, many enterprises produce a large number of process variants, whose traces are recorded in event logs. Unfortunately, most current algorithms try to discover a unified process model from event logs and fail to capture the variants of processes. In this paper, we propose a process mining algorithm that can discover configurable process models. As a basis for our approach, a rule-based configurable process (RCP) model is presented, which comprises two parts, i.e., a baseline process model and a set of ECA(Event-Condition-Action)-based configuration rules. Then, our RCP mining algorithm (RCPM) is aimed at discovering the RCP models from event logs. The RCPM is evaluated on synthetic and real-life event logs, and the experiment results prove its effectiveness.

Keywords: Process mining · Configurable process · Baseline model · ECA rule · Workflow

1 Introduction

Business process management (BPM) [1] can significantly improve efficiency and reduce costs, so it is widely adopted and applied in modern enterprises. Processes can be managed and automated by a business process management system (BPMS) [2] or coordinated by people. Regardless of how it is done, an increasing number of event logs are being recorded, driving the need for process mining [3]. Process mining aims to discover, monitor, and improve real processes by extracting knowledge from these logs [4,5], which can reduce the burden of designing process models or checking the compliance of actual behaviors with process models.

Nowadays, because of complex and rapidly changing environments, the success of enterprises increasingly depends on their ability to respond to changes. To gain a competitive advantage, enterprises have to modify their business processes continuously. So, an event log may contain information about multiple

Y. Sun et al. (Eds.): ChineseCSCW 2022, CCIS 1681, pp. 422–436, 2023.
https://doi.org/10.1007/978-981-99-2356-4_34

variants of the process [6,7]. However, traditional process mining can only mine a unified process model, which cannot represent these variants in the log very well. Mining configurable processes is necessary and presents many challenges.

The result of configurable process mining is a configurable process model. There are several configurable process model representations in the existing research, and they are mainly based on configuration options [8–12]. These representation schemes capture both commonalities and differences in multiple similar process variants, then convert the common parts into a reference model and transform the different parts into variation points [13]. Although these methods simplify the management of process variants to a certain extent, they have several shortcomings:

1. The process models and configuration elements are coupled together, making it more difficult to understand the models [14].
2. The configuration options provide too few functions, and the ability to modify the reference model is limited.
3. Variation points and configuration options are fixed and lack flexibility and scalability.

In this paper, we present a rule-based configuration process (RCP) model which consists of a baseline model and a set of configuration rules. The baseline model represents the commonalities of process variants and defines the logic of process execution. The configuration rules adopt the ECA (Event-Condition-Action) mechanism [15,16], and they can modify all the elements in the model. The RCP model decouples the baseline model and the configuration elements (rules), making it easier to understand. Moreover, the ECA-based configuration rule set is flexible and has strong extensibility, which can cope with unforeseen changes in the future.

More importantly, we propose a configurable process mining algorithm called RCPM. The idea of the approach is to compute the frequency of each branch in the process tree mined from an event log, then cut the branches with low frequency and transform them into ECA rules. Finally, we obtain a high-frequency baseline model and some low-frequency rules.

The contributions of this paper are as follows:

1. We propose the RCP model, which is a more flexible configuration process model.
2. A new configurable process mining algorithm RCPM is proposed to discover the RCP model efficiently.

The rest of this paper is arranged as follows: Sect. 2 introduces the related work on configurable process mining; Sect. 3 describes the representation of the RCP model; Sect. 4 presents our mining algorithm; Sect. 5 demonstrates the effectiveness of the RCPM through experiments; the last part summarizes the paper and presents suggestions for future work.

2   Related Work

Buijs et al. [17] compared four representative methods of configurable process mining, which covered the main existing solutions. In this paper, we divide these into the following two methods:

1. Multiple process variants are mined from the event logs and then merged to produce a configurable process.
2. A configurable process is discovered directly, making full use of behavior information in the event logs.

Li et al. [18–20] studied how to derive a reference model from process variants. The approach measures the distance between two process models using the number of modification operations (e.g., to add, delete, or move activities), and finds the "best" reference model whose average distance to each process variant is the smallest. The work in [21] focuses on configurable processes in the cloud service framework and proposes the concept of cross-organizational process mining, which aims to allow organizations to learn from each other and improve their respective processes. The work in [22] studies how to mine configurations, which can be combined into options for configurable processes, from a given process tree and event logs. The method discovers configuration elements according to the execution frequencies and orderings, which is similar to ours. The work in [14] makes a compromise between process variants and a configurable process. According to business driving strength and process similarity, some parts are integrated into a configurable process, and the other parts are modeled separately, finally forming a hybrid process model.

3   RCP Model: A Rule-based Configurable Process Model

In this section, we introduce the RCP model in detail using a formal notation system. The RCP model includes a baseline model and configurable rules. In theory, our baseline model can be expressed in any general process modeling language, such as Petri net, BPMN[1], BPEL and YAWL, etc. They are the core of the process.

Definition 1 (Baseline Model).   *The process model is a five-tuple $M = (i, o, T, G, F)$, where:*

- *i is a start node, which means the beginning of the process; o is an end node, which means the end of the process.*
- *T is a finite set of activity nodes, G is a finite set of logical nodes, $T \cap G = \emptyset$.*
- *$N = \{i, o\} \cup T \cup G$ are collectively called nodes.*
- *$F \subseteq N \times N$ is a set of control flows, connecting two nodes.*

---

[1] BPMN 2.0 specification http://www.omg.org/spec/BPMN/2.0/.

However, the baseline model can describe only a static process, unable to represent various process variants. We use ECA rules to add variability to the process. The ECA rules originated from research on active databases [23], simple but powerful. Each of them consists of three parts: event, condition, and action. When an event occurs, the system detects the event and judges whether the condition is met. If the result is true, it executes the corresponding action. Since modifying the process may require multiple actions, we propose the concept of an action group which is a list containing several actions.

Definition 2 (ECA Rule). *Each rule is a triple $R = (e, c, \mathscr{A})$, where:*

- *e is an event that triggers the rule, which occurs when the state of the process or activity changes. For example, if activity a ends, event Ended(a) is generated.*
- *c is a logical expression that can make a conditional judgment on the context of the process. If the result is true, execute the action group $\mathscr{A}$. The c can also be empty, and the action group $\mathscr{A}$ should be executed directly in this case.*
- *$\mathscr{A} = [A_1, A_2, A_3, ..., A_n]$ is an action group, which contains several actions, and these actions are executed in sequence. For the definition of action, see Definition 3.*

Definition 3 (Configuration Action). *Let M, M' be two sound baseline models, and let A be a configuration action, then: $M \to M'$ iff A is applicable to M and M' is the (sound) baseline model resulting from the application of A to M. The configuration action is defined as a triple $A = (op, tar, pos)$, where:*

- *op is an operation type of the action.*
- *tar is the activity operated by the action.*
- *pos is the position where the action occurs.*

The operations supported by configuration actions include insert activity, delete activity, move activity, and replace activity. For example, operation (insert, a, before(b)) inserts activity a before activity b; operation (delete, a, -), in turn, deletes activity a; operation (replace, a, b) replaces activity b with activity a. Certainly, configuration actions can support all operations that keep the baseline model sound in theory.

Definition 4 (RCP Model). *The RCP model is a two-tuple $P = (M, \mathscr{R})$, where:*

- *M is a baseline model, defined in Definition 1.*
- *$\mathscr{R}$ is a set of configuration rules, $R \in \mathscr{R}$, defined in Definition 2.*

For the same baseline model, different variants can be obtained by applying different rules. As shown in Fig. 1, rule 1 denotes adding activity e before activity b, and rule 2 denotes deleting activity b. Both the rules are applied to the same model, generating variant 1 and variant 2, respectively. In addition, the RCP model is more flexible and scalable. When requirements change, new configurable

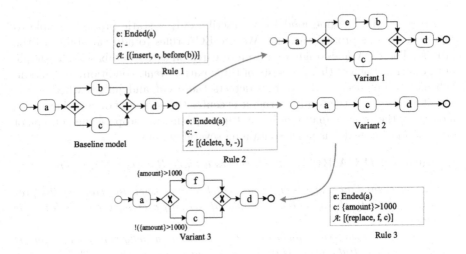

Fig. 1. The example of our RCP model to generate process variants

rules can be added to meet needs in the future. For variant 2 in Fig. 1, we can continue to apply rule 3, whose condition is not empty. The amount in the condition belongs to the context information in the process. When the amount is more than 1000, activity c is replaced by activity f. In turn, when the amount is not more than 1000, rule 3 is not executed and activity c remains. Finally, a new variant (variant 3) is obtained.

4 RCPM: RCP Model Mining Algorithm

4.1 Process Tree

The main idea of the RCPM is to prune a process tree to generate configuration rules, which is illustrated in this subsection. The process tree, a tree-structured process model, is defined as follows:

Definition 5 (Process Tree). *Let $\mathcal{T}$ be a set of activities, and $\tau \notin \mathcal{T}$, where τ is a silent activity, which is used to skip some activities in special scenarios. $\oplus = \{ \rightarrow, \times, \wedge, \circlearrowleft \}$ is the set of operators in the process tree. The recursive definition of the process tree is as follows [3]:*

- *If $t \in \mathcal{T} \cup \{\tau\}$, then $Q = t$ is a process tree.*
- *If $Q_1, Q_2, ..., Q_n$ are all process trees, $n \geqslant 1$, and $\oplus \in \{\rightarrow, \times, \wedge\}$, then $Q = \oplus(Q_1, Q_2, ..., Q_n)$ is a process tree.*
- *If Q_1, Q_2 are two process trees, then $Q = \circlearrowleft (Q_1, Q_2)$ is a process tree.*

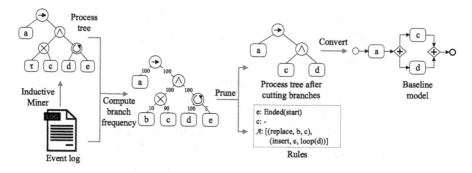

Fig. 2. The framework of our configurable process mining algorithm

From Definition 5, it can be seen that the leaf nodes of the process tree represent activities and the non-leaf nodes represent control operators $\oplus = \{$ $\rightarrow, \times, \wedge, \circlearrowright\}$, where, $\rightarrow$ is a sequential structure, $\times$ is a choice structure, $\wedge$ is a parallel structure, and $\circlearrowright$ is a loop structure. Under the loop operator, there are only two child nodes: the first is the do part, and the second is the redo part. For example, the process tree $\circlearrowright (a, b)$ may produce the following traces: $< a >$, $< a, b, a >$, $< a, b, a, b, a >$.

At present, there are several mining algorithms directly based on process trees, such as ETM (Evolutionary Tree Miner) [24], IM (Inductive Miner) [25], and so on. In this paper, we use the IM algorithm to obtain the process tree from the event log because it has an excellent performance.

4.2 Steps

The mining algorithm is divided into the following four steps, as shown in Fig. 2:

1. Use the IM algorithm to mine a process tree from the event log.
2. Compute the execution frequency of each branch in the process tree by analyzing the event log.
3. Prune the process tree and low-frequency branches in the choice, and transform loop structures into rules.
4. Convert the pruned process tree into a general baseline model.

The second and third steps are the key parts of this algorithm. The following two subsections detail the both steps.

4.3 Computing Branch Frequency

Since an event log only records the traces of executed activities, the frequency of τ cannot be obtained simply by counting the activities in the log. In this paper, we consider directly-follows relationships between activities, which can get the frequencies of general and silent activities. For convenience, we use the directly-follows matrix, which is defined as follows:

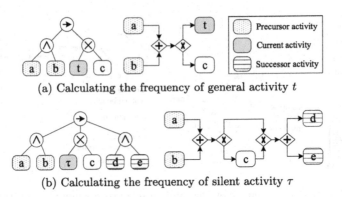

(a) Calculating the frequency of general activity t

(b) Calculating the frequency of silent activity τ

Fig. 3. Example of calculating the frequency of activities

Definition 6 (Directly-Follows Matrix). *L is an event log on $\mathscr{T}$, x and y are two activities in $\mathscr{T}$ ($x, y \in \mathscr{T}$), $|x >_L y|$ indicates the number of situations where y directly follows x in L, that is, $|x >_L y| = \sum_{\sigma \in L} L(\sigma) \times |\{1 \leqslant i \leqslant |\sigma| | \sigma(i) = x \wedge \sigma(i+1) = y\}|$ [3]. D is a square matrix representing the directly-follows relationships between activities, where $D[x, y] = |x >_L y|$.*

To describe how to obtain the frequencies of activities conveniently, we propose the concepts of the predecessor activity set and successor activity set. From the perspective of the process model, they analyze which activities may have a directly-follows relationship with activity t.

Definition 7 (Predecessor Activity Set $\bullet t$, Successor Activity Set $t \bullet$). *L_M is an universal set of possible traces generated by model M in theory, the predecessor activity set $\bullet t$ of an activity t ($t \in \mathscr{T}$) refers to the set of activities that t may directly follow in L_M, namely, $\bullet t = \{x \in \mathscr{T} || x >_{L_M} t| \geqslant 1\}$. Similarly, the successor activity set $t \bullet$ of an activity t refers to the set of activities that t may be followed directly in L_M, that is, $t \bullet = \{x \in \mathscr{T} || t >_{L_M} x| \geqslant 1\}$.*

Without considering the influence of arbitrary order execution brought by parallel structures as shown in Fig. 3a, the predecessor activity set $\bullet t = \{a, b\}$, then the frequency of t is $|a >_L t| + |b >_L t|$, that is, $\sum_{x \in \bullet t} |x >_L t|$. As shown in the Fig. 3b, the predecessor activity set $\bullet \tau = \{a, b\}$, the successor activity set $\tau \bullet = \{d, e\}$. Since the silent activity τ does not produce any activity traces, the activities in the predecessor activity set and successor activity set follow directly, so the frequency of the silent activity τ is $|a >_L d| + |a >_L e| + |b >_L d| + |b >_L e|$, namely, $\sum_{(x,y) \in \bullet \tau \times \tau \bullet} |x >_L y|$.

However, it is well known that activities on different branches of parallel structures are executed in any order, and the aforementioned method of calculating the frequency of the silent activity τ no longer works. Therefore, for each parallel branch, we remove the activities in the other branches from the log to eliminate the impact of parallel structures.

When it comes to logical nodes such as $\rightarrow$-node, $\times$-node, $\wedge$-node, and $\circlearrowright$-node, their frequencies are determined by that of their child nodes.

Algorithm 1. Computing the Frequency of a Process Tree

Require: *root*, a root node of the process tree Q
        L, an event log
Ensure: *freq*, the frequency of the process tree Q
 1: **function** *GetFrequency(root, L)*
 2:     $freq \leftarrow 0$
 3:     **if** $root \in \mathscr{T}$ **then**
 4:         **for all** tp such that $tp \in \bullet root$ **do**
 5:             $freq \leftarrow freq + |tp >_L root|$
 6:         **end for**
 7:     **else if** $root = \tau$ **then**
 8:         **for all** tp such that $tp \in \bullet root$ **do**
 9:             **for all** tn such that $tn \in root \bullet$ **do**
10:                 $freq \leftarrow freq + |tp >_L tn|$
11:             **end for**
12:         **end for**
13:     **else if** $root \in \{\rightarrow, \circlearrowleft\}$ **then**
14:         $fc \leftarrow children(root)[0]$
15:         $freq \leftarrow GetFrequency(fc, L)$
16:     **else if** $root = \times$ **then**
17:         **for all** c such that $c \in children(root)$ **do**
18:             $freq \leftarrow freq + GetFrequence(c, L)$
19:         **end for**
20:     **else if** $root = \wedge$ **then**
21:         **for all** c such that $c \in children(root)$ **do**
22:             $A \leftarrow activities(root) \setminus activities(c)$
23:             $L_p \leftarrow$ Remove A from L
24:             $freq \leftarrow max(freq, GetFrequence(c, L_p))$
25:         **end for**
26:     **end if**
27:     **return** $freq$
28: **end function**

- For the $\rightarrow$-node, since its children are executed in sequence, the frequency of each child node should be the same theoretically. In this paper, we take the frequency of the first child node.
- For the $\times$-node, each child node is mutually exclusive, so the frequency of this node is obtained by summing that of the child nodes.
- For the $\wedge$-node, in theory, the frequency of each child node is the same, and the maximum frequency of the child node is taken.
- For the $\circlearrowleft$-node, its execution frequency is determined by the do part.

The description of the algorithm to obtain branch execution frequency is shown in Algorithm 1.

4.4   Cutting Branches with Low Frequency

In the process tree, three logical nodes can produce branches: ×-node, ∧-node, and ○-node. Since the frequency of the branches under the ∧-node is the same, we only focus on ×- and ○-nodes.

For the ×-node, the child nodes are mutually exclusive, and only one branch is executed at a time. In theory, the average frequency of each branch is $freq_{\times-node}/n$, where $freq_{\times-node}$ is the frequency of the ×-node, and n is the total number of child nodes. In this paper, the average frequency is used as a reference standard, and branches with a frequency lower than a threshold are judged as low-frequency ones, as shown in Formula 1.

$$\frac{freq_c \times n}{freq_{\times-node}} < threshold \tag{1}$$

where $freq_c$ is the frequency of a child node.

For the ○-node, there are only two child nodes: do-node and redo-node. The do-node is executed every time, but the redo-node may not necessarily be executed. Therefore, we take the frequency of the do-node as a reference to judge whether the frequency of the redo-node is too low, as shown in Formula 2.

$$\frac{freq_{redo-node}}{freq_{do-node}} < threshold \tag{2}$$

where $freq_{do-node}$ is the execution frequency of the do-node, and $freq_{redo-node}$ is the execution frequency of the redo-node.

When cutting branches, the pruned branches should be converted into ECA rules. To keep the rules concise and clear, we cut out only those branches that contain a single activity or a sequence of activities. If we cut the branches that contain nodes such as ×-node, ∧-node, and ○-node, the generated rules would be more complicated, which reduces intelligibility. The conversion method is as follows:

- For the event, traverse the log to find out the event that must occur when the pruned activity occurs. If there is no such event, take the start node.
- For the condition, if the event logs contain data flow, we regard it as a binary classification of whether the pruned activity is executed or not and build a decision tree [26] to discover the relationship between the execution of the pruned activity and the context of the process. Then, we traverse the decision tree and select the leaf nodes that represent the existence of the pruned activity. According to the paths from the root node to these leaf nodes, we convert the decision tree into a symbolic representation, which can be used as a condition in the rule.
- For the action, in the ×-node, if branch b is pruned and only branch c is left, the ×-node should be removed, and the action is "(replace, b, c)" ($b \neq \tau$) or "(delete, c)" ($b = \tau$); otherwise, the action is "(insert, b, ×-node)". In the ○-node, after cutting the redo branch, the ○-node is definitely removed and the action is "(insert, $redo$-node, loop(do-node))".

5 Experiment

5.1 Experiment Setup

We used both synthetic and real-life event logs to conduct experiments. The RCPM algorithm are implemented in the ProM framework[2] [27]. The experiments are divided into two parts. The first part compares the RCPM with another configurable process mining algorithm, and the second is to analyze the influence of the threshold value on the mining results of the RCPM.

We selected six criteria to evaluate the results of the experiments, and they are fitness, precision, f-score, complexity, generalization, and the number of rules [3,28]. Fitness evaluates the ability of a model to replay the behaviors in the log, precision indicates the ability of a model to generate only the behaviors in the log, f-score is the harmonic mean of fitness and precision, complexity is measured by counting the total number of activities and gateways in the BPMN model, generalization examines the ability to generalize the example behavior seen in the event log, and the number of rules stands for the complexity of rules.

5.2 Method Comparison

In this section, we used synthetic event logs to compare our RCPM algorithm with the ETMc algorithm [17,29], which is a representative configurable process mining approach. The synthetic data set is from a travel application process, containing four scenarios, as shown in Fig. 4. Figure 4a shows the business trip application process which is applicable to ordinary employees of a branch company, and Fig. 4b shows the situation where managers in the branch company apply for a business trip. Figure 4c and Fig. 4d are the processes of the head company, corresponding to ordinary employees and managers respectively. The event logs with 5% noise were obtained by simulation, a total of 453 traces. In detail, the four scenarios account for 36.7%, 26.5%, 21.3%, and 15.5% separately. The reason why we chose this process is that the results mined are more understandable.

In fact, there are many differences between the RCPM and ETMc algorithm, which are as follows:

1. The configurable process mined by the RCPM uses configuration rules, while that discovered by the ETMc is based on configuration options. The configuration options only support blocking or hiding activities and degrading operators, while the rules can support more modification operations and are more flexible.
2. The RCPM aims to mine a baseline model and configuration rules from the event log in which the execution records of processes corresponding to multiple scenarios are mixed. In contrast, the goal of the ETMc is to mine a configurable process from various logs, and each log file corresponds to one scenario.

---

[2] http://www.promtools.org.

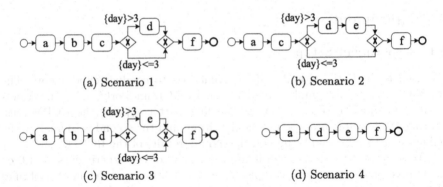

Fig. 4. Four scenarios of a business travel application process (a = travel application, b = review by department head, c = review by branch company head, d = review by business unit head, e = review by group president, f = inform applicant).

3. The ETMc is based on an evolutionary algorithm, which is time-consuming and can not be applied to large data sets.

Figure 5 shows the configurable processes mined by two different methods. In Fig. 5a, a baseline model and a set of ECA-rules are discovered by our RCPM algorithm. Each rule contains an execution condition that will be matched with different scenarios so that the rule can be executed to revise the baseline model. For example, compared with the baseline model, the process for scenario 1 has no activity e. Applying the rule in the upper left corner in Fig. 5a activity e can be deleted from the baseline model. Figure 5b is the result of the ETMc, which is a configurable process tree where each node can be blocked, hidden, or degraded. It can be seen that one activity may appear multiple times in the process tree, such as activity c and d. Thus the size of configurable process trees is often large, reducing their comprehensibility. The precision of ETMc is also lower (as shown in Table 1). In addition, the ETMc only mines a configuration point (in activity d) so that the configurability in this case is relatively weak. Table 1 shows the evaluation results of the two configurable processes over the event logs of each scenario. We can see that the results of the RCPM are generally better than those of the ETMc, because configuration rules are not limited to configurable points, and can be used to add, delete and move activities. They can even be used to change process structure. In particular, the precision and generalization of the RCPM are greatly improved.

5.3   Impact of Threshold Values

The RCPM determines whether to cut a branch in terms of the threshold, which has an important influence on the mining results. This section begins with the impact of different threshold values on each evaluation index.

In the experiment, we used the open-source BPI Challenge 2020 data set, which comes from the real reimbursement process of the Eindhoven University

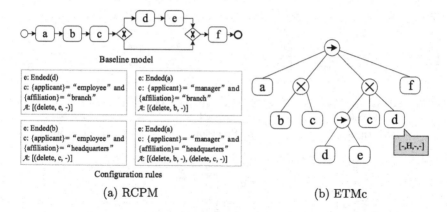

Fig. 5. Configurable process model discovered using the RCPM and ETMc

Table 1. The comparison results of the RCPM and ETMc.

	Method	Fitness	Precision	F-score	Generalization
Combined	RCPM	**0.992**	**0.944**	**0.966**	**0.860**
	ETMc	0.983	0.730	0.838	0.680
Scenario 1	RCPM	**1.000**	**1.000**	**1.000**	**0.921**
	ETMc	0.985	0.714	0.828	0.679
Scenario 2	RCPM	**1.000**	**1.000**	**1.000**	**0.895**
	ETMc	1.000	0.762	0.865	0.747
Scenario 3	RCPM	0.961	**0.857**	**0.906**	**0.794**
	ETMc	1.000	0.763	0.866	0.734
Scenario 4	RCPM	**1.000**	**0.833**	**0.909**	**0.745**
	ETMc	0.929	0.667	0.776	0.496

of Technology (TU/e), including data from 2017 (for only two departments) and 2018 (for the entire university). The range of the threshold is 0–1, and the step was 0.1. By setting different threshold values, the corresponding configurable processes were mined. The performances are shown in Fig. 6. It can be seen from Fig. 6e that when the threshold value is 0, the process tree is not pruned, and the number of rules is 0, which is equivalent to the result directly mined by the IM algorithm. As the threshold value increases, more branches are cut, and the number of rules increases. More importantly, the complexity of the model has been greatly reduced. In addition, as a result of the simplification of the model, the threshold value also has an influence on fitness and precision. That is, precision is improved but fitness decreases. Since the algorithm removes low-frequency branches, the baseline model retains the backbone of the process and fitness decreases slightly, i.e., it can still replay most of the behaviors in the log.

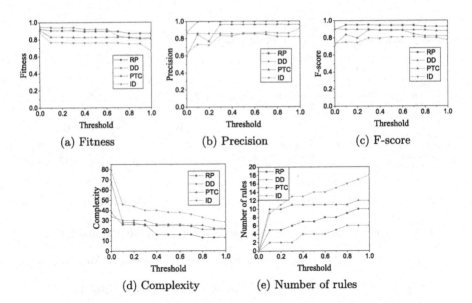

Fig. 6. The curve of each index of the process with different threshold values (RP = Request For Payment, DD = Domestic Declarations, PTC = Prepaid Travel Costs, ID = International Declarations)

6   Conclusion and Future Work

Since multiple process variants produce event logs in competitive environments, it is necessary to mine a configurable process. We introduce a new configurable process model (RCP model), which serves as the basis for configurable process model mining. The RCP model comprises two parts: a baseline model and an ECA-based configuration rule set. The baseline model is the core of the process and the rules are the supplement of the model. Then, we propose a configurable process mining algorithm called RCPM. The experiment results show that the RCPM can mine a baseline model with high frequency and configuration rules that can improve flexibility and scalability.

The RCPM can discover the RCP model from the event logs. However, the baseline model and the rules are not static. When the execution frequency of a rule continues to increase and exceeds the threshold value, it is necessary to incorporate it into the baseline model. Similarly, when the execution frequency of a branch in the model becomes too low, the branch will be cut and transformed into a rule. This will be our future work.

Acknowledgements. This work is partially supported by National Key Research and Development Plan(No. 2019YFB1704405), China National Science Foundation (Granted Number 62072301) and the program of Technology Innovation of the Science and Technology Commission of Shanghai Municipality (Granted No. 21511104700).

References

1. Van der Aalst, W.M.: Business process management: a comprehensive survey. Int. Schol. Res. Not. **2013** (2013)
2. Kir, H., Erdogan, N.: A knowledge-intensive adaptive business process management framework. Inf. Syst. **95**, 101639 (2021)
3. Aalst, W.M.P.: Process Mining: Data Science in Action. Springer, Heidelberg (2016). https://doi.org/10.1007/978-3-662-49851-4
4. van der Aalst, W., et al.: Process mining manifesto. In: Daniel, F., Barkaoui, K., Dustdar, S. (eds.) BPM 2011. LNBIP, vol. 99, pp. 169–194. Springer, Heidelberg (2012). https://doi.org/10.1007/978-3-642-28108-2_19
5. Pery, A., Rafiei, M., Simon, M., van der Aalst, W.M.P.: Trustworthy artificial intelligence and process mining: challenges and opportunities. In: Munoz-Gama, J., Lu, X. (eds.) ICPM 2021. LNBIP, vol. 433, pp. 395–407. Springer, Cham (2022). https://doi.org/10.1007/978-3-030-98581-3_29
6. Taymouri, F., La Rosa, M., Dumas, M., Maggi, F.M.: Business process variant analysis: survey and classification. Knowl.-Based Syst. **311**, 106557 (2020)
7. Augusto, A., Mendling, J., Vidgof, M., Wurm, B.: The connection between process complexity of event sequences and models discovered by process mining. Inf. Sci. **598**, 196–215 (2022)
8. Schunselaar, D.M.M., Verbeek, E., van der Aalst, W.M.P., Raijers, H.A.: Creating sound and reversible configurable process models using CoSeNets. In: Abramowicz, W., Kriksciuniene, D., Sakalauskas, V. (eds.) BIS 2012. LNBIP, vol. 117, pp. 24–35. Springer, Heidelberg (2012). https://doi.org/10.1007/978-3-642-30359-3_3
9. Huang, Y., Feng, Z., He, K., Huang, Y.: Ontology-based configuration for service-based business process model. In: 2013 IEEE International Conference on Services Computing, pp. 296–303. IEEE (2013)
10. Derguech, W., Bhiri, S., Curry, E.: Designing business capability-aware configurable process models. Inf. Syst. **72**, 77–94 (2017)
11. Ait Wakrime, A., Boubaker, S., Kallel, S., Gaaloul, W.: A SAT-based formal approach for verifying business process configuration. In: Younas, M., Awan, I., Benbernou, S. (eds.) Innovate-Data 2019. CCIS, vol. 1054, pp. 47–62. Springer, Cham (2019). https://doi.org/10.1007/978-3-030-27355-2_4
12. Khannat, A., Sbai, H., Kjiri, L.: Event logs pre-processing for configurable process discovery: ontology-based approach. In: 2020 6th IEEE Congress on Information Science and Technology (CiSt), pp. 139–144. IEEE (2021)
13. La Rosa, M., Dumas, M., Ter Hofstede, A.H., Mendling, J.: Configurable multi-perspective business process models. Inf. Syst. **36**(2), 313–340 (2011)
14. Milani, F., Dumas, M., Ahmed, N., Matulevičius, R.: Modelling families of business process variants: a decomposition driven method. Inf. Syst. **56**, 55–72 (2016)
15. Cacciagrano, D.R., et al.: Analysis and verification of ECA rules in intelligent environments. J. Ambient Intell. Smart Environ. **10**(3), 261–273 (2018)
16. Brockhoff, T., et al.: Process prediction with digital twins. In: 2021 ACM/IEEE International Conference on Model Driven Engineering Languages and Systems Companion (MODELS-C), pp. 182–187. IEEE (2021)
17. Buijs, J.C.A.M., van Dongen, B.F., van der Aalst, W.M.P.: Mining configurable process models from collections of event logs. In: Daniel, F., Wang, J., Weber, B. (eds.) BPM 2013. LNCS, vol. 8094, pp. 33–48. Springer, Heidelberg (2013). https://doi.org/10.1007/978-3-642-40176-3_5

18. Li, C., Reichert, M., Wombacher, A.: Discovering reference process models by mining process variants. In: 2008 IEEE International Conference on Web Services, pp. 45–53. IEEE (2008)

19. Li, C., Reichert, M., Wombacher, A.: Discovering reference models by mining process variants using a heuristic approach. In: Dayal, U., Eder, J., Koehler, J., Reijers, H.A. (eds.) BPM 2009. LNCS, vol. 5701, pp. 344–362. Springer, Heidelberg (2009). https://doi.org/10.1007/978-3-642-03848-8_23

20. Li, C., Reichert, M., Wombacher, A.: The minadept clustering approach for discovering reference process models out of process variants. Int. J. Cooper. Inf. Syste. 19(03n04), 159–203 (2010)

21. Aalst, W.M.P.: Configurable services in the cloud: supporting variability while enabling cross-organizational process mining. In: Meersman, R., Dillon, T., Herrero, P. (eds.) OTM 2010. LNCS, vol. 6426, pp. 8–25. Springer, Heidelberg (2010). https://doi.org/10.1007/978-3-642-16934-2_5

22. Oirschot, V.: Using trace clustering for configurable process discovery explained by event log data. Master's thesis, Eindhoven University of Technology (2014)

23. Liu, L., Özsu, M.T.: Encyclopedia of Database Systems, vol. 6. Springer, New York (2009). https://doi.org/10.1007/978-0-387-39940-9

24. Buijs, J.C., van Dongen, B.F., van der Aalst, W.M.: Quality dimensions in process discovery: the importance of fitness, precision, generalization and simplicity. Int. J. Cooper. Inf. Syst. 23(01), 1440001 (2014)

25. Leemans, S.J.J., Fahland, D., van der Aalst, W.M.P.: Discovering block-structured process models from event logs containing infrequent behaviour. In: Lohmann, N., Song, M., Wohed, P. (eds.) BPM 2013. LNBIP, vol. 171, pp. 66–78. Springer, Cham (2014). https://doi.org/10.1007/978-3-319-06257-0_6

26. Lee, C.S., Cheang, P.Y.S., Moslehpour, M.: Predictive analytics in business analytics: decision tree. Adv. Decis. Sci. 26(1), 1–29 (2022)

27. van Dongen, B.F., de Medeiros, A.K.A., Verbeek, H.M.W., Weijters, A.J.M.M., van der Aalst, W.M.P.: The ProM framework: a new era in process mining tool support. In: Ciardo, G., Darondeau, P. (eds.) ICATPN 2005. LNCS, vol. 3536, pp. 444–454. Springer, Heidelberg (2005). https://doi.org/10.1007/11494744_25

28. Buijs, J.C.A.M., van Dongen, B.F., van der Aalst, W.M.P.: On the role of fitness, precision, generalization and simplicity in process discovery. In: Meersman, R., et al. (eds.) OTM 2012. LNCS, vol. 7565, pp. 305–322. Springer, Heidelberg (2012). https://doi.org/10.1007/978-3-642-33606-5_19

29. Buijs, J.: Flexible evolutionary algorithms for mining structured process models. Unpublished Ph. D. Thesis, Eindhoven University of Technology, Netherland 220 (2014)

Popularity Bias Analysis of Recommendation Algorithm Based on ABM Simulation

Cizhou Yu[1,2], Dongsheng Li[1], Tun Lu[1,2(✉)], and Yichuan Jiang[3]

[1] School of Computer Science, Fudan University, Shanghai, China
{dongshengli,lutun}@fudan.edu.cn
[2] Shanghai Key Laboratory of Data Science, Fudan University, Shanghai, China
[3] School of Computer Science and Engineering, Southeast University, Nanjing, China
yjiang@seu.edu.cn

Abstract. With the rapid development of the Internet, recommendation algorithms are increasingly influencing consumers' decision-making. The issue of fairness in recommendation algorithms, especially popularity bias, is also becoming more and more heated. For the research on popularity bias, most existing methods cannot balance long-term interactivity and low cost. Using the ABM simulation method, various variables in the recommender system can be controlled, and the long-term impact of the continuous interaction between the recommender system and the user can be studied, especially the influence of popularity bias.

In this paper, we construct and implement a recommendation algorithm simulation framework based on ABM, and two algorithms, Item-Based CF and SVD, are respectively deployed on it to count item popularity distribution and Gini coefficient under multiple rounds of recommendation. The indicators, combined with the visualization results of user interest offset, are used to explore the popularity bias problem of two classic recommendation algorithms under multiple rounds of interaction. We also summarize the existing problems and make an outlook for future improvements.

Keywords: Recommender systems · Agent-based simulation · Popularity bias

1 Introduction

The problem of information overload brought about by the era of big data has accelerated the development of recommender systems. Although recommender systems alleviate information overload to a great extent, they also bring about fairness issues, such as popularity bias. In the recommendation system, there is a process of continuous interaction between the user and the recommendation algorithm (as shown in the following Fig. 1), and due to the design idea of the recommendation algorithm, the recommendation algorithm tends to recommend

Y. Sun et al. (Eds.): ChineseCSCW 2022, CCIS 1681, pp. 437–448, 2023.
https://doi.org/10.1007/978-981-99-2356-4_35

popular items to users, and more users' clicks and ratings will strengthen the popularity of these items, causing users to see narrow and convergent content, which damages the experience of a diverse user base. Himan et al. classified the biases existing in recommender systems and current improvement methods, and defined popularity bias: Popular items are recommended even more frequently than their popularity would warrant [1].

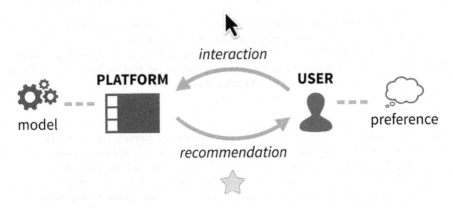

Fig. 1. Schematic diagram of recommendation algorithm and user interaction [2]

In recent years, scholars have used different methods to study and analyze the popularity bias brought by recommendation algorithms. The research methods mainly include static dataset-based methods and multi-round interaction-based methods.

1.1　Methods Based on Static Datasets

The popularity bias of recommendation algorithm was confirmed by Himan [3] et al. in 2019 with experiments based on MovieLens static dataset. In 2020, Himan [1], on the basis of confirming the existence of popularity bias, further analyzed the popularity bias caused by recommendation algorithms based on two static datasets, and analyzed the impact of popularity bias from the perspectives of users and content providers, respectively. Dietmar [4] et al. analyzed the popularity bias of various recommendation algorithms under static large data sets, and compared these recommendation algorithms from different perspectives including accuracy, directory coverage, etc.

However, with methods based on static datasets we cannot study the long-term impact of the recommendation algorithm under the constant interaction with users. Hence, multi-round interaction based approach was born.

1.2　Method Based on Multi-round Interaction

In recent years, some scholars have applied the ABM(Agent-Based Modeling, multi-agent modeling) method to the research of recommendation systems, using each agent in it to simulate human behavior, so as to control microscopic variables and observe macroscopic evolution.

Meizi [5] et al. used the agent-based simulation model framework proposed by Zhang et al. [6] to study the influence of the inherent bias in the system and the bias caused by external disturbance on the preference bias. MLADENOV [7] and others in the Google research team used the multi-agent-based simulation framework RecSim NG to implement the "short-sighted strategy" recommendation algorithm and observed its long-term impact, and found that the "short-sighted" recommendation algorithm would lead to item diversity decrease and increase in popularity bias.

To sum up, existing studies have used the ABM modeling method to analyze the long-term impact of recommendation bias on recommendation systems [5], and the long-term impact of a specific recommendation algorithm on popularity bias [8]. However, for the use of the ABM simulation method to study the popularity bias caused by the classic and commonly used recommendation algorithms, there is no relevant research and conclusion with great influence.

This paper uses the ABM modeling method to simulate the interaction between the two recommendation algorithms and users, and analyzes the long-term change process of the user's overall state and item popularity under the long-term interaction between users and the recommendation system, so as to obtain the evolutionary process of recommendation algorithm popularity bias. Our main contributions and innovations are: (1) Design and implement an ABM-based recommendation system simulation framework; (2) On the simulation framework, two classic recommendation algorithms, Item-Based CF and SVD, are deployed, and based on the MovieLens dataset, the evolution process of indicators such as item popularity and Gini coefficient under the recommendation system and long-term user interaction is calculated; (3) In the simulation framework, the long-term impact of recommendation algorithm on user interest is discussed qualitatively and quantitatively, and the evolution process of user interest vector is visualized.

2   Related Work

ABM Simulation Recommender System. Zhang [9] et al. proposed a multi-agent-based simulation framework, which includes three parts: item population, user population and recommender engine, and studied the Item-Based CF algorithm in the datasets Netflix and Yahoo! Long-term impact on Music. Meizi [5] et al. used the agent-based simulation framework proposed by Zhang et al. [9] to build a simulated recommendation system, and studied the influence of the inherent bias and external disturbance bias on popularity bias influences. MLADENOV [7] and others in the Google team developed the RecSim NG framework based on multi-agent and probabilistic perspectives, and used this framework to simulate the recommendation environment, optimize the recommendation algorithm and other tasks.

2.1   Recommendation Algorithm Popularity Bias

Himan and Mansoury et al. define the popularity bias of recommendation algorithms: a popular item is recommended even more times than its popularity warrants [1]. It has been found that there is a popularity bias problem in many recommender systems [10–12], so that the popularity distribution of items shows an obvious long-tailed distribution trend. In recent years, more and more scholars have attempted to analyze and calculate the popularity bias of recommendation algorithms. In 2019, Himan [3] and others confirmed the existence of popularity bias with experiments on static data sets. In 2020, they further analyzed the reasons for popularity bias caused by recommendation algorithms [1].

3   Construction of ABM-Based Recommendation System Simulation Framework

3.1   System Build

Based on the idea of multi-agent simulation, this paper constructs a simulation framework including user agent, item set, recommendation engine and recommendation environment, as shown in Fig. 2. The specific design of each part is as follows.

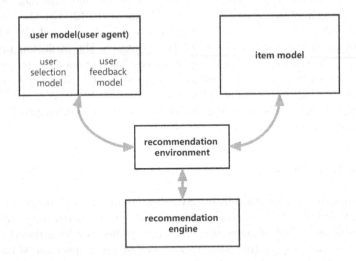

Fig. 2. Recommendation system simulation framework diagram

User Agent. Considering the behavior of real users on a recommendation platform, user behavior is naturally divided into two sub-models: the selection model describes how the user selects an item from the recommended list, and the feedback model determines how the user evaluates (i.e., scores) after interacting with the item.

Selection model: This paper adopts a ranking model (as shown in the Formula 1). The user's probability of selecting an item decreases as the item's ranking in the recommendation list decreases.

$$M_s^{ranked}(v) = (\alpha - 1) \cdot \alpha^{-i}, \alpha > 1 \tag{1}$$

Feedback model: simulate the real-world user rating situation, this paper adopts the real feedback model (as shown in the Formula 2). The user's evaluation of an item is related to his satisfaction with the item, and the satisfaction can be determined by the inner product of the user's interest vector and the item's feature vector. However, according to studies by Cosley [13] et al. and Amatriain [14] et al., users' ratings are often not completely consistent with the above; studies have shown that users tend to give ratings based on a Gaussian distribution [15], and more than 90% inconsistent bias ±1 [9]. Therefore, a Gaussian noise factor (mean 0, variance 1.0) is introduced in the true feedback model to simulate real-world rating bias.

$$M_f^{real}(v) = interest_u \cdot content_i + N(0,1) \tag{2}$$

After the user interacts with the item, the interest vector is offset according to the quality of the item and the degree of preference for the item. The offset formula is shown in the Formula 3, where θ is the user's interest vector decay term, $itemInfluence_u$ is the sensitivity of the user's interest vector to the item, and $feedback_{ui}$ is the user's rating on the item.

$$interest_u = (1 - \theta) \cdot interest_u + itemInfluence_u \cdot feedback_{ui} \cdot content_i \tag{3}$$

Item Set. The properties of the item itself are: item number, feature vector, and item quality.

Each item is modeled as an item object in the simulation framework. Each item object needs to maintain its own number, feature vector, and mass. When the recommendation engine needs to do the recommendation task, the recommendation environment is responsible for counting the item number list and passing it to the recommendation engine.

Recommendation Engine. Two classical recommendation algorithms are used: Item-Based CF algorithm and SVD algorithm. The recommendation engine is responsible for receiving the user's historical rating matrix for items, the list of users who are still active in the system, and the item list, generating a fixed-length recommendation list for each user with a specific recommendation algorithm, and predicting ratings from high to low. The order is sorted, and the recommendation list is handed over to the recommendation environment.

Recommendation Environment. The recommendation environment collects the list of users who are still active in the system, the list of items in the system, and submits it to the recommendation engine together with the user's rating of the item; distributes the recommendation engine's recommendation result to each user; and records user consumption and ratings is added to the scoring matrix.

3.2   System Operation Details

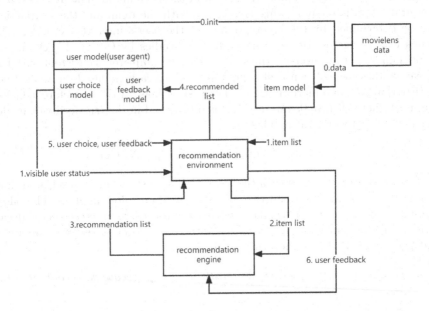

Fig. 3. Framework operation flow chart

The running process of the framework is shown in Fig. 3. Specifically, it can be disassembled into the following steps:

(1) Initialization: Read the movie list of the MovieLens dataset, obtain the item number of the item, and randomly generate the item quality; read the rating matrix of the MovieLens dataset, convert it into the user-item interaction matrix, use SVD to decompose to get the item's the feature vector and the user's interest vector, obtain the user number from the rating matrix, and specify the user selection model and user feedback model at the same time; specify the algorithm type of the recommendation engine and all other hyperparameters.

(2) The recommendation environment obtains the visible part of the user's state and passes it to the recommendation engine together with the visible item information.

(3) The recommendation engine uses the score matrix to generate a fixed number of recommendation lists for each user, and sorts them from high to low by the predicted score;

(4) The recommendation environment distributes the recommendation list to the corresponding users. Each user selects and consumes items according to his own user selection model, user feedback model and his own state; and then according to the quality of the item, his preference for the item and his own sensitivity to the item, the user's interest vector is offset;

(5) The recommendation environment records the selection and rating of items by all users, and incorporates the new rating into the rating matrix. Then go to 2.

Generally speaking, the experiment starts with several rounds of cold start (set the recommendation engine as a random recommendation algorithm). After collecting a sufficient size of the score matrix (so that the subsequent recommendation algorithm has a better effect), set the recommendation engine to other recommendation algorithms such as Item-Based CF algorithm and SVD algorithm.

4   Experimental Validation and Data Analysis

4.1   Experimental Tools and Environment

In experiment, we used software environment of 64-bit Windows10 operating system and virtual python3.8 environment based on Anaconda, with hardware environment of Intel Core i7 CPU and GeForce RTX 2060 graphics card.

4.2   Metrics and Parameter Setting

We use two popularity-related metrics: item popularity and Gini coefficient to measure the popularity bias of recommendation algorithms.

The formula for calculating item popularity is shown in the Formula 4. Among them, $\mathbb{I}$ represents the indicator function.

$$itemPopularity = \sum_{u \in U} \mathbb{I}\left[i \in D_u(t)\right] \tag{4}$$

Gini coefficient (as shown in the Formula 5) is a commonly used indicator to measure distribution differences. Among them, $RP(i,t)$ represents the rank of the number of times the item i is consumed until time t, and $D_u(t)$ represents the set of items consumed by user u until time t. The value of the Gini coefficient is between 0 and 1. The closer it is to 0, the more balanced the distribution is; on the contrary, the closer it is to 1, the more unbalanced the distribution is. We can think that the larger the Gini coefficient, the more obvious the popularity bias phenomenon. There have been many precedents [2,16] to measure the popularity bias of the Gini coefficient user recommendation algorithm, and it has been recognized by everyone. And the hyperparameters used in experiment are shown in Table 1.

$$G(t) = \frac{\sum_{i \in I}(2 \cdot RP(i,t) - |I| - 1)\sum_{u \in U}\mathbb{I}\left[i \in D_u(t)\right]}{|I|\sum_{i \in I}\sum_{u \in U}\mathbb{I}\left[i \in D_u(t)\right]} \tag{5}$$

Table 1. System Hyperparameter Settings

algorithm	dataset	number of recommended items	initial user number	user interest item feature vector dimension	cold-start algorithm	cold-start round
Item-Based CF	MovieLens 1M	10	610	100	random	100
SVD	MovieLens 1M	10	610	100	random	100

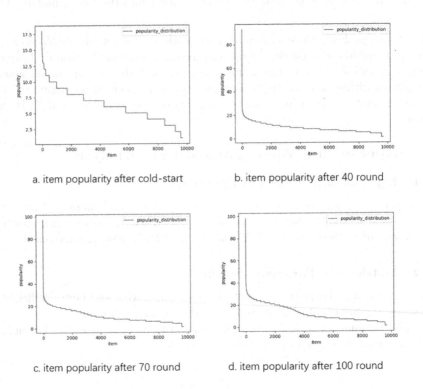

a. item popularity after cold-start   b. item popularity after 40 round

c. item popularity after 70 round   d. item popularity after 100 round

Fig. 4. Evolution of item popularity under Item-Based CF algorithm

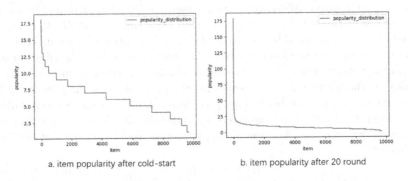

a. item popularity after cold-start   b. item popularity after 20 round

Fig. 5. The evolution process of item popularity under SVD algorithm

4.3   Popularity Bias Analysis of Two Algorithms

Item Popularity Statistics. Figure 4 and Fig. 5 show the change of item popularity with recommendation rounds under Item-Based CF algorithm and SVD algorithm.

It can be seen that with the continuous interaction between users and the two algorithms, the popularity of items presents a long-tailed distribution, and in a longer time span, this distribution imbalance has not been alleviated.

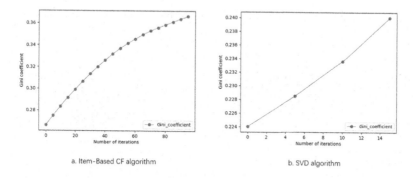

a. Item-Based CF algorithm   b. SVD algorithm

Fig. 6. The evolution process of Gini coefficient under two algorithms

Gini Coefficient Statistics. Figure 6 show the variation of Gini coefficient with recommendation rounds under Item-Based CF algorithm and SVD algorithm. The results show that as the number of recommendation rounds increases, the Gini coefficient is closer to 1; it means that under multiple rounds of interaction between the user and the recommendation system, the distribution of clicked items becomes more and more unbalanced.

Popularity Bias Analysis. Figure 4 and Fig. 5, after using the Item-Based CF algorithm and the SVD algorithm for recommendation, the item popularity distribution presents an obvious long-tailed distribution. Combining Fig. 6, the Gini coefficient keeps increasing, we can infer that under the long-term interaction between users and the recommendation algorithm, popular items are clicked more and more times. At the same time, unpopular items lack attention.

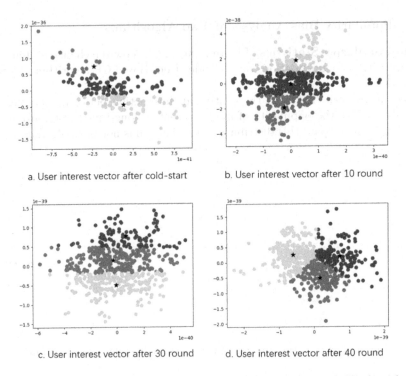

a. User interest vector after cold-start

b. User interest vector after 10 round

c. User interest vector after 30 round

d. User interest vector after 40 round

Fig. 7. Evolution process of user interest vector under Item-Based CF algorithm

User Interest Vector Visualization. Furthermore, we visualizes the changing process of user feature vector. Since the user feature vector is a high-dimensional vector, we uses the t-SNE dimensionality reduction method to reduce the 100-dimensional user interest vector to two-dimensional, and then uses the K-Means method of k = 3 for clustering. The result is shown in the Fig. 7 and Fig. 8. The different colors in the figure represent different categories in the K-Means clustering results, each dot represents a user, and the black five-pointed star represents the cluster center point.

From Fig. 7 and Fig. 8, with the increase of recommendation rounds, the two-dimensional data distribution is more dense; and according to the t-SNE principle, the distribution of low-dimensional can reflect the density of high-dimensional data to a certain extent. Therefore, it is concluded that as the number of recommendation rounds increases, the distribution of user interest vectors gradually becomes denser, that is, users tend to be homogeneous.

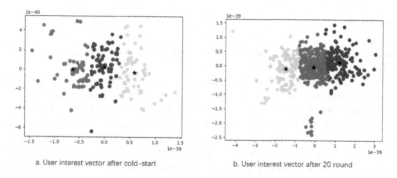

a. User interest vector after cold-start   b. User interest vector after 20 round

Fig. 8. Evolution process of user interest vector under SVD algorithm

5   Summary and Outlook

The specific work of this paper is as follows:

(1) Constructed and implemented an ABM-based recommendation simulation framework, which mainly includes user agent, recommendation engine, item list and interactive environment;
(2) Deploy Item-Based CF and SVD algorithms respectively on this framework, load the MovieLens dataset to initialize the system, and count the changes of various popularity-related indicators such as item popularity distribution and Gini coefficient under multiple rounds of recommendation, and visualize the user interest offset by using t-SNE dimensionality reduction method and K-Means clustering method;
(3) Based on the above indicators, demonstrate the popularity bias problem brought by the two algorithms.

There has also been a lot of research on reinforcement learning recommendation algorithms on simulated systems. Using the reinforcement learning method on the simulated system, it is possible to learn a recommendation algorithm that achieves a better solution under the long-term interaction between the user and the recommendation algorithm. If the recommendation accuracy and recommendation fairness are included in the reinforcement learning goal, the accuracy and fairness can be taken into account in recommendation algorithm.

Acknowledgements. This work was supported by the National Natural Science Foundation of China (NSFC) under Grant No. 62172106 and 62076060, in part by the Key Research and Development Program of Jiangsu Province of China under Grant BE2022157, and in part by the Defense Industrial Technology Development Program under Grant JCKY2021214B002.

References

1. Abdollahpouri, H., Mansoury, M.: Multi-sided exposure bias in recommendation. arXiv preprint arXiv:2006.15772 (2020)
2. Chaney, A.J., Stewart, B.M., Engelhardt, B.E.: How algorithmic confounding in recommendation systems increases homogeneity and decreases utility. In: Proceedings of the 12th ACM Conference on Recommender Systems, pp. 224–232 (2018)
3. Abdollahpouri, H., Mansoury, M., Burke, R., Mobasher, B.: The unfairness of popularity bias in recommendation. arXiv preprint arXiv:1907.13286 (2019)
4. Jannach, D., Lerche, L., Gedikli, F., Bonnin, G.: What recommenders recommend – an analysis of accuracy, popularity, and sales diversity effects. In: Carberry, S., Weibelzahl, S., Micarelli, A., Semeraro, G. (eds.) UMAP 2013. LNCS, vol. 7899, pp. 25–37. Springer, Heidelberg (2013). https://doi.org/10.1007/978-3-642-38844-6_3
5. Zhou, M., Zhang, J., Adomavicius, G.: Longitudinal impact of preference biases on recommender systems' performance. Kelley School of Business Research Paper (2021-10) (2021)
6. Adomavicius, G., Jannach, D., Leitner, S., Zhang, J.: Understanding longitudinal dynamics of recommender systems with agent-based modeling and simulation. arXiv preprint arXiv:2108.11068 (2021)
7. Mladenov, M., et al.: RecSim NG: toward principled uncertainty modeling for recommender ecosystems. arXiv preprint arXiv:2103.08057 (2021)
8. Chen, J., Dong, H., Wang, X., Feng, F., Wang, M., He, X.: Bias and debias in recommender system: a survey and future directions. arXiv preprint arXiv:2010.03240 (2020)
9. Zhang, J., Adomavicius, G., Gupta, A., Ketter, W.: Consumption and performance: Understanding longitudinal dynamics of recommender systems via an agent-based simulation framework. Inf. Syst. Res. 31(1), 76–101 (2020)
10. Abdollahpouri, H., Burke, R., Mobasher, B.: Managing popularity bias in recommender systems with personalized re-ranking. In: The Thirty-Second International Flairs Conference (2019)
11. Bellogín, A., Castells, P., Cantador, I.: Statistical biases in information retrieval metrics for recommender systems. Inf. Retrieval J. 20(6), 606–634 (2017)
12. Channamsetty, S., Ekstrand, M.D.: Recommender response to diversity and popularity bias in user profiles. In: The Thirtieth International Flairs Conference (2017)
13. Cosley, D., Lam, S.K., Albert, I., Konstan, J.A., Riedl, J.: Is seeing believing? How recommender system interfaces affect users' opinions. In: Proceedings of the SIGCHI Conference on Human Factors in Computing Systems, pp. 585–592 (2003)
14. Amatriain, X., Pujol, J.M., Oliver, N.: I like it... I like it not: evaluating user ratings noise in recommender systems. In: Houben, G.-J., McCalla, G., Pianesi, F., Zancanaro, M. (eds.) UMAP 2009. LNCS, vol. 5535, pp. 247–258. Springer, Heidelberg (2009). https://doi.org/10.1007/978-3-642-02247-0_24
15. Pennock, D.M., Horvitz, E.J., Lawrence, S., Giles, C.L.: Collaborative filtering by personality diagnosis: a hybrid memory-and model-based approach. arXiv preprint arXiv:1301.3885 (2013)
16. Jannach, D., Lerche, L., Kamehkhosh, I., Jugovac, M.: What recommenders recommend: an analysis of recommendation biases and possible countermeasures. User Model. User-Adap. Inter. 25(5), 427–491 (2015). https://doi.org/10.1007/s11257-015-9165-3

Cloud-Edge Collaborative Task Scheduling Mechanism Based on Improved Parameter Adaptation Particle Swarm Optimization Algorithm

Haoyang Zeng, Ningjiang Chen[✉], Wanting Li, and Siyu Yu

School of Computer, Electronics and Information, Guangxi University, Nanning 530004, China
chnj@gxu.edu.cn

Abstract. Cloud-edge collaboration can combine large-scale cloud and edge resources to achieve efficient service providing. However, a lot of tasks generated by cloud-edge scenario may cause application service latency and impact Quality of Service (QoS). Thus, efficient task scheduling mechanism is required to achieve load balancing and reduce service latency. The heterogeneity and geographical distribution of edge nodes did not be considered by most existed approaches. The traditional scheduling strategy based on optimization algorithm is easy to fall into local optimization, so as to eventually produce an unsatisfactory scheduling scheme, just like the PSO algorithm (Particle Swarm Optimization). In this paper, a parameter adaptive particle swarm optimization algorithm (PAPSO) is proposed to achieve efficient task scheduling. Its inertia coefficient, local optimal learning factor and global optimal learning factor are dynamically changed in the iterative process, and the velocity update of particles is more suitable for the needs of different stages of iteration, so that the algorithm has better effect on the global search ability. A cloud-edge collaborative task scheduling strategy is designed based on PAPSO. The simulation results show that the proposed method reduces the average time of solving the optimal scheduling strategy by around 10% than the traditional scheduling schemes.

Keywords: Cloud-Edge collaboration · Task scheduling · Particle swarm optimization algorithm

1 Introduction

Cloud-edge collaboration, as a fresh computing paradigm [1], can provide great Quality of Service (QoS) by simultaneously utilizing cloud resources and edge resources to support application tasks [2]. In the cloud-edge collaboration model scenario, edge computing is primarily in charge of processing latency-sensitive data in real-time [3]. Cloud computing handles high-density, high-real-time work [4], and manages the entire life cycle of edge programs [5]. As a result, how to reasonably schedule tasks at cloud nodes and edge nodes become the key to reduce service latency and improve QoS by using cloud-edge collaboration [6].

© The Author(s), under exclusive license to Springer Nature Singapore Pte Ltd. 2023
Y. Sun et al. (Eds.): ChineseCSCW 2022, CCIS 1681, pp. 449–464, 2023.
https://doi.org/10.1007/978-981-99-2356-4_36

To ensure that all users' average completion times are as quick as possible according to the resources pre-allocated on the cloud, main scheduling approaches include heuristic, game theory, and optimization algorithm. For example, HODA [7] is an offloading heuristic judgment process that is semi-distributed. Which can maximize system utility. NE [8] is a wireless computing offloading game which can achieve efficient computing offloading. Furthermore, since the particle swarm optimization algorithm has obvious advantages in solving large-scale task scheduling and combinatorial optimization problems, it has been widely used in task scheduling strategy design [9, 10]. However, the PSO algorithm is also very sensitive to the quality of the initial population, and at the same time, it may drop into the local optimal solution due to the quick convergence speed. Finding the best task scheduling method for the collaborative cloud-edge scenario is insufficient. In summary, scheduling strategies based on traditional optimization algorithm are susceptible to local optimum, the pursuit of global optimality and fast response is still challenging in task scheduling under edge-cloud collaboration.

Based on the particle swarm optimization algorithm, in this paper, a parameter adaptive particle swarm optimization algorithm (PAPSO) is proposed to improve the particle swarm optimization algorithm. PAPSO can enable the inertia coefficient, local and global optimal learning factors to be dynamically adapted during iterative process. In addition, compared with the PSO algorithm, PAPSO algorithm can fully explore the entire search space at the beginning of the iteration and break free of restrictions of the local optimal solution toward the end of the iteration. Through examination of the outcomes of the experiment, the effectiveness of the PAPSO algorithm proposed in this paper when seeking a scheduling scheme that takes the least time to do the assignment in the task scheduling problem in the cloud-edge collaboration scenario, it enables a more adequate search of the search space. Carrying out a more sufficient search can well enhance the PSO scheduling algorithm's flaw that it is simple to settle for the local optimal solution and has a faster optimization speed and optimization accuracy.

To summarize, the following are the paper's contributions:

(1) PAPSO is proposed to improve PSO to avoid falling into the local optimal solution and improve the optimization speed and accuracy. And a edge-cloud collaborative task scheduling mechanism is designed based on the PAPSO, reducing the completion time of tasks, thereby reducing the latency of application services.

(2) Numerous experiments have been carried out to evaluate the ability to find the global optimum of PAPSO, and simulation experiments on ClousSim demonstrate the potential for improved performance of the PAPSO-based task scheduling technique in the cloud-edge collaborative scenario, and its task completion time, optimization speed and global space search ability are better.

2   The Problem's Description and the Modeling

The task's time to completion is one of the most important factors considered in the cloud-edge collaboration scenario's issue with task scheduling [11]. This paper studies the task scheduling problem in the edge-cloud collaboration scenario, aiming to speed up the completion of the work in this scenario, and proposes a cloud-edge collaboration task scheduling model.

2.1 Problem Description

Addressing the issue of task scheduling under cloud-edge collaboration, we only studies how the data center allocates many cloud tasks sent to the edge nodes that are less than the amount of tasks necessary to complete the tasks so that the task completion time is as short as possible and ignores the specific edge nodes for the time being. Temporarily ignoring the number of hotspots and related properties in specific edge nodes. The computing power of edge nodes is unified and abstracted into the computing power of virtual machines and virtual machines are used to represent edge nodes. To understand the content of this article, we need to know:

(1) Each task is the smallest unit and cannot be further divided, and there is no relationship between tasks and tasks, and they exist independently.
(2) To investigate the efficiency of the scheduling strategy, the number of jobs in this paper will be substantially more than the number of virtual machines, and each virtual machine can only process one task at a time, which can focus on the effect of task scheduling on tasks. Impact on completion time.

For several tasks, a task set with n tasks will be created, which is expressed as follows:

$$Tasks = \{t1, t2 \ldots tn\} \tag{1}$$

Each task has information such as its task length. The task length is a parameter for calculating the completion time of the task. It is imported through a text file and used as a parameter of the fitness function of the scheduling algorithm.

Tasks will be assigned to run on edge nodes, so a set of m virtual machines will be created to represent edge nodes, as follows:

$$VM = \{vm1, vm2 \ldots vmm\} \tag{2}$$

Each virtual machine has its own computing power, running memory and other information. We can determine the task's execution time on the virtual machine using the task's length and the virtual machine's capacity to process data.

2.2 Model Building

Collaborative work framework scheduling in the cloud and edge can refer to Fig. 1. When the terminal user application uploads data, the server can divide the task into several parts and send them to several edge clusters around the server for processing. The edge nodes can also continue to upload tasks that cannot be processed to the cloud computing center for processing. The cloud computing center can act as a control center to schedule the overall resources in the network and can also store and process data from the other two layers for a long time.

At present, this paper only studies how the data center allocates many different tasks to the edge nodes far less than the number of tasks to run tasks so that the task completion

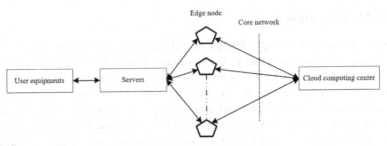

Fig. 1. Cloud-Edge collaborative task scheduling framework

time is as short as possible. When the scheduling strategy assigns the tasks to the relevant virtual machines, their mapping matrix $A(n \times m)$ is expressed as follows:

$$A = \begin{pmatrix} a_{11} & \cdots & a_{1m} \\ \vdots & \ddots & \vdots \\ a_{n1} & \cdots & a_{nm} \end{pmatrix} \tag{3}$$

If the value of the element a_{ij} in the above matrix is 1, it means that the task numbered i will be dispatched to the virtual machine numbered j to run; if its value is 0, then the work representing the number i will not be assigned to the number on the virtual machine of j.

After the simulation is performed, it will be generated on the basis of the above-mentioned mapping matrix. The task completion time matrix $T(n \times m)$ is expressed as follows:

$$T = \begin{pmatrix} time_{11} & \cdots & time_{1m} \\ \vdots & \ddots & \vdots \\ time_{n1} & \cdots & time_{nm} \end{pmatrix} \tag{4}$$

The element $time_{ij}$ in the above matrix represents the length of time that task i runs on VM numbered j. As stated by the computing power of the VM vm_mips and the task length $task\_length$, we can count the latency of each task to calculate the duration of the entire simulation process. The completion time of task i on VM j is expressed as follows:

$$exec\_time_{i,j} = \frac{task\_length_{i,j}}{vm\_mips_j} \tag{5}$$

Following is an expression for the execution time of a single virtual machine, where k is the number of tasks that were assigned to virtual machine j:

$$vm\_time_j = \sum_{i=0}^{k} exec\_time_{i,j} \tag{6}$$

Because different virtual machines are running in parallel, the overall duration of the task is the maximum virtual machine time of completion, as follows:

$$Total\_Time = \max(vm\_time_j) \tag{7}$$

The task scheduling strategy under cloud-edge collaboration is to find the allocation scheme with the least total task completion time. When the intelligent swarm algorithm finds this scheme, this paper uses the fitness to show the effectiveness of the plan. The better the solution, the greater the fitness, so we set the fitness function as:

$$Fitness = \frac{1}{Total\_Time} \tag{8}$$

For the scheduling model described above, we need to encode each particle, and a particle represents a scheduling scheme. For n tasks, m edge nodes (represented by virtual machines), the value of n is much larger than m, we encode the particles as shown in Table 1, indicating which virtual machine each task is assigned to. The following algorithm experiments and simulation experiments are carried out based on the above background and theory.

Table 1. Particle coding style

Task	1	2	3	...	n-2	n-1	N
Vm	3	5	6	...	m	m-5	1

3 Task Scheduling Based on Parameter Adaptive Particle Swarm Optimization Algorithm

PSO is a swarm intelligence-based evolutionary computing technology, which has obvious advantages in solving large-scale task scheduling, combinatorial optimization and other problems [12]. It has few parameters, simple principle, powerful functions and easy implementation, and has been widely used in artificial intelligence and industrial fields. However, the starting population's quality has a significant impact on the PSO as well, and at the same time, it's very easy to fall into a locally optimal solution because the convergence speed is too fast. It is insufficient to find the most suitable task scheduling scheme in a heterogeneous and larger cloud-edge collaborative scenario. This paper improves the PSO algorithm by adaptively changing the inertia coefficient w, the local and global optimal learning factor $c1$ and $c2$ in iterative process and proposes the PAPSO algorithm.

In PSO, its inertia coefficient w, local optimal learning factor $c1$ and global optimal learning factor $c2$ are constant throughout the iterative process. If the value of the inertia coefficient is too large, it is easy to miss the target value because the step size is too long, and a good convergence effect cannot be obtained. On the other hand, if the value of the inertia coefficient is tiny, early in its evolution, the particle lacks a robust capacity for self-exploration and cannot thoroughly investigate the entire search space. The learning factors $c1$ and $c2$ are two non-negative constants, which are the learning factors of the local and global optimal solution in the iterative process, respectively. Appropriate local optimal learning factors and global optimal learning factors will strike a balance between local and global search capabilities, which can speed up the convergence and is difficult to enter the local optimal answer. Therefore, we hope that the inertia coefficient w can be appropriately set to a slightly larger value at the beginning of the iteration to ensure that the exploration range of the entire search space can be as large as possible. At the same time, we hoped that the learning factors $c1$ and $c2$ can also be automatically changed in different periods of iteration to obtain more suitable values, which will have a better impact on the capability of global search and help it to better jump out of the limitations of local optimal solutions. In this paper, the factor P is introduced into the PAPSO algorithm. The expression of the P formula is as follows, and R is the current iteration number:

$$P = 2 - (1.5/R) \tag{9}$$

It is easy to know that the difference between 2 and 0.5 is 1.5. If there is a linear correlation, the result of dividing 1.5 by the number of iterations R is the step size of the parameter change after each iteration, then the value of formula P will increase linearly from 2 with the number of iterations decremented to 0.5; The value of $1/P$ increases linearly from 0.5 to 2 when the quantity of iterations grows. P is multiplied by the parameter to quadruple the value of the parameter at the beginning and end of the iteration.

In PAPSO, according to the inertia coefficient we have analyzed, it should be slightly larger at the beginning of the iteration and slightly smaller toward the end of the iteration. Meanwhile, about local and global optimal learning factor $c1$ and $c2$, we hope that at the beginning of the iteration, the particles can be less restricted by the current global optimal solution and can explore more search spaces by themselves. Reduced search space for exploration and keep moving closer to the global optimal solution. It is easy to find that the ideal parameter change trend proposed above is monotonic, that is, a higher value to a lower value reduction or an increase from a lower value to a higher value are the two possible outcomes.

This paper considers that since the change trend of all parameters is monotonic, the change trend is directly assumed to be linear. If the parameters are monotonically decreasing, we will decrease from twice the initial parameters at the beginning of the iteration to half the initial parameters at the end of the iteration; If the function is monotonically increasing, then we will increment from half the parameter at the start of the iteration to twice the initial parameter at the end of the iteration. Parameters that need to be incremented are multiplied by P, and parameters that need to be decremented are multiplied by $1/P$.

In this paper, for exploring the impact of various parameters on the algorithm's performance, we associate P with the inertia coefficient w, the local and the global optimal learning factor $c1$ and $c2$. We design four PAPSO algorithms, PAPSO_1, PAPSO_2, PAPSO_3, and PAPSO_4, which differ only in the placement of P.

For PAPSO_1, we only associate P with the inertia coefficient w, where $iter$ represents the number of iterations completed so far, and its velocity update formula is as follows:

$$v_{ij}(t+1) = wv_{ij}(t) * P * iter + c_1 r_1(t)\big[p_{ij}(t) - x_{ij}(t)\big]$$
$$+c_2 r_2(t)\big[p_{gj}(t) - x_{ij}(t)\big] \tag{10}$$

For PAPSO_2, we only associate P with the local optimal learning factor $c1$, whose velocity update formula is as follows:

$$v_{ij}(t+1) = wv_{ij}(t) + c_1 * P * iter * r_1(t)\big[p_{ij}(t) - x_{ij}(t)\big]$$
$$+c_2 r_2(t)\big[p_{gj}(t) - x_{ij}(t)\big] \tag{11}$$

For PAPSO_3, we only associate P with the local optimal learning factor $c2$, because $c2$ needs to be monotonically decreasing in the iterative process, so its velocity update formula is as shows:

$$v_{ij}(t+1) = wv_{ij}(t) + c_1 r_1(t)\big[p_{ij}(t) - x_{ij}(t)\big]$$
$$+c_2 * 1/(P * iter)r_2(t)\big[p_{gj}(t) - x_{ij}(t)\big] \tag{12}$$

For PAPSO_4, we associate P with all three parameters, and the velocity update formula is as follows:

$$v_{ij}(t+1) = P * iter(wv_{ij}(t) + c_1 * r_1(t)\big[p_{ij}(t) - x_{ij}(t)\big]$$
$$+c_2/(P * iter)r_2(t)\big[p_{gj}(t) - x_{ij}(t)\big] \tag{13}$$

The purpose of all the above-mentioned versions of the PAPSO algorithm is to allow the initial parameters to be adaptively changed during the iterative process. It expands the search space of particles at the early stage of iteration, so that it can fully explore the solution space, and in the subsequent iteration stage, it can accelerate the convergence rate and let the algorithm jump out of the defect that it is easy to fall into the local optimal solution. Through experiments we will conclude that the factor P associated with all three parameters has the most positive effect on the effectiveness of our approach, which we refer to as the PAPSO algorithm. The implementation steps of the PAPSO algorithm are shown below.

Algorithm : Parametric adaptive particle swarm optimization algorithm
Input: N: Population quantity Individual dimension,
R: Number of iterations,
F: Solve function,
SP: Search space
Output: BestPosition: Optimal solution position, BestFitness: Optimal solution value
1   FOR each particle i
2   FOR each dimension N
3   Initialize position Xi randomly within permissible range
4   Initialize velocity Vi randomly within permissible range
5   END FOR
6   END FOR
7   Iteration k=1
8   DO
9   Update the parameter adaptive factor P according to formula (9)
10   FOR each particle i
11   Calculate fitness value according to the fitness function F
12   IF the fitness value is better than Pi in history
13   Set current fitness value as the Pi
14   END IF
15   END FOR
16   Choose the particle having the best fitness value as the Pg
17   FOR each particle i
18   FOR each dimension N
19   Update the particle velocity according to one of the formulas (10) to (13) and position
20   END FOR
21   END FOR
22   k=k+1
23   WHILE k<=R
24   Output the optimal solution position and optimal solution value

The improvement of PAPSO algorithm does not increase the loop on the basis of the PSO algorithm. Their algorithms' time complexity is determined by the space dimension, population size, and number of iterations. The flowchart of task scheduling strategy based on PAPSO algorithm is depicted in Fig. 2.

4   Experiments and Evaluation

This section will conduct experimental work from the perspective of algorithm and task scheduling strategy.

4.1   Evaluation of Algorithm Performance

In the experiments, we use five different algorithms on MATLABworks to find the minimum value of the set with two special peak functions. The five algorithms to be compared are shown in Table 2. We will set the number of particles N of the population

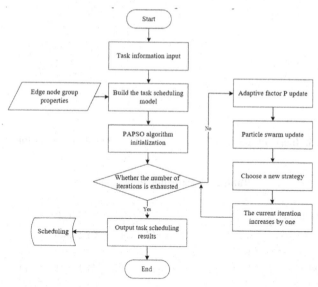

Fig. 2. Flowchart of task scheduling strategy based on PAPSO algorithm

in all algorithms to ten, and the number of iterations R to be 50. Each function is run several times on all algorithms.

Table 2. Basic parameters selected for comparison experiments

Algorithm	P-Associated parameters
PSO	null
PSO_1	w
PSO_2	$c1$
PSO_3	$c2$
PSO_4	$w, c1, c2$

To verify the superiority of the PAPSO_i ($i = 1, 2, 3, 4$) algorithm compared to the traditional PSO algorithm. Two special functions $F1$ and $F2$ with strong fluctuation characteristics are selected in this paper to evaluate the performance of PAPSO. There are many minimum and maximum values in the definition domain of these two functions, indicating that there are many local optimal solutions when finding their minimum or maximum value. Therefore, the global search capability and optimization speed of PSO and PAPSO can be fully verified. The function images of functions $F1$ and $F2$ are depicted in Fig. 3 and Fig. 4.

Table 3 shows the expressions of the functions $F1$ and $F2$, the search area and the function's own minimal value within the defined domain.

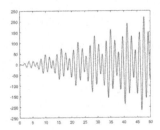

Fig. 3. Image of function *F1*

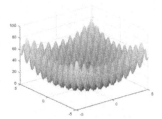

Fig. 4. Image of function *F2*

Table 3. Information of two functions

Function	Formula	Search space	Minimum
F1	$X * sin(x) * cos(2 * x) - 2 * x * sin(3 * x + 3 * x * sin(4 * x)$	$X \in [0,50]$	-215.5683
F2	$20 + x^2 + y^2 - 10 * cos(2 * pi * x) - 10 * cos(2 * pi * y)$	$X \in [-5.12, 5.12]$ $Y \in [-5.12, 5.12]$	0.0

After each algorithm performs multiple consecutive minimums seeking for each function, we will use the computational results to analyze. Table 4 is analysis of the best values from the data of the operating results of PSO, PAPSO_1, PAPSO_2, PAPSO_3, and PAPSO_4 under the given functions *F1* and *F2*. Among them, the average error in the table represents the average error of the optimal value obtained by running the same function multiple times for each algorithm; the standard error is obtained by analyzing the standard deviation of several optimal values and standard errors.

Because in this experiment, we let each function run several times consecutively with each algorithm, we did a mean and standard deviation analysis of the final positions of the 10 particles for each run, and then averaged the mean and standard deviations. The data we obtained is convenient for analysis and comparison, thus proving the conclusion that PAPSO performs well.

Table 5 is the analysis of the average optimal value of these algorithms, the optimal solution value genuinely represents the minimal value of the initial function, and the optimal value of the algorithm is the minimum value searched in the search space.

After comparative experiments, we can see from the data shown in Table 4 that the average and standard deviations of the results run by the PAPSO_4 algorithm are the smallest for either function *F1* or *F2*. Therefore, we analyzed the data and found that the inertia coefficient *w*, the local optimal and the global optimal learning factor *c1* and *c2*. These three parameters have a positive impact on our search results after reasonable changes in the entire iterative process, which also shows that the positive effect of simultaneous function adaptive changes to these three parameters is the most obvious. Therefore, in this paper, we can believe that the PAPSO_4 algorithm has better performance than the other four algorithms, the ease of use and stability of the method are very good, and its robustness is also better than the other algorithms compared. From the average optimal solution of the five algorithms analyzed in Table 4, the optimal solution

Table 4. Operation results

Test function	Algorithm type	Average error	Standard error
F1	PSO	1.05e−14	53.75
	PSO_1	1.27e−14	111.08
	PSO_2	1.07e−14	95.58
	PSO_3	7.39e−15	117.53
	PSO_4	5.72e−15	25.77
F2	PSO	2.33e−16	3.84
	PSO_1	7.05e−16	9.37
	PSO_2	1.59e−16	4.02
	PSO_3	3.38e−16	2.66
	PSO_4	2.02e−17	0.36

Table 5. Average optimum

Function	F1	F2
Minimum	−215.5683	0
PSO	−203.8915	0.71
PSO_1	−215.5591	0.42
PSO_2	−203.9601	0.69
PSO_3	−201.0653	0.29
PSO_4	−215.5619	0

obtained by PAPSO_4 is closest to the maximum value of the function and has stronger search accuracy than the other three algorithms.

Combined with the analysis of the concentration and dispersion of particles in the function of the five algorithms in Fig. 5, Fig. 6, Fig. 7, Fig. 8, Fig. 9 and the evolution curve of the best fitness compared to other algorithms, optimization results of the PAPSO_4 algorithm are closer to the optimal solution value. From the perspective of the evolution process of the most fitness, the optimization curve is the steepest, and the optimization speed is faster, and from the final position dispersion of the particles, the particles of PAPSO_4 are the most concentrated, and most of them are on the optimal solution. It can be shown that the PAPSO_4 algorithm can well jump out of the shortcomings of the local optimal solution, and the optimization speed and the optimization's precision are also dramatically enhanced compared with the PSO algorithm, so it proves that the direction of our improvement on the PSO algorithm is correct. In the following content, we will refer to the PAPSO_4 algorithm as the PAPSO algorithm, which is the new parameter adaptive PAPSO we proposed.

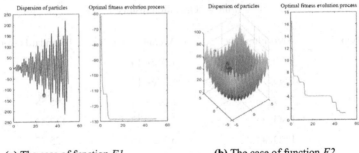

(a) The case of function *F1*   **(b)** The case of function *F2*

Fig. 5. Distribution and evolution of PSO particles

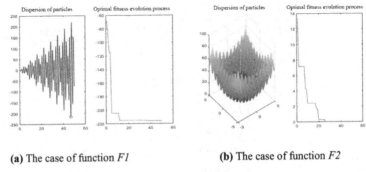

(a) The case of function *F1*   **(b)** The case of function *F2*

Fig. 6. Distribution and evolution of PAPSO_1 particles

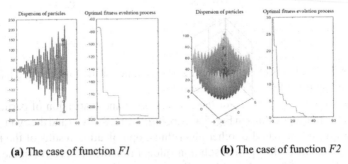

(a) The case of function *F1*   **(b)** The case of function *F2*

Fig. 7. Distribution and evolution of PAPSO_2 particles

4.2   Task Scheduling Simulation Experiment

The experiments using simulation in this paper are carried out on the CloudSim [13] simulation platform. We will use the algorithm for scheduling tasks depending on PAPSO and PSO suggested in this document and the First-Come-First-Served (FCFS) task scheduling algorithm for simulation comparison experiments. Because the FCFS-based

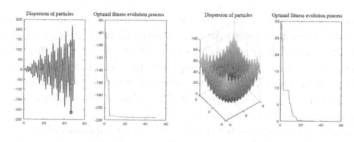

(a) The case of function *F1*   **(b)** The case of function *F2*

Fig. 8. Distribution and evolution of PAPSO_3 particles

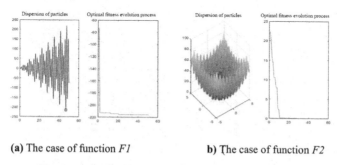

(a) The case of function *F1*   **b)** The case of function *F2*

Fig. 9. Distribution and evolution of PAPSO_4 particles

task scheduling method arranges tasks for the virtual machine sequentially, the task scheduling algorithm's outcomes are same every time, which can be used as a reference.

Before the experiment starts, for the first two intelligent swarm algorithms PAPSO and PSO scheduling algorithm, we set its particle number N to 100, and other parameters are consistent with the parameters used in the previous section, and repeated experiments for each algorithm under different conditions. It is necessary to explain the various attribute parameters or parameter ranges of the virtual machine and the task, as shown in Table 6 below.

Table 6. Parameter description of the virtual machine and the task

Name	Property	Range
Cloudlet	The length of the task. (Millions of instruction lengths)	[1000, 10000]
Vm	MIPS	[500, 5000]
	Number of cores	[1, 2]
	Ram (MB)	512
	Storage (MB)	10000
	Bandwidth (MB/s)	1000

Task completion time is a key issue that should be considered in task scheduling, and it is also a factor used in this paper to compare three cloud-edge collaborative task scheduling strategies. This paper will use two schemes to carry out the task scheduling simulation experiment with the task completion time as the evaluation standard under cloud-edge collaboration. They are the solution of increasing the quantity of tasks with the same quantity of virtual machines and the solution of increasing the quantity of virtual machines with the same quantity of tasks.

In Scheme 1, 10 virtual machines are created, and the quantity of tasks goes up from 200 to 800 in steps of 100. The outcomes of the experiment are displayed in Fig. 10.

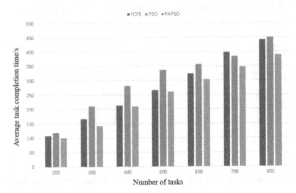

Fig. 10. The experimental results of scheme 1

The test outcomes depicted in Fig. 10 show that, compared with the task scheduling algorithms based on FCFS and PSO, the results of the algorithm for scheduling tasks based on PAPSO to solve optimal scheduling strategy are reduced by 9.51% and 12.66% on average.

In Scheme 2, 500 tasks are created, and the quantity of virtual machines grows in stages of 10 from 10 to 40. The outcomes of the experiment are displayed in Fig. 11.

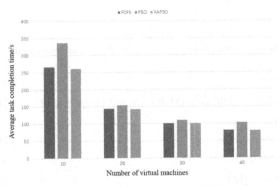

Fig. 11. The experimental results of scheme 2

The test outcomes depicted in Fig. 11 show that, compared to the PSO and FCFS-based task scheduling algorithm, the outcomings of task scheduling algorithm based on PAPSO reduce the average time of solving the optimal scheduling strategy by 7.43% and 1.66% respectively.

On average, for both scenarios, compared to the PSO-based task scheduling algorithm, the results of the task scheduling algorithm based on PAPSO reduce the average time of solving the optimal scheduling strategy by more than 9%.

In summary, the outcomes of the trial indicate the improvement direction of the PAPSO proposed in this paper is correct. By adaptively changing the parameters of the PAPSO algorithm, the algorithm can explore the search area more fully early in the iteration process, speed up the convergence speed and improve the convergence accuracy, try to avoid falling into the local optimal solution in the later iteration. The simulation experiment also shows that the task scheduling algorithm based on PAPSO proposed in this paper is also acceptable for the task scheduling problem under edge-cloud collaboration and has better performance than the other two classical task scheduling algorithms.

5 Conclusion

This paper aims at the task scheduling problem in the cloud-edge collaboration scenario to reduce the time of completion of the task and thus reduce the latency of the application service. Based on the traditional PSO algorithm, a new PAPSO algorithm that can be applied to this scene is proposed. Compared with PSO, the PAPSO algorithm can explore the search space more fully in the early process of iteration and find the optimal results more accurate and faster in subsequent iterations. And through simulation experiments, it is concluded that the task scheduling algorithm based on PAPSO can have better performance in the cloud-edge collaborative scenario, and its task completion time, optimization speed and global space search ability are better. In the future work, a richer scheduling model is planned to be established, and more evaluation indicators, such as usage cost and energy consumption, will be considered, and the algorithm will be optimized.

Acknowledgments. This work is funded by the National Key Research and Development Project of China (No. 2018YFB1404404), and the Natural Science Foundation of China (No. 62162003, No. 61762008).

References

1. Du, B., Huang, R., Xie, Z., et al.: KID model-driven things-edge-cloud computing paradigm for traffic data as a service. IEEE Netw. **32**(1), 34–41 (2018)
2. Shi, W.S., Sun, H., Cao, J., et al.: Edge computing: a new computing model for the Internet era. J. Comput. Res. Dev. **54**(5), 907–924 (2017)
3. Zhang, H., Chen, S., Zou, P., et al.: Research and application of industrial equipment management service system based on cloud-edge collaboration. In: Proceedings of the 2019 Chinese Automation Congress (CAC), China, pp. 5451–5456 (2019)

4. Kumar, M., Sharma, S.C., Goel, A., et al.: A comprehensive survey for scheduling techniques in cloud computing. J. Netw. Comput. Appl. **143**, 1–33 (2019)

5. Muniswamaiah, M., Agerwala, T., Tappert, C.C.: A survey on cloudlets, mobile edge, and fog computing. In: 2021 8th IEEE International Conference on Cyber Security and Cloud Computing (CSCloud)/2021. In: 7th IEEE International Conference on Edge Computing and Scalable Cloud (EdgeCom), Washington, DC, USA, pp. 139–142 (2021)

6. Maenhaut, P.J., Volckaert, B., Ongenae, V., et al.: Resource management in a containerized cloud: status and challenges. J. Netw. Syst. Manage. **28**(2), 197–246 (2020)

7. Lyu, X., Tian, H., Sengul, C., et al.: Multiuser joint task offloading and resource optimization in proximate clouds. IEEE Trans. Veh. Technol. **66**(4), 3435–3447 (2017)

8. Zhang, Y., Dong, X., Zhao, Y.: Decentralized computation offloading over wireless-powered mobile-edge computing networks. In: 2020 IEEE International Conference on Artificial Intelligence and Information Systems (ICAIIS), Dalian, China, pp. 137–140 (2020)

9. Sreelakshmi, S.S.: Multi-objective PSO based task scheduling - a load balancing approach in cloud. In: 2019 1st International Conference on Innovations in Information and Communication Technology (ICIICT), Chennai, India, pp. 1–5 (2019)

10. Liu, S., Yin, Y.: Task scheduling in cloud computing based on improved discrete particle swarm optimization. In: 2019 2nd International Conference on Information Systems and Computer Aided Education (ICISCAE), Dalian, China, pp. 594–597 (2019)

11. Mohapatra, S., Panigrahi, C.R., Pati, B., et al.: MSA: a task scheduling algorithm for cloud computing. Int. J. Comput. **8**(3), 283–297 (2019)

12. Yang, X.S.: Nature-inspired optimization algorithms: challenges and open problems. J. Comput. Sci. **46**(10), 101104 (2020)

13. Santra, S., Mali, K.: A new approach to survey on load balancing in VM in cloud computing: using CloudSim. In: 2015 International Conference on Computer, Indore, India, pp. 1–5 (2015)

An Approach to Assessing the Health of Opensource Software Ecosystems

Ruoxuan Yang[1,2], Yongqiang Yang[1], Yijun Shen[1(✉)], and Hailong Sun[1]

[1] Beihang University, Beijing, China
{yangyongqiang,shenyijun,sunhl}@buaa.edu.cn
[2] Tsinghua University, Beijing, China
yrx22@mails.tsinghua.edu.cn

Abstract. With the development of open-source technology, open-source software ecosystems (OSSECO) have been formed due to various connections between open-source projects and developers. To measure stability and sustainability, the health of an OSSECO is proposed, like the health of ecosystems in nature. Unfortunately, there are not a set of unified and mature OSSECO health evaluation rules yet, nor have effective governance methods. Existing researches mainly analyze the health of a specific open-source ecosystem or design performance indicators related to OSSECO health. This paper combines the classic OSEHO model with the rapidly developing CHAOSS open-source community metrics, establishes an OSSECO health evaluation model that can provide specific scores based on Entropy Method, and develops an open-source ecosystem health evaluation system based on the model. To the best of our knowledge, we are the first to propose a qualitative and quantitative model to show the health status of open-source ecosystems. Meanwhile, we conduct the automatic evaluation of the health of an OSSECO. Finally, we analyze the software ecosystem health of 10 open-source projects on GitHub by the established evaluation system. The result can prove the effectiveness of the system and provide data support for developers to make governance decisions.

Keywords: open-source software · ecosystem · health assessment

1 Introduction

The concept of 'Free Open-Source Software (FOSS)' was proposed as early as the 1980s. In the late 1990s, the term 'open-source' was born [1]. Different from traditional commercial software, the open-source mode attracts and converges developers around the world to collaboratively and competitively develop products that meet diverse needs. With the development of the open-source community, the scale of open-source developers is continuously increasing, while the number of open-source projects also rises rapidly. The complex network structure of open-source software (OSS) systems is formed due to the interaction of developers, the dependencies of components or modules, and the sharing of developing tools, which is also called the Open-Source Software Ecosystem [2].

© The Author(s), under exclusive license to Springer Nature Singapore Pte Ltd. 2023
Y. Sun et al. (Eds.): ChineseCSCW 2022, CCIS 1681, pp. 465–480, 2023.
https://doi.org/10.1007/978-981-99-2356-4_37

A complete OSSECO health evaluation system can help users comprehensively understand the health of an OSSECO. While the results of the evaluation can also provide strong scientific theoretical support for the risk early warning and dynamic governance of the OSSECO, leading to a benign open-source ecological cycle of evaluation early-warning-governance, and providing a more stable, reliable, and sustainable development environment for numerous open-source projects.

Unfortunately, the current open-source ecosystem is characterized by the uncertainty of project evolution and developer behavior, which makes it difficult to sustain the established open-source ecosystem. For example, researches show that even in successful open-source ecosystems such as Linux [3] and OpenStack [4], there are still problems such as insufficient developer communication and loss of participating companies.

At present, the researchers are actively exploring the health assessment mechanism of the open-source ecosystem. However, existing studies often carry out case studies for specific open-source projects, resulting in low evaluation efficiency, lack of universality in the evaluation method, and difficulty in automating the evaluation process. There is still not a suitable quantification method for the health of an open-source ecosystem, which is hard to support scientific and effective decisions when leaders manage an OSSECO, when developers and users choose an OSSECO, and when investors evaluate an OSSECO.

In response to these problems, this paper propose a qualitative and quantitative model and system to measure the health of an open-source ecosystem. To be specific, the contributions of this paper are summarized as follows:

- We design a qualitative and quantitative health assessment model for OSSECOs based on the OSEHO model and CHAOSS Metrics.
- We design and implement an automatic OSSECO health assessment system to conduct the evaluating process and visualize the result of the health assessment.
- We analyze 10 typical OSSECO health to evaluate the applicability of the model and system.

2   Related Work

2.1   Software Ecosystem Health

For the measurement and governance of software ecosystems, some researchers used 'Health' [5] to describe the state of the software ecosystem, and research on 'health' became an emerging hotspot. Jansen et al. [6] defined software ecosystem health as a metric that could help decision-makers judge whether a software ecosystem is worth joining. Manikas et al. [7] compared the related concepts in natural ecosystems and commercial ecosystems and defined software ecosystem health as the sustainable and flexible capability of the system. Gamalielsson et al. [8] found that software ecosystem health is an important factor when considering OSS adoption or testing a seed project. Yvonne [9] qualitatively analyzed the common characteristics of a set of product development and evolution in a software ecosystem. Further, Iuri et al. [10] proposed the HEAL ME model for evaluating software ecosystem health, which captured SECO data in a semi-automated manner and presented SECO health scenarios by using predefined metrics. However, because the concept of a software ecosystem is too broad, it is difficult for these models to take the unique characteristics of OSSECOs into account.

2.2   Open-Source Software Ecosystem Health

For the OSSECO, *Open-source Community Maturity Research Report* [11], published by CAICT in 2021, defined the open-source community maturity curve graph and the open-source community maturity quadrant graph to describe the changes in the open-source community over time. Wang et al. [12] evaluated the activity of developers and projects in open-source communities and estimated the number of developers using different development languages. However, as mentioned by Goggins et al. [13] - the current measurement metrics for open-source projects are limited to the internal scope of the project, ignoring the project's sustainability in an environment where competition and dependencies coexist.

For the qualitative evaluation of the OSSECO, Jansen [14] proposed the OSEHO model in 2014, which built a table through 3 layers: theory layer, network layer, and project layer, and 3 dimensions: productivity, robustness, and niche. The multi-dimensional evaluation model was formed by filling each unit with relevant metrics of the OSSECO.

For the quantitative evaluation of the OSSECO, CHAOSS (Community Health Analytics Open-source Software) [15], which is an open-source project of Linux Foundation, focused on creating metrics on open-source community health. Its latest publication *CHAOSS Metrics* [16] was released in April 2022, including a total of 75 metrics that could be used to measure the health of the open-source community. However, it has the problem of different granularity for the division of metrics, which leads to the detailed and clear description of some of the metrics, while the other metrics are too vague. Meanwhile, the publication only listed all the metrics without illustrating the connection among them, which failed to propose a general evaluation method for OSSECO health.

3   Qualitative and Quantitative Evaluation Methods of Open-Source Software Ecosystem Health

3.1   Data Acquisition Method

This paper completes the acquisition and storage of data through Augur, including the number of issues, stars, and pull requests. Augur [17] is a suite developed by CHAOSS to collect structured data about the FOSS software community. It can build a set of relational repositories to collect trace data, normalize it into a designed data model, and provide API for data access.

After the collection, we use the REST API provided by Augur to obtain 43 metrics, including 42 integer metrics and 1 string metrics badge_level (CII best practice badge). For the badge_level metrics, we define the value 'in_progess' as 0 and the value 'passing' as 1, which allows it to be converted into an integer metric.

In addition, based on the analysis of Augur's data model, this paper adds four integer metrics - active_subs, tag_count, language_count and con-trb_location_count. The active_subs metric counts the number of sub projects with commit behavior in the past month, tag_count counts the number of keywords displayed by the project, language_count counts the number of programming languages used by the project, and contrb_location_count counts the number of cities where project contributors are located. **In the end, 47 integer metrics were formed.**

The later analysis also used Augur's data model as an important reference to lay the data foundation for the final system development.

3.2   Qualitative Evaluation Method

We build the final qualitative model based on the OSEHO (Open-source Ecosystem Health Operationalization) model proposed by Jansen et al. [14] in 2014. Some metrics in the old model are out-of-date for today's open-source ecosystem, with new concepts and technologies emerging in recent years needing to be supplemented. Furthermore, some metrics in the model are of relatively large granularity, making it difficult to find specific definitions and descriptions in real projects. Therefore, further refinement is required for the ultimate automated analysis system.

Fortunately, the metrics released by CHAOSS give the answer to the real-time and granularity problems of OSEHO. In addition, in response to the continuous introduction of new functions and services by major open-source platforms, the metrics of CHAOSS are also constantly being updated.

Modifications to OSEHO. This paper mainly analyzes and deletes the metrics of the network layer and project layer in OSEHO. The modified OSEHO model is shown in Table 1.

Table 1. Modified OSEHO

	Productivity	Robustness	Niche
Network Layer	New related projects	Total number of active projects	Variety in Projects
	Added knowledge about ecosystem	Network connectivity	
	Events		
Project Layer	KLOC/time period added	Active contributors	Variation in contributor type
	New by-products	Number of users	Variation in project applications
	Bug fix time	Contributor rating and reputation	Supported languages
		User satisfaction and ratings	Variation in technologies
		Downloads and usage	

Network Layer. The productivity of the network layer also represents the productivity of the ecosystem. The number of downloads of new projects was a metric of network productivity in OSEHO. But as a criterion for evaluating project quality, it is relatively weak in terms of productivity, and is transferred to the robustness evaluation index in this paper; other metrics are reserved.

The robustness of the network layer represents the anti-interference ability of the ecosystem. The cohesion between projects, the consistency of the core network, and the number of connections with other software ecosystems are used to represent the connectivity of the network. And the cost of converting to other software ecosystems represents the difficulty for participants in one software ecosystem to transfer to another software ecosystem, which does not explicitly indicate the strength of the system's anti-interference ability, so this metric is deleted.

The niche of the network layer contains only one metric of project diversity, which describes the size of the opportunity for the system to open up new markets. A more diverse system of projects corresponds to the possibility of opening up more markets and attracting more potential users.

Project Layer. Productivity metrics at the project layer can indicate a project's contribution to the entire ecosystem. As a direct product of productivity, the various by-products newly added by the project mark the status of productivity, including work orders, technical branches, partners, and patents, while downloads and usage are the evaluation of project quality rather than productivity. It is an indicator of the robustness of the project, so it is transferred. And the current email response time is less indicative of productivity, so this metric is deleted.

Analogous to natural ecosystems, ecosystems with more active components are generally more robust, and the robustness of a project can also be measured in terms of components' quality and quantity: the number of active developers and the number of end users represent the level of quantity, with various ratings, downloads, and usage reflecting the quality of the project. Several evaluation metrics based on the organizational level in the original OSEHO have been deleted because the organization-based activities in the open-source ecosystem are far less than the individual-based activities, the same as the network layer.

Project-level niche value metrics refer to whether the project allows enough degrees of freedom and variation. Market diversity actually refers to niche markets, which are too macroscopic and empty. It can be approximated by project application diversity, that is, projects with rich application scenarios must correspond to their rich markets; other metrics are reserved.

Analysis and Selection of CHAOSS Metrics. After careful observation, it is not difficult to find that most of the CHAOSS metrics overlap or are similar to OSEHO's. For those metrics that are similar, we will choose the more clearly-described one. At the same time, CHAOSS Metrics also includes some metrics that cannot be classified into any category in OSEHO. Based on the classic framework, we just dump these metrics that cannot be classified. The final finished model is shown in Table 2.

Table 2. The qualitative evaluation model for OSSECO health

	Productivity	Robustness	Niche
Network Layer	New related projects Added knowledge about ecosystem Events	Total number of active projects Network connectivity	Variety in Projects
Project Layer	KLOC/time period added New by-products Bug fix time	Active contributors Number of users Contributor rating and reputation User satisfaction and ratings Downloads and usage License coverage	Variation in contributor type Variation in project applications Programming language distribution Variation in technologies

The productivity of the open-source ecosystem has always been indicated by the number of products, so OSEHO and CHAOSS are basically the same in terms of productivity. The security-related license coverage metric was added to the robustness of the project layer, and the 'supported languages' metric was changed to the 'programming language distribution' metrics supported by CHAOSS in the niche of the project layer.

3.3 Quantitative Evaluation Model

The mathematical evaluation model of open-source ecosystem health needs not only to undertake the qualitative evaluation model constructed in the previous section, but also consider the feasibility of the final implementation. It means that if the statistical data used in the model is difficult to obtain in reality (e.g. the cost of converting an open-source ecosystem to other software ecosystems is an objective quantity, but it is difficult to obtain specific data in reality), then the availability and feasibility of the model are insufficient. Therefore, when selecting the metrics involved in the final mathematical model, all metrics must be obtained in actual statistical operations.

This paper adopts the method of layered weighting and multi-dimensional display. First, each grid in the table is weighted by one layer to obtain the evaluation score of a certain layer and a certain dimension (e.g. the robustness score of the network layer is 78.67 points), and then The three dimensions of each layer are weighted to obtain the evaluation score of each layer (e.g. the health score of the project layer is 90.33 points), and finally, the two evaluation scores of the network layer health degree and the project layer health degree are used as the evaluation result. The health of the network layer reflects the overall health of the community and ecosystem where the project is a part of the open-source ecosystem, while the health of the project layer reflects the health of the project in the actual development and application process.

Selection of Quantified Metrics. This paper focuses on the data model and REST API provided by Augur in the selection of quantitative metrics, and obtains 47 mathematical metrics as a candidate. The 47 metrics corresponding to the health evaluation model are classified by the category of Table 2. After removing the relatively redundant metrics, we obtain the metrics in Table 3, which is the final mathematical evaluation metrics used in the model.

Table 3. The evaluation model for OSSECO health

	Productivity	Robustness	Niche
Network Layer	sub_project_count release_count	active_subs	tag_count
Project Layer	fork_count pull_request_count	watchers_count stars_count	language_count contrib_location_ counts
	commits_count patch_count issues_count	commiters_count new_contributors avg_issue_response_ time(negative)	
	avg_issue_resolution_ time(negative) line_additions	issues_active	
		pull_request_acceptance_ rate number_of_license badge_level	

Hierarchical Weighting. The Entropy Method is to determine the amount of information contained in an index described by the information entropy and then determine the importance of the index to the entire system. The larger the entropy value, the smaller the amount of information, and the smaller the impact on the entire system [18].

Assuming that the data of n example repositories is obtained through Augur, the 22 secondary metrics in Table 3 are extracted and exported, and the values of the metrics corresponding to the repository are shown in Table 4 respectively.

Table 4. Alphabetical representation of the metrics

First-level metrics name	Alphabetical representation	Second-level metrics name	Alphabetical representation
Productivity of network layer	NP_i	sub_project_count release_count	np_{i1} np_{2i}

The calculation method of the secondary weight corresponding to each second-level metric is as follows (take the metrics 'sub_project_count' as an example):

1) Normalize all values corresponding to the metrics.
   When the metrics is positive:

$$np_{1i} = \frac{np_{1i} - min(np_{11}, np_{12}, ..., np_{1n})}{max(np_{11}, np_{12}, ..., np_{1n}) - min(np_{11}, np_{12}, ..., np_{1n})} \quad (1)$$

When the metrics is negative:

$$np_{1i} = \frac{max(np_{11}, np_{12}, ..., np_{1n}) - np_{1i}}{max(np_{11}, np_{12}, ..., np_{1n}) - min(np_{11}, np_{12}, ..., np_{1n})} \quad (2)$$

2) Calculate the information entropy E_{np_1}.

$$E_{np_1} = -\frac{1}{\ln n} \sum_{i=1}^{n} p_{np_{1i}} \ln p_{np_{1i}} \quad (3)$$

in which

$$p_{np_{1i}} = \frac{np_{1i}}{\sum_{i=1}^{n}} \quad (4)$$

3) Calculate the second-level weight W_{np_1}.

$$W_{np_1} = \frac{1 - E_{np_1}}{2 - \sum_{j=1}^{2} E_{np_j}} \quad (5)$$

The calculation method of the first-level weight corresponding to each first-level indicator is as follows (take 'network layer productivity' as an example):

1) Based on the known second-level weights, calculate the network layer productivity score of each repository.

$$NP_i = \sum_{j=1}^{2} np_{ji} * W_{np_j} \quad (6)$$

2) Normalize all values (there would be no negative metrics at this time)

$$NP_i = \frac{NP_i - min(NP_1, NP_2, ..., NP_n)}{max(NP_1, NP_2, ..., NP_n) - min(NP_1, NP_2, ..., NP_n)} \quad (7)$$

3) Calculate the information entropy E_{NP}

$$E_{NP} = -\frac{1}{\ln n} \sum_{i=1}^{n} p_{NP_i} \ln p_{NP_i} \quad (8)$$

in which

$$p_{NP} = -\frac{NP_i'}{\sum_{i=1}^{n} NP_i'} \quad (9)$$

4) Calculate the first-level weight W_{NP}

$$W_{NP} = -\frac{1 - E_{NP}}{3 - (E_{NP} + E_{NR} + E_{NN})} \tag{10}$$

Finally, we get the network layer health and the project layer health of the repository.

$$N_i = NP_i * W_{NP} + NR_i * W_{NR} + NN_i * W_{NN} \tag{11}$$

$$P_i = PP_i * W_{PP} + PR_i * W_{PR} + PN_i * W_{PN} \tag{12}$$

3.4   Score Conversion

The scores and weights calculated under formulas (1)–(12) will change according to the original data, so there is no upper and lower limit for the score. Sometimes it is difficult to judge whether the OSSECO is good or bad by just looking at the score. Therefore, we need to convert the score to allow a higher reference value, that is, every score is mapped to a 0–100 percentile score.

We consider fitting a normal distribution with the calculated scores, standardize it, and then use the probability distribution of each score as its final percentile score which can reflect the ranking level of the item in all items.

Assuming that the scores of n example repositories are $(s_1, s_2, ..., s_n)$, the score normalization method used in this paper is as follows:

1) Calculate the mean μ and standard deviation σ of n samples as two parameters of the normal distribution.

$$\mu = \frac{s_1 + s_2 + ... + s_n}{n} \tag{13}$$

$$\sigma = \sqrt{(s_1 - \mu)^2 + (s_2 - \mu)^2 + ... + (s_n - \mu)^2} \tag{14}$$

2) Do the standard transformation of s_i and convert it to the value μ_i on the standard normal distribution.

$$\mu_i = \frac{s_i - \mu}{\sigma} \tag{15}$$

3) Get the final percentile score by looking up the standard normal distribution table.

$$s_i = P\{x \le \mu_i\} * 100\% \tag{16}$$

4   System Design and Implementation

Based on the established OSSECO health evaluation method, this paper designs and implements an OSSECO health evaluation system, which can realize the automatic evaluation of the OSSECO health degree on the Internet, and supports additional functions such as login and collection.

4.1   System Design

The target OSSECO health assessment system should include an account system, search and display system, and collection system. The system architecture diagram of this system is shown in Fig. 1.

The platform used to display the mathematical model of OSSECO health assessment is positioned as a Web system. Since its main function is displaying, the overall structure is relatively simple and can be developed using a general request-response model.

The front-end uses the current mainstream Vue3.0 framework and Vuetify component library for page development, and the data visualization part uses Apache Echarts visual components. The back-end is developed using the Python-based lightweight microservice framework flask, which is easy to add functions and iterative optimization later. At the same time, the back-end also needs to control Augur's configuration and data collection. Consistent with Augur, we use PostgreSQL to ensure good data transfer, access, and manipulation.

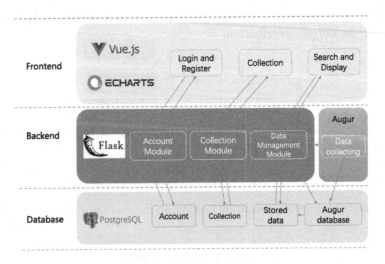

Fig. 1. System Architecture

Table 5. Sample repositories

Repository name	Address
chaoss/augur	https://github.com/chaoss/augur
chaoss/grimoirelab	https://github.com/chaoss/grimoirelab
flutter/flutter	https://github.com/flutter/flutter
Azure/azure-rest-api-specs	https://github.com/Azure/azure-rest-api-specs
huggingface/transformers	https://github.com/huggingface/transformers
alibaba/fastjson2	https://github.com/alibaba/fastjson2
jojoldu/junior-recruit-scheduler	https://github.com/jojoldu/junior-recruit-scheduler
tokyo-metropolitan-gov/covid19	https://github.com/tokyo-metropolitan-gov/covid19
FarbstoffRSL/RSL-Helper	https://github.com/FarbstoffRSL/RSL-Helper
https://github.com/FarbstoffRSL/RSL-Helper	https://github.com/gustavoguanabara/html-css

4.2   Back-End Implementation

Data Acquisition. The goal of this section is to find open-source data acquisition channels and build a suitable database for storing data. The acquired data is required to be real-time and comprehensive and to support the later system platform development. In this paper, the data of 10 typical projects on Github were successfully collected as a reference for applying the Entropy Method in the mathematical model establishment stage. Sample repositories are shown in Table 5.

The selection of sample repositories is required to be representative and extensive. We select two, Augur and GrimoreLab, as representatives of ordinary repositories with general maintenance conditions, while the remaining 8 repositories are recommended by GitHub's Trendings, representing more active projects. The active 8 repositories include 3 English repositories, 1 Chinese repository, 1 Japanese repository, 1 Korean repository, 1 German repository, and 1 Portuguese repository, which ensures the extensiveness of sample selection.

Implementation of Back-End Key Modules. The back-end of the OSSECO health evaluation system established in this paper includes three modules: account module, collection module, and data management module. The account module and the collection module are mainly composed of API interfaces, which are used to respond to the HTTP requests related to login, registration, and collection sent by the front-end. The key module of the back-end is the data management module, and its main components are database management service, evaluation service, Augur control service, and API interface.

4.3   Web-Based Front-End Implementation

This paper made a prototype of the system and completed the development of the front-end of the whole system according to the prototype.

The system consists of 6 pages and a navigation bar. The basic components of the page are developed based on Vue.js, all styles are carefully designed, and the styles are unified and reusable. Charts are developed by Echarts, which configures the chart by the data sent from the back-end. The front-end uses HTTP to request and send data to the back-end (Fig. 2).

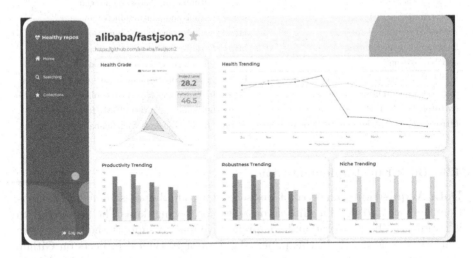

Fig. 2. Screenshot of the evaluation result

The evaluation result page above mainly displays the analysis results of the target project, including real-time health scores and trends. The radar chart in the upper left corner of the page shows the scores of the three dimensions in the two layers(blue is the project layer, and green is the network layer). The line chart in the upper right corner of the page shows the health trend of the project over the past eight months. The three bar charts at the bottom of the page respectively show the trend of the score in three different dimensions in the past six months. Users can follow or unfollow a project by clicking the yellow star button next to the item title.

5   Experiment on Open-Source Software Ecosystem Health Evaluation

In order to verify the accuracy of the established OSSECO health assessment method, this paper uses the data from obtained 10 sample repositories to conduct OSSECO health evaluation experiments, simulate the entire evaluation process, and analyze the evaluation results.

5.1   Data Acquisition and Score Calculation

Obtain the data of 10 example repositories in Table 5 through Augur, extract 22 first-level metrics in Table 3, and divide them into 6 groups according to the classification of Table 3. For each group of data, calculate the first-level weight corresponding to each first-level metric under formula (1)-formula (5). Then, according to the obtained first-level weights, the first-level scores of each repository are calculated respectively. Finally, the scores are converted under formula (13)-formula (15). The obtained percentile scores are shown in Fig 3 (the result is kept to one decimal place).

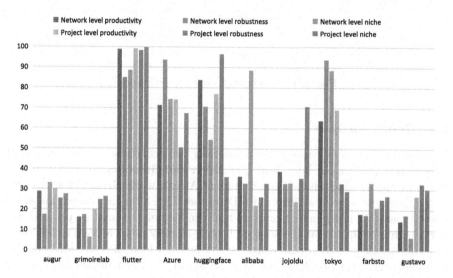

Fig. 3. Second-Level scores of sample repositories

The scores before conversion are divided into 2 groups according to the network layer and the project layer. For each group of data, the first-level weight corresponding to each first-level metric is calculated under formula (6)-formula (10), and under formula (11)–(12) we calculate the health score of each repository. Finally, we convert the scores under formula (13)-formula (15), and the obtained percentile score is shown in Fig. 4 (retain 1 decimal place for the result).

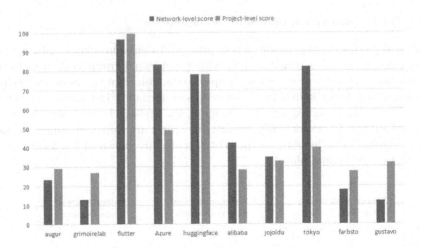

Fig. 4. Final scores of sample repositories

5.2   Result Analysis

It is not difficult to find that even as ordinary projects, there is still a relatively large gap in the project layer health of Augur and GrimoireLab. This is due to the more timely maintenance and update of Augur, while GrimoireLab has had a significant decrease in activity since December 2021 after the completion of the development. As independent projects that are less related to other projects, the performance of the two at the network layer is slightly poor, revealing the potential vulnerability of the open-source ecosystem in which they are located. The same network layer problems can be reflected in the German-language project Farbsto and the Portuguese-language project Gustavo.

As a recent phenomenon-level open-source UI development tool, Flutter has been well received by developers since its launch. The number of contributors to open-source repositories is also increasing month by month, indicating that its ecological environment is growing.

The cloud computing service Azure launched by Microsoft ranks second only to Flutter in the network layer, showing its advantages as a product of a large company - a complete product chain, rich related products, and excellent compatibility, and at the same time, higher projects layer health can also show its good pace of development.

The same can explain the high network-level score of the tokyo-metropolitan-gov project. The project is in charge of the Tokyo government and is connected to many subordinate subsystems. Its user scale is larger than ordinary organizations and projects.

As a large-scale company project similar to Azure, Alibaba's FastJSON project is also relatively healthy at the network layer, because it has a relatively close connection with many other projects of Alibaba, and Alibaba's software ecosystem has been developed for a long time with considerable scale and stability. But the project-level score points out that the current development and maintenance pace of the project still requires further governance.

Huggingface and Jojoldu are representatives of English and Korean Trending projects respectively. Considering the characteristics of the number of people using natural language, their scores are relatively good among similar language projects, and they can be used as project representatives with a relatively healthy network layer and project layer.

Through the above analysis, it can be found that the OSSECO health evaluation system proposed in this paper already has a certain usability, and with the increase of data recorded in the database in the later stage, the calculated weights will be more accurate, which can provide developers and managers with strong data support for project and ecosystem governance decisions.

6 Conclusion

In view of the current health measurement problem of open-source ecosystems, the quantitative models in the existing research results are often not applicable to most ecosystems, and the descriptions of qualitative models are too vague and general, neither of which can directly give an open-source ecosystem. Universal Health Assessment Program. This paper combines the classic OSEHO model and the rapidly developing CHAOSS open-source community metrics, establishes an OSSECO health evaluation model that can provide specific scores based on Entropy Method, and develops an OSSECO health evaluation system based on this model. It can automatically evaluate the health of open-source projects on GitHub and GitLab, two open-source code hosting platforms, and analyze the software ecosystem health of 10 open-source projects on GitHub.

In the future, while continuously improving the OSSECO health assessment model that has been built, we will also independently define indicative OSSECO health metrics based on the current performance of open-source projects and ecology (especially ecological aspects).

Acknowledgements. This paper was supported partly by National Natural Science Foundation of China under Grant Nos (62141209, 61932007, 61972013), and partly by Ministry of Industry and Information Technology.

References

1. Gonzalez-Barahona, J.M.: A brief history of free, open-source software and its communities. Computer **54**(2), 75–79 (2021)
2. Zhi, J., Minghui, Z., Yuxia, Z.: Open source software and its eco-systems: today and tomorrow. Sci. Technol. Rev. **34**(14), 42–48 (2016)
3. Tan, X., Zhou, M.: How to communicate when submitting patches: an empirical study of the Linux Kernel. In: Proceedings of the ACM on Human-Computer Interaction 2019, CSCW, vol. 3, pp. 1–26 (2019)

4. Zhang, Y., Zhou, M., Mockus, A., et al.: Companies' participation in OSS development-an empirical study of OpenStack. IEEE Trans. Software Eng. **47**(10), 2242–2259 (2021)
5. Liao, Z., Deng, L., Fan, X., et al.: Empirical research on the evaluation model and method of sustainability of the open-source ecosystem. Symmetry **10**(12), 747 (2018)
6. Jansen, S., Finkelstein, A., Brinkkemper, S.: A sense of community: a research agenda for software ecosystems. In: 2009 31st International Conference on Software Engineering-Companion Volume, pp. 187–190 (2009)
7. Manikas, K., Hansen, K.: Reviewing the health of software ecosystems - a conceptual framework proposal. In: CEUR Workshop Proceedings, p. 987 (2013)
8. Gamalielsson, J., Lundell, B., Lings, B.: Responsiveness as a measure for assessing the health of OSS ecosystems. In: Proceedings of International Workshop on Building Sustainable Open Source Communities (2010)
9. Yvonne, D.: Software engineering beyond the project - sustaining software ecosystems. Inf. Softw. Technol. **56**(11), 1436–1456 (2011)
10. Iuri, A., Fernanda, C., Regina, M., et al.: HEAL ME - an architecture for health software ecosystem evaluation. In: 2017 IEEE/ACM Joint 5th International Workshop on Software Engineering for Systems-of-Systems and 11th Workshop on Distributed Software Development, Software Ecosystems and Systems-of-Systems (JSOS), pp. 59–65 (2017)
11. Open-source Community Maturity Research Report. http://doc.opensourcecloud.cn/2021/0724.pdf. Accessed 27 Sept 2022
12. Wang, W., Zhou, T., Zhao, S., et al.: Research on the development of global open-source ecology. Inf. Commun. Technol. Policy **46**(5), 38–44 (2020)
13. Goggins, S., Lumbard, K., Germonprez, M.: Open-source community health: analytical metrics and their corresponding narratives. In: 2021 IEEE/ACM 4th International Workshop on Software Health in Projects, Ecosystems and Communities (SoHeal), pp. 25–33 (2021)
14. Jansen, S.: Measuring the health of open-source software ecosystems: moving beyond the project scope. Inf. Softw. Technol. **56**(11), 1508–1519 (2014)
15. CHAOSS. https://chaoss.community. Accessed 27 Sept 2022
16. CHAOSS Metrics. https://chaoss.community/wp-content/uploads/2022/04/English-Release-2022-04-18v2.pdf. Accessed 27 Sept 2022
17. Augur. https://github.com/chaoss/augur. Accessed 27 Sept 2022
18. Yuxin, Z., Dazuo, T., Feng, Y.: Effectiveness of entropy weight method in decision-making. Math. Problems Eng. **2020**, 5 (2020). Article ID 3564835

Topic Discovery in Scientific Literature

Yujian Huang, Qiang Liu, Jia Liu, and Yanmei Hu[(✉)]

Chengdu University of Technology, Chengdu, China
{huangyj,huyanmei}@cdut.edu.cn, liujia0833@stu.cdut.edu.cn

Abstract. With the progress of society and science, various fields have achieved unprecedented development. Various research directions and problems have blossomed, and a huge amount of scientific literature has emerged. Scientific literature contains rich "knowledge", e.g., research hotspots and topics. If those "knowledge" can be obtained from scientific literature, it would be of great practical significance to both government and researchers. The existing methods generally obtain "knowledge" by analyzing the semantics of scientific literature, which is complex and time-consuming. In this paper, we aim to explore new methods of research hot word extraction and research topic discovery from the perspective of network. Firstly, the word network is constructed based on the text of scientific literature. Next, a research hot word extraction method based on node centrality and a structural topic discovery method are proposed on the word network. Then, the consistency between structural topics and semantic topics is explored. Finally, the proposed methods are experimentally verified on a real dataset. The experimental results show that the proposed centrality based hot word extraction method can effectively extract research hot words, and the topics obtained by the structural topic discovery method are consistent with the semantic topics in some cases, providing a new way to textual knowledge discovery.

Keywords: topic discovery · network structure · centrality · clustering · community discovery

1 Introduction

Scientific literature is the main manifestation of scientific research carried out by scientific and technical workers, and it condenses the highest wisdom of human beings, gathers the concerns of various research fields and even the whole human society, and contains the intricate relationships between research problems and key technologies. Therefore, by observing and analyzing scientific literature, we can understand the concerns and key technologies of different research fields and capture the correlation between them, and even find interesting patterns which would give us a deeper insight on the development of science and technology. For instance, mining research hotspots and topics hidden in scientific literature is significantly important to researchers and governments, since research hotspots and topics can tell what the concerns are in different fields. In recent years, the scientific literature has shown a rapid growth and a large number of scientific articles have been appearing, since many countries pay more and more attention to scientific research. Taking China as an example, it has ushered in the peak period of rapid

© The Author(s), under exclusive license to Springer Nature Singapore Pte Ltd. 2023
Y. Sun et al. (Eds.): ChineseCSCW 2022, CCIS 1681, pp. 481–491, 2023.
https://doi.org/10.1007/978-981-99-2356-4_38

growth of scientific articles since the reform and open policy was executed. According to reports from China Science and Technology Network, the total number of scientific papers indexed by SCI, SSCI and the Humanities and Arts Citation Index (A&HCI) from China exceeded 10,000 in 1995; the number of scientific articles from China was nearly 140,000 in 2010; and the annual output of scientific articles is nearly 290,000 in 2015. Obviously, to observe and analyze "knowledge" from such a large amount of scientific literature, it is extremely unrealistic to only rely on manual labour.

Fortunately, data mining has been developed widely and the related technologies are more and more mature, making it possible to automatically accomplish a lot of tasks using machines. Data mining refers to the process of extracting hidden rules and valuable information from a large amount of data by algorithms, involving mathematical statistics, machine learning, pattern recognition, etc. A natural way to apply data mining to exploring "knowledge" from scientific literature is performing text mining on a collection of articles, since each article in the scientific literature is essentially a document. For example, we can use clustering to categorize articles into different groups, and many methods, e.g., traditional clustering algorithms such as K-means [1] and its variants, and ontology-based clustering [2], are available to text clustering. We can also use topic models such as Probabilistic Latent Semantic Analysis (PLSA) [3], Latent Dirichlet Allocation (LDA) [4], and their variants to detect research topics. We can also simply count word and take the words with high frequency as research hot words. However, regarding to the traditional clustering methods, each article (or the used text of each article) is required to be represented as numerical vector using techniques such as coding or Doc2vec [5]. The former one must use an element to represent each word appearing in the corpus, i.e., the length of the numerical vector is equal to the number of words, consuming a huge amount of memory and computation time; the later one is developed based on Word2vec and is much more complicated, and it also requires a corpus large enough to obtain good representation. Regarding to topic models, they can automatically extract topics as well as the belongingness of each article to each topic based on text information, but the quality of the model is not guaranteed and the major problem is that the topic result is not visual and may not reflect the difference between topics. In addition, word frequency indicates the number of times that a word appears in the used articles and reflects word's popularity, but it does not consider the interaction and similarity between words.

In this paper, we mine "knowledge", specifically hot words and topics, in scientific literature from the perspective of network, and study the consistency between structural topics and semantic topics for the first time, with the aim of exploring a more visual and effective method to mine the main research contents and concerns in scientific literature. First, a word network is constructed to represent the collection of scientific literature. Second, a method of hot word extraction based on node centrality is proposed to identify research hot words from the word network. Then, a structural topic discovery method is proposed to detect research topics according to the topological structure of the word network. The consistency between structural topics and semantic topics is also explored. Finally, experiments are conducted on a collection of scientific literature in the field of computer science to test the proposed methods. Experimental results show that the research hot words can be effectively extracted by the proposed hot word extraction method, and the obtained structural topics can be consistent with semantic topics. This result implies that it is feasible to discover the main contents and concerns in scientific literature from the perspective of network, providing a new way to "knowledge" discovery in text.

The organization of rest part is as follows. The most related work is described in Sect. 2. Section 3 presents the hot word extraction method based on node centrality. Section 4 presents the structural topic discovery method and analyzes the consistency between structural topics and semantic topics. Experiments are presented in Sect. 5, and Sect. 6 concludes the work.

2 Related Work

To detect research hot words in scientific literature, one can simply count each word appears in articles. However, for an article not each word is informative to the main content. It is thus more realistic to only count the keywords since they condense the most concerned content of article. There are commonly keywords explicitly provided for an article, but one may perform keyword extraction to obtain more objective and suitable keywords. As a fundamental problem in text mining, keyword extraction has been researched widely and there are many ways to extract keywords. For example, one can train a machine learning model on a set of documents where the keywords are known and then used the resulting model to obtain keywords for documents where the keywords are not known [6]. One can also apply statistical methods to obtain keywords. The n-gram statistics [7], word frequency, TF-IDF [8], word co-occurrence, and PAT tree [9] can all be used as statistics of words. Particularly, Biswas et al. proposed KECNW, which is based on node edge rank centrality with node weight depending on various parameters, to extract keywords [10].

To detect research topics in scientific literature, one can use topic models. LDA [11] is a classical model for topics mining in a set of documents. It applies statistics to obtain the topics and the distribution of each document on the topics. LDA can efficiently infer topics, but the number of topics is artificially preset. The HDP model overcomes this limitation by automatically determining the number of topics, but the number of hidden parameters in HDP increases with the data size [12]. The related topic model (CTM) represents another extension of LDA, and it uses a logistic normal distribution to model the variability in the topic proportions of each document to discover related topics [13]. Linstead et al. first used LDA to extract topics in source code and visualize software similarity [14]. Zhao et al. proposed a personalized topic recommendation method based on LDA, called hashtag-LDA, to discover latent topics in microblog [15]. Yin et al. propose a topic model named as LGTA, which is a combination of topic modeling and geographic clustering, to detect topics from geographic information and GPS related documents [16]. Link-LDA is extended from LDA to discover latent topics in a collection of articles by combining citation structures and textual information [17]. Some researchers also integrate author information into LDA, PLSA or HDP to solve the problem of mining author-topic distribution [18]. Cuietal utilizes TextFlow to show the split and fusion of themes [19]. Liu developed a method for mapping technological evolutionary paths using a novel nonparametric topic model named as CIHDP, which adds citation information to the topic model to determine the number of topics for better dynamic topic detection and track scientific literature [20]. BALILI et al. proposed the TermBall framework, which can simulate the knowledge structure of research topics and track or predict the evolution of research topics [21]. TermBall represents research topics as communities of keywords in a dynamic co-occurrence network.

3   Research Hot Word Extraction Based on Node Centrality

Two problems need to be solved to extract research hot words from the perspective of network. One is how to construct a network based on text data of scientific literature. The other one is how to use the structure of word network to determine hot words. To solve these two problems, we propose a research hot word extraction method based on node centrality. The method consists of two steps: 1) construct a word network according to the adjacent positions of words; 2) apply a centrality metric to calculate each node's centrality value in the word network, and then select the words corresponding to nodes with high centrality value as hot words. Next, we will describe the two steps in detail.

3.1   The Construction of Word Network

For a collection of scientific literature, we first extract each article's abstract and concatenate all the abstracts to form a text. Here we only consider abstract for each article because abstract condenses the research content of a article. Then, we preprocess the text by removing meaningless words and irrelevant words. Meaningless words refer to words without specific meanings such as conjunctions, prepositions and modal verbs. Irrelevant words refer to unimportant words. For a word, its importance is measured as.

$$R(id) = atf_{id} * log(\frac{N}{n_{id}}) \tag{1}$$

where atf_{id} is the times of word id (each word is assigned a unique id) appearing in the text, N is the number of articles, n_{id} is the number of articles where word id appears. After the importance of each word is evaluated by Eq. 1, the words with small importance are considered as unimportant nodes and are eliminated. Actually, we find that the distribution of word importance follows a long tail distribution, i.e., a lot of words have small importance while a few words have extremely large importance.

After the preprocessing above, we construct the word network as follows: each word in the text is represented as a node, and if two words are adjacent to each other in the same sentence, a directed edge is established between the corresponding two nodes. For example, given a text with only one sentence "w1 w2 w1 w3." where w1, w2, and w3 are three different words, the word network constructed from this text contains 3 nodes with each one representing one word; and because w1 and w2 are adjacent to each other in this sentence, there is a directed edge from w1 to w2. Similarly, there are directed edges from w2 to w1 and from w1 to w3.

3.2 Node Centrality Calculation and Hot Words Selection

The centrality of a node is used to evaluate the importance or influence of the node, generally according to the network structure [22]. Thus, we can utilize the centrality of nodes in word network to extract the hot words in scientific literature. There are many centrality metrics in the literature, e.g., degree centrality, betweenness centrality [23, 24], closeness centrality [25], PageRank centrality [26], eigenvector centrality [27]. Some metrics based on local structure such as local clustering coefficient [28] and neighborhood conductance [29] can be used as local centrality. Among these centralities, which one is more suitable for our case? First, hot words should appear frequently; second, hot words should span multiple domains. Moreover, we find that the word network is very dense, and most nodes have relatively high degree and all nodes have a degree more than 50 (see experimental part for details). It means that most nodes meet the first condition. For a node v_i, its betweenness centrality is calculated as:

$$(v_i) = \sum_{s \neq t \neq v_i} \frac{\sigma_{st(v_i)}}{\sigma_{st}} \tag{2}$$

where σ_{st} is the number of shortest paths from node s to node t, and $\sigma_{st(v_i)}$ is the number of shortest paths through v_i. It can be seen from Eq. 2 that if a node frequently appears on the shortest paths between other nodes, its betweenness centrality is high, implying that nodes with high betweenness centrality are important bridges connecting other nodes. This meets the second condition. Therefore, we calculate the betweenness centrality of each node in the word network, and then select as hot words the words corresponding to nodes with high centrality value. Specifically, nodes are sorted in descending order of centrality value, and the top k nodes are selected to obtain hot words.

4 Structural Topic Discovery and Consistence Analysis

4.1 Structural Topic Discovery

The word network reflects the contextual relationship between words, and the nodes that are densely connected in the word network are context-dependent on each other. We call the context-dependent words as a structural topic, since they are grouped together through the topology of word network. Discovering structural topics is essentially the task of community detection, since each structural topic corresponds to a group of densely connected nodes in the word network. Thus, we can perform community detection on the word network to complete the discovery of structural topics.

Community detection is to find out the subsets of densely connected nodes and take each of these subsets as a community [30], and is a fundamental problem in network science. There have been a large number of community detection algorithms proposed in the literature [31], we can choose one of them to perform on the word network, and take each obtained community as a structural topic.

4.2 Consistence Analysis

Further, it is interesting to explore whether the structural topic is consistent with the semantic topic obtained through semantics (e.g., the topic obtained by LDA). If the structural topic is consistent with the semantic topic, then we can discover topics through word network, without using more complex methods such as topic models. Then, how to analyze the consistence between structural topics and sematic topics? After obtaining the structural topics as described in the previous subsection, we follow three steps to fulfil this task: 1) cluster words into different groups to obtain sematic topics; 2) analyze the connectivity within each semantic topic; 3) analyze the distribution of each cohesive sematic topic on structural topics.

Sematic Topics. To obtain sematic topics, we first apply the technique of Word2vec to represent each word as a vector, then use K-means to cluster the word vectors into different groups. Each group is taken as a sematic topic.

Connectivity within a Semantic Topic. For a semantic topic ST_i, we randomly choose a word in it, and take the node corresponding to the chosen word as starting node to perform the breadth-first search algorithm on the word network, with the constrain of ST_i. In particular, for a node encountered by the breadth-first search algorithm, if the corresponding word belongs to ST_i, then the breadth-first search will continue on this node; otherwise, the breadth-first search is truncated at this node. If the corresponding node of each word in ST_i has been visited after the breadth-first search terminates, ST_i is cohesive; otherwise, it is not.

Distribution of a Cohesive Semantic Topic on Structural Topics. For a cohesive semantic topic ST_i, , find the structural topics that overlap with it (two topics are overlapped if they have at least one common word), and evaluate the degree of overlap between ST_i and each of these structural topics.

5 Experimental Results and Analysis

In this section, the proposed methods are tested, and the consistency between structural topics and semantic topics is analyzed. The used dataset is obtained by crawling articles published in ACM and IEEE (only the articles related to computer science are considered in this publisher) from 2015 to 2019, and a total of 11,592 articles are contained.

Word Network. Following the method described in Sect. 3.1, we construct the word network corresponding to the dataset, and its structural information is as follows: the word network contains 849 nodes and more than 100,000 edges, and the average degree is 135.11, the average length of the shortest paths is 1.84, the density is 0.159, and the average clustering coefficient is 0.333, implying that the word network is relatively dense and nodes can easily reach each other. In addition, the degree distribution of the word network is shown in Fig. 1. It can be seen that this distribution is quite different from the well-known power-law distribution, and even the minimum degree is larger than 50.

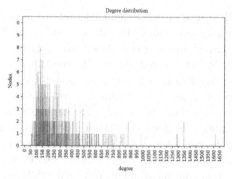

Fig. 1. Degree distribution of word network

Hot Words. The betweenness centrality distribution is shown in the left figure in Fig. 2. It can be seen that the range of the centrality values is [12.8, 30654.5] which is a relatively large span; this distribution follows a power-law distribution, which implies that only a few nodes have a very high centrality value and most nodes have a very low centrality value. We empirically take the top 30 words as hot words and show them separately in the right figure of Fig. 2. It can be seen that the hot words are common technical terms such as model, algorithm and graph, and there are also some words related to research topics such as recommendation, classification and cluster.

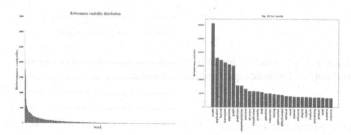

Fig. 2. Betweenness centrality distribution (left) and the top 30 hot words (right).

In addition, we analyze the neighborhood of hot words. Specifically, for each hot word, we get the neighbor nodes of its corresponding node, and sort these neighbor nodes in descending order of centrality value. We find that all the hot words have very similar neighbors with high centrality, which are further very similar to the hot word set. Taking "graph" as an example, the first 30 neighbor nodes are exactly the same to the top 30 hot words (the ones shown in the right figure in Fig. 2). This implies that all the hot words are highly connected. Further, it seems that the word network is composed of highly connected hot words and marginal words closely surrounding the hot words.

Structural Topics and Consistence with Semantic Topics. To obtain the structural topics on the word network, we apply a very popular algorithm of community detection, named as Louvain [32], to perform community discovery on the word network, and each community is taken as a structural topic. In order to evaluate the quality of the obtained structure topics from network structure (i.e., the quality of the discovered communities), we apply two metrics: conductance and density. The conductance of a community is the proportion of out-going edges to the total edges induced by the nodes in this community, and density is the ratio of edges in the community to the ones in the complete graph containing the same nodes. Lower conductance indicates better community while higher density indicates better one. The details of the two metrics are referred to [33]. The left figure in Fig. 3 shows the evaluation result (isolated nodes are not shown); each node represents a community and the node size is proportional to the community size, the value on the left of "-" is conductance and the one on the right is density. It can be seen that the connections within communities are relatively dense (high density), but there are also many connections between communities (high conductance). It can be inferred that the boundary between communities is blurred, which is reasonable in dense networks.

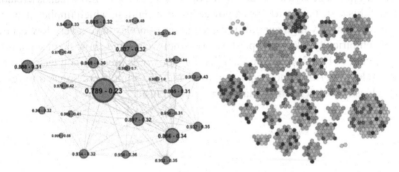

Fig. 3. The quality of the structural topics from the perspective of network structure (left) and the obtained structural and semantic topics and their distribution (right)

To obtain the sematic topics, we apply Word2vec to convert each word into a vector of 100 dimensions, and then use K-means to cluster the word vectors into different groups. Consequently, 35 semantic topics are obtained. After checking the connectivity of semantic topics, we find that the semantic topics to which the hot words belong are all cohesive. This means that the hot words have good connectivity in the word network, which is consistent with the definition of betweenness centrality. Besides, there are three semantic topics that are not cohesive, but they are also semantically unimportant. To analyze the consistence between structural topics and semantic topics, we compare structural topics and semantic topics from a macro perspective, and the results are shown in the right figure of Fig. 3, where each separated part indicates a structural topic, and each color indicates a semantic topic. It can be seen that there are three types of semantic topics that are relatively tight in structure, and most words of them are within the same structural topic. The first type is related to proper nouns (such as GPU, disk, file, etc.), including three semantic topics. Most words in them are distributed within one structural topic (the largest structural topic in the upper left corner), and they are the main members of that structural topic. The second type mainly involves business and market media (such as amazon, commerce, sale, profit, market, twitter, etc.), including three semantic topics. Most words in them are also within the same structural topic (the largest structural topic in the lower right corner). The third type also includes three sematic topics, mainly involving expressions related to daily life (such as traffic, taxi, bus, GPS, home, car, vehicle, weather, etc.). To these three types of sematic topics, each of them concentrates on one structural topic, indicating that these sematic topics are similar to structural topics. Furthermore, the words belonging to semantic topics related to graph theory are basically distributed in the leftmost structural topic, but this structural topic also contains other words such as bridge, connectivity, neighbor, and motif, which are all related to graph theory. This indicates that in this case the structural topic is better than the semantic topic. In addition, there are eight isolated nodes (upper left corner) corresponding to words of model, framework, application, machine, feature, recommendation, graph and algorithm, respectively. There are also 4 semantic topics scattered in multiple structural topics, which are pink-purple, green, orange, and brown, and we find that the words of these sematic topics are unimportant in terms of centrality. From the discussion above, it can be inferred that in some cases the structural topics and the semantic topics are consistent.

6 Conclusion

From the perspective of network, this paper explores the methods of extracting research hot words and discovering research topics in scientific literature. Specifically, a word network is constructed to represent the contextual relationship of words in abstracts of articles. Based on the word network, we propose to extract hot words by node centrality and discover structural topics by community detection. Moreover, we analyze the consistency between structural topics and sematic topics. Experimental results on a collection of articles show that the proposed hot word extraction method can effectively extract research hot words, and the structural topics are consistent with semantic topics in some cases. This provides a potential way to mine research hot words and topics. However, this work is preliminary and requires more study in the future. For example, testing the methods on large datasets to obtain pervasive conclusion, trying or designing more suitable methods to discover structural topics, and designing suitable metrics to improve consistence analysis.

References

1. Yildirim, M.E., Kaya, M., Ince, L.F.: A case study: unsupervised approach for tourist profile analysis by k-means clustering in turkey. Internet Comput. Serv. **23**(1), 11–17 (2022)
2. Dou, D.J., Wang, H., Liu, H.S.: Semantic data mining: a survey of ontology-based approaches. In: IEEE ICSC (2015) 978–1–4799–7935–6
3. Bassiou, N.K., Kotropoulos, C.L.: online plsa: batch updating techniques including out-of-vocabulary words. IEEE Trans. Netw. Learn. Syst. **25**(11), 1953–1966 (2014)
4. Li, X., Ouyang, J., Zhou, X., Lu, Y., Liu, Y.: Supervised labeled latent Dirichlet allocation for document categorization. Appl. Intell. **42**(3), 581–593 (2014). https://doi.org/10.1007/s10 489-014-0595-0

5. Hernández-Castañeda, Á., García-Hernández, R.A., Ledeneva, Y., Millán-Herná-Ndez, C.E.: Extractive automatic text summarization based on lexical-semantic keywords. IEEE Access **8**, 49896–49907 (2020)
6. Beliga, S., Meštrović, A., Martinčić-Ipšić, S.: Selectivity-based keyword extraction method. Int. J. on Semantic Web Inf. Syst. **12**(3), 1–26 (2016)
7. Tripathy, A., Agrawal, A., Rath, S.K.: Classification of sentiment reviews using n-gram machine learning approach. Expert Syst. Appl. **57**, 117–126 (2016)
8. Zhang, Y.T., Gong, L., Wang, Y.C.: An improved TF-IDF approach for text classlncatlon. Zhejiang Univ. Sci. **6**(1), 49–55 (2005)
9. Kang, D.-K., Sohn, K.: Learning decision trees with taxonomy of propositionalized attributes. Pattern Recogn. **42**(1), 84–92 (2009)
10. Biswas, S.K., Bordoloi, M., Shreya, J.: A graph based keyword extraction model using collective node weight. Expert Syst. Appl. **97**, 51–59 (2018)
11. Li, X., Ouyang, J., Lu, Y., Zhou, X., Tian, T.: Group topic model: organizing topics into groups. Inf. Retrieval J. **18**(1), 1–25 (2014). https://doi.org/10.1007/s10791-014-9244-9
12. Teh, Y.W., Jordan, M.I., Beal, M.J., Blei, D.M.: Hierarchical dirichlet processes. J. Am. Stat. Assoc. **101**(476), 1566–1581 (2006)
13. Blei, D.M., Lafferty, J.D.: A correlated topic model of science. Annal. Appli. Stat. **1**(1), 17–35 (2007)
14. Jelodar, H., et al.: Latent Dirichlet allocation (LDA) and topic modeling: models,applications, a survey. Multimedia Tools Appli. **78**(11), 15169–15211 (2019)
15. Zhao, F., Zhu, Y.J., Jin, H., Yang, L.T.: A personalized hashtag recommendation approach using LDA-based topic model in microblog environment. Futur. Gener. Comput. Syst. **65**, 196–206 (2016)
16. Yin, Z.J., Cao, L.L., Han, J.W., Zhai, C.X., Huang, T.: Geographical topic discovery and comparison. In: Proceedings of the 20th International Conference on World Wide Web, pp. 247–256. ACM (2011)
17. Nallapati, R., Ahmed, A., Xing, E.P., Cohen, W.W.: Joint latent topic models for text and citations. In: Conference on knowledge Discovery Data Mining (KDD), vol. 14, pp. 542–550 (2008)
18. Shi, Q.W., Li, Y.N., Guo, P.L.: Dynamic finding of authors' research interests in scientific literature. J. Comput. Appli. **33**(11), 3080–3083 (2013)
19. Cui, W.W., et al.: Textfow: Towards better understanding of evolving topics in text. IEEE Trans. Visual Comput. Graph. **17**(12), 2412–2421 (2011)
20. Liu, H., Chen, Z., Tang, J., Zhou, Y., Liu, S.: Mapping the technology evolution path: a novel model for dynamic topic detection and tracking. Scientometrics **125**(3), 2043–2090 (2020). https://doi.org/10.1007/s11192-020-03700-5
21. Balili, C., Lee, U., Segev, A., Kim, J., Ko, M.: TermBall: tracking and predicting evolution types of research topics by using knowledge structures in scholarly big data. IEEE Access **8**, 108514–108529 (2020)
22. Borgatti, S.P., Everett, M.G.: A graph-theoretic perspective on centrality. Social networks **28**(4), 466–484 (2006)
23. Freeman, L.C.: A Set of measures of centrality based on betweenness. Sociometry **40**(1), 35–41 (1997)
24. Tsalouchidou, I., Baeza-Yates, R., Bonchi, F., Liao, K., Sellis, T.: Temporal betweenness centrality in dynamic graphs. Int. J. Data Sci. Analyt. **9**(3), 257–272 (2019). https://doi.org/10.1007/s41060-019-00189-x
25. Adebayo, I.G., Sun, Y.X.: A novel approach of closeness centrality measure for voltage stability analysis in an electric power grid. Int. J. Emerging Electric Power Syst. 3 (2020)
26. Hashemi, A., Dowlatshahi, M.B., Nezamabadi-pour, H.: MGFS: A multi-label graph-based feature selection algorithm via PageRank centrality. Expert Syst. Appl. **142**, 113024 (2019)

27. Cheung, K.F., Bell, M.G.H., Pan, J.J., Perera, S.: An eigenvector centrality analysis of world container shipping network connectivity. Transp. Res. Part E **140**, 101991 (2020)
28. Yin, H., Benson, A.R., Leskovec, J.: The local closure coefficient: a new perspective on network clustering. In: Proceedings of the Twelfth ACM International Conference on Web Search and Data Mining, pp. 303–311 (2019)
29. Hu, Y.M., Yang, B., Wong, H.S.: A weighted local view method based on observation over ground truth for community detection. Inf. Sci. **355**, 37–57 (2016)
30. Fortunato, S.: Community detection in graphs. Phys. Report **486**(3–5), 75–174 (2010)
31. Souravlas, S., Sifaleras, A., Tsintogianni, M., Katsavounis, S.: A classification of community detection methods in social networks: a survey. Int. J. Gen Syst **50**(1), 63–91 (2021)
32. Blondel, V.D., Guillaume, J-L., Lambiotte, R., Lefebvre, E.:Fast unfolding of communities in large networks. J. Statistical Mech. Theory Experim., P10008 (2008)
33. Hu, Y.M., Yang, B., Duo, B., Zhu, X.: Exhaustive exploitation of local seeding algorithms for community detection in a unified manner. Mathematics **10**(15), 2807 (2022)

Multi-agent Adversarial Reinforcement Learning Algorithm Based on Reward Query Attention Mechanism

Liwei Chen[1], Dingquan Jin[1], Tong Wang[1], and Yuan Chang[2(✉)]

[1] Harbin Engineering University, Harbin 150001, China
[2] Heilongjiang Branch of the National Computer Network Emergency Response Technical Team/Coordination Center of China, Harbin 150028, China
a15104536677@163.com

Abstract. In the multi-agent adversarial scenario, there are problems such as partial observability, exponential increase in the state space and action space of agents, non-stationary environment, and credit allocation. In order to solve the above problems,this paper proposes a value decomposition deep reinforcement learning algorithm QMIX-NA based on the reward query attention mechanism.The algorithm introduces batch regularization and attention mechanism to reduce the complexity of the algorithm and improve the performance of the algorithm. Finally, simulation experiments are carried out in the StarCraft 2 micro-management environment SMAC. The results show that the performance of the QMIX-NA algorithm is better than the traditional value decomposition deep reinforcement learning algorithm.

Keywords: Multi-agent reinforcement learning · Attention mechanism · Batch regularization

1 Introduction

Reinforcement learning plays an important role in the field of agents today. Reinforcement learning has good applications in Atari games [1], Go games [2], intelligent transportation [3] and resource allocation [4]. Traditional reinforcement learning algorithms such as Q-learning [5] and policy gradient learning [6] are difficult to meet today's task requirements,especially in the multi-agent field.With the increase of the number of agents, the state space and the action space will expand exponentially, the data will become difficult to process, and the complexity also will be increased [7]. Agents may also influence each other's policies, and problems such as environmental non-stationarity and credit assignment [8] also make it difficult for the learned agent policies to converge.

Partially observable and adversarial multi-agent problem requires that a single agent can only observe and make decisions within the observation range, which is more similar to the adversarial environment in the real world. Currently, the main solution to this problem is centralised training with decentralised execution framework[9]. This framework requires agents to use global information during training, and communication constraints between agents are removed. During testing, the agent communication constraints was turned on, and the agent also changed back to a partially observable setting. The centralized training with decentralised execution framework can be simulated in the laboratory.

At present, partially observable multi-agent algorithms mainly include COMA, IQL [10], VDN [11] and QIMX [12]. COMA is an algorithm based on policy gradients, all agents share a critic network, the output policies and output actions of the actor network of all agents are input into the critic network for training, and the algorithm proposes a counterfactual baseline to solve credit allocation problem. The IQL algorithm utilizes an actor-critic architecture, where each agent has an actor-critic trained to derive a policy.VDN and QMIX are based on value decomposition to solve the multi-agent adversarial problem. The action value function of each agent is mixed to the total action value function for training, and then decentralised for testing.

Traditional deep reinforcement learning algorithms based on value decomposition cannot effectively use sample information. Algorithms fail to optimize observations and global state, resulting in increased computational complexity and redundancy. To solve such problems, this paper proposes a value decomposition reinforcement learning algorithm QMIX-NA based on reward query attention mechanism, which extends QMIX. Firstly, the algorithm inputs the observations and actions into the batch regularization layer to obtain the data,then the data is passed through the agent network to get the action value function of the agent, and the greedy strategy is used to get the action of the agent in the current time step. Second, the global state and the reward value in the observation range are passed through the attention mechanism layer, where the reward value in the observation range is used as the query, and then calculate the correlation between the global state and the reward value to obtain the attention value.Finally, the attention value is input into the hypernetwork to get the parameter of the mixing network. The QMIX-NA algorithm is simulated in the SMAC environment. The experimental results show that the QMIX-NA algorithm is better than the traditional reinforcement learning algorithm based on value decomposition in both the average winning rate and the average return.

The main contributions of this paper are as follows:

1. A value decomposition reinforcement learning algorithm based on reward query attention mechanism is proposed. The attention value is obtained by calculating the correlation between the reward of the agent and the global state, where the reward is used as the query. Input the attention value into the hypernetwork to get the parameters of the mixing network. This approach can obtain more important state information in the current time step,and improves the efficiency of the algorithm.
2. The observations and actions are input into the batch regularization layer for batch regularization, and their output is input into the agent network. The agent network obtains the action value function of the agent. This approach improves convergence speed.
3. The algorithm proposed in this paper is simulated in StarCraft II micromanagement. Experimental results show that the new algorithm performs better than other reinforcement learning algorithms.

2 Background

A fully cooperative adversarial multi-agent task can be described as a decentralised partially observable Markov model (Dec-POMDP), it consists of a tuple $G = \langle S, n, A, P, r, U, O, \gamma \rangle$, $s \in S$ describes the global state of the environment [13]. n is the number of all agents, where $i \in n$. A represents the set of action spaces, agent i selects an action a^i, and the actions selected by all agents are combined into a joint action value $a \in A$. P represents the state transition function, which means that the system selects a joint action at a certain time step to make the multi-agent system transfer from one state to another state, and its expression is $P(s'|s, a) : S \times A \times S \rightarrow [0, 1]$. r is the value of the reward function shared by the agents, $r(s, a) : S \times A \rightarrow \mathbb{R}$. $\gamma \in [0, 1)$ is a discount factor. U is the individual agent observations according to observation function $U(s, a) : S \times A \rightarrow O$. Each agent has an action observation history value $\tau^i \in T \equiv (O \times A)^*$, which conditions a stochastic policy $\pi^i(a^i|\tau^i) : T \times A \rightarrow [0, 1]$. The joint action value function is $Q^\pi(s_t, a_t) = \mathbb{E}_{s_{t+1:\infty}, a_{t+1:\infty}}[R_t|s_t, a_t]$, where $R_t = \sum_{k=0}^{\infty} \gamma^i r_{t+k}$ is the discounted return.

2.1 Deep Q-Learning

Deep Q-learning refers to the combination of neural network and reinforcement learning, and uses neural network to learn action value function [2]. In order to make better use of samples, deep Q learning uses experience replay pool to store sample $\langle s, a, r, s' \rangle$, and extracts samples during training. s' is the new state generated after state s selects action a. θ is learned by taking samples in batches of transition tuples in the experience replay pool and minimizing the TD squared error. The TD error loss function of the action value function is given by the following expression:

$$L(\theta) = \sum_{j=1}^{b}\left[\left(y_j^{DQN} - Q(s, a; \theta)\right)^2\right] \tag{1}$$

$$y^{DQN} = r + \gamma \max_{a'} Q(s', a'; \theta^-) \tag{2}$$

θ^- is the parameter of the target network, this target network parameter is updated by the value of θ in each epoch and keeps its value unchanged for many times of training.

2.2 Value Decomposition Network

VDN is a reinforcement learning algorithm based on value decomposition. In this algorithm, the action value function of each agent is summed to obtain Q_{tot}, and the action value function of each agent can only be learned through its own observations:

$$Q_{tot}(\tau, a) = \sum_{k=1}^{n} Q_k\left(\tau^k, a^k; \theta^k\right) \tag{3}$$

The loss function of VDN is the same as Eq. (1), except that Q is replaced by Q_{tot}.

2.3 Batch Regularization

During the training process of the neural network, the parameters of network layer also change with the update of input data [14]. This phenomenon causes the network to be extremely unstable, which leads to the failure of the algorithm to converge. In order to solve the above problems, batch regularization method is proposed to alleviate the variation of the input data distribution. The idea is that the input data will be processed at each network layer so that the mean is zero and the variance is one. In this way, the problem that the input data distribution is always changing and affecting the training of the later layer network is avoided.

2.4 Attention Mechanism

The attention mechanism is mainly based on the way of human cognition [15]. When processing information, humans focus on the information they need and ignore the information that is not important. This is an important way for humans to find valuable parts in a large amount of information with limited processing resources. Attention mechanisms improve the ability to process data and increase efficiency. In the attention mechanism, a query vector q is defined, and some information in the vector X is selected by q.

3 QMIX-NA Algorithm

In this paper, we propose a multi-agent adversarial reinforcement learning algorithm based on the reward query attention mechanism(QMIX-NA). Based on QMIX, the algorithm introduces reward query attention mechanism method and batch regularization method.

QMIX is a deep reinforcement learning algorithm based on value decomposition, which extends the constraints of VDN so that Q_{tot} and Q_k only need to satisfy the monotonic condition. QMIX consists of individual agent networks and mixing networks. Individual agent network is used to generate action value function and action. The mixing network mixes the Q_k of each agent to Q_{tot} and its parameters are mainly generated by the global state and then input into the hypernetwork.

It is difficult for QMIX to effectively use the global state information of the environment. The global state includes all the state information of the ally and the enemy, and the data is very large. Not all of the global states have an impact on the current decision task. We input all the global state information into the system, which will cause the increase of algorithm complexity and computation cost. This paper proposes the QMIX-NA algorithm to solve the problem that global state information cannot be effectively utilized. Compared with QMIX algorithm, the new algorithm adds a network layer of reward query attention mechanism.This layer calculates the correlation between the reward of the agent within the observation range and the global state of the environment, and obtains a new global state value, where the reward value is used as a query. This process focuses on the states that have the most impact on the decision in the current time step. The new state is input into the hypernetwork to get the parameters of the mixing network, which reduces the computational complexity and improves the performance of the algorithm. The algorithm also inputs the observation and the action of the agent into the batch regularization layer for batch regularization, which improves the convergence speed and the robustness of the network. The algorithm was simulated in StarCraft 2 Micromanagement.

The overall structure of the network is shown in Fig. 1. Environment part represents the system environment. The multi-agent extracts observations and actions at the current time step from the Environment. The composition of QMIX-NA network is shown in Fig. 1 as follows: (1) Attention part on the right represents the network layer based on reward query attention mechanism.(2) Agent part is the network of individual agents, which outputs action value function of individual agents. (3) The Mixing Network part is a network that mixes individual agent value functions Q_k into Q_{tot}.(4) Input the Q_{tot} into the target network for training to get a good model.

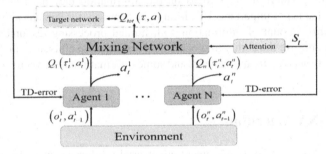

Fig. 1. The structure of QMIX-NA.

3.1 Individual Agent Network

The individual agent network is used to obtain the action value function of the agent, and uses the greedy strategy to select an action. The input of the individual agent network is the agent's current step observation o_t^k and the previous step's action a_{t-1}^k. The instability of the inputs will affect the convergence of the network parameters and the subsequent network training.Therefore, we add a batch regularization layer to process the input data, so that the mean value of the data is zero and the variance is one.Then the data is input to the fully connected layer. The input values are partially observable,so a GPU recurrent neural network is added. Finally, the greedy strategy is used to select the action value function $Q_k(\tau^k, a_t^k)$ and action a_t^k at the current time.

3.2 Attention Mechanism Network Layer

Hypernetwork generates mixing network parameters. In QMIX, the input of the hypernetwork is global state s_t. s_t is all unit information in the environment, this includes both ally and enemy forces. But not all of this information is what we need to pay attention to. A lot of state information is not important in the current task decision, and it will reduce the efficiency of training and cause information overload. We propose a reward query attention mechanism network layer. Figure 2 shows the structure of the attention mechanism network layer. First, we pass s_t through the encoder to get f_t^i. The encoder is a fully connected network layer. f_t^i is the global state information of agent i. Scores function uses the additive model to calculate the correlation between reward matrix r_{t-1} and state information f_t^i, r_{t-1} is reward matrix of all agents within the observation range of agent i at the previous time step. Scores function β_t^i is:

$$\beta_t^i = V_1^T \tanh\left(W_1 f_t^i + W_2 r_{t-1}\right) \tag{4}$$

V_1, W_1, W_2 are learnable parameter matrices.
The distribution of attention is:

$$\alpha_t^i = \frac{\exp\left(\beta_t^i\right)}{\sum_{j=1}^N \exp\left(\beta_t^j\right)} \tag{5}$$

α_t^i is the probability of each value in the global state at the current time step, which α_t^i can be obtained by the softmax function. Its main role is which information is more important in the current system. Finally, state f_t^i of agent i and attention distribution are weighted sum to obtain the attention value G_t^i:

$$G_t^i = \sum \alpha_t^i f_t^i \tag{6}$$

The new global state G_t is obtained by merging the output. The dimension of G_t is mainly determined by the number of agents.

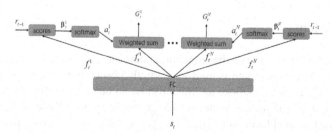

Fig. 2. Attention mechanism layer network structure. The reward matrix in the previous time step is used as query vector to calculate the correlation with global state of the agent to obtain attention distribution α_t^i. α_t^i is the probability of information in the global state. The higher the probability, the more information we need to pay attention to. Finally, the weighted sum is performed to obtain the attention value.

3.3 Mixture of Action Value Functions

Figure 3 shows the structure of the mixing network. The action value function of the individual agents Q_k is input into the mixing network. The mixing network is a feedforward neural network,its parameters are mainly determined by the hypernetwork. The input G_t of the hypernetwork can obtain W_a and W_b by the softmax function, which satisfy the non-negativity condition. Softmax function is verified to be better than abs function. G_t obtains the deviation value through the relu function and the activation function, and the deviation value does not need to satisfy the non-negativity condition. Finally, the state value function of each agent is input into the mixing network to get Q_{tot}. Q_{tot} is input into the target network for loss value calculation. The loss value is input into the individual agent network to minimize the loss value, and its loss value is:

$$L(\theta) = \sum_{j=1}^{b} \left[\left(y_j^{tot} - Q_{tot}(\tau, a; \theta) \right)^2 \right] \tag{7}$$

$y_j^{tot} = r_{all} + \gamma \max_{a'} Q_{tot}(\tau', a'; \theta')$. r_{all} is the total reward in the whole environment.

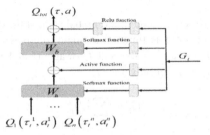

Fig. 3. Structure diagram of the mixing network

4   Experiments

In this paper, SMAC is used as the simulation platform. The platform is based on Star-Craft II micromanagement and is used for partially observable multi-agent adversarial simulation [16]. The observations are the information obtained by the agent within the observation range. The feature vectors observed by the agent include: distance,relative x,relative y,health,shield,and unit_type. The agent can also observe the surrounding terrain information. Using this terrain information, the agent can reduce the disadvantage in terms of numbers and improve the probability of defeating the enemy.The global state includes all the unit information on the scenario. Actions that the agent can choose include: move [direction], attack [enemy_id],stop,and no-op. The maximum value of actions that an individual agent can perform is between 7 and 40, depending on the scenario. The default value of the reward is set to the health damage dealt and the number of enemy units killed. The system also provides a sparse reward with +1 for winning and −1 for losing.

We simulate experiments in 8m_vs_9m homogeneous scenario and 3s5z_vs_3s6z heterogeneous scenario. The scenario is shown in Fig. 4 m_vs_9m is 8 marines units fighting with 9 marines units. 3s5z_vs_3s6z is a battle between 3 skulks, 5 zealots and

Fig. 4. Scenarios of 8 m_vs_9 m and 3s5z_vs_3s6z

3 skulks, 6 zealots. The system is trained centrally for 200 rounds and then performs decentralised testing. The mean win rate is the number of rounds the ally beats the enemy in a certain period of time divided by the total number of rounds. We use VDN, QMIX, QMIX-NA three algorithms to experiment and compare their mean win rate and mean return.

Fig. 5. Shows the performance of the three algorithms on the 8m_vs_9m scenario. The horizontal axis is the time step, while the vertical axis is the test mean win rate and test mean return, respectively. The convergence speed of VDN is the slowest. The mean win rate of VDN is stable at 80%. The mean return is similar, converging after 4 million time steps of training. Compared with VDN, the convergence speed of QMIX is fast. But in the end, the mean win rate and the mean return are almost the same as the VDN. In QMIX-NA, the convergence speed is almost the same with QMIX in 2 million time steps. However, in later training, it converges quickly and has excellent stability. The mean win rate and the mean return of QMIX-NA are better than those of QMIX and VDN, indicating that QMIX-NA has the best performance in this scenario.

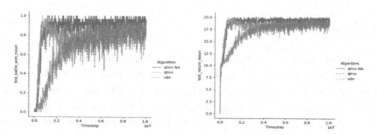

Fig. 5. The mean win rate and the mean return of the algorithm on the 8m_vs_9m scenario.

Fig. 6. Shows the performance of the three algorithms on 3s5z_vs_3s6z. The convergence speed of VDN algorithm is very slow, and the mean win rate can only reach 60%. This indicates that the performance of VDN is not good in this scenario. The convergence speed of QMIX is faster than VDN, and the mean win rate and the mean return are also higher than VDN. The convergence speed of QMIX-NA is obviously better than that of QMIX in the initial stage. The mean win rate and the mean return are also the highest.

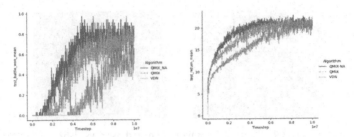

Fig. 6. The average win rate and the average return of the algorithm on 3s5z_vs_3s6z scenario.

The winning rate and the mean return of the three algorithms in the 8m_vs_9m scenario and in the 3s5z_vs_3s6z scenario are shown in Table 1. QMIX-NA is better than the other two algorithms in both the winning rate and the mean return.

Table 1. Table of the winning rate and mean return statistics for the three algorithms..

Scenario	Indicator	VDN	QMIX	QMIX-NA
8m_vs_9m	Winning rate	80%	85%	95%
	Mean return	17.7	18.1	20.9
3s5z_vs_3s6z	Winning rate	60%	70%	85%
	Mean return	14.1	16.2	19.2

5 Conclusion

This paper proposes a value decomposition deep reinforcement learning algorithm QMIX-NA based on the reward query attention mechanism. First, observations and actions are batch regularized. Then, the reward value of the agent is input as the query and the global state to the attention mechanism layer for calculation. The obtained attention value can reflect the more important state information in the current time decision. The algorithm is simulated in the homogeneous and heterogeneous scenarios of SMAC. The results show that the QMIX-NA algorithm is better than VDN and QMIX in mean win rate and mean return. However, the winning rate of QMIX-NA is the same as that of QMIX after training for a certain number of times in heterogeneous scenarios. How to further improve the winning rate in longer training is also a problem that needs to be solved, and it is also the main research work in the future.

References

1. Silver, D., Schrittwieser, J., Simonyan, K., et al.: Mastering the game of go without human knowledge. Nature **550**(7676), 354–359 (2017)

2. Mnih, V., Kavukcuoglu, K., Silver, D., et al.: Human-level control through deep reinforcement learning. Nature **518**(7540), 529–533 (2015)
3. Kim, S., Kim, B.J., Park, B.B.: Environment-adaptive multiple access for distributed V2X network: A reinforcement learning framework. In: 2021 IEEE 93rd Vehicular Technology Conference (VTC2021-Spring), pp. 1–7. IEEE (2021)
4. Burgueño, J., Adeogun, R., Bruun, R L., et al.: Distributed deep reinforcement learning resource allocation scheme for industry 4.0 device-to-device scenarios. In: 2021 IEEE 94th Vehicular Technology Conference (VTC2021-Fall), pp. 1–7. IEEE (2021)
5. Peters, J., Bagnell, J.A.: Policy gradient methods. Scholarpedia **5**(11), 3698 (2010)
6. Watkins, C.J.C.H., Dayan, P.: Q-learning. Mach. Learn. **8**(3), 279–292 (1992)
7. Zhang, K., Yang, Z., Başar. T.: Multi-agent reinforcement learning: A selective overview of theories and algorithms. In: Handbook of Reinforcement Learning and Control, pp. 321–384 (2021)
8. Foerster, J., Farquhar, G, Afouras, T., et al.: Counterfactual multi-agent policy gradients. In: Proceedings of the AAAI Conference on Artificial Intelligence, vol. 32(1) (2018)
9. Zhang, Y., Ma, H., Wang, Y.: Avd-net: Attention value decomposition network for deep multi-agent reinforcement learning. In: 2020 25th International Conference on Pattern Recognition (ICPR), pp. 7810–7816. IEEE (2021)
10. Tampuu, A., Matiisen, T., Kodelja, D., et al.: Multiagent cooperation and competition with deep reinforcement learning. PLoS ONE **12**(4), e0172395 (2017)
11. Sunehag, P., Lever, G., Gruslys, A., et al.: Value-decomposition networks for cooperative multi-agent learning. arXiv preprint arXiv:1706.05296, (2017)
12. Rashid, T., Samvelyan, M., Schroeder, C., et al.: Qmix: Monotonic value function factorisation for deep multi-agent reinforcement learning. In: International conference on machine learning, pp. 4295–4304. PMLR (2018)
13. Oliehoek, F.A., Amato, C.A.: concise introduction to decentralized POMDPs. Springer, (2016). https://doi.org/10.1007/978-3-319-28929-8
14. Ioffe, S., Szegedy. C.: Batch normalization: Accelerating deep network training by reducing internal covariate shift. In: International Conference on Machine Learning, pp. 448–456. PMLR (2015)
15. Niu, Z., Zhong, G., Yu, H.: A review on the attention mechanism of deep learning. Neurocomputing **452**, 48–62 (2021)
16. Samvelyan, M., Rashid, T., De Witt, C.S., et al.: The starcraft multi-agent challenge. arXiv preprint arXiv:1902.04043, (2019)

UAV Target Roundup Strategy Based on Wolf Pack Hunting Behavior

Tong Wang[1], Jianchao Wang[1], Min Ouyang[1], and Yu Tai[2(✉)]

[1] Harbin Engineering University, Harbin 150001, China
[2] Heilongjiang Province Big Data Center for Government Affairs, Harbin 150001, China
hrbtaiyu@126.com

Abstract. In nature, in order to hunt prey more efficiently, animals often adopt the method of group cooperation. By analyzing the similarity between the behavior of biological clusters and the control of unmanned aerial vehicle (UAV) clusters, this paper proposes a distributed hunting algorithm based on the hunting behavior of wolves to solve the target hunting problem in the cooperative combat of UAV clusters. Firstly, the chase and escape model of UAV is established, and the escape mode of the target is designed according to the artificial potential field method. Secondly, the hunting strategy of UAV clusters is determined by imitating the behavior characteristics of wolves during hunting. Finally, it is verified by simulation experiment. In this paper, the simulation hunting environment and multi-agent reinforcement learning environment are respectively verified, the UAV clusters can realize the target hunting, which proves the effectiveness of the algorithm.

Keywords: Cluster · cooperative rounding · wolf pack hunting behavior · distributed

1 Introduction

In the military and civil fields, UAV has been widely used because of its small size, low risk, strong concealment and mobility, and low cost [1]. Militarily, as the application scenarios of UAVs become more and more complex, the mission requirements of UAVs are also becoming higher and higher. The efficiency and success rate of a single UAV is low, and it cannot cope with some battlefield situations or complete some more complex tasks. Therefore, more UAVs are needed to cooperate with each other to meet the mission needs on the battlefield [2]. In recent years, multi-UAV cooperative control has been the focus of research [3]. The coordinated capture of multiple UAVs means that in the battlefield, UAVs can round up enemy targets according to a pre-designed hunting strategy. This kind of research has important value and broad application prospect [4].

In related research on roundup strategies. Reference [5] proposed a method for multi-robot cooperative pursuit of multi-moving targets. The method divides the search process into two parts: forming the pursuit group and capturing the target. By doping the target position, the pursuit is transformed into multi-robot path planning. Reference [6] proposed a new method based on particle swarm optimization, which enables particles to

Y. Sun et al. (Eds.): ChineseCSCW 2022, CCIS 1681, pp. 502–515, 2023.
https://doi.org/10.1007/978-981-99-2356-4_40

search and capture targets while bypassing obstacles. Reference [7] proposed a multi-underwater robot round-up strategy based on the wolf pack algorithm. Considering the environmental factors, the objective adaptive function is set. Each catcher optimizes task assignment through cooperative feedback, which greatly improves the convergence performance of the algorithm. Reference [8] introduces some models related to pursuit and escape. These models reveal a variety of general statistical features and show that small changes in behavioral rules or interaction parameters can lead to very different statistical behaviors. Reference [9] aims at the problems of slow convergence speed, poor stability and low positioning accuracy in the current multi-robot cooperative hunting process. A new roundup strategy is proposed, and a Cross-EKF positioning algorithm is designed to achieve accurate roundup of the target. This method has high practical value. Reference [10] studied the problem of target search and cooperative roundup of multi-robot fish swarms, and discussed the influence of the size of multi-robot fish swarms on target search and roundup success. Reference [11] proposed a collaborative roundup algorithm in which the roundup robot can predict the escaper's route in advance according to the target's trajectory. Reference [12] proposed the motion control of unmanned underwater vehicle (UUV) teams and an algorithm to predict the location of evaders in real time. In this method, only the central UUV needs to measure the relative positions of other UUVs through sensors. Inspired by the siege behavior of group animals during predation, Reference [13] proposed an effective strategy for faster target handling situations, and verified its effectiveness. Reference [14] designed a distributed controller to surround a moving target with a fixed radius and uniformly distributed phase angle. Reference [15] designed a distributed control method to make the agent globally converge to the desired circular formation around the moving target.

In the related research of multi-agent cooperative roundup and formation control problems. Reference [16] uses deep reinforcement learning to track an omnidirectional moving target and uses shared experience to train a policy for a given number of roundups. The strategy is executed by each agent individually and successfully applied to the pursuit scenarios of three motion-constrained pursuit UAV. Reference [17] introduced the concept of delay in multi-agent reinforcement learning, and proposed the Lenient DQN model, which made the learning speed of multi-agent cooperation converge faster. Reference [18] proposes a new method to quantitatively evaluate the collaboration of multi-agent reinforcement learning in continuous spatial tasks. Such a metric is useful for measuring collaboration between computational agents, and could serve as a collaborative training signal in future reinforcement learning paradigms involving humans. In the formation tracking problem, reference [19] designed a robust control strategy for the robust control problem of networked robot swarms under nonlinear dynamics and unknown disturbances. Reference [20] proposes a distributed adaptive backstepping control method for cooperative tracking of moving targets, which keeps the system asymptotically stable during the tracking process. Reference [21] proposed a relational forward model (RFM) for multi-agent learning. The network can learn to accurately predict the future behavior of agents in a multi-agent environment. After learning better feature representations, it can be applied to Multi-agents learn and collaborate more efficiently.

Among the existing methods, there are few studies on UAV rounding based on biological group behavior. Many strategies fail to account for situations in which some of the pursuit UAVs cannot continue their mission in special environments such as the battlefield (such as being shot down by enemy forces or malfunctioning). At this point the original strategy is not effective due to the number of pursuit UAVs lost. In view of the above situation, this paper proposes a roundup algorithm based on the hunting behavior of wolves [22]. There are no lead UAVs in the cluster. All pursuit UAVs are equivalent. In the process of encircling the target, there is no need to observe the global information, and only need to sense the coordinates of the escape UAV and the nearest pursuit UAV to successfully round up the target. It is verified by simulation experiments, and the results prove the effectiveness of the algorithm.

2   Task Description

In this paper, the scene of UAV cluster rounding up the escaping UAV in a two-dimensional simulation environment is adopted. The pursuit UAVs and escape UAVs are treated as particles, while ignoring the size and shape of the UAVs, each UAV can sense the location of other UAVs in real time. Based on the distributed characteristics, no leading UAV is set. Each pursuit UAV does not need to communicate with other UAVs, and plans its following pursuit direction according to its own perception of the surrounding environment. The escape UAV can also sense the location of other pursuit UAVs and plan its next escape direction. When the pursuit UAVs can be evenly distributed around the target and meet the prescribed distance, it is regarded as a successful roundup.

3   Hunting Algorithm Based on Wolf Pack Hunting Behavior

3.1   Brief Description of Hunting Behavior of Wolves

Wolves hunt differently than lions and tigers. Due to the relatively small size of wolves, in the process of hunting, they will not directly conflict with large prey, but adopt a roundabout way of group cooperation. While encircling the prey, it continued to fight the war of attrition with the prey, and finally succeeded in the predation. In the process of hunting, wolves do not rely on the mutual communication between hunting individuals, nor do they need to cooperate according to the hierarchical division of labor in the group to correctly complete the task. The hunting process of wolves is mainly divided into two stages: approaching the prey and encircling the prey. When approaching the prey, each wolf moves towards the prey. When the distance from the prey reaches a safe distance, in order to prevent the target prey from being hurt by counterattack, keep this safe distance and do not continue to approach the prey. At this time, wait for other wolves to encircle the prey. In the stage of encircling the prey, in addition to maintaining a safe distance from the prey, each wolf should keep away from other hunting wolves, and attack the prey during this period until the hunt is successful.

3.2   A Roundup Strategy Based on the Hunting Behavior of Wolves

In the roundup algorithm based on the hunting behavior of wolves. The rounding up of the target by the UAVs is divided into two stages: the approaching stage and the encircling stage. During the pursuit, the escape target can plan its next behavior based on the movement information of all the pursuit UAVs. When the target perceives the pursuit UAV, according to the principle of repulsion between itself and each pursuit UAV, the direction of escape selects the combined velocity direction of all the pursuit UAVs. As shown in Fig. 1, the dot is the current position of the target UAV. All solid lines represent the speed direction of the pursuit UAV, and the dashed line direction is the combined speed direction of all solid lines, that is, the escape direction of the target. The escape angle of the target is as follows:

$$\alpha = \arctan\left(\frac{\sum\limits_{i=1}^{n} v_i \sin\theta_i}{\sum\limits_{i=1}^{n} v_i \cos\theta_i}\right) + m\pi,\ m = \begin{cases} 0, & \text{combined speed in one and four quadrants} \\ 1, & \text{combined speed in two and three quadrants} \end{cases}$$

$$(1)$$

In the formula, v_i is the speed of the i-th pursuit UAV, and θ_i is the angle between the speed direction of the i-th UAV and the x-axis.

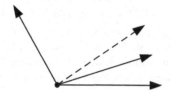

Fig. 1 Escape strategy of the target

When the pursuit UAV finds the target UAV, it enters the approaching stage of the roundup process. In this stage, the UAV cluster first maintains the original formation method to approach the target. After reaching a certain distance, in order to continue to make the pursuit UAV approach the target from multiple directions and maintain a certain safe distance from the target, the following strategy is adopted. As shown in Fig. 2, multiple circles are made with target A as the center, and the innermost solid circle represents the safe distance of the target UAV. All pursuit UAVs should try to avoid entering the circle and colliding with the target during this process. The moving direction of the pursuit UAV is the tangent direction formed by the current position and the dotted circle. In order to approach the target as soon as possible and prevent the pursuit UAV from being too close to cause a collision, the radius of all dotted circles changes dynamically with the distance of the pursuit UAV relative to the target. The line connecting the target UAV and the center of the pursuit UAV cluster is a straight line AB, and the pursuit UAV decides which tangential direction to move along according to its position relative to the straight line AB.

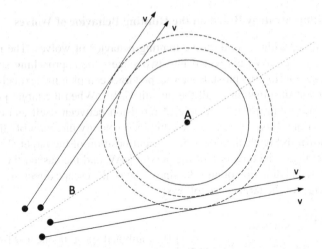

Fig. 2 Movement strategy for pursuit UAVs in the approach phase.

When a certain number of pursuit UAVs reach the safe range of the target UAV, it enters the encirclement stage of the roundup process. In this stage, in addition to moving to a designated position with a safe distance from the target as soon as possible, all the pursuit UAVs should also be distributed evenly around the target as much as possible. The movement strategy of the pursuit UAV is shown in Fig. 3. In Fig. 3, A is the target UAV, B1, B2, and B3 are the pursuit UAVs, and R is the safety distance of the target. When the position of the pursuit UAV is outside a safe distance, such as B1, the movement strategy of B1 is as follows. First, find the closest pursuit UAV B2. According to the relative position of B2 and the straight line AB1, B1 selects the direction away from B2 in the two tangential directions, that is, the V1 direction, to ensure that it can be evenly distributed around the target. When the position of the pursuit UAV B3 enters the safe range of target A, in order to ensure a certain safe distance, the moving direction selected by B3 is the direction of V3 away from target A.

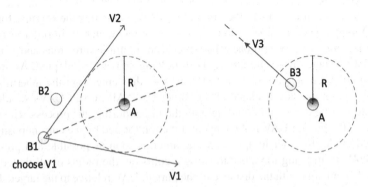

Fig. 3 Movement strategy for pursuit UAVs in the encirclement phase.

In the encirclement stage, the roundup strategy based on the allocation of encirclement sites is not adopted. All pursuit UAVs are equivalent in the encirclement phasephase. Each pursuit UAV only needs the perceived target A and the position coordinates of the nearest pursuit UAV to make the action choice autonomously. This allows no matter how many pursuit UAVs there are, they can be evenly distributed in a circle with the target as the center and a safe distance as the radius. To a great extent, it satisfies the needs of the roundup task for escape targets in special environments such as the battlefield. The overall process of the roundup strategy based on the hunting behavior of wolves is shown in Fig. 4.

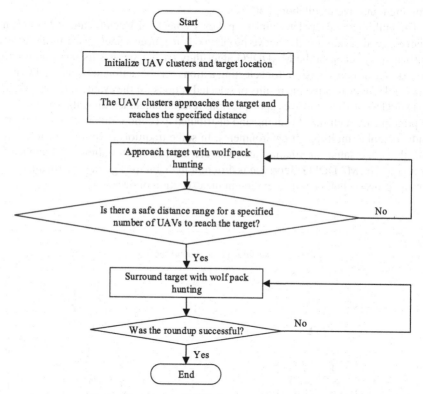

Fig. 4 Flow chart of UAV clusters rounding up target

3.3 Wolf Pack Hunting Behavior Combined with Reinforcement Learning

Reinforcement learning is a type of machine learning. Unlike supervised learning and unsupervised learning, reinforcement learning learns through the constant interaction of the agent with the environment to achieve specified goals or maximize reward returns. Multi-agent reinforcement learning extends Markov property to the field of multi-agent. Suppose there are some agents in the environment, each agent chooses an action according to its own strategy, enters the next state after executing the action, and obtains a reward according to the current state. In this process, each agent will try to get itself a higher expected return.

Multi-agent scenarios are very common in life. In the same environment, there are multiple agents interacting with the current environment at the same time. In this environment, each agent's own policy actions will also become part of the environment and continue to affect the learning of other agents. Due to the dynamic nature of the environment caused by the above situation, it will be very difficult to achieve a feasible and effective reinforcement learning algorithm. Assuming that only centralized learning methods are used, an exponentially growing complex space will be faced, and if completely independent algorithms are used, it is difficult to achieve good results for training involving multi-agent collaboration.

The multi-agent deep deterministic policy gradient (MADDPG) algorithm [23] has achieved good results for the above problems. It has been widely used in the field of multi-agent systems. In the MADDPG algorithm, each agent has its own Actor-Critic network, Actor is responsible for selecting actions for the action network, and Critic is responsible for evaluating the results of selected actions for the evaluation network. The MADDPG algorithm improves upon previous reinforcement learning algorithms. Using the principle of centralized training and distributed execution, this feature enables it to handle complex multi-agent environments. In some traditional reinforcement learning algorithms, the same information and data are used for both training and application execution. The MADDPG algorithm is different in that it uses global information in the learning process, but local information in the execution of decisions.

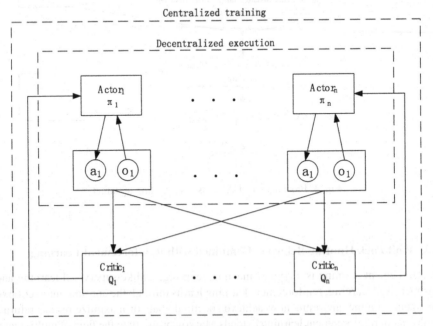

Fig. 5 MADDPG algorithm framework

The framework of the MADDPG algorithm is shown in Fig. 5. As can be seen from the figure, in centralized training, the training basis of the evaluation network is to obtain the gradient between the square variance of Q estimation and the Q actual, while the policy network is to update the strategy more accurately according to the feedback information of the global evaluation network that can be observed. When it is actually executed, a single agent cannot obtain the actions of other agents, and thus cannot obtain all the state information. Therefore, after the network is trained, in the process of decentralized execution, each agent only needs the observed local information to decide what action to choose, without knowing the action state values of other agents.

In reinforcement learning, through the reward function, the reward obtained by the agent after selecting an action can be obtained. This reward value is the most direct evaluation of the outcome of the agent's interaction with the environment. The design of a reasonable reward function can enable the agent to more accurately perceive the state of the surrounding environment, thereby speeding up its learning speed. In the environment of cooperative pursuit of UAVs, in order to enable the UAV cluster to round up the target as soon as possible, the following two aspects are mainly considered in the design of the reward function. The safe distance between the pursuit UAV and the target, and the anti-collision problem between the UAVs. Therefore, for the design of the reward function, the distance between the UAVs is an important factor.

In this paper, the wolf pack hunting behavior is integrated into a multi-agent reinforcement learning algorithm, and the pursuit UAV is regarded as the hunting wolf, and the escaped UAV is regarded as the escaped prey. According to the characteristics of wolves' hunting behavior in Sect. 3.1, multiple agents representing the pursuit of UAVs keep a safe distance from the target while continuously approaching the target, and finally form a uniform distribution state around the target. The agent representing the target UAV will select appropriate actions according to the training strategy, in order to be rounded up by other agents as late as possible. Combined with the feature that the reward function in reinforcement learning can be used to guide the agent to achieve the goal, the reward of pursuit UAV is as follows.

$$reward = \alpha_1 \times |d_1 - d_{safe}| + \alpha_2 \times d_2 \times flag + \sum_{i=1}^{n} \beta_i \times d_i \qquad (2)$$

The reward of UAV is mainly divided into three parts, where α_1, α_2 and β_i are the weight coefficients of each part. The first part is designed according to the safety distance of the escape UAV, where $d_1 = \sqrt[2]{(x_1 - x_0)^2 + (y_1 - y_0)^2}$ represents the Euclidean distance between the current pursuit UAV and the target UAV, and d_{safe} represents the safety distance of the escape UAV. The second part is designed according to the pursuit UAV and the closest other pursuit UAV, where $d_2 = \sqrt[2]{(x_1 - x_2)^2 + (y_1 - y_2)^2}$ represents the Euclidean distance between the current pursuit UAV and the nearest pursuit UAV, and $flag$ represents whether the two UAVs currently calculated are in the specified area, where the value of $flag$ is 0 or 1. If there are obstacles in the environment, the third part is designed according to the pursuit UAV and the obstacle area, where $d_i = \sqrt[2]{(x_1 - x_i)^2 + (y_1 - y_i)^2}$ represents the Euclidean distance between the current pursuit UAV and the center of the obstacle area.

4 Simulation Experiment and Result Analysis

In order to verify the effectiveness of the roundup algorithm proposed in this paper, the following simulation experiments are carried out in the Windows10 environment.

4.1 Experimental Simulation and Analysis of Wolves' Hunting Behavior Roundup Strategy

In the two-dimensional environment, there is a cluster of eight pursuit UAVs, and one escape UAV. Where the red circle represents the pursuit UAV in the cluster, and the green circle represents the escape UAV. When the escaping UAV is found, the pursuit.

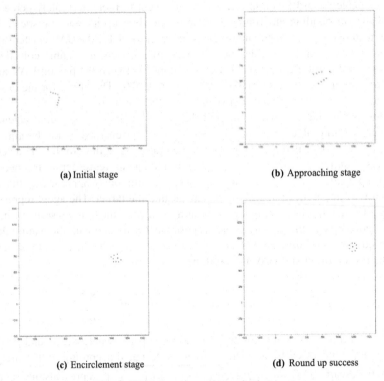

(a) Initial stage   **(b)** Approaching stage

(c) Encirclement stage   **(d)** Round up success

Fig. 6 UAV cluster rounds up single target

UAV cluster adopts a hunting strategy based on the hunting behavior of wolves to approach and round up the target. Since there is no boundary limit in the environment, in order to ensure that the pursuit UAV cluster can successfully approach and round up the target, the speed parameters of the UAV cluster and the target UAV speed are set as follows: In the approaching stage, the speed of each pursuit UAV in the cluster is 1.2 times the target; in the encirclement stage, the speed of the pursuit UAV is 1.5 times the target. The pursuit process is shown in Fig. 6. When the pursuit UAVs form a uniform distribution on the circle with the target UAV as the center and the safety distance as the radius, it means the pursuit is successful.

It can be seen from Fig. 6 that after adopting the roundup strategy proposed in this paper, the UAV cluster successfully rounded up the target UAV, which proves the effectiveness and feasibility of the algorithm. Next, the distributed characteristics of the algorithm are verified. It is assumed that in the UAV cluster, a certain number of pursuit UAVs are damaged or other malfunction in the battlefield environment, which makes it impossible to continue to perform the roundup mission. Test whether.

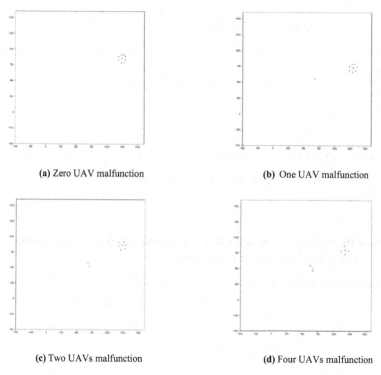

(a) Zero UAV malfunction

(b) One UAV malfunction

(c) Two UAVs malfunction

(d) Four UAVs malfunction

Fig. 7 The roundup of targets after some UAVs malfunction

the remaining cluster of pursuit UAVs can effectively round up the target. This paper assumes that 1, 2, and 4 UAVs malfunction during the roundup due to other reasons and cannot continue the roundup task. Test the roundup effect of the remaining pursuit UAVs, and the simulation results are shown in Fig. 7.

It can be seen from the simulation results in Fig. 7 that when 1, 2, and 4 UAVs malfunction, the remaining pursuit UAVs can still be evenly distributed around the target. It is proved that in the complex environment such as battlefield, when some UAVs cannot continue to carry out the mission due to other reasons, the remaining UAVs can still effectively round up the escaping UAVs by sensing the surrounding environment information and deciding their own movement strategy according to the rounding algorithm in the paper.

Finally, this paper conducts a simulation verification of the multi-escaping UAVs that the UAV cluster rounds up and escapes. It is assumed that there are 15 pursuit UAVs in the UAV cluster, which are represented by red circles, and three escape UAVs are represented by green circles. The following three scenarios are verified respectively: all UAVs can carry out the roundup mission normally, 3 UAVs and 6 UAVs malfunction. The simulation results are shown in Fig. 8, and it can be seen from the simulation results that according to the roundup strategy in this paper, the pursuit UAVs can realize the roundup of multiple scattered escape UAVs.

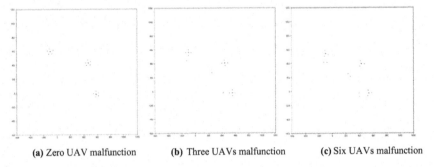

(a) Zero UAV malfunction   (b) Three UAVs malfunction   (c) Six UAVs malfunction

Fig. 8 UAV cluster rounds up multiple scattered targets

4.2 Simulation Experiment of Wolf Pack Hunting Behavior Combined with Multi-agent Reinforcement Learning

In the simulation environment of multi-agent reinforcement learning, this paper sets.

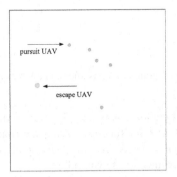

Fig. 9 Simulation experiment scene

up multiple pursuit UAVs, one escape UAV, and all the agents move simultaneously at the same time. As shown in Fig. 9, the smallest red circle represents the pursuit UAV, and the slightly larger green circle represents the escape UAV. All UAVs move at a set speed. In order to enable the UAV cluster to form a uniform roundup on the target as soon as possible, the speed of the pursuit UAV is set to be 1.5 times that of the escape UAV. The main hyperparameters of the environmental neural network are set as follows: the learning rate of network Actor and network Critic is 0.008, discount factor is 0.95, and batch-size is 1024.

In order to verify the effectiveness and feasibility of the method in this paper, simulation experiments were carried out on the following scenarios. Four pursuit UAVs round up an escape UAV, and five pursuit UAVs round up an escape UAV. The simulation test is carried out on whether there is a UAV malfunction in each scenario. The experimental results are shown in Fig. 10.

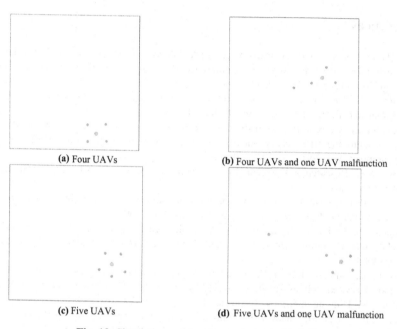

(a) Four UAVs

(b) Four UAVs and one UAV malfunction

(c) Five UAVs

(d) Five UAVs and one UAV malfunction

Fig. 10 Simulation results of round-up escape UAV

According to the simulation results, when all the four UAVs can execute the task normally to chase a target, the target UAV can be effectively rounded up. When one of the UAVs cannot execute the task due to a malfunction, the remaining three UAVs can still effectively round up the target. When five pursuit UAVs are used in the simulation experiment, no matter the five pursuit UAVs can carry out the task normally, or one of the UAVs can not carry out the task normally due to a malfunction, the target UAV can also be effectively rounded up. Therefore, using the training strategy in this paper, no matter whether there are UAVs in the UAV cluster that cannot perform the task normally, they can eventually be evenly distributed around the target, and the target UAV can be successfully rounded up. This strategy satisfies the need for rounding up targets in complex battlefield environments.

5 Conclusion

With the development of modern computer, network and other technologies, UAVs will play an increasingly important role in war. Multi-UAV cooperative roundup is one of the most significant applications of UAV cluster in war. By analyzing the hunting behavior of wolves, this paper proposes a distributed hunting algorithm based on the hunting behavior of wolves, which is verified by simulation experiments. The experiment proves that the UAV cluster can effectively capture the escaping target in the complex environment such as battlefield.

References

1. Nikolic, J., Leutenegger, S., Burri, M., et al.: A UAV System for Inspection of Industrial Facilities[C]. In: 2013 IEEE Aerospace Conference. [V.4].:Institute of Electrical and Electronics Engineers, pp. 2638–2645 (2013)
2. Duan, H., Pei, L.I.: Autonomous control for unmanned aerial vehicle swarms based on biological collective behaviors. Sci. Technol. Rev. (2017)
3. Kendra, Lt., Cook, L.B.: The institute of electrical and electronics engineers,inc. the silent force multiplier: the history and role of UAVs in warfare. In: 2007 IEEE Aerospace Conference, vol. 7(9), pp. 3194–3200 (2007)
4. Huang, C.: Research on key technology of future air combat process Intelligentization. Aero Weaponry (2019)
5. Li, J., Pan, Q., Hong, B.: A new approach of multi-robot cooperative pursuit based on association rule data mining. Int. J. Adv. Robotic Syst. (2009)
6. Uehara, S., Takimoto, M., Kambayashi, Y.: Mobile Agent Based Obstacle Avoidance in Multi-robot Hunting. Springer International Publishing (2017). Doi: https://doi.org/10.1007/978-3-319-49049-6_32
7. Luan, X., Sun., Y.: Research on cooperative encirclement strategy of multiple underwater robots based on wolf swarm algorithm. J. Phys. Conf. Ser. **1570**(1), 012017 (6pp) (2020)
8. Dutta, K.: Hunting in groups. Resonance **19**(10), 936–957 (2014)
9. Cai, Y.F., Tang, Z.M., Zhang, H.F:. Multi-robots cooperative hunting strategy based on Cross-EKF localization. Kongzhi yu Juece/Control Decision **25**(9), 1313–1317+1323 (2010)
10. An, Y., Li, S., Da, L.: Multiple Robotic Fish's Target Search and Cooperative Hunting Strategies. TELKOMNIKA Indonesian J. Electrical Eng. **12**(1) (2014)
11. Chen, S., Chen, X., Mei, Y., et al.: A cooperative hunting algorithm of multi-robot based on dynamic prediction of the target via consensus-based kalman filtering. Journal of Information and Computational Science **12**(4), 1557–1568 (2015)
12. Choi, S., Kim, J.: Three dimensional formation control to pursue an underwater evader utilizing underwater robots measuring the sound generated from the evader. IEEE Access **7**, 150720–150728 (2019)
13. Jin, L., Li, S., La, H.M., et al.: Dynamic task allocation in multi-robot coordination for moving target tracking: A distributed approach. Automatica **100**, 75–81 (2019)
14. Xum B., Zhang, H.T., Meng, H., et al.: Moving target surrounding control of linear multiagent systems with input saturation. IEEE Trans. Syst. Man Cybern. Syst. (2020)
15. Dou, L., Song, C., Wang, X., et al.: Target localization and enclosing control for networked mobile agents with bearing measurements. Automatica **118**, 109022 (2020)
16. De Souza, C., Newbury, R., Cosgun, A., et al.: Decentralized multi-agent pursuit using deep reinforcement learning. IEEE Robot. Automat. Lett. **6**(3), 4552–4559 (2021)

17. Palmer, G., Tuyls, K., Bloembergen, D., et al.: Lenient multi-agent deep reinforcement learning. arXiv preprint arXiv:1707.04402 (2017)
18. Barton, S.L., Waytowich, N.R., Zaroukian, E., et al.: Measuring collaborative emergent behavior in multi-agent reinforcement learning. In: International Conference on Human Systems Engineering and Design: Future Trends and Applications. Springer, Cham, pp. 422–427 (2018)
19. Hu, J., Turgut, A.E., Lennox, B., et al.: Robust formation coordination of robot swarms with nonlinear dynamics and unknown disturbances: Design and experiments. IEEE Trans. Circuits Syst. II Express Briefs **69**(1), 114–118 (2021)
20. Zhang, P., Xue, H., Gao, S., et al.: Distributed adaptive consensus tracking control for multi-agent system with communication constraints. IEEE Trans. Parallel Distrib. Syst. **32**(6), 1293–1306 (2020)
21. Tacchetti, A., Song, H.F., Mediano, P.A.M., et al.: Relational forward models for multi-agent learning. arXiv preprint arXiv:1809.11044 (2018)
22. Muro, C., Escobedo, R., Spector, L., et al.: Wolf-pack (Canis lupus) hunting strategies emerge from simple rules in computational simulations. Behav. Proc. **88**(3), 192–197 (2011)
23. Lowe, R., Wu, Y., Tamar, A., et al.: Multi-agent actor-critic for mixed cooperative-competitive environments. In: Proceedingsof the Advances in Neural Information Processing Systems, pp. 6379 - 6390 (2017)

Prediction of New Energy Vehicles via ARIMA-BP Hybrid Model

Beiteng Yang[1], Jianjun Liu[2], and Dongning Liu[1(✉)]

[1] School of Computer Science and Technology, Guangdong University of Technology, Guangzhou 510006, China
liudn@gdut.edu.cn
[2] School of Electromechanical Engineering, Guangdong University of Technology, Guangzhou 510006, China

Abstract. An important measure of the development of the new energy vehicle market is the prediction of vehicle sales. It is of great significance to complete the construction of relevant supporting facilities, according to the predicted sales volume for the development of the Chinese new energy vehicle industry. Based on this, this paper proposes a combined model that organically combines a single prediction model. Firstly, the ARIMA model is used to predict the linear information in the sales data, and BP neural network model is used to predict the residual sequence between the previous prediction and the actual value. After that, it adds the prediction results to get the final prediction results of new energy vehicle sales. The results verified with the actual sales data show that the prediction accuracy of the ARIMA-BP Residual Optimization Combination model used in this paper is 85.07%. Compared with the single prediction model and the simple weighted combination prediction model, there are general advantages, which can be used for the actual monthly sales prediction of new energy vehicles.

Keywords: New energy vehicles · ARIMA model · BP neural network model · ARIMA-BP Residual Optimization Combination model

1 Introduction

As one of the strategic emerging industries proposed to grow and develop during the "14th Five-Year Plan" period in my country, the development and progress of the new energy vehicle industry not only conforms to the global green development trend, but also involves the adjustment and transformation of related industries in the country. The accuracy of the sales forecast is related to the manufacturer's judgment of the market and the control of production and sales. An accurate forecast can help manufacturers

Fund Project: This work was supported in part by the R&D Projects in Key Area of Guangdong Province No. 2021B0101200003, National Natural Science Foundation of China under Grants No. 62072120, Guangdong Provincial Key Laboratory of Cyber-Physical System No. 2020B1212060069.

Y. Sun et al. (Eds.): ChineseCSCW 2022, CCIS 1681, pp. 516–527, 2023.
https://doi.org/10.1007/978-981-99-2356-4_41

formulate development strategies and have important guiding significance for enhancing the competitiveness of products.

At present, the methods commonly used for prediction mainly include the ARIMA model [1–3], the Neural Network prediction model [4–6], and Gray prediction. Such as Yang Jun, Li Lei [7] and others used the ARIMA model. Wu Qiang, Wang Yu [8] and others adopted the BP neural network model to solve their problem. Feng Zhipeng, Zhang Yuanyang, and Ge Fengyi [9] used the grey prediction method. All of the above are predicted using a single model. The sales data of new energy vehicles contains linear information and nonlinear information. If only a single model is used for prediction, the information will become incomplete.

Therefore, in order to avoid the lack of information, based on two single methods commonly used in the sales forecast of new energy vehicles, this paper proposes a residual optimization combined forecasting method to improve the accuracy. Experiments using this combined prediction method show that it can effectively predict the overall trend of sales. Compared with single models, it can effectively extract the information of linear and nonlinear contained in it, which has a higher prediction accuracy.

2 Linear Prediction

Linear forecasting methods usually use time series and statistical methods to explore the laws contained in time series by observing the change characteristics of time series, and then make a statistical description of them, establish corresponding models, and estimate the future trend of new energy vehicle sales time series more accurately. Therefore, linear models are generally used to predict the trend of car sales. Common linear prediction methods include the ARIMA model, Arch model [10, 11], the Stochastic Volatikity model, etc.

ARIMA model is used in linear prediction model. It is a time series prediction model with a very wide range of use. It mainly uses difference operations to process non-stationary data to make it stable data, and then uses dependent variables to fit the backward values. Then, it builds a model according to the lag value and the present value of random error obtained by model simulation, and finally carries out experimental verification. The specific methods are as follows:

2.1 Stationarity Test of Time Series

According to the broken line chart of the original data, it can be found that the time series of sales volume of new energy vehicles shows an upward trend. Although it can be preliminarily determined that the sales volume data is not a stable time series, the ADF test should be conducted on the original sales volume data to determine whether the sales volume data is stable. The ADF test results were shown in Table 1:

Through the ADF test, it is found that the ADF values are all larger than the standard value, indicating that there is a unit root in the ADF test, so the second difference is performed, and the results are shown in the following Table 2:

The experimental results show that the tesr value is less than 0.05, so the time series after the difference is stationary.

Table 1. ADF test table of the original sequence

Augmented Dickey-Fuller Test	
Data	Total
Dickey-Fuller	1.478
Critical Value (1%)	−3.546
Critical Value (5%)	−2.912
Critical Value (10%)	−2.594
P-value	0.997

Table 2. ADF test table after differential sequence

Augmented Dickey-Fuller Test	
Data	Total
Dickey-Fuller	−7.183
Critical Value (1%)	−3.654
Critical Value (5%)	−2.957
Critical Value (10%)	−2.618
P-value	2.615e−10

2.2 White Noise Series

This paper mainly uses Python software to obtain the test probability of the last column, and use this to determine whether the residual sequence belongs to the white noise sequence. The results are shown in the following Table 3:

Table 3. Ljung-Box test table after differential sequence

Ljung-Box Test	
Data	Total
LB test p-value	0.012

It can be seen from Table 3. In the above white noise test, the test value is less than 0.05. So the test passes.

2.3 Determine the Order of Model

ACF test and PACF test were conducted, and the corresponding diagram were shown in Fig. 1:

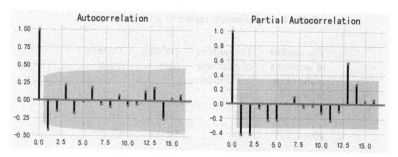

Fig. 1. ACF diagram and PACF diagram

Based on the specific situation of ACF and PACF and fitting [12], take $p = 1, q = 0$. Since the judgment by looking at the picture may not be accurate, the AIC rule [13] is used to traverse the value of p and q on Python. Several experiments based on the AIC rule have obtained the optimal parameters in the current experiment, namely $p = 1, q = 0$. The ARIMA $(1, 2, 0)$ model was constructed.

3 Nonlinear Prediction

The new energy vehicle market is very complex and will be interfered with by many factors, such as policy systems, economic environment, enterprise development and consumer psychology. Therefore, the new energy vehicle market is a complex non-linear market. However, the traditional prediction model based on linear assumption often performs poorly when forecasting the sales volume of new energy vehicles. The non-linear model is based on non-linear assumptions, thus it has certain advantages in sales volume prediction. Nonlinear prediction methods include Neural Network prediction, Wavelet Analysis [14–16], Grey prediction [17, 18], etc.

In this paper, BP neural network model is used in nonlinear prediction. Methods as follows:

3.1 Determine the Number of Neurons and Hidden Layer Nodes

In the modeling process, there are often cases of inadequate fitting, and overfitting. Therefore, it is crucial to choose the appropriate parameters through continuous experiments.

In this paper, different numbers of neurons are selected for experiments. The results are shown in the following Table 4:

From the Table 4, the appropriate neurons in the input layer and hidden layer in the experiment is 300 and 150, respectively.

Because there are many methods for determining hidden layer nodes at present, and there is no consensus. In this paper, a more commonly used method is selected, which can be roughly used as a reference for the value of the number of nodes.

$$m = \sqrt{nl} \tag{1}$$

Table 4. Experimental results of different neurons

The number of neurouns in the input layer	The number of neurouns in the hidden layer	Training error	Training times
50	25	2.0094	40
100	50	3.4188	43
150	75	1.4229	53
200	100	1.9530	40
250	125	2.0384	57
300	150	1.2337	37
350	175	1.7773	36
400	200	2.5746	29
450	225	2.8522	35

where m is the number of hidden layer nodes, n is the number of input layer nodes, l is the number of output layer nodes, and a is a constant between 1–10. This paper chooses formula (1). Since $n = 6$, $l = 1$, and m is 2.65, thus the value of the hidden layer is 3 to 13. When the input layer is 300 and the hidden layer is 150, the results of different values of the number of hidden layer nodes are compared, as shown in Table 5:

Table 5. Experimental results of different numbers of hidden layer nodes

The number of hidden layer nodes	Training error	Training times
3	1.8672	55
4	2.2256	40
5	1.8796	50
6	1.2337	37
7	2.4264	44
8	2.4926	39
9	2.6614	28
10	2.0999	22
11	2.2762	39
12	2.0868	43
13	2.0761	34

In the experiment, the input layer is 300, and the hidden layer is 150, so we start training, When the value of the loss function no longer decreases after training, the final training times can be confirmed. The result that can be drawn from multiple experiments is that the training error is smaller and nodes corresponding to fewer times is 6. The Loss diagram at this time as follows Fig. 2:

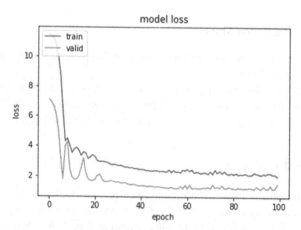

Fig. 2. Loss graph (When the number of hidden layer nodes is 6)

3.2 Select Activation Function

The activation function adopts the Relu function. The Relu function has the following advantages: it can perform efficient gradient descent and backpropagation, effectively avoiding the problem of gradient explosion and disappearance, and the calculation process is also simplified, and there are no other complex activation functions. Influences such as exponential functions in the neural network, at the same time, the dispersion of activities reduces the overall computational cost of the neural network.

$$f(x) = relu(x) = \max(x, 0) \tag{2}$$

3.3 Data Normalization

Normalizing the data can control the range of the sales sequence between $[-1, 1]$, and the data will not fluctuate greatly, effectively eliminating the existence of singular samples in the training samples, so as to achieve the purpose of removing noise.

Next, the data needs to be normalized, and the normalization formula is as follows:

$$x'_t = \frac{x_t - x_{min}}{x_{max} - x_{min}} \tag{3}$$

Through normalization, after the result is obtained, de-normalization is performed to obtain a predicted value with basically no noise. The inverse normalization formula is as follows:

$$x_t = x'_t(x_{max} - x_{min}) + x_{min} \tag{4}$$

3.4 Establish Prediction Model

The model parameters corresponding to the data in this paper determined after the test, the settings are as follows:

The number of nodes in both input and hidden layers is 6, and the output layer nodes is 1. The ReLU activation function is adopted, the loss function is the mean absolute error function, the training times is 50, and the training samples each time is 32.

4   Combined Forecast

There are both regular linear information and irregular nonlinear information in the sales data of new energy vehicles. A single forecasting method has certain limitations in the forecasting of new energy vehicle sales. Theoretical and empirical research results show that the integration of different models can be an effective method to improve their effectiveness [19, 20]. Therefore, if the advantages of the single models can be combined, the accuracy of China's new energy vehicle sales forecast can be effectively improved.

4.1   ARIMA-BP Weighted Combination Model

Let the prediction result be Ft, α_1 and α_2 are the weights of the ARIMA model and BP model in the weighted combination model, expressed as:

$$F_t = \alpha_1 F_{1t} + \alpha_2 F_{2t} \tag{5}$$

$$\alpha_1 + \alpha_2 = 1 \quad \alpha_1 \geq 0\alpha_2 \geq 0$$

Firstly, the weights of the root mean square error of the two single models are calculated, and the weights α_1 and α_2 in the weighted combination model are obtained.

Next, two single models were used to predict the original data respectively, and then the weighted method is used to process them.

Finally, the predicted value of the ARIMA-BP weighted combination model is obtained through calculation.

4.2 ARIMA-BP Residual Optimization Combination Model

This paper assumes that the original data is composed of linear part L_t and nonlinear part N_t, which can be expressed as:

$$Y_t = L_t + N_t = \text{ARIMA} + \text{BP} \tag{6}$$

First, the ARIMA model is used for modeling and prediction, and the prediction result of linear information in sales volume can be obtained, expressed by $\hat{L}_t$. And the nonlinear residual sequence can be obtained. The difference between the original sequence and the ARIMA model prediction result is the residual sequence e_t, expressed as:

$$e_t = Y_t - \hat{L}_t \tag{7}$$

Next, the BP neural network model is used to model and predict the residual sequence e_t, the first n values of the predicted value are selected as the input variables of the neural network, and the predicted value is put into the output layer as the output variable of the neural network to obtain the predicted value $\hat{e}_t$ of the residual sequence.

Finally, the predicted values can be directly added to obtain the final predicted results $\hat{Y}_t$, which are shown as follows:

$$\hat{Y}_t = \hat{L}_t + \hat{e}_t \tag{8}$$

5 Experimental Analysis

Based on the Passenger Vehicle Market Information Joint Conference, this paper collects the sales data of new energy vehicles in my country for 72 consecutive months from January 2016 to December 2021. The data for 60 months from 2016 to 2020 is used as a sample to build a model, and the model prediction and verification are carried out on the sales data for the whole year of 2021.

5.1 Evaluation Indicators

In this experiment, RMSE, MAE and MAPE are selected as indicators to evaluate the performance of the model, and the calculation formulas are as follows (9)–(11). The smaller the values of the above three indicators, the better the prediction performance [21–25].

$$\text{RMSE} = \sqrt{\frac{1}{n} \sum_{i=1}^{n} \left(Y_{\text{pred}} - Y_{\text{test}} \right)^2} \tag{9}$$

$$\text{MAE} = \frac{1}{n} \sum_{i=1}^{n} \left| Y_{\text{pred}} - Y_{\text{test}} \right| \tag{10}$$

$$\text{MAPE} = \frac{100\%}{n} \sum_{i=1}^{n} \left| \frac{Y_{\text{pred}} - Y_{\text{test}}}{Y_{\text{test}}} \right| \tag{11}$$

5.2　Model Evaluation

Based on the constructed model, the sales forecast is carried out. Since vehicle sales are greatly affected by environmental factors such as policies and the new crown epidemic, only from January to December 2021 are selected for forecasting. The result is shown in Figs. (3, 4, 5 and 6):

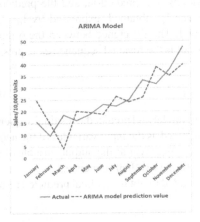

Fig. 3.　ARIMA model prediction

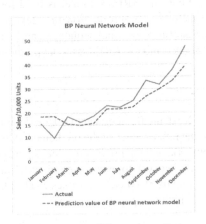

Fig. 4.　BP Neural Network prediction

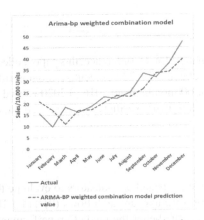

Fig. 5.　ARIMA-BP weighted combination model prediction

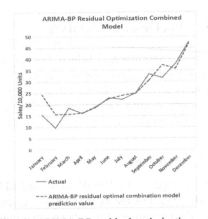

Fig. 6.　ARIMA-BP residual optimization combined model prediction

From Figs. (3, 4, 5 and 6), it can be seen that the three models are not accurate enough for the prediction of January to March. Those who pay more attention to cars at ordinary times know that January, February, and March in 2021 belong to the off-season of car sales. Moreover, in January 2021, the Ministry of Finance and other four departments jointly issued the policy that the subsidy standard for new energy vehicles in 2022 will be reduced by 30% on the basis of the previous year, which will undoubtedly greatly affect the enthusiasm of users who are still on the sidelines.

In order to more intuitively select a model with a better prediction effect, this paper evaluates the model by calculating the indicators. As shown in Table 6:

Table 6. Evaluation Metrics for Different Prediction Models

Predictive model	MAE	MAPE	RMSE
ARIMA (1, 2, 0) model	5.62	27.21%	6.71
BP neural network model	3.74	18.77%	4.56
ARIMA-BP weighted combination model	4.08	20.29%	4.86
ARIMA-BP residual optimization combined model	2.63	14.93%	3.77

As can be seen from the above three indicators and prediction results, in a single model, the ARIMA (1, 2, 0) model has the worst prediction effect. This is because the ARIMA model is a linear prediction-based model that cannot effectively predict nonlinear information in car sales data, so it performs the worst. The BP model has better nonlinear prediction ability, and it will automatically learn to predict during the training process, so it performs better. In the combination model, the weighted combination method simply adds the values of the linear prediction and the nonlinear prediction according to the weight, so the error is larger than the ARIMA-BP residual optimization combination model. Finally, from the perspective of indicators and predicted values, the ARIMA-BP residual optimization combined model is obviously the best in terms of the error and the distribution of the error.

The experimental results show that the ARIMA-BP residual optimization combination model has certain advantages in the sales forecast. It can not only extract linear information, but also fully extract nonlinear information. This results in higher prediction accuracy and more uniform error distribution than the predictions of the single model and the ARIMA-BP weighted combination model.

6 Conclusion

The ARIMA-BP residual optimization combined model used in this paper can intuitively predict the trend of sales from a strategic perspective. In this paper, the sales in China is predicted by the combined prediction model: the overall trend of sales volume is rising, but it will enter a cold period in January and February of each year. At the same time, the Spring Festival is about to start, and manufacturers will stop working one after another.

The residual optimization combination prediction method can appropriately provide reference opinions for new energy vehicle manufacturers. For example, how to formulate production and sales strategies, how to timely and appropriately adjust the production and marketing, and how to make relevant sales plans to meet the national preferential policies and the needs of the people as much as possible. At the same time, it can also provide a reference for the government to adjust the new energy industry policy in line with my country's national conditions, and for enterprises to grasp the industry development trend and adjust their strategic planning promptly.

References

1. Sharma, R.R., Kumar, M., Maheshwari, S., Ray, K.P.: EVDHM-ARIMA-based time series forecasting model and its application for COVID-19 cases. IEEE Trans. Instrum. Meas. **70**, 1–10 (2021)
2. Guo, J., He, H., Sun, C.: ARIMA-based road gradient and vehicle velocity prediction for hybrid electric vehicle energy management. IEEE Trans. Veh. Technol. **68**(6), 5309–5320 (2019)
3. Biernacki, A.: Improving quality of adaptive video by traffic prediction with (F)ARIMA models. J. Commun. Netw. **19**(5), 521–530 (2017)
4. Chen, M., Challita, U., Saad, W., Yin, C., Debbah, M.: Artificial neural networks-based machine learning for wireless networks: a tutorial. IEEE Commun. Surv. Tutorials **21**(4), 3039–3071 (2019)
5. Tanaka, T., Kawakami, W., Kuwabara, S., Kobayashi, S., Hirano, A.: Intelligent monitoring of optical fiber bend using artificial neural networks trained with constellation data. IEEE Network. Lett. **1**(2), 60–62 (2019)
6. Tanaka, T., Inui, T., Kawai, S., Kuwabara, S., Nishizawa, H.: Monitoring and diagnostic technologies using deep neural networks for predictive optical network maintenance. J. Opt. Commun. Network. **13**(10), E13–E22 (2021)
7. Yang, J., Li, L., Shi, Y., Xidie, X.: An ARIMA model with adaptive orders for predicting blood glucose concentrations and hypoglycemia. IEEE J. Biomed. Health Inform. **23**(3), 1251–1260 (2019)
8. Qiang, W., et al.: Ablation state assessment of SF6 circuit breaker contacts based on BP neural network and mean impact value. Energy Rep. **8**(S5), 874–883 (2022)
9. Feng, Z., Zhang, Y.: Demand forecasting of vegetable logistics in Shouguang based on grey forecasting model. Logistics Eng. Manag. **44**(5). 73–75+126 (2022)
10. Chen, E., Ye, Z., Wang, C., Xu, M.: Subway passenger flow prediction for special events using smart card data. IEEE Trans. Intell. Transp. Syst. **21**(3), 1109–1120 (2020)
11. Ding, C., Duan, J., Zhang, Y., Wu, X., Yu, G.: Using an ARIMA-GARCH modeling approach to improve subway short-term ridership forecasting accounting for dynamic volatility. IEEE Trans. Intell. Transp. Syst. **19**(4), 1054–1064 (2018)
12. Bayer, F.M., Bayer, D.M., Marinoni, A., Gamba, P.: A novel Rayleigh dynamical model for remote sensing data interpretation. IEEE Trans. Geosci. Remote Sens. **58**(7), 4989–4999 (2020)
13. Weng, Y., Wang, X., Hua, J., Wang, H., Kang, M., Wang, F.: Forecasting horticultural products price using ARIMA model and neural network based on a large-scale data set collected by web crawler. IEEE Trans. Comput. Soc. Syst. **6**(3), 547–553 (2019)
14. Jun, X., Xuesong, M., Wang Xiao, F., Yumeng, Z.Y., Junping, W.: A relative state of health estimation method based on wavelet analysis for lithium-ion battery cells. IEEE Trans. Industr. Electron. **68**(3), 6973–6981 (2021)
15. Mizeva, I., Dremin, V., Potapova, E., Zherebtsov, E., Kozlov, I., Dunaev, A.: Wavelet analysis of the temporal dynamics of the laser speckle contrast in human skin. IEEE Trans. Biomed. Eng. **67**(7), 1882–1889 (2020)
16. Kalra, M., Kumar, S., Das, B.: Seismic signal analysis using empirical wavelet transform for moving ground target detection and classification. IEEE Sens. J. **20**(14), 7886–7895 (2020)
17. Xia, H., Zhang, S.F., Sun, Y.C., Xiao, P., Li, Y., Cheng, X.Z.: Design of 'trust-based secure multicast routing protocol in VANETs. Chin. J. Comput. **42**(05), 961–979 (2019)
18. Zhou, D., Al-Durra, A., Zhang, K., Ravey, A., Gao, F.: A robust prognostic indicator for renewable energy technologies: a novel error correction grey prediction model. IEEE Trans. Industr. Electron. **66**(12), 9312–9325 (2019)

19. Kavousi-Fard, A.: A hybrid accurate model for tidal current prediction. IEEE Trans. Geosci. Remote Sens. **55**(1), 112–118 (2017)
20. Bowen, T., Zhe, Z., Yulin, Z.: Forecasting method of e-commerce cargo sales based on ARIMA-BP model. In: 2020 IEEE International Conference on Artificial Intelligence and Computer Applications (ICAICA), pp. 133–136, Dalian, China (2020)
21. Pan, Y.F., He, F.Z., Yu, H.P.: Social recommendation algorithm using implicit similarity in trust. Chin. J. Comput. **41**(01), 65–81 (2018)
22. Zhu, H.L., Yun, X.C., Han, Z.S.: Weibo popularity prediction method based on propagation acceleration. J. Comput. Res. Dev. **55**(06), 1282–1293 (2018)
23. Wu, F., Jing, R., Zhang, X.-P., Wang, F., Bao, Y.: A combined method of improved grey BP neural network and MEEMD-ARIMA for day-ahead wave energy forecast. IEEE Trans. Sustain. Energy. **12**(4), 2404–2412 (2021)
24. Li, Y., Yang, Y., Zhu, K., Zhang, J.: Clothing sale forecasting by a composite GRU-prophet model with an attention mechanism. IEEE Trans. Ind. Inf. **17**(12), 8335–8344 (2021)
25. Huang, H.Y., Liu, X.W., Ding, Z.H.: Sales forecasting based on multi-dimensional grey model and neural network. Ruan Jian Xue Bao/J. Softw. **30**(4), 1031–1045 (2019)

Author Index

Printed in the United States
by Baker & Taylor Publisher Services